Consolidated Ontario Education Statutes and Regulations 1995

Consulting Editor

PETER MONASTYRSKYJ

of the Ontario Bar

CARSWELL

© 1995 Thomson Canada Limited

All rights reserved. No part of this publication may be reproduced, stored in a retrieval system, or transmitted, in any form or by any means, electronic, mechanical, photocopying, recording, or otherwise, without the prior written permission of the publisher.

This publication is designed to provide accurate and authoritative information. It is sold with the understanding that the publisher is not engaged in rendering legal, accounting or other professional advice. If legal advice or other expert assistance is required, the services of a competent professional should be sought. The analysis contained herein should in no way be construed as being either official or unofficial policy of any governmental body.

ISBN 0-459-55918-4

This work reproduces official English language versions of Ontario statutes and regulations. As the Revised Statutes of Ontario, 1990 and many Ontario Regulations also have official French versions, the reader is advised that reference to the official French language material may be warranted in appropriate circumstances.

The paper used in this publication meets the minimum requirements of the American National Standard for Information Sciences – Permanence of Paper for Printed Library Materials, ANSI Z39. 48-1984.

CARSWELL
Thomson Professional Publishing

One Corporate Plaza, 2075 Kennedy Road, Scarborough, Ontario M1T 3V4
Customer Service:
Toronto 1-416-609-3800
Elsewhere in Canada/U.S. 1-800-387-5164
Fax 1-416-298-5094

Table of Contents

Introduction	v
Education Act — Concordance	vii
Education Act — Table of Contents	1
Education Act	37
Regulations under the Education Act	235
Immunization of School Pupils Act	401
Regulation under the Immunization of School Pupils Act	409
Municipal Conflict of Interest Act	417
Local Government Disclosure of Interest Act, 1994 (Not yet in force)	425
School Boards and Teachers Collective Negotiations Act	437
Teaching Profession Act	463
Regulation Made Under the Teaching Profession Act	469
Index	481

Introduction

This book contains a collection of the statutes and regulations that govern primary- and secondary-level education in the province of Ontario. It is a handy, up-to-date, comprehensive and time-saving desk-top reference for teachers, student teachers, principals, administrators, trustees, parents and lawyers.

The core statute is the Education Act. A table of contents and a detailed table of contents allows readers to focus on a specific provision in this large and complex Act without referring to text. A table of concordance between the present Act and its predecessors allows readers to trace the history of a provision.

Other statutes and regulations, however, expand on, add to and overlap with the Education Act in many areas. Readers need to refer not just to the Education Act, but also to the appropriate regulation and perhaps even to a different statute. The index provided in this book allows for cross-reference between the various statutes and regulations.

Except for the two regulations discussed below, all of the regulations included in this book have been issued under the authority of the Education Act.

This book also includes R.R.O. 1990 Regulation 645 (General) made under the authority of the Immunization of School Pupils Act.

The 1995 edition also introduces the Regulation Made Under the Teaching Profession Act. This regulation is different from the others included in this work in that it is not covered by the Regulation Act, R.S.O. 1990, c. R.21. The practical significance of this exemption is that any amendments to the regulation are not required to be published in the Ontario Gazette, as set out in section 5 of that Act. This regulation is also different in that it has not been made directly by the Ontario Lieutenant Governor in Council (that is, the provincial Cabinet). Rather, it has been made by the Board of Governors of the Ontario Teachers' Federation pursuant to authority granted to the Board by section 12 of the Teaching Profession Act.

A number of regulations issued annually under the authority of the Education Act have not been included because they are of limited and short-term interest.

In preparing the 1995 edition, the Ontario Gazette was reviewed up to and including the December 31, 1994 edition, covering all regulations issued up to and including O. Reg. 800/94. Statutes were updated to the end of Votes and Proceedings No. 169, dated December 8, 1994.

The Regulation Made Under the Teaching Profession Act has been updated to December 31, 1994.

Amending citations have been inserted at the end of the affected sections, as well as summarized at the beginning of each statute and regulation. Amendments which have yet to be proclaimed or are not yet in force have been included. In places, this has resulted in the inclusion of both the repealed section as well as its replacement.

Where applicable, the index has been updated to reflect the amendments.

French versions have not been included, except where it has been incorporated into the body of the English text, for example, the French version of a form. However, the citations as to where they can be found have been included.

January 1995

EDUCATION ACT

CONCORDANCE

The following concordance shows the interrelationship of the Education Act as it exists in its current form (referred to as "1994", reflecting the cut-off date for updates for this edition), in R.S.O. 1990, c. E.2 (referred to as "1990"), in R.S.O. 1980, c. 129 (referred to as "1980") and in S.O. 1974, c. 109 (referred to as "1974").

1994	1990	1980	1974
1(1),(2)	1(1),(2)	1(1),(2)	1(1),(2)
1(3)	1(3)	1(3)	1(4)
1(4)	1(4)	1(4)	1(6)
1(5)	1(5)	1(5)	-
1(6)	-	-	-
2(1)-(3)	2(1)-(3)	2(1)-(3)	2(1)-(3)
2(4)-(6)	2(4)-(6)	2(4)-(6)	-
3-7	3-7	3-7	3-7
8(1)¶1-3	8(1)¶1-3	8(1)(a-c)	8(1)(a-c)
8(1)¶3.1	-	-	-
8(1)¶4	8(1)¶4	8(1)(d)	8(1)(d)
8(1)¶5	8(1)¶5	8(1)(e)	-
8(1)¶6-22	8(1)¶6-22	8(1)(f-v)	8(1)(e-u)
8(1)¶23	8(1)¶23	8(1)(w)	-
8(1)¶23.1	-	-	-
8(1)¶24-25	8(1)¶24-25	8(1)(x-y)	-
8(1)¶26	8(1)¶26	8(1)(z)	-
8(1)¶27-29	8(1)¶27-29	8(1)(za-zc)	-
8(1)¶29.1	-	-	-
8(1)¶29.2	-	-	-
8(1)¶30-33	8(1)¶30-33	8(1)(zd-zg)	-
8(1)¶34-35	-	-	-
8(2)	8(2)	8(1a)	-
8(3)	8(3)	8(2)	-
8(4)	8(4)	8(3)	8(2)
9	9	8a	-
10	10	9	9
11(1)¶1-5	11(1)¶1-5	10(1)¶1-5	10(1)¶1-5
11(1)¶6	11(1)¶6	10(1)¶6	-
11(1)¶7-11	11(1)¶7-11	10(1)¶7-11	10(1)¶6-10
11(1)¶12	11(1)¶12	10(1)¶11a	-
11(1)¶13-16	11(1)¶13-16	10(1)¶12-15	10(1)¶11-14
11(1) ¶17-18	11(1) ¶17-18	10(1)¶15a-15b	-
-	-	10(1)¶16	10(1)¶15

vii

CONCORDANCE

1994	1990	1980	1974
11(1)¶19-21	11(1)¶19-21	10(1)¶17-19	10(1)¶16-18
11(1)¶21.1	-	-	-
11(1)¶22-27	11(1)¶22-27	10(1)¶20-25	10(1)¶19-24
11¶28 [Repealed]	11(1)¶28	10(1)¶26	10(1)¶25
11(1)¶29-34	11(1)¶29-34	11(1)¶27-32	10(1)¶26-31
11(1)¶35	11(1)¶35	10(1)¶33	-
11(1)¶36	11(1)¶36	10(1)¶34	-
11(2) [Repealed]	11(2)	10(2)	10(2)
11(3)	11(3)	10(3)	10(3)
11(4)	11(4)	10(3a)	-
11(5)-(10)	11(5)-(10)	10(4)-(9)	10(4)-(9)
11(11),(12)	11(11),(12)	10(10),(11)	-
11(13)-(15)	11(13)-(15)	10(11a-11c)	-
11(15.1)	-	-	-
11(16)	11(16)	10(11d)	-
11(17) [Repealed]	11(17)	10(11e)	-
11(18)	11(18)	10(12)	-
12(1),(2)	12(1),(2)	11(1),(2)	11(1),(2)
12(3)	12(3)	11(2a)	-
12(4),(5)	12(4),(5)	11(3),(4)	11(3),(4)
13(1)	13(1)	12(1), pt	12(1), pt
13(2)	13(2)	12(2), pt	12(2), pt
13(3)	13(3)	12(1),(2), pt	12(1),(2), pt
13(4)	13(4)	12(3)	12(3)
13(4.1)	-	-	-
13(5)	13(5)	12(4)	-
13(6)	13(6)	12(5)	-
13(7)	13(7)	12(6)	12(4)
-	-	12(7)	12(5)
14(1)-(3)	14(1)-(3)	13(1)-(3)	13(1)-(3)
-	-	13(4)	13(4)
14(4)	14(4)	13(5)	13(5)
15	15	14(1)	14(1)
-	-	14(2)	14(2)
16	16	15	15
17	17	16	16
17.1	-	-	-
18	18	17	17
19	19	18	18
20	20	19	19
21	21	20	20
22	22	21	21
23(1)-(1.2)	23(1)	22(1)	22(1)
23(2)	23(2)	22(2)	22(2)

CONCORDANCE

1994	1990	1980	1974
23(2.2)	-	-	-
23(3)-(5)	23(3)-(5)	22(3)-(5)	22(3)-(5)
24	24	23	23
25	25	24	24
26	26	25	25
27	27	26	26
28	28	27	27
29	29	28	28
30	30	29	29
31	31	30	30
32	32	31	31
33(1)-(4)	33(1)-(4)	32(1)-(4)	32(1)-(4)
33(5)-(6) [Repealed]	33(5)-(6)	32(5)-(6)	32(5)-(6)
34(1)-(2)	34(1)-(2)	33(1)-(2)	33(1)-(2)
34(2.1)-(2.2) [To be repealed on September 1, 1997]	-	-	-
34(3)	34(3)	33(3)	33(3)
35 [Repealed]	35	34	34
36	36	35	-
37	37	36	-
38	38	37	35
39	39	38	36
40(1)-(2)	40(1)-(2)	39(1)-(2)	37(1)-(2)
40(3)	40(3)	39(3)	37(3)
-	-	39(4)	37(4)
40(4),(5)	40(4),(5)	39(5),(6)	37(5),(6)
41	41	40	38
42	42	41	39
43	43	42	40
44	44	43	41
45	45	44	42
46	46	45	43
47	47	46	44
48(1) [Repealed]	48(1)	47(1)	-
-	-	47(2)-(5)	45(1)-(5)
48(2),(3)	48(2),(3)	47(4a),(4b)	-
49(1)-(5)	49(1)-(5)	48(1)-(5)	46
49(6)	49(6)	48(6)	-
49(7)	49(7)	48(7)	-
49.1	-	-	-
50	50	49	47
51	51	50	48
52	52	51	49

CONCORDANCE

1994	1990	1980	1974
53	53	52	50
54(1),(2)	54(1),(2)	53(1),(2)	51(1),(2)
54(3)	54(3)	53(2a)	-
54(4)-(6)	54(4)-(6)	53(3)-(5)	51(3)-(5)
55(1)-(7)	55(1)-(7)	54(1)-(7)	52
55(8)	55(8)	54(8)	-
56(1)-(4)	56(1)-(4)	55(1)-(4)	53(1)-(4)
-	-	55(5)	53(5)
57(1)-(3)	57(1)-(3)	56(1)-(3)	54(1)-(3)
-	-	56(4)-(8)	54(4)-(8)
-	-	57,58	55,56
-	-	59(1)-(9)	57(1)-(9)
-	-	59(10)	-
-	-	59(11)-(14)	57(10)-(13)
-	-	59(15)	-
-	-	59(16)-(34)	57(14)-(32)
58	58	60	58
-	-	61	59
59(1)-(3)	59(1)-(3)	62(1)-(3)	60(1)-(3)
-	-	-	60(4)
59(4),(5)	59(4),(5)	62(4),(5)	60(5)-(6)
60	60	63	61
61	61	64	62
62	62	65	63
63	63	66	64
64	64	66a	-
65(1)-(6)	65(1)-(6)	67(1)-(6)	65(1)-(6)
-	-	67(7)-(11)	65(7)-(11)
65(7)	65(7)	67(12)	65(12)
66(1)-(4)	66(1)-(4)	68(1)-(4)	66(1)-(4)
-	-	-	66(5)
66(5)	66(5)	68(5)	66(6)
67	67	69	67
68	68	70	68
69 [Repealed]	69	71	69
70(1),(2) [Repealed]	70(1),(2)	72(1),(2)	70(1),(2)
-	-	-	70(3)
72(3) [Repealed]	72(3)	72(3)	-
-	-	72(4)	-
71 [Repealed]	71	73	71
72(1) [Repealed]	72(1)	74(1)	72(1)
74(2),(3) [Repealed]	74(2),(3)	74(2),(3)	-
74(4)-(8) [Repealed]	74(4)-(8)	74(4)-(8)	72(2)-(6)
73 [Repealed]	73	75	73

CONCORDANCE

1994	1990	1980	1974
74 [Repealed]	74	76	74
-		-	75
-	-	-	76
75 [Repealed]	75	77	77(1)
	-	-	77(2),(3)
76 [Repealed]	76	78	78
77	77	79	79
78(1)-(4)	78(1)-(4)	80(1)-(4)	80(1)-(4)
-	-	80(5)-(9)	80(5)-(9)
-	-	81(1)-(3),(5)	81(1)-(3),(5)
79	79	81(4)	81(4)
-	-	82	82
80(1)-(5)	80(1)-(5)	83(1)-(5)	83(1)-(5)
-	-	83(6)	83(6)
80(6),(7)	80(6),(7)	83(7),(8)	83(7)-(8)
-	-	84(1),(2)	84(1),(2)
81	81	84(3),(4)	84(3),(4)
82	82	85	85
83	83	86	86
84	84	87	87
85	85	88(1)-(3)	88(1)-(3)
-	-	88(4)	88(4)
86	86	89	89
-	-	90(1),(2)	90(1),(2)
-	-	90(2a)	-
-	-	90(3)	90(3)
-	-	91	91
-	-	92	92
-	-	93	93
-	-	94	94
87	87	95	95
88	88	96	96
89	89	97	97
90(1),(2)	90(1),(2)	98(1),(2)	98
90(3)	90(3)	98(3)	-
91	91	99	99
92(1)-(10)	92(1)-(10)	100(1)-(10)	100(1)-(10)
92(11)	92(11)	100(10a)	-
92(12),(13)	92(12),(13)	100(11),(12)	100(11),(12)
92(14)	92(14)	100(13)	100(13)
92(15)-(22)	92(15)-(22)	100(14)-(21)	100(14)-(21)
93(1)	93(1)	101(1)	100a
93(2)	93(2)	101(2)	-
94(1)	94(1)	102(1)	100b

CONCORDANCE

1994	1990	1980	1974
94(2),(3)	94(2),(3)	102(2),(3)	-
95(1)-(8)	95(1)-(8)	103(1)-(8)	101(1)-(8)
-	-	103(9)	101(9)
95(9)	95(9)	103(10)	101(10)
96	96	104	102
97(1)-(4)	97(1)-(4)	105(1)-(4)	103(1)-(3)
97(5),(6)	97(5),(6)	105(4a),(4b)	-
97(7)	97(7)	105(5)	103(4)
98	98	106	103a
-	-	107	104
-	-	108	105
99	99	109	106
100(1)-(3)	100(1)-(3)	110(1)-(3)	107(1)-(3)
-	-	110(4)-(8)	107(4)-(8)
100(4)	100(4)	110(9)	107(9)
101	101	110a	-
102(1)-(4)	102(1)-(4)	111(1)-(4)	108
102(5)	102(5)	111(5)	-
103(1),(2)	103(1),(2)	112(1),(2)	109(1),(2)
103(3)	103(3)	112(2a)	-
-	-	112(3)	109(3)
103(4)	103(4)	112(4)	109(4)
-	-	113	110
-	-	114	111
104(1),(2)	104(1),(2)	115(1),(2)	112(1),(2)
-	-	115(3)	112(3)
104(3)	104(3)	115(4)	112(4)
-	-	116	113
-	-	117	114
-	-	118(1)	115(1)
105	105	118(2)	115(2)
106(1),(2)	106(1),(2)	119(1),(2)	116(1),(2)
106(3)	106(3)	119(2a)	-
106(4)-(8)	106(4)-(8)	119(3)-(7)	116(3)-(7)
107	107	120	117
-	-	121	118
108	108	122	119
108(Form 1)	108(Form 1)	122(Form 1)	-
109	109	123	120
110	110	124	121
111	111	125	122
112(1)	112(1)	126(1)	123(1)
112(2),(3)	112(2),(3)	126(1a),(1b)	-
112(4)-(7)	112(4)-(7)	126(2)-(5)	123(2)-(5)

CONCORDANCE

1994	1990	1980	1974
112(7.1)-(7.2)	-	-	-
112(8)	112(8)	126(6)	123(6)
112(9)	112(9)	126(6a)	-
112(10)	112(10)	126(7)	-
-	-	126(8)	-
112(11)	112(11)	126(9)	-
113(1)-(8)	113(1)-(8)	126a(1)-(8)	-
113(8.1)	113(8.1)	-	-
113(9)	113(9)	126a(9)	-
113(9.1) [In force December 1, 1995]	-	-	-
113(10)	113(10)	126a(10)	-
114	114	127	124
115	115	128	125
116	116	129	126
117(1)-(5)	117(1)-(5)	130(1)-(5)	127(1)-(5)
117(6)-(9)	117(6)-(9)	130(5a)-(5d)	-
117(10)-(13)	117(10)-(13)	130(6)-(9)	127(6)-(9)
117(14)	117(14)	130(10)	-
118	118	131	128
119	119	132	129
120	120	133	130
121	121	134	131
122	122	135	132
123	123	136	133
124	124	136a	-
125	125	136b	-
126	126	136c	-
127	127	136d	-
128	128	136e	-
-	-	136f	-
129	129	136g	-
130	130	136h	-
131(1)	131(1)	136i(1)	-
131(2),(3)	131(2),(3)	136i(1a),(1b)	-
-	-	136i(2)	-
131(4)	131(4)	136i(3)	-
-	132	136j(1),(2)	-
-	-	136j(3)	-
-	133	136k(1),(2)	-
-	-	136k(3)	-
134(1)-(9)	134(1)-(9)	136ka(1)-(9)	-
134(9.1)-(9.3)	-	-	-
134(10)-(15)	134(10)-(15)	136ka(10)-(15)	-

CONCORDANCE

1994	1990	1980	1974
135(1)-(20)	135(1)-(20)	136l(1)-(20)	136l(1)-(20)
135(21)-(26)	135(21)-(26)	136l(21a)-(26f)	136¶(20a)-(20f)
135(26.1)	-	-	-
135(27)	135(27)	136l(20g)	-
135(28)-(30)	135(28)-(30)	136l(21)-(23)	-
136	136	136la	-
137	137	136m	-
138	138	136ma	-
139	139	136mb	-
140	140	136mc	-
141	141	136md	-
142	142	136me	-
143	143	136n	-
144	144	136o	-
145	145	136p	-
146	146	136q	-
*147	147	136r	-
*148	148	136s	-
*149	149	136t	-
*150	150	136u	-
*151	151	136v	-
*152	152	136w	-
*153	153	136x	-
154	154	-	-
155	155	136xa	-
156	156	136xb	-
157	157	136y	-
158	158	137	134
159	159	138	135
160	160	139	136
161	161	140	137
162	162	141	138
163	163	142	139
164	164	143	140
165	165	144	141
166	166	145	142
167	167	146	143
168	168	147	144
169	169	148	145
170(1)¶1-6	170¶1-6	149¶1-6	146
170(1)¶6.1-6.2	-	-	-

* Sections 147 to 153 are to be repealed on July 1, 1995. See R.S.O. 1990, c. E.2, s. 154.

CONCORDANCE

1994	1990	1980	1974
170(1)¶7-12	170¶7-12	149¶7-12	146
170(1)¶12.1	-	-	-
170(1)¶13-17	170¶13-17	149¶13-17	146
170(1)¶18	170¶18	149¶18	-
170(2)	-	-	-
170(3) [To be repealed September 1, 1997]	-	-	-
171(1)¶1	171(1)¶1	150(1)¶1	147(1)¶1
171(1)¶2	171(1)¶2	150(1)¶1a	-
171(1)¶3-14	171(1)¶3-14	150(1)¶2-13	147(1)¶2-13
171(1)¶15 [To be repealed September 1, 1997]	171(1)¶15	150(1)¶14	147(1)¶14
171(1)¶16-20	171(1)¶16-20	150(1)¶15-19	147(1)¶15-19
171(1)¶21	171(1)¶21	150(1)¶19a	-
171(1)¶22	171(1)¶22	150(1)¶20	147(1)¶20-45
171(1)¶23	171(1)¶23	150(1)¶21	-
171(1)¶24-30	171(1)¶24-30	150(1)¶22-28	-
171(1)¶31	171(1)¶31	150(1)¶29	-
171(1)¶31.1	-	-	-
171(1)¶32-39	171(1)¶32-39	150(1)¶30-37	-
171(1)¶40, pt	171(1)¶40, pt	150(1)¶38	-
171(1)¶41	171(1)¶41	150(1)¶39	-
171(1)¶40, pt	171(1)¶40, pt	150(1)¶40	-
171(1)¶42-46	171(1)¶42-46	150(1)¶41-45	-
171(1)¶47	171(1)¶47	150(1)¶46	-
171(1)¶48-49	-	-	-
171¶50	-	-	-
171(2)	171(2)	150(2)	147(2)
171(3)	-	-	-
171(4)-(5)	-	-	-
171.1	-	-	-
172	172	150a	-
173	173	151	148
174	174	152	149
175	175	153	150
176	176	154	151
177	177	155	152
178	178	156(1)-(5)	153(1)-(5)
-	-	156(6)	153(6)
179(1)-(4)	179(1)-(4)	157(1)-(4)	154(1)-(4)
-	-	157(5)	154(5)
-	180(1)	158(1)	155(1)

xv

CONCORDANCE

1994	1990	1980	1974
-	180(2)	158(1a)	-
-	180(3)	158(1b)	-
180(4)-(7)	180(4)-(7)	158(2)-(5)	155(2)-(5)
180(8) [Repealed]	180(8)	158(6)	155(6)
180(9) [Repealed]	180(9)	158(7)	155(7)
180(10)	180(10)	158(8)	155(8)
-	-	158(9)	155(9)
181	181	159	156
182	182	159a	-
183	183	160	157
184	184	161	158
185	185	162	159
186	186	163	160
187	187	164	161
188(1)	188(1)	165(1)	162(1)
188(2)	188(2)	165(1a)	-
188(3)-(7)	188(3)-(7)	165(2)-(6)	163(2)-(6)
188(8)	188(8)	165(6a)	-
188(9)-(11)	188(9)-(11)	165(7)-(9)	163(7)-(9)
188(12),(13)	188(12),(13)	165(10),(11)	-
189	189	165a	-
190(1)	190(1)	166(1)	163(1)
190(2)	190(2)	166(1a)	-
190(3)-(14)	190(3)-(14)	166(2)-(13)	163(2)-(13)
191(1),(2)	191(1),(2)	167(1),(2)	164(1),(2)
-	-	167(1a)-(1c)	-
191(3)	191(3)	167(2a)	-
191(4)	191(4)	167(2b)	-
191(5)-(9)	191(5)-(9)	167(2c)-(2g)	-
191(10)-(13)	191(10)-(13)	167(3)-(6)	164(3)-(6)
192	192	168	165
193	193	169	166
194	194	170	167
195(1),(2)	195(1),(2)	171(1),(2)	168(1),(2)
-	-	171(3),(5)	168(3),(5)
195(3)	195(3)	171(4)	168(4)
195(4)-(6)	195(4)-(6)	171(6)-(8)	168(6)-(8)
196	196	172	169
197(1)	197(1)	173(1)	170(1)
197(2)	197(2)	173(1a)	-
197(3)	197(3)	173(1b)	-
197(4)	197(4)	173(1c)	-
197(5)-(6)	197(5)-(6)	173(2),(3)	170(2),(3)
197(7)-(10)	197(7)-(10)	173(4)-(7)	170(4)-(7)

xvi

CONCORDANCE

1994	1990	1980	1974
198	198	174	171
199	199	175	172
200	200	176	173
201	201	177	174
202	202	178	175
203	203	179	176
204	204	180	177
205	205	181	178
206(1)-(6)	206(1)-(6)	182(1)-(6)	178a(1)-(6)
206(7) [Repealed]	206(7)	182(7)	178a(7)
206(8)-(11)	206(8)-(11)	182(8)-(11)	178a(8)-(11)
207(1)	207(1)	183(1)	179(1)
207(2)	207(2)	183(1a)	-
207(3),(4)	207(3),(4)	183(2),(3)	179(2),(3)
208	208	184	180
209	209	185	181
210	210	186	182
211	211	187	183
212	212	188	184
213	213	189	185
214	214	190	186
215	215	191	187
216	216	192	188
217	217	193	189
218	218	194	190
219	219	195	191
220(1)	220(1)	196(1)	192(1)
220(2)	220(2)	196(1a)	-
220(3)-(6)	220(3)-(6)	196(2)-(5)	192(2)-(5)
-	-	-	192(6)
221	221	197	193
222	222	198	194
223	223	199	195
224	224	200	196
-	-	201	197
225	225	202	198
226	226	203	199
227(1)	227(1)	204(1)	200
227(2)	227(2)	204(2)	-
228	228	205	201
229	229	206	202
230(1)-(4)	230(1)-(4)	206a(1)-(4)	-
230(5),(6)	230(5),(6)	206a(4a),(4b)	-
230(7)-(11)	230(7)-(11)	206a(5)-(9)	-

CONCORDANCE

1994	1990	1980	1974
230(12),(13)	230(12),(13)	206a(9a),(9b)	-
230(14)	230(14)	206a(10)	-
230(14.1-14.4)	-	-	-
230(15)-(28)	230(15)-(28)	206a(11)-(24)	-
231	231	206b	-
232	232	206c	-
233	233	206d	-
234	234	207(1)-(9)	203(2)-(10)
235(1)-(2)	235(1)-(2)	208(1)-(2)	204(1)-(2)
235(2.1)	-	-	-
235(3)-(6)	235(3)-(6)	208(3)-(6)	204(3)-(6)
235.1	-	-	-
235.2	-	-	-
235.3	-	-	-
236(1)-(2)	236(1)-(2)	209(1)-(2)	205(1)-(2)
236(3) [Repealed]	236(3)	209(3)	205(3)
236(4)-(10)	236(4)-(10)	209(4)-(10)	205(4)-(10)
236(11) [Repealed]	236(11)	209(11)	205(11)
236(12)-(13)	236(12)-(13)	209(12)-(13)	205(12)-(13)
237	237	210	205a
238	238	211	205b
239	239	212	205c
-	-	213(1)-(8)	206(1)-(8)
-	-	213(9)	206(8a)
-	-	213(10),(11)	206(9),(10)
-	-	213(12),(13)	206(11),(12)
240(1)-(5)	240(1)-(5)	214(1)-(5)	207
240(6)	240(6)	214(6)	-
-	-	214(7)	-
240(7)-(16)	240(7)-(16)	214(8)-(17)	-
241	241	214a	-
242(1)-(4)	242(1)-(4)	214b(1)-(4)	-
243(1)-(8)	243(1)-(8)	215(1)-(8)	208(1)-(8)
243(9)-(11)	243(9)-(11)	215(9)-(11)	-
244	244	216	209
245(1)-(6)	245(1)-(6)	217	210
245(7)-(8)	-	-	-
246	246	218	211
247	247	219	212(1)-(3)
-	-	-	212(4)
248	248	220	213
249	249	221	214
250(1)-(3)	250(1)-(3)	222(1)-(3)	215
250(4)	250(4)	222(4)	-

CONCORDANCE

1994	1990	1980	1974
251	251	223	216
252	252	224	217
253	253	225	218
254	254	226	219
255	255	227	220
256	256	228(1)-(7)	221(1)-(7)
-	-	-	221(8)
257	257	229	222
-	-	-	223
258	258	230	224
259	259	230a	-
260(1)	260(1)	231(1)	225(1)
260(2)	260(2)	231(1a)	-
260(3)-(8)	260(3)-(8)	231(2)-(7)	225(2)-(7)
261	261	232	226
262	262	233	227
263	263	234	228
264(1)	264(1)	235(1)	229(1)
264(1.1)	-	-	-
264(2)-(3)	264(2)-(3)	235(2)-(3)	229(2)-(3)
265	265	236	230
266(1)-(2)	266(1)-(2)	237(1)-(2)	231(1)-(2)
266(2.1)	-	-	-
266(3)-(13)	266(3)-(13)	237(3)-(13)	231(3)-(13)
267	267	238	232
268	268	239	233
269	269	240	234
270	270	241	235
271	271	242	236
272	272	243	237
273	273	244	238
274	274	245	239
275	275	246	240
276	276	247	241
277	277	248	242
278	278	249	243
279	279	250	244
280	280	251	245
281(1) [Repealed]	281(1)	252(1)	246
281(2),(3)	281(2),(3)	252(2),(3)	-
282(1)	282(1)	252a(1)	-
282(2)	282(2)	252a(2)	-
283(1),(2)	283(1),(2)	253(1),(2)	247
283(3)	283(3)	253(3)	-

CONCORDANCE

1994	1990	1980	1974
284(1)	284	254	248
284(2)	-	-	-
284.1	-	-	-
285(1)(a)	285(1)(a)	255(1)(a)	249(1)(a)
-	285(1)(b)	255(1)(b)	249(1)(b)
285(1)(b)	285(1)(c)	255(1)(c)	249(1)(c)
286	286	256	250
287	287	257	251
288	288	257a	-
-	-	258(1)	252(1)
289(1)-(5)	289(1)-(5)	258(2)-(6)	252(2)-(6)
289(6)	289(6)	258(6a)	-
289(7),(8)	289(7),(8)	258(7),(8)	252(7),(8)
290	290	259	259
-	-	260	254
291	291	261(1)-(3)	255(1)-(3)
-	-	261(4),(5)	255(4),(5)
292(1)	292(1)	262(1)	256(1)
292(2)	292(2)	262(1a)	
-	-	262(1b)	-
292(3)-(6)	292(3)-(6)	262(1c)-(1f)	-
292(7),(8)	292(7),(8)	262(2),(3)	256(2),(3)
-	-	262(3a)	-
292(9)-(13)	292(9)-(13)	262(4)-(8)	256(4)-(8)
292(14),(15)	292(14),(15)	262(9),(10)	-
293(1)	293(1)	263(1)	257
293(2)	293(2)	263(2)	-
294	294	264	258
295	295	265	259
296	296	266	260
297	297	267	261
298(1)	298(1)	268(1)	262(1)
298(2)-(5)	298(2)-(5)	268(1a)-(1d)	-
298(6)-(8)	298(6)-(8)	268(2)-(4)	262(2)-(4)
298(9)-(11)	298(9)-(11)	268(5)-(7)	-
299(1)-(2)	299(1)-(2)	269(1)-(2)	263(1)-(2)
299(2.1)	-	-	-
299(3)	299(3)	269(3)	263(3)
300	300	270	264
-	-	271	265
301(1),(2)	301(1),(2)	272(1),(2)	266(1),(2)
301(3),(4)	301(3),(4)	272(3),(4)	-
-	-	272(5)	-
302	302	273	267

CONCORDANCE

1994	1990	1980	1974
303	303	274	268
304(1)-(7)	304(1)-(7)	275(1)-(7)	269(1)-(7)
304(7.1)	-	-	-
304(8)-(15)	304(8)-(15)	275(8)-(15)	269(8)-(15)
305	305	276	270
306(1),(2)	306(1),(2)	277(1),(2)	271
306(3)-(5)	306(3)-(5)	277(3)-(5)	-
307	307	277a	-
308	308	277b	-
309(1)	309(1)	277c(1)	-
309(2)-(3)	-	-	-
310	310	277ca	-
311(1)-(4)	311(1)-(4)	277d(1)-(4)	-
-	-	277d(5)	-
311(5)	311(5)	277d(6)	-
312	312	277e	-
-	-	277f	-
313	313	277g	-
314	314	277h	-
315(1),(2)	315(1),(2)	277i(1),(2)	
-	-	277i(3)	-
315(3)-(9)	315(3)-(9)	277(4)-(10)	-
-	-	277i(11)	-
315(10)-(12)	315(10)-(12)	277i(12)-(14)	-
315.1	-	-	-
316	316	277j	-
317	317	277k	-
-	-	277l	-
318	318	277m	-
319(1)	319(1)	277n(1)	-
-	-	277n(2)	-
319(2)-(5)	319(2)-(5)	277n(3)-(6)	-
320	320	277o	-
321(1)	321(1)	277p(1)	-
321(2)	321(2)	277p(2)	-
322	322	277q(1)-(6)	-
-	-	277q(7)-(10)	-
323	323	277r	-
324(1)-(3)	324(1)-(3)	277s(1)-(3)	-
324(4)	324(4)	277s(3a)	-
324(5)	324(5)	277s(4)	-
325(1)(a)-(c)	325(1)(a)-(c)	277t(1)(a)-(c)	-
325(1)(c.1)	-	-	-
325(2)(a)-(c)	325(2)(a)-(c)	277t(2)(a)-(c)	-

CONCORDANCE

1994	1990	1980	1974
325(2)(c.1)	-	-	-
325(3)	325(3)	277t(3)	-
325.1	-	-	-
326	326	277u	-
-	-	277(v-za)	-
-	-	278(1)-(2)	-
-	-	278(3), pt	-
-	236(11)	278(3), pt	-

EDUCATION ACT

TABLE OF CONTENTS

DEFINITIONS

1.	**(1)**	Definitions	37
	(2)	Authority or obligation of parent vested in pupil of 18 years of age	43
	(3)	Questions re proceeding as to formation of school section	43
	(4)	Effect on separate schools	43
	(5)	Existing school arrangements continued	43
	(6)	Deemed adjustment of boundaries	43

PART I

MINISTRY OF EDUCATION

2.	**(1)**	Ministry continued	44
	(2)	Minister to have charge	44
	(3)	Administration	44
	(4)	Delegation of powers and duties	44
	(5)	Limitations	44
	(6)	Application of *Executive Council Act*, s. 6	44
3.		Annual report	44
4.		Additions to enrolment in special cases	44
5.	**(1)**	Closing of school or class	44
	(2)	Pupils deemed in attendance	44
6.	**(1)**	Guarantee of debentures	44
	(2)	Form of guarantee	44
	(3)	Validity of guaranteed debentures	45
7.		Fixing rate of interest on debentures, etc., held by Treasurer	45
8.	**(1)**	Powers of Minister	45
	(2)	Additional powers of Minister	49
	(3)	Identification programs and special education programs and services	49
	(4)	Application	49
9.		Accounting statement related to assistance by Ministry	49
10.		Powers of Minister	49
11.	**(1)**	Regulations	49
	(2)	[Repealed]	52
	(3)	Regulations, grants	52
	(4)	Idem	53
	(5)	Application to previous year	53
	(6)	Estimates and expenditures	53
	(7)	School year, terms and holidays	53

	(8)	Exceptions: compulsory attendance	53
	(9)	Regulations	54
	(10)	Metropolitan Toronto School Board	54
	(11)	Regulations	54
	(12)	Consistency with *Municipal Elections Act*	55
	(13)	French-language school boards	55
	(14)	Idem	55
	(15)	Idem	55
	(15.1)	Ottawa-Carleton French-language School Boards	56
	(16)	Consultation before regulation under subs. (13)	56
	(17)	[Repealed]	56
	(18)	Metropolitan Toronto School Board	56
12.	(1)	Agreements with Canada re: physical fitness	56
	(2)	Pupils at Indian schools	56
	(3)	Non-Indian pupils at Indian schools	56
	(4)	Bursaries and scholarships	56
	(5)	Learning materials	57
13.	(1)	Continuation of school for deaf	57
	(2)	Continuation of school for blind	57
	(3)	Administration	57
	(4)	Additional schools	57
	(4.1)	Idem	57
	(5)	Demonstration schools	57
	(6)	Idem	57
	(7)	Regulations	57
14.	(1)	Teacher education	58
	(2)	Practice teaching	58
	(3)	Idem	58
	(4)	Idem	58
15.		Leadership training camps	58
16.	(1)	Intention to operate private school	58
	(2)	Idem	58
	(3)	Idem	58
	(4)	Offence to operate private school without filing notice of intent to operate	59
	(5)	Return	59
	(6)	Inspection of school	59
	(7)	Inspection on request	59
	(8)	Inspection of teachers	59
	(9)	Offence for false statement	59
17.	(1)	Variation of scholarships and awards	59
	(2)	Where award is repayable loan	60
17.1	(1)	Ontario Parent Council	60
	(2)	Eligibility for appointment	60
	(3)	Eligibility criteria established by Minister	60

TABLE OF CONTENTS

(4)	Non-application of *Regulations Act*		60
(5)	Term of office		60
(6)	Same		60
(7)	Chair		60
(8)	Remuneration and expenses		60
(9)	Staff and accommodation		60
(10)	Mandate		60
(11)	Annual report		60
(12)	Additional reports		60

PART II

SCHOOL ATTENDANCE

18.		Definition	61
19.		Closing of school or class by board	61
20.		Closing of schools on civic holiday	61
21.	(1)	Compulsory attendance	61
	(2)	When attendance excused	61
	(3)	Blind, deaf or mentally handicapped children	62
	(4)	Child under compulsory age	62
	(5)	Duty of parent, etc.	62
	(6)	Separate school supporters	62
22.		Where school year varied	62
23.	(1)	Suspension of pupil	62
	(1.1)	Period of suspension	62
	(1.2)	Notice	62
	(2)	Appeal against suspension	62
	(2.1)	Effect of appeal	62
	(2.2)	Review of suspensions	63
	(3)	Expulsion of pupil	63
	(4)	Parties to hearing	63
	(5)	Readmission of pupil	63
	(6)	Committee to perform board functions	63
24.	(1)	Provincial School Attendance Counsellor	63
	(2)	Inquiry by Provincial Counsellor	63
	(3)	Powers of Provincial Counsellor	64
25.	(1)	Appointment of school attendance counsellors	64
	(2)	Idem	64
	(3)	Vacancies	64
	(4)	Notice of appointment	64
	(5)	Jurisdiction and responsibility of school attendance counsellor	64
26.	(1)	Powers of counsellors	64
	(2)	Reports	64

	(3)	To act under appropriate supervisory officer and provincial counsellor	64
	(4)	Inquiry by counsellor and notice	64
27.		Census	65
28.	(1)	Reports and information	65
	(2)	Where no school attendance counsellor	65
29.		Provincial counsellor as trustee	65
30.	(1)	Liability of parent or guardian	65
	(2)	Bond for attendance	65
	(3)	Employment during school hours	65
	(4)	Offences by corporations	65
	(5)	Habitually absent from school	66
	(6)	Proceedings under subs. (5)	66
	(7)	Reference to provincial counsellor for inquiry	66
31.	(1)	Proceedings to be taken by attendance counsellors	66
	(2)	Certificate of principal as proof in the absence of evidence to the contrary	66
	(3)	Proof of age	66
	(4)	Order re school attendance	66
32.	(1)	Resident pupil right to attend school	66
	(2)	Admission without fee	66
33.	(1)	Resident pupil public school qualification	66
	(2)	Resident pupil separate school qualification	67
	(3)	Evidence as to right to attend	67
	(4)	Resident pupil, elementary	67
	(5)	[Repealed]	67
	(6)	[Repealed]	67
34.	(1)	Kindergarten	67
	(2)	Junior kindergarten	68
	(2.1)	Same	68
	(2.2)	Same	68
	(3)	Beginners class	68
35.		[Repealed]	68
36.	(1)	Establishment of Special Education Tribunal	68
	(2)	Procedures of Special Education Tribunals	68
37.	(1)	Leave to appeal	68
	(2)	Establishment of regional tribunal	68
	(3)	Hearing by Special Education Tribunal	68
	(4)	Regulations	68
	(5)	Decision final	69
	(6)	Disposition	69
38.		Admission where pupil moves into residence not assessed in accordance with his or her school support	69
39.		Resident pupil's right to attend more accessible school in adjoining school section or separate school zone	69
40.	(1)	Resident pupil secondary school qualification	69
	(2)	Resident pupil, secondary	70

TABLE OF CONTENTS

	(3)	[Repealed]	70
	(4)	Admission of adult resident who is not a resident pupil	70
	(5)	Limitation on right to attend without payment of fee	70
41.	(1)	Resident pupil	70
	(2)	Restrictions	71
	(3)	Where agreement between boards	71
42.	(1)	Admission of resident pupil from other district	71
	(2)	Notice of admission	71
43.	(1)	Admission to secondary school	71
	(2)	Idem	71
	(3)	Where admission denied	71
	(4)	Alternative course or program	72
	(5)	Admission to continuing education class	72
44.		Admission where one parent is sole support	72
45.	(1)	Tax exempt land	72
	(2)	Resident on land exempt from taxation	72
46.	(1)	Admission of ward, etc., of children's aid society or training school to an elementary school	72
	(2)	Admission of ward, etc., of children's aid society or training school to a secondary school	73
47.		Where fee payable	73
48.	(1)	[Repealed]	73
	(2)	Idem	73
	(3)	Agreement re transportation	73
49.	(1)	Fees payable	73
	(2)	Idem	73
	(3)	Idem	73
	(4)	Admission of resident pupil to another school by reason of distance to school	73
	(5)	Admission of qualified non-resident pupil	74
	(6)	Fees for pupils	74
	(7)	Application of subs. (6)	74
49.1		Persons unlawfully in Canada	74

PART III

PUBLIC AND SECONDARY SCHOOLS

Tax Exemption of Separate School Supporters

| 50. | | Exemption of supporters of separate schools | 75 |

Religious Instruction

| 51. | (1) | Religious instruction | 75 |
| | (2) | Religious exercises | 75 |

Visitors

52.		Visitors	75

Divisional Boards

53.	(1)	Application to schools on exempt land	75
	(2)	Essex county	75
	(3)	Territory without municipal organization deemed district municipality	75
54.	(1)	Powers and duties of divisional board re territory without municipal organization	76
	(2)	Parts of territory without municipal organization attached to municipality	76
	(3)	Application of *Municipal Act*, s. 363	76
	(4)	Estimates to include expenses of collection, etc., and allowances to be made	77
	(5)	Where attached territory not included with municipality for election	77
	(6)	Elections in improvement districts	77
55.	(1)	School divisions, formation and alteration	77
	(2)	Adjustment of assets and liabilities on formation	78
	(3)	Dissolution of board	78
	(4)	Name of board: defined city	78
	(5)	County	78
	(6)	Regional municipality and counties	78
	(7)	Territorial districts	79
	(8)	Bilingual	79
56.	(1)	Divisional boards establishment	79
	(2)	Deemed public school section and secondary school district	79
	(3)	Powers and duties	79
	(4)	Members to be trustees	79
57.	(1)	Alteration of boundaries: disposition of assets and liabilities	79
	(2)	Dispute	80
	(3)	Employment contracts	80

Boards of Education

58.	(1)	Definition	80
	(2)	Establishment and status of board	80
	(3)	Name of board	80
	(4)	Idem	80
	(5)	Members to be trustees	80
	(6)	Assets, liabilities, etc.	80

District School Area Boards

59.	(1)	School section to be district school area	80
	(2)	Formation and alteration of district school area	80
	(3)	Notification of assessment commissioner	81

TABLE OF CONTENTS

	(4)	Arbitration	81
	(5)	Name of board	81
60.	(1)	New district school areas	81
	(2)	Alteration and formation: disposition of assets and liabilities	81
61.	(1)	Definition	81
	(2)	Composition of board	81
	(3)	Idem	82
	(4)	Increase in number of members	82
	(5)	Election year end term of office	82
	(6)	Term of office	82

Elections and Meetings of Electors

62.	(1)	Election date	82
	(2)	Notice of meeting	82
	(3)	Meeting	82
	(4)	First meeting	83
	(5)	Minutes to be sent to Ministry	83
	(6)	Special meetings	83
	(7)	Declaration where right to vote objected to	83
	(8)	Election procedures	83
63.	(1)	Elections	83
	(2)	Idem	83
	(3)	Idem	83
64.	(1)	Elections	84
	(2)	Validity of election	84
65.	(1)	Powers and duties	84
	(2)	Auditors and financial matters	84
	(3)	Rates in municipality	84
	(4)	Debentures	84
	(5)	Collection of taxes	84
	(6)	Tax sales officer	85
	(7)	Rates for first year to be levied on current assessment	85
66.	(1)	District school area board to be inactive	85
	(2)	Accounts in inactive area	85
	(3)	Board dissolved	85
	(4)	Records to be forwarded to Ministry	85
	(5)	Closing of school by Minister	85

Secondary Schools Outside School Divisions in Territorial Districts

67.	(1)	In territorial districts	85
	(2)	Board in territorial districts outside school divisions	85
	(3)	Powers and duties	86
	(4)	Auditors and estimates	86
	(5)	Rates in municipality	86

	(6)	Collection of taxes	86
	(7)	Board of education	86

Boards on Tax Exempt Land

68.	**(1)**	Public school on Crown lands	86
	(2)	Secondary school on exempt land	86
	(3)	Board of education on exempt land	86
	(4)	Section not to be included in district school area or school division	87
	(5)	Fee payable by non-resident	87
	(6)	Revocation of order	87
69.		[Repealed]	87
70.		[Repealed]	87
71.		[Repealed]	87
72.		[Repealed]	87
73.		[Repealed]	87
74.		[Repealed]	87
75.		[Repealed]	87
76.		[Repealed]	87

PART IV

ROMAN CATHOLIC SEPARATE SCHOOLS

77.	Application of Part	87

Zones

78.	**(1)**	Boundaries of zones	87
	(2)	Zones not in municipalities or geographic townships	88
	(3)	Zone description	88
	(4)	Deemed inclusion to zones	88
79.		Rates in unorganized territory in combined zone	88

Formation and Discontinuance of Zones

80.	**(1)**	Meeting to establish a separate school zone	88
	(2)	Procedure	88
	(3)	Certification	89
	(4)	Notification	89
	(5)	Corporate name	89
	(6)	Formation not rendered invalid by reason only of vacancy in office of trustee	89
	(7)	Roman Catholic deemed separate school elector	89
81.	**(1)**	Powers of trustees	89
	(2)	Where school not united	89
82.		Right to vote in year of establishment of zone	89

TABLE OF CONTENTS

83.		Legislative grants	89
84.	(1)	Formation of combined separate school zones in non-designated areas	90
	(2)	Adjustment of rights	90
	(3)	Dissolution of boards	90
	(4)	Corporate name of trustees	90
85.	(1)	Detaching school zone from combined school zone	90
	(2)	Qualified voters detaching a separate school zone	90
	(3)	When school zone detached	90
86.	(1)	Discontinuing board by a vote of the supporters	90
	(2)	Other conditions under which a separate school board is discontinued	91
	(3)	Notification of Minister, etc., when board discontinued	91
	(4)	Settling accounts	91
	(5)	Records	91
	(6)	Boundaries to be revised	91
	(7)	Sale of real property	91
	(8)	Deposit of funds from sale	91
	(9)	Re-establishing a board	91

Separate School Electors

87.		Residents other than supporters entitled to vote	92
88.		Where person residing out of urban municipality to vote	92

Rural Separate Schools

89.	(1)	Trustees term of office	92
	(2)	Term of office	92
	(3)	Idem	92
	(4)	Organization and quorum	92
	(5)	Regularity	92
	(6)	Electors, qualifications	92
	(7)	Idem	93
90.	(1)	Duties of rural boards	93
	(2)	Appointment of auditor by the Minister	93
	(3)	Approval of new school site	93
91.	(1)	Appointment of collector	93
	(2)	Powers and duties of collectors	93
92.	(1)	Annual meeting	93
	(2)	Election of board	94
	(3)	Idem	94
	(4)	Organization of meeting	94
	(5)	Order of business	94
	(6)	Duties of presiding officer	94
	(7)	Granting poll and proceedings in case of a poll	94
	(8)	Entries in poll book	94
	(9)	Form of ballot paper	94

EDUCATION ACT

	(10)	Marking of ballot paper	94
	(11)	Number of votes	95
	(12)	Manner of voting	95
	(13)	Appointment of scrutineer	95
	(14)	Declaration where right to vote objected to	95
	(15)	When poll shall close	95
	(16)	Polling at afternoon meetings	95
	(17)	Counting votes, tie vote	95
	(18)	Declaration of result	95
	(19)	Statement of result of poll	96
	(20)	Secretary to transmit minutes to Ministry	96
	(21)	Meetings called in default of first or annual meeting	96
	(22)	Validity of election	96
93.	(1)	Where municipality may conduct election	96
	(2)	Application of *Municipal Elections Act*	96

Separate Schools — General

94.	(1)	Secretary of board as returning officer	96
	(2)	Reporting of vote	97
	(3)	Reporting if no municipality	97

Combined Separate School Zones

95.	(1)	Trustees	97
	(2)	Trustee in office until organization of new board	97
	(3)	First trustees	97
	(4)	Trustees in combined separate school zone including urban municipality	97
	(5)	Resolution providing for trustees	97
	(6)	Election and term of office	98
	(7)	Voters list for areas in combined zone	98
	(8)	Copy of resolution to be sent to Minister	98
	(9)	Electors' qualifications, rural combined separate school zone	98

Duties and Powers of Separate School Boards

96.	(1)	Duties of board	98
	(2)	Religious education	98

County and District Combined Roman Catholic Separate School Zones

97.	(1)	Separate school zones	99
	(2)	Regulations	99
	(3)	Dissolution of board	99
	(4)	Establishment of boards	99
	(5)	Idem	99
	(6)	Idem	99
	(7)	Separate school zones	99

10

TABLE OF CONTENTS

98.	(1)	Designation of a combined separate school board as a district combined separate school board	99
	(2)	Regulation	100
99.	(1)	Arbitration where boundaries of designated areas are altered	100
	(2)	Appointment of additional arbitrator	100
	(3)	Referral to judge	100
100.	(1)	Alteration of boundaries: disposition of assets and liabilities	100
	(2)	Dispute	101
	(3)	Employment contracts	101
	(4)	Area added to Scarborough to be under Metropolitan Separate School Board	101
101.		School to remain school of board	101
102.	(1)	Name of board in one county	101
	(2)	Name of county combined board	101
	(3)	Name of board in territorial districts	101
	(4)	Name of board in regional municipality	101
	(5)	Bilingual	101
103.	(1)	Deemed district municipalities	102
	(2)	Powers and duties of combined board re territory without municipal organization	102
	(3)	Application of *Municipal Act*, s. 363	102
	(4)	Election in improvement district	102
104.	(1)	Number of votes to be cast	102
	(2)	Retiring trustees eligible for re-election	102
	(3)	Person not to be candidate for more than one seat on board	102
105.		Application of ss. 234, 235	103

Rates, Borrowing Powers and Grants

106.	(1)	Exemption of supporters from public school rates	103
	(2)	No renewal required	103
	(3)	Exemption from public school rates for other separate school supporters	103
	(4)	Who may be supporters of separate schools	103
	(5)	Rights of non-residents to be assessed for separate school	103
	(6)	Certificate of notice	103
	(7)	Penalty for wilful false statements in notice	103
	(8)	As to rates imposed before separate school established	103
107.	(1)	Notice of withdrawal of support	103
	(2)	Exception	104
108.	(1)	Clerk to keep index book	104
	(2)	Entries	104
	(3)	Inspection	104
	(4)	Filings	104
	(5)	Clerk to be guided by index book	104
109.	(1)	Correction of mistakes in assessing	105
	(2)	Liability	105

110.	(1)	Distinguishing the school rates	105
	(2)	Idem	105
111.	(1)	Case of owner and occupant	105
	(2)	When owner may exercise option	105
112.	(1)	Definition	105
	(2)	Application	105
	(3)	Right of corporation to support separate schools	105
	(4)	Copy of notice to clerk	105
	(5)	Duty of assessment commissioner	105
	(6)	Duty of clerk	106
	(7)	Proportion of assessment	106
	(7.1)	Application	106
	(7.2)	Transition	106
	(8)	Effect of notice	106
	(9)	Idem	106
	(10)	Filing notice	106
	(11)	Secondary school purposes	106
113.	(1)	Definitions	106
	(2)	Interpretation	108
	(3)	Assessment of designated ratepayer for separate school purposes [To be repealed December 1, 1995]	108
	(3)	Assessment of designated ratepayer [In force December 1, 1995]	108
	(4)	Idem [To be repealed December 1, 1995]	108
	(4)	Same [In force December 1, 1995]	108
	(4.1)	Same [In force December 1, 1995]	108
	(5)	Duty of assessment commissioner [To be repealed December 1, 1995]	108
	(5)	Duty of assessment commissioner [In force December 1, 1995]	109
	(6)	Supplementary or omitted assessments	109
	(7)	Regulations	109
	(8)	Idem	109
	(8.1)	Exemption from taxation	109
	(9)	Idem [To be repealed December 1, 1995]	109
	(9)	Same [In force December 1, 1995]	109
	(9.1)	Same [In force December 1, 1995]	109
	(10)	Same	109
114.	(1)	Estimates	110
	(2)	Where cost of separate levy payable by board	110
	(3)	Application of *Municipal Act*	110
115.	(1)	Powers of trustees	110
	(2)	Land on which there are rates uncollected	110
	(3)	Return	110
	(4)	Collection of rates	110
	(5)	Deficiency	110
116.		Levy for costs for transportation and board and lodging of secondary school pupils not resident in secondary school district	110

TABLE OF CONTENTS

117.	**(1)**	Determining school rates by equalizing factor	111
	(2)	Adoption of rate	111
	(3)	Arbitrators, appointment	111
	(4)	Meeting	111
	(5)	Determination of factors	111
	(6)	Apportionment under s. 240	111
	(7)	Resolution of board	111
	(8)	Notice	111
	(9)	Non-application	111
	(10)	When factors to be determined	111
	(11)	Appeal to board	112
	(12)	Use of factors	112
	(13)	Cost of arbitration	112
	(14)	Non-application	112
118.		Trustees may copy assessment roll of municipality	112
119.		Clerk to give trustees annual statement of supporters of separate schools	112
120.	**(1)**	Request for collection of separate school rates by the municipality	112
	(2)	Expenses of collection	112
121.	**(1)**	Borrowing powers of separate school trustees	113
	(2)	Terms of payment	113
	(3)	Debentures	113
	(4)	Maturity	113
	(5)	Sinking fund	113
	(6)	Investment of fund	113
	(7)	Publication of notice of by-law	113
	(8)	Amounts	114
122.	**(1)**	Share of legislative grants	114
	(2)	Right of separate schools to a share of municipal grants	114
	(3)	Apportionment	114
	(4)	Not to share in public school assessment	114

Visitors

123.		Separate school visitors	114

Secondary School Education

124.	**(1)**	Election re secondary school	114
	(2)	By-law	114
	(3)	Approval	114
	(4)	Transmittal	114
	(5)	Notice	114
125.	**(1)**	Effective date	115
	(2)	Election after 30th day of June	115
126.		Powers and duties of Roman Catholic school board	115
127.	**(1)**	Agreement for education at other school	115

	(2)	Calculation of fees	115
128.	(1)	Legislative grants	115
	(2)	Conditions	115
	(3)	Apportionment and distribution	115
	(4)	Compliance	115
	(5)	Regulations	115
129.	(1)	Secondary school grades	115
	(2)	Grades nine and ten	115
	(3)	Additional grades	116
	(4)	All services provided by agreement	116
	(5)	Restrictions when subs. (4) applies	116
130.	(1)	French language schools	116
	(2)	Entitlement	116
131.	(1)	Membership on public board	116
	(2)	Application of subs. (1)	116
	(3)	Idem	116
	(4)	Eligibility of separate school elector	117
132.	(1)	Payment of public secondary school rates	117
	(2)	Application of subs. (1)	117
133.	(1)	Estimates and rates for separate secondary school purposes	117
	(2)	Elementary and secondary estimates	117
134.	(1)	Mandatory joint committees	117
	(2)	Multiple committees	117
	(3)	Combined joint committee	117
	(4)	Composition	117
	(5)	French-language representative	117
	(6)	Idem	118
	(7)	Idem	118
	(8)	Term of office	118
	(9)	Vacancies	118
	(9.1)	Quorum	118
	(9.2)	Chair	118
	(9.3)	Chair voting	118
	(10)	Personnel and services	118
	(11)	Public meetings	118
	(12)	Recommendations	118
	(13)	Consideration of recommendations by boards	118
	(14)	Reconsideration of recommendations	118
	(15)	Annual report	119
135.	(1)	Teaching and other staff	119
	(2)	Contents of regulations and agreements	119
	(3)	Idem	119
	(4)	Collective agreements	119
	(5)	Affirmative action	119
	(6)	Yearly designations for ten years	119

TABLE OF CONTENTS

	(7)	Idem	119
	(8)	Maximum limit	120
	(9)	Date for designations	120
	(10)	Transfer of employment if subs. 129(4) does not apply	120
	(11)	Transfer of employment if cl. 129(5)(a) applies	120
	(12)	Idem	120
	(13)	Objectors	120
	(14)	Second transfer of employment if cl. 129(5)(b) applies	120
	(15)	Similar employment	120
	(16)	Training assistance	120
	(17)	Seniority	121
	(18)	Transmittal of lists	121
	(19)	Compensation rate	121
	(20)	Seniority and employment status	121
	(21)	Sick leave credits	121
	(22)	Credit for total accumulation	122
	(23)	Accumulation and use of sick leave credits	122
	(24)	Gratuity	122
	(25)	Idem	122
	(26)	Idem	122
	(26.1)	Idem	122
	(27)	Non-application of subss. (24) to (26)	122
	(28)	Employment, advancement and promotion	123
	(29)	Definition	123
	(30)	Deemed designated persons	123
136.	(1)	Hiring after ten-year period	123
	(2)	Application of *Human Rights Code* s. 5	123
	(3)	Repeal	123
137.	(1)	Staff dispute resolution	123
	(2)	Parties	123
	(3)	Notice to arbitrate	123
	(4)	Name of appointee	124
	(5)	Response	124
	(6)	Chair	124
	(7)	Failure to act	124
	(8)	Hearing	124
	(9)	Majority	124
	(10)	Decision is final	124
	(11)	Examination of documentary evidence	124
	(12)	Prior knowledge	124
	(13)	Notice of communication	124
	(14)	Participation in decision	124
	(15)	Release of documentary evidence	124
	(16)	Collective agreement	124
138.	(1)	Vacancy on arbitration board	124

	(2)	Chair unable to act	125
	(3)	Arbitrator unable to act	125
139.		Matters that may be considered by arbitrator or arbitration board	125
140.		Report of arbitrator or arbitration board	125
141.		Arbitration fees and expenses	125
142.		Application of *Arbitrations Act*	126
143.	(1)	Right to continue in public secondary school	126
	(2)	Fee	126
144.	(1)	Right to receive secondary school instruction from Roman Catholic school board	126
	(2)	Right to receive secondary school instruction from public board	126
	(3)	Fee	126
	(4)	Amount	126
	(5)	Exemption from religious studies	126
	(6)	Idem	127
	(7)	Additional exemptions	127
145.		Interpretation	127
146.		Enforcement	127

Planning and Implementation Commission

147.	(1)	Commission continued	127
	(2)	Chair and vice-chair	127
	(3)	Term of office	127
	(4)	Authority of vice-chair	127
	(5)	Remuneration and expenses	127
	(6)	Quorum	127
	(7)	Applications before Divisional Court	127
	(8)	Staff and accommodation	127
148.	(1)	Advice to Minister	127
	(2)	Annual report	128
	(3)	Additional reports	128
	(4)	Consultation	128
	(5)	Matters to be considered by Commission	128
	(6)	Non-application of subss. (4, 5)	128
	(7)	Non-application of *Regulations Act*	128
149.	(1)	Implementation plans	128
	(2)	Public board	128
	(3)	Format	128
	(4)	Compliance	129
	(5)	Non-application of *Regulations Act*	129
150.	(1)	Public meetings	129
	(2)	Notice	129
151.	(1)	Negotiations	129
	(2)	Criteria	129
	(3)	Good faith	129

TABLE OF CONTENTS

152.	**(1)**	Assistance by Commission	129
	(2)	Appointment of mediator	129
	(3)	Duties of mediator	130
	(4)	Duties of boards	130
	(5)	Remuneration and expenses	130
153.	**(1)**	Appointment of tribunal to resolve matters	130
	(2)	Head of tribunal	130
	(3)	Eligibility of members	130
	(4)	Replacement of members	130
	(5)	Notice	130
	(6)	Parties	130
	(7)	Criteria	130
	(8)	Decisions	130
	(9)	Delivery of decision	131
	(10)	Order by Minister	131
	(11)	Retransfer	131
	(12)	Application of *Expropriations Act*	131
	(13)	Enforcement of order	131
	(14)	L.G. in C. may confirm, vary or rescind order	131
	(15)	No further petition	131
	(16)	Filing of documents on petition	131
	(17)	Hearing by L.G. in C.	131
	(18)	Remuneration and expenses	131
154.		Repeal	132
155.		Limitation on real property transfers	132
156.		Regulations	132
157.		Conflict	132

PART V

PROTESTANT SEPARATE SCHOOLS

158.	**(1)**	Application to establish Protestant separate school	132
	(2)	Permission to establish	132
	(3)	Restrictions on establishment	132
	(4)	Effective date	132
159.	**(1)**	Notice to be supporter, exemption from public school rates	132
	(2)	No renewal required	133
	(3)	Certificate of notice	133
	(4)	Penalty for wilful false statements in notice	133
	(5)	As to rates imposed before Protestant separate school established	133
160.		Withdrawal of support	133
161.	**(1)**	Index book	133
	(2)	Inspection	133

EDUCATION ACT

	(3)	Filing of notices	133
	(4)	Clerk to be guided by index book	133
162.	(1)	Not to share in public school assessment	133
	(2)	Share of legislative grants	133
163.	(1)	Reports	133
	(2)	Use of assessor's roll by board	133
164.		Qualification of a voter	134
165.	(1)	Qualification of a trustee	134
	(2)	Election of trustees	134
	(3)	Idem	134
166.		Corporate name of board	134
167.		Powers of board	134
168.		Discontinuing board	134
169.		Application of other sections	134

PART VI

BOARDS

Duties and Powers

170.	(1)	Duties of boards	134
	(2)	S. 67 school districts	136
	(3)	Regulations [To be repealed September 1, 1997]	136
171.	(1)	Powers of boards	136
	(2)	Collection of rates in territory without municipal organization by action	141
	(3)	Child care facilities	141
	(4)	Definitions	141
	(5)	Regulations re: paragraph 49	141
171.1		Effect of joint investment agreements	141
172.		Board name	141
173.	(1)	Establishment of scholarships, etc.	141
	(2)	Idem	141

Vocational Courses

174.	(1)	Vocational courses	142
	(2)	Courses of study	142
	(3)	Admission procedures	142
	(4)	Admission of adult	142
175.	(1)	Advisory committee	142
	(2)	Allowance	142

TABLE OF CONTENTS

Benefits

176.		Powers of board	142
177.	(1)	Insurance, hospital and health services	143
	(2)	Contributions re insured services	143
	(3)	Participation of retired person in contract	143
178.	(1)	Pensions	143
	(2)	Idem	143
	(3)	Definition	143
	(4)	Employees of newly organized board	144
	(5)	Assumption of board of rights and obligations of former board	144
179.	(1)	Retirement allowances	144
	(2)	Widow or widower	144
	(3)	Definition	144
	(4)	Limitation on application of section	144
180.	(1)	Sick leave credits	145
	(2)	Idem	145
	(3)	Idem	145
	(4)	Allowing of credits on transfer of employment	145
	(5)	Where transferred because of change in jurisdiction of board	145
	(6)	Idem	145
	(7)	Limitation	145
	(8)	[Repealed]	145
	(9)	[Repealed]	145
	(10)	Applicability of sick leave credits	146

Agreements

181.	(1)	Agreements to provide accommodation or services for another board	146
	(2)	Where building, additions, etc., required	146
	(3)	Where cost borne by board not providing accommodation	146
	(4)	Fees, exception	146
182.	(1)	Transfer of French-language instructional unit	146
	(2)	Transfer not a closing	146
183.	(1)	Definitions	146
	(2)	Agreements for joint use of facilities, etc.	146
	(3)	Approval of Minister	147
	(4)	Previous agreement	147
	(5)	Facilities deemed community recreation centre	147
184.	(1)	Agreement between public school boards	147
	(2)	Agreement between separate school boards	147
	(3)	Admission of pupils to Indian schools	148
	(4)	Levy for fees, transportation, etc.	148
	(5)	Closing of school by board	148
185.		Agreements for education of public and separate school pupils	148

EDUCATION ACT

186.	(1)	Secondary school agreements	148
	(2)	Agreements for education at outside schools	148
187.		Agreements re pupils in federal establishments	148
188.	(1)	Agreements re education of Indian pupils	148
	(2)	Agreements re instruction in Indian schools	149
	(3)	Agreements re accommodation for Indian pupils	149
	(4)	Cost of special services	149
	(5)	Appointment of representative of Indian pupils	149
	(6)	Additional representative	150
	(7)	Where appointment in discretion of board	150
	(8)	When Indian school enrolment included	150
	(9)	Enrolment	150
	(10)	Appointed members in addition to elected members	150
	(11)	Exception re subss. (5-10)	150
	(12)	Vacancy in office	150
	(13)	Representative of Indian pupils on Roman Catholic separate school board to be Roman Catholic	150
189.	(1)	Definition	150
	(2)	Agreements for adult basic education	150
	(3)	Idem	150

Transportation

190.	(1)	Transportation of pupils	151
	(2)	Idem	151
	(3)	Idem	151
	(4)	Idem	151
	(5)	Purchase of bus	151
	(6)	Agreements	151
	(7)	Agreements not exceeding five years	151
	(8)	Boarding of secondary school pupils residing in territorial district	151
	(9)	Idem	151
	(10)	Idem	152
	(11)	Boarding and transportation of secondary school pupils in a territorial district taking ''francais'' subject	152
	(12)	Boarding of elementary school pupils residing in territorial districts	152
	(13)	Boarding of elementary school pupils where transportation impracticable	152
	(14)	Certification of attendance	153

Allowances

191.	(1)	Allowance for members	153
	(2)	Chair and vice-chair	153
	(3)	Different allowances	153
	(4)	Basis of allowance	153
	(5)	Idem	153

TABLE OF CONTENTS

	(6)	Decrease in allowance 153
	(7)	Chair and vice-chair of council or section 153
	(8)	Idem 153
	(9)	Allocation of cost 153
	(10)	Travel expenses to attend board meetings 153
	(11)	Expenses for authorized travel on board business 154
	(12)	Deduction because of absence 154
	(13)	Advisory committee members 154

Property

192.	(1)	School lands granted before 1850 vested in board for school purposes 154
	(2)	Property in trust vested in board 154
193.	(1)	Possession of property 154
	(2)	Idem 154
	(3)	Appropriation of property 154
194.	(1)	Disposal of realty 155
	(2)	Application for removal of restrictions on use of school lands 155
	(3)	Lease or sale of site or property 155
	(4)	Disposal of buildings 155
	(5)	Exceptions 155
195.	(1)	Board may purchase or expropriate within its jurisdiction 155
	(2)	Purchase or lease of site in adjoining jurisdiction 155
	(3)	School outside designated area 155
	(4)	Buildings on land owned by board 156
	(5)	Buildings on leased land 156
	(6)	Additions or alterations 156
196.		Agreement for multi-use building 156

Out-of-Classroom Programs

197.	(1)	Acquisition of land for natural science program 156
	(2)	Application 156
	(3)	Idem 156
	(4)	Approval not required 156
	(5)	Agreement between boards 156
	(6)	Taxation 157
	(7)	Agreements with conservation authorities, etc. 157
	(8)	Idem 157
	(9)	Idem 157
	(10)	Board and lodging for courses in conservation 157

Officers

198.	(1)	Duties of secretary 157
	(2)	Security by officers 158
	(3)	Form of security 158

21

		(4) Failure to take security	158
		(5) Duties of treasurer	158
		(6) Business administrator	158
199.		Responsibility of officers	158

School Board Advisory Committees

200.		Definition	158
201.		Committee establishment	158
202.	(1)	Composition	158
	(2)	Separate school board	159
	(3)	Board of education	159
	(4)	Notice of teacher appointees	159
	(5)	Appointment and term of office	159
	(6)	Reappointment	159
	(7)	Vacancies	159
203.	(1)	First meeting	160
	(2)	Chair	160
	(3)	Quorum	160
	(4)	Sub-committees	160
204.	(1)	Recording secretary	160
	(2)	Budget	160
	(3)	Expenditures	160
205.	(1)	Powers of committee	160
	(2)	Limitation	160
	(3)	Consideration of reports	160

Special Education Advisory Committee

206.	(1)	Definitions	160
	(2)	Advisory committee	160
	(3)	Idem	161
	(4)	Application of s. 229	161
	(5)	Members of committee	161
	(6)	Ontario Association for Community Living	161
	(7)	[Repealed]	161
	(8)	Recommendations	161
	(9)	Opportunity to be heard	161
	(9.1)	Vacancies, quorum, chair	161
	(9.2)	Personnel and facilities	161
	(10)	Members of committee	161
	(11)	Selection by board	162

Access to Meetings and Records

207.	(1)	Open meetings of boards	162
	(2)	Closing of certain committee meetings	162

TABLE OF CONTENTS

	(3)	Exclusion of persons	162
	(4)	Inspection of books and accounts	162

Board Meetings

208.	(1)	When board deemed constituted	162
	(2)	First meeting	162
	(3)	Supervisory officer may provide for calling first meeting	162
	(4)	Presiding officer	163
	(5)	Election of chair	163
	(6)	Subsequent meetings	163
	(7)	Vice-chair	163
	(8)	Where equality of votes	163
	(9)	Temporary chair	163
	(10)	Temporary secretary	163
	(11)	Quorum	163
	(12)	Chair, voting; equality of votes	163
	(13)	Special meetings	163
209.	(1)	Declaration	163
	(2)	Idem	164
	(3)	Oath of allegiance	164
	(4)	Filing of declaration and oath	164

Arbitrators

210.	(1)	Arbitrators to send copy of award to board, etc.	164
	(2)	Liability of parties for costs	164
	(3)	Expenses	164
	(4)	Fees	165
	(5)	Application	165
	(6)	Application to treasurers	165
	(7)	Exception	165

Offences and Penalties

211.		False declaration	165
212.	(1)	Disturbances	165
	(2)	Idem	165
213.	(1)	Acting while disqualified	165
	(2)	False reports and registers	165
214.		Information to auditors	165
215.	(1)	Delivery up of books and money	165
	(2)	Summons for appearance	166
	(3)	Service of summons	166
	(4)	Order to account	166
	(5)	Other remedy not affected	166

EDUCATION ACT

216.	(1)	Compelling delivery of books, money, etc., on dissolution of school board	166
	(2)	Application of subs. (1)	166
217.	(1)	Promotion or sale of books, etc., by employees of board or Ministry to board, pupil, etc., prohibited	166
	(2)	Exception for authors	166
	(3)	Employment of employee of board or Ministry to promote sale of books, etc., to board, pupil, etc., prohibited	167
	(4)	Penalty	167

Validity of Elections

218.	(1)	Action for declaration that seat vacant	167
	(2)	Time for bringing action	167
	(3)	Power of court	167
	(4)	Application of *Municipal Elections Act*	167
	(5)	Joining of claims	167
	(6)	Validity of elections and corrupt practices	167

PART VII

BOARD MEMBERS — QUALIFICATIONS, RESIGNATIONS AND VACANCIES

219.		Employee disqualified	167
220.	(1)	Qualifications of members	167
	(2)	Idem	168
	(3)	Members eligible for re-election	168
	(4)	Disqualification	168
	(5)	Qualification to act as member	168
	(6)	Person not to be candidate for more than one seat	168
221.	(1)	Members to remain in office	169
	(2)	Board not to cease for want of members	169
	(3)	Resignation of members	169
	(4)	Resignation to become candidate for some other office	169
222.	(1)	Definition	169
	(2)	Vacancies	169
	(3)	Optional election	169
	(4)	Idem	169
	(5)	Term of office	169
223.	(1)	Elections for three member boards	169
	(2)	Time of meeting	170
	(3)	Notice of meeting	170
	(4)	Election at meeting	170
224.	(1)	Vacancy in rural separate school board before incorporation	170
	(2)	Manner of election	170

TABLE OF CONTENTS

225.		Vacancy on board	170
226.	**(1)**	Election to fill vacancy	170
	(2)	Extension of time limits	170
227.	**(1)**	Appointment of trustees on failure of qualified person	170
	(2)	Interim administration pending new elections	170
228.		Tie vote	170
229.	**(1)**	Seat vacated by conviction	171
	(2)	Proviso	171

PART VIII

TRUSTEE REPRESENTATION

Public and Separate School Boards

230.	**(1)**	Definitions	171
	(2)	Elections	172
	(3)	Change of boundaries	172
	(4)	New city	173
	(5)	Determination of population of electoral groups	173
	(6)	Idem	173
	(7)	Number of members on a board	173
	(8)	Rules for determination	173
	(9)	Number of members for each electoral group of a board	175
	(10)	Rules for determination	175
	(11)	Calculation of members for the purpose of rule 5 of subs. (10)	176
	(12)	Calculation of members for the purposes of rules 6 and 7 of rule (10)	176
	(13)	Idem	176
	(14)	Rounding off	176
	(14.1)	Decrease in numbers of members for an electoral group	176
	(14.2)	Same	176
	(14.3)	Same	177
	(14.4)	Same	177
	(15)	Distribution of members	177
	(16)	Rules for distribution	177
	(17)	Alternative distribution	177
	(18)	Idem	178
	(19)	Effect of resolution	178
	(20)	Idem	178
	(21)	Distribution of members	178
	(22)	Rules for distribution	178
	(23)	Effect of alternative distribution	179
	(24)	Election by general vote	179
	(25)	Electoral areas in a municipality	179
	(26)	Time for passing by-law	179

EDUCATION ACT

	(27)	Wards in electoral areas	179
	(28)	Election in combined municipalities	179

Appeal

231.	(1)	Appeal	179
	(2)	Idem	179
	(3)	Appeal on distribution	180
	(4)	Time for appeal	180
	(5)	Time for decision	180
	(6)	Decision of judge on appeal	180
	(7)	Idem	180
	(8)	Where no appeal	180

Applications

232.	(1)	Application for determination or distribution	180
	(2)	Idem	180
	(3)	Time for application	180
	(4)	Time for determination	180
	(5)	Determination or distribution final	180
	(6)	No determination or distribution	180
233.	(1)	Electoral areas	181
	(2)	Limitation	181
	(3)	Election	181
	(4)	Petition	181
	(5)	Electoral area	181

PART IX

FINANCE

234.	(1)	Auditor	181
	(2)	Disqualification of auditor	181
	(3)	Duties of auditor	182
	(4)	Rights of auditor	182
	(5)	Auditor may take evidence	182
	(6)	Auditor may attend meetings	182
	(7)	Publication of financial statements	182
	(8)	Idem	182
	(9)	Filing of financial statements	182
235.	(1)	Debentures	182
	(2)	Temporary advances pending issue and sale of debentures	182
	(2.1)	Temporary borrowing	183
	(3)	Notification of debt charges	183
	(4)	Payment of debt charges for debentures not issued by the board	183

TABLE OF CONTENTS

	(5)	Withholding from debenture levy	183
	(6)	Deficiency payable by board	183
235.1	**(1)**	Where other board has divisional board powers	183
	(2)	Non-application of subs. (1)	183
235.2		Payment by treasurer	183
235.3	**(1)**	Regulations	184
	(2)	O.M.B. approval not required	184
236.	**(1)**	Estimates	184
	(2)	Definition	185
	(3)	[Repealed]	185
	(4)	Reserve fund limitation exception	185
	(5)	Same	185
	(6)	Expenditure of reserve fund money	185
	(7)	Where estimates submitted after March 1st	185
	(8)	Where cost of separate levy payable by divisional board	185
	(9)	Requirement re estimates	186
	(10)	Application to board of education	186
	(11)	[Repealed]	186
	(12)	Application to public school board	186
	(13)	Application to secondary school board	186
237.	**(1)**	Limitation	186
	(2)	Money raised locally not spent for salaries because of strike or lock-out to be used to reduce taxes	186
	(3)	Statement	186
	(4)	Notice	186
	(5)	Cost of preparing notices	186
	(6)	Board providing statements	187
238.	**(1)**	Definitions	187
	(2)	Money raised not spent for salaries because of strike or lock-out to be used to reduce taxes	187
	(3)	Information	187
	(4)	Adjustment of monthly instalments	187
	(5)	Statement	187
	(6)	Idem	188
	(7)	Notice	188
	(8)	Cost of notice	188
239.		Regulations	188
240.	**(1)**	Regulations for apportionment in any year	188
	(2)	Review	188
	(3)	Where estimated data used	189
	(4)	Application of grants	189
	(5)	Meeting	189
	(6)	Review by treasurers	189
	(7)	Decision	189
	(8)	Idem	189

EDUCATION ACT

	(9)	Decision final	189
	(10)	Effect of decision	189
	(11)	Apportionment where unorganized territory becomes part of school division	189
	(12)	Territory without municipal organization	189
	(13)	Idem	189
	(14)	Levy despite review	189
	(15)	Adjustment where apportionment altered	189
	(16)	Non-application	190
241.	(1)	Regulations for apportionment, Sudbury District Roman Catholic Separate School Board	190
	(2)	Idem	190
	(3)	Where estimated data used	190
242.	(1)	Regulations for separate school board apportionment	190
	(2)	Application	190
	(3)	Application of regulation	190
	(4)	Where estimated data used	190
243.	(1)	Rates	190
	(2)	Payment to boards	191
	(3)	Agreement	191
	(4)	Termination of agreement	191
	(5)	Where instalment due before requisition received	191
	(6)	Application to separate schools	191
	(7)	Application to public school board	192
	(8)	Application to secondary school board	192
	(9)	Transfer of payments	192
	(10)	Definition	192
	(11)	Business days	192
244.	(1)	Tax notices	192
	(2)	Municipality to account for money	192
	(3)	Correction of errors in collection of rates in previous years	192
245.	(1)	Current borrowing	192
	(2)	Debt charges	193
	(3)	Limitation	193
	(4)	When limitation calculated on estimated revenue	193
	(5)	Copy of resolution authorizing borrowing	193
	(6)	Estimated revenues	193
	(7)	Board administered by Ministry of Municipal Affairs	193
	(8)	Approval of Minister	193
246.		When fees payable by boards	193
247.	(1)	Reduction of requisition or rates	193
	(2)	Adjustment of rates where under- or over-levy	194
	(3)	Levy for difference	194
248.		Definitions	194
249.		Data furnished by the municipality	195

250.	(1)	Determination of rates	195
	(2)	Who to determine rates	195
	(3)	Idem	195
	(4)	Non-application	195
251.		Assessments for school purposes	195
252.		Levying of school rates	196
253.		Conflict	196
254.		Rates for public library in unorganized territory in school division	196
255.	(1)	Definitions	196
	(2)	Share of licence fees for trailers to be paid to boards	196
	(3)	Idem	197
	(4)	Licence fees not part of annual rates	197
	(5)	Application to municipally operated trailer camps	197
256.	(1)	Levy on trailer in public school section in unorganized territory	197
	(2)	Levy on trailer re separate school in unorganized territory	197
	(3)	Levy on trailer in secondary school district in unorganized territory	197
	(4)	Notice	198
	(5)	Content of notice	198
	(6)	No levy where trailer assessed	198
	(7)	Offence	198
257.	(1)	School rate where no public school in municipality	198
	(2)	Reserve account	198
	(3)	Use of money in account	198
	(4)	Application in a school division	198

PART X

TEACHERS

Contracts

258.	(1)	Full-time or part-time teacher	199
	(2)	Memorandum of contract	199
259.	(1)	Continuing education teachers	199
	(2)	Application of subs. (1)	199
	(3)	Contract	199
	(4)	Full-time or part-time teacher and continuing education teacher	199
	(5)	Permanent or probationary teacher and continuing education teacher	199
	(6)	Permanent or probationary teacher as continuing education teacher only	199
260.	(1)	Salary of teacher	199
	(2)	School days and school year	200
	(3)	Payment for absence due to illness or dental condition	200
	(4)	Part-time teacher	200
	(5)	Absence of teacher in quarantine	200
	(6)	Absence by reason of being a juror or witness	200

EDUCATION ACT

	(7)	Award of salary by way of penalty	200
	(8)	Failure of board to pay salary when no written agreement or contract	200
261.		Probationary teacher	200
262.	(1)	Teachers to be qualified	201
	(2)	Certificates	201
	(3)	Idem	201
263.		Termination of contract where welfare of school involved	201

Duties

264.	(1)	Duties of teacher	201
	(1.1)	Sign language	202
	(2)	Refusal to give up school property	202
	(3)	Teachers, conferences	202
265.		Duties of principal	202

Pupil Records

266.	(1)	Definition	203
	(2)	Pupil records privileged	204
	(2.1)	Information to medical officer of health	204
	(3)	Right of parent and pupil	204
	(4)	Idem	204
	(5)	Reference where disagreement	204
	(6)	Use re further education or employment	204
	(7)	Information for Minister or board	204
	(8)	No action re content	205
	(9)	Testimony re content	205
	(10)	Secrecy re contents	205
	(11)	Definition	205
	(12)	Application to former records	205
	(13)	Use of record in disciplinary cases	205

Boards of Reference

267.		Definitions	205
268.	(1)	Termination of contract by board	205
	(2)	Termination of contract by teacher	205
	(3)	Application for board	205
	(4)	Service of notice	206
269.	(1)	Appointment in place of teacher dismissed	206
	(2)	New contract after termination of contract by teacher	206
270.	(1)	Application for Board of Reference	206
	(2)	Appointment	206
	(3)	Naming of representatives	207
	(4)	Failure to name representatives	207
	(5)	Idem	207

30

TABLE OF CONTENTS

	(6)	Failure of representatives to appear	207
	(7)	Applicant deemed eligible	207
	(8)	Death or withdrawal of representative	207
	(9)	Death, etc., of chair before hearing	207
	(10)	New Board of Reference after hearing commences	207
	(11)	Procedure at new Board of Reference	208
271.		Place and time of hearing	208
272.		Duty to inquire and powers of judge	208
273.	(1)	Direction of Board of Reference to report	208
	(2)	Chair of Board of Reference to report	208
274.		New Board of Reference provided	208
275.	(1)	Direction of Board	208
	(2)	Failure to comply with direction of Board	208
	(3)	Idem	208
276.		Payment of costs	208
277.		Regulations	208

PART XI

SUPERVISORY OFFICERS

278.		Qualifications of supervisory officers	209
279.		Director of education	209
280.		Director of education for separate school board	209
281.	(1)	[Repealed]	209
	(2)	Idem	209
	(3)	Idem	209
282.	(1)	Abolition of position	209
	(2)	Idem	209
283.	(1)	Chief executive officer	210
	(2)	Idem	210
	(3)	General report of chief executive officer	210
284.	(1)	Supervisory officers and director of education	210
	(2)	English and French	210
284.1	(1)	Supervisory officers, enrolment under 2,000	210
	(2)	Agreements	210
	(3)	Same	210
285.	(1)	Responsibility of supervisory officers	210
	(2)	Confirmation by Minister	210
286.	(1)	Duties of supervisory officers	211
	(2)	Responsibility to Minister	211
	(3)	Responsibility to board	211
	(4)	Full-time position	211
	(5)	Access to books and records, etc.	211

EDUCATION ACT

| 287. | (1) | Suspension or dismissal of supervisory officer by board | 211 |
| | (2) | Notice re suspension or dismissal | 211 |

PART XII

FRENCH LANGUAGE INSTRUCTION

Elementary

288.		Definitions	212
289.	(1)	Right to instruction in French-language instructional unit	212
	(2)	Duty of board to provide French-language instructional unit	212
	(3)	Meals, lodging and transportation	213
	(4)	English as a subject of instruction	213
	(5)	Idem, grades 5, 6, 7 and 8	213
	(6)	Admission of pupils other than French-speaking pupils	213
	(7)	Where board has no French-speaking supervisory officer	213
	(8)	English-language schools or classes	213
290.		Duties and responsibilities of advisory committee in elementary schools	213

Secondary

291.	(1)	Right to instruction in French-language instructional unit	214
	(2)	Duty of board to provide French-language instructional unit	214
	(3)	Meals, lodging and transportation	214
292.	(1)	French-language advisory committee	214
	(2)	Definitions	214
	(3)	Resolution	214
	(4)	Composition of committee	214
	(5)	Qualifications	215
	(6)	Disqualification	215
	(7)	Committee of less than nine members	215
	(8)	Application of s. 229	215
	(9)	Term of office	215
	(10)	Apportionment of members	215
	(11)	Meetings of French-speaking ratepayers to elect committee members	215
	(12)	Idem	215
	(13)	Consultation with committee re apportionment	215
	(14)	Idem	215
	(15)	Dissolution	215
293.	(1)	French-speaking ratepayers to elect subsequent members to committee	216
	(2)	Idem	216
294.	(1)	Election of chair of meeting	216
	(2)	Secretary of meeting	216

TABLE OF CONTENTS

	(3)	Procedure at meeting	216
	(4)	Notice of result of election	216
295.	(1)	Chair and vice-chair of committee	216
	(2)	Quorum	216
	(3)	Vote of chair, equality of votes	216
	(4)	Special meeting	216
296.	(1)	Vacancies	216
	(2)	Application of s. 221(3)	216
297.	(1)	Recommendations	217
	(2)	Committee report to board	217
	(3)	Board to seek advice of committee	217
	(4)	Consideration of recommendations by board	217
	(5)	Referral by committee to Languages of Instruction Commission	217
298.	(1)	Attendance of committee chair at board meetings	217
	(2)	Presentation of recommendations	218
	(3)	Designation of member by chair	218
	(4)	Attendance of committee chair at board committee meeting	218
	(5)	Confidentiality	218
	(6)	Distribution of administrative materials	218
	(7)	Formation of sub-committees	218
	(8)	Committee may hold public meetings	218
	(9)	Declaration	218
	(10)	Resignation	218
	(11)	Filing	218
299.	(1)	Resources and services to be provided by board	218
	(2)	Annual report of committee	219
	(2.1)	Same	219
	(3)	Services of professional staff to be provided	219
300.	(1)	Allowance	219
	(2)	Attendance at meetings and conferences	219
	(3)	Provincial association membership fee	219
301.	(1)	English-language classes where French-language school or classes established	219
	(2)	English-language advisory committee	219
	(3)	Application of ss. 291 to 302	219
	(4)	Definitions	219
302.	(1)	Admission of pupils other than French-speaking pupils	219
	(2)	Where board has no French-speaking supervisory officer	220

Languages of Instruction Commission of Ontario

303.		Definitions	220
304.	(1)	Commission continued	220
	(2)	Term, reappointment and remuneration	220
	(3)	Vacancies	220
	(4)	Commission is responsible to the Minister	220

	(5)	Quorum	220
	(6)	Recommendation	220
	(7)	Duties of commission	220
	(7.1)	Same	221
	(8)	Person to speak for group	221
	(9)	Referral to Commission by Minister	221
	(10)	Determination by Commission re establishment of advisory committee	221
	(11)	Investigation of irregularity	221
	(12)	Deferral of action by board	221
	(13)	Commission shall request mediation or reject referral	221
	(14)	Where referral rejected	221
	(15)	Notice of appointment of mediator	221
305.	(1)	Remuneration	222
	(2)	Who not eligible as mediator	222
	(3)	Duties of mediator	222
	(4)	Extension of period of mediation	222
306.	(1)	Duties of Commission	222
	(2)	Resolution by board	222
	(3)	Notice to Commission	222
	(4)	Where board resolves not to implement recommendation	222
	(5)	Time for notices and reasons	222
307.	(1)	Second resolution	222
	(2)	Conflict with by-law	222
	(3)	Time for second resolution	222
308.	(1)	Reconsideration by Commission	222
	(2)	Order by Minister	223
	(3)	Report and recommendation not binding on Minister	223
	(4)	Enforcement of order	223
	(5)	Service of order	223

PART XIII

GOVERNANCE OF FRENCH-LANGUAGE INSTRUCTION

309.	(1)	Definitions	223
	(2)	French day nurseries	224
	(3)	Corporation	224
310.		Regulations	224
311.	(1)	French-language section	224
	(2)	300 resident pupils	224
	(3)	10 per cent enrolment	224
	(4)	Minority	224
	(5)	Exception	224
312.		Authority of French-language section	224

TABLE OF CONTENTS

313.		Qualifications of members of French-language section	224
314.	**(1)**	Elector	225
	(2)	Idem	225
315.	**(1)**	Election	225
	(2)	General vote	225
	(3)	Idem	225
	(4)	Public meeting	225
	(5)	Final determination	225
	(6)	Idem	225
	(7)	Idem	225
	(8)	Boundaries	225
	(9)	Election officers	226
	(10)	Idem	226
	(11)	Information	226
	(12)	Application of section 230	226
315.1	**(1)**	Application of section	226
	(2)	Special election of French-language section	226
	(3)	Same	226
	(4)	Same	226
	(5)	Non-application of sections 313 to 315	226
	(6)	Qualifications of members of French-language section	226
	(7)	Electors	226
	(8)	Whether members to be apportioned by area	226
	(9)	Apportionment of members	227
	(10)	Consultation with French-language advisory committee	227
	(11)	Meetings to elect French-language section members	227
	(12)	Same	227
	(13)	Same	227
	(14)	Procedure at meeting	227
	(15)	Appointments to French-language section by Minister	227
	(16)	Term of office	227
	(17)	When French-language section deemed constituted	227
	(18)	Taking office	227
	(19)	Same	227
	(20)	Dissolution of French-language advisory committee	228
316.		Meetings, etc.	228
317.	**(1)**	Areas of representation	228
	(2)	Limitation	228
318.	**(1)**	Jurisdiction	228
	(2)	Excluded matters	228
	(3)	Common jurisdiction	229
	(4)	Quorum	229
	(5)	Change of jurisdiction	229
	(6)	Reversion of jurisdiction	229
319.	**(1)**	Application	229

	(2)	Allocation of estimated revenues	229
	(3)	Schools and classes	230
	(4)	Balance of schools and classes	230
	(5)	Definition	230
320.	(1)	Duty of board	230
	(2)	Variation	230
321.	(1)	Annual filing by boards	230
	(2)	Counting date	230
322.	(1)	Calculated enrolment	231
	(2)	When calculation made	231
	(3)	Approval of calculation	231
	(4)	Referral to the Languages of Instruction Commission of Ontario	231
	(5)	Idem	231
	(6)	Idem	231
323.	(1)	Liaison committee	231
	(2)	Function	231
324.	(1)	Notice to Minister	231
	(2)	Dissolution	231
	(3)	Revocation of notice	232
	(4)	Section 182 agreement distinguished	232
	(5)	Deemed application	232
325.	(1)	English as language of instruction	232
	(2)	Interpretation	232
	(3)	French as majority	233
325.1	(1)	Definitions	233
	(2)	Application of section	233
	(3)	Special election of English-language section	233
	(4)	Same	233
	(5)	Same	233
	(6)	Qualifications of members of English-language section	233
	(7)	Electors	233
	(8)	Application of subsections 315.1(5) and (8) to (20)	233
	(9)	Same	233
	(10)	Non-application of subsection 325(3)	234
326.	(1)	Forms	234
	(2)	Application of *Regulations Act*	234

EDUCATION ACT

R.S.O. 1990, c. E.2, as am. S.O. 1991, Vol. 2, c. 10 and 15; 1992, c. 15, ss. 85-89; c. 16; c. 17, ss. 1-3; c. 27, s. 59; c. 32, s. 9; 1993, c. 11, ss. 8-43; c. 23, s. 67; c. 26, ss. 44-45; c. 27, Schedule; c. 41; 1994, c. 1, s. 22; c. 17, ss. 48, 51; c. 23, s. 65 (not yet in force).

DEFINITIONS

1. (1) Definitions.—In this Act and the regulations, except where otherwise provided in the Act or regulations.

"adjoining".—"adjoining" means touching at any point; ("voisin")

"assessment commissioner".—"assessment commissioner" means the assessment commissioner appointed under the *Assessment Act* for the region in which the board is situated; (commissaire à l'évaluation")

"average daily enrolment".—"average daily enrolment" for a calendar year means the average daily enrolment calculated in accordance with the regulations; ("effectif quotidien moyen")

"band".—"band" and "council of the band" have the same meaning as in the *Indian Act* (Canada); ("bande", "conseil de bande")

"board".—"board" means a board of education, public school board, secondary school board, Roman Catholic separate school board or Protestant separate school board; ("conseil")

"board of education".—"board of education" includes a divisional board' ("conseil de l'éducation")

"city".—"city" includes a separated town and the portion of a city that is in one school division; ("cité")

"combined separate school zone".—"combined separate school zone" means a union of two or more separate school zones; ("zone fusionnée d'écoles séparées")

"continuing education instructor".—"continuing education instructor" means a person employed to provide instruction in a continuing education course or class established in accordance with the regulations other than those courses or classes for which a valid certificate of qualification or a letter of standing as a teacher is required by the regulations; ("instructeur de l'éducation permanente")

"continuing education teacher".—"continuing education teacher" means a teacher employed to teach a continuing education course or class established in accordance with the regulations for which a valid certificate of qualification or a letter of standing as a teacher is required by the regulations; ("enseignant de l'éducation permanente")

"county".—"county" includes united counties; ("comté")

"county combined separate school board".—"county combined separate school board" means a separate school board established for a county combined separate school zone; ("conseil fusionné d'écoles séparées de comté") "**county combined separate school zone**".—"county combined separate school zone" means a separate school zone that is an area designated by the regulations that is not in a territorial district; ("zone fusionnée d'écoles séparées de comté")

"**county municipality**".—"county municipality" means a municipality, other than a city, that forms part of a county or regional municipality that is not in the territorial districts; ("municipalité de comté")

"**credit**".—"credit" means recognition granted to a pupil by a principal as proof, in the absence of evidence to the contrary, that the pupil has successfully completed a quantity of work that,
  (a) has been specified by the principal in accordance with the requirements of the Minister, and
  (b) is acceptable to the Minister as partial fulfilment of the requirements for the Ontario secondary school diploma, the secondary school graduation diploma or the secondary school honour graduation diploma, as the case may be; ("crédit")

"**current expenditure**".—"current expenditure" means an expenditure for operating purposes or a permanent improvement from funds other than those arising from the sale of a debenture, from a capital loan or from a loan pending the sale of a debenture; ("dépenses courantes")

"**current revenue**".—"current revenue" means all amounts earned by a board, together with the amounts to which it becomes entitled, other than by borrowing, that may be used to meet its expenditures; ("recettes courantes")

"**debt charge**".—"debt charge" means the amount of money necessary annually,
  (a) to pay the principal due on long-term debt not payable from a sinking fund,
  (b) to provide a fund for the redemption of debentures payable from a sinking fund, and
  (c) to pay the interest due on all debt referred to in clauses (a) and (b); ("service de la dette")

"**defined city**".—"defined city" means,
  (a) the City of Hamilton,
  (b) the City of London, and
  (c) the City of Windsor; ("cité désignée")

"**district combined separate school board**".—"district combined separate school board" means a separate school board established for a district combined separate school zone; ("conseil fusionné d'écoles séparées de district")

"**district combined separate school zone**".—"district combined separate school zone" means a separate school zone that is an area designated by the regulations in a territorial district; ("zone fusionnée d'écoles séparées de district")

"**district municipality**".—"district municipality" means a municipality, except a city, in a territorial district; ("municipalité de district")

"**district school area**".—"district school area" means a school section in the territorial districts that is not a school division or a school section designated under section 68; ("secteur scolaire de district")

"**divisional board**".—"divisional board" means a divisional board of education; ("conseil de division scolaire")

DEFINITIONS   S. 1

"**education authority**".—"education authority" means a corporation that is incorporated by one or more bands or councils of bands for the purpose of providing for the educational needs of the members of the band or bands.

"**elementary school**".—"elementary school" means a public school, Roman Catholic separate school or Protestant separate school; ("école élémentaire")

"**exceptional pupil**".—"exceptional pupil" means a pupil whose behavioural, communicational, intellectual, physical or multiple exceptionalities are such that he or she is considered to need placement in a special education program by a committee, established under subparagraph iii of paragraph 5 of subsection 11(1), of the board,

(a) of which the pupil is a resident pupil,
(b) that admits or enrols the pupil other than pursuant to an agreement with another board for the provision of education, or
(c) to which the cost of education in respect of the pupil is payable by the Minister; ("élève en difficulté")

"**guardian**".—"guardian" means a person who has lawful custody of a child, other than the parent of the child; ("tuteur")

"**head office**".—"head office" of a board means the place at which the minute book, financial statements and records, and seal of the board are ordinarily kept; ("siège")

"**Indian**".—"Indian" has the same meaning as in the *Indian Act* (Canada); ("Indien")

"**intermediate division**".—"intermediate division" means the division of the organization of a school comprising the first four years of the program of studies immediately following the junior division; ("cycle intermédiaire")

"**judge**".—"judge" means a judge of the Ontario Court (General Division); ("juge")

"**junior division**".—"junior division" means the division of the organization of an elementary school comprising the first three years of the program of studies immediately following the primary division; ("cycle moyen")

"**locality**".—"locality" means a part of territory without municipal organization that is deemed to be a district municipality for the purposes of a divisional board or of a district combined separate school board; ("localité")

"**Minister**".—"Minister" means the Minister of Education; ("ministre")

"**Ministry**".—"Ministry" means the Ministry of Education; ("ministère")

"**municipality**".—"municipality" means a city, town, village, township or improvement district; ("municipalité")

"**occasional teacher**".—"occasional teacher" means a teacher employed to teach as a substitute for a permanent, probationary, continuing education or temporary teacher who has died during the school year or who is absent from his or her regular duties for a temporary period that is less than a school year and that does not extend beyond the end of a school year; ("enseignant suppléant")

"**parcel of land**".—"parcel of land" means a parcel of land that by the *Assessment Act* is required to be separately assessed; ("parcelle de terrain")

"**part-time teacher**".—"part-time teacher" means a teacher employed by a board on a regular basis for other than full-time duty; ("enseignant à temps partiel")

"permanent improvement".—"permanent improvement" includes,
- (a) a school site and an addition or an improvement to a school site,
- (b) a building used for instructional purposes and any addition, alteration or improvement thereto,
- (c) an administration office, a residence for teachers or caretakers and a storage building for equipment and supplies, and any addition, alteration or improvement thereto,
- (c.1) a child care facility on a school site and any addition, alteration or improvement to such a facility,
- (d) furniture, furnishings, library books, instructional equipment and apparatus, and equipment required for maintenance of the property,
- (e) a bus or other vehicle, including watercraft, for the transportation of pupils,
- (f) the obtaining of a water supply or an electrical power supply on the school property or the conveying of a water supply or an electrical power supply to the school from outside the school property,
- (g) initial payments or contributions for past service pensions to a pension plan for officers and other employees of the board; ("améliorations permanentes")

"permanent teacher".—"permanent teacher" means a teacher employed by a board under a permanent teacher's contract made in accordance with the regulations and includes a teacher whose contract is deemed to include the terms and conditions contained in the form of contract prescribed in the regulations for a permanent teacher; ("enseignant permanent")

"Planning and Implementation Commission".—"Planning and Implementation Commission" means the Planning and Implementation Commission continued under section 147; ("Commission de planification et de mise en oeuvre")

"polling list".—"polling list" means a polling list as defined in the *Municipal Elections Act*; ("liste électorale")

"population".—"population" means the population as determined by the assessment commissioner from the last municipal enumeration as updated under the provisions of the *Assessment Act*; ("population")

"primary division".—"primary division" means the division of the organization of an elementary school comprising junior kindergarten, kindergarten and the first three years of the program of studies immediately following kindergarten; ("cycle primaire")

"principal".—"principal" means a teacher appointed by a board to perform in respect of a school the duties of a principal under this Act and the regulations; ("directeur d'école")

"private school".—"private school" means an institution at which instruction is provided at any time between the hours of 9 a.m. and 4 p.m. on any school day for five or more pupils who are of or over compulsory school age in any of the subjects of the elementary or secondary school courses of study and that is not a school as defined in this section; ("école privée")

"probationary teacher".—"probationary teacher" means a teacher employed by a board under a probationary teacher's contract made in accordance with the regulations; ("enseignant stagiaire")

DEFINITIONS **S. 1**

"provincial supervisory officer".—"provincial supervisory officer" means a supervisory officer employed in the Ministry; ("agent provincial de supervision")

"public board".—"public board" means a board of education or a secondary school board established under section 67; ("conseil public")

"public school elector".—"public school elector", in respect of an area for which one or more members of a board are to be elected by public school electors, means a public school elector under the *Municipal Elections Act*, who is qualified to vote at the election for such members in such area; ("électeur des écoles publiques")

"regulations".—"regulations" means the regulations made under this Act; ("règlements")

"reserve fund".—"reserve fund" means a reserve fund established under section 163 of the *Municipal Act*; ("fonds de réserve")

"Roman Catholic".—"Roman Catholic" includes a Catholic of the Greek or Ukrainian Rite in union with the See of Rome; ("catholique")

"Roman Catholic school board".—"Roman Catholic school board" means a separate school board that has made an election under section 124 that has been approved by the Minister; ("conseil d'écoles catholiques")

"rural separate school".—"rural separate school" means a separate school for Roman Catholics that is not part of a county or district combined separate school zone; ("école séparée rurale")

"rural separate school zone".—"rural separate school zone" means a separate school zone in respect of a rural separate school; ("zone d'écoles séparées rurales")

"salary".—"salary" means all payments and benefits paid or provided to or for the benefit of a person who is designated under section 135; ("salaire")

"school".—"school" means,
(a) the body of public school pupils or separate school pupils or secondary school pupils that is organized as a unit for educational purposes under the jurisdiction of the appropriate board, or
(b) the body of pupils enrolled in any of the elementary or secondary school courses of study in an educational institution operated by the Government of Ontario,

and includes the teachers and other staff members associated with such unit or institution and the lands and premises used in connection therewith; ("école")

"school day".—"school day" means a day that is within a school year and is not a school holiday; ("jour de classe")

"school division".—"school division" means the area in which a divisional board has jurisdiction; ("division scolaire")

"school section".—"school section" means the area in which a public school board or board of education has jurisdiction for public school purposes; ("circonscription scolaire")

"school site".—"school site" means land or interest therein or premises required by a board for a school, school playground, school garden, teacher's residence, caretaker's residence, gymnasium, offices, parking areas or for any other school purpose; ("emplacement scolaire")

"school year".—"school year" means the period prescribed as such by, or approved as such under, the regulations; ("année scolaire")

"secondary school".—"secondary school" means a school that is under the jurisdiction of a secondary school board; ("école secondaire")

"secondary school district".—"secondary school district" means the area in which a secondary school board or a board of education has jurisdiction for secondary school purposes; ("district d'écoles secondaires")

"secretary".—"secretary" and "treasurer" includes a secretary-treasurer; ("secrétaire", "trésorier")

"senior division".—"senior division" means the division of the organization of a secondary school comprising the three years of the program of studies following the intermediate division; ("cycle supérieur")

"separated town".—"separated town" means a town separated for municipal purposes from the county in which it is situated; ("ville séparée")

"separate school board".—"separate school board" means a board that operates a separate school for Roman Catholics; ("conseil d'écoles séparées")

"separate school elector".—"separate school elector", in respect of an area for which one or more members of a board are to be elected by separate school electors, means a separate school elector under the *Municipal Elections Act*, who is qualified to vote at the election of such members in such area; ("électeur des écoles séparées")

"separate school supporter".—"separate school supporter" means a Roman Catholic ratepayer,
- (a) in respect of whom notice of school support has been given in accordance with section 106 and notice of withdrawal of support has not been given under section 107,
- (b) who is shown as a separate school supporter on the school support list as prepared or revised by the assessment commissioner under section 16 of the *Assessment Act*, or
- (c) who is declared to be a separate school supporter as a result of a final decision rendered in proceedings commenced under the *Assessment Act*,

and includes the Roman Catholic spouse of such ratepayer; ("contribuable des écoles séparées")

"separate school zone".—"seperate school zone" means the area in which property may be assessed to support a separate school or schools for Roman Catholics under the jurisdiction of one separate school board; ("zone d'écoles séparées")

"special education program".—"special education program" means, in respect of an exceptional pupil, an educational program that is based on and modified by the results of continuous assessment and evaluation and that includes a plan containing specific objectives and an outline of educational services that meets the needs of the exceptional pupil; ("programme d'enseignement à l'enfance en difficulté")

"special education services".—"special education services" means facilities and resources, including support personnel and equipment, necessary for developing and implementing a special education program; ("services à l'enfance en difficulté")

DEFINITIONS **S. 1**

"**supervisory officer**".—"supervisory officer" means a person who is qualified in accordance with the regulations governing supervisory officers and who is employed,

(a) by a board, or

(b) in the Ministry and designated by the Minister,

to perform such supervisory and administrative duties as are required of supervisory officers by this Act and the regulations; ("agent de supervision")

"**support staff**".—"support staff" means staff other than supervisory officer staff or teaching staff; ("personnel de soutien")

"**teacher**".—"teacher" means a person who holds a valid certificate of qualification or a letter of standing as a teacher in an elementary or a secondary school in Ontario; ("enseignant")

"**temporary teacher**".—"temporary teacher" means a person employed to teach under the authority of a letter of permission; ("enseignant temporaire")

"**urban municipality**".—"urban municipality" means a city, town or village; ("municipalité urbaine")

"**urban school section**".—"urban school section" means a school section, except a school division or a district school area, that includes a municipality; ("circonscription scolaire urbaine")

"**vocational school**".—"vocational school" includes a special vocational school. ("école professionnelle")

(2) **Authority or obligation of parent vested in pupil of 18 years of age.**—Where by or under this Act any authority or right is vested in, or any obligation is imposed upon, or any reimbursement may be made to, a parent or guardian of a pupil, such authority, right, obligation or reimbursement shall, where the pupil is an adult, be vested in or imposed upon or made to the pupil, as the case may be.

(3) **Questions re proceeding as to formation of school section.**—Where any question arises touching the validity of any proceeding with respect to the formation, alteration or dissolution of a school section or touching any by-law with respect to any of such matters, the question shall be raised, heard and determined upon a summary application to a judge, and no proceeding or by-law with respect to the formation, alteration or dissolution of a school section is invalid or shall be set aside because of failure to comply with the provisions of any Act applicable to the proceeding or by-law, unless, in the opinion of the judge before whom the proceeding or by-law is called in question, the proceeding or by-law, if allowed to stand, would cause substantial injustice to be done to any person affected thereby.

(4) **Effect on separate schools.**—This Act does not adversely affect any right or privilege respecting separate schools enjoyed by separate school boards or their supporters under the predecessors of this Act as they existed immediately prior to the 1st day of January, 1975.

(5) **Existing school arrangements continued.**—Until altered under the authority of this or any other Act, all school jurisdictions and boards, including the names of the boards, as they existed on the 31st day of July, 1981, are continued subject to the provisions of this Act.

(6) **Deemed adjustment of boundaries.**—If, before the 1st day of January, 1993, an alteration is made in the boundaries of a county, regional municipality or defined city, the

boundaries of a school division in the county, regional municipality or defined city shall be deemed to be adjusted accordingly from the date of the alteration. 1992, c. 16, s. 1; 1993, c. 11, ss. 8, 9; c. 23, s. 67(1).

PART I

MINISTRY OF EDUCATION

2. (1) **Ministry continued.**—The ministry of the public service known in English as the Ministry of Education and in French as ministère de l'Éducation is continued.

(2) **Minister to have charge.**—The Minister shall preside over and have charge of the Ministry.

(3) **Administration.**—The Minister is responsible for the administration of this Act and the regulations and of such other Acts and the regulations thereunder as may be assigned to the Minister by the Lieutenant Governor in Council.

(4) **Delegation of powers and duties.**—The Minister may in writing authorize the Deputy Minister or any other officer or employee in the Ministry to exercise any power or perform any duty that is granted to or vested in the Minister under this or any other Act.

(5) **Limitations.**—The Minister may in writing limit an authorization made under subsection (4) in such manner as he or she considers advisable.

(6) **Application of *Executive Council Act*, s. 6.**—Section 6 of the *Executive Council Act* does not apply to a deed or contract that is executed under an authorization made under subsection (4).

3. Annual report.—The Minister shall, after the close of each fiscal year, submit to the Lieutenant Governor in Council a report upon the affairs of the Ministry for the immediately preceding fiscal year and shall then lay the report before the Assembly if it is in session or, if not, at the next session.

4. Additions to enrolment in special cases.—The Minister may, in respect of a school, require to be included in the enrolment on any date the number of pupils who were absent from school because of any condition considered by the Minister to constitute a special circumstance or an emergency.

5. (1) **Closing of school or class.**—Subject to the approval of the Lieutenant Governor in Council, the Minister may order the closing of a school or any class thereof for a specified period.

(2) **Pupils deemed in attendance.**—Where a school or class is closed for a specified period under subsection (1), the pupils in such school or class shall for all purposes, including the calculation of general legislative grants and fees, be deemed to be in attendance.

6. (1) **Guarantee of debentures.**—The Lieutenant Governor in Council may authorize the Treasurer of Ontario to guarantee payment by the Province of any debentures issued by a board in Ontario for any school purpose for which the board is authorized to issue debentures.

(2) **Form of guarantee.**—The form of the guarantee and the manner of its execution shall be determined by the Lieutenant Governor in Council, and every guarantee given or

purporting to be given under this section is binding upon the Province and is not open to question upon any ground whatsoever.

(3) **Validity of guaranteed debentures.**—Any debenture issued by a board, payment of which is guaranteed by the Province under this section, is valid and binding upon the board by which it is issued and the ratepayers thereof, according to its terms, and the validity of any debenture so guaranteed is not open to question upon any ground whatsoever.

7. Fixing rate of interest on debentures, etc., held by Treasurer.—Despite anything in any Act fixing the rate of interest to be paid or credited to any board by the Treasurer of Ontario upon school securities, sinking funds or debentures deposited with or in the hands of the Treasurer of Ontario either as an investment by the Province or for investment on behalf of a board, the rate at which interest shall be allowed to, paid by or credited to a board upon any such securities, sinking funds or debentures heretofore or hereafter deposited with or purchased by the Treasurer of Ontario shall be the current rate of interest as fixed from time to time by the Lieutenant Governor in Council, to be based upon the average rate of interest actually payable upon the money borrowed on behalf of Ontario as a provincial loan and then outstanding.

8. (1) **Powers of Minister.**—The Minister may,

1. **diplomas and certificates.**—name the diplomas and certificates that are to be granted to pupils and prescribe their form and the conditions under which they are to be granted;
2. **courses of study.**—prescribe the courses of study that shall be taught and the courses of study that may be taught in the primary, junior, intermediate and senior divisions;
3. **courses and areas of study.**—in respect of schools under the jurisdiction of a board,
3.1 **reviews of effectiveness.**—conduct reviews of classroom practices and the effectiveness of educational programs and require a board or a private school inspected under subsection 16(7) to participate in the reviews and to provide information to the Minister for that purpose in such form as the Minister may prescribe;
    (a) issue curriculum guidelines and require that courses of study be developed therefrom and establish procedures for the approval of courses of study that are not developed from such curriculum guidelines,
    (b) prescribe areas of study and require that courses of study be grouped thereunder and establish procedures for the approval of alternative areas of study under which courses of study shall be grouped, and
    (c) approve or permit boards to approve,
        (i) courses of study that are not developed from such curriculum guidelines, and
        (ii) alternative areas of study under which courses of study shall be grouped, and authorize such courses of study and areas of study to be used in lieu of or in addition to any prescribed course of study or area of study;
4. **procedures.**—establish procedures by which and the conditions under which books and other learning materials are selected and approved by the Minister;
5. **textbooks and other learning materials.**—purchase and distribute textbooks and other learning materials for use in schools;

6. **textbooks, reference books, etc.**—select and approve for use in schools textbooks, library books, reference books and other learning materials;
7. **publication of book lists.**—cause to be published from time to time lists of textbooks, learning materials, reference books and library books, selected and approved by the Minister for use in elementary and secondary schools;
8. **daily register.**—prescribe the form of the register of attendance and the manner of its use in recording the daily attendance of pupils of schools, or approve the use of an alternate method of recording such daily attendance, and prescribe the form in which enrolment and attendance data shall be submitted to the Minister;
9. **application of *Workers' Compensation Act.***—prescribe the conditions under which and the terms upon which pupils of boards shall be deemed to be workers for the purpose of coverage under the *Workers' Compensation Act*, deem pupils to be workers for such purpose and require a board to reimburse Ontario for payments made by Ontario under that Act in respect of a pupil of the board deemed by the Minister to be a worker employed by Ontario;
10. **letter of permission.**—grant a letter of permission to a board authorizing the board to employ as a teacher a person not qualified as such if the Minister is satisfied that no teacher is available, but a letter of permission shall be effective only for the period, not exceeding one year, that the Minister may specify therein;
11. **letter of approval.**—grant a temporary letter of approval to a board authorizing the board to appoint or assign, for a period not exceeding one year, a teacher to teach a subject or hold a position where the teacher does not hold the certificate required for teaching the subject;
12. **withdraw letter.**—withdraw any letter of permission or temporary letter of approval granted under this Act;
13. **suspend or cancel.**—suspend or cancel and reinstate any certificate of qualification or letter of standing;
14. **accept equivalent qualification.**—accept in lieu of any requirement prescribed for a teacher, head of a department, principal, director, supervisor or supervisory officer, or for a candidate for a certificate or for admission to a school, such experience, academic scholarship or professional training as the Minister considers equivalent thereto, and may require such evidence thereof as the Minister considers necessary;
15. **medical examinations.**—require employees of school boards to submit to medical examinations;
16. **courses.**—provide or approve and review courses for teachers, principals, supervisory officers, attendance counsellors and native counsellors and grant certificates in respect of the successful completion of such courses;
17. **correspondence courses.**—provide for the development, distribution and supervision by the Ministry of correspondence courses;
18. **scholarships, bursaries.**—provide for, and prescribe the conditions of, the granting of scholarships, bursaries and awards to pupils and the granting of bursaries to teachers;
19. **teachers' colleges.**—in respect of teachers' colleges,
    (a) define courses of study and subjects to be taught,
    (b) recommend reference books and library books,

PART I — MINISTRY OF EDUCATION S. 8

(c) approve textbooks,

(d) determine the number of terms and the dates upon which each term begins and ends, and

(e) grant Bachelor of Education degrees;

20. **provincial schools.**—in respect of schools for the deaf and the blind, determine the number of terms and the dates upon which each term begins and ends;

21. **apportion federal grants.**—apportion and pay all sums received for educational purposes from the Government of Canada or any source other than an appropriation by the Legislature, in accordance with the terms of the grant, if any, and otherwise in any manner the Minister considers proper;

22. **educational advancement programs, activities and projects and accountable advances.**—make payments out of funds appropriated therefor by the Legislature to a board, an individual, a voluntary association or a corporation without share capital having objects of a charitable or educational nature,

    (a) to assist or advance programs, activities or projects for students that involve a cultural and educational exchange with other provinces and countries, provincial or interprovincial travel, school twinning and related assistance, leadership training, or summer employment, and

    (b) to foster and promote educational advancement by means of programs, activities or projects that are provided for visiting educational officials, designed to further the professional development of teachers and supervisory officers including exchange of such personnel, or considered by the Minister to be valuable in advancing a particular area of study,

    and, subject to the terms and conditions that are approved for such purpose by the Lieutenant Governor in Council, make an accountable advance to the recipient of a payment under this clause or to an individual, not being a member of the public service, who conducts or assists in conducting or participates in any such program, activity or project;

23. **agreements concerning learning materials.**—enter into an agreement with any board, person or organization in respect of the development and production of learning materials, and pay all or part of the costs in connection therewith;

23.1 **copyright licence agreements.**—enter into a licence agreement to permit boards to copy, under the terms of the licence agreement, works protected by copyright, and to,

    (a) extend the rights under the licence agreement to boards, and

    (b) require boards to comply with the terms of the licence agreement;

24. **educational research and grants for promotion of advancement of education.**—initiate educational research and make grants to a board, an individual, a voluntary association or a corporation for educational research programs, activities or projects to promote the advancement of education;

25. **discretion to establish French-language programs for English-speaking pupils.**—permit a board to establish for English-speaking pupils programs involving varying degrees of the use of the French language in instruction, provided that programs in which English is the language of instruction are made available to pupils whose parents desire such programs for their children;

26. **guidelines respecting school closings.**—in respect of schools under the jurisdiction of a board, issue guidelines respecting the closing of schools and require that boards develop policies therefrom with respect to procedures to be followed prior to the closing of a school by decision of the board;
27. **guidelines respecting keeping of pupil records.**—issue guidelines respecting pupil records and require boards to comply with the guidelines;
28. **approve awards.**—approve awards for the purpose of subclause 49(7)(f)(iv);
29. **employment equity.**—require boards to develop and implement a policy on employment equity for women and other groups designated by the Minister, to submit the policy to the Minister for approval and to implement changes to the policy as directed by the Minister;
29.1 **ethnocultural equity.**—require boards to develop and implement an ethnocultural equity and antiracism policy, to submit the policy to the Minister for approval and to implement changes to the policy as directed by the Minister;
29.2 **drug education.**—establish a drug education policy framework and require boards to develop and implement a policy on drug education in accordance with the framework.
30. **assessment equalization factors.**—provide an assessment equalization factor,
    (a) for each municipality or part thereof including, for public and secondary school purposes, any part of territory without municipal organization that is deemed to be attached thereto for such purposes and, for public school purposes, any part of territory without municipal organization that is deemed to be annexed thereto for public school purposes,
    (b) for each locality,
    (c) for each public school section that comprises only territory without municipal organization, and
    (d) for each separate school zone that comprises only territory without municipal organization,
    and determine the assessment roll to which each such factor applies;
31. **weighting and adjustment factors.**—provide interim and final weighting and adjustment factors for the purposes of the regulations;
32. **payment of instalments of legislative grants.**—prescribe the number of instalments in which payments of legislative grants shall be paid to boards, the dates upon which the payments shall be made and the amounts of the payments as a percentage of the total amount estimated by the Minister to be payable to the boards;
33. **approval of agreements.**—approve the entering into of an agreement by boards under subsection 182(1).
34. **capital allocations.**—make allocations in respect of the construction of child care facilities on school sites.
35. **education costs outside Ontario.**—make payments towards the cost of elementary or secondary education that a person receives outside Ontario, if the person is outside Ontario for the purpose of receiving insured services within the meaning of the *Health Insurance Act* and the cost of the insured services is paid for in whole or in part by the Ontario Health Insurance Plan.

(2) **Additional powers of Minister.**—The Minister may, for the purposes of the calculation and payment of legislative grants,

   (a) approve classes, courses and programs;
   (b) approve adult basic education as defined in subsection 189(1) provided for boards by,
      (i) colleges of applied arts and technology, and
      (ii) community groups; and
   (c) prescribe the standards that shall be attained by a community group in respect of the provision of adult basic education under subsection 189(3) and the criteria that shall be used to determine whether the standards are attainable.

(3) **Identification programs and special education programs and services.**—The Minister shall ensure that all exceptional children in Ontario have available to them, in accordance with this Act and the regulations, appropriate special education programs and special education services without payment of fees by parents or guardians resident in Ontario, and shall provide for the parents or guardians to appeal the appropriateness of the special education placement, and for these purposes the Minister shall,

   (a) require school boards to implement procedures for early and ongoing identification of the learning abilities and needs of pupils, and shall prescribe standards in accordance with which such procedures be implemented; and
   (b) in respect of special education programs and services, define exceptionalities of pupils, and prescribe classes, groups or categories of exceptional pupils, and require boards to employ such definitions or use such prescriptions as established under this clause.

(4) **Application.**—An act of the Minister under this section is not a regulation within the meaning of the *Regulations Act*.

1991, Vol. 2, c. 10, s. 1; 1992, c. 16, s. 2; c. 27, s. 59; 1993, c. 11, s. 10.

9. Accounting statement related to assistance by Ministry.—The Minister may require a person or organization that has received financial assistance under this Act or the regulations to submit to the Minister a statement prepared by a person licensed under the *Public Accountancy Act* that sets out the details of the disposition of the financial assistance by the person or organization.

10. Powers of Minister.—The Minister may,

   (a) **advisory body.**—appoint such advisory or consultative bodies as may be considered necessary by the Minister from time to time;
   (b) **commission of inquiry.**—appoint as a commission one or more persons, as the Minister considers expedient, to inquire into and report upon any school matter, and such commission has the powers of a commission under Part II of the *Public Inquiries Act*, which Part applies to such inquiry as if it were an inquiry under that Act;
   (c) **secure legal opinion.**—submit a case on any question arising under this Act to the Divisional Court for opinion and decision.

11. (1) **Regulations.**—Subject to the approval of the Lieutenant Governor in Council, the Minister may make regulations in respect of schools or classes established under this Act, or any predecessor of this Act, and with respect to all other schools supported in whole or in part by public money,

1. **general.**—for the establishment, organization, administration and government thereof;
2. **admit pupils.**—governing the admission of pupils;
3. **pupil records.**—prescribing the manner in which records in respect of pupils of elementary and secondary schools shall be established and maintained, including the forms to be used therefor and the type of information that shall be kept and recorded, and providing for the retention, transfer and disposal of such records;
4. **disposition of present pupil records.**—providing for the disposition of records established prior to the 1st day of September, 1972, in respect of pupils;
5. **special education programs.**—governing the provision, establishment, organization and administration of,
    i. special education programs,
    ii. special education services, and
    iii. committees to identify exceptional pupils and to make and review placements of exceptional pupils;
6. **identification and placement appeals.**—governing procedures with respect to parents or guardians for appeals in respect of identification and placement of exceptional pupils in special education programs;
7. **evening classes.**—defining and governing evening classes;
8. **purchase books.**—requiring boards to purchase books for the use of pupils;
9. **accommodation and equipment.**—prescribing the accommodation and equipment of buildings and the arrangement of premises;
10. **recreation programs.**—defining and governing programs of recreation, camping, physical education and adult education;
11. **certificates and letters of standing.**—governing the granting, suspending and cancelling of certificates of qualification, and letters of standing;
12. **teacher's qualifications record cards.**—providing for the issuing of teacher's qualifications record cards and governing the professional qualifications that may be recorded on such record cards;
13. **letter of permission.**—governing the granting to a board of a letter of permission and a temporary letter of approval and providing for the withdrawal of such letters;
14. **teacher's contract.**—prescribing the form of contract that shall be used for every contract entered into between a board and a permanent, probationary or continuing education teacher for the services of the teacher, and prescribing in the form of contract the terms and conditions of the contract;
15. **schools on Crown lands.**—governing the establishment and operation of public and secondary schools on lands held by the Crown in right of Canada or Ontario or by an agency thereof, or on other lands that are exempt from taxation for school purposes;
16. **supervisory officers, examinations.**—providing for the holding of examinations for persons to become supervisory officers and governing such examinations;
17. **continuing education courses and classes.**—defining and governing continuing education courses and classes;

PART I — MINISTRY OF EDUCATION **S. 11**

18. **idem.**—prescribing the continuing education courses and classes for which a valid certificate of qualification or a letter of standing as a teacher is required;
19. **fees of examiners.**—prescribing the fees to be paid to presiding officers and examiners in connection with examinations and by whom and in what manner such fees and other expenses in connection with such examinations shall be borne and paid;
20. **religious exercises and education.**—governing the provision of religious exercises and religious education in public and secondary schools and providing for the exemption of pupils from participating in such exercises and education and of a teacher from teaching, and a public school board or a secondary school board from providing, religious education in any school or class;
21. **language of instruction.**—prescribing the language or languages in which any subject or subjects shall be taught in any year of the primary, junior, intermediate or senior division;
21.1 **sign language.**—respecting the use of American Sign Language and Quebec Sign Language as languages of instruction.
22. **exchange teachers.**—providing for and governing the exchange of teachers between Ontario and other parts of Canada and between Ontario and other jurisdictions;
23. **school libraries.**—governing school libraries;
24. **textbooks.**—listing the textbooks that are selected and approved by the Minister for use in schools;
25. **practice teaching.**—respecting observation and practice teaching by student teachers;
26. **powers and duties of teachers, etc.**—prescribing the powers, duties and qualifications, and governing the appointment of teachers, supervisors, directors, supervisory officers, heads of departments, principals, superintendents, residence counsellors, school attendance counsellors and other officials;
27. **pupils.**—prescribing the duties of pupils;
28. [Repealed 1993, c. 11, s. 11(2).]
29. **qualification to teach.**—prescribing the qualifications and experience required for the purpose of qualifying a person to teach;
30. **forms.**—prescribing forms and providing for their use;
31. **transportation.**—governing the transportation of pupils;
32. **practice and procedure.**—regulating the practice and procedure to be followed at any hearing provided for by or under this Act;
33. **duties of supervisory officers.**—governing the assignment by a board of duties to directors of education and other supervisory officers and prescribing the procedures in respect thereof, and defining any word or expression used in such regulation;
34. **suspension or dismissal of supervisory officers.**—prescribing the practices and procedures to be followed by a board in the case of suspension or dismissal of a director of education or other supervisory officer;
35. **competition with private sector.**—despite paragraph 28 of subsection 171(1), prohibiting or regulating and controlling any program or activity of a board that is or may be in competition with any business or occupation in the private sector and providing that such regulations have general application or application to a particular board;

36. **language programs.**—requiring boards to offer programs that deal with languages other than English or French and governing the establishment and operation of such programs.

(2) [Repealed 1993, c. 11, s. 11(3).]

(3) **Regulations, grants.**—Subject to the approval of the Lieutenant Governor in Council, the Minister may make regulations,

- (a) governing the apportionment and distribution of money appropriated or raised by the Legislature for educational purposes;
- (a.1) governing the apportionment and distribution of money appropriated or raised by the Legislature for the construction of child care facilities in schools;
- (b) prescribing the conditions governing the payment of legislative grants;
- (c) for the purposes of legislative grants,
    - (i) defining any word or expression,
    - (ii) requiring the approval of the Minister to any amount of money, enrolment, portion, number, estimate, facility, unit, project or rate used in determining the amount of such grants,
    - (iii) prescribing the portions of any expenditure to which such grants apply,
    - (iv) respecting the application of any part of such grants,
    - (v) applying factors in the calculation of the grants, and
    - (vi) authorizing the Minister to adjust amounts of assessment;
- (d) providing an assessment equalization factor,
    - (i) for each municipality, including, for public and secondary school purposes, any part of territory without municipal organization that is deemed to be attached thereto for such purposes and, for public school purposes, any part of territory without municipal organization that is deemed to be annexed thereto for public school purposes,
    - (ii) for each part of territory without municipal organization that is deemed to be a district municipality for the purposes of Part III,
    - (iii) for each part of territory without municipal organization that is deemed to be a district municipality for the purposes of Part IV,
    - (iv) for each public school section that comprises only territory without municipal organization, and
    - (v) for each separate school zone that comprises only territory without municipal organization,

    and may determine the assessment roll to which each such factor applies;
- (e) prescribing the method of determining the amount of the fee receivable by a board in respect of elementary or secondary school pupils or any class or group thereof, where the board provides education for one or more pupils in respect of whom a fee is payable under this Act, and defining any word or expression used in such regulation;
- (f) prescribing the method of calculating average daily enrolment;
- (g) providing for the payment of money to assist in the cost of the establishment and maintenance of schools referred to in paragraph 15 of subsection (1);

PART I — MINISTRY OF EDUCATION   **S. 11**

   (h) providing for assistance in the payment of board, lodging and transportation costs of elementary and secondary school pupils;

   (i) governing the provision of assistance for the payment of the cost of education of pupils who,

        (i) reside in the territorial districts, on lands held by the Crown in right of Canada or Ontario or by an agency of Canada or Ontario or on other lands that are exempt from taxation for school purposes,

        (ii) are qualified to be resident pupils in respect of a school section, separate school zone or secondary school district in Ontario and receive elementary or secondary education in Manitoba or Quebec, as the case may be, where, in the opinion of the Minister, daily transportation to a school in Ontario or the provision of board, lodging and transportation to and from a school in Ontario once a week is impracticable,

        (iii) are wards of or in care of a children's aid society, or

        (iv) are admitted to a centre, facility, home, hospital or institution that is approved, designated, established, licensed or registered under any Act;

   (j) providing for payments to a board for the purpose of limiting in a year the amount of the requisition for public or secondary school purposes or the increase in the mill rate for separate school purposes in respect of,

        (i) a municipality or part thereof, or

        (ii) a part of territory without municipal organization that is deemed to be a district municipality,

under the jurisdiction of the board.

(4) **Idem.**—A regulation made under subsection (3) may,

(a) be general or particular in its application;

(b) with respect to clause (3)(e), prescribe the maximum amount of any fee that may be charged; or

(c) with respect to clause (3)(e), provide for the determination of fees by boards.

    (5) **Application to previous year.**—A regulation made in any year under subsection (3) may be made to apply in its operation to that year, to a previous year, or to both.

    (6) **Estimates and expenditures.**—Subject to the approval of the Lieutenant Governor in Council and to section 121, the Minister may make regulations governing estimates that a board is required to prepare and adopt and expenditures that may be made by a board for any purpose.

    (7) **School year, terms and holidays.**—Subject to the approval of the Lieutenant Governor in Council, the Minister may make regulations,

(a) prescribing and governing the school year, school terms and school holidays;

(b) authorizing a board to vary one or more school terms or school holidays as designated by the regulations; and

(c) permitting a board to designate, and to implement with the prior approval of the Minister, a school year, school terms and school holidays for one or more schools under its jurisdiction that are different from those prescribed by the regulations.

    (8) **Exceptions: compulsory attendance.**—Subject to the approval of the Lieutenant Governor in Council, the Minister may make regulations prescribing the conditions under

which, and establishing the procedures by which, a child who is otherwise required to attend school under Part II and who has attained the age of fourteen years may be excused from attendance at school or required to attend school only part-time.

(9) **Regulations.**—Subject to the approval of the Lieutenant Governor in Council, the Minister may make regulations,

- (a) **fee for transcripts.**—prescribing the fee to be paid to the Ministry for a transcript of standing obtained in Ontario by a pupil;
- (b) **fee for certificates and letters of standing.**—prescribing the fee to be paid to the Ministry for duplicates of certificates of qualification, letters of standing and Ontario Teacher's Qualifications Record Cards;
- (c) **fee for statement of standing.**—prescribing the fee to be paid to the Ministry by a teacher for the preparation at the teacher's request of a statement of standing obtained, or a description of courses completed, at a teacher education institution in Ontario, and the forwarding thereof to a certification authority outside Ontario or to an educational institution;
- (d) **fees for evaluations.**—prescribing the conditions under which fees shall be paid to the Ministry for the evaluation of academic certificates, transcripts and other documents of educational standing, and prescribing the amounts of the fees;
- (e) **fees for duplicates of certificates.**—prescribing the fees to be paid for duplicates of diplomas and certificates granted to pupils;
- (f) **fees for courses.**—prescribing the fees to be paid for courses provided by the Ministry for teachers, principals and supervisory officers or any class thereof;
- (g) **admission to teachers' college.**—prescribing the terms and conditions upon which students may be admitted to a teachers' college, remain therein and be dismissed therefrom;
- (h) **tuition fee teachers' college.**—requiring the payment of a tuition fee by students attending a teachers' college, fixing the amount and manner of payment thereof and prescribing the conditions under which a student is entitled to a refund of the fee or part thereof.

(10) **Metropolitan Toronto School Board.**—A regulation made under this section may be made to apply to The Metropolitan Toronto School Board.

(11) **Regulations.**—The Lieutenant Governor in Council may make regulations,

- (a) prescribing the persons who shall make the determinations that are required to be made under subsections 230(7) and (9) and the distribution that is required to be made under subsection 230(15) and an alternative distribution that is required to be made under subsection 230(21) and the manner in which and the time by which they shall be made;
- (b) governing the distribution of information that relates to the determinations that are required to be made under subsections 230(7) and (9) and distributions that are required to be made under subsection 230(15) and an alternative distribution that is required to be made under subsection 230(21) and information that relates to appeals and applications with respect to such determinations and distributions;
- (c) governing the nomination procedures for the election of members to boards from

areas, including electoral areas established under subsection 315(3), that are composed of all or part of two or more municipalities;
(d) prescribing the duties to be performed by the clerks of the municipalities referred to in clause (c) and by the secretaries of boards in respect of nominations and elections.

(12) **Consistency with *Municipal Elections Act*.**—A regulation made under clause (11)(c) or (d) shall not be inconsistent with the *Municipal Elections Act* except to the extent necessary to ensure that the nominations and the election referred to in those clauses are carried out in an efficient and orderly manner.

(13) **French-language school boards.**—The Lieutenant Governor in Council may make regulations establishing French-language school boards.

(14) **Idem.**—A regulation under subsection (13) may include provisions respecting.
(a) the area of jurisdiction of a French-language school board;
(b) the structure and membership of a French-language school board and, if the board has more than one component, the jurisdiction of each component;
(c) the powers and duties of a French-language school board or a component of a French-language school board;
(d) attendance at schools operated by a French-language school board or a component of a French-language school board;
(e) the assessment and payment of rates in respect of a French-language school board or a component of a French-language school board;
(f) the election of members of a French-language school board or a component of a French-language school board, including the qualifications of electors and members;
(g) the resolutions of disputes between the components of a French-language school board and between a French-language school board and other boards;
(h) the transfer of real and personal property of other boards to a French-language school board or a component of a French-language school board.
(i) the transfer of employees of other boards to a French-language school board or a component of a French-language school board, including the rights of transferred employees;
(j) the dissolution and winding up of another board or a component of another board.
(k) the transfer or adjustment of assets and liabilities of a board affected by the establishment of a French-language school board.
(l) the continuation of legal and other proceedings commenced by or against a board or component of a board before the establishment of a French-language school board and the enforcement of court orders made before the establishment of a French-language school board in favour of or against a board or component of a board; and
(m) any other matter that the Lieutenant Governor in Council considers necessary or advisable in connection with the establishment of a French-language school board.

(15) **Idem.**—A regulation under subsection (13) may,
(a) deem a French-language school board or a component of a French-language school board to be a board for the purpose of any provision of this Act;
(b) modify or exclude the application of any provision of this Act, the *Assessment Act* or the *Municipal Elections Act*;

(c) deem a French-language school board or a component of a French-language school board to be a board for the purpose of the *School Boards and Teachers Collective Negotiations Act*, and deem classes of persons who are members of the Association des enseignantes et des enseignants franco-ontariens or The Ontario Secondary School Teachers' Federation to be branch affiliates for the purpose of that Act; and

(d) deem classes of transferred employees to have been intermingled for the purpose of section 64 of the *Labour Relations Act* and make any provision of that section applicable to the affected boards and their employees.

(15.1) **Ottawa-Carleton French-language School Board.**—A regulation under subsection (13) that dissolves The Ottawa-Carleton French-language School Board may provide that the order made by the Ontario Municipal Board under Part III of the *Municipal Affairs Act* on September 13, 1991 (Order Number M910066) applies with necessary modifications to a French-language school board.

(16) **Consultation before regulation under subs. (13).**—A regulation may not be made under subsection (13) unless there has been consultation with boards and employee groups that will be directly or indirectly affected by the creation of a French-language school board under the regulation.

(17) [Repealed 1993, c. 41, s. 1(1).]

(18) **Metropolitan Toronto School Board.**—A regulation made under this section that applies to The Metropolitan Toronto School Board may,

(a) deem The Metropolitan Toronto School Board and the boards of education in The Municipality of Metropolitan Toronto to be one divisional board of education; and

(b) deem the area municipalities in The Municipality of Metropolitan Toronto to be one urban municipality. 1991, Vol. 2, c. 10, s. 2; 1993, c. 11, s. 11; c. 41, s. 1(1); 1994, c. 1, s. 22(1)-(6).

12. (1) **Agreements with Canada re: physical fitness.**—The Crown in right of Ontario, represented by the Minister, with the approval of the Lieutenant Governor in Council, may make agreements with the Crown in right of Canada, represented by the Minister of National Health and Welfare of Canada respecting physical fitness, and the Minister may authorize a board to provide training in physical fitness.

(2) **Pupils at Indian schools.**—The Crown in right of Ontario, represented by the Minister, may make agreements with the Crown in right of Canada, represented by the Minister charged with the administration of the *Indian Act* (Canada), for the admission of pupils, other than Indians, to schools for Indians operated under that Act.

(3) **Non-Indian pupils at Indian schools.**—The Crown in right of Ontario, represented by the Minister, may enter into an agreement with a band, the council of the band or an education authority where such band, council of the band or education authority is authorized by the Crown in right of Canada to provide education for Indians, for the admission of pupils who are not Indians to a school operated by the band, council of the band or education authority.

(4) **Bursaries and scholarships.**—The Crown in right of Ontario, represented by the Minister, may make agreements with the Crown in right of Canada, represented by the Minister of Manpower and Immigration, respecting the establishment, awarding and payment of bursaries and scholarships to students eligible therefor under the regulations.

PART I — MINISTRY OF EDUCATION   S. 13

(5) **Learning materials.**—The Crown in right of Ontario, represented by the Minister, may enter into an agreement with the Crown in right of Canada in respect of the development and production of learning materials and the sharing of the costs thereof.

13. (1) **Continuation of school for deaf.**—The Ontario School for the Deaf for the education and instruction of the deaf and partially deaf is continued under the name Ontario School for the Deaf in English and École provinciale pour sourds in French.

(2) **Continuation of school for blind.**—The Ontario School for the Blind for the education and instruction of the blind and partially blind is continued under the name Ontario School for the Blind in English and École provinciale pour aveugles in French.

(3) **Administration.**—Both schools are under the administration of the Minister.

(4) **Additional schools.**—Subject to the approval of the Lieutenant Governor in Council, the Minister may establish, maintain and operate one or more additional schools for the deaf or schools for the blind.

(4.1) **Idem.**—A demonstration school may provide, in a residential or non-residential setting, special education programs and special education services for exceptional pupils with learning disabilities or with hearing or visual impairments.

(5) **Demonstration schools.**—Subject to the approval of the Lieutenant Governor in Council, the Minister may,

- (a) establish, maintain and operate one or more demonstration schools; or
- (b) enter into an agreement with a university to provide for the establishment, maintenance and operation by the university, under such terms and conditions as the Minister and the university may agree upon, of a demonstration school,

for exceptional pupils whose learning disabilities are such that a residential setting is required.

(6) **Idem.**—A demonstration school referred to in subsection (5) that was established by the Minister before the 12th day of December, 1980 is deemed not to be a school operated by the Ministry of Education for the purposes of the *Provincial Schools Negotiations Act*, and the provincial schools authority is not responsible for any matter relating to the employment of teachers at a demonstration school.

(7) **Regulations.**—Subject to the approval of the Lieutenant Governor in Council, the Minister may, in addition to his or her powers under section 11, make regulations with respect to schools continued or established under this section,

- (a) prescribing the terms and conditions upon which pupils may,
    - (i) be admitted to, and remain in, a school,
    - (ii) reside in homes approved by a superintendent, and
    - (iii) be discharged from a school;
- (b) authorizing the Minister to appoint a committee to determine any question concerning the eligibility for admission of an applicant;
- (c) prescribing the fees, if any, that shall be paid in respect of pupils or any class or classes thereof;
- (d) authorizing the payment of part or all of the transportation costs of pupils whose parents or guardians reside in Ontario, and fixing the maximum amount that may be paid;

(e) authorizing a superintendent to establish rules in respect of pupils admitted to the school;
(f) authorizing a superintendent to specify the type and minimum amount of clothing that a parent or guardian shall provide for a pupil;
(g) requiring a parent or guardian to deposit a sum of money with the business administrator of a school for the purpose of defraying the personal incidental expenses of a pupil, and fixing the amount of the deposit;
(h) authorizing a superintendent to dismiss a pupil and prescribing procedures in respect thereof;
(i) authorizing the Minister to provide training for, and certification of, teachers of the deaf and of the blind;
(j) designating the name of each school continued or established under this section. 1991, Vol. 2, c. 10, s. 3.

14. (1) **Teacher education.**—Subject to the approval of the Lieutenant Governor in Council, the Minister may,
(a) establish, maintain and conduct a college for the professional education of teachers;
(b) enter into an agreement with a university, a college of a university or a college to provide for the professional education of teachers by the university or college, under such terms and conditions as the Minister and the university or college may agree upon.

(2) **Practice teaching.**—Where the Minister conducts a teacher education program, a board that operates a public, separate or secondary school shall permit its schools to be used for observation and practice teaching purposes and shall provide for the services of any of its teachers in accordance with a schedule of payments to boards that provide accommodation for practice teaching purposes and to their principals and teachers who participate therein, and such schedule shall be approved by the Lieutenant Governor in Council.

(3) **Idem.**—Where a teacher education program is conducted pursuant to an agreement under clause (1)(b), a board that operates a public, separate or secondary school shall permit its schools to be used for observation and practice teaching purposes and shall provide for the services of any of its teachers under such terms and conditions as may be agreed upon between the board and the institution conducting the program and failing agreement in accordance with the schedule of payments to boards, principals and teachers referred to in subsection (2).

(4) **Idem.**—The cost of providing the professional education of teachers by a university, a college of a university or a college under an agreement referred to in clause (1)(b) shall be payable out of money appropriated therefor by the Legislature.

15. Leadership training camps.—The Minister may establish, maintain and conduct camps for leadership training.

16. (1) **Intention to operate private school.**—No private school shall be operated in Ontario unless notice of intention to operate the private school has been submitted in accordance with this section.

(2) **Idem.**—Every private school shall submit annually to the Ministry on or before the 1st day of September a notice of intention to operate a private school.

(3) **Idem.**—A notice of intention to operate a private school shall be in such form and shall include such particulars as the Minister may require.

PART I — MINISTRY OF EDUCATION **S. 17**

(4) **Offence to operate private school without filing notice of intent to operate.**—Every person concerned in the management of a private school that is operated in contravention of subsection (1) is guilty of an offence and on conviction is liable to a fine of not more than $50 for every day such school is so operated.

(5) **Return.**—The principal, headmaster, headmistress or person in charge of a private school shall make a return to the Ministry furnishing such statistical information regarding enrolment, staff, courses of study and other information as and when required by the Minister, and any such person who fails to make such return within sixty days of the request of the Minister is guilty of an offence and on conviction is liable to a fine of not more than $200.

(6) **Inspection of school.**—The Minister may direct one or more supervisory officers to inspect a private school, in which case each such supervisory officer may enter the school at all reasonable hours and conduct an inspection of the school and any records or documents relating thereto, and every person who prevents or obstructs or attempts to prevent or obstruct any such entry or inspection is guilty of an offence and on conviction is liable to a fine of not more than $500.

(7) **Inspection on request.**—The Minister may, on the request of any person operating a private school, provide for inspection of the school in respect of the standard of instruction in the subjects leading to the Ontario secondary school diploma, the secondary school graduation diploma and to the secondary school honour graduation diploma, and may determine and charge a fee for such inspection.

(8) **Inspection of teachers.**—The Minister may, on the request of a person operating a private school or of a person in charge of a conservation authority school or field centre, provide for the inspection of a teacher in such school or centre who requires the recommendation of a supervisory officer for certification purposes.

(9) **Offence for false statement.**—Every person who knowingly makes a false statement in a notice of intention to operate a private school or an information return under this section is guilty of an offence and on conviction is liable to a fine of not more than $500.

17. (1) **Variation of scholarships and awards.**—Where the educational object of a gift or bequest accepted by the Treasurer of Ontario under section 6 of the *Financial Administration Act* is the establishment of a scholarship or an award that is available to one or more students in an elementary or a secondary school or a teacher training institution and,

(a) the selection of the recipient of the scholarship or award is based upon an examination which is no longer given;

(b) the school or teachers' college at which attendance is required for eligibility is no longer operated;

(c) reference to a county or a board in the terms and conditions of the gift or bequest is no longer appropriate by reason of the establishment of a regional municipality or a divisional board of education; or

(d) the course or program of instruction specified in the terms and conditions is no longer available, or is no longer available at the school or teachers' college,

the Lieutenant Governor in Council on the recommendation of the Minister may, from time to time, vary the terms and conditions of the gift or bequest in respect of the qualifications for eligibility for the scholarship or award so as to ensure that such scholarship or award will be granted or given under such terms and conditions as in the opinion of the Minister most nearly approximate those of the original gift or bequest, and the Minister may delegate his or her powers under the original terms and conditions of such gift or bequest to a representative of the board, or the educational institution, granting the scholarship or making the award, pursuant to any variation in the terms and conditions of the gift or bequest made under this section.

(2) **Where award is repayable loan.**—In the case of an award in the form of a repayable loan for which no person has made application for seven consecutive years, the Lieutenant Governor in Council, on the recommendation of the Minister and with the written consent of the person making the gift or the trustee of the person making the bequest, may capitalize the fund and any interest accrued thereon held by the Treasurer of Ontario, and may change the educational object of the gift or bequest to another object of an educational nature, in which case the provisions of subsection (1) shall apply with necessary modifications.

17.1 (1) **Ontario Parent Council.**—The council known in English as the Ontario Parent Council and in French as Conseil ontarien des parents is continued and shall be composed of not more than eighteen members appointed by the Minister.

(2) **Eligibility for appointment.**—A person is eligible for appointment to the Council if the person,

(a) is a parent or guardian of a child enrolled in an elementary or secondary school in Ontario; and

(b) meets the eligibility criteria established under subsection (3).

(3) **Eligibility criteria established by Minister.**—The Minister may establish such eligibility criteria for appointment to the Council as the Minister considers advisable.

(4) **Non-application of *Regulations Act*.**—The *Regulations Act* does not apply to criteria established under subsection (3).

(5) **Term of office.**—Members of the Council shall be appointed for a term of two years and may be reappointed for further terms, except that no person shall be appointed for three or more consecutive terms.

(6) **Same.**—Despite subsection (5), members appointed to the Council before the coming into force of this section are appointed for the term specified in the appointment.

(7) **Chair.**—The Minister shall designate a chair from among the members of the Council.

(8) **Remuneration and expenses.**—The members of the Council shall be paid such remuneration and expenses as are determined by the Lieutenant Governor in Council.

(9) **Staff and accommodation.**—The Ministry shall provide the Council with such staff and accommodation as the Minister considers necessary for the purposes of the Council.

(10) **Mandate.**—The Council shall advise the Minister on,

(a) issues related to elementary and secondary school education; and

(b) methods of increasing parental involvement in elementary and secondary school education.

(11) **Annual report.**—The Council shall report on its activities annually to the Minister.

(12) **Additional reports.**—In addition to its annual report, the Council may report to the Minister at any time and shall comply with any requests made by the Minister for additional reports. 1993, c. 41, s. 2.

PART II
SCHOOL ATTENDANCE

18. Definition.—In sections 21, 23, 26, 28 and 30, "guardian", in addition to having the meaning ascribed in section 1, includes any person who has received into his or her home a child of compulsory school age who is not the person's child but resides with the person or is in his or her care.

19. Closing of school or class by board.—A board may close or authorize the closing of a school or class for a temporary period where such closing appears unavoidable because of,
   (a) failure of transportation arrangements; or
   (b) inclement weather, fire, flood, the breakdown of the school heating plant, the failure of an essential utility or a similar emergency.

20. Closing of schools on civic holiday.—Where the head of the council of a municipality in which a school is situate proclaims a school day as a civic holiday for the municipality, the board may, by resolution, close any of the schools under its jurisdiction on such day.

21. (1) **Compulsory attendance.**—Unless excused under this section,
   (a) every child who attains the age of six years on or before the first school day in September in any year shall attend an elementary or secondary school on every school day from the first school day in September in that year until the child attains the age of sixteen years; and
   (b) every child who attains the age of six years after the first school day in September in any year shall attend an elementary or secondary school on every school day from the first school day in September in the next succeeding year until the last school day in June in the year in which the child attains the age of sixteen years.

(2) **When attendance excused.**—A child is excused from attendance at school if,
   (a) the child is receiving satisfactory instruction at home or elsewhere;
   (b) the child is unable to attend school by reason of sickness or other unavoidable cause;
   (c) transportation is not provided by a board for the child and there is no school that the child has a right to attend situated,
      (i) within 1.6 kilometres from the child's residence measured by the nearest road if the child has not attained the age of seven years on or before the first school day in September in the year in question, or
      (ii) within 3.2 kilometres from the child's residence measured by the nearest road if the child has attained the age of seven years but not the age of ten years on or before the first school day in September in the year in question, or
      (iii) within 4.8 kilometres from the child's residence measured by the nearest road if the child has attained the age of ten years on or before the first school day in September in the year in question;
   (d) the child has obtained a secondary school graduation diploma or has completed a course that gives equivalent standing;
   (e) the child is absent from school for the purpose of receiving instruction in music and the period of absence does not exceed one-half day in any week;

(f) the child is suspended, expelled or excluded from attendance at school under any Act or under the regulations;
(g) the child is absent on a day regarded as a holy day by the church or religious denomination to which the child belongs; or
(h) the child is absent or excused as authorized under this Act and the regulations.

(3) **Blind, deaf or mentally handicapped children.**—The fact that a child is blind, deaf or mentally handicapped is not of itself an unavoidable cause under clause (2)(b).

(4) **Child under compulsory age.**—Where a child under compulsory school age has been enrolled as a pupil in an elementary school, this section applies during the period for which the child is enrolled as if the child were of compulsory school age.

(5) **Duty of parent, etc.**—The parent or guardian of a child who is required to attend school under this section shall cause the child to attend school as required by this section.

(6) **Separate school supporters.**—Nothing in this section requires the child of a Roman Catholic separate school supporter to attend a public school or a Protestant separate school, or requires the child of a public school supporter to attend a Roman Catholic separate school.

22. Where school year varied.—Where a school year approved by the Minister does not commence on the day following Labour Day, references to the first school day in September and the last school day in June in section 21 shall be read as the first school day in the school year and the last school day in the school year respectively for the purpose of compulsory attendance of pupils of the school or schools or parts thereof to which the school year applies.

23. (1) **Suspension of pupil.**—A principal may suspend a pupil because of persistent truancy, persistent opposition to authority, habitual neglect of duty, the wilful destruction of school property, the use of profane or improper language, or conduct injurious to the moral tone of the school or to the physical or mental well-being of others in the school.

(1.1) **Period of suspension.**—A suspension under subsection (1) shall be for a period fixed by the principal, not exceeding twenty school days or such shorter period as may be established by the board as the maximum period for suspensions under subsection (1).

(1.2) **Notice.**—When a pupil is suspended under subsection (1), the principal shall,

(a) notify forthwith in writing the pupil, the pupil's parent or guardian, the pupil's teachers, the board, the appropriate school attendance counsellor and the appropriate supervisory officer of the suspension and the reasons for the suspension; and
(b) notify forthwith in writing the pupil and the pupil's parent or guardian of the right of appeal under subsection (2).

(2) **Appeal against suspension.**—The parent or guardian of a pupil who has been suspended or the pupil, where the pupil is an adult, may, within seven days of the commencement of the suspension, appeal to the board against the suspension and the board, after hearing the appeal or where no appeal is made, may remove, confirm or modify the suspension and, where the board considers it appropriate, may order that any record of the suspension be expunged.

(2.1) **Effect of appeal.**—An appeal under subsection (2) does not stay the suspension and, if the suspension expires before the appeal is determined, the board shall determine whether the suspension should be confirmed or whether the record of the suspension should be removed or modified.

PART II — SCHOOL ATTENDANCE   **S. 24**

(2.2) **Review of suspensions.**—If the pupil is suspended for the maximum period allowed under subsection (1.1) or is suspended more than once during a school year, the board shall ensure that a guidance counsellor or other appropriate resource person employed by the board,

(a) reviews the circumstances of the suspension or suspensions, as the case may be; and
(b) where appropriate, informs the pupil and, if the pupil is not an adult, the pupil's parent or guardian, of services that are available from the board or elsewhere in the community to assist the pupil.

(3) **Expulsion of pupil.**—A board may expel a pupil from its schools on the ground that the pupil's conduct is so refractory that the pupil's presence is injurious to other pupils or persons, if,

(a) the principal and the appropriate supervisory officer so recommend;
(b) the pupil and the pupil's parent or guardian have been notified in writing of,
 (i) the recommendation of the principal and the supervisory officer, and
 (ii) the right of the pupil where the pupil is an adult and otherwise of the pupil's parent or guardian to make representations at a hearing to be conducted by the board;
(c) the teacher or teachers of the pupil have been notified; and
(d) such hearing has been conducted.

(4) **Parties to hearing.**—The parties to a hearing under this section shall be the parent or guardian of the pupil or the pupil, where the pupil is an adult, the principal of the school that the pupil attends and, in the case of an expulsion, the appropriate supervisory officer.

(5) **Readmission of pupil.**—A board may at its discretion readmit to school a pupil who has been expelled.

(6) **Committee to perform board functions.**—The board, by resolution, may direct that the powers and duties of the board under subsections (2) to (5) shall be exercised and performed by a committee of at least three members of the board named in the resolution or designated from time to time in accordance with the resolution. 1993, c. 11, s. 12.

24. (1) **Provincial School Attendance Counsellor.**—The Lieutenant Governor in Council may appoint an officer, to be the Provincial School Attendance Counsellor, who shall, under the direction of the Minister, superintend and direct the enforcement of compulsory school attendance.

(2) **Inquiry by Provincial Counsellor.**—Where the parent or guardian of a child considers that the child is excused from attendance at school under subsection 21(2), and the appropriate school attendance counsellor or the Provincial School Attendance Counsellor is of the opinion that the child should not be excused from attendance, the Provincial School Attendance Counsellor shall direct that an inquiry be made as to the validity of the reason or excuse for non-attendance and the other relevant circumstances, and for such purpose shall appoint one or more persons who are not employees of the board that operates the school that the child has the right to attend to conduct a hearing and to report to the Provincial School Attendance Counsellor the result of the inquiry and may, by order in writing signed by him or her, direct that the child,

(a) be excused from attendance at school; or

(b) attend school,

and a copy of the order shall be delivered to the board and to the parent or guardian of the child.

(3) **Powers of Provincial Counsellor.**—The Provincial School Attendance Counsellor has all the powers of a school attendance counsellor and may exercise such powers anywhere in Ontario.

25. (1) **Appointment of school attendance counsellors.**—Every board shall appoint one or more school attendance counsellors.

(2) **Idem.**—Two or more boards may appoint the same school attendance counsellor or counsellors.

(3) **Vacancies.**—Where the office of a school attendance counsellor becomes vacant, it shall be filled forthwith by the board.

(4) **Notice of appointment.**—Notice of the appointment of a school attendance counsellor shall be given in writing by the board to the Provincial School Attendance Counsellor and to the supervisory officers concerned.

(5) **Jurisdiction and responsibility of school attendance counsellor.**—A school attendance counsellor appointed by a board has jurisdiction and is responsible for the enforcement of compulsory school attendance in respect of every child who is required to attend school and who,

(a) is qualified to be a resident pupil of the board; or

(b) is or has been enrolled during the current school year in a school operated by the board, except a child who is under the jurisdiction of a person appointed under section 119 of the *Indian Act* (Canada).

26. (1) **Powers of counsellors.**—Where a school attendance counsellor has reasonable and probable grounds for believing that a child is illegally absent from school, he or she may, at the written request of the parent or guardian of the child or of the principal of the school that the child is required to attend, take the child to the child's parent or guardian or to the school from which the child is absent provided that, if exception is taken to the school attendance counsellor entering a dwelling place, he or she shall not enter therein.

(2) **Reports.**—A school attendance counsellor shall report to the board that appointed him or her as required by the board.

(3) **To act under appropriate supervisory officer and provincial counsellor.**—A school attendance counsellor is responsible to the appropriate supervisory officer, and shall carry out the instructions and directions of the Provincial School Attendance Counsellor.

(4) **Inquiry by counsellor and notice.**—A school attendance counsellor shall inquire into every case of failure to attend school within his or her knowledge or when requested so to do by the appropriate supervisory officer or the principal of a school or a ratepayer, and shall give written warning of the consequences of such failure to the parent or guardian of a child who is not attending school as required, and shall also give written notice to the parent or guardian to cause the child to attend school forthwith, and shall advise the parent or guardian in writing of the provisions of subsection 24(2).

PART II — SCHOOL ATTENDANCE S. 30

27. Census.—A board may make or obtain a complete census of all persons in the area in which the board has jurisdiction who have not attained the age of twenty-one years.

28. (1) **Reports and information.**—The principal of every elementary and secondary school shall,

(a) report to the appropriate school attendance counsellor and supervisory officer the names, ages and residences of all pupils of compulsory school age who have not attended school as required;

(b) furnish the school attendance counsellor with such other information as the counsellor requires for the enforcement of compulsory school attendance; and

(c) report in writing to the school attendance counsellor every case of expulsion and readmission of a pupil.

(2) **Where no school attendance counsellor.**—Where a child of compulsory school age has not attended school as required and there is no school attendance counsellor having jurisdiction in respect of the child, the appropriate supervisory officer shall notify the parent or guardian of the child of the requirements of section 21.

29. Provincial counsellor as trustee.—Where it appears to the Minister that the board of a district school area is not providing accommodation or instruction for its resident pupils either in schools operated by the board or under an agreement with another board in schools operated by such other board, has neglected or failed to raise the necessary funds for the provision of such accommodation and instruction or has in other respects failed to comply with this Act and the regulations, or that the election of members of the board has been neglected and no regular board is in existence, the Minister may authorize and direct the Provincial School Attendance Counsellor to do all things and exercise all powers that may be necessary for the provision and maintenance of accommodation and instruction for the resident pupils of the board including the erection of school buildings and the conduct of schools and for the levying of all sums of money required for the purposes of the board, and generally whatever may be required for the purpose of establishing, maintaining and conducting schools in accordance with this Act and the regulations, and thereupon the Provincial School Attendance Counsellor has, for such period as authorized by the Minister, all the authority and powers vested in, and may, during such period perform the duties of, the board.

30. (1) **Liability of parent or guardian.**—A parent or guardian of a child of compulsory school age who neglects or refuses to cause the child to attend school is, unless the child is legally excused from attendance, guilty of an offence and on conviction is liable to a fine of not more than $200.

(2) **Bond for attendance.**—The court may, in addition to or instead of imposing a fine, require a person convicted of an offence under subsection (1) to submit to the Treasurer of Ontario a personal bond, in a form prescribed by the court, in the penal sum of $200 with one or more sureties as required, conditioned that the person shall cause the child to attend school as required by this Part, and upon breach of the condition the bond is forfeit to the Crown.

(3) **Employment during school hours.**—A person who employs during school hours a child who is required to attend school under section 21 is guilty of an offence and on conviction is liable to a fine of not more than $200.

(4) **Offences by corporations.**—Subsections (1) and (3) apply with necessary modifications to a corporation and, in addition, every director and officer of the corporation who

authorizes, permits or acquiesces in the contravention is guilty of an offence and on conviction is liable to the same penalty as the corporation.

(5) **Habitually absent from school.**—A child who is required by law to attend school and who refuses to attend or who is habitually absent from school is guilty of an offence and, subject to the *Provincial Offences Act*, on conviction is liable to the penalties that were provided immediately before the 2nd day of April, 1984 for children adjudged to be juvenile delinquents under the *Juvenile Delinquents Act* (Canada), and subsection 266(2) applies in any proceeding under this section.

(6) **Proceedings under subs. (5).**—Proceedings in respect of offences under subsection (5) shall be proceeded with only in accordance with such subsection.

(7) **Reference to provincial counsellor for inquiry.**—Where, in a proceeding under this section, it appears to the court that the child may have been excused from attendance at school under subsection 21(2), the court may refer the matter to the Provincial School Attendance Counsellor who shall direct that an inquiry shall be made as provided in subsection 24(2) which subsection shall apply with necessary modifications except that the Provincial School Attendance Counsellor shall, in lieu of making an order, submit a report to the court.

31. (1) **Proceedings to be taken by attendance counsellors.**—Prosecutions under section 30 shall be instituted by the school attendance counsellor concerned.

(2) **Certificate of principal as proof in the absence of evidence to the contrary.**—In prosecutions under section 30, a certificate as to the attendance or non-attendance at school of any child, signed or purporting to be signed by the principal of the school, is proof in the absence of evidence to the contrary of the facts stated therein without any proof of the signature or appointment of the principal.

(3) **Proof of age.**—Where a person is charged under section 30 in respect of a child who is alleged to be of compulsory school age and the child appears to the court to be of compulsory school age, the child shall, for the purposes of such prosecution, be deemed to be of compulsory school age unless the contrary is proved.

(4) **Order re school attendance.**—An order made under subsection 24(2) shall be admitted in evidence in a prosecution only where the prosecution is in respect of the school year for which the order was made. 1993, c. 27, *Schedule.*

32. (1) **Resident pupil right to attend school.**—A person has the right, without payment of a fee, to attend a school in a school section, separate school zone or secondary school district, as the case may be, in which the person is qualified to be a resident pupil.

(2) **Admission without fee.**—Despite the other provisions of this Part, except subsection 49(6), where it appears to a board that a person who resides in the area of jurisdiction of the board is denied the right to attend school without the payment of a fee, the board, at its discretion, may admit the person from year to year without the payment of a fee.

33. (1) **Resident pupil public school qualification.**—Subject to sections 35, 38 and 45, a person who attains the age of six years in any year is, after the 1st day of September in such year, qualified to be a resident pupil in respect of a school section until the last school day in June in the year in which the person attains the age of twenty-one years, if,

(a) the person resides in the school section in which the person's parent or guardian who is not a separate school supporter resides; or
(b) the person or the person's parent or guardian is assessed for public school purposes in the school section,
   (i) as an owner, or
   (ii) for business assessment, or
   (iii) as an owner and for business assessment,

for an amount that, when adjusted by the latest assessment equalization factor applicable thereto that is provided by the Minister, is not less than the quotient obtained by dividing the total equalized assessment, for the year next preceding, of property rateable for public school purposes in that school section, by the average daily enrolment of pupils resident in that school section in such year.

(2) **Resident pupil separate school qualification.**—Subject to sections 35, 38 and 45, a person who attains the age of six years in any year is, after the 1st day of September in such year, qualified to be a resident pupil in respect of a separate school zone until the last school day in June in the year in which he attains the age of twenty-one years, if,

(a) the person resides in the separate school zone in which the person's parent or guardian who is a separate school supporter resides; or
(b) the person or the person's parent or guardian is assessed for separate school purposes in the zone,
   (i) as an owner, or
   (ii) for business assessment, or
   (iii) as an owner and for business assessment,

for an amount that, when adjusted by the latest assessment equalization factor applicable thereto that is provided by the Minister, is not less than the quotient obtained by dividing the total equalized assessment, for the year next preceding, of property rateable for separate school purposes in that zone, by the average daily enrolment of pupils resident in that zone in such year.

(3) **Evidence as to right to attend.**—It is the responsibility of the parent or guardian to submit evidence that the child has a right to attend an elementary school, including proof of age.

(4) **Resident pupil, elementary.**—A person who is qualified to be a resident pupil in respect of a school section or a separate school zone is a resident pupil if the person enrols in a school operated by the board of the school section or separate school zone, as the case may be, or in a school operated by another board to which the board of such school section or separate school zone pays fees on the person's behalf.

(5) [Repealed 1993, c. 11, s. 13.]

(6) [Repealed 1993, c. 11, s. 13.]

34. (1) **Kindergarten.**—If a board operates a kindergarten in a school, a child who is otherwise qualified may become a resident pupil at an age one year lower than that referred to in section 33. 1993, c. 11, s. 14(1).

(2) **Junior kindergarten.**—If a board operates a junior kindergarten in a school, a child who is otherwise qualified may become a resident pupil at an age two years lower than that referred to in section 33. 1993, c. 11, s. 14(2).

(2.1) **Same.**—Subsection (2) does not apply to a board that is exempt from paragraph 6.2 of subsection 170(1). 1993, c. 11, s. 14(2). [To be repealed on September 1, 1997. 1993, c. 11, s. 14(3).]

(2.2) **Same.**—If a board that is exempt from paragraph 6.2 of subsection 170(1) operates a junior kindergarten in a school, a child who is otherwise qualified and who resides within the attendance area of that school may become a resident pupil at an age two years lower than that referred to in section 33. 1993, c. 11, s. 14(2). [To be repealed on September 1, 1997. 1993, c. 11, s. 14(3).]

(3) **Beginners class.**—A board may provide a class or classes for children to enter school for the first time on or after the first school day in January and, where the board so provides, a child whose birthday is on or after the 1st day of January and before the 1st day of July, who resides in an area determined by the board and who is eligible to be admitted to an elementary school or kindergarten, as the case may be, on the first school day in the following September, may become a resident pupil in respect of such class. 1993, c. 11, s. 14.

35. [Repealed 1993, c. 11, s. 15(1). *But see 1993, c. 11, s. 15(2).*]

36. (1) **Establishment of Special Education Tribunal.**—The Lieutenant Governor in Council shall establish one or more Special Education Tribunals, provincial or regional, and appoint a secretary of such tribunals.

(2) **Procedures of Special Education Tribunals.**—The Lieutenant Governor in Council may by order,

(a) establish the procedures that shall apply; and
(b) authorize Special Education Tribunals to fix and assess costs,

with respect to matters dealt with by Special Education Tribunals. 1993, c. 11, s. 16.

37. (1) **Leave to appeal.**—Where a parent or guardian of a pupil has exhausted all rights of appeal under the regulations in respect of the identification or placement of the pupil as an exceptional pupil and is dissatisfied with the decision in respect of the identification or placement, the parent or guardian may apply to the secretary of a Special Education Tribunal for a hearing for leave to appeal to a regional tribunal established by the Minister under subsection (2) in respect of the identification or placement.

(2) **Establishment of regional tribunal.**—Where leave to appeal is granted under subsection (1), a regional tribunal shall be established by the Minister to hear the appeal of the parent or guardian.

(3) **Hearing by Special Education Tribunal.**—Despite subsection (1), a Special Education Tribunal may with the consent of the parties before it in lieu of granting leave to appeal to a regional tribunal hear and dispose of the appeal of the parent or guardian.

(4) **Regulations.**—The Lieutenant Governor in Council may make regulations governing the provision, establishment, organization and administration of a regional tribunal and regulating and controlling the practice and procedure before such tribunal including the costs of persons before such tribunal.

(5) **Decision final.**—The decision of a Special Education Tribunal or of a regional tribunal under this section is final and binding upon the parties to any such decision.

(6) **Disposition.**—The tribunal hearing the appeal may,
- (a) dismiss the appeal; or
- (b) grant the appeal and make such order as it considers necessary with respect to the identification or placement of the pupil.

38. Admission where pupil moves into residence not assessed in accordance with his or her school support.—Where a child who would otherwise have the right to attend school in a school section or separate school zone moves with his or her parent or guardian,
- (a) who is not a separate school supporter, into a residence that is assessed to the support of separate schools; or
- (b) who is a separate school supporter, into a residence that is assessed to the support of public schools,

and the latest date upon which the assessment of the residence may be changed from,
- (c) separate to public school support; or
- (d) public to separate school support,

has passed, upon the filing of a notice of change of support for the following year with the clerk of the municipality, the child shall be admitted, without the payment of a fee, to a public or separate school, as the case may be, that will be supported by the assessment of the residence on the effective date of the change of school support.

39. Resident pupil's right to attend more accessible school in adjoining school section or separate school zone.—Where a resident pupil of a school section or separate school zone resides,
- (a) more than 3.2 kilometres by the shortest distance by road from the school that the pupil is required to attend;
- (b) more than 0.8 kilometres by the shortest distance by road from any point from which transportation is provided to the school that the pupil is required to attend; and
- (c) nearer by the shortest distance by road to another public school in another school section in the case of a public school pupil, or of another separate school in another separate school zone in the case of a separate school pupil, than to the school that the pupil is required to attend,

the pupil shall be admitted to the nearer public school or the nearer separate school, as the case may be, referred to in clause (c), where the appropriate supervisory officer for the school section or separate school zone, as the case may be, in which such school is situate, certifies that there is sufficient accommodation for the pupil in such school, and where the pupil is admitted to such school, the board of the school section or separate school zone of which the pupil is a resident pupil shall pay in respect of the pupil a fee calculated in accordance with the regulations.

40. (1) **Resident pupil secondary school qualification.**—A person is qualified to be a resident pupil in respect of a secondary school district if,
- (a) the person and the person's parent or guardian reside in the secondary school district; or
- (b) the person or the person's parent or guardian is assessed in the secondary school district,

(i) as an owner, or
(ii) for business assessment, or
(iii) as an owner and for business assessment,

for an amount that, when adjusted by the latest assessment equalization factor applicable thereto that is provided by the Minister, is not less than the quotient obtained by dividing the total equalized assessment, for the year next preceding, of property rateable for secondary school purposes in that secondary school district, by three times the average daily enrolment of pupils resident in that secondary school district in such year; or

(c) the person resides in the secondary school district and is the owner or tenant of property therein that is separately assessed; or

(d) the person is over eighteen years of age and has resided in the secondary school district for the twelve months immediately before the person's admission to a secondary school in the secondary school district or to a secondary school operated by another secondary school board to which the board of such secondary school district pays fees on the person's behalf.

(2) **Resident pupil, secondary.**—A person who is qualified to be a resident pupil in respect of a secondary school district is a resident pupil if the person enrols in a secondary school operated by the board of the secondary school district or in a secondary school operated by another secondary school board to which the board of such secondary school district pays fees on the person's behalf.

(3) [Repealed 1993, c. 11, s. 17.]

(4) **Admission of adult resident who is not a resident pupil.**—Despite any general or special Act, a person who resides in a secondary school district and who, except as to residence, is qualified to be a resident pupil in another secondary school district shall be admitted, without the payment of a fee, to a secondary school operated by the board of the secondary school district in which the person resides if,

(a) the person has attained the age of eighteen years and has been promoted or transferred to a secondary school; and

(b) the appropriate supervisory officer certifies that there is adequate accommodation in the secondary school.

(5) **Limitation on right to attend without payment of fee.**—Despite section 32, where a pupil,

(a) has completed elementary school; and
(b) has attended one or more secondary schools for a total of seven or more years,

the board of the secondary school that the pupil attends may charge a fee calculated in accordance with the regulations. 1993, c. 11, s. 17.

41. (1) **Resident pupil.**—Subject to subsections (2) and (3), a person who is qualified to be a resident pupil of a secondary school district has the right to attend any secondary school,

(a) that is more accessible to the person than any secondary school in the secondary school district of which the person is qualified to be a resident pupil;

(b) to take, for the purpose of obtaining the secondary school honour graduation diploma, a subject or subjects not available in the secondary school district of which the person

is qualified to be a resident pupil but required by the person for admission to any university or teacher-training course or for entry into any trade, profession or calling;
(c) to take a program of study that includes the subject of French for French-speaking pupils in the intermediate or senior division and that is not available in the secondary school district of which the person is qualified to be a resident pupil, where such program of study is required by the person for admission to any university of teacher-training course or college of applied arts and technology or for entry into any trade, profession or calling; or
(d) to take a program in a French-language school or class if a French-language school or class is not provided by the board of the secondary school district of which the person is qualified to be a resident pupil.

(2) **Restrictions.**—Subsection (1) applies to a person who is qualified to be a resident pupil of a secondary school district only if the appropriate supervisory officer certifies that there is adequate accommodation for the person in the school.

(3) **Where agreement between boards.**—Clauses (1)(b), (c) and (d) do not apply to a person who is qualified to be a resident pupil of a secondary school district if the board of the secondary school district has entered into an agreement with another secondary school board under section 186 and the programs and subjects referred to in such clauses are offered in the schools covered by the agreement.

42. (1) **Admission of resident pupil from other district.**—A person who is qualified to be a resident pupil of a secondary school district and who applies for admission to a secondary school situated in another secondary school district shall furnish the principal of the school to which admission is sought with a statement signed by the person's parent or guardian or by the pupil where the pupil is an adult, stating,

(a) the name of the secondary school district in respect of which the person is qualified to be a resident pupil;
(b) whether or not the pupil or the pupil's parent or guardian is assessed in the secondary school district in which the school is situated, and if so assessed the amount of such assessment; and
(c) the authority, under this Act, under which the pupil claims to have a right to attend the school.

(2) **Notice of admission.**—The principal of the school shall forward the statement to the chief executive officer of the board that operates the school and, if the pupil is admitted, the chief executive officer of the board shall forthwith notify the chief executive officer of the board of the secondary school district of which the pupil is qualified to be a resident pupil of the fact of the admission and of the information included in the statement.

43. (1) **Admission to secondary school.**—Where a pupil has been promoted from elementary school, the pupil shall be admitted to secondary school.

(2) **Idem.**—A person who has not been promoted from elementary school shall be admitted to a secondary school if the principal of the secondary school is satisfied that the applicant is competent to undertake the work of the school.

(3) **Where admission denied.**—Where an applicant for admission to a secondary school under subsection (2) is denied admission by the principal, the applicant may appeal to the board

and the board may, after a hearing, direct that the applicant be admitted or refused admission to a secondary school.

(4) **Alternative course or program.**—Where the pupil has clearly demonstrated to the principal that the pupil is not competent to undertake a particular course or program of studies, the principal shall not permit the pupil to undertake such course or program, in which case the pupil may take a prerequisite course, or select with the approval of the principal an appropriate alternative course or program provided that, where the pupil is a minor, the consent of the pupil's parent or guardian has been obtained.

(5) **Admission to continuing education class.**—A person is entitled to enrol in a continuing education course or class that is eligible for credit towards a secondary school diploma if the principal is satisfied that the person is competent to undertake the work of the course or class. 1993, c. 11, s. 18.

44. Admission where one parent is sole support.—Where, for any reason, one parent of a person is the sole support of the person, and that parent,

(a) resides in Ontario;
(b) is not assessed for school purposes in Ontario; and
(c) boards the person in a residence that is not a children's residence as defined in Part IX (Licensing) of the *Child and Family Services Act,*

the person shall, if otherwise qualified to be a resident pupil, be deemed to be qualified to be a resident pupil in respect of,

(d) a school section, if such residence is situate in the school section and is assessed to the support of public schools; or
(e) a separate school zone, if the person is a Roman Catholic and such residence is situate in the separate school zone and is assessed to the support of separate schools; or
(f) a secondary school district, if such residence is situate in the secondary school district and is assessed to the support of secondary schools.

45. (1) **Tax exempt land.**—A person who resides in a school section, separate school zone or secondary school district in which the person's parent or guardian resides, on land that is exempt from taxation for school purposes, is not qualified to be a resident pupil of the school section, separate school zone or secondary school district, unless the person or his or her parent or guardian is assessed and pays taxes for school purposes in such school section, separate school zone or secondary school district.

(2) **Resident on land exempt from taxation.**—A person who is otherwise qualified to attend an elementary or secondary school and who resides on land that is exempt from taxation for school purposes shall be admitted to a school that is accessible to the person where the appropriate supervisory officer has certified that there is sufficient accommodation for the person in the school for the current year, and fees calculated in accordance with the regulations shall, except where the regulations provide otherwise in respect of such fees, be prepaid monthly by the person or by his or her parent or guardian.

46. (1) **Admission of ward, etc., of children's aid society or training school to an elementary school.**—A child who is a ward of a children's aid society or in the care of a children's aid society or a ward of a training school, and who is otherwise qualified to be admitted to an elementary school, shall be admitted without the payment of a fee to an elementary school operated by the board of the school section or separate school zone, as the case may be, in which the child resides.

(2) **Admission of ward, etc., of children's aid society or training school to a secondary school.**—A child who is a ward of a children's aid society or in the care of a children's aid society or a ward of a training school, and who is otherwise qualified to be admitted to a secondary school, shall be admitted without the payment of a fee to a secondary school operated by the board of the secondary school district in which the child resides.

47. Where fee payable.—Where a child who is in the custody of a corporation, society or person, has not the right under the other provisions of this Part to attend the school that the corporation, society or person elects that the child attend, and the appropriate supervisory officer certifies that there is sufficient accommodation in such school for the current school year, the board that operates such school shall, where the child is otherwise qualified to attend such school, admit the child to the school upon the prepayment monthly by the corporation, society or person of a fee calculated in accordance with the regulations.

48. (1) [Repealed 1993, c. 11, s. 19(1). *But see 1993, c. 11, s. 19(2).*]

(2) **Idem.**—If on the 31st day of December, 1989 a pupil is enrolled in a school that the pupil has a right to attend and on the 1st day of January, 1990 the pupil, because of alterations to school board boundaries, no longer has a right to attend the school under any other provision of this Part, the pupil has the right to attend the school until the pupil completes his or her education in the school.

(3) **Agreement re transportation.**—The board of which a pupil referred to in subsection (2) is qualified to be a resident pupil may enter into an agreement with the board that operates the school, referred to in subsection (2), in respect of the transportation of the pupil to and from the school. 1993, c. 11, s. 19.

49. (1) **Fees payable.**—Where a person qualified to be a resident pupil of a secondary school district attends a secondary school that the person has a right to attend under subsection 41(1), the board of the secondary school district of which the person is qualified to be a resident pupil shall pay to the board that operates the secondary school attended by the pupil a fee calculated in accordance with the regulations.

(2) **Idem.**—Where a person qualified to be a resident pupil of a school division attends a public or secondary school in another school division under section 48, the divisional board of which the person is qualified to be a resident pupil shall pay to the divisional board that operates the school attended by the pupil a fee calculated in accordance with the regulations.

(3) **Idem.**—Where a separate school pupil resident in a county or district combined separate school zone attends a separate school in another combined separate school zone under section 48, the board of the combined separate school zone in which the pupil resides shall pay to the combined separate school board that operates the separate school attended by the pupil a fee calculated in accordance with the regulations.

(4) **Admission of resident pupil to another school by reason of distance to school.**—A child who resides with his or her parent or guardian in a residence that is assessed to the support of public schools and who may be excused from attendance under clause 21(2)(c) may be admitted to a public school in another school section if the appropriate supervisory officer certifies that there is sufficient accommodation for the child, and the board of the section in

which the child resides shall pay to the board of the other school section a fee calculated in accordance with the regulations.

(5) **Admission of qualified non-resident pupil.**—A board may admit to a school that it operates a person whose admission with or without the payment of a fee is not otherwise provided for in this Act but who, except as to residence, is qualified to attend such school, and may, at its discretion, require the payment by or on behalf of the person of a fee calculated in accordance with the regulations.

(6) **Fees for pupils.**—Despite any other provision of this Part, if a board admits to a school that it operates a person who is a visitor within the meaning of the *Immigration Act* (Canada) or a person who is in possession of a student authorization issued under that Act, the board shall charge the person the maximum fee calculated in accordance with the regulations.

(7) **Application of subs. (6).**—Subsection (6) does not apply to,

(a) a person who is a participant in an educational exchange program under which a pupil of the board attends a school outside Canada without a fee;
(b) a person who enrolled in an elementary school or a secondary school prior to the 1st day of July, 1982;
(c) a person who is a dependant within the meaning of the *Visiting Forces Act* (Canada);
(d) a person who is in Canada under a diplomatic, consular or official acceptance issued by the Department of External Affairs;
(e) a person who claims to be or is found to be a convention refugee under the *Immigration Act* (Canada);
(f) a person who is in Canada while the person's parent or other person who has lawful custody of the person is in Canada,
   (i) pursuant to employment authorization or ministerial permit issued by the Department of Employment and Immigration,
   (ii) under a diplomatic, consular or official acceptance issued by the Department of External Affairs,
   (iii) awaiting determination of a claim to be found a convention refugee under the *Immigration Act* (Canada),
   (iv) as a graduate student who is the recipient of an award approved by the Minister for the purposes of this clause and who is in attendance at a university or institution in Ontario, including its affiliated or federated institutions, that receives operating grants from the Ministry of Colleges and Universities, or
   (v) in accordance with an agreement with a university outside Canada to teach at an institution in Ontario, including its affiliated or federated institutions, that receives operating grants from the Ministry of Colleges and Universities; or
(g) a person who is in Canada while the person's parent or other person who has lawful custody of the person is in Canada as a convention refugee under the *Immigration Act* (Canada). 1993, c. 11, s. 20.

49.1 Persons unlawfully in Canada.—A person who is otherwise entitled to be admitted to a school and who is less than eighteen years of age shall not be refused admission because the person or the person's parent or guardian is unlawfully in Canada. 1993, c. 11, s. 21.

PART III

PUBLIC AND SECONDARY SCHOOLS

Tax Exemption of Separate School Supporters

50. Exemption of supporters of separate schools.—Nothing in this Act authorizing the levying or collecting of taxes on property rateable for public school purposes applies to the supporters of Roman Catholic separate schools or Protestant separate schools, except that the taxable property in respect of which a person gives notice under section 106 or 159 or under section 15 of the *Assessment Act* is not exempt from taxation for public school purposes imposed before the person becomes a separate school supporter in respect of such property.

Religious Instruction

51. (1) **Religious instruction.**—Subject to the regulations, a pupil shall be allowed to receive such religious instruction as the pupil's parent or guardian desires or, where the pupil is an adult, as the pupil desires.

(2) **Religious exercises.**—No pupil in a public school shall be required to read or study in or from a religious book, or to join in an exercise of devotion or religion, objected to by the pupil's parent or guardian, or by the pupil, where the pupil is an adult.

Visitors

52. Visitors.—A parent or guardian of a child attending a public or secondary school and a member of the board that operates the school may visit such school, and a member of the Assembly and a member of the clergy may visit a public and secondary school in his or her constituency or in the area where he or she has pastoral charge, as the case may be.

Divisional Boards

53. (1) **Application to schools on exempt land.**—A school section or a secondary school district that is designated as such by the Minister on lands held by the Crown in right of Canada or Ontario or by an agency thereof, or on any lands that are exempt from taxation for school purposes, shall not be included in a school division.

(2) **Essex county.**—For divisional board purposes, the County of Essex includes Pelee Island.

(3) **Territory without municipal organization deemed district municipality.**—In respect of divisional boards of education,

    (a) every school section in existence on the 31st day of December, 1968 that comprises only territory without municipal organization, except a school section established under section 67 or 68;

    (b) any part of territory without municipal organization that on the 31st day of December, 1968 was part of a high school district but was not in a school section; and

    (c) any part of territory without municipal organization that is designated by a regulation made under subsection 55(1), or a predecessor thereof, as a district municipality or

S. 54 EDUCATION ACT

that is added to a school division without being so designated and that on the 31st day of December, 1968 was not in a school section or in a high school district, shall be deemed to be a district municipality unless and until it becomes or is included in a municipality.

54. (1) **Powers and duties of divisional board re territory without municipal organization.**—Subject to subsection (2), the divisional board of a school division that includes territory without municipal organization that is deemed a district municipality shall, for public school purposes and for secondary school purposes, exercise the powers and duties of a municipal council for such district municipality with respect to preparing estimates, levying rates, collecting, cancelling, reducing or refunding taxes and issuing debentures for the purposes of the divisional board, and with respect thereto and to the election of members of the divisional board all the officers appointed by the divisional board have the same powers and duties, including the powers and duties with respect to the sale of land for tax arrears, as similar officers in an organized municipality and the provisions of subsections 65(5), (6) and (7) apply with necessary modifications, and the expenses incurred by the board in connection therewith except the issuing of debentures shall be apportioned to the property rateable for public school purposes and to the property rateable for secondary school purposes in such district municipality in the ratio that the assessment of such property rateable for public school purposes bears to the assessment of such property rateable for secondary school purposes, and shall be included in the levy imposed for school purposes on such property.

(2) **Parts of territory without municipal organization attached to municipality.**—Except as provided in subsection (5), where any part of territory without municipal organization that is included in a school division is attached to a municipality for public school purposes or is deemed to be attached to a municipality for public and secondary school purposes, such part shall continue to be deemed to be attached to such municipality for the purposes of the divisional board, and the officers of such municipality shall collect all taxes and do all such other acts and perform all such duties and be subject to the same liabilities with respect to such part of territory without municipal organization that forms part of the school division as with respect to any part of the school division that is within the municipality, and the expenses incurred in connection therewith shall be apportioned to the property rateable for public school purposes and to the property rateable for secondary school purposes in such territory without municipal organization in the ratio that the assessment of such property rateable for public school purposes bears to the assessment of such property rateable for secondary school purposes and shall be included in the levy imposed for school purposes on such property, but the divisional board may, by resolution passed before the 1st day of July in any year effective on the 1st day of January next following, a copy of which resolution shall be given forthwith to the Minister, the clerk of the municipality and the appropriate assessment commissioner, detach such territory from the municipality for school purposes and deem such territory to be a district municipality whereupon subsection (1) applies thereto.

(3) **Application of *Municipal Act*, s. 363.**—Section 363 of the *Municipal Act* applies to territory without municipal organization that is deemed a district municipality under this Act, and the divisional board has the powers of a municipal council under the said section 363 in respect of any such territory that is not attached to a municipality for school purposes, and the council of the municipality to which any such territory is attached for public school purposes

and for secondary school purposes under subsection (2) has the powers of a municipal council under the said section 363 in respect of the territory so attached.

(4) **Estimates to include expenses of collection, etc., and allowances to be made.**—The divisional board in preparing estimates of the sums required to be raised under subsection (1) or (2) shall,

- (a) make allowance for the abatement of and discount on taxes, for uncollectable taxes and for taxes that it is estimated will not be collected during the year in such part of the territory without municipal organization;
- (b) include the proper proportion of the salaries and expenses of the officers involved, having regard to the time spent by such officers on their duties under subsection (1) or (2); and
- (c) include the cost of providing elections of members of the board in such territory.

(5) **Where attached territory not included with municipality for election.**—Where any part of territory without municipal organization is attached to a municipality for public school purposes, or is deemed to be attached to a municipality for public and secondary school purposes, and such part is included, under subsection 230(15) or (21), with one or more municipalities in a combined area for the election of one or more members of the divisional board and the combined area does not include the municipality to which such part is so attached, such part shall be deemed to be attached for election purposes to the municipality that has the greatest residential and farm assessment in the combined area according to the last revised assessment roll as adjusted by the latest assessment equalization factor applicable thereto for each such municipality, provided by the Minister, and subsection (2) applies with necessary modifications.

(6) **Elections in improvement districts.**—The secretary-treasurer of an improvement district that forms all or part of a school division, in each year in which an election for members of the divisional board is to be held, shall provide for such election in the improvement district in the same manner as for the election of members of a divisional board in a municipality and shall have all the powers and shall perform all the duties of the clerk and returning officer of a municipality in relation to the election of members of a divisional board under the *Municipal Elections Act*.

55. (1) **School divisions, formation and alteration.**—The Lieutenant Governor in Council may, by regulation,

- (a) designate as a school division all or part of one or more municipalities, localities, counties, regional municipalities, district municipalities or territory without municipal organization or a combination thereof;
- (b) assign a name to a divisional board that has jurisdiction in a territorial district;
- (c) dissolve a board of a school division or of a school section that is included in a school division;
- (d) combine two or more adjoining school divisions to form one school division and provide that the board of the combined school division shall be a divisional board of education;
- (e) alter the boundaries of a school division and, where any part of territory without municipal organization is attached to a school division, designate such part as a district municipality or attach it to a district municipality;

(f) provide for representation if the boundaries of a school division are altered.

(2) **Adjustment of assets and liabilities on formation.**—Upon the formation of a new school division,

   (a) all lands and premises that become part of a new school division, including the personal property therein or thereon and that, on the last school day immediately prior to such formation, were used as school sites and vested in the board of a school division or school section affected by such formation, become vested in the board of such new school division, and no compensation or damages are payable in respect of such lands, premises and personal property;

   (b) all debts, contracts, agreements and liabilities for which a board or former board was liable in respect of that portion of its area of jurisdiction that becomes part of a new school division become obligations of the board of such new school division unless otherwise determined under clause (c);

   (c) the boards affected by such formation shall, in respect of the area that becomes part of a new school division, adjust in such manner as may be agreed upon by such boards, the assets and liabilities of such boards as of the date of such formation, except the property referred to in clause (a), and, where the boards are unable to agree, any matter in disagreement shall be referred by a board affected to the Ontario Municipal Board, whose decision is final;

   (d) the Minister may, by order, provide for the first election of the divisional board of a new school division, for a new election of the divisional board or board of a school section of an altered school division or school section, for the right of pupils affected by such formation to continue to attend schools that they were attending immediately prior to the formation and for any matter not specifically provided for in this section that the Minister considers necessary or advisable to carry out the intent and purposes of this Part.

(3) **Dissolution of board.**—No regulation made under this section has the effect of dissolving a board unless so provided in the regulation.

(4) **Name of board: defined city.**—Except where expressly provided in any other Act, the name of a divisional board that has jurisdiction in a defined city is ''The Board of Education for the City of ....'' or ''Conseil de l'éducation de la cité de ....'' or both (*inserting the name of the defined city*).

(5) **county.**—The name of a divisional board that has jurisdiction in one county is ''The .... County Board of Education'' or ''Conseil de l'éducation du comté de ....'' or both (*inserting the name of the county*).

(6) **regional municipality and counties.**—Except where expressly provided in any other Act, the name of a divisional board that has jurisdiction in,

   (a) all or part of a regional municipality;
   (b) all or parts of two or more counties; or
   (c) all or part of a regional municipality and all or part of one or more counties,

is ''The .... Board of Education'' or ''Conseil de l'éducation de ....'' or both (*inserting the name selected by the board and approved by the Minister*).

PART III — PUBLIC AND SECONDARY SCHOOLS   **S. 57**

(7) **territorial districts.**—The name of a divisional board that has jurisdiction in the territorial districts is "The .... Board of Education" or "Conseil de l'éducation de ...." or both (*inserting the name assigned by the regulations*).

(8) **bilingual.**—The name of a divisional board may be as follows where approved by the Minister:

> "Conseil de l'éducation de .... Board of Education" (*inserting the name of the county or defined city or the name approved by the Minister or assigned by the regulations*).

56. (1) **Divisional boards establishment.**—A divisional board of education shall be established in each school division, and the members of the board shall be elected and the board organized in accordance with sections 53 to 57, section 131, and Parts VIII and XIII.

(2) **Deemed public school section and secondary school district.**—For the purposes of every Act, a school division shall be deemed to be a school section and a secondary school district.

(3) **Powers and duties.**—Every divisional board is a corporation and has all the powers and shall perform all the duties that by this or any other Act are conferred or imposed upon,

(a) a public school board for public school purposes; and
(b) a secondary school board for secondary school purposes.

(4) **Members to be trustees.**—A member of a divisional board, other than a member of a French-language or English-language section, who is,

(a) elected by separate school electors; or
(b) appointed, in the case of a vacancy, by the remaining members elected to the divisional board by separate school electors,

is a trustee for secondary school purposes only and shall not move, second or vote on a motion that affects public schools exclusively, and all other members of a divisional board are trustees for public and secondary school purposes.

57. (1) **Alteration of boundaries: disposition of assets and liabilities.**—Where the boundaries of a school divisional are altered, except by reason of the formation of a new school division, all lands and premises that,

(a) are situate in an area that is added to a school section or secondary school district by such alteration;
(b) are used as school sites on the last school day preceding the effective date of such alteration; and
(c) immediately prior to the effective date of such alteration are vested in another board of education, public school board or secondary school board except a board appointed or formed under section 68,

shall, on and after such effective date, be vested without compensation, subject to all existing debts, contracts, agreements and liabilities that pertain to such lands and premises, in the board of the school section or secondary school district to which such area is added, and the boards concerned shall agree upon the disposition of all other property situate upon, or used in connection with, such lands and premises.

(2) **Dispute.**—Any dispute as to the disposition of property under subsection (1) may be referred by one or more of the boards concerned to the Ontario Municipal Board, which shall determine the matters in dispute, and its decision is final.

(3) **Employment contracts.**—The employment contract of every employee of a board who, immediately before the effective date of the alteration of the boundaries of a school division, was required to perform his or her duties in a school that is vested under subsection (1) in the board of a school division, school section or secondary school district becomes an obligation of the board in which the school is vested.

Boards of Education

58. (1) **Definition.**—In this section, "board of education" means a board of education other than a divisional board of education.

(2) **Establishment and status of board.**—A board of education may be established in a secondary school district that is not a school division to perform the duties of a secondary school board for the district and the duties of a public school board for the school section or sections situated within the boundaries of the district and, where a board of education is established, subsection 56(3) applies, with necessary modifications.

(3) **Name of board.**—The name of a board of education that has jurisdiction in one municipality is "The Board of Education for the .... of ...." or "Conseil de l'éducation de ...." or both (*inserting the name of the municipality*).

(4) **Idem.**—The name of a board of education that has jurisdiction in more than one municipality is "The .... Board of Education" or "Conseil de l'éducation de ...." or both (*inserting a name selected by the board and approved by the Minister*).

(5) **Members to be trustees.**—A member of a board of education elected by separate school electors or, in the case of a vacancy, by the remaining members elected by separate school electors is a trustee for secondary school purposes only and shall not move, second or vote on a motion that affects public schools exclusively and all other members of a board of education are trustees for public and secondary school purposes.

(6) **Assets, liabilities, etc.**—Upon the organization of a board of education,

(a) the secondary school board and all public school boards in the secondary school district are dissolved;
(b) all the property vested in such boards becomes vested in the board of education; and
(c) all debts, contracts, agreements and liabilities for which such boards were liable become obligations of the board of education.

District School Area Boards

59. (1) **School section to be district school area.**—Every school section that is in a territorial district but is not in a school division or designated as a school section under section 68 is a district school area, and the board of each such school section is a public school board and shall be known as a district school area board.

(2) **Formation and alteration of district school area.**—In respect of the territorial districts, the Lieutenant Governor in Council may, by regulation,

PART III — PUBLIC AND SECONDARY SCHOOLS **S. 61**

- (a) form any part thereof that is not in a school section into a district school area;
- (b) combine two or more district school areas into one district school area;
- (c) add a part thereof that is not in a school division to a district school area;
- (d) detach a portion thereof from one district school area and attach it to another district school area or form it into a new district school area; or
- (e) detach a portion thereof from a district school area.

(3) **Notification of assessment commissioner.**—Where a district school area is formed or altered under subsection (2), the appropriate provincial supervisory officer shall notify the assessment commissioner concerned.

(4) **Arbitration.**—Where the boundaries of a district school area are altered in accordance with clause (2)(b) or (d), the Minister shall, by order, provide for arbitration of the assets and liabilities of the boards concerned.

(5) **Name of board.**—The board of a district school area is a corporation by the name of "The .... District School Area Board" or "Conseil du secteur scolaire de district de ...." or both (*inserting a name selected by the board and approved by the Minister*).

60. (1) **New district school areas.**—Where a district school area is formed under clause 59(2)(b), upon the effective date of such formation the existing public school boards in the new district school area are dissolved, and, subject to subsection 59(4),

- (a) the property vested in such boards is vested in the new district school area board; and
- (b) all debts, contracts, agreements and liabilities for which such boards were liable become obligations of the district school area board.

(2) **Alteration and formation: disposition of assets and liabilities.**—Where the boundaries of a district school area are altered or a new district school area is formed under clause 59(2)(d), upon the effective date of such alteration or formation, and, subject to subsection 59(4),

- (a) all real and personal property of the board situate in the part of the district school area that is detached is vested in the board of the district school area to which such part is attached, or in the board of the new district school area, as the case may be; and
- (b) all debts, contracts, agreements and liabilities of the board in respect of the part of the district school area that is detached become obligations of the board of the district school area to which such part is attached or of the board of the new district school area, as the case may be.

61. (1) **Definition.**—In this section and in sections 62 and 63, "public school electors" in respect of territory without municipal organization means,

- (a) owners and tenants of property in such territory without municipal organization; and
- (b) the spouses of such owners and tenants,

who are Canadian citizens and of the full age of eighteen years and who are not separate school supporters.

(2) **Composition of board.**—Subject to subsections (3) and (4), a district school area board shall be composed of three members.

(3) **Idem.**—Where a school section that became a district school area on the 1st day of January, 1975, had a board of five members, the district school area board shall be composed of five members.

(4) **Increase in number of members.**—Before the 1st day of July of an election year, the board of a district school area that is not an improvement district may, by resolution approved at a meeting of the public school electors, determine that the number of members to be elected shall be increased from three to five and, at the next following election, five members shall be elected.

(5) **Election year end term of office.**—The election of members of the board of a district school area that is not an improvement district shall be held in each year in which a regular election is held under the *Municipal Elections Act* and the members shall hold office until the next regular election is held under that Act and their successors are elected under this Act and the new board is organized except that,

(a) where a new district school area is formed to take effect on the 1st day of January in a year that is not a year of a regular election under the *Municipal Elections Act*, the first members of such board shall be elected in the year preceding such 1st day of January and shall hold office until the next regular election is held under the *Municipal Elections Act* and their successors are elected under this Act and the new board is organized; or

(b) where the boundaries of a district school area are altered to take effect on the 1st day of January in a year that is not a year in which a regular election is held under the *Municipal Elections Act*, a new district school area board shall be elected in the year preceding such 1st day of January and the members so elected shall hold office until the next regular election is held under the *Municipal Elections Act* and their successors are elected under this Act and the new board is organized.

(6) **Term of office.**—The term of office of members of the board of a district school area that is not an improvement district shall commence on the 1st day of December in the election year.

Elections and Meetings of Electors

62. (1) **Election date.**—Except as provided in section 63 and subject to subsection (4), a district school area board shall be elected at a meeting of the public school electors held on the second Monday in November or, where that day is Remembrance Day, on the next succeeding day in the year of an election at a time and place selected by the board.

(2) **Notice of meeting.**—At least six days before a meeting under subsection (1) or (6), the secretary of the board shall post notice of the meeting, including notice of any resolution required to be approved by the electors, in three or more of the most prominent places in the district school area and may advertise the meeting in such other manner as the board considers expedient.

(3) **Meeting.**—Meetings of public school electors shall be conducted in the manner determined by the public school electors present at the meeting by a presiding officer selected by such electors, but the election of members of the board shall be by ballot, and the minutes of the meeting shall be recorded by a secretary selected by such electors.

PART III — PUBLIC AND SECONDARY SCHOOLS   S. 63

(4) **First meeting.**—Despite subsection 61(5), the first meeting for the election of a board of a district school area formed or altered under subsection 59(2) shall be held at a time and place named by a person, designated by the Minister, who shall make the necessary arrangements for the meeting and the person so elected shall hold office until the date the next regular election is held under the *Municipal Elections Act* and their successors are elected under this Act and the new board is organized.

(5) **Minutes to be sent to Ministry.**—A correct copy of the minutes of every meeting of the public school electors, signed by the presiding officer and the secretary of the meeting, shall, within ten days after the meeting, be transmitted by the presiding officer to the Ministry.

(6) **Special meetings.**—A special meeting of the public school electors shall be called by the secretary when directed by the board or upon the request in writing of five public school electors of the area, by posting notice of the meeting in three or more of the most prominent places in the district school area, and such notice shall include a clear statement of the date, time, place and objects of the meeting, and the meeting may be advertised in such other manner as is deemed necessary.

(7) **Declaration where right to vote objected to.**—If objection is made to the right of a person in territory without municipal organization to vote at a meeting under this section, or at an election under section 63, the presiding officer or the returning officer, as the case may be, shall require the person to make the following declaration in English or in French:

I, ... , declare and affirm that:
1. I am the owner (*or* tenant) of property in the .... District School Area; *or*, I am the spouse of the owner (*or* tenant) of property in The .... District School Area;
2. I am of the full age of eighteen years;
3. I am a Canadian citizen;
4. The property in respect of which I claim the right to vote is not assessed to the support of separate schools;
5. I have a right to vote at this election (*or* on the question submitted to this meeting),

and after making such declaration the person making it is entitled to vote.

(8) **Election procedures.**—Subsections 92(8), (9), (10), (11), (12), (13), (15), (16), (17), (18), (19), (21) and (22) apply with necessary modifications to an election under this section.

63. (1) **Elections.**—Despite section 62, before the 1st day of July in an election year, the board of a district school area may, by resolution approved at a meeting of the public school electors, determine that the board shall conduct the elections in the same manner as for the members of a divisional board of education, except that the members shall be elected by a general vote of the public school electors of the district school area and for such purposes subsection 54(1) applies with necessary modifications to the district school area board and to the officers of such board.

(2) **Idem.**—The board shall give notice of the determination made under subsection (1) to the electors in the same manner as provided in subsection 62(2).

(3) **Idem.**—Where a district school area comprises,

(a) a municipality other than an improvement district;

(b) a municipality and territory without municipal organization;
(c) all or part of two or more municipalities; or
(d) all or parts of two or more municipalities and territory without municipal organization,

the election of the board of such district school area shall be conducted under the *Municipal Elections Act*, and for the purposes of an election under this section in an improvement district or in territory without municipal organization the secretary of the board shall be the returning officer in respect of the improvement district or territory without municipal organization and shall perform all the duties that are required of a municipal clerk in relation to the election of members of a divisional board.

64. (1) **Elections.**—Despite subsection 62(3) and (8) and section 63, where a district school area is formed under clause 59(2)(b), the Lieutenant Governor in Council may make regulations,

(a) determining the number of members to be elected to the board of the district school area;
(b) determining the areas each member referred to in clause (a) shall represent;
(c) providing for the nomination of candidates to be elected; and
(d) prescribing the manner in which the election of the members shall be conducted,

and the election of the members shall be in accordance with such regulations.

(2) **Validity of election.**—No election under this section is invalid by reason of noncompliance with the provisions of the regulations made under subsection (1) or by reason of any mistake or irregularity if it appears that the election was conducted in accordance with the principles laid down in the regulations and that the non-compliance, mistake or irregularity did not affect the result of the election.

65. (1) **Powers and duties.**—The board of a district school area that includes territory without municipal organization shall, for public school purposes and in accordance with the regulations for community recreation purposes, exercise the powers and duties of a municipal council for such territory in respect of levying rates and collecting taxes, and the officers appointed by the board have the same powers and duties, including the powers and duties with respect to the sale of land for tax arrears, as similar officers in a municipality, and the expenses in connection therewith shall be raised by a levy imposed by the board on the property rateable for public school purposes in such territory without municipal organization.

(2) **Auditors and financial matters.**—Subject to subsection (4), the provisions of sections 234, 235 and 236 respecting auditors, debentures and estimates apply with necessary modifications in respect of a district school area and to the board thereof.

(3) **Rates in municipality.**—Where a district school area includes a municipality, section 243 applies with necessary modifications to the council of the municipality.

(4) **Debentures.**—A district school area board in territory without municipal organization may not apply to the Ontario Municipal Board in respect of the issue of debentures for a permanent improvement until such issue has been sanctioned at a special meeting of the public school electors.

(5) **Collection of taxes.**—The board of a district school area may appoint a tax collector who has in that part of the district school area that is not a municipality the same powers in

collecting the school rate or subscriptions, and is under the same liabilities and obligations and shall proceed in the same manner in the school section, as a township collector in collecting rates in a township.

(6) **Tax sales officer.**—The board of a district school area shall name one of its officers as the officer of the board responsible for the sale of land for tax arrears and that officer has the same powers and duties as a treasurer under the *Municipal Tax Sales Act* and the board has the same powers and duties as a council under that Act.

(7) **Rates for first year to be levied on current assessment.**—In the first year that any territory without municipal organization is included in a district school area, the rates for that year shall be levied on the assessment of the property in such territory made for that year.

66. (1) **District school area board to be inactive.**—Where the number of public school pupils of compulsory school age residing in a district school area is fewer than ten and the board has ceased to operate a school, the Minister may declare the district school area board inactive as of the 31st day of December in any year.

(2) **Accounts in inactive area.**—When a district school area board is declared to be inactive, the board shall liquidate its assets, settle its accounts and have them audited, and forward to the Ministry the audited statement of accounts, the auditor's report and the balance of the funds for deposit in the Consolidated Revenue Fund.

(3) **Board dissolved.**—If the Minister is satisfied that the board has carried out its duties under subsection (2), the Minister shall dissolve the board and the district school area shall cease to exist as of the date that the district school area board was declared inactive under subsection (1).

(4) **Records to be forwarded to Ministry.**—The records of the dissolved board of the district school area shall be filed as the Minister may direct and, for the purposes of this Act, the pupils resident in such area shall be deemed not to reside in a school section.

(5) **Closing of school by Minister.**—Where in any district school area there are for two consecutive years fewer than eight persons between the ages of five and fourteen years residing therein, the Minister may direct that the public school of the area shall no longer remain open, and the school shall thereupon be closed until the Minister otherwise directs.

Secondary Schools Outside School Divisions in Territorial Districts

67. (1) **In territorial districts.**—The Lieutenant Governor in Council may establish any area in the territorial districts that is not part of a school division as a secondary school district and may discontinue or decrease or increase the area of any such secondary school district and, if any such secondary school district is discontinued, or the area is decreased or increased, the assets and liabilities of the board shall be adjusted or disposed of as determined by the Ontario Municipal Board.

(2) **Board in territorial districts outside school divisions.**—Where a secondary school district is established under subsection (1), the Lieutenant Governor in Council may make regulations providing for,

    (a) the formation and composition of a secondary school board and for the dissolution thereof;

    (b) the apportionment of costs within the secondary school district; and

(c) the issuing of debentures by the board for permanent improvements,

and the board is a corporation by the name designated by the Lieutenant Governor in Council.

(3) **Powers and duties.**—The board shall exercise the powers and duties of a municipal council for that part of the secondary school district that comprises territory without municipal organization in respect of levying rates and collecting taxes for secondary school purposes, and the officers appointed by the board have the same powers and duties, including the powers and duties with respect to the sale of land for tax arrears, as similar officers in a municipality, and the expenses in connection therewith shall be raised by a levy imposed on the property rateable for secondary school purposes in such territory without municipal organization.

(4) **Auditors and estimates.**—The provisions of sections 234 and 236 respecting auditors and estimates apply with necessary modifications to the board of a secondary school district established under this section.

(5) **Rates in municipality.**—Where a secondary school district established under this section includes a municipality, section 243 applies with necessary modifications to the council of the municipality.

(6) **Collection of taxes.**—Subsections 65(5), (6) and (7) apply with necessary modifications in respect of a secondary school district established under this section and to the board thereof.

(7) **Board of education.**—The Lieutenant Governor in Council may establish a board of education for a secondary school district established under subsection (1), in which case the other provisions of this section and subsections 58(5) and (6) apply with necessary modifications to the board of education for public school purposes and for secondary school purposes.

Boards on Tax Exempt Land

68. (1) **Public school on Crown lands.**—Where, in the opinion of the Minister, it is desirable to establish and maintain a public school board on lands held by the Crown in right of Canada or Ontario, or by an agency thereof, or on other lands that are exempt from taxation for school purposes, the Minister may by order designate any portion of such lands as a school section and may appoint as members of the board such persons as the Minister considers proper, and the board so appointed is a body corporate by the name indicated in the order establishing the school section and has all the powers and duties of a divisional board for public school purposes.

(2) **Secondary school on exempt land.**—Where, in the opinion of the Minister, it is desirable to establish and maintain a secondary school board on lands held by the Crown in right of Canada or Ontario, or by an agency thereof, or on other lands that are exempt from taxation for school purposes, the Minister may by order designate any portion of such lands as a secondary school district, and may appoint as members of the board such persons as the Minister considers proper, and the board so appointed is a corporation by the name indicated in the order establishing the secondary school district and has all the powers and duties of a divisional board for secondary school purposes.

(3) **Board of education on exempt land.**—Where a secondary school district has been designated under subsection (2), the Minister may authorize the formation of a board of education for the district and may provide for the name of the board, its composition and the

term or terms of office of the members thereof, and for all other purposes the provisions in respect of divisional boards apply to the board.

(4) **Section not to be included in district school area or school division.**—No school section or secondary school district designated under this section shall be included in a district school area or a school division.

(5) **Fee payable by non-resident.**—Where a pupil attends a school that is operated by a board appointed under this section in a centre for the treatment of cerebral palsy, a crippled children's treatment centre, a hospital or a sanatorium and is not a resident pupil of such board, the board of which the pupil is a resident pupil or is qualified to be a resident pupil shall pay to the board that operates the school a fee calculated under the regulations and, where the pupil is not a resident pupil or qualified to be a resident pupil of a board and the pupil's cost of education is not payable by the Minister under the regulations, the pupil's parent or guardian shall pay to the board that operates the school a fee fixed by such board, but such fee shall not be greater than the fee calculated under the regulations.

(6) **Revocation of order.**—If an order under subsection (1) or (2) is to be revoked on the 1st day of January next following a regular election under the *Municipal Elections Act*, the order shall, for the purpose of the election, be deemed to have been revoked.

69. [Repealed 1993, c. 11, s. 22.]
70. [Repealed 1993, c. 11, s. 22.]
71. [Repealed 1993, c. 11, s. 22.]
72. [Repealed 1993, c. 11, s. 22.]
73. [Repealed 1993, c. 11, s. 22.]
74. [Repealed 1993, c. 11, s. 22.]
75. [Repealed 1993, c. 11, s. 22.]
76. [Repealed 1993, c. 11, s. 22.]

PART IV

ROMAN CATHOLIC SEPARATE SCHOOLS

77. Application of Part.—This Part applies to separate schools for Roman Catholics now or hereafter established and shall have the same effect as if this Part were a special Act respecting separate schools for Roman Catholics.

Zones

78. (1) Boundaries of zones.—Unless otherwise determined in accordance with regulations made under subsections 97(2) and 98(2), the boundaries of a separate school zone shall, in accordance with sections 80 and 84, be the boundaries of,

(a) a municipality;
(b) a geographic township;
(c) a combination of municipalities;

(d) a combination of geographic townships; or

(e) a combination of the areas referred to in clauses (a) to (d).

(2) **Zones not in municipalities or geographic townships.**—The boundaries of a separate school zone, in those parts of the territorial districts that are neither geographic townships nor municipalities, shall be the boundaries of a 9.6 kilometre square of land of which two sides are parallel to a line of latitude.

(3) **Zone description.**—If a separate school zone is a 9.6 kilometre square of land, the location of the zone shall be determined by the latitude and longitude of its northwest corner.

(4) **Deemed inclusion to zones.**—If on the 31st day of December, 1989 no part of a separate school zone is a part of an area designated under subsection 97(2) and if the separate school zone includes a part of a municipality or geographic township, the separate school zone shall be deemed to include all of the municipality or geographic township.

79. Rates in unorganized territory in combined zone.—Where a combined separate school zone includes a former zone in territory without municipal organization and a former zone in a municipality, the combined separate school board is responsible for the levying and collecting of rates for separate schools in the territory without municipal organization and the board and the council of the municipality may enter into an agreement providing for the officers of the municipality to levy and collect rates for separate schools in such territory without municipal organization.

Formation and Discontinuance of Zones

80. (1) **Meeting to establish a separate school zone.**—A public meeting of persons desiring to establish a separate school zone may be convened by,

(a) not fewer than five heads of families, being Roman Catholics and being householders or freeholders resident within a municipality or a geographic township that is not within an area designated by the regulations made under subsection 97(2), who desire to establish the area of the municipality or geographic township as a separate school zone;

(b) not fewer than ten heads of families being Roman Catholics and being householders or freeholders resident within a 9.6 kilometre square of land, that is not part of a municipality, a geographic township, a separate school zone established under this subsection or a combined separate school zone, who desire to establish the square of land as a separate school zone; or

(c) not fewer than five heads of families being Roman Catholics and being householders or freeholders resident within a 9.6 kilometre square of land, that is not part of a municipality, a geographic township, a separate school zone established under this subsection or a combined separate school zone, who desire to establish the square of land as a separate school zone and unite the zone with one or more separate school zones.

(2) **Procedure.**—Where such a meeting is held, the persons present shall,

(a) elect a chair and a secretary for the meeting;

(b) pass a motion to determine that the area of the municipality or geographic township, as the case requires, be established as a separate school zone;

(c) if clause (1)(a) or (b) applies, elect the required number of trustees; and

(d) require the chair of the meeting to transmit notice in writing of the holding of the meeting and of the election of trustees to the clerks of the municipalities and to the chief executive officer of the divisional board or the secretary of the public school board, as the case may be, for the area in which the separate school zone is to be established designating by name and residence each of the persons elected as trustees.

(3) **Certification.**—Each of the officers receiving the notice shall certify thereon the date of its receipt, and shall transmit a copy of the notice so certified to the chair of the meeting.

(4) **Notification.**—The chair of the meeting shall forthwith transmit the copy of the certified notice, a copy of the minutes of the meeting, and of the notice calling it, to,

(a) the Minister; and

(b) the appropriate assessment commissioner.

(5) **Corporate name.**—On and after transmission to the Minister of the documents referred to in subsection (4), the separate school zone is established and the trustees named therein are a body corporate under the name of "The .... Roman Catholic Separate School Board" or "Conseil des écoles séparées catholiques de ...." or both (*inserting the name selected by the board and approved by the Minister*).

(6) **Formation not rendered invalid by reason only of vacancy in office of trustee.**—The formation of a separate school is not rendered invalid by reason only of a vacancy in the office of a trustee occurring before the trustees become a body corporate, provided that the vacancy is filled forthwith and the Minister is provided with the information required under clause (2)(d) in respect of the filling of the vacancy.

(7) **Roman Catholic deemed separate school elector.**—For the purpose of qualifying to be elected as a trustee at a meeting to establish a separate school zone, a Roman Catholic who is otherwise qualified under subsection 220(1) is deemed to be a separate school elector.

81. (1) **Powers of trustees.**—The trustees elected at a meeting convened under subsection 80(1) have all the powers of a public school board in territory without municipal organization and are in all other respects subject to the provisions of this Act that apply to rural separate school boards.

(2) **Where school not united.**—Where in any year a separate school zone is established by not fewer than five heads of families under clause 80(1)(c), the public meeting for the election of trustees shall be held before the 1st day of June in that year, and the only powers and duties of the separate school board so formed are to proceed in the same year to implement the provisions of section 84, and if the separate school zone is not united with one or more separate school zones to form a combined separate school zone before the 1st day of August in that year under section 84, the board is dissolved on that date.

82. Right to vote in year of establishment of zone.—A Roman Catholic who is a householder or freeholder, who is eighteen years of age and who desires to establish the area in which the Roman Catholic is resident as a separate school zone under section 80, is entitled, in the year in which the separate school zone is established, to vote on any matter that relates to the separate school.

83. Legislative grants.—On receipt by the Minister of the documents required under section 80 that a separate school zone has been established and suitable accommodation provided for school purposes, the Minister may pay to the board out of the appropriation made by the Legislature for public and separate schools such sums as may be approved by the Lieutenant Governor in Council.

84. (1) **Formation of combined separate school zones in non-designated areas.**—A separate school board or five supporters of a separate school that is not within an area designated by the regulations made under subsection 97(2) may, before the 1st day of July in any year, hold a meeting of the supporters of such separate school to consider the question of uniting the separate school zone with one or more other separate school zones in such area to form a combined separate school zone and, where the majority of such supporters present at each such meeting who vote on the question, vote in favour of the union and of the adjustments referred to in subsection (2), each such board shall give notice of the decision, before the 1st day of August of the same year, to the Minister, the clerks of the municipalities affected, and the appropriate assessment commissioner, and the combined separate school zone thus formed shall be deemed to be one zone for all Roman Catholic separate school purposes on the 1st day of December of the same year, except that, for the purposes of the election of trustees, it shall be deemed to be one zone on the day of nomination for trustees of the combined separate school board.

(2) **Adjustment of rights.**—In order to adjust the rights and claims of the combining boards, the supporters of any school may offer to assume and may assume a differential in rates for a stated period of time.

(3) **Dissolution of boards.**—When a combined separate school zone is formed, the board of each zone forming part of the union is dissolved, and all the real and personal property vested in such board is vested in the board of the combined separate school zone.

(4) **Corporate name of trustees.**—The trustees of a combined separate school board are a corporation by the name of "The .... Combined Roman Catholic Separate School Board" or "Conseil fusionné des écoles séparées catholiques de ...." or both (*inserting the name selected by the board and approved by the Minister*).

85. (1) **Detaching school zone from combined school zone.**—Where, in an area not designated by the regulations made under subsection 97(2), a petition of ten heads of families, being householders or freeholders who are supporters of a combined separate school, to detach a separate school zone from the combined separate school zone is submitted in any year to the combined separate school board, the board shall provide for a vote on the question within ninety days of the receipt of the petition.

(2) **Qualified voters detaching a separate school zone.**—The persons who are entitled to vote on the question are the supporters of the combined separate school who reside in the portion of the combined separate school zone that it is proposed to detach.

(3) **When school zone detached.**—If, before the 1st day of July in any year, a majority of the supporters who are entitled to vote on the question vote in favour of detaching the zone it is detached on the 1st day of January of the following year, except that, for the purposes of the election of trustees, it shall be deemed to be detached on the day of nomination for trustees, and the requisite number of trustees of the separate school zone so detached shall be elected as provided in section 92 or subsection 230(8), as the case may be.

86. (1) **Discontinuing board by a vote of the supporters.**—In an area not designated by the regulations made under subsection 97(2), a separate school board or five supporters of such board may, before the 1st day of July in any year, hold a meeting of the separate school supporters to consider the question of discontinuing the separate school board and, where the majority of the supporters vote in favour of discontinuing and fewer than five supporters vote in opposition, the board shall within thirty days notify the Minister, the clerk of each municipality concerned and the secretary of any school board that may be affected thereby and, for assessment purposes, the zone shall be discontinued on the 30th day of September following the meeting.

(2) **Other conditions under which a separate school board is discontinued.**—A separate school board is discontinued on the 30th day of November in any year,
- (a) if, for any continuous four month period in a school year, after the year in which the board was established, the board,
    - (i) fails to operate a school, or
    - (ii) fails to make an agreement with another separate school board for the education of its pupils and fails to provide transportation for the pupils who would otherwise be excused from attendance under clause 21(2)(c); or
- (b) if no one is assessed as a separate school supporter in the separate school zone in relation to property in respect of which taxes are to be levied in the following year; or
- (c) if the supporters fail to elect the required number of trustees in two successive regular elections.

(3) **Notification of Minister, etc., when board discontinued.**—When a board is discontinued under subsection (2), the appropriate supervisory officer for separate schools shall forthwith notify the Minister, the clerks of the municipalities concerned and the secretaries of the public school boards affected thereby.

(4) **Settling accounts.**—The trustees who are in office in the year in which the board is discontinued under this section shall remain in office for the purpose of settling the accounts and outstanding debts of the board and, following an audit by an auditor licensed under the *Public Accountancy Act*, shall forward the balance of its funds to the Minister for deposit in the Consolidated Revenue Fund for safekeeping.

(5) **Records.**—The records of a board that has been discontinued under this section shall be filed with the Ministry.

(6) **Boundaries to be revised.**—The boundaries of the zones that are altered as a result of discontinuing a separate school zone shall be revised by the appropriate supervisory officer.

(7) **Sale of real property.**—Where a board that has been discontinued fails to dispose of its real property in the year in which it was discontinued and the appropriate separate school supervisory officer is notified that an offer to purchase the real property has been made, he or she shall cause notices to be posted to call a meeting of the persons who were supporters in the year in which the board was discontinued to elect three persons who, when elected, are a board for the purpose of selling the property.

(8) **Deposit of funds from sale.**—When the board has sold the real property, it shall, after paying any outstanding debts, forward the balance of the money received from the sale to the Minister for deposit in the Consolidated Revenue Fund for safekeeping.

(9) **Re-establishing a board.**—A separate school board that has been discontinued in any year may, in any subsequent year, be re-established in the manner provided in section 80,

and the funds that were deposited by the board that was discontinued shall be returned to the board. 1993, c. 11, s. 23.

Separate School Electors

87. Residents other than supporters entitled to vote.—Despite the provisions of this or any other Act, including *The Metropolitan Separate School Board Act, 1953*, a Roman Catholic who is not an owner or tenant as defined in the *Municipal Elections Act* but who,
   (a) is a Canadian citizen;
   (b) has attained the age of eighteen years or on or before polling day will attain the age of eighteen years; and
   (c) resides within a separate school zone,
and who wishes to be a separate school elector at an election may cause his or her name to be entered on the preliminary list of electors of the polling subdivision in which he or she resides as a separate school elector, and for such purpose is entitled to be enumerated as such and to have entered opposite his or her name on the preliminary list of electors for the polling subdivision in which he or she resides that he or she is a separate school elector and, where the name of such person appears on the polling list, the person shall be deemed to be a separate school elector for the purpose of voting at such election.

88. Where person residing out of urban municipality to vote.—When a supporter of a separate school in an urban municipality resides outside the municipality, he or she is entitled to vote int he ward or polling subdivision in which the separate school nearest to his or her residence is situate.

Rural Separate Schools

89. (1) Trustees term of office.—The board of a rural separate school shall consist of three trustees who, subject to subsection (3), shall be elected in each year in which a regular election is held under the *Municipal Elections Act* and shall hold office until the date the next regular election is held under that Act and their successors are elected under this Act and the new board is organized.

(2) **Term of office.**—The term of office of trustees of a rural separate school board shall commence on the 1st day of December in the year of a regular election.

(3) **Idem.**—Where the first election of a newly established rural separate school board is held in a year in which no regular election is held under the *Municipal Elections Act*, the trustees so elected shall hold office until the date upon which the next regular election is held under that Act and their successors are elected under this Act and the new board is organized.

(4) **Organization and quorum.**—A majority of the trustees is a quorum, and the board shall be organized by the election of a chair and by the appointment of a secretary and a treasurer or of a secretary-treasurer.

(5) **Regularity.**—No act or proceeding is valid that is not adopted at a regular or special meeting of the board of which notice has been given as required under section 90 and at which at least two trustees are present.

(6) **Electors, qualifications.**—Every householder or freeholder of the full age of eighteen years, who is a Canadian citizen and who is a supporter of a rural separate school, is entitled

to vote at any election for school trustee or on any school question at any annual or special meeting of the supporters of the school.

(7) **Idem.**—Every person who is a Roman Catholic and is the spouse of a supporter of a rural separate school who is entitled to vote under subsection (6), and where elections are held under the *Municipal Elections Act*, every person who is a separate school elector in the area of jurisdiction of the board of such school, is entitled to vote at the election of trustees of such school and on any question submitted to a meeting of the supporters, except a question involving the selection of a school site or an expenditure for a permanent improvement.

90. (1) **Duties of rural boards.**—It is the duty of every rural separate school board and it has power,

    (a) **time and place of meetings.**—to appoint the place of each annual school meeting of the supporters of the school, and the time and place of any special meeting for,
        (i) filling any vacancy in the board,
        (ii) the approval of a site selected by the board for a new school,
        (iii) the appointment of a school auditor, or
        (iv) any other school purpose,

and to cause notices of the time and place and of the objects of such meetings to be posted in three or more public places of the neighbourhood in which the school is situate at least six days before the time of holding the meeting;

    (b) **annual report.**—to cause to be prepared and read at the annual school meeting a report for the year then ending, containing among other things a summary of the proceedings of the board during the year, together with a full and detailed account of the receipts and expenditures of all school money during such year, and signed by the chair and by one or both of the school auditors.

(2) **Appointment of auditor by the Minister.**—Where a rural separate school board neglects or the supporters at an annual or special meeting neglect to appoint an auditor, or an auditor appointed refuses or is unable to act, the Minister, upon the request in writing of any five supporters of the school, may make the appointment.

(3) **Approval of new school site.**—No site for a new school shall be acquired by a rural separate school board without approval of the site by the majority of the supporters of the rural separate school who are present at an annual or a special meeting of the board.

91. (1) **Appointment of collector.**—A separate school board in territory without municipal organization may appoint a person, who may be one of the trustees, to collect the rates imposed upon the supporters of the school or the sums that the inhabitants or others have subscribed or a rate-bill imposed upon any person and may pay to the collector at the rate of not less than 5 and not more than 10 per cent on the money collected by the collector, and every collector shall give such security as may be required by the board.

(2) **Powers and duties of collectors.**—Every collector has the same powers in collecting the school rate, rate-bill or subscription and is under the same liabilities and obligations and shall proceed in the same manner as a township collector in collecting rates in a township and has the same powers and duties as a treasurer under the *Municipal Tax Sales Act* and the board by which the collector is employed has the same powers and duties as a council under that Act.

92. (1) **Annual meeting.**—An annual meeting of the supporters of a rural separate school shall be held on the last Wednesday in December or, if that day is a holiday, on the next day following, commencing at the hour of 10 o'clock in the forenoon, or if the board by resolution so directs, at the hour of 1 o'clock or 8 o'clock in the afternoon, at such place as the board by resolution determines or, in the absence of such resolution, at the separate school.

(2) **Election of board.**—A rural separate school board shall be elected at a meeting of the separate school supporters held on the second Monday in November or, where that day is Remembrance Day, on the next succeeding day, in the year of a municipal election at a time and place selected by the board.

(3) **Idem.**—Where the annual meeting of supporters of the school cannot conveniently be held as provided for in subsection (1), the supporters, at a regular meeting or at a special meeting called for that purpose, may pass a resolution naming another day for the holding of the annual meeting, which shall be held on that day in each year thereafter until some other day is similarly named.

(4) **Organization of meeting.**—The supporters of the school present at a meeting shall elect one of themselves to preside over its proceedings and shall also appoint a secretary who shall record the proceedings of the meeting and perform such other duties as are required of the secretary by this section.

(5) **Order of business.**—The business of the annual meeting may be conducted in the following order,

(a) receiving and dealing with the annual report of the trustees;
(b) receiving and dealing with the annual report of the auditors;
(c) appointing one or more auditors for the current year;
(d) electing a trustee or trustees to fill any vacancy or vacancies; and
(e) miscellaneous business.

(6) **Duties of presiding officer.**—The presiding officer shall submit all motions to the meeting in the manner desired by the majority, and is entitled to vote on any motion, and,

(a) in the case of an equality of votes with respect to the election of two or more candidates, the presiding officer shall provide for drawing lots to determine which of the candidates is elected; and
(b) in the case of an equality of votes on a motion, the motion is lost.

(7) **Granting poll and proceedings in case of a poll.**—Where a poll is demanded by two supporters of the school at a meeting for the election of a trustee, the presiding officer shall forthwith grant the poll.

(8) **Entries in poll book.**—Where a poll is granted, the secretary shall enter in a poll book the name and residence of each qualified supporter of the school offering to vote within the time prescribed and shall furnish him or her, at the time of voting, with a ballot paper on the back of which the secretary has placed his or her initials, and shall provide a pencil for the marking of the ballot paper.

(9) **Form of ballot paper.**—Ballot papers shall be pieces of plain white paper of uniform size.

(10) **Marking of ballot paper.**—A voter shall make his or her ballot,

(a) in the election of a trustee, by marking the name of the trustee thereon; and
(b) on a question, by marking thereon "for" or "pour" if in favour or "against" or "contre" if opposed.

PART IV — ROMAN CATHOLIC SEPARATE SCHOOLS   **S. 92**

(11) **Number of votes.**—A voter is entitled to as many votes as there are trustees to be elected, but may not give more than one vote to any one candidate.

(12) **Manner of voting.**—Each voter shall make his or her ballot paper in a compartment or other place provided for the purpose that is so arranged that the manner in which the voter marks the ballot is not visible to other persons and shall thereupon fold it so that the initials of the secretary can be seen without opening it and hand it to the secretary who shall, without unfolding it, ascertain that the secretary's initials appear upon it and shall then in full view of all present, including the voter, place the ballot in a ballot box or other suitable container that has been placed and is kept upon a table for the purpose.

(13) **Appointment of scrutineer.**—Every candidate may appoint a person to act as the candidate's scrutineer during the election.

(14) **Declaration where right to vote objected to.**—When an objection is made to the right of a person to vote at a meeting of the supporters of a rural separate school, either for trustee or upon a school question, the presiding officer shall require the person whose right to vote is objected to to make the following declaration in English or in French, whereupon the person making the declaration is entitled to vote:

I, ..., declare,

    (a) that I am a Roman Catholic and a householder or freeholder assessed to the support of .... ; or

                               (*insert name of board*)

    (b) that I am a Roman Catholic and the spouse of a supporter of ....;
and   (*insert name of board*)

    (c) that I am of the full age of eighteen years;

  (c.1) that I am a Canadian citizen; and

    (d) that as such supporter or spouse of a supporter I have the right to vote at this meeting.

(15) **When poll shall close.**—The poll shall not close before noon, but shall close at any time thereafter when a full hour has elapsed without any vote being polled, and shall not be kept open later than 4 o'clock in the afternoon.

(16) **Polling at afternoon meetings.**—When a meeting for the election of one or more trustees is held at 8 o'clock in the afternoon the supporters present may decide by resolution that the polling shall take place forthwith or at 10 o'clock on the following morning, and if it takes place forthwith the poll shall close when ten minutes have elapsed without any vote being recorded.

(17) **Counting votes, tie vote.**—When the poll is closed, the presiding officer and secretary shall count the votes polled for the respective candidates or affirmatively and negatively upon the question submitted, and,

    (a) in the case of an equality of votes with respect to the election of two or more candidates, the presiding officer shall provide for drawing lots to determine which of the candidates is elected; and

    (b) in the case of an equality of votes on a motion, the motion is lost.

(18) **Declaration of result.**—In the case of an election of trustees, the presiding officer shall then declare the candidate elected for whom the highest number of votes has been polled,

and in case of a vote on a motion the presiding officer shall declare it carried or lost as the majority of votes is in favour of or against the motion.

(19) **Statement of result of poll.**—A statement of the result of the vote shall be certified by the presiding officer and secretary and in the case of an election of trustees the statement shall be signed by any scrutineers present at the counting of the ballots and a copy thereof shall be delivered to each candidate.

(20) **Secretary to transmit minutes to Ministry.**—A correct copy of the minutes of every meeting, signed by the presiding officer and secretary of the meeting, shall be transmitted forthwith by the secretary to the Ministry.

(21) **Meetings called in default of first or annual meeting.**—If from want of proper notice or other cause any meeting for the election of trustees is not held at the proper time, the appropriate separate school supervisory officer or any two supporters of the school may call a meeting by giving six days notice posted in at least three of the most public places in the locality in which the school is situate.

(22) **Validity of election.**—No election under this section is invalid by reason of non-compliance with the provisions of this section as to the taking of the poll or the counting of the votes, or by reason of any mistake in the use of forms, or of any irregularity, if it appears that the election was conducted in accordance with the principles laid down in this section, and that the non-compliance or mistake or irregularity did not affect the result of the election. 1993, c. 11, s. 24.

93. (1) **Where municipality may conduct election.**—Despite section 92, if the rural separate school zone is a municipality or combination of municipalities, the board of the rural separate school may, by resolution passed before the 1st day of July in the year of an election and approved at a meeting of the supporters of the rural separate school, determine that the election of trustees of the board shall be conducted by the municipality having the greatest population under the *Municipal Elections Act*, and the trustees shall be elected by general vote of the separate school electors of the separate school zone.

(2) **Application of *Municipal Elections Act*.**—Despite section 92, if the area of a rural separate school zone is not in a township or territory without municipal organization, in the year of a regular election the *Municipal Elections Act* applies with necessary modifications to the election of trustees of the rural separate school board, except that the voter shall take the following oath or make the following affirmation in English or French:

> You swear (*or* affirm) that you are the person named (*or* intended to be named) in the list of voters now shown to you (*showing the list to the voter*); That you are eighteen years of age; That you are a Roman Catholic separate school elector; That you have not voted before at this election; That you have not, directly or indirectly, received any reward or gift and do not expect to receive any for the vote which you tender at this election. So help you God. (*delete this sentence in an affirmation*).

Separate Schools – General

94. (1)— **Secretary of board as returning officer.**—If territory without municipal organization is part of a combined separate school zone and the election of trustees of the board

PART IV — ROMAN CATHOLIC SEPARATE SCHOOLS   **S. 95**

for a part of the combined zone is conducted under the *Municipal Elections Act*, the secretary of the board shall be the returning officer and shall perform all the duties of a municipal clerk in the election for the territory without municipal organization.

(2) **Reporting of vote.**—The secretary of the board shall report forthwith the vote recorded in the territory to the returning officer for the municipality having the greatest population in the electoral area, of which the territory without municipal organization forms part.

(3) **Reporting if no municipality.**—If there is no municipality in the electoral area, the secretary of the board shall report to the returning officer of the municipality that has the greatest population in the area of jurisdiction of the board and the returning officer shall prepare the final summary and announce the result of the vote.

Combined Separate School Zones

95. (1) **Trustees.**—Where a combined separate school zone is formed or where another separate school zone is added to or detached from a combined separate school zone, the trustees in office shall retire on the 1st day of December following the election of trustees of the combined separate school zone and, subject to the number of trustees being determined under subsection (5), five trustees shall be elected by the supporters of the newly-created or altered combined separate school zone,

    (a) as provided in section 92, where the combined separate school zone is formed, or where another separate school zone is added to or detached from a combined separate school zone in the year next following the year in which a regular election was held under the *Municipal Elections Act*, in which case the provisions of section 89 apply; or

    (b) as provided in subsection 230(2), where the combined separate school zone is formed or where another separate school zone is added to or detached from a combined separate school zone in the year in which a regular election is to be held under the *Municipal Elections Act*.

(2) **Trustee in office until organization of new board.**—Every trustee shall continue in office until his or her successor has been elected and the new board is organized.

(3) **First trustees.**—For the purpose of electing the first trustees for a combined separate school zone, the boards of the separate schools forming the combined separate school zone shall, before the 1st day of September, each appoint a person to a committee, which shall arrange for the election of trustees in accordance with section 92 or subsection 230(2), as the case may be.

(4) **Trustees in combined separate school zone including urban municipality.**—Where a combined separate school zone includes one or more urban municipalities, the board shall be composed of the same number of trustees as the separate school board of the urban municipality having the greatest population would have under subsection 230(8) and the zone shall be deemed to be one separate school zone.

(5) **Resolution providing for trustees.**—Despite subsections (1) and (4), the board of a combined separate school zone may be composed of such number of trustees, not fewer than five or more than nine, representing such municipalities or parts thereof, or separate school

zones in territory without municipal organization, within the combined separate school zone as is provided for in a resolution passed by the board, or, in the case of a newly-formed combined separate school zone, by the committee formed under subsection (3).

(6) **Election and term of office.**—Where a resolution is passed under subsection (5), the trustees shall be elected at large in the areas within the combined separate school zone that they respectively represent, and section 87 and subsections 93(2) and 230(2) apply with necessary modifications, provided that, where a municipality is divided into wards, the resolution may provide for representation by wards.

(7) **Voters list for areas in combined zone.**—Where one or more trustees represent two or more municipalities or parts thereof, or two or more municipalities or parts thereof and one or more separate school zones in territory without municipal organization, and the election is conducted under subsection 230(2), subsection 230(15) or (21) applies with necessary modifications.

(8) **Copy of resolution to be sent to Minister.**—The board or committee that passes a resolution under subsection (5) shall forthwith send a copy thereof to the Minister.

(9) **Electors' qualifications, rural combined separate school zone.**—Every person who resides in a rural combined separate school zone and is entitled to vote at the election of trustees under section 89 is entitled to vote at the election of trustees of the combined separate school zone and, subject to subsection 89(7), on any school question.

Duties and Powers of Separate School Boards

96. (1) **Duties of board.**—It is the duty of a separate school board and it has power,

(a) **appointment of officers.**—to appoint, where required, one or more collectors of school fees or rate-bills, who may be members of the board, and who shall discharge all duties, have powers similar to those of like officers of a municipality, and be subject to the obligations of and the penalties applicable to such officers;

(b) **collection of rates.**—where the board does not appoint a collector, to apply to the municipal council, on or before the 1st day of March in each year, for the levying and collecting of all rates for the support of the board's schools, and for any other school purposes authorized by this Act to be collected from the supporters of the separate schools under the control of the board;

(c) **appointment of auditors.**—to appoint an auditor or auditors;

(d) **accounts.**—to lay all the accounts of the board before the auditors, together with the agreements, vouchers, contracts and books in its possession, and to afford the auditors all the information in its power as to the receipt and expenditure of school money; and

(e) **other powers and duties.**—to exercise all such other powers and perform all such other duties of boards as are applicable to public school boards, except where otherwise expressly provided in this Act.

(2) **Religious education.**—A separate school board may establish and maintain programs and courses of study in religious education for pupils in all schools under its jurisdiction.

PART IV — ROMAN CATHOLIC SEPARATE SCHOOLS **S. 98**

County and District Combined Roman Catholic Separate School Zones

97. (1) **Separate school zones.**—Each area that prior to the 31st day of December, 1989 is designated by the regulations under subsection (2) shall be one separate school zone.

(2) **Regulations.**—The Lieutenant Governor in Council may make regulations,

(a) designating, as a county or district combined separate school zone, all or part of one or more municipalities, localities, counties, regional municipalities, district municipalities or territory without municipal organization or a combination thereof and designating the name of the area;

(b) altering the boundaries of a designated area, referred to in clause (a) and, if any part of territory without municipal organization is attached to the area, designating the part as a district municipality or attaching it to a district municipality;

(c) respecting any matter necessary or advisable to carry out effectively the intent and purpose of sections 97 to 105;

(d) providing for representation if the boundaries of a designated area are altered;

(e) combining two or more adjoining county or district combined separate school zones and providing that the board of the combined zone shall be a county or district combined separate school board;

(f) providing for the initial composition of a board to which subsection (6) applies and for the initial appointment or election of members of the board to hold office until the next regular election under the *Municipal Elections Act*.

(3) **Dissolution of board.**—Where an area that is designated under clause (2)(a) includes an existing separate school zone, the board of such zone is dissolved effective upon such date as may be set out in the regulation designating the area.

(4) **Establishment of boards.**—A separate school board shall be established for each county and district combined separate school zone and, except as otherwise provided under section 98 or a regulation made under subsection (2), the trustees of the board shall be elected and the board organized in accordance with sections 104 and 230.

(5) **Idem.**—If a county or district combined separate school zone is to be designated by a regulation under subsection (2) on the 1st day of January next following a regular election under the *Municipal Elections Act*, the county or district combined separate school zone shall, for the purpose of the election, be deemed to have been designated.

(6) **Idem.**—If a county or district combined separate school zone is designated by a regulation under subsection (2) and subsection (5) does not apply, the composition of the board and the appointment or election of members of the board shall be in accordance with the regulations.

(7) **Separate school zones.**—Where a separate school zone is within an area designated by the regulations made under subsection (2), the separate school zone shall forthwith become a part of the county or district combined separate school zone in that area.

98. (1) **Designation of a combined separate school board as a district combined separate school board.**—The Lieutenant Governor in Council on the recommendation of the Minister may, by regulation, designate a combined separate school zone as a district combined separate school zone, and upon such designation,

(a) the board of the combined separate school zone is dissolved and a separate school board for the district combined separate school zone is established, composed of the trustees of the board of the combined separate school zone who shall remain in office as trustees of the board of the district combined separate school zone until the board is organized following the next regular election of trustees;

(b) all property, including the employment contracts of the employees, of the combined separate school board becomes vested in the district combined separate school board; and

(c) all debts, contracts, agreements and liabilities of the combined separate school board become obligations of the district combined separate school board,

and except as provided by or under this section, the provisions of this Act shall apply in respect of the district combined separate school board and the zone designated under this section as if the designation of the zone and the formation of the board had been made under section 97.

(2) **Regulation.**—If the board of a combined separate school zone in the territorial districts applies to the Minister to extend the boundaries of the combined separate school zone so as to include parcels of land on which a separate school zone cannot be established because of the operation of subsection 80(1), the Lieutenant Governor in Council may by regulation extend the boundaries of the combined separate school zone.

99. (1) **Arbitration where boundaries of designated areas are altered.**—Where the boundaries of an area designated by the regulations under subsection 97(2) are altered to include,

(a) one or more separate school zones established under section 80; or

(b) part or all of one or more separate school zones that form part or all of another county or district combined separate school zone,

each of the boards concerned shall appoint one arbitrator who, subject to subsection (2), shall forthwith value and adjust in an equitable manner the assets and liabilities of the boards affected by the alteration of the boundaries and the decision of the arbitrators is final and binding upon the boards concerned.

(2) **Appointment of additional arbitrator.**—Where the number of arbitrators appointed under subsection (1) is an even number, the arbitrators so appointed shall appoint an additional arbitrator.

(3) **Referral to judge.**—Where a majority of the arbitrators appointed under subsections (1) and (2) is unable to reach a decision on any matter, such matter shall be referred by the arbitrators to a judge whose decision is final.

100. (1) **Alteration of boundaries: disposition of assets and liabilities.**—Where the boundaries of an area designated by the regulations under subsection 97(2) are altered, all lands and premises that,

(a) are situate in a municipality or part thereof or territory without municipal organization that is added to the designated area by such alteration;

(b) are used as separate schools on the last school day preceding the effective date of such alteration; and

(c) immediately prior to the effective date of such alteration are vested in a separate school board,

shall, on and after such effective date, be vested without compensation, but subject to all existing debts, contracts, agreements and liabilities that pertain to such lands and premises, in

PART IV — ROMAN CATHOLIC SEPARATE SCHOOLS   **S. 102**

the county or district combined separate school board for the designated area to which the municipality or part thereof or territory without municipal organization is added, and the separate school boards concerned shall agree upon the disposition of all other property situate upon, or used in connection with, such lands and premises.

(2) **Dispute.**—Any dispute as to the disposition of property under subsection (1) may be referred by one or more of the boards concerned to the Ontario Municipal Board, which shall determine the matters in dispute and its decision is final.

(3) **Employment contracts.**—The employment contract of every employee of a separate school board who, immediately before the effective date of the alteration of the boundaries of an area designated by the regulations under subsection 97(2) was required to perform his or her duties in a separate school that is vested under subsection (1) in the county or district combined separate school board for such designated area becomes an obligation of such county or district combined separate school board.

(4) **Area added to Scarborough to be under Metropolitan Separate School Board.**—The area added to the Borough of Scarborough by subsection 175(2) of the *Municipality of Metropolitan Toronto Act* is part of the district of which the separate schools are administered by The Metropolitan Separate School Board.

101. School to remain school of board.—Despite sections 99 and 100, a school that was in the area of jurisdiction of a county or district combined separate school board on the 31st day of December, 1989 shall be a school of the board and shall so remain unless otherwise determined by the board.

102. (1) **Name of board in one county.**—A county combined separate school board that has jurisdiction in an area that includes only one county is a corporation by the name of "The .... County Roman Catholic Separate School Board" or "Conseil des écoles séparées catholiques du comté de ...." or both (*inserting the name of the county*).

(2) **Name of county combined board.**—A county combined separate school board that has jurisdiction in an area that includes two or more counties, or one county and a defined city, is a corporation by the name of "The .... County Roman Catholic Separate School Board" or "Conseil des écoles séparées catholiques du comté de ...." or both (*inserting the names of the counties, the name of the city and of the county or a name selected by the board and approved by the Minister*).

(3) **Name of board in territorial districts.**—A district combined separate school board that has jurisdiction in the territorial districts is a corporation by the name of "The .... District Roman Catholic Separate School Board" or "Conseil des écoles séparées catholiques du district de ...." or both (*inserting the name of the area designated by the regulations*).

(4) **Name of board in regional municipality.**—Despite subsections (2) and (3), a combined separate school board that has jurisdiction in all or part of a regional municipality is a corporation by the name of "The .... Roman Catholic Separate School Board" or "Conseil des écoles séparées catholiques de ...." or both (*inserting a name selected by the board and approved by the Minister*).

(5) **Bilingual.**—The name of a county or district combined separate school board by be as follows where approved by the Minister:

"Conseil des écoles séparées catholiques du (comté ou district) de ....
(County or District) Roman Catholic Separate School Board (*inserting the name of the county or counties, district or districts, name selected by the board and approved by the Minister or name of area designated by the regulations*). 1993, c. 27, *Schedule*.

103. (1) **Deemed district municipalities.**—A part of territory without municipal organization that is in an area designated by the regulations made under subsection 97(2) shall be deemed to be a district municipality for district combined separate school purposes.

(2) **Powers and duties of combined board re territory without municipal organization.**—The board of a district combined separate school zone that includes territory without municipal organization that is deemed a district municipality for separate school purposes shall exercise the powers and duties of a municipal council for such district municipality in respect of preparing estimates, levying rates, collecting, cancelling, reducing or refunding taxes and issuing debentures for the purposes of the district combined separate school board and in respect of the preparation of a list of voters and the election of members of such board, and all the officers appointed by such board have the same powers and duties, including the powers and duties with respect to the sale of land for tax arrears, as similar officers in an organized municipality except that the provisions of subsections 65(5), (6) and (7) apply with necessary modifications, and the expenses incurred by the board in connection therewith except the issuing of debentures shall be raised by a levy imposed by the district combined separate school board on all property rateable for separate school purposes in such district municipality.

(3) **Application of *Municipal Act*, s. 363.**—Section 363 of the *Municipal Act* applies to territory without municipal organization that is deemed a district municipality under subsection (1), and the district combined separate school board has the powers of a municipal council under the said section 363 in respect of any such territory.

(4) **Election in improvement district.**—The secretary-treasurer of an improvement district that forms part of a district combined separate school zone, in each year in which an election for members of the district combined separate school board is to be held, shall provide for such election in the improvement district in the same manner as for the election of trustees in a municipality, and the secretary-treasurer of the improvement district shall be the clerk and returning officer and has all the powers and shall perform all the duties of the clerk and returning officer of a municipality in relation to the election of members of a district combined separate school board under the *Municipal Elections Act*.

104. (1) **Number of votes to be cast.**—Every person in a municipality or in a part thereof or in a combination of municipalities who is qualified to vote for trustees of a separate school board under sections 97 to 105 and section 230 is entitled to as many votes as there are trustees to be elected in such municipality or part or combination of municipalities, but may not give more than one vote to any one candidate.

(2) **Retiring trustees eligible for re-election.**—A trustee of a county or district combined separate school board is eligible for re-election if otherwise qualified.

(3) **Person not to be candidate for more than one seat on board.**—No person shall qualify himself or herself as a candidate for more than one seat on a county or district combined separate school board, and any person who so qualifies and is elected to hold one or more seats on the county or district combined separate school board is not entitled to sit as a trustee of the board by reason of the election, and the person's seat or seats are thereby vacated.

PART IV — ROMAN CATHOLIC SEPARATE SCHOOLS   S. 107

105. Application of ss. 234, 235.—Sections 234 and 235 apply with necessary modifications to the City of Windsor and The Windsor Roman Catholic Separate School Board.

Rates, Borrowing Powers and Grants

106. (1) **Exemption of supporters from public school rates.**—Every person paying rates in a separate school zone on property that the person occupies as owner or tenant or on unoccupied property that the person owns, who personally or by his or her agent, on or before the 30th day of September in any year, gives to the clerk of the municipality notice in writing that the person is a Roman Catholic and wishes to be a separate school supporter, is exempt from the payment of all rates imposed on such property in the separate school zone for public school purposes for the following year and every subsequent year while the person continues to be a separate school supporter with respect to such property.

(2) **No renewal required.**—The notice is not required to be renewed annually.

(3) **Exemption from public school rates for other separate school supporters.**—Every person paying rates in a separate school zone on property that the person occupies as owner or tenant or on unoccupied property that the person owns, who in the year becomes a separate school supporter within the meaning of clause (b) or (c) of the definition of "separate school supporters" in subsection 1(1), is exempt from the payment of all rates imposed on such property in the separate school zone for public school purposes for the following year and every subsequent year while the person continues to be a separate school supporter with respect to such property.

(4) **Who may be supporters of separate schools.**—Any person who is a Roman Catholic and resident on a parcel of land that is within a separate school zone may be a separate school supporter in that zone.

(5) **Rights of non-residents to be assessed for separate school.**—Any person who, if he or she were resident in a separate school zone, would be entitled to be a supporter of a separate school and who is the owner of unoccupied land situate in the separate school zone, may, on or before the 30th day of September in any year, by written notice to the clerk of the municipality in which the land is situate or, where the land is not in a municipality, to the secretaries of the public and separate school boards, direct that all such land in the separate school zone shall be assessed for the purposes of the separate school.

(6) **Certificate of notice.**—Every clerk of a municipality, upon receiving the notice, shall deliver a certificate to the person giving the notice to the effect that the notice has been given and showing the date thereof.

(7) **Penalty for wilful false statements in notice.**—Any person who fraudulently gives such notice, or wilfully makes any false statement therein, does not thereby secure any exemption from the rates, and in addition is guilty of an offence and on conviction is liable to a fine of not more than $100.

(8) **As to rates imposed before separate school established.**—Nothing in this section exempts any person from paying any rate for public school purposes imposed before the establishment of the separate school zone.

107. (1) **Notice of withdrawal of support.**—A Roman Catholic who desires to withdraw his or her support from a separate school shall, on or before the 30th day of September in any year, give notice in writing that he or she desires to withdraw his or her support for the following year,

    (a) where the separate school is situated in a municipality, to the clerk of the municipality; or

    (b) where the separate school is situated in territory without municipal organization,

        (i) if he or she resides in a school section, to the secretary of the public school board of the section and to the secretary of the separate school board, or

        (ii) if he or she does not reside in a school section, to the secretary of the separate school board,

otherwise he or she shall be deemed to be a supporter of the separate school.

(2) **Exception.**—A person who withdraws his or her support from a Roman Catholic separate school is not exempt from paying rates for separate school purposes imposed before the date on which the withdrawal of such support is effective.

108. (1) **Clerk to keep index book.**—The clerk of every municipality shall keep entered in an index book (Form 1) and in alphabetical order, the name of every person who has given to the clerk, or to any former clerk of the municipality, notice in writing that such person is a Roman Catholic and a supporter of a separate school in or contiguous to the municipality, as provided by sections 106, 111 and 112 or by former Acts respecting separate schools.

(2) **Entries.**—The clerk shall enter opposite the name, in a column for that purpose, the date on which the notice was received, and in a third column opposite the name any notice by such person of withdrawal from supporting a separate school, as provided by section 107, or by any such other Act, with the date of the withdrawal, or any disallowance of the notice by the Assessment Review Board, the Ontario Municipal Board or a court, with the date of the disallowance.

(3) **Inspection.**—The index book shall be open to inspection by any ratepayer.

(4) **Filings.**—The clerk shall file and carefully preserve all such notice heretofore or hereafter received.

(5) **Clerk to be guided by index book.**—The clerk and the appropriate assessment commissioner shall be guided by the entries in the index book in ascertaining those who have given the prescribed notices.

FORM 1
FORM OF INDEX BOOK
[*Section 108(1)*]

Names/Noms	Date notice received/Date de réception de l'avis	Remarks/Remarques
Allen, John	3rd February 19....	Notice of withdrawal received in January, 19....
Ardagh, Joseph	3rd February 19....	
Ashbridge, Robert	3rd February 19....	Disallowed by Assessment Review Board, 1st June, 19....

PART IV — ROMAN CATHOLIC SEPARATE SCHOOLS **S. 112**

109. (1) **Correction of mistakes in assessing.**—If, after the return of the assessment roll, it appears to the council of any municipality that through mistake or inadvertance a ratepayer has been entered on the list prepared by the assessment commissioner under section 16 of the *Assessment Act* either as a supporter of separate schools or as a supporter of public schools, the council after due inquiry and notice may correct the error by directing the school taxes of the ratepayer to be paid to the proper school board, but the council is not competent to reverse the decision of the Assessment Review Board, the Ontario Municipal Board or a court on appeal.

(2) **Liability.**—In case of such action by a council, the ratepayer is liable for the same amount of school taxes as if the ratepayer had in the first instance been properly entered on the roll.

110. (1) **Distinguishing the school rates.**—The clerk of every municipality, in making out the collector's roll, shall place columns therein so that under a heading for school rates the public school rate may be distinguished from the separate school rate, and that under a heading for special rate for school debts public school purposes may be distinguished from separate school purposes.

(2) **Idem.**—The proceeds of any such rate shall be kept distinguished by the collector and accounted for accordingly.

111. (1) **Case of owner and occupant.**—The occupant or tenant of land shall be deemed to be the person primarily liable for the payment of school rates and for determining whether those rates shall be applied to public or separate school purposes, and no agreement between the owner or tenant as to the payment of taxes as between themselves alters or affects this provision.

(2) **When owner may exercise option.**—Where, as between the owner and tenant or occupant, the owner is not to pay taxes, if by the default of the tenant or occupant to pay the same, the owner is compelled to pay such school rate, the owner may direct the same to be applied to either public or separate school purposes, and if the public school rate and the separate school rate are not the same the owner is only liable to pay the amount of the rate of the schools to which the owner directs money to be paid.

112. (1) **Definition.**—In this section, "partnership" means partnership within the meaning of the *Partnerships Act*.

(2) **Application.**—This section does not apply to a corporation that is a designated ratepayer within the meaning of section 113.

(3) **Right of corporation to support separate schools.**—Subject to subsection (7), a corporation or partnership by notice to the assessment commissioner in a form prescribed under the *Assessment Act* may require the whole or any part of its assessment to be entered, rated and assessed for separate school purposes.

(4) **Copy of notice to clerk.**—The assessment commissioner shall thereupon forward a copy of such notice to the clerk of the municipality in which the land referred to in the said notice is situate.

(5) **Duty of assessment commissioner.**—The assessment commissioner, upon receipt of the notice from the corporation or partnership, shall enter the corporation or partnership on the assessment roll to be next returned as a separate school supporter with respect to the assessment

designated in the notice, and the assessment so designated shall be assessed accordingly for separate school purposes and the remainder, if any, of the assessment of the corporation or partnership shall be separately entered and assessed for public school purposes.

(6) **Duty of clerk.**—The clerk, upon receipt of the notice from the assessment commissioner, shall enter the corporation or partnership as a separate school supporter in the collector's roll in respect of the assessment designated in the notice and the proper entries shall be made in the prescribed column for separate school rates, and the assessment so designated shall be assessed accordingly for separate school purposes and the remainder, if any, of the assessment of the corporation or partnership shall be separately entered and assessed for public school purposes.

(7) **Proportion of assessment.**—The portion of an assessment that is designated by a corporation or partnership under this section shall not bear a greater proportion to the whole of the assessment than,

(a) in the case of a corporation, the number of shares held by separate school supporters in the corporation bears to the total number of shares of the corporation issued and outstanding; and

(b) in the case of a partnership, the interest of partners who are separate school supporters in the assets giving rise to the assessment bears to the whole interest of the partnership in the assets giving rise to the assessment.

(7.1) **Application.**—Clause (7)(a) does not apply to a corporation without share capital or a corporation sole.

(7.2) **Transition.**—The assessment of a corporation without share capital or corporation sole that gave notice under subsection (3) before subsection (7.1) comes into force is not open to challenge on the ground that the assessment does not comply with clause (7)(a).

(8) **Effect of notice.**—A notice given by a corporation under this section pursuant to a resolution of the directors or other persons having control or management over the affairs of the corporation is sufficient and shall continue in force and be acted upon until it is withdrawn, varied or cancelled by a notice subsequently given pursuant to a resolution of the corporation, its directors or such other persons.

(9) **Idem.**—A notice given by a partnership under this section is sufficient if signed by a partner and shall continue in force and be acted upon until it is withdrawn, varied or cancelled by a notice subsequently given by a partner.

(10) **Filing notice.**—Every notice so given shall be kept by the assessment commissioner in his or her office, and shall at all convenient hours be open to inspection and examination.

(11) **Secondary school purposes.**—The assessment of a corporation or partnership for separate school purposes under subsections (1) to (10) in respect of a Roman Catholic school board applies in the same manner in relation to secondary school purposes as to elementary school purposes. 1992, c. 17, s. 1.

113. (1) **Definitions.**—In this section and in section 112,

"assessment".—"assessment", in respect of a designated ratepayer, corporation or partnership, means the assessment of land under the *Assessment Act* of which the designated ratepayer, corporation or partnership is either the owner and occupant, or, not being the owner, is the tenant, occupant or actual possessor, and includes the business or other

PART IV — ROMAN CATHOLIC SEPARATE SCHOOLS   S. 113

assessment of the designated ratepayer, corporation or partnership made under that Act; ("évaluation")

"**common jurisdictional area**", in respect of two or more boards, means the area within the territorial jurisdiction of both or all of those boards, and for the purpose The Metropolitan Toronto School Board shall be included as a board and the boards of education for the area municipalities in The Municipality of Metropolitan Toronto shall not be included as boards; ("secteur commun de compétence") [1994, c. 17, s. 48(3). In force December 1, 1995: 1994, c. 17, s. 51]

"**designated enrolment**" means a number of pupils of a board resident in a common jurisdictional area, calculated by the Minister in accordance with the regulations; ("effectif désigne") [1994, c. 17, s. 48(3). In force December 1, 1995: 1994, c. 17, s. 51]

"**designated ratepayer**".—"designated ratepayer" means the Crown in right of Canada or a province, a corporation without share capital or corporation sole that is an agency, board or commission of the Crown in right of Canada or a province, a municipal corporation, a corporation without share capital that is a local board as defined in the *Municipal Affairs Act*, a conservation authority established by or under the *Conservation Authorities Act* or a predecessor of that Act, or a public corporation; ("contribuable désigné")

"**municipality**".—"municipality" means a city, town, village, township or a public school section, separate school zone or secondary school district that is in territory without municipal organization or that portion of a public school section, separate school zone or secondary school district that is in territory without municipal organization; ("municipalité")

"**public corporation**".—"public corporation" means,
(a) a body corporate that is, by reason of its shares, a reporting issuer within the meaning of the *Securities Act* or that has, by reason of its shares, a status comparable to a reporting issuer under the law of any other jurisdiction,
(b) a body corporate that issues shares that are traded on any market if the prices at which they are traded on that market are regularly published in a newspaper or business or financial publication of general and regular paid circulation, or
(c) subject to subsection (2), a body corporate that is, within the meaning of subsections 1(1) and (2), clause 1(3)(a) and subsections 1(4), (5) and (6) of the *Securities Act*, controlled by or is a subsidiary of a body corporate or two or more bodies corporate described in clause (a) or (b); ("sociètè ouverte")

"**residential and farm assessment**".—"residential and farm assessment" means residential and farm assessment as defined in section 248 but,
(a) for assessment in 1990, 1991 or 1992 for taxation in 1991, 1992 or 1993, does not include the assessment of real property of public corporations, and
(b) for assessment in 1993 for taxation in 1994 and for later years, does not include the assessment of real property of designated ratepayers. ("évaluation résidentielle et agricole") [To be repealed December 1, 1995: 1994, c. 17, ss. 48(1), 51 *but see* 1994, c. 17, s. 48(2)]

S. 113 EDUCATION ACT

"**total designated enrolment**" means a number of pupils resident in a common jurisdictional area, calculated by the Minister in accordance with the regulations. ("effectif désigné total") [1994, c. 17, s. 48(3). In force December 1, 1995: 1994, c. 17, s 51]

(2) **Interpretation.**—For the purposes of this section, the expression "more than 50 per cent of the votes" in the second and third lines of clause 1(3)(a) of the *Securities Act* shall be deemed to read "50 per cent or more of the votes".

(3) **Assessment of designated ratepayer for separate school purposes.**—An assessment of a designated ratepayer in a municipality shall be rated and assessed for separate school purposes in the same proportion to the total assessment of the designated ratepayer in the municipality as the residential and farm assessment rated and assessed for separate school purposes in the municipality bears to the total residential and farm assessment in the municipality. [To be repealed December 1, 1995: 1994, c. 17, ss. 48(4), 51].

(3) **Assessment of designated ratepayer.**—An assessment of a designated ratepayer in a common jurisdictional area shall be rated and assessed for the purposes of each board in the same proportion to the total assessment of the designated ratepayer in the common jurisdictional area as the designated enrolment of the board for that common jurisdictional area bears to the total designated enrolment in the common jurisdictional area. [1994, c. 17, s. 48(4). In force December 1, 1995: 1994 c. 17, s. 51]

(4) **Idem.**—For the purposes of subsection (3), if more than one public school board has jurisdiction in the same municipality, the proportion to be determined shall be the proportion of the assessment in the portion of the municipality within the jurisdiction of each board. [To be repealed December 1, 1995: 1994, c. 17, ss. 48(5), 51]

(4) **Same.**—On or before October 15 in each year the Minister shall provide to each assessment commissioner the following information for each common jurisdictional area in the assessment region for which the commissioner is appointed:
1. The total designated enrolment for the area.
2. The designated enrolment for each board in the area. [1994, c. 17, s. 48(5). In force December 1, 1995: 1994, c. 17, s. 51]

(4.1) **Same.**—On receipt of the information, the assessment commissioner shall, for each common jurisdictional area, provide to the clerk of each municipality situate in that area the information received under subsection (4) for that area. [1994, c. 17, s. 48(5). In force December 1, 1995: 1994, c. 17, s. 51]

(5) **Duty of assessment commissioner.**—The assessment commissioner shall enter the designated ratepayer on the assessment roll to be next returned as a separate school supporter with respect to the proportion of its assessment in the municipality determined by subsection (3) and the remainder of the assessment of the designated ratepayer shall be separately entered

PART IV — ROMAN CATHOLIC SEPARATE SCHOOLS **S. 113**

and assessed for public school purposes. [To be repealed December 1, 1995: 1994, c. 17, ss. 48(6), 51]

(5) **Duty of assessment commissioner.**—The assessment commissioner shall enter each designated ratepayer on the assessment roll to be next returned as a supporter of each board having territorial jurisdiction in the common jurisdictional area in which the property assessed is situate, in the proportions established under subsection (3). [1994, c. 17, s. 48(6). In force December 1, 1995: 1994, c. 17, s. 51]

(6) **Supplementary or omitted assessments.**—An assessment of a designated ratepayer made under section 33 or 34 of the *Assessment Act* shall be rated and assessed for public and separate school purposes in the manner set out in subsections (3) and (5).

(7) **Regulations.**—The Lieutenant Governor in Council may make regulations adjusting the proportions of assessment rated and assessed for public and separate school purposes under this section in each municipality in each year until the end of 1995 and requiring the assessment commissioner to adjust the rolls accordingly. [To be amended on December 1, 1995 by substituting "1995" in the third line with "1998": 1994, c. 17, ss. 48(7), 51.]

(8) **Idem.**—Despite subsections (3) and (5), the proportions of assessment rated and assessed for public and separate school purposes in any year for which a regulation made under subsection (7) is applicable shall be those proportions determined in accordance with such regulation.

(8.1) **Exemption from taxation.**—Subsections (3) to (8) do not apply to an assessment of real property or business assessment in respect of which an exemption from taxation for school purposes applies.

(9) **Idem.**—The Lieutenant Governor in Council may make regulations adjusting the allocation or payment of the tax levied in each year under subsections 159(12) and (13) of the *Municipal Act* to each board, until the end of 1995 and requiring the council of the municipality that levied the tax to allocate or pay the tax accordingly. [To be repealed December 1, 1995: 1994, c. 17, ss. 48(8), 51]

(9) **Same.**—The Lieutenant Governor in Council may make regulations,
(a) prescribing the method of calculating designated enrolment and total designated enrolment;
(b) adjusting the allocation or payment of the tax levied in each year under subsections 159 (12) and (13) of the *Municipal Act* to each board, until the end of 1998 and requiring the council of the municipality that levied the tax to allocate or pay the tax accordingly. [1994, c. 17, s. 48(8). In force December 1, 1995: 1994, c. 17, s. 51]

(9.1) **Same.**—A regulation made under clause (9) (a) may be general or particular in its application. [1994, c. 17, s. 48(8). In force December 1, 1995: 1994, c. 17, s. 51]

(10) **Same.**—Despite subsections 159(22) and 379(4) of the *Municipal Act*, subsection 135.12(2.1) of the *Regional Municipalities Act*, subsection 84.9(2.1) of the *County of Oxford*

Act and subsection 79(2.1) of the *District Municipality of Muskoka Act*, the allocation or payment determined for each board for any year to which a regulation made under subsection (9) is applicable shall be that determined in accordance with the regulation. [Subsection to be amended on December 1, 1995 by striking out ''subsection (9)'' in the last line and substituting ''clause (9)(b)''. 1994, c. 17, ss. 48(9), 51.]

1992, c. 17, s. 2; 1993, c. 11, s. 25; 1994, c. 1, s. 22; c. 17, s. 48.

114. (1) **Estimates.**—Every separate school board shall prepare and adopt estimates of all sums required during the year for separate school purposes, and the provisions of section 236 in respect of the preparation and adoption of the estimates of all sums required for public school purposes by a divisional board of a school division apply with necessary modifications to a separate school board for separate school purposes.

(2) **Where cost of separate levy payable by board.**—Where rates or taxes in respect of separate schools are levied and collected by the council of a municipality under section 120 and the separate school board is unable in any year to submit to the council on or before the 1st day of March the rates required by the separate school board to be levied and collected in the municipality for separate school purposes, the later submission thereof does not relieve the council of its duty under section 120 to levy and collect such rates, and, where the municipality is required, by reason of such later submission, to levy such rates by a separate levy from the amount levied for municipal purposes, the separate school board on the request of the treasurer of the municipality shall pay to the treasurer the cost of levying such rates.

(3) **Application of *Municipal Act*.**—Subsection 162(5) of the *Municipal Act* does not apply to a separate school board.

115. (1) **Powers of trustees.**—The board of a separate school may in respect of the estimates adopted under section 114 impose and levy school rates and collect school rates and subscriptions upon and from persons sending children to or subscribing towards the support of such schools, and may appoint collectors for collecting the school rates or subscriptions who shall have all the powers in respect thereof possessed by collectors of taxes in municipalities.

(2) **Land on which there are rates uncollected.**—If a collector appointed by the board is unable to collect any part of a school rate charged on land liable to assessment by reason of there being no person resident thereon or no goods and chattels to distrain, the board shall make a return to the clerk of the municipality before the end of the then current year of such land and the uncollected rates thereon.

(3) **Return.**—The clerk shall make a return of such land and the arrears of separate school rates thereon to the appropriate municipal treasurer.

(4) **Collection of rates.**—The arrears shall be collected and accounted for by the treasurer in the same manner as the arrears of other taxes.

(5) **Deficiency.**—The council of the township, village, town or city in which the separate school zone is situate shall make up the deficiency arising from such uncollected rates out of the general funds of the municipality.

116. Levy for costs for transportation and board and lodging of secondary school pupils not resident in secondary school district.—Where some of the supporters in a separate school zone reside in a municipality or in territory without municipal organization and in a secondary school district and other supporters in the separate school zone reside in another

PART IV — ROMAN CATHOLIC SEPARATE SCHOOLS   **S. 117**

municipality or in territory without municipal organization and not in a secondary school district, and the separate school board,

(a) provides daily transportation; or

(b) reimburses the parents or guardians for the cost of board, lodging and transportation once a week under subsection 190(11),

for secondary school pupils whose parents or guardians are separate school supporters who do not reside in the secondary school district, such separate school board may levy the cost of such transportation or reimbursement for the preceding year, less the legislative grants paid thereon, on the supporters who do not reside in the secondary school district.

117. (1) **Determining school rates by equalizing factor.**—Where a separate school zone includes territory in two or more municipalities, the board shall, when it is setting the rates to be levied in any year, use an equalizing factor for each municipality in the zone which, when applied to the local assessment of properties in a municipality, would increase or decrease the local assessment on such properties to a sum equal to the local assessment on similar properties in the municipality in which the greatest number of its pupils reside.

(2) **Adoption of rate.**—The board shall adopt a tax rate to be levied in the municipality in which the greatest number of its pupils reside and multiply that rate by the factor determined for each municipality in the zone, and the resulting rates calculated to the nearest tenth of a mill shall be the rates in the respective municipalities for separate school purposes in the zone.

(3) **Arbitrators, appointment.**—For the purpose of determining the factors, the board shall appoint three arbitrators who are not trustees who shall meet and determine the factors.

(4) **Meeting.**—The secretary of the board shall call the meeting of the arbitrators.

(5) **Determination of factors.**—The arbitrators shall base their decision on a comparison of the local assessment on sample properties that are assessed to the support of the separate schools in the municipality in which the greatest number of its pupils reside with the local assessment on similar properties in the other municipalities in which any part of the separate school zone is situated, and the factors so determined shall be used by the board when it sets its rates at any time following the decision of the arbitrators and until the factors are altered by arbitration.

(6) **Apportionment under s. 240.**—Where the arbitrators conclude that it would be more just and equitable in the interests of the supporters of the board for the board when setting the rates to be levied in a year to have apportioned its requirements in accordance with a regulation made under section 240 in respect of the year, the arbitrators shall so advise the board when they have determined and reported the factors under subsection (5).

(7) **Resolution of board.**—After being advised under subsection (6), the board may resolve to apportion its requirements in accordance with the regulation that applies for the year.

(8) **Notice.**—A board that resolves to apportion under subsection (7) shall forthwith notify the Minister of its decision.

(9) **Non-application.**—The review referred to in section 240 does not apply in the case of a board that acts under subsection (7).

(10) **When factors to be determined.**—The factors shall be determined,

(a) in the year in which the separate school is formed;

(b) in any year that is divisible evenly by 5;

(c) in any year in which the basis of assessing has been changed in any of the municipalities in which part of the separate school zone is situate; and

(d) in any year if the board so directs.

(11) **Appeal to board.**—Five supporters of the separate school in the separate school zone or the majority of the supporters who reside in one municipality in the zone may, on or before the 1st day of November in any year, appeal to the board against the last determination of the factors, and the decision of the board is final.

(12) **Use of factors.**—The factors determined in any year shall be used for the purposes of taxation in the following and subsequent years until the year following the next determination of the factors.

(13) **Cost of arbitration.**—The cost of the arbitration shall be paid by the separate school board.

(14) **Non-application.**—This section does not apply to,

(a) The Haldimand-Norfolk Roman Catholic Separate School Board;
(b) The Waterloo Region Roman Catholic Separate School Board;
(c) The Sudbury District Roman Catholic Separate School Board in respect of the portion of its zone in The Regional Municipality of Sudbury; or
(d) as separate school board in respect of any portion of its zone in a county, regional or district municipality or the County of Oxford where an assessment update has been carried out under subsection 371(2) of the *Municipal Act*, subsection 135.3(1) of the *Regional Municipalities Act*, subsection 81(1) of the *District Municipality of Muskoka Act* or subsection 84.13(1) of the *County of Oxford Act*. 1992, c. 15, s. 85; 1993, c. 11, s. 26.

118. Trustees may copy assessment roll of municipality.—The clerk or other officer of a municipality within or adjoining which a separate school is established, having possession of the assessor's or collector's roll of the municipality, shall permit any trustee or the collector of the board to make a copy of the roll in so far as it relates to the persons supporting the separate school.

119. Clerk to give trustees annual statement of supporters of separate schools.—The clerk of a municipality in which there is a separate school board shall, once in each year, upon the written request of the board, deliver to it a statement in writing showing the names of all persons who are separate school supporters with the amount for which each person has been rated upon the assessment roll.

120. (1) **Request for collection of separate school rates by the municipality.**—The council of a municipality, if so requested on or before the 1st day of February in any year by a separate school board having jurisdiction in the municipality, shall levy and collect upon the property rateable for separate school purposes in the municipality and within the jurisdiction of the board, the rates or taxes imposed thereon by the board, and such request shall be deemed to continue from year to year unless terminated by the board giving notice to the council on or before the 1st day of February in any year.

(2) **Expenses of collection.**—Any expenses attending the assessment, collection or payment of school rates by the municipal corporation shall be borne by the corporation, and the

PART IV — ROMAN CATHOLIC SEPARATE SCHOOLS S. 121

rates and taxes collected for separate school purposes shall be paid by the corporation to the treasurer of the board and section 243 applies with necessary modifications to such rates and taxes.

121. (1) **Borrowing powers of separate school trustees.**—The board of a separate school may pass by-laws for borrowing money, by mortgages or other instruments, upon the security of the schoolhouse property and premises and any other real or personal property vested in the board and upon the separate school rates for the purpose of paying the cost of school sites, school buildings or additions or repairs thereto or for any other school purposes.

(2) **Terms of payment.**—The principal money may be made payable in annual or other instalments, with or without interest, and the board, in addition to all other rates or money that it may levy in any one year, may levy and collect in each year such further sum as may be requisite for paying all principal money and interest falling due in that year, and the same shall be levied and collected in each year in the same manner and from the like persons and property by, from, upon or out of which other separate school rates may be levied and collected.

(3) **Debentures.**—Such mortgages and other instruments may in the discretion of the board be made in the form of debentures, and the debentures are a charge on the same property and the rates as in the case of mortgages thereof made by the board.

(4) **Maturity.**—The debt to be so incurred and the debentures to be issued therefor may be made payable in thirty years at the furthest, and in equal annual instalments of principal and interest, or in any other manner authorized by the *Municipal Act* in the case of debentures issued under that Act.

(5) **Sinking fund.**—Where the debt is not payable by instalments, the board shall levy in each year during the currency of the debt in addition to the amount required to pay the interest falling due in such year a sum such that the aggregate amount so levied during the currency of the debt, with the estimated interest on the investments thereof, will be sufficient to discharge the debt when it becomes payable.

(6) **Investment of fund.**—The sum referred to in subsection (5) shall be deposited with a bank listed in Schedule I or II to the *Bank Act* (Canada) or a trust corporation that is registered under the *Loan and Trust Corporations Act*, and such sum and any income resulting therefrom shall be invested by such bank or trust corporation in the manner provided in the *Municipal Act* for sinking funds, and subsections 144(4) to (9) of the *Municipal Act* apply with necessary modifications except that reference therein to the Ministry of Municipal Affairs shall be deemed to be a reference to the Ministry of Education.

(7) **Publication of notice of by-law.**—Before a by-law for borrowing money for a permanent improvement is acted upon, notice of the passing of the by-law shall be published for three consecutive weeks in a newspaper having general circulation within the separate school zone stating,

(a) the purpose for which the money is to be borrowed;
(b) the amount to be borrowed and the security therefor;
(c) the terms of repayment including the rate of interest,

and, if no application to quash the by-law is made for three months after publication of notice of the passing thereof, the by-law is valid despite any want of substance or form in the by-law or in the time or manner of passing the by-law.

(8) **Amounts.**—The debentures issued under the by-law may be for such amounts as the board considers expedient. 1993, c. 11, s. 27.

122. (1) **Share of legislative grants.**—Every separate school shall share in the legislative grants in like manner as a public school.

(2) **Right of separate schools to a share of municipal grants.**—Every separate school is entitled to share in all grants, investments and allotments for public school purposes made by any municipal authority according to the average number of pupils enrolled at the school during the next preceding twelve months, or during the number of months that may have elapsed from the establishment of a new separate school, as compared with the whole average number of pupils enrolled at school in the same city, town, village or township.

(3) **Apportionment.**—Where the grant is made by a council of a county or a regional municipality it shall be apportioned in like manner as the legislative grant.

(4) **Not to share in public school assessment.**—A separate school is not entitled to share in any school money arising or accruing from local assessment for public school purposes within the city, town, village or township in which the school is situate.

Visitors

123. Separate school visitors.—A parent or guardian of a child attending a separate school and a member of the board that operates the school may visit such school, and a member of the Assembly and a member of the clergy of the Roman Catholic Church may visit a separate school in his or her constituency or in the area where he or she has pastoral charge, as the case may be.

Secondary School Education

124. (1) **Election re secondary school.**—A separate school board may elect to perform the duties of a secondary school board for the area of jurisdiction of the board.

(2) **By-law.**—An election under subsection (1) shall be by by-law approved by the Minister.

(3) **Approval.**—The Minister may approve a by-law under subsection (2) upon receiving the advice of the Planning and Implementation Commission that the Commission is of the opinion that the first annual implementation plan formulated by the separate school board for the purpose of providing secondary school education and filed with the Commission will permit the separate school board to provide secondary school education and will promote the best interests of public education in Ontario.

(4) **Transmittal.**—The secretary of a separate school board that makes an election under subsection (1) shall forthwith transmit to the Ministry a copy of the by-law certified by the secretary.

(5) **Notice.**—Upon approval of a by-law by the Minister, the Ministry shall transmit notice of the approval to the board that passed the by-law and shall transmit a copy of the by-law and notice of approval,

(a) to the Planning and Implementation Commission;

PART IV — ROMAN CATHOLIC SEPARATE SCHOOLS S. 129

(b) to the secretary of every board of education that has jurisdiction in the same area as the separate school board;

(c) to the clerk of every municipality all or part of which is within the area of jurisdiction of the separate school board; and

(d) to the appropriate assessment commissioner.

125. (1) **Effective date.**—An election under section 124 is effective on the first day of the school year specified in the by-law approved by the Minister.

(2) **Election after 30th day of June.**—A by-law approved by the Minister after the 30th day of June in a year shall not take effect before the school year that commences in the next following year.

126. Powers and duties of Roman Catholic school board.—A Roman Catholic school board has all the powers and shall perform all the duties that are conferred or imposed by this Act on a secondary school board in respect of the secondary school grades for which the Roman Catholic school board is entitled to share in the legislative grants.

127. (1) **Agreement for education at other school.**—A Roman Catholic school board and a public board may enter into an agreement to provide secondary school instruction of pupils of the one board in a school or schools operated by the other board, upon payment of fees by the board requesting the instruction to the board that provides the instruction.

(2) **Calculation of fees.**—The fees for the provision of the instruction shall be calculated in accordance with the regulations.

128. (1) **Legislative grants.**—A Roman Catholic school board is entitled to share in the legislative grants for secondary school purposes.

(2) **Conditions.**—The payment of legislative grants to a Roman Catholic school board is subject to the conditions prescribed by the regulations, in addition to conditions that may be made under clause 11(3)(b).

(3) **Apportionment and distribution.**—The apportionment and distribution of legislative grants to a Roman Catholic school board is subject to the regulations.

(4) **Compliance.**—The payment and apportionment of legislative grants to a Roman Catholic school board is subject to compliance by the Roman Catholic school board with sections 124 to 157.

(5) **Regulations.**—A regulation made for the purposes of this section,

(a) may be general or particular in its application; or

(b) may provide for the withholding or repayment of all or part of a grant where a condition of the grant is not satisfied.

129. (1) **Secondary school grades.**—For the first school year in respect of which an election is effective, the entitlement of a Roman Catholic school board under section 128 applies in respect of the secondary school grade or grades, not exceeding grades nine and ten, in which the board is providing instruction in the immediately preceding school year and in respect of the next higher grade.

(2) **Grades nine and ten.**—The entitlement of a Roman Catholic school board under section 128 applies in respect of grade nine or grade ten, or both, provided for the first time in the first school year in respect of which the election of the Roman Catholic school board is effective.

(3) **Additional grades.**—For each subsequent school year, the board's entitlement under section 128 applies in respect of the same secondary school grades as in the previous school year and in respect of the next higher grade until the entitlement applies in respect of all secondary school grades.

(4) **All services provided by agreement.**—Despite subsections (1) to (3), for the first school year in which an election is effective and for every subsequent year, the entitlement of a Roman Catholic school board under section 128 applies in respect of all secondary school grades if, in the first school year, the board provides instruction in all secondary school grades and the instruction is provided in accordance with the board's first annual implementation plan in a school operated by another board by means of an agreement with the other board.

(5) **Restriction when subs. (4) applies.**—A Roman Catholic school board to which subsection (4) applies may provide instruction in a secondary school grade only if,

(a) the instruction is provided in a school operated by another board by means of an agreement referred to in subsection (4); or
(b) after the first school year in which the election under section 124 is effective,
   (i) the Roman Catholic school board to which subsection (4) applies files with the Planning and Implementation Commission a plan to provide instruction in all secondary school grades in a school operated by the board, and
   (ii) the Minister approves the provision of instruction in a school operated by the board after receiving the advice of the Planning and Implementation Commission that the Commission is of the opinion that the plan will permit the board to provide instruction in all secondary school grades and will promote the best interests of public education in Ontario.

130. (1) **French language schools.**—A Roman Catholic school board is entitled to share in the legislative grants as provided in section 128 in respect of a secondary school established and operated under Part XII by a public board and transferred to and operated by the Roman Catholic school board.

(2) **Entitlement.**—The entitlement under subsection (1) is in addition to the entitlement under section 129 (secondary school grades).

131. (1) **Membership on public board.**—No member shall be elected by separate school electors to a public board that has the same or part of the same area of jurisdiction as a Roman Catholic school board.

(2) **Application of sub. (1).**—Subsection (1) does not apply where a public board has part of the same area of jurisdiction as a Roman Catholic school board as a result of the fact that a separate school zone that comprises part of the county or district combined Roman Catholic separate school zone for which the Roman Catholic school board was established has a centre that is situate within 4.8 kilometres of the boundary of the public board and is not situate within the area of jurisdiction of the public board.

(3) **Idem.**—Part VIII applies with respect to the election of members elected by separate school electors to a public board to which subsection (2) applies as if the coterminous Roman Catholic separate school board as defined in subsection 230(1) was not a Roman Catholic school board.

PART IV — ROMAN CATHOLIC SEPARATE SCHOOLS **S. 134**

(4) **Eligibility of separate school elector.**—After the end of the first calendar year in which a Roman Catholic school board performs the duties of a secondary school board in accordance with an election under section 124, no member elected by separate school electors and no separate school supporter or separate school elector is eligible to be a member of a public board that has the same or part of the same area of jurisdiction as the Roman Catholic school board.

132. (1) **Payment of public secondary school rates.**—Every separate school supporter paying rates on property in the area of jurisdiction of a Roman Catholic school board is exempt from the payment of all rates imposed for secondary school purposes of a public board to the same extent that the person is exempt from payment of rates imposed for public elementary school purposes.

(2) **Application of subs. (1).**—The exemption under subsection (1) commences in respect of the year following the year in which the election of the Roman Catholic school board becomes effective under section 125.

133. (1) **Estimates and rates for separate secondary school purposes.**—The provisions of this Part that apply to the preparation and adoption of estimates and the levying and collection of rates or taxes for separate school purposes apply with necessary modifications for secondary school purposes in respect of a Roman Catholic school board.

(2) **Elementary and secondary estimates.**—Every Roman Catholic school board shall continue to prepare and adopt the estimates required of it for elementary school purposes and must prepare and adopt estimates for secondary school purposes in the same manner as is required of a public board.

134. (1) **Mandatory joint committees.**—If the area of jurisdiction of a public board is substantially the same as the area of jurisdiction of a Roman Catholic school board or if their common area of jurisdiction includes the whole of a municipality, the two boards shall establish a joint committee.

(2) **Multiple committees.**—If a board is required under subsection (1) to establish more than one joint committee, the board shall ensure that at least one member of each such joint committee is a member of the other joint committee or committees.

(3) **Combined joint committee.**—If a Roman Catholic school board is required to establish more than one joint committee and all of the public boards concerned agree, the boards concerned may establish a single combined joint committee instead of the joint committees required under subsection (1).

(4) **Composition.**—Each joint committee and combined joint committee shall consist of such number of members as the boards concerned may agree upon and, if the boards are unable to agree, shall be composed of,

  (a) three members of each public board concerned, appointed by their respective boards; and
  (b) three members of the Roman Catholic school board, appointed by that board.

(5) **French-language representative.**—If a board that appoints members to a joint committee or a combined joint committee is required to have a French-language section or a French-

language education council, at least one appointee of that board shall be a member of such section or council.

(6) **Idem.**—Subsection (5) applies with necessary modifications if a board is required to have an English-language section or an English-language education council.

(7) **Idem.**—Nothing in Part XIII applies so as to restrict the participation of a member of a joint committee or combined joint committee in any meeting of the committee or so as to prevent the member from voting on any matter at a meeting of the committee.

(8) **Term of office.**—A member of a joint committee or a combined joint committee shall hold office during the term of the members of his or her respective board and until a new board is organized and a successor is appointed or elected, as the case may be.

(9) **Vacancies.**—If a position on a joint committee or combined joint committee becomes vacant, the board that appointed the person whose position has become vacant shall appoint a qualified person to fill the vacancy for the remainder of the term of the person whose position has become vacant.

(9.1) **Quorum.**—A majority of the members of a joint committee or combined joint committee is a quorum, and a vote of a majority of the members present at a meeting is necessary to bind the committee.

(9.2) **Chair.**—The members of a joint committee or combined joint committee shall, at their first meeting, elect one of the members as chair who shall preside at all meetings and, if at any meeting the chair is not present, the members present may elect a chair for that meeting.

(9.3) **Chair voting.**—On every motion, the chair may vote with the other members of a joint committee or combined joint committee, and any motion on which there is an equality of votes is lost.

(10) **Personnel and services.**—The boards concerned shall make available to the joint committee or combined joint committee such personnel and services as the boards consider necessary for the proper functioning of the joint committee or combined joint committee.

(11) **Public meetings.**—A joint committee or combined joint committee shall hold public meetings to report upon its work.

(12) **Recommendations.**—A joint committee or combined joint committee is responsible for exploring opportunities for transferring facilities, leasing facilities or sharing services, facilities, resources and staff, and may make recommendations in respect of the implementation of programs for such purpose.

(13) **Consideration of recommendations by boards.**—A public board and a Roman Catholic school board shall consider any recommendation submitted to it in writing by a joint committee or combined joint committee and shall not refuse its approval without having given the committee an opportunity to be heard by the board or by the board and any committee of the board to which such recommendation is referred.

(14) **Reconsideration of recommendations.**—If a recommendation requires the approval of two or more boards to be effective and one or more of the boards concerned rejects the recommendation, the board or boards that approved the recommendation may make representations to the board or boards that rejected the recommendation, in which case the board or boards that rejected the recommendation shall reconsider the recommendation and may approve or reject it.

PART IV — ROMAN CATHOLIC SEPARATE SCHOOLS   S. 135

(15) **Annual report.**—Each joint committee and combined joint committee shall report annually upon its proceedings and the disposition of its recommendations to the public board, the Roman Catholic school board and to the Planning and Implementation Commission which shall review and comment upon the reports as part of its annual report to the Minister. 1993, c. 11, s. 28.

135. (1) **Teaching and other staff.**—A public board that has jurisdiction in an area that is also part or all of the area of jurisdiction of a Roman Catholic school board shall designate, in accordance with the regulations or by agreement between the boards, the persons on its supervisory officers staff, elementary teaching staff, secondary teaching staff and support staff whose services will not be required by the public board consequent on,

(a) the election of the Roman Catholic school board to perform the duties of a secondary school board; or

(b) the provision of instruction by the Roman Catholic school board under clause 129(5)(b).

(2) **Contents of regulations and agreements.**—The regulations or agreement referred to in subsection (1) shall provide for,

(a) the exchange of enrolment and other data between the boards so as to enable the public board to make the calculations necessary to determine the designation referred to in subsection (1);

(b) methods for encouraging voluntary transfers of public board teachers and supervisory officers to positions with the Roman Catholic school board and for treating a person so transferred as a designated person with all rights and entitlements provided by this Act; and

(c) a right of first refusal, on the basis of seniority, for designated persons with respect to positions that become vacant in the public board.

(3) **Idem.**—The regulations or agreement referred to in subsection (1) may contain provisions in addition to those required by subsection (2), including provisions related to the encouragement of the secondment and assignment of services of teachers and supervisory officers of the public board to positions with the Roman Catholic school board.

(4) **Collective agreements.**—No agreement under subsection (1) renders inoperative any provision in a collective agreement unless the branch affiliate or affiliates concerned agree in writing to an amendment to the collective agreement.

(5) **Affirmative action.**—In determining the designations referred to in subsection (1) and in implementing its employment policy thereafter, the public board shall endeavour to maintain and promote affirmative action with respect to the employment of women on its teaching staff.

(6) **Yearly designations for ten years.**—The public board shall make the designations referred to in subsection (1) in each of the first ten school years during which the Roman Catholic school board performs the duties of a secondary school board.

(7) **Idem.**—Subject to subsection (8), the public board shall make the designations referred to in subsection (1) in each of the first ten school years during which the Roman Catholic school board provides instruction under clause 129(5)(b).

(8) **Maximum limit.**—No designations shall be made under subsection (1) after the twentieth school year during which the Roman Catholic school board performs the duties of a secondary school board.

(9) **Date for designations.**—Designations shall be made under subsection (1) not later than the date prescribed by the regulations for each year.

(10) **Transfer of employment if subs. 129(4) does not apply.**—If subsection 129(4) does not apply to the Roman Catholic school board referred to in subsection (1), the teaching contract, employment contract or employment relationship, as the case may be, of a person designated by a public board under subsection (1) is transferred to, and assumed by, the Roman Catholic school board referred to in subsection (1), effective on the 1st day of September next following the date on which the public board makes the designation or on such earlier date as the boards concerned may agree on.

(11) **Transfer of employment if cl. 129(5)(a) applies.**—If subsection 129(4) applies to the Roman Catholic school board referred to in subsection (1) and the board provides instruction in accordance with clause 129(5)(a), the teaching contract, employment contract or employment relationship, as the case may be, of a person designated by a public board under subsection (1) is transferred to, and assumed by, the board that operates the school in which the instruction is provided under the agreement referred to in clause 129(5)(a), effective the 1st day of September next following the date on which the public board makes the designation or on such earlier date as the boards concerned may agree on.

(12) **Idem.**—If more than one board operates schools in which instruction is provided under an agreement referred to in clause 129(5)(a), the board to which a contract or relationship shall be transferred under subsection (11) shall be,

(a) one of the boards that operates the schools, as determined by agreement of those boards; or

(b) in the absence of an agreement, the Roman Catholic school board referred to in subsection (1).

(13) **Objectors.**—If a designated person objects for reasons of conscience to the transfer of employment to a Roman Catholic school board under subsection (10) or (11), he or she may so advise the public board and, unless it is of the opinion that the objection is not made in good faith, the public board shall designate another person in place of the person making the objection.

(14) **Second transfer of employment if cl. 129(5)(b) applies.**—If subsection 129(4) applies to the Roman Catholic school board referred to in subsection (1) and the Minister approves the provision of instruction in a school operated by the board under clause 129(5)(b), a teaching contract, employment contract or employment relationship transferred under subsection (11) to another board is transferred to, and assumed by, the Roman Catholic school board referred to in subsection (1), effective on the date the board begins to provide instruction under clause 129(5)(b) or on such earlier date as the boards concerned may agree on.

(15) **Similar employment.**—A board to which the teaching contract, employment contract or employment relationship of a person is transferred under subsection (10), (11) or (14) shall employ the person in a position substantially similar to the position in which the person was employed immediately before the transfer.

(16) **Training assistance.**—If the board to which the teaching contract, employment contract or employment relationship of a person is transferred under subsection (10), (11) or

(14) has no position as provided under subsection (15) for the person on the appropriate staff of the board, the person is entitled to receive training assistance, as prescribed by the regulations, for an alternate position on the appropriate staff, and the board to which the contract or relationship is transferred shall maintain the person in its employ, provide the assistance and offer to the person employment in a position appropriate to either his or her previous or newly acquired qualifications.

(17) **Seniority.**—Subject to any collective agreement in effect, the public board shall designate, on the basis of seniority, the persons on its support staff whose services will not be required by the public board consequent on,

    (a) the election of the Roman Catholic school board to perform the duties of a secondary school board; or

    (b) the provision of instruction by the Roman Catholic school board under clause 129(5)(b).

(18) **Transmittal of lists.**—Each public board that designates persons under this section shall transmit to the Planning and Implementation Commission in each year, not later than the date for each year fixed by the Commission, a list of the names and positions of persons that it has designated.

(19) **Compensation rate.**—A designated person employed by a board to which the person's teaching contract, employment contract or employment relationship is transferred under subsection (10), (11) or (14) has the right in the first year that the person is employed by the board to an annual rate of salary of not less than the annual rate of salary that would have applied to the person if the contract or relationship had not been transferred, but if the annual rate of salary of the position in which the person is employed by the board to which the contract or relationship is transferred is lower than such first-mentioned annual rate of salary, the person is not entitled to any increase in annual rate of salary until the annual rate of salary of the position becomes equal to such first-mentioned annual rate of salary.

(20) **Seniority and employment status.**—A designated person employed by a board to which the person's teaching contract, employment contract or employment relationship is transferred under subsection (10), (11) or (14) has the right to commence the employment with seniority and with probationary and permanent status with the board equal to the seniority and the probationary or permanent status the person would have had if the contract or relationship had not been transferred.

Education Amendment Act (Miscellaneous), 1991

Editor's Note: S.O. 1991, Vol. 2, c. 10, s. 4(3) states:

    Boards to which former subsection 135(20) of the Act applied before the 20th day of December, 1990 shall, despite that subsection, be deemed to have had the authority to agree to share the amount of a payment under former subsection 135(18) or (19) of the Act in any manner, including the payment of the entire amount by one of the boards.

(21) **Sick leave credits.**—Sick leave credits standing to a designated person's credit immediately before the person's teaching contract, employment contract or employment rela-

tionship is transferred under subsection (10), (11) or (14) shall be transferred to the plan maintained by the board to which the contract or relationship is transferred at the time the contract or relationship is transferred.

(22) **Credit for total accumulation.**—If the number of sick leave credits transferred exceeds the total number of sick leave credits that may be accumulated under the plan to which they are transferred, the designated person shall be given credit in the plan for the number transferred but is not entitled to accumulate further sick leave credits under the plan unless the plan is amended to permit greater accumulation.

(23) **Accumulation and use of sick leave credits.**—Subject to subsection (22), a designated person employed by a board to which the person's teaching contract, employment contract or employment relationship is transferred under subsection (10), (11) or (14) is entitled to accumulate and to use sick leave credits in accordance with the plan maintained by the board to which the contract or relationship is transferred.

(24) **Gratuity.**—On termination of employment with the board to which a designated person's teaching contract, employment contract or employment relationship is transferred under subsection (10), (11) or (14), the person is entitled to payment of an amount calculated in accordance with,

(a) the collective agreement that applied on the last date the person was employed by the public board that designated the person, as though the person had been in the continuous employ of the public board, if a collective agreement applied in respect of the person on that date; or

(b) the policy of the public board that designated the person as of the last date he or she was employed by the public board, as though the person had been in the continuous employ of the public board, if no collective agreement applied in respect of the person on that date.

(25) **Idem.**—In lieu of the payment under subsection (24), the designated person is entitled to require payment of an amount calculated in accordance with,

(a) the collective agreement that applies in respect of the person on the last date the person is employed before the termination of employment, if a collective agreement applies in respect of the person on that date; or

(b) the policy of the board with which the person is employed as of the last date he or she is employed by that board, if no collective agreement applies in respect of the person on that date.

(26) **Idem.**—The amount of the payment under subsection (24) or (25) shall be shared by the public board that designated the person and the board or boards to which the person's employment was transferred under this section in the ratio that the number of years of service of the person with each board bears to the total number of years of service of the person with such boards.

(26.1) **Idem.**—Despite subsection (26), the boards concerned may agree to share the amount of the payment under subsection (24) or (25) in any manner, including the payment of the entire amount by one of the boards. 1991, Vol. 2, c. 10, s. 4(1).

(27) **Non-application of subss. (24) to (26).**—Subsections (24) to 26(1.1) do not apply to a termination of employment with a board that occurs when the teaching contract, employ-

ment contract or employment relationship of the person is transferred to another board under subsection (10), (11) or (14).

(28) **Employment, advancement and promotion.**—Section 5 of the *Human Rights Code* applies to designated persons employed by a Roman Catholic school board in respect of their employment, advancement and promotion by the Board, despite section 23 of the said Code.

(29) **Definition.**—In this section, "seniority" means seniority as agreed upon between the public board that employed the designated person and the organization that entered into a collective agreement with the public board in respect of the designated person, or, where there is no collective agreement, in accordance with the policy of the public board.

(30) **Deemed designated persons.**—This section applies with necessary modifications in respect of entitlements of teachers who were employed by a public board that has jurisdiction in an area that is also the area or part of the area of jurisdiction of a Roman Catholic school board and who subsequent to a report to the Minister by the Commission under subsection 136f(1) as enacted by the Statutes of Ontario, 1986, chapter 21, section 2, but before the 24th day of June, 1986 accepted employment with the Roman Catholic school board. 1991, Vol. 2, c. 10, s. 4.

136. (1) **Hiring after ten-year period.**—For the purpose of maintaining the distinctiveness of separate schools, the Roman Catholic school board may require as a condition of employment that teachers hired by the board after the ten school year period mentioned in subsection 135(6) agree to respect the philosophy and traditions of Roman Catholic separate schools in the performance of their duties.

(2) **Application of *Human Rights Code* s. 5.**—Subject to subsection (1), and despite section 24 of the *Human Rights Code*, section 5 of the said Code applies to ensure that such teachers employed by a Roman Catholic school board will enjoy equal opportunity in respect of their employment, advancement and promotion by the board.

(3) **Repeal.**—If it is finally determined by a court that subsection (1) or (2) prejudicially affects a right or privilege with respect to denominational schools guaranteed by the Constitution of Canada, subsections (1) and (2) are repealed, it being the intention of the Legislature that the remaining provisions of the Act are separate from and independent of the said subsections.

137. (1) **Staff dispute resolution.**—A dispute in respect of the designation of or the failure to designate a person on the teaching or other staffs of a public board, or in respect of any matter arising under section 135 in the employment relationship between a designated person and a board to which the person's teaching contract, employment contract or employment relationship was transferred under that section, may be resolved by a grievance arbitration procedure in accordance with this section.

(2) **Parties.**—The parties to the arbitration are the public board or the board to which the contract or relationship was transferred, as the case requires, and the person or, if the person is employed in accordance with the terms of a collective agreement, the organization that represents the person under the collective agreement.

(3) **Notice to arbitrate.**—Either party to the dispute may notify the other party in writing of intention to submit the dispute to arbitration.

(4) **Name of appointee.**—The notice shall contain the name of the first party's appointee to an arbitration board.

(5) **Response.**—The second party shall, within five days after receiving the notice, notify the first party either that the second party accepts the appointee as a single arbitrator or notify the first party of the name of the second party's appointee to the arbitration board.

(6) **Chair.**—The two appointees shall, within five days after the appointment of the second of them, appoint a third person who shall be the chair of the arbitration board.

(7) **Failure to act.**—If the second party fails to give notice accepting a single arbitrator or appointing a second arbitrator, or if the two appointees fail to appoint a chair, the appointment shall be made by the Education Relations Commission upon the request of either party to the dispute.

(8) **Hearing.**—The single arbitrator or the arbitration board, as the case may be, shall hear the parties and issue a decision.

(9) **Majority.**—The decision of a majority is the decision of the arbitration board, but if there is no majority, the decision of the chair is the decision of the arbitration board.

(10) **Decision is final.**—The decision is final and binding upon the parties to the dispute and upon the person in respect of whom the dispute has been arbitrated and who is represented by the organization that is a party.

(11) **Examination of documentary evidence.**—A party to an arbitration proceeding shall be afforded an opportunity to examine before the hearing any written or documentary evidence that will be produced or any report the contents of which will be given in evidence at the hearing.

(12) **Prior knowledge.**—A single arbitrator or a member of an arbitration board shall not have taken part before the hearing in an investigation or consideration of the subject-matter of the hearing.

(13) **Notice of communication.**—A single arbitrator or a member of an arbitration board shall not communicate directly or indirectly in relation to the subject-matter of the hearing with any person or party or the representative of a party except upon notice to and opportunity for all parties to participate.

(14) **Participation in decision.**—No member of an arbitration board shall participate in a decision of the board unless the member was present throughout the hearing and heard the evidence and argument of the parties and, except with the consent of the parties, a decision of the board shall not be given unless all members so present participate in the decision.

(15) **Release of documentary evidence.**—Documents and things put in evidence at an arbitration hearing shall, upon the request of the person who produced them, be released to the person by the board within a reasonable time after the matter in issue has been finally determined.

(16) **Collective agreement.**—If there is a collective agreement between the parties to the dispute and the collective agreement does not provide for arbitration of such a dispute, the collective agreement shall be deemed to include subsections (1) to (15).

138. (1) **Vacancy on arbitration board.**—If a member of an arbitration board is unable to enter on or to carry on his or her duties so as to enable a decision to be made within sixty days after the date of appointment of the chair, or within such longer period of time as may be fixed in writing by the arbitration board and consented to by the Education Relations Commission, or ceases to act by reason of withdrawal or death before the arbitration board has completed its work, a replacement shall be appointed by the person or body that appointed the member, and the arbitration board shall continue to function as if such member were a member of the arbitration board from the beginning.

(2) **Chair unable to act.**—If the chair of an arbitration board is unable to enter on or to carry on his or her duties so as to enable a decision to be rendered within sixty days after his or her appointment, or within such longer period of time as may be fixed in writing by the arbitration board and consented to by the Education Relations Commission, or ceases to act by reason of withdrawal or death, the Education Relations Commission shall give notice thereof to the members of the arbitration board who shall within seven days of the giving of the notice appoint a person to be the chair and if the appointment is not so made by the members, it shall be made by the Education Relations Commission, and after the chair is appointed the arbitration shall begin anew.

(3) **Arbitrator unable to act.**—If an arbitrator is unable to enter on or to carry on his or her duties so as to enable a decision to be rendered within sixty days after his or her appointment, or within such longer period of time as may be fixed in writing by the arbitrator and consented to by the Education Relations Commission, or ceases to act by reason of withdrawal or death, the Education Relations Commission shall give notice thereof to the parties who shall within seven days of the giving of the notice appoint a person to be the arbitrator and if the appointment is not so made, it shall be made by the Education Relations Commission, and after the arbitrator is appointed the arbitration shall begin anew.

139. Matters that may be considered by arbitrator or arbitration board.—For the purpose of the arbitration and in order to reach a decision in respect of the dispute, the arbitrator or arbitration board,

(a) may inquire into and consider any matter that the arbitrator or arbitration board considers relevant to the arbitration; and

(b) subject to such conditions as the arbitrator or arbitration board may establish, may permit persons who are not parties to the arbitration to participate at the hearing of the matter.

140. Report of arbitrator or arbitration board.—The arbitrator or arbitration board shall complete the consideration of the dispute and shall report the decision to the parties, the Education Relations Commission and the Planning and Implementation Commission in writing within sixty days after the giving of notice of the appointment of the arbitrator or within sixty days of the appointment of the chair of the arbitration board, as the case may be, or within such longer period of time as may be fixed in writing by the arbitrator or arbitration board and consented to by the Education Relations Commission.

141. Arbitration fees and expenses.—Each of the parties to an arbitration shall pay one-half of the fees and expenses of the arbitrator or, in the case of an arbitration board, of the members and chair of the arbitration board, except that if one of the parties is a natural person and not an organization, the board that is the other party shall pay all of the fees and expenses of the arbitrator or of the members and chair of the arbitration board.

142. Application of *Arbitrations Act*.—The *Arbitrations Act* does not apply to an arbitration of a dispute mentioned in section 137, except if there is no agreement with respect to the fees of the arbitrator or of the members and chair of an arbitration board, the fees prescribed under that Act shall be charged.

143. (1) Right to continue in public secondary school.—If a pupil or the parent or other person who has lawful custody of a pupil becomes exempt from payment of rates imposed for public secondary school purposes by reason of an election made under section 124 by a Roman Catholic school board and the pupil is a pupil in a public secondary school operated by a public board that receives a fee in respect of the pupil from a public board that has jurisdiction in whole or in part in the same area of jurisdiction as that of the Roman Catholic school board, the pupil is entitled to continue to be a pupil in the public secondary school.

(2) **Fee.**—If a pupil exercises the right under subsection (1), the Roman Catholic school board shall pay to the public board that operates the secondary school a fee in respect of the pupil calculated in accordance with the regulations. 1993, c. 11, s. 29.

144. (1) Right to receive secondary school instruction from Roman Catholic school board.—A person who is qualified to be a resident pupil of a public board and to receive instruction in a secondary school grade is entitled to receive instruction provided in a secondary school operated by a Roman Catholic school board if the area of jurisdiction of the public board is in whole or in part the same as the area of jurisdiction of the Roman Catholic school board.

(2) **Right to receive secondary school instruction from public board.**—A person who is qualified to be a resident pupil of a Roman Catholic school board and to receive instruction in a secondary school grade is entitled to receive instruction provided in a secondary school operated by a public board if the area of jurisdiction of the Roman Catholic school board is in whole or in part the same as the area of jurisdiction of the public board.

(3) **Fee.**—The public board shall pay the fee to which the Roman Catholic school board is entitled for providing secondary school education under subsection (1), and the Roman Catholic school board shall pay the fee to which the public board is entitled for providing secondary school education under subsection (2).

(4) **Amount.**—The fee to which a board is entitled under this section is the lesser of the fee set by the board or the fee calculated in accordance with the regulations.

(5) **Exemption from religious studies.**—Upon written application, a Roman Catholic school board shall exempt a person who is qualified to be a resident pupil in respect of a secondary school operated by a public board from programs and courses of study in religious education if,

(a) the person is enrolled in a program that is not otherwise available to the person in a secondary school operated by a public board within the area of jurisdiction of the Roman Catholic school board;
(b) it is impractical by reason of distance or terrain or by reason of physical handicap, mental handicap or multihandicap for the person to attend a secondary school operated by a public board; or
(c) the person is enrolled in an instructional unit of the Roman Catholic school board under Part XII.

PART IV — ROMAN CATHOLIC SEPARATE SCHOOLS   S. 148

(6) **Idem.**—A person who is qualified to be a resident pupil in respect of a secondary school operated by a public board who attends a secondary school operated by a Roman Catholic school board for a reason other than the one mentioned in clause 144(5)(a), (b) or (c) is considered to have enrolled in all of the school's programs and courses of study in religious education.

(7) **Additional exemptions.**—In addition to the exemptions provided for in subsection (5), no person who is qualified to be a resident pupil in respect of a secondary school operated by a public board who attends a secondary school operated by a Roman Catholic school board shall be required to take part in any program or course of study in religious education where a parent or guardian of the person, or the person where the person is an adult, applies in writing to the Roman Catholic school board for exemption of the person therefrom.

145. Interpretation.—Other provisions of this Act shall be construed with necessary modifications in order to give effect to and be consistent with sections 124 to 157.

146. Enforcement.—A right or duty under sections 124 to 157 may be enforced by order of the Divisional Court upon application to the court.

Planning and Implementation Commission

147. (1) **Commission continued.**—The Planning and Implementation Commission is continued under the name Planning and Implementation Commission in English and Commission de planification et de mise en oeuvre in French and shall be composed of not more than eight members appointed by the Lieutenant Governor in Council.

(2) **Chair and vice-chair.**—The Lieutenant Governor in Council shall designate a chair and a vice-chair from among the members of the Commission.

(3) **Term of office.**—The members of the Commission shall be appointed for such terms as may be determined by the Lieutenant Governor in Council and may be reappointed for further terms.

(4) **Authority of vice-chair.**—If the chair is absent or unable to act or if there is a vacancy in the office of chair, the vice-chair shall act as and have all the powers of the chair.

(5) **Remuneration and expenses.**—The members of the Commission shall be paid such remuneration and expenses as are determined by the Lieutenant Governor in Council.

(6) **Quorum.**—A majority of the members of the Commission, including the chair or vice-chair, constitutes a quorum.

(7) **Applications before Divisional Court.**—The Commission, in its name, may be a party to any application before the Divisional Court.

(8) **Staff and accommodation.**—The Ministry shall provide the Commission with such staff and accommodation as the Minister considers necessary for the purposes of the Commission.

148. (1) **Advice to Minister.**—The Planning and Implementation Commission shall advise the Minister in respect of specific means by which the extension of the Roman Catholic school system to include secondary school education may best be carried out.

(2) **Annual report.**—The Commission shall make an annual report to the Minister and the Minister shall submit the report to the Lieutenant Governor in Council and shall then lay the report before the Assembly if it is in session or, if not, at the next session.

(3) **Additional reports.**—In addition to its annual report, the Commission may report to the Minister at any time and shall report to the Minister in such form and manner, with such information and at such times as the Minister requires.

(4) **Consultation.**—For the purposes of preparing its advice and reports to the Minister, the Commission shall consult with organizations that have a direct interest in the subject-matter of the particular advice and report, organizations and persons that the Commission considers it appropriate to consult and organizations and persons specified by the Minister.

(5) **Matters to be considered by Commission.**—For the purpose of preparing its advice and reports to the Minister, the Commission shall establish criteria in respect of and, in accordance with the criteria, shall evaluate,

- (a) plans formulated by Roman Catholic school boards to provide secondary school education;
- (b) plans formulated by public boards in relation to the extension of the Roman Catholic school system to include secondary school education;
- (c) plans for new or altered areas of jurisdiction of Roman Catholic school boards in relation to separate secondary schools;
- (d) the effect on the employment of supervisory officers, teachers and other persons employed in secondary schools consequent upon the extension of the Roman Catholic school system and the plans formulated by Roman Catholic school boards and public boards in relation to the employment of such persons; and
- (e) any other subject specified by the Minister.

(6) **Non-application of subss. (4, 5).**—Subsections (4) and (5) do not apply in respect of annual reports.

(7) **Non-application of *Regulations Act*.**—The *Regulations Act* does not apply to criteria established under subsection (5).

149. (1) **Implementation plans.**—The Planning and Implementation Commission may require a Roman Catholic school board to formulate and file with the Commission each year an implementation plan setting out details of education programs, facilities, and supervisory officers, teaching staff and other staff required by the board for the purpose of providing the secondary school education until the Roman Catholic school board has filed implementation plans in respect of all secondary school grades.

(2) **Public board.**—The Commission may require a public board that is affected or that is likely to be affected by the provision of secondary school education by a Roman Catholic school board to formulate and file with the Commission annually, not later than the date specified by the Commission, a plan setting out details of changes in education programs, facilities and supervisory officers, teaching staff and other staff that will be or that are likely to be necessary in response to the provision of secondary school education by the Roman Catholic school board.

(3) **Format.**—The Commission may specify the format to be used in plans to be filed by Roman Catholic school boards and public boards and may specify time limits for the filing of plans requested by the Commission.

PART IV — ROMAN CATHOLIC SEPARATE SCHOOLS S. 152

(4) **Compliance.**—Every Roman Catholic school board and every public board shall comply with a request by the Commission for the formulation and filing of a plan under subsections (1) to (3).

(5) **Non-application of *Regulations Act*.**—The *Regulations Act* does not apply to any matter specified under subsection (3).

150. (1) **Public meetings.**—For the purpose of ensuring that it receives adequate information, the Planning and Implementation Commission may hold public meetings in respect of the provision of secondary school education by individual Roman Catholic school boards.

(2) **Notice.**—Where the Commission decides to hold a meeting mentioned in subsection (1), the Commission shall give notice of the meeting to the organizations it is required to consult, to such other persons or organizations as the Commission specifies and shall give public notice of the meeting.

151. (1) **Negotiations.**—Where the Planning and Implementation Commission is of the opinion that the implementation plans of one or more Roman Catholic school boards and one or more public boards that have jurisdiction in the same or part of the same area of jurisdiction as the Roman Catholic school board or boards do not together provide a method that meets the criteria set out in subsection (2), the Commission shall so notify the boards and shall specify for them the matters that must be resolved in order to meet the criteria.

(2) **Criteria.**—The criteria are that the method,

(a) must permit the Roman Catholic school board to provide viable secondary school education;
(b) must promote the best interests of public education in Ontario;
(c) must ensure the viability of the secondary school program offered by the public board especially in single secondary school communities; and
(d) must ensure, in a community that has only one secondary school operated by a public board, that the secondary school will continue to be operated by the public board despite the election to provide secondary education by a Roman Catholic school board having jurisdiction in the community, unless the public board decides otherwise.

(3) **Good faith.**—Upon receipt of the notice, the boards shall negotiate in good faith in respect of the matters specified by the Commission in order to meet the criteria set out in subsection (2).

152. (1) **Assistance by Commission.**—A public board or a Roman Catholic school board, or the Minister, may request the Planning and Implementation Commission to arrange or assist in, or both, negotiations between or among the boards respecting any one or more of,

(a) the transfer of the use of real or personal property;
(b) the transfer of the ownership of real or personal property; or
(c) the joint use or ownership of real or personal property.

(2) **Appointment of mediator.**—The Minister, on the recommendation of the Planning and Implementation Commission, may appoint a mediator to confer with one or more public boards and one or more Roman Catholic school boards and to endeavour to effect an agreement between or among the boards on the matters that the Commission has specified must be resolved between them.

(3) **Duties of mediator.**—The mediator shall confer with the boards and endeavour to effect an agreement and shall report the result to the Minister.

(4) **Duties of boards.**—Each board shall co-operate with the mediator and shall provide forthwith to the mediator such information as is requested by the mediator, and the mediator may request the provision of such information as the mediator considers relevant to the matters to be resolved.

(5) **Remuneration and expenses.**—The mediator shall be paid such remuneration as may be fixed by the Lieutenant Governor in Council, and subject to the approval of Management Board of Cabinet, the reasonable expenses incurred in the course of his or her duties.

153. (1) **Appointment of tribunal to resolve matters.**—If a mediator reports to the Minister that the mediator was unable to effect an agreement, the Minister shall appoint a tribunal of not more than three persons to hear and decide the matters that must be resolved.

(2) **Head of tribunal.**—The Minister shall designate one of the members of the tribunal to be the head of the tribunal.

(3) **Eligibility of members.**—No person is eligible to be a member of a tribunal who is or has been a member of a board that is a party to the proceeding before the tribunal or who is acting or has, within a period of six months preceding the date of the designation of the head of the tribunal, acted as solicitor, counsel or agent of either of the parties.

(4) **Replacement of members.**—If a member of the tribunal is unable to enter on or to carry on his or her duties so as to enable a decision to be made within sixty days after the date of the designation of the head of the tribunal, or within such longer period of time as may be fixed in writing by the tribunal and consented to by the Minister, or ceases to act by reason of withdrawal or death before the tribunal has completed its work, a replacement shall be appointed by the Minister and the tribunal shall continue to function as if the replacement member were a member of the tribunal from the beginning.

(5) **Notice.**—The tribunal shall appoint a time and place for a hearing and shall give notice thereof to the parties.

(6) **Parties.**—The parties to the hearing are the public board or public boards and the Roman Catholic school board or Roman Catholic school boards that are unable to effect an agreement on the matters that must be resolved between or among them.

(7) **Criteria.**—In deciding the matters that must be resolved, the tribunal shall endeavour to permit the Roman Catholic school board or Roman Catholic school boards to provide secondary education and shall endeavour to promote the best interests of public education in Ontario.

(8) **Decisions.**—The tribunal, in its decision, may provide for,

(a) the transfer of the use of real property or personal property, or both, from a public board that is a party to a Roman Catholic school board that is a party;

(b) the transfer of the ownership of real property or personal property, or both, from a public board that is a party to a Roman Catholic school board that is a party;

(c) the joint use of real property or personal property, or both, by a public board that is a party and a Roman Catholic school board that is a party in such proportions as the tribunal specifies, or any combination of them.

(9) **Delivery of decision.**—The tribunal shall give to the Minister its decision in writing, together with written reasons therefor, and the record of the proceeding forthwith after making the decision.

(10) **Order by Minister.**—The Minister shall issue and transmit to the parties an order in the terms of the decision, together with a copy of the decision and the written reasons for the decision.

(11) **Retransfer.**—Real property that is the subject of an order under subsection (10) is not subject to expropriation by a public board, but upon application the Minister with the approval of the Lieutenant Governor in Council may,

    (a) order the retransfer, subject to such conditions as are specified in the retransfer order, of the use or ownership of all or part of the real property or personal property, or both, that was transferred in accordance with an order under subsection (10);

    (b) by order vary or rescind an order under subsection (10) that provides for the joint use of any real property or personal property.

(12) **Application of *Expropriations Act*.**—The *Expropriations Act* does not apply in respect of the transfer or retransfer of real property or personal property in accordance with an order under this section.

(13) **Enforcement of order.**—The Minister shall cause a copy of an order made under this section to be filed in the Ontario Court (General Division), exclusive of the reasons therefor, and the order shall be entered in the same way as a judgment of the court and is enforceable as such.

(14) **L.G. in C. may confirm, vary or rescind order.**—Upon the petition of a party to a proceeding under this section, filed with the Clerk of the Executive Council within twenty-eight days after the date of an order by the Minister in the proceeding, the Lieutenant Governor in Council may,

    (a) confirm, vary or rescind the whole or any part of the order; or

    (b) require the Minister to appoint a new tribunal to hold a new hearing of the whole or any part of the matter upon which the order of the Minister was based.

(15) **No further petition.**—The order of the Minister after a new hearing ordered by the Lieutenant Governor in Council is not subject to petition under this section.

(16) **Filing of documents on petition.**—Upon the filing of a petition, the Minister shall file with the Clerk of the Executive Council the decision and written reasons therefor of the tribunal and a copy of the order of the Minister.

(17) **Hearing by L.G. in C.**—The Lieutenant Governor in Council is not required to hold or to afford to any person an opportunity for a hearing before deciding upon a petition under this section.

(18) **Remuneration and expenses.**—The head of the tribunal and the other members of the tribunal who are not officers in the Public Service of Ontario shall be paid such remuneration as may be fixed by the Lieutenant Governor in Council and, subject to the approval of Management Board of Cabinet, the reasonable expenses incurred by them in the course of their duties under this Act.

154. Repeal.—Sections 147 to 153 are repealed on the 1st day of July, 1995.

155. Limitation on real property transfers.—Despite any other provision of this Act, the ownership of real property used for purposes of a public secondary school shall not be transferred to a Roman Catholic school board before the 24th day of June, 1991 and no mediator under section 152 or tribunal under section 153 shall make a decision affecting the ownership of any such real property before that date but this section does not apply so as to prevent such a transfer before that date if the public board and the Roman Catholic school board agree and the Minister approves of the transfer.

156. Regulations.—The Lieutenant Governor in Council may make regulations,

(a) prescribing any matter that is referred to in sections 124 to 157 as prescribed by the regulations;

(b) prescribing the method of determining persons to be designated under subsection 135(1) and the matters referred to in subsections 135(2) and (3);

(c) requiring public boards and Roman Catholic school boards to confer with the Planning and Implementation Commission and branch affiliates on such matters as may be prescribed.

157. Conflict.—The resolution of a matter between a public board and a Roman Catholic school board under sections 124 to 156, except as specifically provided for in those sections, is a nullity if the result is inconsistent with any other Act, any other provision of this Act or a regulation under any Act.

PART V

PROTESTANT SEPARATE SCHOOLS

158. (1) Application to establish Protestant separate school.—Subject to subsection (3), five or more heads of families resident in a municipality and being Protestants may, before the 1st day of July in any year, apply in writing, in the case of a township, to the council of the township or, in the case of an urban municipality, to the public school board for permission to establish in the municipality one or more separate schools for Protestants.

(2) **Permission to establish.**—Subject to subsection (3), the council or the public school board, as the case may be, within thirty days of the receipt of a proper application shall grant permission to the applicants to establish in the municipality one or more separate schools for Protestants.

(3) **Restrictions on establishment.**—A Protestant separate school shall not be established in a municipality except where the teacher or teachers in the public school or schools in the municipality are Roman Catholics.

(4) **Effective date.**—A Protestant separate school is established on the day following the granting of permission to establish the school by the council or public school board, as the case may be.

159. (1) Notice to be supporter, exemption from public school rates.—Every person paying rates on property that the person occupies as owner or tenant in a municipality in which a Protestant separate school is established, who, personally or by his or her agent, on or before the 30th day of September in any year, gives to the clerk of the municipality notice in writing

PART V — PROTESTANT SEPARATE SCHOOLS **S. 163**

that the person is a Protestant and wishes to be a Protestant separate school supporter, is exempt from the payment of all rates imposed on such property for the support of public schools or for the purchase of land or the erection of buildings for public school purposes for the following year and every subsequent year while the person continues to be a Protestant separate school supporter with respect to such property.

(2) **No renewal required.**—The notice is not required to be renewed annually.

(3) **Certificate of notice.**—Every clerk of a municipality, upon receiving the notice shall deliver a certificate to the person giving the notice to the effect that the notice has been given and showing the date thereof.

(4) **Penalty for wilful false statements in notice.**—Any person who fraudulently gives such notice, or wilfully makes any false statement therein, does not thereby secure any exemption from the rates and in addition is guilty of an offence and liable to a fine of not more than $100.

(5) **As to rates imposed before Protestant separate school established.**—Nothing in this section exempts any person from paying any rate for public school purposes imposed before the establishment of the Protestant separate school.

160. Withdrawal of support.—A Protestant separate school supporter who desires to withdraw his or her support from a Protestant separate school shall give notice thereof in writing to the clerk of the municipality in which he or she resides on or before the 30th day of September in any year, otherwise he or she shall be deemed to be a Protestant separate school supporter.

161. (1) **Index book.**—The clerk of each municipality in which a Protestant separate school is established shall keep an index book to record the name of each Protestant who has declared himself or herself to be a supporter of a Protestant separate school in the same manner with necessary modifications as is provided for the keeping of an index of each Roman Catholic who has declared himself or herself to be a supporter of a Roman Catholic separate school.

(2) **Inspection.**—The index book shall be open to inspection by any ratepayer.

(3) **Filing of notices.**—The clerk shall file and carefully preserve all notices given to the clerk of the municipality under sections 159 and 160.

(4) **Clerk to be guided by index book.**—The clerk and the appropriate assessment commissioner shall be guided by the entries in the index book in ascertaining those who have given the prescribed notices.

162. (1) **Not to share in public school assessment.**—Protestant separate schools shall not share in money raised by local municipal assessment for public school purposes.

(2) **Share of legislative grants.**—Every Protestant separate school shall share in the legislative grants in like manner as a public school.

163. (1) **Reports.**—Every Protestant separate school board and principal of a Protestant separate school in a municipality shall transmit reports to the Ministry in such form and at such times as may be required by the Minister.

(2) **Use of assessor's roll by board.**—The clerk or other officer of the municipality in which a Protestant separate school is established who has possession of the assessor's or collector's roll of the municipality shall allow any trustee or the authorized collector of the board to make a copy of the roll.

164. Qualification of a voter.—Every person who is assessed as a Protestant separate school supporter and whose name appears on the list of voters of the municipality in which the land in respect of which he or she is assessed is situate, and the wife or husband of such supporter, if she or he is a Protestant, is entitled to vote at the election of trustees for the Protestant separate school board and on any school question having to do with the Protestant separate school or board.

165. (1) **Qualification of a trustee.**—A Protestant separate school trustee shall have the same qualifications as a public school trustee, except that he or she shall be a supporter of a Protestant separate school.

(2) **Election of trustees.**—A Protestant separate school board shall have the same number of trustees as a Roman Catholic separate school board would have if established in the same municipality, and the trustees may be elected in the same manner as Roman Catholic separate school trustees may be elected, and the provisions of Part IV with respect to the election of trustees of Roman Catholic rural separate schools apply with necessary modifications to the election of trustees of Protestant rural separate school boards.

(3) **Idem.**—Despite subsection (2), Part VIII applies to the election of trustees of a Protestant separate school board that is situated in an urban municipality.

166. Corporate name of board.—The trustees of every Protestant separate school board are a body corporate under the name of "The Protestant Separate School Board of the ...." or "Conseil des écoles séparées protestantes de ...." or both (*inserting the name of the city, town, village or township*).

167. Powers of board.—A Protestant separate school board has the same powers as a district school area board.

168. Discontinuing board.—A Protestant separate school board is discontinued in the same manner as a Roman Catholic separate school board is discontinued and may be re-established in the manner provided in section 158.

169. Application of other sections.—Subsections 89(3) and (4), subsection 90(2), sections 109, 110 and 111 and clause 198(1)(d) apply in respect of Protestant separate schools and Protestant separate school boards.

PART VI

BOARDS

Duties and Powers

170. Duties of boards:—Every board shall,

1. **appoint secretary-treasurer.**—appoint a secretary and a treasurer or a secretary-treasurer who, in the case of a board of not more than five elected members, may be a member of the board;
2. **security of treasurer.**—take proper security from the treasurer or secretary-treasurer;
3. **order payment of bills.**—give the necessary orders on the treasurer for payment of all money expended for school purposes and of such other expenses for promoting

the interests of the schools under the jurisdiction of the board as may be authorized by this Act or the regulations and by the board;

4. **meetings.**—fix the times and places for the meetings of the board and the mode of calling and conducting them, and ensure that a full and correct account of the proceedings thereat is kept;

5. **head office.**—establish and maintain a head office and notify the Ministry of its location and address and notify the Ministry of any change in the location or address of the head office within ten days of such change;

6. **provide instruction and accommodation.**—provide instruction and adequate accommodation during each school year for the pupils who have a right to attend a school under the jurisdiction of the board;

6.1 **kindergarten.**—operate kindergartens;

6.2 **junior kindergarten.**—after the 31st day of August, 1994, operate junior kindergartens;

7. **special education programs and services.**—provide or enter into an agreement with another board to provide in accordance with the regulations special education programs and special education services for its exceptional pupils in the English language or, where the pupil is enrolled in a school or class established under Part XII, the French language, as the case may be;

8. **repair property.**—keep the school buildings and premises in proper repair and in a proper sanitary condition, provide suitable furniture and equipment and keep it in proper repair, and protect the property of the board;

9. **insurance.**—make provision for insuring adequately the buildings and equipment of the board and for insuring the board and its employees and volunteers who are assigned duties by the principal against claims in respect of accidents incurred by pupils while under the jurisdiction or supervision of the board;

10. **conduct schools.**—ensure that every school under its charge is conducted in accordance with this Act and the regulations;

11. **school open.**—keep open its schools during the whole period of the school year determined under the regulations, except where it is otherwise provided under this Act;

12. **appoint principal and teachers.**—appoint for each school that it operates a principal and an adequate number of teachers, all of whom shall be qualified according to this Act and the regulations;

12.1 **notice of offences.**—promptly notify the Minister in writing when the board becomes aware that a teacher who is or has been employed by the board has been convicted of an offence under the *Criminal Code* (Canada) involving sexual conduct and minors, or of any other offence that in the opinion of the board indicates that pupils may be at risk;

13. **provide textbooks.**—subject to paragraph 31.1 of subsection 171(1) provide, without charge, for the use of the pupils attending the school or schools operated by the board, the textbooks that are required by the regulations to be purchased by the board;

14. **vehicle insurance.**—where it furnishes transportation for pupils in a vehicle that is owned by the board, provide and carry with an insurer licensed under the *Insurance*

Act for each such vehicle at least the amount of insurance that is required to be provided in respect of such a vehicle by the licensee of a school vehicle under the *Public Vehicles Act*;

15. **report children not enrolled.**—ascertain and report to the Ministry at least once in each year in the manner required by the Minister the names and ages of all children of compulsory school age within its jurisdiction who are not enrolled in any school or private school and the reasons therefor;
16. **reports.**—transmit to the Minister all reports and returns required by this Act and the regulations;
17. **statement of sick leave credits.**—issue to an employee, upon the termination of his or her employment with the board, a statement of the sick leave credits standing to the employee's credit with the board at the time of such termination;
18. **requirements.**—do anything that a board is required by the Minister to do under subsection 8(1).

(2) **s. 67 school districts.**—Paragraphs 6.1 and 6.2 of subsection (1) do not apply to the board of a secondary school district established under section 67.

(3) **Regulations.**—The Lieutenant Governor in Council may make regulations exempting a board from paragraph 6.2 of subsection (1), subject to conditions established by the regulations, for a period specified in the regulations that ends not later than the 31st day of August, 1997. [To be repealed on September 1, 1997. 1993, c. 11, s. 30(5)].

1993, c. 11, s. 30.

171. (1) **Powers of boards:**—A board may,

1. **committees.**—establish committees composed of members of the board to make recommendations to the board in respect of education, finance, personnel and property;
2. **idem.**—establish committees that may include persons who are not members of the board in respect of matters other than those referred to in paragraph 1;
3. **appoint employees.**—subject to Part XI, appoint and remove such officers and servants and, subject to Part X, appoint and remove such teachers, as it considers expedient, determine the terms on which such officers, servants and teachers are to be employed, prescribe their duties and fix their salaries, except that in the case of a secretary of a board who is a member of the board, the board may pay only such compensation for his or her services as is approved by the electors at a meeting of the electors;
4. **voluntary assistants.**—permit a principal to assign to a person who volunteers to serve without remuneration such duties in respect of the school as are approved by the board and to terminate such assignment;
5. **supervisors.**—appoint supervisors of the teaching staff for positions that are provided for in any Act or regulation administered by the Minister and every appointee shall hold the qualifications and perform the duties required in the Act or regulations;
6. **psychiatrist or psychologist.**—appoint one or more,
    i. psychiatrists who are on the register of specialists in psychiatry of The Royal College of Physicians and Surgeons of Canada or of the College of Physicians and Surgeons of Ontario,

PART VI — BOARDS S. 171

ii. psychologists who are legally qualified medical practitioners or hold a certificate of registration under the *Psychologists Registration Act*;

7. **schools and attendance areas.**—determine the number and kind of schools to be established and maintained and the attendance area for each school, and close schools in accordance with policies established by the board from guidelines issued by the Minister;

8. **courses of study.**—provide instruction in courses of study that are prescribed or approved by the Minister, developed from curriculum guidelines issued by the Minister or approved by the board where the Minister permits the board to approve courses of study;

9. **computer programming.**—in lieu of purchasing a computer or system of computer programming, enter into an agreement for the use thereof by the board;

10. **playgrounds, parks, rinks.**—operate the school ground as a park or playground and rink during the school year or in vacation or both, and provide and maintain such equipment as it considers advisable, and provide such supervision as it considers proper, provided the proper conduct of the school is not interfered with;

11. **gymnasiums.**—organize and carry on gymnasium classes in school buildings for pupils or others during the school year or in vacation or both, and provide supervision and training for such classes, provided the proper conduct of the school is not interfered with;

12. **milk.**—purchase milk to be consumed by the pupils in the schools under the jurisdiction of the board during school days in accordance with the terms and conditions prescribed by the regulations;

13. **provision of supplies, etc.**—provide school supplies, other than the textbooks that it is required to provide under paragraph 13 of section 170, for the use of pupils;

14. **libraries.**—establish and maintain school libraries and resource centres;

15. **junior kindergartens.**—operate junior kindergartens, if the board is not required to do so under section 170 [To be repealed on September 1, 1997. 1993, c. 11, s. 31(2).];

16. **signatures mechanically reproduced.**—provide that the signature of the treasurer and of any other person authorized to sign cheques issued by the treasurer may be written or engraved, lithographed, printed or otherwise mechanically reproduced on cheques;

17. **membership fees and travelling expenses.**—pay the travelling expenses and membership fees of any member of the board, or of any teacher or officer of the board, incurred in attending meetings of an educational association and may make grants and pay membership fees to any such organization;

18. **legal costs.**—pay the costs, or any part thereof, incurred by any member of the board or by any teacher, officer or other employee of the board in successfully defending any legal proceeding brought against him or her,

  i. for libel or slander in respect of any statements relating to the employment, suspension or dismissal of any person by the board published at a meeting of the board or of a committee thereof, or

  ii. for assault in respect of disciplinary action taken in the course of duty;

S. 171　　　　　　　　　　EDUCATION ACT

19. **invest funds.**—invest funds received from an insurance claim, gift, legacy or sale of property in such securities as a trustee may invest in under the *Trustee Act*;
20. **idem.**—invest money other than money held in a reserve fund and that is not required immediately by the board in,
    i. bonds, debentures or other evidences of indebtedness of, or guaranteed by, the Government of Canada or the Province of Ontario, or any other province of Canada,
    ii. debentures, notes or guaranteed investment certificates of or term deposits with any trust corporation or loan corporation that is registered under the *Loan and Trust Corporations Act*,
    iii. term deposits, deposit receipts, deposit notes, certificates of deposit, acceptances and other similar instruments issued, accepted, guaranteed or endorsed by any bank listed in Schedule I or II to the *Bank Act* (Canada),
    iv. promissory notes of a municipality as defined in the *Municipal Affairs Act*, and promissory notes of a metropolitan municipality, a regional municipality, the District Municipality of Muskoka and the County of Oxford, and
    v. term deposits accepted by a credit union as defined in the *Credit Unions and Caisses Populaires Act*,

    provided that the investments become due and payable by the day on which the money is required by the board, and all interest thereon shall be credited to the fund from which the money is invested;
21. **idem.**—invest money held in a reserve fund in,
    i. guaranteed contracts issued by an insurer licensed under the *Insurance Act*, and
    ii. such securities as a trustee may invest in under the *Trustee Act* provided that all interest and gain thereon is credited to the fund from which the money is invested;
22. **borrowing from funds.**—despite any other Act, borrow, for any purpose for which the board has authority to spend money, any money in any fund established by the board that is not immediately required by the board for the purposes of such fund, but such borrowing shall not extend beyond the term of office of the members of the board and, where secondary school money is borrowed for public school purposes or public school money is borrowed for secondary school purposes, the board shall pay interest to the fund from which such money is borrowed at a rate not less than that being earned by the fund at the date of borrowing;
23. **student fees.**—subject to the provisions of this Act and the regulations, fix the fees to be paid by or on behalf of pupils, and the times of payment thereof, and when necessary enforce payment thereof by action in the Small Claims Court, and exclude any pupil by or on behalf of whom fees that are legally required to be paid are not paid after reasonable notice;
24. **permit use of school and school buses.**—permit the school buildings and premises and school buses owned by the board to be used for any educational or other lawful purpose;
25. **surgical treatment.**—provide for surgical treatment of children attending the school

PART VI — BOARDS   S. 171

who suffer from minor physical defects, where in the opinion of the teacher and, where a school nurse and medical officer are employed, of the nurse and medical officer, the defect interferes with the proper education of the child, and include in the estimates for the current year the funds necessary for cases where the parents are not able to pay, provided that no such treatment shall be undertaken without the consent of the parents or guardian of the child; [To be repealed on proclamation. 1992, c. 32, s. 9.];

25. **surgical treatment.**—provide for surgical treatment of children attending the school who suffer from minor physical defects, where in the opinion of the teacher, and where a school nurse and medical officer are employed, of the nurse and medical officer, the defect interferes with the proper education of the child, and includes in the estimates for the current year the funds necessary for cases where the parents are not able to pay, provided that not such treatment shall be undertaken without consent that complies with the *Consent to Treatment Act, 1992*; 1992, c. 32, s. 9 [*Not yet proclaimed.*];

26. **cadet corps.**—establish and maintain cadet corps;
27. **athletics.**—provide for the promotion and encouragement of athletics and for the holding of school games;
28. **activities.**—provide, during the school year or at other times, activities and programs on or off school premises, including field trips, and exercise jurisdiction over those persons participating therein;
29. **guidance.**—appoint one or more teachers qualified in guidance according to the regulations to collect and distribute information regarding available occupations and employments, and to offer such counsel to the pupils as will enable them to plan intelligently for their educational and vocational advancement;
30. **public lectures.**—conduct free lectures open to the public and include in the estimates for the current year the expenses thereof;
31. **continuing education.**—establish continuing education courses and classes.
31.1 **deposit for continuing education textbooks.**—require a pupil enrolled in a continuing education course or class that is eligible for credit towards a secondary school diploma to pay a nominal deposit for a textbook provided by the board that will be forfeited to the board in whole or in part if the textbook is not returned or is returned in a damaged condition; 1993, c. 11, s. 31(3).
32. **courses for teachers.**—establish and conduct during the school year courses for teachers;
33. **evening classes.**—establish evening classes;
34. **erect fences.**—erect and maintain any wall or fence considered necessary by the board for enclosure of the school premises;
35. **school fairs.**—contribute toward the support of school fairs;
36. **student activities.**—authorize such school activities as pertain to the welfare of the pupils and exercise jurisdiction in respect thereof;
37. **cafeteria.**—operate a cafeteria for the use of the staff and pupils;

S. 171 EDUCATION ACT

38. **records management.**—institute a program of records management that will, subject to the regulations in respect of pupil records,
    i. provide for the archival retention by the board or the Archivist of Ontario of school registers, minute books of the board and its predecessors, documents pertaining to boundaries of school sections, separate school zones and secondary school districts, original assessment and taxation records in the possession of the board and other records considered by the board to have enduring value or to be of historical interest, and
    ii. establish, with the written approval of the auditor of the board, schedules for the retention, disposition and eventual destruction of records of the board and of the schools under its jurisdiction other than records retained for archival use;
39. **education of children in charitable organizations.**—employ and pay teachers, when so requested in writing by a charitable organization having the charge of children of school age, for the education of such children, whether such children are being educated in premises within or beyond the limits of the jurisdiction of the board, and pay for and furnish school supplies for their use;
40. **programs in detention homes.**—with the approval of the Minister, conduct an education program in a centre, facility, home, hospital or institution that is approved, designated, established, licensed or registered under any Act and in which the Ministry does not conduct an education program, or in a demonstration school for exceptional pupils;
41. **maternity leave.**—provide for maternity leave for a teacher, not exceeding two years for each pregnancy;
42. **assumption of treatment centres, etc.**—when requested by the board of a cerebral palsy treatment centre school, a crippled children's treatment centre school, a hospital school or a sanatorium school, and with the approval of the Minister, by agreement, assume the assets and liabilities of such board and continue to operate such a school, and, upon the effective date of the agreement between the two boards, the board making the request is dissolved;
43. **recreation committees.**—where a recreation committee or a joint recreation committee has been appointed for territory without municipal organization within the jurisdiction of the board, exercise the powers and duties of a municipal council with respect to preparing estimates of the sums required during the year for the purposes of the committee or joint committee, and levying rates and collecting taxes for such purposes on the rateable property supporting the board in such territory, and where such a joint recreation committee has been appointed, apportion the costs of such committee by agreement with the other board concerned;
44. **agreement for provision and use of recreational facilities.**—with the approval of the Minister, enter into an agreement with a university, college of a university, or the board of governors of a polytechnical institute or of a college of applied arts and technology, in respect of the provision, maintenance and use of educational or recreational facilities on the property of either of the parties to the agreement;
45. **election recounts.**—pass a resolution referred to in subsection 88(2) of the *Municipal Elections Act*;

PART VI — BOARDS S. 173

46. **insurance.**—provide for insurance against risks that may involve pecuniary loss or liability on the part of the board, and for paying premiums therefor;
47. **designation of expenditures.**—designate portions of current expenditure of the board as ordinary expenditures for the purposes of legislative grants provided for by a regulation made under subsection 11(3).
48. **Child care facilities.**—construct and renovate child care facilities in any school. 1991, Vol. 2, c. 10, s. 5(1).
49. **day nurseries.**—establish, operate and maintain day nurseries within the meaning of the *Day Nurseries Act*, subject to that Act. 1993, c. 11, s. 31(3).
50. subject to paragraphs 19, 20 and 21, enter into agreements with any other board, or with a municipality, hospital, university or college, or their agents, for the joint investment of money. 1993, c. 26, s. 44(1).

(2) **Collection of rates in territory without municipal organization by action.**—In addition to any other remedy possessed by a board in territory without municipal organization for the recovery of rates imposed under the authority of this Act, the board, with the approval of the Minister, may bring an action in a court of competent jurisdiction for the recovery of any rates in arrear against the person assessed therefor.

(3) **Child care facilities.**—For the purpose of subsection 236(1), the construction or renovation of child care facilities under paragraph 48 of subsection (1),

(a) in a public school is deemed to be a public school purpose; and
(b) in a secondary school is deemed to be a secondary school purpose. 1991, Vol. 2, c. 10, s. 5(2).

(4) **Definitions.**—For the purpose of paragraph 50 of subsection (1),

"college" means a board of governors of a college of applied arts and technology established in accordance with section 5 of the *Ministry of Colleges and Universities Act*; ("collège")

"hospital" has the same meaning as "board" in section 1 of the *Public Hospitals Act*; ("hôpital")

"municipality" includes a county and a metropolitan, regional and district municipality and the County of Oxford; ("municipalité")

"university" means a degree granting institution as authorized under section 3 of the *Degree Granting Act*. ("université")

(5) **Regulations re: paragraph 49.**—The Minister of Municipal Affairs may prescribe additional persons, or classes of them, with which a board may enter into agreements authorized by paragraph 50 of subsection (1). 1993, c. 26, s. 44(2).

171.1 Effect of joint investment agreements.—No agreement entered into under paragraph 50 of subsection 171(1) may affect an education development charges account, as defined in subsection 29(1) of the *Development Charges Act*. 1993, c. 26, s. 45.

172. Board name.—If another Act gives a board a name in English only, the board may also be known by such French name as it chooses by resolution and the Minister approves.

173. (1) **Establishment of scholarships, etc.**—Any person may, with the approval of the board concerned, establish scholarships, bursaries or prizes.

(2) **Idem.**—A board may award bursaries or prizes to its pupils under such terms and conditions as the board may prescribe.

S. 174 EDUCATION ACT

Vocational Courses

174. (1) **Vocational courses.**—A secondary school board may provide vocational courses of study in one or more of its schools.

(2) **Courses of study.**—Vocational courses of study may comprise,

(a) full-time day courses of study;
(b) part-time day courses of study; and
(c) evening courses of study.

(3) **Admission procedures.**—A secondary school board may provide for the admission of a pupil to a vocational course and may determine the procedures for admission to such course.

(4) **Admission of adult.**—Where a principal of a school is satisfied that an adult is competent to receive instruction in a vocational course, the adult may, without regard to his or her school standing, be admitted to,

(a) a special full-time day course of study;
(b) a part-time day course of study; or
(c) an evening course of study,

in the school.

175. (1) **Advisory committee.**—A secondary school board that provides or plans to provide a vocational course may, by resolution, appoint an advisory committee to be known as the advisory committee for .... (*inserting the name of the vocational course*) and composed of such persons, all or any of whom may be members of the board, appointed for such term, not extending beyond the term of office of the members of the board, as the board considers necessary to advise the board on matters relating to the vocational course.

(2) **Allowance.**—A secondary school board may pay to each person appointed under subsection (1) who is not a member of the board such allowance as the board may determine for each month for which the person is appointed.

Benefits

176. Powers of board.—A board may,

1. **accident, etc., insurance.**—provide, by contract with an insurer licensed under the *Insurance Act*,

    i. group accident insurance to indemnify a member of a board or of an advisory committee appointed by a board or his or her estate against loss in case he or she is accidentally injured or killed, and

    ii. group public liability and property damage insurance to indemnify a member of a board or of an advisory committee appointed by a board or his or her estate in respect of loss or damage for which he or she has become liable by reason of injury to persons or property or in respect of loss or damage suffered by him or her by reason of injury to his or her own property,

    while travelling on the business of the board or in the performance of duties as a

member of the board or of an advisory committee either within or outside the area over which the board has jurisdiction;
2. **benefits.**—provide for any or all of the members of the board any benefit that may be provided for the employees of the board under section 177 and any other benefits of a like nature that the board considers appropriate;
3. **accident and public liability insurance re work-experience programs.**—where, in co-operation with business, industry or other enterprise, it provides for pupils training programs designed to supplement the courses given in its schools, provide, by contract with an insurer under the *Insurance Act*, accident insurance to indemnify such pupils against loss in case they are accidentally injured while participating in such a program and public liability insurance to insure such pupils and the board against loss or damage to the person or property of others while the pupils are participating in such a program;
4. **insurance for pupils.**—provide, by contract with an insurer under the *Insurance Act*, accident and life insurance for pupils, the cost of which is to be paid on a voluntary basis by the parents or guardians.

177. (1) **Insurance, hospital and health services.**—Subject to the *Health Insurance Act*, a board by resolution may provide,

(a) by contract either with an insurer licensed under the *Insurance Act* or with an association registered under the *Prepaid Hospital and Medical Services Act*,

   (i) group life insurance for its employees or any class thereof and their spouses and children,

   (ii) group accident insurance or group sickness insurance for its employees or any class thereof and their spouses and children, and

   (iii) hospital, medical, surgical, nursing or dental services, or payment therefor, for employees or any class thereof and their spouses and children; and

(b) for payment by the board of the whole or part of the cost of any insurance or services provided under this subsection.

(2) **Contributions re insured services.**—A board may by resolution provide for paying the whole or part of the cost to employees of insured services under the *Health Insurance Act*.

(3) **Participation of retired person in contract.**—A board may retain a person who retires from employment with the board before he or she attains the age of sixty-five years in a group established for the purposes of a contract referred to in clause (1)(a) until the person attains such age if the person pays the full premium required to be paid to retain his or her participation in the contract.

178. (1) **Pensions.**—A board, by resolution, may provide pensions for employees or any class thereof under the *Ontario Municipal Employees Retirement System Act*.

(2) **Idem.**—Despite subsection (1), a board that makes contributions to an approved pension plan, as defined in subsection 117(1) of the *Municipal Act*, may continue to provide pensions under such plan, and the said section 117 applies with necessary modifications.

(3) **Definition.**—In this section, ''employee' does not include a teacher or supervisory officer or an administrative officer who holds a certificate of qualification as a teacher and who

is eligible to contribute to the pension fund maintained to provide benefits in respect of The Ontario Teachers' Pension Plan.

(4) **Employees of newly organized board.**—An employee of a divisional board who was a contributor or who was entitled to be a contributor under the *Ontario Municipal Employees Retirement System Act*, by reason of his employment with a former board on the 31st day of December, 1968, shall continue to be a contributor or to be entitled to be a contributor, as the case may be, and the divisional board shall assume in respect of such employee all the rights and obligations of the former board, but in respect of other employees, the divisional board, before such employees may participate under such Act, shall pass a resolution electing to become a participant under such Act, as required by the regulations made thereunder, and stating the effective date.

(5) **Assumption of board of rights and obligations of former board.**—A divisional board that is required to make the contribution of a former board to an approved pension plan, as defined in section 117 of the *Municipal Act*, in respect of an employee who was a contributor to such approved pension plan on the 31st day of December, 1968, shall assume all the rights and obligations of such former board under the approved pension plan in respect of such employee.

179. (1) **Retirement allowances.**—A board may grant an annual retirement allowance, payable weekly, monthly or otherwise for such period as the board may determine, to any employee of the board who has been in the service of the board for at least twenty years and who,

(a) is retired because of age; or
(b) while in the service has become incapable through illness or otherwise of efficiently discharging his or her duties,

provided that no retirement allowance shall be granted under this section which, together with the amount of any pension payments payable to the employee in any year under a pension plan of the board or any municipality or under the *Teachers' Pension Act*, will exceed three-fifths of the employee's average annual salary for the preceding three years of his or her service.

(2) **Widow or widower.**—Where an employee,

(a) has been granted an annual retirement allowance under subsection (1) and subsequently dies; or
(b) would have been eligible, except for his or her death, for such an allowance,

the board may grant to the widow or widower of such employee for such period as the board may determine an annual allowance, not exceeding one-half of the maximum allowance that may be granted under subsection (1).

(3) **Definition.**—In subsection (1), "pension payments" means, in the case of pension payments under a board or municipal plan, only such payments that result from joint contributions of the employer and employee and does not include any such payments that result solely from contributions of the employee.

(4) **Limitation on application of section.**—Where the board has a pension plan in operation, or where a municipality has a pension plan in operation in which the employees of the board are included, this section applies only to employees who were in the employ of the

board on or before the 1st day of July, 1954, and in any event does not apply to any employee who enters the service of the board after the 1st day of July, 1956.

180. (1) **Sick leave credits.**—A board, by resolution, may establish a system of sick leave credit gratuities for employees or any class thereof provided that on the termination of his or her employment no employee is entitled to more than an amount equal to the employee's salary, wages or other remuneration for one-half the number of days standing to the employee's credit and, subject to subsection (3), in any event not in excess of the amount of one-half year's earnings at the rate received by the employee immediately prior to termination of employment.

(2) **Idem.**—Where a sick leave gratuity is paid upon termination of employment, the number of days used to calculate the amount of the gratuity ceases to stand to the credit of the employee and is not available for transfer or reinstatement of credits under subsection (4).

(3) **Idem.**—Where, pursuant to a collective agreement, or a policy of the board, an employee to whom subsection (1) applies has elected to accept a reduction in employment from full-time to part-time employment in respect of one or more years or school years, as the case may be, including the year or school year immediately preceding the employee's termination of employment by reason of retirement, the limitation upon the amount of the gratuity payable under subsection (1) does not apply to the employee and, in lieu thereof, the maximum amount receivable by the employee shall not be in excess of an amount equal to one-half of the full-time annual rate of the earnings received by the employee for the last complete year or school year, as the case may be, in which the employee was employed by the board.

(4) **Allowing of credits on transfer of employment.**—Where an employee of a board that has established a sick leave credit plan under this or any other general or special Act becomes an employee of another board that has also established a sick leave credit plan under this or any other general or special Act, the latter board shall, subject to the limitation in subsection (7), place to the credit of the employee the sick leave credits standing to the credit of the employee in the plan of the first-mentioned board.

(5) **Where transferred because of change in jurisdiction of board.**—Despite subsection (4), where the contract of employment of an employee of a board has become an obligation of another board by or under any Act, the latter board shall place to the credit of the employee the sick leave credits and the termination of employment benefits standing to the employee's credit in the system of sick leave credit gratuities of the first-mentioned board.

(6) **Idem.**—Where an employee of a municipality or a local board, as defined in the *Municipal Affairs Act*, except a school board, that has established a sick leave credit plan under any general or special Act, becomes an employee of a board that has established a sick leave credit plan under this or any other general or special Act, the board shall, subject to the limitation in subsection (7), place to the credit of the employee the sick leave credits standing to the credit of the employee in the plan of such municipality or local board.

(7) **Limitation.**—The amount of sick leave credits placed to the credit of an employee under subsection (4) or (6) shall not exceed the amount of cumulative sick leave credits permitted under the plan to which the credits are placed.

(8) [Repealed 1993, c. 11, s. 32.]

(9) [Repealed 1993, c. 11, s. 32.]

(10) **Applicability of sick leave credits.**—Where an employee of a board that, before the 1st day of June, 1968, had established a sick leave credit plan became, on the 1st day of January, 1969, an employee of a divisional board or of a county or district combined separate school board, such board shall place to the credit of the employee the sick leave credits and the termination of employment benefits standing to the employee's credit in the plan of the first-mentioned board. 1993, c. 11, s. 32.

Agreements

181. (1) **Agreements to provide accommodation or services for another board.**—A board may, subject to subsection (2), enter into an agreement with another board to provide, for the other board for such periods and under such conditions as are specified in the agreement,

    (a) accommodation and equipment for administrative purposes;
    (b) accommodation and equipment for instructional purposes;
    (c) the services of teachers and other personnel; or
    (d) the transportation of pupils,

that the board by this Act is authorized or required to provide for its own pupils.

(2) **Where building, additions, etc., required.**—Where the construction of a school building or an addition, alteration or improvement to a school building is required under an agreement made under subsection (1), the agreement shall make provision for the payment of the cost of such building, addition, alteration or improvement and is not effective until approved by the Minister.

(3) **Where cost borne by board not providing accommodation.**—Where, under an agreement, the board that does not provide the additional accommodation is required to bear and pay the cost thereof, the additional accommodation shall, for the purposes of issuing debentures, be deemed to be a permanent improvement of such board.

(4) **Fees, exception.**—An agreement under this section may, despite the regulations, provide for the calculation and payment of fees in respect of pupils covered by the agreement.

182. (1) **Transfer of French-language instructional unit.**—A public board that has jurisdiction in an area that is also the area or part of the area of jurisdiction of a Roman Catholic school board may, with the approval of the Minister, enter into an agreement with the Roman Catholic school board to transfer a secondary school established and operated under Part XII or a French-language instructional unit as defined in section 309 to the Roman Catholic school board.

(2) **Transfer not a closing.**—A transfer of a secondary school referred to in subsection (1) is not a closing of the secondary school.

183. (1) **Definitions.**—In this section,

"**board**".—"board" includes The Metropolitan Toronto School Board; ("conseil")

"**municipality**".—"municipality" includes a county and a district, metropolitan or regional municipality and a local board of a municipality or county or of a district, metropolitan or regional municipality, except a school board. ("municipalité")

(2) **Agreements for joint use of facilities, etc.**—One or more boards and the council of a municipality or the councils of two or more municipalities may enter into an agreement,

PART VI — BOARDS S. 184

    (a) in respect of the use of existing facilities owned by one of such parties; or

    (b) for the purpose of establishing and providing for the maintenance and operation of facilities on the property of any of the parties to such agreement,

for such cultural, recreational, athletic, educational, administrative or other community purposes as are set out in the agreement, and such agreement shall include provision for,

    (c) the acquisition of any land that may be required for the purposes of the agreement, and the manner of approving and the method of apportioning the cost thereof;

    (d) the manner of approving and the method of apportioning the cost of the construction, maintenance and operation of the facilities;

    (e) the manner in which each party to the agreement shall pay its portion of the costs referred to in clauses (c) and (d) and the times when such costs shall be paid;

    (f) the regulation, control and use of the facilities including the charging of fees for admission thereto; and

    (g) the duration of the agreement and the manner in which and the terms upon which it may be terminated.

(3) **Approval of Minister.**—Where, pursuant to an agreement made under this section, a permanent improvement is required, it shall not be proceeded with until such plans and specifications therefor as are required by the Minister have been approved by the Minister.

(4) **Previous agreement.**—This section does not affect an agreement entered into before the 23rd day of June, 1972,

    (a) under subsection 168(2) of the *Municipality of Metropolitan Toronto Act*; or

    (b) between a board and the council of a municipality, including a regional municipality or a county, or a local board thereof, for fulfilling, executing or completing, at their joint expense or at the expense of either of the parties to the agreement, any undertaking for the joint benefit of the parties to the agreement, including the joint use of educational and municipal facilities,

but an amendment to an agreement referred to in clause (a) or (b) or an agreement to which the said subsection 145(2) applies may be made only in accordance with this section.

(5) **Facilities deemed community recreation centre.**—Where an agreement under this section or an agreement referred to in subsection (4) between one or more boards and one or more municipalities provides for the use of existing facilities or for the establishment of facilities, such facilities or any of them that come within the definition of community recreation centre under the *Community Recreation Centres Act* may be considered by the Minister of Community and Social Services as a community recreation centre for the purposes of making grants under section 6 of that Act.

184. (1) **Agreement between public school boards.**—A public school board may enter into an agreement with another public school board under which one public school board shall furnish education for pupils of the other upon payment by such other public school board on behalf of such pupils of fees calculated in accordance with the regulations.

(2) **Agreement between separate school boards.**—A separate school board may enter into an agreement with another separate school board under which one separate school board shall furnish education for pupils of the other upon payment by such other separate school board on behalf of such pupils of fees calculated in accordance with the regulations.

(3) **Admission of pupils to Indian schools.**—The board of an elementary school may provide for the admission of one or more of its pupils to a school for Indian children established, operated and maintained under the *Indian Act* (Canada), subject to the approval of the authority having control of such school, and the accommodation provided under such arrangement shall be in lieu of the accommodation that the board is required by this Act to provide for such pupils.

(4) **Levy for fees, transportation, etc.**—The board of an elementary school may levy and collect upon the property rateable for the purposes of the board such sum as may be necessary to pay the fees of its pupils who attend schools for Indian children pursuant to subsection (3) and to pay for the transportation of such pupils to and from such schools as well as such other sums as the board considers expedient or as may be required by this Act.

(5) **Closing of school by board.**—Where a board has arranged under this section for the admission of all its pupils to a school or schools that the board does not operate, the board may close its schools for the period during which such arrangement or arrangements are in effect.

185. Agreements for education of public and separate school pupils.—A public school board and a separate school board may enter into an agreement in respect of the provision of education in a public or separate school under the jurisdiction of either board for pupils of the other board in a course or courses that are not available in a school under the jurisdiction of the board requiring the provision of education or that are considered by such board to be not readily accessible to the pupils in respect of whom the agreement is made where,

(a) the appropriate supervisory officer of the board providing education certifies that accommodation is available in such school for such pupils; and
(b) the board requiring the provision of education pays for each such pupil a fee calculated in accordance with the regulations.

186. (1) **Secondary school agreements.**—The board of a secondary school district that is not a school division may, in lieu of establishing and maintaining a school, enter into an agreement with another secondary school board to provide for the instruction of its pupils in the schools under the jurisdiction of that board and for the payment in respect of such pupils of fees calculated in accordance with the regulations.

(2) **Agreements for education at outside schools.**—A secondary school board that has established one or more secondary schools may enter into an agreement with another secondary school board to provide for the instruction, in the school or schools maintained by the latter board, of resident pupils of the first-mentioned board and for the payment in respect of such pupils of fees calculated in accordance with the regulations.

187. Agreements re pupils in federal establishments.—A board may enter into an agreement with the Crown in right of Canada for such periods and under such conditions as are specified in the agreement whereby the board may provide for the education of pupils who reside on land held by the Crown in right of Canada in a school or schools operated by the board on land owned by the board or held by the Crown in right of Canada.

188. (1) **Agreements re education of Indian pupils.**—A board may enter into an agreement with,

(a) the Crown in right of Canada; or
(b) a band or the council of the band or an education authority where such band, the

PART VI — BOARDS **S. 188**

council of the band or education authority is authorized by the Crown in right of Canada to provide education for Indians,

to provide for Indian pupils, for the period specified in the agreement, accommodation, instruction and special services in the schools of the board, and such agreement shall provide for the payment by the Crown in right of Canada, the band, the council of the band or the education authority, as the case may be, of fees calculated in accordance with the regulation governing the fees payable by Canada.

(2) **Agreements re instruction in Indian schools.**—A board may enter into an agreement with,

(a) the Crown in right of Canada; or

(b) a band, the council of the band or an education authority referred to in clause (1)(b),

to provide for Indian pupils, for the period specified in the agreement, instruction and special services in schools provided by the Crown in right of Canada, the band, the council of the band or the education authority, as the case may be, and such agreement shall provide for the payment by the Crown in right of Canada, the band, the council of the band or the education authority, as the case may be, of the full cost of the provision of the instruction and special services.

(3) **Agreements re accommodation for Indian pupils.**—A board may enter into an agreement with the Crown in right of Canada for a period specified in the agreement to provide for a payment from the Crown in right of Canada to provide additional classroom accommodation and to provide tuition for a maximum of thirty-five Indian pupils for each additional classroom so provided, and the fees therefor shall be calculated in accordance with the regulations, but exclusive of expenditures for the erection of school buildings for instructional purposes and additions thereto.

(4) **Cost of special services.**—A board shall not enter into an agreement under subsection (1), (2) or (3) that requires the board to provide special services for Indian pupils that it does not provide for its resident pupils unless, in addition to the fees referred to in subsection (1) or (3), the cost of such services is payable by the Crown in right of Canada.

(5) **Appointment of representative of Indian pupils.**—Where a board has entered into one or more agreements under this section, the council of the band, or the councils of the bands, to which the Indian pupils, or a majority of the Indian pupils, who are, pursuant to the agreement or agreements, enrolled in the schools operated by the board or in the schools in which the board provides all the instruction, belong, may, subject to subsection (6), name one person to represent on the board the interests of the Indian pupils and, where a person is so named, the board shall, subject to subsection (7), appoint the person a member of the board, and the member so appointed shall be deemed to be an elected member of the board, except that,

(a) where the agreement or agreements under this section are in respect of secondary school pupils only, the member so appointed is a trustee for secondary school purposes only and shall not vote on a motion or otherwise take part in any proceedings that affect public schools exclusively; and

(b) where the agreement or agreements under this section are in respect of elementary school pupils only, the member so appointed is a trustee for elementary school purposes only and shall not vote on a motion or otherwise take part in any proceedings that affect secondary schools exclusively.

(6) **Additional representative.**—Where the number of Indian pupils enrolled in the schools under the jurisdiction of a board pursuant to one or more agreements made under this section exceeds 25 per cent of the average daily enrolment in the schools of the board, two persons may be named under subsection (5), and subsection (5) applies with necessary modifications in respect of such persons.

(7) **Where appointment in discretion of board.**—Where the number of Indian pupils enrolled in the schools under the jurisdiction of the board pursuant to one or more such agreements is fewer than the lesser of 10 per cent of the average daily enrolment in the schools of the board and 100, the appointment under subsection (5) may be made at the discretion of the board.

(8) **When Indian school enrolment included.**—For the purpose of determining the number of Indian pupils enrolled in the schools under the jurisdiction of a board referred to in subsection (6) or (7), the number of Indian pupils in Indian schools in which the board provides all the instruction shall be included.

(9) **Enrolment.**—Where the agreement is, or the agreements are, in respect of elementary school pupils only or secondary school pupils only, the enrolment referred to in subsections (6) and (7) shall be that of elementary school pupils only or secondary school pupils only, as the case may be.

(10) **Appointed members in addition to elected members.**—A member of the board appointed under subsection (5), (6) or (7) is in addition to the number of members of the board otherwise provided for in this Act and the term of office of such member terminates on the same date as the term of office of the elected members.

(11) **Exception re subss. (5-10).**—Where a regulation made under clause 67(2)(a) provides for the appointment of one or more members to represent on the board the interests of Indian pupils, subsections (5) to (10) do not apply.

(12) **Vacancy in office.**—Where the office of a member of a board appointed under this section becomes vacant for any reason, it shall be filed in accordance with subsection (5), and the person so appointed shall hold office for the remainder of the term of his predecessor.

(13) **Representative of Indian pupils on Roman Catholic separate school board to be Roman Catholic.**—Where a person is chosen by a band to represent the interests of Indian pupils on a Roman Catholic separate school board, such person shall be a Roman Catholic and of the full age of eighteen years.

189. (1) **Definition.**—In this section, "adult basic education" means programs and courses that are designed to develop and improve the basic literacy and numeracy skills of adults.

(2) **Agreements for adult basic education.**—Subject to the approval of the Minister, a board may, in respect of persons who reside in the area of jurisdiction of the board, enter into an agreement in writing with a college of applied arts and technology for the area in which the board has jurisdiction under which the college of applied arts and technology provides for the board such adult basic education as is specified in the agreement.

(3) **Idem.**—A board may, in respect of persons who reside in the area of jurisdiction of the board, enter into an agreement in writing with a community group for the provision by the group of adult basic education that is approved by the Minister.

PART VI — BOARDS S. 190

Transportation

190. (1) **Transportation of pupils.**—A board may provide for,

(a) a resident pupil of the board who is enrolled in a school that the board operates or in a school operated by another board to which the board pays fees in respect of such pupil;

(b) a pupil in respect of whom the Minister pays the cost of education under the regulations; and

(c) a child over two years of age who may, under the regulations, be admitted to a program for hearing-handicapped children,

transportation to and from the school that the pupil attends.

(2) **Idem.**—A board may provide for a pupil who is enrolled in a school that the board operates transportation to and from an activity that is part of the program of such school.

(3) **Idem.**—A board may provide for a person who is qualified to be a resident pupil of the board transportation to and from the Ontario School for the Blind, an Ontario School for the Deaf, a demonstration school established by or operated under an agreement with the Minister for pupils with severe communicational exceptionalities, a centre classified as a Group K hospital under the *Public Hospitals Act*, a facility designated under the *Developmental Services Act*, a psychiatric facility designated as such under the *Mental Health Act* and a place where an agency approved under subsection 8(1) of Part I (Flexible Services) of the *Child and Family Services Act* provides a child development service, a child treatment service or a child and family intervention service.

(4) **Idem.**—A secondary school board may assist in the provision of transportation for children who are qualified to be resident pupils of the board to and from a centre operated by a local association that is affiliated with the Ontario Association for Community Living.

(5) **Purchase of bus.**—For the purposes of this section, a board may purchase a vehicle either from current revenue or from a debenture issued for that purpose.

(6) **Agreements.**—Subject to subsection (7), for the purposes of this section, a board may make an agreement or agreements for one school year or less with a corporation, commission or person for the transportation of such pupils.

(7) **Agreements not exceeding five years.**—Where a board provides transportation for more than thirty pupils, the board may, with the approval of the Ontario Municipal Board, make an agreement for a term not exceeding five years for the transportation of such pupils.

(8) **Boarding of secondary school pupils residing in territorial district.**—Where a pupil resides in a school section or separate school zone in a territorial district but not in a school division with his or her parent or guardian in a residence that is twenty-four kilometres or more by road or rail from a secondary school that the pupil is eligible to attend, an elementary school board may reimburse the parent or guardian at the end of each month for the cost of providing for such pupil, board, lodging, and transportation once a week from his or her residence to school and return, in an amount set by the board for each day of attendance as certified by the principal of the secondary school that the pupil attends.

(9) **Idem.**—Where a pupil resides in a territorial district but not in a school section, a separate school zone or a school division, with his or her parent or guardian in a residence that

is twenty-four kilometres or more by road or rail from a secondary school that the pupil is eligible to attend, the board of the secondary school that the pupil attends may reimburse the parent or guardian at the end of each month for the cost of providing for such pupil, board, lodging, and transportation once a week from his or her residence to school and return, in an amount set by the board for each day of attendance as certified by the principal of the secondary school that the pupil attends.

(10) **Idem.**—Where a pupil resides with his or her parent or guardian in a school division or a secondary school district in a residence that,

(a) in a territorial district is twenty-four kilometres or more; or
(b) in a county or regional municipality that is not in a territorial district is forty-eight kilometres or more,

by road or rail from a secondary school that the pupil attends, or where a pupil resides with his or her parent or guardian on an island in a school division or a secondary school district the board of the school division or secondary school district of which the pupil is a resident pupil may reimburse the parent or guardian at the end of each month for the cost of providing for such pupil, board, lodging, and transportation once a week from his or her residence to school and return, in an amount set by the board for each day of attendance as certified by the principal of the secondary school that the pupil attends.

(11) **Boarding and transportation of secondary school pupils in a territorial district taking "francais" subject.**—Where a secondary school pupil resides in a territorial district in a school division with his or her parent or guardian in a residence that is twenty-four kilometres or more by road or rail from a secondary school in which the subject of French, taught as a subject for students who normally speak the French language, is offered as one of the subjects of the courses of study, an elementary school board may reimburse the parent or guardian at the end of each month for the cost of providing for such pupil, when not so provided by the secondary school board, board, lodging, and transportation once a week from his or her residence to school and return, in an amount set by the board for each day of attendance as certified by the principal of the secondary school that the pupil attends, or may furnish transportation for such pupil in lieu thereof.

(12) **Boarding of elementary school pupils residing in territorial districts.**—Where a pupil resides in a territorial district but not in a school section or a separate school zone, with his or her parent or guardian in a residence from which daily transportation to and from an elementary school that the pupil may attend is impracticable due to distance or terrain, as certified by the appropriate supervisory officer of the elementary school nearest such residence, the board of the elementary school that the pupil attends may reimburse the parent or guardian at the end of each month for the cost of providing for such pupil, board, lodging, and transportation once a week from his or her residence to school and return, in an amount set by the board for each day of attendance as certified by the principal of the elementary school that the pupil attends.

(13) **Boarding of elementary school pupils where transportation impracticable.**—Where a pupil resides in a school section or a separate school zone with his or her parent or guardian in a residence from which daily transportation to and from an elementary school that the pupil may attend is impracticable due to distance or terrain, as certified by the supervisory officer who has jurisdiction in the school section or the separate school zone, the

board of the elementary school of which the pupil is a resident pupil may reimburse the parent or guardian at the end of each month for the cost of providing for such pupil, board, lodging, and transportation once a week from his or her residence to school and return, in an amount set by the board for each day of attendance as certified by the principal of the elementary school that the pupil attends.

(14) **Certification of attendance.**—For the purpose of certifying attendance under subsections (8) to (13), the principal may add to the number of days of attendance of a pupil the number of days the pupil is excused from attendance under the regulations or is absent by reason of being ill or is absent for any other cause if the principal is of the opinion that the absence was unavoidable.

Allowances

191. (1) **Allowance for members.**—A board may pay to each member of the board an allowance in such amount that is determined by the board to be payable to the members thereof.

(2) **Chair and vice-chair.**—A board may pay an allowance in such amount as is determined by the board in addition to the allowance payable under subsection (1) to the chair and vice-chair of the board and to the chairs of committees of the board.

(3) **Different allowances.**—The additional allowance payable to the chair may differ from the additional allowance payable to the vice-chair.

(4) **Basis of allowance.**—A member of a board of education elected by separate school electors, a member of the board elected for the purposes of Part XIII and a member appointed to the board are entitled to an allowance on the same basis as a member of the board elected by public school electors.

(5) **Idem.**—A trustee of a separate school board elected for the purposes of Part XIII or appointed to the board is entitled to an allowance on the same basis as a trustee who is elected, other than for the purposes of Part XIII, by separate school electors.

(6) **Decrease in allowance.**—A board may at any time decrease any allowance payable to members, the chair or the vice-chair of the board.

(7) **Chair and vice-chair of council or section.**—Where the French-language education council, English-language education council, French-language section or English-language section of a board has a chair or a vice-chair of the council or section, as the case may be, the council or section may authorize an additional allowance, not to exceed that paid to the chair or vice-chair of the board under subsection (2), to be paid to the chair or vice-chair of the council or section.

(8) **Idem.**—A chair or vice-chair of a council or section may only be paid one additional allowance.

(9) **Allocation of cost.**—An allowance payable under subsection (1), (2) or (7) with respect to a French-language education council or French-language section shall be included as part of centralized services for the purposes of allocating amounts under section 319.

(10) **Travel expenses to attend board meetings.**—In respect of travel of a member of the board to and from his or her residence to attend a meeting of the board, or a committee thereof, that is held within the area of jurisdiction of the board, the board may,

(a) reimburse the member for his or her expenses necessarily incurred therefor or such lesser amount as may be determined by the board; or

(b) pay the member an allowance at a rate per kilometre determined by the board.

(11) **Expenses for authorized travel on board business.**—A board may authorize a member, teacher or official of the board to travel on designated business of the board, and may reimburse the member, teacher or official for his or her actual expenses incurred on business of the board, or such lesser amount as may be determined by the board.

(12) **Deduction because of absence.**—A board may provide for a deduction of a reasonable amount from the allowance of a member because of absence from regular or committee meetings of the board.

(13) **Advisory committee members.**—Subsections (10), (11) and (12) apply with necessary modifications to members of a committee established by the board who are not members of the board.

Property

192. (1) **School lands granted before 1850 vested in board for school purposes.**—All lands that before the 24th day of July, 1850, were granted, devised or otherwise conveyed to any person or persons in trust for common school purposes and held by such person or persons and their heirs or other successors in the trust, and have been heretofore vested in a public school board or a board of education having jurisdiction in the municipality in which the lands are situate, continue to be vested in such board, and continue to be held by it and its successors upon the like trusts and subject to the same conditions and for the estates upon or subject to or for which the lands are respectively held.

(2) **Property in trust vested in board.**—All property heretofore granted or devised to, acquired by or vested in any person or corporation,

(a) for the secondary school purposes of a secondary school district or any part thereof; or

(b) for the separate school purposes in a separate school zone,

is vested in the board having jurisdiction in the secondary school district or separate school zone, as the case may be.

193. (1) **Possession of property.**—A board may take possession of all property acquired or given for school purposes and hold and apply it according to the terms on which it was acquired or given.

(2) **Idem.**—A separate school board has power to acquire and hold as a corporation, by any title whatsoever, land, movable property, money or income given to or acquired by the board at any time for school purposes and hold or apply the same according to the terms on which it was acquired or received.

(3) **Appropriation of property.**—A board of education may appropriate any property acquired by it or in its possession or control for any of the purposes of the board but, where public school property is appropriated for secondary school purposes, the value of the property so appropriated or the revenue derived therefrom shall be applied for public school purposes and, where secondary school property is appropriated for public school purposes, the value of

the property so appropriated or the revenue derived therefrom shall be applied for secondary school purposes.

194. (1) **Disposal of realty.**—A board that is in possession of real property that was originally granted by the Crown for school purposes and that has reverted or may have reverted to the Crown may continue in possession of the real property for school purposes and when the board determines that the real property is no longer required for school purposes, the board may, with the approval of the Lieutenant Governor in Council and subject to such conditions as are prescribed by the Lieutenant Governor in Council, sell, lease or otherwise dispose of the real property.

(2) **Application for removal of restrictions on use of school lands.**—Where land, the use of which is restricted by deed in any manner to school purposes so as to appear that some other person may have an interest therein, has been vested in a board for at least fifty years, the board may apply to the Ontario Court (General Division) to remove the restriction, and the court may make such order on the application as it considers just including, where the land adjoins land being used as a farm, a requirement that the board shall, where the board intends to sell the land, first offer it at a reasonable price to the owner or owners of such adjoining land.

(3) **Lease or sale of site or property.**—Subject to subsection (4), a board has power to sell, lease or otherwise dispose of any school site or part thereof or property of the board upon the adoption of a resolution that such site or part or property is not required for the purposes of the board, and the board shall apply the proceeds thereof for the purposes of the board and shall advise the Minister of the sale, conveyance or transfer, or of the lease where the term thereof exceeds one year, of any of its schools.

(4) **Disposal of buildings.**—Despite any general or special Act, including *The Metropolitan Separate School Board Act, 1953*, a board shall not sell, lease or otherwise dispose of a building or part thereof other than to another board or demolish a building, unless, in addition to any other approval that may be required, the board has obtained the approval of the Minister.

(5) **Exceptions.**—Subsection (4) does not apply,

(a) to the use of a building or part thereof pursuant to an agreement under section 183; or

(b) where a building or part thereof is in use as a school, to the use of the building or part for any purpose that does not interfere with the proper conduct of the school.

195. (1) **Board may purchase or expropriate within its jurisdiction.**—Subject to the provisions of section 90 as to the approval of the site of a new school by a rural separate school board, every board may select and may acquire, by purchase or lease, or may expropriate, a school site that is within its area of jurisdiction.

(2) **Purchase or lease of site in adjoining jurisdiction.**—A public school board, board of education or secondary school board may, with the approval of the Minister, acquire by purchase or lease a school site in an adjoining school section or secondary school district, as the case may be, for the purpose of operating a school thereon, but the board shall not expropriate any such site.

(3) **School outside designated area.**—A county or district combined separate school board may, with the approval of the Minister, acquire by purchase or lease a school site that is

outside the area designated in respect of such board by regulation made under subsection 97(2) and may operate thereon a separate school, but a county or district combined separate school board shall not expropriate any such site.

(4) **Buildings on land owned by board.**—Subject to section 196 or subsection 197 (1), a board may erect, add to or alter buildings for its purposes on land owned by the board.

(5) **Buildings on leased land.**—A board may erect a school building on land that is leased by the board where the term of the lease, the school site and the plans of the school building are approved by the Minister.

(6) **Additions or alterations.**—A board may, with the approval of the Minister, make an addition, alteration or improvement to a school building that is acquired by the board under a lease.

196. Agreement for multi-use building.—Where a board plans to provide, other than by way of a lease, accommodation for pupils on a school site that is not to be occupied or used exclusively by the board, the board shall obtain the prior approval of the Minister to enter into negotiations with a person, other than a board or a municipality, in respect of the provision of such accommodation, and an agreement for such purposes may be entered into with such person only after the proposed agreement, the plans of the school and of the building of which it may be a part and the site have been approved by the Minister.

Out-of-Classroom Programs

197. (1) **Acquisition of land for natural science program.**—Where a board acquires a school site under subsection 195(1), (2) or (3) for the purpose of conducting thereon a natural science program and other out-of-classroom programs, the board shall obtain the approval of the Minister before it erects, adds to or alters buildings on or makes other improvements to the school site for such purpose.

(2) **Application.**—Subsection (1) does not apply with respect to a school site acquired by a separate school board under subsection 195(1) where the cost of the erection of, the addition to or the alteration of the buildings on the school site or of making other improvements to the school site is provided entirely by the separate school board.

(3) **Idem.**—A board may, with the approval of the Minister, acquire by purchase or lease for the purpose of conducting a natural science program and other out-of-classroom programs a school site in Ontario that it does not have the authority to acquire under section 195, and the board shall obtain the approval of the Minister before it erects, adds to or alters buildings on or makes other improvements to the school site for such purpose.

(4) **Approval not required.**—An approval of the Minister is not required under subsection (2) or (5) for normal maintenance to a building or site.

(5) **Agreement between boards.**—Two or more boards may enter into an agreement for a period specified therein for the shared use of a school site in Ontario for conducting natural science programs and other out-of-classroom programs but, where under such agreement one of the boards may acquire or is to acquire by purchase or lease a school site for such purpose or is to erect, add to or alter a building on or make other improvements to such site, the agreement is not effective until it is approved by the Minister, and a school site situate outside

the jurisdiction of the boards that are parties to the agreement shall not be acquired without the prior approval of the Minister.

(6) **Taxation.**—All land acquired by a board for the purpose of conducting a natural science program and other out-of-classroom programs, so long as it is held by the board and is not situated,
- (a) within the jurisdiction of the board or within the jurisdiction of another board with which the board has entered into an agreement under subsection (5); or
- (b) in the case of a separate school board, within the area designated in respect of such board by regulation made under subsection 97(2),

is subject to taxation for municipal and school purposes in the municipality in which it is situate.

(7) **Agreements with conservation authorities, etc.**—A board may enter into an agreement with a conservation or other appropriate authority under which the board may, with the approval of the Minister, construct and maintain on lands owned by the authority the necessary facilities for the purpose of conducting a natural science program or other out-of-classroom program.

(8) **Idem.**—A board that conducts a natural science, conservation or other out-of-classroom program may enter into an agreement with a conservation or other appropriate authority for the use of the facilities and personnel of such authority for the purpose of conducting such a program as directed by the board.

(9) **Idem.**—One or more boards may enter into an agreement with a conservation or other appropriate authority to provide for the construction, furnishing and equipping by the authority on lands owned by the authority of facilities for the purposes of conducting a natural science, conservation or other out-of-classroom program as directed by the board or one or more of the boards and, where under the agreement a board is required to pay all or part of the cost of the facilities, the construction of the facilities shall be first approved by the Minister, and the amount paid therefor by the board shall be deemed to be an expenditure made by the board for a permanent improvement.

(10) **Board and lodging for courses in conservation.**—A board may provide or pay for board and lodging for a pupil for a period not exceeding two weeks in any year while the pupil participates, with the consent of his or her parent or guardian and with the permission of the board, in a natural science, conservation or other out-of-classroom program.

Officers

198. (1) **Duties of secretary.**—The secretary of a board is responsible for,
- (a) keeping a full and correct record of the proceedings of every meeting of the board in the minute book provided for that purpose by the board and ensuring that the minutes when confirmed are signed by the chair or presiding member;
- (b) transmitting to the Ministry copies of reports requested by the Ministry;
- (c) giving notice of all meetings of the board to each of the members by notifying the member personally or in writing or by sending a written notice to his or her residence;
- (d) calling a special meeting of the board on the request in writing of the majority of the members of the board; and

(e) performing such other duties as may be required of the secretary by the regulations, by this Act or by the board.

(2) **Security by officers.**—Every treasurer and collector of a board and, if required by the board, any other officer of a board shall give security for the faithful performance of his or her duties, and the security shall be deposited for safe-keeping as directed by the board.

(3) **Form of security.**—The security to be given shall be by the bond, policy or guarantee contract of a guarantee company as defined in the *Guarantee Companies Securities Act*.

(4) **Failure to take security.**—If a board refuses or neglects to take proper security from the treasurer or other person to whom it entrusts money of the board and any of the money is forfeited or lost in consequence of the refusal or neglect, every member of the board is personally liable for such money, which may be recovered by the board or by any ratepayer assessed for the support of the school or schools under the jurisdiction of the board suing personally and on behalf of all other such ratepayers in a court of competent jurisdiction, but no member is liable if the member proves that he or she made reasonable efforts to procure the taking of the security.

(5) **Duties of treasurer.**—Every treasurer of a board shall,

(a) receive and account for all money of the board;
(b) open an account or accounts in the name of the board in such place of deposit as may be approved by the board;
(c) deposit all money received by the treasurer on account of the board, and no other money, to the credit of such account or accounts;
(d) disburse all money as directed by the board; and
(e) produce, when required by the board or by auditors or other competent authority, all papers and money in the treasurer's possession, power or control belonging to the board.

(6) **Business administrator.**—Where a board determines that one or more persons should be employed full time to carry out the duties of a secretary or treasurer or both, it may appoint one or more business administrators and one or more assistant business administrators and may assign to a person so appointed any of the duties of the secretary, treasurer and supervisor of maintenance of school buildings.

199. Responsibility of officers.—Every officer appointed by a board is responsible to the board through its chief executive officer for the performance of the duties assigned to him or her by the board.

School Board Advisory Committees

200. Definition.—In sections 201 to 205, "committee" means a school board advisory committee established under section 201.

201. Committee establishment.—A board of education, a county or district combined separate school board or The Metropolitan Separate School Board may establish a school board advisory committee.

202. (1) **Composition.**—The committee shall be composed of,

(a) three members of the board appointed by the board;
(b) the chief education officer of the board or his or her nominee;

PART VI — BOARDS **S. 202**

    (c) six teachers employed by the board, appointed by the teachers in the employ of the board;

    (d) four persons appointed by the board who are neither teachers nor members of a board, but who are resident within the jurisdiction of the board; and

    (e) the persons appointed under subsections (2) and (3).

(2) **Separate school board.**—In the case of a separate school board,

    (a) where the Diocesan Council or Councils of the Federation of Catholic Parent-Teacher Associations of Ontario organized in the area of jurisdiction of the board so recommend, the board shall appoint to the committee one person selected by the Council or Councils;

    (b) where the Fédération des associations de parents francophones de l'Ontario organized in the area of jurisdiction of the board so recommends, the board shall appoint one person selected by the regional section and, where there is no regional section, by the local section of such Fédération; and

    (c) where no recommendation and appointment is made under clause (a), a recommendation and appointment of two persons may be made under clause (b) and, where no recommendation and appointment is made under clause (b), a recommendation and appointment of two persons may be made under clause (a).

(3) **Board of education.**—In the case of a board of education,

    (a) where the Diocesan Council or Councils of the Federation of Catholic Parent-Teacher Associations of Ontario organized in the area of jurisdiction of the board so recommends, the board shall appoint to the committee one person selected by the Council or Councils;

    (b) where the Home and School Council organized in the area of jurisdiction of the board so recommends, the board shall appoint to the committee one person selected by the Council;

    (c) where the Fédération des associations de parents francophones de l'Ontario organized in the area of jurisdiction of the board so recommends, the board shall appoint one person selected by the regional section and, where there is no regional section, by the local section of such Fédération; and

    (d) where no appointment is made under any two of clause (a), (b) or (c), two members may be appointed under the remaining clause.

(4) **Notice of teacher appointees.**—The teachers shall submit to the board, not later than the 31st day of December in each year, the names of the appointees under clause (1)(c).

(5) **Appointment and term of office.**—Members of the committee shall be appointed on or before the 31st day of December in each year and shall hold office for one year.

(6) **Reappointment.**—Except for the chief education officer, a member of the committee shall not hold office for more than three years in succession.

(7) **Vacancies.**—Every vacancy on a committee occasioned by the death or resignation of a member, or by any other cause, shall be filled by a person qualified under subsection (1) and appointed by the body or person that appointed the member whose office has become vacant, and every person so appointed shall hold office for the unexpired portion of the term of such member. 1993, c. 27, *Schedule*.

203. (1) **First meeting.**—The chair of the board shall call the first meeting of the committee not later than the 31st day of January in each year, and shall preside at such meeting until the chair of the committee is elected.

(2) **Chair.**—The chair of the committee shall be elected by the committee at its first meeting in each year.

(3) **Quorum.**—Eight members of the committee constitute a quorum and a vote of the majority of the members present is necessary to bind the committee.

(4) **Sub-committees.**—The committee may establish such sub-committees as it considers necessary.

204. (1) **Recording secretary.**—The board shall provide a recording secretary for the committee.

(2) **Budget.**—The committee shall, as required by the board, submit to the board for approval a budget of its estimated expenditures for the calendar year.

(3) **Expenditures.**—The board shall pay such expenditures of the committee as are approved by the board.

205. (1) **Powers of committee.**—The committee may make reports and recommendations to the board in respect of any educational matter pertaining to the schools under the jurisdiction of the board.

(2) **Limitation.**—Despite subsection (1), the committee shall not concern itself with salaries of employees of the board or with matters pertaining to personnel problems and policies relating to personnel.

(3) **Consideration of reports.**—The board shall consider any report or recommendation submitted to it by the committee and shall not refuse its approval without having given the committee, or its representatives, an opportunity to be heard by the board.

Special Education Advisory Committee

206. (1) **Definitions.**—In this section,

"**board**".—"board" means a divisional board of education, a county and district combined Roman Catholic separate school board, a board of education in The Municipality of Metropolitan Toronto, The Metropolitan Separate School Board and The Windsor Roman Catholic Separate School Board; ("conseil")

"**committee**".—"committee" means a special education advisory committee; ("comité")

"**local association**".—"local association" means an association or organization of parents that operates locally within the area of jurisdiction of a board and that is affiliated with an association or organization that is not an association or organization of professional educators but that is incorporated and operates throughout Ontario to further the interests and well-being of one or more groups of exceptional children or adults. ("association locale")

(2) **Advisory committee.**—Every board shall, subject to subsection (6), establish a special educational advisory committee that shall consist of,

(a) one representative from each of the local associations, not to exceed twelve, in the

PART VI — BOARDS   **S. 206**

      area of jurisdiction of the board, as nominated by the local association and appointed by the board;
- (b) where the board provides a French-language instructional unit as defined in section 288, one or more members who are French-speaking appointed by the board as representative of the French-speaking ratepayers or supporters of the board;
- (c) where the board provides English-language schools or classes under sections 289 and 301, one or more members who are English-speaking appointed by the board as representative of the English-speaking ratepayers or supporters of the board; and
- (d) three members appointed by the board from among its members.

and, in addition to the members referred to in clauses (a), (b), (c) and (d), the board may appoint one or more additional members who are not representative of either a local association or the French-speaking community and are not members of the board or of a committee of the board.

    (3) **Idem.**—Each of the persons appointed under subsection (2) who are not members of the board shall have the qualifications required for members of the board that appointed them and shall hold office during the term of the members of the board and until the new board is organized.

    (4) **Application of s. 229.**—Section 229 applies with necessary modifications to a member of a committee established under subsection (2).

    (5) **Members of committee.**—One of the members of a committee appointed by a board of education under clause (2)(d) shall be a member of the board of education elected by separate school electors.

    (6) **Ontario Association for Community Living.**—A board that establishes a committee under subsection (2) shall select as one of the local associations for the purpose of clause (2)(a) a parents' group that is affiliated with the Ontario Association for Community Living and that operates within the area of jurisdiction of the board. [To be repealed on September 1, 1996. 1993, c. 11, s. 33(2).]

    (7) [Repealed 1993, c. 11, s. 33(1).]

    (8) **Recommendations.**—A committee established under subsection (2) may make recommendations to the board in respect of any matter affecting the establishment and development of special education programs and services in respect of exceptional pupils of the board.

    (9) **Opportunity to be heard.**—Before making a decision on a recommendation of the committee established under subsection (2), the board shall provide an opportunity for the committee to be heard before the board and before any committee of the board to which the recommendation is referred.

    (9.1) **Vacancies, quorum, chair.**—Subsections 134(9) to (9.3) apply with necessary modifications to a committee established under subsection (2).

    (9.2) **Personnel and facilities.**—The board shall make available to a committee established under subsection (2) such personnel and facilities as the board considers necessary for the proper functioning of the committee.

    (10) **Members of committee.**—A district school area board, a Protestant separate school board, a combined separate school board and a rural separate school board shall appoint a committee consisting of two members appointed by the school board from among its members and two members appointed by the local associations in the area of jurisdiction of the school

board, or where no such local association or associations have been established, two members appointed by the school board who are not members of such board.

(11) **Selection by board.**—For the purposes of subsection (2), where there are more than twelve local associations in the area of jurisdiction of the board, the board shall select the twelve local associations that shall be represented. 1993, c. 11, s. 33.

Access to Meetings and Records

207. (1) **Open meetings of boards.**—The meetings of a board and, subject to subsection (2), meetings of a committee of the board, including a committee of the whole board, shall be open to the public, and no person shall be excluded from a meeting that is open to the public except for improper conduct.

(2) **Closing of certain committee meetings.**—A meeting of a committee of a board, including a committee of the whole board, may be closed to the public when the subject-matter under consideration involves,

(a) the security of the property of the board;
(b) the disclosure of intimate, personal or financial information in respect of a member of the board or committee, an employee or prospective employee of the board or a pupil or his or her parent or guardian;
(c) the acquisition or disposal of a school site;
(d) decisions in respect of negotiations with employees of the board; or
(e) litigation affecting the board.

(3) **Exclusion of persons.**—The presiding officer may expel or exclude from any meeting any person who has been guilty of improper conduct at the meeting.

(4) **Inspection of books and accounts.**—Any person may, at all reasonable hours, at the head office of the board inspect the minute book, the audited annual financial report and the current accounts of a board, and, upon the written request of any person and upon the payment to the board at the rate of 25 cents for every 100 words or at such lower rate as the board may fix, the secretary shall furnish copies of them or extracts therefrom certified under the secretary's hand.

Board Meetings

208. (1) **When board deemed constituted.**—A board shall be deemed to be constituted when a majority of the members to be elected or appointed has been elected or appointed.

(2) **First meeting.**—A board that is elected at a regular election under the *Municipal Elections Act* and a board that is appointed or elected other than at a regular election under the *Municipal Elections Act* shall hold its first meeting not later than seven days after the day on which the term of office of the board commences on such date and at such time and place as the board determines and, failing such determination, at 8 p.m. at the head office of the board on the first Wednesday following the commencement of the term of office.

(3) **Supervisory officer may provide for calling first meeting.**—Despite subsection (2), on the petition of a majority of the members of a newly elected or appointed board, the

appropriate supervisory officer may provide for calling the first meeting of the board at some other time and date.

(4) **Presiding officer.**—At the first meeting in December of each year, the chief executive officer shall preside until the election of the chair or, if there is no chief executive officer or in his or her absence, the members present shall designate who shall preside at the election of the chair and if a member of the board is so designated, he or she may vote at the election of the chair.

(5) **Election of chair.**—At the first meeting in December of each year and at the first meeting after a vacancy occurs in the office of chair, the members shall elect one of themselves to be chair, and the chair shall preside at all meetings.

(6) **Subsequent meetings.**—Subsequent meetings of the board shall be held at such time and place as the board considers expedient.

(7) **Vice-chair.**—The members of the board may also elect one of themselves to be vice-chair and he or she shall preside in the absence of the chair.

(8) **Where equality of votes.**—In the case of an equality of votes at the election of a chair or vice-chair, the candidates shall draw lots to fill the position of chair or vice-chair, as the case may be.

(9) **Temporary chair.**—If at any meeting there is no chair or vice-chair present, the members present may elect one of themselves to be chair for that meeting.

(10) **Temporary secretary.**—In the absence of the secretary from any meeting, the chair or other member presiding may appoint any member or other person to act as secretary for that meeting.

(11) **Quorum.**—The presence of a majority of all the members constituting a board is necessary to form a quorum, except that when a board of education is dealing with matters that affect public schools exclusively, the presence of a majority of the members elected to the board of education by the public school electors is necessary to form a quorum.

(12) **Chair, voting; equality of votes.**—Subject to subsection 56(4), the presiding officer, except where he or she is the chief executive officer of the board and is not a member, may vote with the other members of the board upon all motions, and any motion on which there is an equality of votes is lost.

(13) **Special meetings.**—Special meetings of the board may be called by the chair and in such other manner as the board may determine.

209. (1) **Declaration.**—Except as provided in subsection (2), every person elected or appointed to a board, on or before the day fixed for the first meeting of the new board, or on or before the day of the first meeting that the person attends, shall make and subscribe the following declaration in English or French before the secretary of the board or before any person authorized to administer an oath or affirmation and in default the person shall be deemed to have resigned:

DECLARATION

1. I am not disqualified under any Act from being a member of (*name of board*).
2. I will truly, faithfully, impartially and to the best of my ability execute the

S. 210   EDUCATION ACT

office of trustee, and that I have not received and will not receive any payment or reward or promise thereof for the exercise of any partiality or malversation or other undue execution of the said office and that I will disclose any pecuniary interest, direct or indirect, as required by and in accordance with the *Municipal Conflict of Interest Act.*

Declared before me at .... in the Province of Ontario .... this .... day of .... , 19 .....   A.B.

[Substitute *"Municipal Conflict of Interest Act"* with *"Local Government Disclosure of Interest Act, 1994"*. 1994, c. 23, s. 65 (*not yet proclaimed*). See Editor's Notes on pages 419 and 427].

(2) **Idem.**—Where a person is elected or appointed to fill a vacancy on a board, the person shall make such declaration on or before the day fixed for holding the first meeting of the board after his or her election or appointment or on or before the day of the first meeting that the person attends and in default the person shall be deemed to have resigned.

(3) **Oath of allegiance.**—Every person elected or appointed to a board, before entering on his or her duties as a trustee, shall take and subscribe before the secretary of the board or before any person authorized to administer an oath the oath or affirmation of allegiance in the following form, in English or French:

I, ...$A.B.$....., do (*swear* or *affirm*) that I will be faithful and bear true allegiance to Her Majesty, Queen Elizabeth II (*or the reigning soverign for the time being*).

(*Sworn* or *affirmed*) before me at .... in the Province of Ontario .... this .... day of .... , 19 .....   A.B.

(4) **Filing of declaration and oath.**—The declaration and oath or affirmation of allegiance shall be filed with the secretary of the board within eight days after the making or taking thereof, as the case may be.

Arbitrators

210. (1) **Arbitrators to send copy of award to board, etc.**—Arbitrators acting under this Act shall send a copy of their award forthwith after the making thereof to the chief executive officer of the board and to the clerk of each municipality affected.

(2) **Liability of parties for costs.**—Such arbitrators shall determine the costs of the arbitration and shall direct to whom and by whom and in what manner such costs or any part thereof, and the fees under subsection (4), shall be paid, and such determination and direction is final.

(3) **Expenses.**—An arbitrator is entitled to an allowance of 10 cents for each kilometre necessarily travelled by the arbitrator to and from his or her residence to attend meetings of arbitrators together with his or her actual expenses for room and meals, incurred while attending such meetings, and such costs shall be included in the costs of the arbitration.

PART VI — BOARDS S. 215

(4) **Fees.**—Each arbitrator shall be paid a fee,

(a) in the case of the Ontario Municipal Board, as determined by the Board;
(b) in the case of an arbitrator other than a supervisory officer, judge or member of the Ontario Municipal Board, at the rate of $20 for each sitting of a half-day or fraction thereof.

(5) **Application.**—This section does not apply to a Board of Reference or the members thereof.

(6) **Application to treasurers.**—This section, except subsection (4), applies to treasurers of municipalities who meet to arbitrate the apportionment of costs within a school division.

(7) **Exception.**—This section does not apply to arbitrations under section 137.

Offences and Penalties

211. False declaration.—Every person who wilfully makes a false statement in a declaration required to be made under this Act is guilty of an offence and on conviction is liable to a fine of not more than $200.

212. (1) **Disturbances.**—Every person who wilfully interrupts or disquiets the proceedings of a school or class is guilty of an offence and on conviction is liable to a fine of not more than $200.

(2) **Idem.**—Every person who, with intent to prevent the discussion of any matter or the passing of any motion at a meeting of a board, or a committee of a board including a committee of the whole board disrupts or endeavours to disturb or interrupt the meeting after having been expelled or excluded from the meeting is guilty of an offence and on conviction is liable to a fine of not more than $200.

213. (1) **Acting while disqualified.**—Every member of a board who sits or votes at any meeting of the board after becoming disqualified from sitting is guilty of an offence and on conviction is liable to a fine of not more than $200 for every meeting at which he or she so sits or votes.

(2) **False reports and registers.**—Every member of a board who knowingly signs a false report and every teacher who keeps a false school register or makes a false return is guilty of an offence and on conviction is liable to a fine of not more than $200.

214. Information to auditors.—Every member of a board and every officer thereof who,

(a) withholds from the auditor access, at all reasonable hours, to the books, records, documents and vouchers of the board; or
(b) refuses or neglects to provide such information and explanations as the auditor may require,

is guilty of an offence and on conviction is liable to a fine of not more than $200, but no person is liable if he or she proves that he or she has made reasonable efforts to procure the furnishing of the papers or information.

215. (1) **Delivery up of books and money.**—A person who holds or has held the office of treasurer, secretary or secretary-treasurer, and a member or other person who has in his or her possession any book, paper, chattel or money that came into his or her possession as such

S. 216 EDUCATION ACT

treasurer, secretary, secretary-treasurer, member or otherwise shall not wrongfully withhold, or neglect or refuse to deliver up, or account for and pay over the same to the person and in the manner directed by the board or by other competent authority.

(2) **Summons for appearance.**—Upon application to a judge by the board, supported by affidavit, showing such wrongful withholding or refusal, the judge may summon the treasurer, secretary, secretary-treasurer, member or person to appear before the judge at a time and place appointed by the judge.

(3) **Service of summons.**—A bailiff of the Small Claims Court, upon being required so to do by the judge, shall serve the summons or a true copy thereof on the person complained against personally or by leaving it with a person apparently not under the age of sixteen years.

(4) **Order to account.**—At the time and place so appointed, the judge, if satisfied that service has been made, shall, in a summary manner, and whether the person complained against does or does not appear, hear the complaint, and if the judge is of the opinion that it is well founded may order the person complained against to deliver up, account for and pay over such book, paper, chattel or money by a day to be named by the judge in the order, together with such reasonable costs incurred in making the application as the judge may allow.

(5) **Other remedy not affected.**—The proceeding before the judge does not impair or affect any other remedy that the board or other competent authority may have against the person complained against or against any other person.

216. (1) **Compelling delivery of books, money, etc., on dissolution of school board.**—Section 215 applies to the case of any person who has in his or her possession any books, paper, chattel or money that came into his or her possession as secretary or treasurer, or member, or otherwise, of a board that has been dissolved, and every such person shall deliver up, account for and pay over every such book, paper, chattel and all such money as provided in this Act and failing any such provision, as directed by the Minister, and in default thereof, a proceeding may be commenced against the person by two ratepayers in the same manner as in the case provided for by section 215 and that section applies with necessary modifications.

(2) **Application of subs. (1).**—Subsection (1) applies to every person who has received from such secretary, treasurer, member or other person any book, paper, chattel or money, which by subsection (1) it is declared to be the duty of such secretary, treasurer, member or other person to deliver up, and a like proceeding may be commenced against such first-mentioned person.

217. (1) **Promotion or sale of books, etc., by employees of board or Ministry to board, pupil, etc., prohibited.**—No teacher, supervisory officer or other employee of a board or of the Ministry shall, for compensation of any kind other than his or her salary as such employee, promote, offer for sale or sell, directly or indirectly, any book or other teaching or learning materials, equipment, furniture, stationery or other article to any board, provincial school or teachers' college, or to any pupil enrolled therein.

(2) **Exception for authors.**—Subsection (1) does not apply to a teacher, supervisory officer or any other employee in respect of a book or other teaching or learning materials of which he or she is an author where the only compensation that he or she receives in respect thereof is a fee or royalty thereon.

(3) **Employment of employee of board or Ministry to promote sale of books, etc., to board, pupil, etc., prohibited.**—No person or organization or agent thereof shall employ a teacher, supervisory officer or other employee of a board or of the Ministry to promote, offer for sale or sell, directly or indirectly, any book or other teaching or learning materials, equipment, furniture, stationery or other article to any board, provincial school or teachers' college, or to any pupil enrolled therein, or shall, directly or indirectly, give or pay compensation to any such teacher, supervisory officer or employee for such purpose.

(4) **Penalty.**—Every person who contravenes any provision of subsection (1) or (3) is guilty of an offence and on conviction is liable to a fine of not more than $1,000.

Validity of Elections

218. (1) **Action for declaration that seat vacant.**—Any person entitled to vote at the election of members of a board may commence an action in the Ontario Court (General Division) for a declaration that the office of a member of such board has become vacant under section 104, 209, 220, 221 or 229.

(2) **Time for bringing action.**—No action shall be commenced under this section more than ninety days after the facts alleged to cause the vacancy in the board came to the knowledge of the person bringing such action.

(3) **Power of court.**—Where in an action under this section the court finds that the office of a member of the board has become vacant, the court may order that the member be removed from office and declare that the office is vacant.

(4) **Application of *Municipal Elections Act*.**—The provisions of sections 123 to 126 and 130 of the *Municipal Elections Act* apply with necessary modifications to an action brought under this section.

(5) **Joining of claims.**—A claim in an action under this section may be joined with a claim in an action under section 122 of the *Municipal Elections Act*, and such claim may be heard and disposed of in the same action.

(6) **Validity of elections and corrupt practices.**—The provisions of the *Municipal Elections Act* in respect of the validity of elections and corrupt practices apply to an election of trustees that is not conducted under the *Municipal Elections Act*.

PART VII

BOARD MEMBERS—QUALIFICATIONS, RESIGNATIONS AND VACANCIES

219. Employee disqualified.—An employee of a board is not eligible to be elected a member of the board by which the employee is employed or entitled to sit or vote thereon.

220. (1) **Qualifications of members.**—A person is qualified to be elected as a member of a board if the person is,

(a) A Canadian citizen;
(b) of the full age of eighteen years;
(c) a resident within the area of jurisdiction of the board; and

(d) in the case of,
- (i) a public school board, a public school elector,
- (ii) a Roman Catholic separate school board, a separate school elector,
- (iii) a member of a board of education to be elected by public school electors, a public school elector, and
- (iv) a member of a board of education to be elected by separate school electors, a separate school elector.

(2) **Idem.**—A person who is an elector, as defined in the *Municipal Elections Act* in respect of an area for which one or more members of a board are to be elected, is qualified to be elected as a member of the board for any area within the jurisdiction of the board,

- (a) by public school electors if the person is a public school elector in the area in which he or she is an elector; or
- (b) by separate school electors if the person is a separate school elector in the area in which he or she is an elector,

if such person is otherwise qualified under subsection (1) and is not disqualified under subsection (4).

(3) **Members eligible for re-election.**—A member of a board is eligible for re-election if otherwise qualified.

(4) **Disqualification.**—A person is not qualified to be elected or to act as a member of a board,

- (a) who is,
    - (i) a member of any other board, or
    - (ii) a member of the council or an elected member of a local board as defined in the *Municipal Affairs Act*, of a municipality, including a metropolitan or regional municipality and The District Municipality of Muskoka, all or part of which is included in the area of jurisdiction of the board,

  and whose term of office has at least two months to run after the last day for filing nominations for a new election unless before the closing of nominations the person has filed his or her resignation with the secretary of the other board or with the clerk of the municipality, as the case may be;
- (b) who is the clerk or treasurer or deputy clerk or deputy treasurer or a county or municipality, including a metropolitan or regional municipality and The District Municipality of Muskoka, all or part of which is included in the area of jurisdiction of the board;
- (c) who is a member of the Assembly or of the Senate or House of Commons of Canada; or
- (d) who is otherwise ineligible or disqualified under this or any other Act.

(5) **Qualification to act as member.**—A person is qualified to act as a member of a board during the term for which the person was elected so long as the person continues to hold the qualifications required for election as a member of the board and does not become disqualified under subsection (4).

(6) **Person not to be candidate for more than one seat.**—No person shall qualify himself or herself as a candidate for more than one seat on a board, and any person who so qualifies

PART VII — BOARD MEMBERS S. 223

and is elected to hold one or more seats on the board is not entitled to sit as a member of the board by reason of the election, and his or her seat or seats are thereby vacated.

221. (1) **Members to remain in office.**—The members of a board shall remain in office until their successors are elected and the new board is organized.

(2) **Board not to cease for want of members.**—A board does not cease to exist by reason only of the lack of members.

(3) **Resignation of members.**—A member of a board, with the consent of a majority of the members present at a meeting, entered upon the minutes of it, may resign as a member, but he or she shall not vote on a motion as to his or her own resignation and may not resign as a member if the resignation will reduce the number of members of the board to less than a quorum.

(4) **Resignation to become candidate for some other office.**—Despite subsection (3), where it is necessary for a member of a board to resign to become a candidate for some other office, the member may resign by filing his or her resignation, including a statement that the resignation is for the purpose of becoming a candidate for some other office, with the secretary of the board and the resignation shall become effective on the 30th day of November after it is so filed or the day preceding the day upon which the term of such office commences, whichever is the earlier.

222. (1) **Definition.**—In this section, "electoral group" means,
   (a) in respect of a board of education or a county or district combined separate school board, an electoral group as defined in Part VIII; and
   (b) in respect of any other board, the persons qualified to be electors of the board.

(2) **Vacancies.**—Subject to section 225, if the office of a member of a board elected by an electoral group becomes vacant before the end of the member's term,
   (a) the remaining members elected by the electoral group shall appoint a qualified person to fill the vacancy within sixty days after the office becomes vacant, if a majority of the members elected by the electoral group remain in office; or
   (b) a new election shall be held to fill the vacancy, in the same manner as an election of the board, if a majority of the members elected by the electoral group do not remain in office.

(3) **Optional election.**—Despite clause (2)(a), if elections of the board are held under the *Municipal Elections Act* and the vacancy occurs in a year in which no regular election is held under that Act or before the 1st day of April in the year of a regular election, the remaining members elected by the electoral group may by resolution require that an election be held in accordance with the *Municipal Elections Act* to fill the vacancy.

(4) **Idem.**—The secretary of the board shall forthwith send to the clerk of the appropriate municipality a certified copy of the resolution under subsection (3).

(5) **Term of office.**—A member appointed or elected to fill a vacancy shall hold office for the remainder of the term of the member who vacated the office.

223. (1) **Elections for three member boards.**—If an election is required to fill a vacancy on a board that is composed of three members and there are fewer than two remaining members of the board, a meeting of the electors may be called by any two electors of the board or by the appropriate supervisory officer.

(2) **Time of meeting.**—The meeting shall take place within sixty days of the date on which the last office became vacant.

(3) **Notice of meeting.**—At least six days before the meeting, the person or persons calling the meeting shall post a notice of the meeting in at least three public places within the area of jurisdiction of the board.

(4) **Election at meeting.**—The electors at the meeting shall elect the required number of board members to fill the vacancies.

224. (1) **Vacancy in rural separate school board before incorporation.**—If a vacancy occurs in the office of a trustee of a rural separate school before the trustees become a body corporate, the remaining trustees shall forthwith take steps to hold a new election to fill the vacancy, and the person elected shall hold office for the remainder of the term of the trustee who vacated the office.

(2) **Manner of election.**—The new election shall be conducted in the same manner as an election of the whole board.

225. Vacancy on board.—Where a vacancy occurs on a board.

(a) within one month before the next election, it shall not be filled; or
(b) after the election, but before the new board is organized, it shall be filled immediately after the new board is organized in the same manner as for a vacancy that occurs after the board is organized.

226. (1) **Election to fill vacancy.**—Where an election is required to fill a vacancy on a board that is composed of more than three members and whose elections are not conducted under the *Municipal Elections Act*, the nomination shall be held on the third Monday following the day on which the office becomes vacant and the polling shall be held on the second Monday following the day of nomination, and the nomination and polling shall be held in the same manner and at the same times as for the office that became vacant.

(2) **Extension of time limits.**—The remaining members of the board may extend the time for the nomination and the polling under subsection (1), but the polling shall be held no later than sixty days after the office becomes vacant.

227. (1) **Appointment of trustees on failure of qualified person.**—Where the appropriate supervisory officer reports that no persons duly qualified are available or that the electors have failed to elect members of a district school area board, the Minister may appoint as members of the board such persons as the Minister may consider proper, and the persons so appointed have, during the term of such appointment, all the authority of a board as though they were eligible and duly elected according to this Act.

(2) **Interim administration pending new elections.**—Where under this Act vacancies on a board are required to be filled by an election to be conducted under the *Municipal Elections Act* and no election can be held under that Act, the Minister may by order provide for the fulfilling of the duties and obligations of the board until such time as a new election is held in accordance with the *Municipal Elections Act* and the members so elected have taken office.

228. Tie vote.—If two or more candidates receive an equal number of votes at a meeting held under clause 222(2)(a) to appoint a person to fill a vacancy or at a meeting to elect a person to fill a vacancy, the chair of the meeting shall provide for the drawing of lots to determine which of the candidates shall be appointed or elected.

229. (1) **Seat vacated by conviction.**—If a member of a board is convicted of an indictable offence, or absents himself or herself without being authorized by resolution entered in the minutes, from three consecutive regular meetings of the board, or ceases to hold the qualifications required to act as a member of the board or becomes disqualified under subsection 220(4), the member thereby vacates his or her seat, and the provisions of this Act with respect to the filling of vacancies apply. 1993, c. 11, s. 34.

(2) **Proviso.**—Despite subsection (1), where a member of a board is convicted of an indictable offence, the vacancy shall not be filled until the time for taking any appeal that may be taken from the conviction has elapsed, or until the final determination of any appeal so taken, and in the event of the quashing of the conviction the seat shall be deemed not to have been vacated.

PART VIII

TRUSTEE REPRESENTATION

Public and Separate School Boards

230. (1) **Definitions.**—In this Part,

"**board**".—"board" means a board of education, a district combined separate school board or a county combined separate school board; ("conseil")

"**coterminous Roman Catholic separate school board**".—"coterminous Roman Catholic separate school board" means a Roman Catholic separate school board that has jurisdiction in an area that is also the area or part of the area of jurisdiction of a public board; ("conseil d'écoles séparées catholiques coincident")

"**electoral group**".—"electoral group" of a board means a category of persons that reside within the area of jurisdiction of the board; ("groupe électoral")

"**public school electoral group**".—"public school electoral group" means, with respect to a board, the electoral group that comprises exclusively persons who are public school supporters or public school electors and includes the dependants of the public school supporters and public school electors of the board; ("groupe électoral des écoles publiques")

"**public school English-language electoral group**".—"public school English-language electoral group" means the part of the public school electoral group that comprises exclusively persons who are not members of the public school French-language electoral group; ("groupe électoral de langue anglaise des écoles publiques")

"**public school French-language electoral group**".—"public school French-language electoral group" means the part of the public school electoral group that comprises exclusively persons who have the right under subsection 23(1) or (2), without regard to subsection 23(3) of the *Canadian Charter of Rights and Freedoms* to have their children receive their primary and secondary school instruction in the French language in Ontario and who choose to vote only for the members of the French-language component of the board and includes the dependants of these persons; ("groupe électoral de langue française des écoles publiques") "**public school supporter**".—"public school supporter" means a ratepayer who is not a separate school supporter; ("contribuable des écoles publiques")

"**separate school electoral group**".—"separate school electoral group" means, with respect to a board, the electoral group that comprises exclusively persons who are separate school supporters or separate school electors and includes the dependants of the separate school supporters and separate school electors of the board; ("groupe électoral des écoles séparées")

"**separate school English-language electoral group**".—"separate school English-language electoral group" means the part of the separate school electoral group that comprises exclusively persons who are not members of the separate school French-language electoral group; ("groupe électoral de langue anglaise des écoles séparées")

"**separate school French-language electoral group**".—"separate school French-language electoral group" means the part of the separate school electoral group that comprises exclusively persons who have the right under subsection 23(1) or (2), without regard to subsection 23(3) of the *Canadian Charter of Rights and Freedoms*, to have their children receive their primary and secondary school instruction in the French language in Ontario and who choose to vote only for the members of the French-language component of the board and includes the dependants of these persons; ("groupe électoral de langue française des écoles séparées")

"**total English-language electoral group**".—"total English-language electoral group" means,

(a) for a public board where the coterminous Roman Catholic separate school board is not a Roman Catholic school board, the electoral group comprising the public school English-language electoral group and the separate school English-language electoral group,

(b) for a public board where the coterminous Roman Catholic separate school board is a Roman Catholic school board, the public school English-language electoral group,

(c) for a separate school board, the separate school English-language electoral group; ("groupe électoral de langue anglaise total")

"**total French-language electoral group**".—"total French-language electoral group" means,

(a) for a public board where the coterminous Roman Catholic separate school board is not a Roman Catholic school board, the electoral group comprising the pubic school French-language electoral group and the separate school French-language electoral group,

(b) for a public board where the coterminous Roman Catholic separate school board is a Roman Catholic school board, the public school French-language electoral group,

(c) for a separate school board, the separate school French-language electoral group. ("groupe électoral de langue française total")

(2) **Elections.**—The election of members of a board shall be conducted by the same officers and in the same manner as the election of members of the council of a municipality.

(3) **Change of boundaries.**—The boundaries of the area of jurisdiction of a board or of a municipality that are to be altered as a result of,

(a) a regulation made under subsection 55(1) or 97(2) or 98(1) or 98(2);

PART VIII — TRUSTEE REPRESENTATION   **S. 230**

    (b) an order of the Ontario Municipal Board;

    (c) an order of the Lieutenant Governor in Council under the *Municipal Boundary Negotiations Act*; or

    (d) any other Act,

on or before the 1st day of January next following a regular election under the *Municipal Elections Act* shall be deemed, for the purposes of this Part, to have been so altered.

(4) **New city.**—A new city that is to be erected on or before the 1st day of January next following a regular election under the *Municipal Elections Act* shall be deemed, for the purposes of this Part, to have been so erected.

(5) **Determination of population of electoral groups.**—The assessment commissioner shall determine the populations of the electoral groups for the purposes of this Part on the 1st day of January in the year of a regular election under the *Municipal Elections Act*.

(6) **Idem.**—The assessment commissioner shall provide the results of the determination of the population of a board's electoral groups made under subsection (5) to the secretary of the board and to the clerk of each municipality in the jurisdiction of the assessment commissioner by the 15th day of February in the year of a regular election.

(7) **Number of members on a board.**—Subject to the increased number of members that may result from the application of rules 8, 9 and 10 of subsection (10) and the additional person that may be appointed by the board under section 188 to represent the interests of Indian pupils, the number of members on a board shall be determined in accordance with subsection (8) by the person prescribed by the regulations.

(8) **Rules for determination.**—A determination of the number of members on a board shall be made using the following rules, that shall be applied in order beginning with rule 1:

1. For a public board where the coterminous Roman Catholic separate school board is a Roman Catholic school board, the population of the separate school electoral group shall be deemed to be zero.
2. For a separate school board, the population of the public school electoral group shall be deemed to be zero.
3. The total population of all electoral groups of the board shall be equal to the sum of the populations of the public school electoral group and the separate school electoral group.
4. Subject to rule 6, the total number of members of a divisional board, a district combined separate school board or a county combined separate school board shall be the number of members set out in column 2 of the following table opposite the total population of all electoral groups of the board set out in column 1 of the following table:

EDUCATION ACT

TABLE

Column 1	Column 2
Total population of all electoral groups of the board	Total number of members
Less than 5,000 persons	8
5,000 or more, up to and including 8,999 persons	10
9,000 or more, up to and including 14,999 persons	12
15,000 or more, up to and including 49,999 persons	14
50,000 or more, up to and including 115,999 persons	15
116,000 or more, up to and including 182,999 persons	17
183,000 or more, up to and including 282,999 persons	18
283,000 or more, up to and including 382,999 persons	19
383,000 or more, up to and including 482,999 persons	20
483,000 or more persons	21

5. Subject to rule 6, the total number of members on a board of education that is not a divisional board shall be the number of members as set out in column 2 of the following table opposite the total population of all electoral groups of the board set out in column 1 of the following table:

TABLE

Column 1	Column 2
Total population of all electoral groups of the board	Total number of members
Less than 140,000 persons	8
140,000 or more, up to and including 234,999 persons	10
235,000 or more, up to and including 329,999 persons	13
330,000 or more, up to and including 424,999 persons	16
425,000 or more persons	19

6. If a board approves an increase of either one or two in the number of members of the board by resolution passed by three-quarters of the members of the board before the date mentioned in rule 7, the number of members of the board shall be deemed to be increased in accordance with the resolution for the next regular election.
7. Rule 6 applies if the resolution is passed before the 31st day of March in the year of

PART VIII — TRUSTEE REPRESENTATION   **S. 230**

the regular election or, if the determination of the calculated enrolment and the total calculated enrolment of the board is referred to the Languages of Instruction Commission of Ontario under subsection 322(4), before the 30th day of April in the year of the regular election.

(9) **Number of members for each electoral group of a board.**—The number of members to be elected at each regular election under the *Municipal Elections Act* by the electors for each of the electoral groups of a board shall be determined in accordance with subsection (10) by the person prescribed by the regulations.

(10) **Rules for determination.**—A determination referred to in subsection (9) shall be made using the following rules, that shall apply in order starting with rule 1:

1. For a public board, where the coterminous Roman Catholic separate school board is a Roman Catholic school board, the population of the separate school electoral group shall be deemed to be zero.
2. For a separate school board, the population of the public school electoral group shall be deemed to be zero.
3. If the board is not required to establish either a French-language or English-language section under Part XIII then,
    i. the population of the public school French-language electoral group shall be added to the population of the public school English-language electoral group and this total population shall be deemed to be the population of the public school English-language electoral group for the purposes of the subsequent rules in this subsection.
    ii. the population of the separate school French-language electoral group shall be added to the population of the separate school English-language electoral group and this total population shall be deemed to be the population of the separate school English-language group for the purposes of the subsequent rules in this subsection, and
    iii. the population of the total French-language electoral group shall be deemed to be zero.
4. If the board is required to establish an English-language section under Part XIII, a reference in rule 5, 6 or 7 to English-language shall be deemed to be a reference to French-language and a reference to French-language shall be deemed to be a reference to English-language.
5. The number of members to be elected by the total French-language electoral group shall be calculated in accordance with the formula set out in subsection (11).
6. The number of members to be elected by the electors of the public school English-language electoral group shall be calculated in accordance with subsection (12) or (13), as the case requires.
7. The number of members to be elected by the electors of the separate school English-language electoral group shall be calculated in accordance with subsection (12) or (13), as the case requires.
8. Where the number of members calculated under rule 5 is less than three but greater than zero, then the number of members shall be deemed to be three.

9. Where the number of members calculated under rule 6 is less than three but greater than zero, then the number of members shall be deemed to be three.
10. Where the number of members calculated under rule 7 is less than one but greater than zero, then the number of members shall be deemed to be one.

(11) **Calculation of members for the purpose of rule 5 of subs. (10).**—For the purpose of rule 5 of subsection (10), the number of members shall be calculated using the following formula:

$$\text{number of members} = \frac{a \times b}{c}$$

where a = the total number of members of the board determined by the rules in subsection (8)
b = the calculated enrolment of the board as determined under section 322
c = the total calculated enrolment of the board as determined under section 322.

(12) **Calculation of members for the purposes of rules 6 and 7 of subs. (10).**—For the purposes of rules 6 and 7 of subsection (10), if there is only one English-language electoral group, the number of members of that electoral group is calculated by subtracting from the total number of members of the board determined by the rules in subsection (8), the number of members calculated in subsection (11).

(13) **Idem.**—For the purposes of rules 6 and 7 of subsection (10), if there are two English-language electoral groups, the number of members shall be calculated using the following formula:

$$\text{number of members} = \frac{(a - b) \times e}{(c - d)}$$

where a = the total number of members of the board determined by the rules in subsection (8)
b = the number of members calculated under subsection (11)
c = the total population of all electoral groups of the board determined under rule 3 of subsection (8)
d = the population of the total French-language electoral group
e = the population of the electoral group to which rule 6 or 7 applies.

(14) **Rounding off.**—For the purposes of rules 5, 6 and 7 of subsection (10) and rule 2 of subsection (22), the calculation shall be correct to the nearest integer with the fraction one-half being raised to the next higher integer.

(14.1) **Decrease in number of members for an electoral group.**—Despite subsections (8) to (14), if the members who represent an electoral group of the board approve, by resolution passed by a majority of those members, a decrease in the number of members to be elected by the electoral group, the number of members to be elected by the electoral group shall be decreased in accordance with the approval for the next regular election and the total number of members for the whole board, whether there is one or more than one electoral group of the board, shall be decreased by the same number for the next regular election.

(14.2) **Same.**—A member who represents an electoral group shall not vote to approve a decrease under subsection (14.1) that in his or her opinion would have the effect of preventing the board, or the part of the board that represents the electoral group, from carrying out any of its duties.

PART VIII — TRUSTEE REPRESENTATION S. 230

(14.3) **Same.**—An approval given under subsection (14.1) applies only if it is given before March 31 in the year of the regular election or, if the determination of the calculated enrolment and the total calculated enrolment of the board is referred to the Languages of Instruction Commission of Ontario under subsection 322(4), before April 30 in the year of the regular election.

(14.4) **Same.**—Despite subsection (14.1), the number of members of a French-language or English-language section established under Part XIII shall not be decreased to fewer than three.

(15) **Distribution of members.**—After the determinations required under this section are made, a distribution of those members that represent the electors of an electoral group of the board shall be made in accordance with subsection (16) by the person prescribed by the regulations to,

(a) the municipalities or combination of municipalities that comprise the area of jurisdiction of a board; or

(b) the electoral areas established under subsection (25) or combination of such electoral areas in a municipality.

(16) **Rules for distribution.**—A distribution shall be made separately for each electoral group for which a distribution is not otherwise provided under section 315 or subsection 325(1) according to the following rules that shall be applied in order beginning with rule 1:

1. Calculate the electoral quotient for each municipality and electoral area using the following formula:

    $$\text{electoral quotient} = \frac{a \times b}{c}$$

    where a = the population of the electoral group resident in the municipality or electoral area

    b = the total number of members that represents the electors of the electoral group calculated by the rules in subsection (10)

    c = the total populations of the electoral group.

2. The number of members that represent the electors of the electoral group for a municipality or electoral area shall be, as nearly as practicable, its electoral quotient.

3. Two or more adjoining municipalities or two or more adjoining electoral areas within a municipality may be combined so that the sum of the electoral quotients of the municipalities or electoral areas so combined is as nearly as practicable an integer.

4. The number of members that represent the electors of the electoral group for a combination of municipalities or for a combination of electoral areas within a municipality shall be as nearly as practicable, the sum of the electoral quotients of the municipalities or electoral areas so combined.

(17) **Alternative distribution.**—The members of the board who represent an electoral group may by resolution passed by an affirmative vote of three-quarters of those members,

(a) designate one or more municipalities within the board's jurisdiction as low population municipalities; and

(b) direct an alternative distribution of those members that represent the electors of the electoral group.

(18) **Idem.**—If an alternative distribution is directed under clause (17)(b), the resolution shall provide that the sum of the electoral quotients for the municipality or municipalities designated under clause (17)(a) shall be increased by either one or two.

(19) **Effect of resolution.**—A resolution passed under subsection (17) shall be effective only for the next regular election.

(20) **Idem.**—A resolution under subsection (17) has no effect unless it is passed before the 31st day of March in the year of the next regular election or, if the determination of the calculated enrolment and the total calculated enrolment of the board is referred to the Languages of Instruction Commission of Ontario under subsection 322(4), before the 30th day of April in the year of the next regular election.

(21) **Distribution of members.**—If a resolution is passed under subsection (17), an alternative distribution of those members that represent the electors of the electoral group shall be made in accordance with subsection (22) by the person prescribed by the regulations to,

(a) the municipalities or combination of municipalities that comprise the area of jurisdiction of a board; or

(b) the electoral areas established under subsection (25) or combination of such electoral areas in a municipality.

(22) **Rules for distribution.**—An alternative distribution for an electoral group shall be made according to the following rules that shall be applied in order beginning with rule 1:

1. Place the municipalities in two groups, one of which shall be comprised of the municipality or municipalities designated under subsection (17) and one of which shall be comprised of the remaining municipalities.

2. Calculate the sum of the electoral quotients, determined under subsection (16), for each group of municipalities.

3. For the group of municipalities that is designated under subsection (17), add to the sum of the electoral quotients the number one or two as determined by resolution of the electoral group passed under subsection (18).

4. For the group of the remaining municipalities, subtract from the sum of the electoral quotients one or two, as the case may be.

5. Calculate the alternative electoral quotient for each municipality and electoral area using the following formula:

$$\text{alternative electoral quotient} = \frac{a \times b}{c}$$

where a = the population of the electoral group resident in the municipality or electoral area

b = the number calculated by rule 3 or 4, as the case requires

c = the total population of the electoral group resident in the group of municipalities to which the municipality or electoral area belongs.

6. The number of members that represent the electors of the electoral group for a municipality or electoral area shall be, as nearly as practicable, its alternative electoral quotient.

7. Two or more adjoining municipalities that were placed under rule 1 in the same group or two or more adjoining electoral areas within a municipality may be combined

so that the sum of the alternative electoral quotients of the municipalities or electoral areas so combined is as nearly as practicable an integer.
8. The number of members that represent the electors of the electoral group for a combination of municipalities or for a combination of electoral areas shall be, as nearly as practicable, the sum of the alternative electoral quotients of the municipalities or electoral areas so combined.

(23) **Effect of alternative distribution.**—An alternative distribution of those members that represent the electors of an electoral group that is made under subsection (21) shall, in lieu of the distribution that is required to be made under subsection (15), be the distribution for those members at the next regular election under the *Municipal Elections Act* and for the purposes of sections 231 and 232 shall be deemed to be a distribution made under subsection 230(15).

(24) **Election by general vote.**—The members representing an electoral group for a municipality shall be elected by general vote of the electors eligible to vote in the municipality for those members.

(25) **Electoral areas in a municipality.**—Despite subsection (24), where the number of members representing an electoral group to be elected under that subsection may be two or more, the council of the municipality may, where so requested by the board, by by-law divide the municipality into two or more electoral areas for the purposes of an election under the *Municipal Elections Act* and a member representing an electoral group for an electoral area shall be elected by general vote of the electors eligible to vote in the electoral area for that member.

(26) **Time for passing by-law.**—A by-law referred to in subsection (25) and a by-law repealing any such by-law shall not be passed later than the 1st day of February in the year of a regular election under the *Municipal Elections Act* and shall take effect for the purpose of the regular election next following the passing of the by-law and remain in force until repealed.

(27) **Wards in electoral areas.**—Despite section 315, where a municipality is divided into wards, an electoral area may include one or more wards but each ward shall be located entirely within the electoral area.

(28) **Election in combined municipalities.**—Where two or more municipalities or electoral areas are combined for the election of one or more members who represent an electoral group, the member or members shall be elected by a general vote of the electors eligible to vote in the combined municipalities or combined electoral areas, as the case may be, for those members. 1993, c. 41, s. 3.

Appeal

231. (1) **Appeal.**—After the determinations are made as required under subsections 230(7) and (9) and the distribution is made as required under subsection 230(15) with respect to a board, the determinations and the distribution or the distribution may be appealed to a judge.

(2) **Idem.**—An appeal under this section shall be made by the council of any municipality concerned or a board on behalf of any territory without municipal organization that is deemed a district municipality.

(3) **Appeal on distribution.**—An appeal on a distribution only may be made only where the distribution allots to a municipality or to a combination of municipalities a number of members to be elected by the electors of an electoral group that is different from the electoral quotient of the municipality or the sum of the electoral quotients for the combined municipalities by an amount that is greater than 0.05 times the total number of members to be elected by the electoral group.

(4) **Time for appeal.**—An appeal shall be made within twenty days after the date prescribed by the regulations for a determination to be made.

(5) **Time for decision.**—The judge shall make a decision with respect to an appeal within thirty days after the appeal is commenced.

(6) **Decision of judge on appeal.**—The judge on an appeal under this section may,

(a) vary a determination or distribution that is the subject of the appeal; or

(b) confirm that a determination or distribution that is the subject of the appeal was made in accordance with section 230.

(7) **Idem.**—The decision of a judge on an appeal under this section is final and the appropriate person prescribed by the regulations to make the determination or distribution shall forthwith make such changes as the judge requires.

(8) **Where no appeal.**—Where an appeal is not made or is not made within a time referred to in subsection (4), a board shall be deemed to be properly constituted despite any defect in a determination or distribution.

Applications

232. (1) **Application for determination or distribution.**—An application may be made to a judge to make,

(a) the determinations that are required to be made under subsections 230(7) and (9) and the distribution that is required to be made under subsection 230(15); or

(b) the distribution that is required to be made under subsection 230(15),

where the determinations and the distribution are not made or a distribution is not made.

(2) **Idem.**—An application under this section shall be made by the council of any municipality concerned or a board on behalf of any territory without municipal organization that is deemed a district municipality.

(3) **Time for application.**—An application shall be made within twenty days after the date prescribed by the regulations for a determination to be made.

(4) **Time for determination.**—The judge shall make the determinations and distribution or the distribution, as the case requires, within thirty days after the application is commenced.

(5) **Determination or distribution final.**—A determination or distribution made by a judge under subsection (4) is not subject to appeal and shall be deemed to be a determination or distribution made under section 230.

(6) **No determination or distribution.**—Where,

(a) determinations and distributions are not made;

(b) a distribution is not made; or

(c) the judge does not deal with the application within the thirty day time period required, the determinations and distribution or the distribution, as the case may be, at the last regular election under the *Municipal Elections Act* shall be deemed to be the determinations and distribution or the distribution for the purposes of the next regular election.

233. (1) **Electoral areas.**—Upon the application of a board authorized by a resolution thereof, or upon the application of petitioners in accordance with subsection (4), the Ontario Municipal Board may, by order,

- (a) divide or redivide a municipality within the area of jurisdiction of a school board into electoral areas and shall designate the name or number each electoral area shall bear and shall declare the date the division or redivision shall take effect;
- (b) alter or dissolve any or all of the electoral areas created by an order under clause (a) and shall declare the date when such alterations or dissolutions shall take effect; and
- (c) despite the *Municipal Elections Act* or section 230 or the regulations, make such provisions as are considered necessary for the holding of elections of members to the board by electors in electoral areas created or altered under this subsection.

(2) **Limitation.**—Despite clause (1)(a) or (b), the Ontario Municipal Board may not create an electoral area under those clauses that contains part only of a ward.

(3) **Election.**—While a provision of an order of the Ontario Municipal Board authorized by subsection (1) is in effect for the purposes of an election, the members of the board to be elected at the election by electors shall be elected in accordance with the provision of the order and not in accordance with subsection 230(25).

(4) **Petition.**—A petition of 150 or more persons who are qualified to elect members to the board may be presented to a school board requesting the board to apply to the Ontario Municipal Board to divide or redivide a municipality within the area of jurisdiction of the board into electoral areas or to alter or dissolve any or all of the existing electoral areas created by order of the Ontario Municipal Board, and if the board refuses or neglects to make the application within one month after receipt by the board of the petition, the petitioners or any of them may apply to the Ontario Municipal Board for the division, redivision, alteration or dissolution, as the case may be.

(5) **Electoral area.**—An electoral area established by the Ontario Municipal Board under this section shall be deemed to be an electoral area referred to in subsection 230(25).

PART IX

FINANCE

234. (1) **Auditor.**—Every board shall appoint an auditor who shall hold office during good behaviour and be removable for cause and who, except in the case of a board established under section 68, shall be a person licensed under the *Public Accountancy Act*.

(2) **Disqualification of auditor.**—No person shall be appointed as an auditor of a board who is or during the preceding year was a member of the board or who has or during the preceding year had any direct or indirect interest in any contract or any employment with the board other than for services within the person's professional capacity, and every auditor, upon appointment, shall make and subscribe a declaration to that effect.

S. 235 EDUCATION ACT

(3) **Duties of auditor.**—An auditor of a board shall perform such duties as are prescribed by the Minister and by the Minister of Municipal Affairs and also such duties as may be required by the board that do not conflict with the duties prescribed by the Minister and by the Minister of Municipal Affairs.

(4) **Rights of auditor.**—An auditor of a board has the right of access at all reasonable hours to all books, records, documents, accounts and vouchers of the board and is entitled to require from the members and officers of the board such information and explanation as in the auditor's opinion may be necessary to enable the auditor to carry out his or her duties.

(5) **Auditor may take evidence.**—An auditor of a board may require any person to give evidence on oath touching on any such matters, and for such purpose has the powers of a commission under Part II of the *Public Inquiries Act*, which Part applies to such inquiry as if it were an inquiry under that Act.

(6) **Auditor may attend meetings.**—An auditor of a board is entitled to attend any meeting of the board or of a committee thereof and to receive all notices relating to any such meeting that any member is entitled to receive and to be heard at any such meeting that the auditor attends on any part of the business of the meeting that concerns him or her as auditor.

(7) **Publication of financial statements.**—The treasurer of every board in every year shall, within one month after receiving the auditor's report on the financial statements of the board, cause to be published or to be mailed or delivered to each ratepayer a copy of the financial statements of the board for the preceding year in such form as the Minister may prescribe, together with a copy of the report of the auditor.

(8) **Idem.**—Where in any year a tax notice is mailed to each ratepayer before the 30th day of June, the treasurer may, in lieu of publishing, mailing or delivering a copy or summary and the report under subsection (7), cause to be included with such notice the copy or summary and the report.

(9) **Filing of financial statements.**—The treasurer of every board in every year shall prepare the financial statements of the board and, upon receiving the auditor's report thereon, shall forthwith submit two copies of the financial statements together with a copy of the auditor's report to the Ministry. 1991, Vol. 2, c. 15, s. 36; 1993, c. 27, *Schedule*.

235. (1) **Debentures.**—Subject to the limitations and restrictions in this Act and the *Ontario Municipal Board Act*, the sums required by a divisional board for permanent improvements may be raised by the issue of debentures by the divisional board in the manner provided for the issue of municipal debentures in the *Municipal Act*, and for the purposes of this section the duties imposed and powers conferred under the *Municipal Act* regarding the issuing of debentures and the use of money received from the sale or hypothecation of debentures, upon the Corporation, the head of council and the treasurer respectively are imposed and conferred upon the divisional board, the chair of the divisional board and the treasurer of the divisional board respectively.

(2) **Temporary advances pending issue and sale of debentures.**—The power conferred on a divisional board to issue debentures includes, pending the issue and sale of the debentures, the power to agree with a person for temporary advances from time to time to meet expenditures incurred up to the total of the amount of the debentures authorized by the Ontario Municipal

Board and any further amount that has been authorized by the Ontario Municipal Board or, if the authorization of the Ontario Municipal Board is not required, up to the total of the amount of the debentures authorized by the divisional board.

(2.1) **Temporary borrowing.**—If the Minister agrees to pay to the divisional board the amounts required to meet the principal and interest payments on debentures to be issued under subsection (1) in respect of a permanent improvement, the divisional board may by by-law authorize temporary borrowing to meet expenditures incurred in respect of the permanent improvement up to the total amount approved by the Minister.

(3) **Notification of debt charges.**—The clerk-treasurer or treasurer of each county and municipality in which a divisional board has jurisdiction shall notify the treasurer of the divisional board before the 1st day of January in each year of the amount of the principal and interest due and payable in that year in respect of debentures issued for school purposes by such county or municipality and the dates on which payments are due.

(4) **Payment of debt charges for debentures not issued by the board.**—The treasurer of the divisional board shall pay to every county and municipality on or before the due date of payment the amount of the principal and interest as notified under subsection (3).

(5) **Withholding from debenture levy.**—The council of each municipality, except a municipality in a school division, shall withhold from the amount levied and collected for a board sufficient funds to meet the annual debt charges payable in the current year by the municipality in respect of debentures issued for the purposes of the board.

(6) **Deficiency payable by board.**—Where the debt charges payable by a municipality referred to in subsection (5) on behalf of a board are more than the amount levied by the municipality for the cost of operation of the board, the board shall make a payment equal to the deficiency to the municipality on or before the date or dates on which the debt charges are payable. 1993, c. 23, s. 67(2), (3).

235.1 (1) **Where other board has divisional board powers.**—A board that does not otherwise have the powers of a divisional board under section 235 has those powers for the purpose of financing a permanent improvement if the Minister agrees to pay to the board the amounts required to meet the principal and interest payments on a proposed loan or issue of debentures in respect of the permanent improvement.

(2) **Non-application of subs. (1).**—Subsection (1) does not apply to the Metropolitan Toronto French-Language School Council and to the following boards of education:

1. The Board of Education for the Borough of East York.
2. The Board of Education of the City of Etobicoke.
3. The Board of Education for the City of North York.
4. The Board of Education for the City of Scarborough.
5. The Board of Education for the City of Toronto.
6. The Board of Education for the City of York. 1993, c. 23, s. 67(4).

235.2 Payment by treasurer.—If the Minister has paid to a board an amount required to meet a principal and interest payment coming due on a debenture issued by the board, the treasurer of the board shall pay that amount to the holder of the debenture on or before the due date. 1993, c. 23, s. 67(4).

235.3 (1) Regulations.—The Lieutenant Governor in Council may make regulations prescribing debt and financial obligation limits for public school boards, secondary school boards and boards of education including,

(a) defining the types of debt, financial obligation or liability to which the limit applies and prescribing the matters to be taken into account in calculating the limit;
(b) prescribing the amount to which the debts, financial obligations and liabilities under clause (a) shall be limited;
(c) requiring a board to apply for the approval of the Ontario Municipal Board for each specific work, the amount of debt for which, when added to the total amount of any outstanding debt, financial obligation or liability under clause (a), causes the limit under clause (b) to be exceeded;
(d) prescribing rules, procedures and fees for the determination of the debt, financial obligation and liability limit of a board;
(e) establishing conditions that must be met by any board or class of board before undertaking any debt, financial obligation or liability or class thereof.

(2) **O.M.B. approval not required.**—Sections 65 and 66 of the *Ontario Municipal Board Act* do not apply to any debt, financial obligation or liability defined under clause (1)(a) if it does not cause the board to exceed the limit prescribed under clause (1)(b). 1993, c. 23, s. 67(4).

236. (1) Estimates.—Every divisional board in each year shall prepare and adopt estimates of all sums required during the year for public school purposes and for secondary school purposes respectively, and such estimates,

(a) shall set forth the estimated revenues and expenditures of the board including debt charges payable by the divisional board or on its behalf by the council of a municipality or a county;
(b) shall make due allowance for a surplus of any previous year that will be available during the current year;
(c) shall provide for any deficit of any previous year;
(d) may provide for expenditures for permanent improvements and for an allocation to a reserve fund, provided that the total of expenditures for permanent improvements referred to in clauses (a), (b) and (c) of the definition of ''permanent improvement'' in subsection 1(1) and any sum allocated to a reserve fund do not exceed,
   (i) for secondary school purposes, an amount that would increase the sum that would be required to be raised by levy for secondary school purposes in the school division if no such provision for expenditures and allocation were made, by an amount calculated at one mill in the dollar upon the total of the equalized assessments of the municipalities and localities in the school division, and
   (ii) for public school purposes, an amount that would increase the sum that would be required to be raised by levy for public school purposes in the school division if no such provision for expenditures and allocation were made, by an amount calculated at one mill in the dollar upon the total of the equalized assessments of the property rateable for public school purposes in the municipalities and localities in the school division; and
(e) may provide for a reserve for working funds of a sum not in excess of 5 per cent of the expenditures of the board for the preceding year, but, where the sum accumulated

in the reserve is equal to or more than 20 per cent of such expenditures, no further sum shall be provided,

and shall submit to the council of each municipality all or part of which is in the school division on or before the 1st day of March in each year a statement indicating the amount of the estimates for public school purposes and for secondary school purposes to be raised by each council and a requisition of the amount of the estimates for public school purposes and for secondary school purposes required to be raised by the council in respect of the municipality or part thereof.

(2) **Definition.**—In subsection (1), "equalized assessment" for a municipality or a locality means the assessment upon which taxes are levied in the municipality or locality, as the case may be, in the year for which the estimates are adopted as adjusted by the latest assessment equalization factor applicable thereto that is provided by the Minister.

(3) [Repealed 1993, c. 11, s. 35.]

(4) **Reserve fund limitation exception.**—The limitation on the sum that a board may allocate to a reserve fund under clause (1)(d) does not apply to revenue received by a board in any year from the sale or disposal of, or insurance proceeds in respect of, permanent improvements.

(5) **Same.**—The limitation on the sum that a board may include in its estimates for permanent improvements under clause (1)(d) does not apply to the following:

1. Revenue received by a board in any year from the sale or disposal of permanent improvements or from insurance proceeds in respect of permanent improvements.

2. An expenditure from a reserve fund for the purpose for which the fund was established.

3. The portion of an expenditure for a permanent improvement receivable by way of a grant under section 9 of the *Community Recreation Centres Act* or receivable from a municipality pursuant to an agreement under section 183.

4. The amount of principal and interest payable under a debenture issued by the board if the Minister agrees to pay that amount to the board to enable it to meet the principal and interest payments.

(6) **Expenditure of reserve fund money.**—The money raised for, or held in, a reserve fund by a board shall not be expended, pledged or applied to any purpose other than that for which the fund was established without the approval of the Minister and subsection 163(4) of the *Municipal Act* does not apply to such money.

(7) **Where estimates submitted after March 1st.**—Where, in any year, a divisional board is unable to submit the statement and requisition required under subsection (1) of the council of each municipality in the school division on or before the 1st day of March, the later submission thereof does not relieve the council of its duty under subsection 243(1) to levy and collect the amount required by the divisional board.

(8) **Where cost of separate levy payable by divisional board.**—Where, in any year, the council of a municipality is required, by reason of receiving the requisition of a divisional board under subsection (1) after the 1st day of March, to levy the amount required by the divisional board by a separate levy from the amount levied for municipal purposes, the divisional board, on the request of the treasurer of the municipality, shall pay to the treasurer the cost of levying the amount required by the divisional board.

(9) **Requirement re estimates.**—Subsection 162(5) of the *Municipal Act* does not apply to divisional boards.

(10) **Application to board of education.**—Except where inconsistent with the provisions of the *Municipality of Metropolitan Toronto Act*, this section applies with necessary modifications to a board of education for an area municipality under such Act.

(11) [Repealed 1993, c. 11, s. 35.]

(12) **Application to public school board.**—The provisions of this section that apply in respect of the public school purposes of a divisional board apply to a public school board.

(13) **Application to secondary school board.**—The provisions of this section that apply in respect of the secondary school purposes of a divisional board apply to a secondary school board. 1993, c. 11, s. 35; c. 23, s. 67 (5).

237. (1) **Limitation.**—This section does not apply to The Metropolitan Toronto School Board or to a board of education in The Municipality of Metropolitan Toronto.

(2) **Money raised locally not spent for salaries because of strike or lock-out to be used to reduce taxes.**—Where, in any year, any money that was provided in the estimates of a board for payment of salaries and wages of teachers and other employees in relation to employment in that year is not paid by reason of a strike by or lock-out of such teachers and other employees, or any of them, an amount of money calculated in accordance with the regulations shall in that year be placed in a reserve, and the estimates of the board for the next following year shall make due allowance for the amount in the reserve to reduce the sum that would otherwise be required for such following year for public, secondary or separate school purposes, as the case may be.

(3) **Statement.**—When in any year a board submits to a municipality a requisition of the amount of the board's estimates for public or secondary school purposes to be raised by that municipality or the rates required for separate school purposes in that municipality, the board shall also submit a statement setting out,

(a) the amount of money placed in a reserve for which due allowance is made under subsection (2) in that year;

(b) where estimates of the board for that year exclude an amount of money that would normally be paid as salaries and wages of teachers and other employees and that was not paid in that year because of a strike or lock-out of such teachers and other employees, or any of them, that occurred prior to the adoption of the estimates in that year, the amount of money calculated in accordance with the regulations; and

(c) the portion of the amounts set out pursuant to clauses (a) and (b) that is applied to reduce the sum required for that year to be raised by that municipality for public, secondary or separate school purposes, as the case may be.

(4) **Notice.**—A collector of a municipality to which subsection (3) applies shall send with the notice of taxes to each ratepayer affected in that municipality a notice showing the amount of money applied to reduce the sum required to be raised in that municipality for public, secondary or separate school purposes and the effect of such reduction upon the mill rate.

(5) **Cost of preparing notices.**—Where the collector of a municipality is required to send notices under subsection (4), the municipality shall be reimbursed by the board for the reasonable expenses incurred by that municipality for preparing and printing such notices.

PART IX — FINANCE **S. 238**

(6) **Board providing statements.**—In the case of,
(a) each locality or part of territory without municipal organization that is within the area of jurisdiction of a board; and
(b) a separate school board that appoints a collector under section 115,

the board shall provide the statements referred to in subsection (3) to the officer of the board who performs in the locality or part of territory without municipal organization the duties of a collector in a municipality, or to the collector appointed by the separate school board, as the case may be, and subsection (4) applies with necessary modifications to such officer or collector in respect of the municipality, locality, territory without municipal organization, or part thereof, in which he or she collects taxes or rates.

238. (1) **Definitions.**—For the purposes of this section,

"**area municipality**".—"area municipality" means an area municipality as defined in the *Municipality of Metropolitan Toronto Act*; ("municipalité de secteur")

"**board**".—"board" means a board of education of an area municipality; ("conseil")

"**Metropolitan Council**".—"Metropolitan Council" means the council of The Municipality of Metropolitan Toronto; ("Conseil de la communauté urbaine")

"**School Board**".—"School Board" means The Metropolitan Toronto School Board. ("Conseil scolaire")

(2) **Money raised not spent for salaries because of strike or lock-out to be used to reduce taxes.**—Where, in any year, any money that was provided in the estimates of the School Board for payment of salaries and wages of teachers and other employees in relation to employment in that year by a board or the School Board is not paid by reason of a strike by or lock-out of such teachers and other employees, or any of them, an amount of money calculated in accordance with the regulations shall in that year be placed in a reserve by the School Board, and the estimates of the School Board for the next following year shall make due allowance for the amount in the reserve to reduce the sum that would otherwise be required for such following year by the School Board for public or secondary school purposes, as the case may be.

(3) **Information.**—Each board shall provide to the School Board, at the time required by the School Board, such information as the School Board may require for the purposes of subsection (2).

(4) **Adjustment of monthly instalments.**—Where in any year the School Board has, by reason of the information given by a board pursuant to subsection (3), placed an amount of money in a reserve under subsection (2), it shall thereafter adjust in the manner determined by the School Board, one or more of the monthly instalments payable to such board in that year under subsection 153(2) of the *Municipality of Metropolitan Toronto Act* so that the amount paid to the board for that year is reduced by the amount placed in the reserve.

(5) **Statement.**—When in any year the School Board submits to the Metropolitan Council its estimates for public and secondary school purposes, the School Board shall also submit statements setting out for public and for secondary school purposes,
(a) the amount of money placed in a reserve for which due allowance is made under subsection (2) in that year; and
(b) where estimates of the School Board for that year exclude an amount of money that

would normally be paid as salaries and wages of teachers and other employees of a board or the School Board and that was not paid in that year because of a strike or lock-out of such teachers and other employees, or any of them, that occurred prior to the adoption of the estimates in that year, the amount of money calculated in accordance with the regulations.

(6) **Idem.**—The Metropolitan Council, when it levies against an area municipality the amount that it apportions for public school purposes and for secondary school purposes to such area municipality, shall submit a statement setting out the portions of the amounts referred to in clauses (5)(a) and (b) that are applied to reduce the sum required to be raised by the area municipality for public or secondary school purposes, as the case may be.

(7) **Notice.**—The collector of each area municipality shall send with the notice of taxes to each ratepayer affected in that area municipality a notice showing the amount of money applied to reduce the sum required to be raised in that area municipality for public or secondary school purposes and the effect of such reduction upon the mill rate.

(8) **Cost of notice.**—Where the collector of an area municipality is required to send notices under subsection (7) in respect of a statement received from the Metropolitan Council under subsection (6), The Municipality of Metropolitan Toronto shall reimburse the area municipality for the reasonable expenses incurred by that area municipality for preparing and printing such notices, and The Municipality of Metropolitan Toronto shall deduct the total amount of such reimbursements from the sums payable to the School Board under subsection 153(1) of the *Municipality of Metropolitan Toronto Act*.

239. Regulations.—The Minister, subject to the approval of the Lieutenant Governor in Council, may make regulations, that may be of general or particular application, providing for the calculation of the amounts of money,

(a) to be placed in a reserve under subsection 237(2) and subsection 238(2); and

(b) for the purposes of statements required under clause 237(3)(b) or clause 238(5)(b).

240. (1) **Regulations for apportionment in any year.**—The Lieutenant Governor in Council may make regulations providing for the apportionment of the sums required by a divisional board for secondary school purposes and for public school purposes for any year among the municipalities or parts thereof and localities in the school division.

(2) **Review.**—Where, in respect of any year, the council of a municipality is of the opinion that the apportionment made under a regulation made under subsection (1) is incorrect because of,

(a) an error or omission in the determination of the amount of the assessment of one or more municipalities or localities in the school division;

(b) an error or omission in the application of a factor used to equalize the assessment of one or more municipalities or localities in the school division;

(c) an error or omission in a calculation; or

(d) the failure to apply one or more provisions of the regulation,

the council may apply to the divisional board within thirty days after receiving the apportionment from the divisional board for a review to determine the correct proportion of the sums required for public school purposes and for secondary school purposes that each municipality or part thereof or locality shall bear in each year.

PART IX — FINANCE   S. 240

(3) **Where estimated data used.**—Where, in making the apportionment in accordance with a regulation made under this section, estimates data are used, an overpayment or an underpayment by a municipality or part thereof or a locality, determined on the basis of actual data, shall be adjusted in the levy for the following year.

(4) **Application of grants.**—Where the regulations provide for a grant to a divisional board on behalf of a part of a territorial district that in the year 1968 was not included in a secondary school district, such grant shall be applied to reduce the sum required to be raised under this section in such part of the territorial district.

(5) **Meeting.**—Upon receipt of the application referred to in subsection (2), the divisional board shall direct its chief executive officer to call a meeting of the treasurer of the county or the regional municipality and the treasurers of the municipalities within the school division.

(6) **Review by treasurers.**—At the meeting, the treasurers shall review and, where appropriate, revise the proportion of the amounts to be raised by each municipality or part thereof or locality in accordance with the regulation.

(7) **Decision.**—The treasurers shall make their decision in writing and shall file a copy of the decision with the chief executive officer of the divisional board.

(8) **Idem.**—Upon receipt of the decision, the chief executive officer shall forthwith send a copy of the decision to the clerk of each municipality by registered mail.

(9) **Decision final.**—The decision of the treasurers is final.

(10) **Effect of decision.**—The decision of the treasurers is effective only in respect of the year for which the decision is made.

(11) **Apportionment where unorganized territory becomes part of school division.**—Where, in any year, territory without municipal organization is included in a school division and property therein is assessed for the first time for the purpose of levying rates and collecting taxes for school purposes, such assessment shall, for the purposes of apportionment of costs for that year under this section, be the assessment on which taxes are levied in that year and an application for a review under subsection (2) may be made within thirty days after receiving the apportionment from the divisional board.

(12) **Territory without municipal organization.**—In territory without municipal organization that is deemed to be a district municipality in a school division, five ratepayers resident in such district municipality have the same powers as the council of a municipality under subsection (2) and may appoint one ratepayer to act as treasurer for the purposes of this section.

(13) **Idem.**—Where the ratepayers cannot agree as to who shall be the treasurer, the chief executive officer of the divisional board shall designate a person to act as treasurer.

(14) **Levy despite review.**—An application for a review under this section does not relieve the council of a municipality of its duty to levy and collect the amounts requisitioned by the board as apportioned to the municipality.

(15) **Adjustment where apportionment altered.**—Where, in respect of any year, a municipality in a school division has, under section 243, levied the amounts that were requisitioned by the divisional board and the amounts are altered as a result of the decision of the treasurers, the provisions of subsections 247(2) and (3) apply in respect of the alteration.

S. 241

(16) **Non-application.**—Subsections (2) to (15) do not apply to an area or local municipality in a county, a regional or district municipality or the County of Oxford where an assessment update has been carried out by the Minister of Revenue under the relevant provision described in subsection 117(14). 1992, c. 15, s. 86.

241. (1) **Regulations for apportionment, Sudbury District Roman Catholic Separate School Board.**—The Lieutenant Governor in Council may make regulations providing for the apportionment of the sums required by The Sudbury District Roman Catholic Separate School Board for separate school purposes for any year among the municipalities or parts thereof and localities in the district combined separate school zone.

(2) **Idem.**—In any year in which a regulation made under subsection (1) is in force, the sums mentioned in that subsection shall be apportioned among the municipalities or parts thereof and localities in the district combined separate school zone in accordance with the regulation.

(3) **Where estimated data used.**—Where, in making the apportionment in accordance with a regulation made under this section, estimated data are used, an overpayment or an underpayment by a municipality or part thereof, other than an area municipality as defined in the *Regional Municipality of Sudbury Act* or by a locality, determined on the basis of actual data, shall be adjusted in the levy for the following year.

242. (1) **Regulations for separate school board apportionment.**—The Lieutenant Governor in Council may make regulations providing for the apportionment of the sums required by a separate school board to which this section applies among the local municipalities or parts thereof that are situate wholly or partly within its area of jurisdiction.

(2) **Application.**—This section applies to those separate school boards having jurisdiction wholly or partly within and partly outside a county, a regional or district municipality or the County of Oxford where an assessment update has been carried out by the Minister of Revenue under the relevant provision described in subsection 117(14).

(3) **Application of regulation.**—In any year in which a regulation made under subsection (1) is in force, the sums mentioned in that subsection shall be apportioned among the local municipalities or parts thereof in accordance with the regulation.

(4) **Where estimated data used.**—Where, in making the apportionment in accordance with a regulation made under this section, estimated data are used, an overpayment or underpayment by a local municipality determined on the basis of actual data, shall be adjusted in the levy for the following year but this subsection does not apply to a local or area municipality situate in a county, a regional or district municipality or the County of Oxford where an assessment update has been carried out by the Minister of Revenue under the relevant provision described in subsection 117(14). 1992, c. 15, s. 87.

243. (1) **Rates.**—The council of each municipality in a school division in each year shall levy and collect,

(a) upon all the property rateable for public school purposes in the municipality the amount that it is required by the divisional board to raise for public school purposes; and

(b) upon all the property rateable for secondary school purposes in the municipality the

PART IX — FINANCE S. 243

amount that it is required by the divisional board to raise for secondary school purposes.

(2) **Payment to boards.**—Subject to subsection (3), the council of each municipality in a school division in each year shall pay to the divisional board the amounts required to be raised by the municipality for public school purposes and for secondary school purposes, in the following instalments:

1. 25 per cent of such amounts on the 31st day of March;
2. 25 per cent of such amounts on the 30th day of June;
3. 25 per cent of such amounts on the 30th day of September; and
4. 25 per cent of such amounts on the 15th day of December,

and in case of non-payment of such instalments or any portion thereof on such dates, the municipality so in default shall pay to the board interest thereon from the day of default to the date that the payment is made at the minimum lending rate of the majority of banks listed in Schedule I or II to the *Bank Act* (Canada) on the day of default and where, with the consent of the board, such instalments or any portion thereof are paid in advance of such dates, the board shall allow to the municipality a discount thereon from the date of payment to the date upon which the payment is due at the minimum lending rate of the majority of banks listed in Schedule I or II to the *Bank Act* (Canada) on the date of payment.

(3) **Agreement.**—A divisional board may, by agreement with a majority of the municipalities in the school division where such municipalities represent at least two-thirds of the equalized assessment in the school division as determined under the regulation made under subsection 240(1), provide for any number of instalments and the amounts and due dates thereof other than those provided in subsection (2), which shall be applicable to all municipalities in the school division and otherwise subsection (2) applies with necessary modifications.

(4) **Termination of agreement.**—Where an agreement under subsection (3) does not provide for its termination, it shall continue in force from year to year until it is terminated on the 31st day of December in any year by notice given before the 31st day of October in such year,

(a) by the chief executive officer of the divisional board as authorized by a resolution of the divisional board; or

(b) by the clerks of the majority of the municipalities which represent at least two-thirds of the equalized assessment in the school division as determined under the regulation made under subsection 240(1),

and where no agreement is in effect under subsection (3), the payments shall be made as provided in subsection (2).

(5) **Where instalment due before requisition received.**—Where, in any year, for any reason, the amounts required to be raised under subsection (1) have not been requisitioned before the date upon which an instalment is due, the amount of the instalment shall be based upon the requisition of the previous year and paid on the due date, and in the case of late payment or prepayment of all or part of such instalment the interest or discount under subsection (2) shall apply thereto, and the necessary adjustment shall be made in the instalment due next following the date upon which the requisition of the divisional board is received.

(6) **Application to separate schools.**—Where a combined separate school board has requested the municipalities that are in whole or in part within the combined separate school

zone to levy and collect the rates or taxes imposed by the board, the provisions of subsections (1) to (5) apply with necessary modifications to such board and such municipalities except that reference to equalized assessment in the school division shall be deemed to refer to equalized assessment rateable for separate school purposes in the combined zone.

(7) **Application to public school board.**—The provisions of this section that apply in respect of the public school purposes of a divisional board apply in respect of a public school board.

(8) **Application to secondary school board.**—The provisions of this section that apply in respect of the secondary school purposes of a divisional board apply in respect of a secondary school board.

(9) **Transfer of payments.**—The council of each municipality shall cause each instalment that the council is required by subsections (1) to (8) to pay to a board to be delivered to the board not later than noon on, or deposited in the board's bank account for credit to the board not later than, the date on which the council is required by those subsections to pay the instalment.

(10) **Definition.**—In this section, "bank account", in relation to a board, means the account kept in a bank listed in Schedule I or II to the *Bank Act* (Canada) in the name of the board and designated by the board for the purpose of this section.

(11) **Business days.**—The council of a municipality that is required by subsection (1) to (10) to pay an instalment on a date that falls on a Saturday, a Sunday or any other day on which the offices of the board are not open for business shall comply with subsection (9) on the day on which the offices of the board are open for business next preceding the instalment due date.

244. (1) **Tax notices.**—Where taxes are collected by a municipal council for the purposes of a board, the notice of taxes given by the collector under section 392 of the *Municipal Act* shall be given separately in relation to taxes imposed for public, secondary or separate school purposes or in such manner as will clearly indicate the taxes imposed for such school purposes.

(2) **Municipality to account for money.**—The council of a municipality shall annually account for all money collected for school purposes, and any sum collected in excess of the amount required by a board to be raised by the municipality for such purposes shall, except as provided in subsection 35(3) of the *Assessment Act*, be retained by the municipality and applied to reduce the amount that the municipality is required by such board to raise for such purposes in the year next following.

(3) **Correction of errors in collection of rates in previous years.**—The council of a municipality shall correct any errors or omissions that may have been made within the three years next preceding such correction in the collection of any school rate duly imposed or intended so to be, to the end that no property shall escape from, or be compelled to pay more than, its proper proportion of the rate.

245. (1) **Current borrowing.**—Despite the provisions of any general or special Act, a board may by resolution authorize the treasurer and the chair or vice-chair to borrow from time to time by way of a promissory note or a banker's acceptance that is drawn as a bill of exchange under the *Bills of Exchange Act* (Canada) on a bank to which the *Bank Act* (Canada) applies such sums as the board considers necessary to meet the current expenditures of the board until the current revenue has been received, provided that the interest and any other charges connected therewith do not exceed the interest that would be payable at the prime lending rate on the date of borrowing of the banks listed in Schedule I to the *Bank Act* (Canada).

(2) **Debt charges.**—A board may also borrow, in the manner provided in subsection (1), such sums as the board considers necessary to meet debt charges payable in any year until the current revenue has been received.

(3) **Limitation.**—The amounts that may be borrowed at any one time for the purposes mentioned in subsections (1) and (2), together with the total of any similar borrowings that have not been repaid, shall not exceed the unreceived or uncollected balance of the estimated revenues of the board, as set forth in the estimates adopted for the year.

(4) **When limitation calculated on estimated revenue.**—Until such estimates are adopted, the limitations upon borrowing prescribed in this section shall temporarily be calculated upon the estimated revenues of the board, as set forth in the estimates adopted for the next preceding year, less the amount of revenues of the current year already collected.

(5) **Copy of resolution authorizing borrowing.**—At the time, in any year, that any amount is borrowed under this section, the treasurer shall furnish to the lender a copy of the resolution authorizing the borrowing, unless the treasurer has previously done so, and as frequently as required by the lender, a statement showing the amount of the estimated revenues of the current year not yet collected or, where the estimates for the current year have not been adopted, a statement showing the amount of the estimated revenues of the board as set forth in the estimates adopted for the next preceding year and the amount of revenues of the current year already collected, and also showing the total amounts borrowed under this section in the current year that have not been repaid.

(6) **Estimated revenues.**—For the purposes of this section, estimated revenues do not include revenues derivable or derived from the sale of assets, borrowings or issues of debentures or from a surplus including arrears to taxes and proceeds from the sale of assets.

(7) **Board administered by Ministry of Municipal Affairs.**—A board may borrow more than the amount authorized to be borrowed under the other provisions of this section if,

(a) at the time of the borrowing, control over the administration of the board is vested in the Ministry of Municipal Affairs under Part III of the *Municipal Affairs Act*; and
(b) the Minister of Education approves the borrowing.

(8) **Approval of Minister.**—The Minister of Education may make his or her approval under subsection (7) subject to such terms as the Minister considers appropriate. 1992, c. 17, s. 3.

246. When fees payable by boards.—The fees payable by a board for the education of pupils shall be paid, when requested by the treasurer of the board that provides the education, on an estimated basis at least quarterly during the year in which the education is provided, with such adjustment as may be required when the actual financial data and enrolment for the year have been finally determined, and the estimate shall be not less than the rate per pupil chargeable for a similar period in the preceding year times 90 per cent of the number of such pupils enrolled at the beginning of the current school year.

247. (1) **Reduction of requisition or rates.**—Where, in any year, provision is made by regulation for a grant to a board for the purpose of limiting in such year the amount of the

requisition for public or secondary school purposes or the increase in the mill rate for separate school purposes in respect of,
- (a) a municipality or part thereof; or
- (b) a part of territory without municipal organization that is deemed to be a district municipality,

under the jurisdiction of the board, the board shall, in such year, despite the provisions of any other Act, apply the grant to reduce the amount of the requisition that otherwise would be required for public or secondary school purposes or to reduce the mill rate that otherwise would be required to be levied for separate school purposes, as the case may be, in respect of the municipality or part thereof, or the district municipality.

(2) **Adjustment of rates where under- or over-levy.**—Where a board that has jurisdiction in more than one municipality or in one municipality and territory without municipal organization ascertains that,
- (a) the sum that the board requisitioned for public or secondary school purposes from, or levied for separate school purposes in, a municipality or a part thereof or part of territory without municipal organization that is deemed to be a district municipality under Part III for public and secondary school purposes or under Part IV for separate school purposes,

differs from,
- (b) the sum that the board ought to have requisitioned for public or secondary school purposes from, or levied for separate school purposes in, such municipality or part thereof or part of territory without municipal organization in such year in accordance with the provisions of this Act after the application of the grant referred to in subsection (1) that is receivable by the board in such year in respect of such municipality or part thereof or part of territory without municipal organization,

the difference shall be added to or subtracted from the sum that is estimated to be required for public or secondary school purposes from, or levied for separate school purposes in, such municipality or part thereof or part of territory without municipal organization in the year in which, or in the year next following the year in which, the existence of the difference is ascertained.

(3) **Levy for difference.**—Despite subsection (2), a board may, with the approval of the Minister, add to or subtract from the sum that is estimated to be required from or levied in a municipality or part thereof or part of territory without municipal organization in each of two or three years, commencing in the year in which, or in the year next following the year in which, the difference referred to in subsection (2) is ascertained, a portion of such difference, so as to make up the total thereof.

248. Definitions.—In sections 249, 250 and 251,

"**commercial assessment**".—"commercial assessment" means the total, according to the last returned assessment roll, of,
- (a) the assessment of real property that is used as the basis for computing business assessment including the assessment for real property that is rented and occupied or used by the Crown in right of Canada or any province or any board, commission, corporation or other agency thereof, or by any municipal or regional corporation or local board thereof,

PART IX — FINANCE S. 251

(b) business assessment, and
(c) the assessment for mineral lands, pipe lines and railway lands, other than railway lands actually in use for residential and farming purposes; ("évaluation des industries et des commerces")

"**residential and farm assessment**".—"residential and farm assessment" means the total assessment for real property according to the last returned assessment roll, except the assessments for real property mentioned in clauses (a) and (c) of the definition of "commercial assessment". ("évaluation résidentielle et agricole")

249. Data furnished by the municipality.—The clerk of a municipality shall in each year furnish to each board having jurisdiction in the municipality, or any parts thereof, information respecting the total of the commercial assessments and of the residential and farm assessments on which rates for the support of the board will be levied in that year and the amount due and payable in the current year for debt charges on debentures issued by the municipality in respect of the board.

250. (1) **Determination of rates.**—Rates to be levied for each board in each municipality or part thereof or part of territory without municipal organization shall be determined in the following manner:

1. Add 85 per cent of the residential and farm assessment in the municipality or part or part of territory without municipal organization to the commercial assessment thereof.
2. Multiply the amount estimated by the board to be raised by levy on the assessment according to the last revised assessment roll for the municipality or part or part of territory without municipal organization by 1,000 and divide the product by the total determined under paragraph 1.
3. The rate to be levied on commercial assessment shall be the rate determined under paragraph 2.
4. The rate to be levied on residential and farm assessment shall be 85 per cent of the rate determined under paragraph 2.

(2) **Who to determine rates.**—Subject to subsection (3), the rates shall be determined by the council of each municipality for each board that has jurisdiction in the municipality.

(3) **Idem.**—A separate school board shall determine the rates to be levied for separate school purposes, and a public or secondary school board shall determine the public or secondary school rates to be levied in respect of territory without municipal organization that is within its area of jurisdiction.

(4) **Non-application.**—Subsection (2) does not apply to a local or area municipality in a county or a regional or district municipality where an assessment update has been carried out by the Minister of Revenue under the relevant provision described in subsection 117(14). 1992, c. 15, s. 88.

251. Assessments for school purposes.—The clerk of each municipality and each secretary of a board in territory without municipal organization, in addition to the particulars required under subsection 14(1) of the *Assessment Act*, shall prepare the following particulars:

1. The commercial assessment for public school purposes.
2. The residential and farm assessment for public school purposes.
3. The commercial assessment for separate school purposes.

4. The residential and farm assessment for separate school purposes.
5. Where two or more school jurisdictions, or parts thereof, are situated in the municipality, the school jurisdiction and the commercial assessment and residential and farm assessment in each such jurisdiction.

252. Levying of school rates.—The council of every local municipality, every public school board that has jurisdiction only in territory without municipal organization, every secondary school board that has jurisdiction only in territory without municipal organization, every divisional board that has jurisdiction in any territory without municipal organization that is deemed a district municipality in a school division, and every separate school board in each year shall levy or cause to be levied on the whole of the assessment for real property and business assessment for public, secondary and separate school purposes, as the case may be, according to the last revised assessment roll, the rates determined for each public, secondary and separate school board having jurisdiction in the municipality, or a part thereof, or in territory without municipal organization, as the case may be.

253. Conflict.—In the event of a conflict between sections 248 to 252 and a provision of any other Act, other than section 373 of the *Municipal Act* or a provision authorizing the Minister of Revenue to carry out an assessment update throughout a regional or district municipality or the County of Oxford, sections 248 to 252 prevail. 1992, c. 15, s. 89.

254. Rates for public library in unorganized territory in school division.—Where a public library has been established for a school section in territory without municipal organization that is deemed a district municipality within a school division under subsection 53(3), the divisional board of the school division shall be deemed to be a municipal council for such district municipality under section 22 of the *Public Libraries Act*, and the amount of the estimates of the board of the public library appropriated for such board by the divisional board of the school division shall be raised by a levy imposed by the divisional board on all the rateable property in the district municipality.

255. (1) **Definitions.**—In this section and in section 256,

"trailer".—"trailer" means any vehicle, whether self-propelled or so constructed that it is suitable for being attached to a motor vehicle for the purpose of being drawn or propelled by the motor vehicle, that is capable of being used for the living, sleeping or eating accommodation of persons, although such vehicle is jacked-up or its running gear is removed; ("roulotte")

"trailer camp".—"trailer camp" or "trailer park" means land in or upon which any trailer is placed, located, kept or maintained, but not including any vehicle unless it is used for the living, sleeping or eating accommodation of persons therein. ("parc à roulottes")

(2) **Share of licence fees for trailers to be paid to boards.**—Except as provided in subsection (3), where a trailer is located in a trailer camp or elsewhere in a municipality and licence fees are collected for the trailer or for the land occupied by the trailer in a trailer camp in any year, the council of the municipality shall pay,

(a) to the public school board having jurisdiction in the school section in which the trailer is located a share of the licence fees collected in the same proportion as the rate levied in that part of the municipality for public school purposes bears to the total of the rates levied in that part of the municipality for public and secondary school purposes and municipal purposes; and

(b) to the secondary school board having jurisdiction in the secondary school district in which the trailer is located a share of the licence fees collected in the same proportion as the rate levied in that part of the municipality for secondary school purposes bears to the total of the rates levied in that part of the municipality for public and secondary school purposes and municipal purposes.

(3) **Idem.**—Where the occupant of a trailer has given to the clerk of the municipality in which the trailer is located a notice in writing stating that the occupant is a Roman Catholic and desires to be a supporter of a separate school that is operated by the separate school board of the separate school zone in which the trailer is located, the council of the municipality shall pay,

(a) to the board of the separate school a share of the licence fees collected with respect to such trailer in the same proportion as the rate levied for separate school purposes in that part of the municipality that is in the separate school zone bears to the total of the rates levied in such part of the municipality for separate and secondary school purposes and municipal purposes; and

(b) to the secondary school board having jurisdiction in the secondary school district in which the trailer is located a share of the licence fees collected with respect to such trailer in the same proportion as the rate levied for secondary school purposes in such district bears to the total of the rates levied for separate and secondary school purposes and municipal purposes in that part of the district in the separate school zone.

(4) **Licence fees not part of annual rates.**—The share of the licence fees payable to a board by the council of a municipality under this section shall be in addition to any other amount that is payable to the board by the municipality, and shall be paid to the board on or before the 15th day of December in the year for which the licence fees are collected.

(5) **Application to municipally operated trailer camps.**—This section does not apply to trailer camps and trailer parks operated by a municipality.

256. (1) **Levy on trailer in public school section in unorganized territory.**—Except as provided in subsection (2), the owner, lessee or person having possession of a trailer that is located in territory without municipal organization in a public school section shall pay to the public school board, on or before the first day of each month, a fee of $5 in respect of such trailer for each month or part thereof, except July and August, that the trailer is so located.

(2) **Levy on trailer re separate school in unorganized territory.**—Where the occupant of a trailer that is located in territory without municipal organization is a Roman Catholic and signifies in writing to the separate school board and if the trailer is located in a public school section to the chief executive officer of the public school board that the occupant is a Roman Catholic and wishes to be a supporter of the separate school that is operated by the separate school board of the separate school zone in which the trailer is located, the owner or lessee of the trailer shall pay to the separate school board, on or before the first day of each month, a fee of $5 in respect of such trailer for each month or part thereof, except July and August, that the trailer is so located.

(3) **Levy on trailer in secondary school district in unorganized territory.**—The owner, lessee or person having possession of a trailer that is located in territory without municipal organization in a secondary school district shall pay to the secondary school board, on or before

the first day of each month, a fee of $5 in respect of such trailer for each month or part thereof, except July and August, that the trailer is so located.

(4) **Notice.**—No person is required to pay a fee under this section until the person has been notified in writing by the secretary of the board concerned or the tax collector that the person is liable to pay such fee, and upon receipt of such notice the person shall forthwith pay all fees for which the person has been made liable under this section before receipt of the notice and shall thereafter pay fees in accordance with subsections (1) to (3).

(5) **Content of notice.**—Every notice under this section shall make reference to this section and shall specify,

(a) the amount of fees for which the person is liable on receipt of the notice;
(b) the amount of the monthly fee to be paid thereafter;
(c) the date by which payment is required to be made;
(d) the place at which payment may be made; and
(e) the fine provided under this section.

(6) **No levy where trailer assessed.**—No fees shall be charged in respect of a trailer assessed under the *Assessment Act*.

(7) **Offence.**—Every owner or lessee or person having possession of a trailer who permits the trailer to be located in any part of territory without municipal organization in which the owner, lessee or person is liable for any fee under this section without paying the fee as required under this section is guilty of an offence and on conviction is liable to a fine of not less than $20 and not more than $100 and each day that this subsection is contravened shall be deemed to constitute a separate offence.

257. (1) **School rate where no public school in municipality.**—Where, in a municipality, a person is entered on the collector's roll as a public school supporter and there is no public school board to which public school rates, if levied in any year on the taxable property of such person in the municipality, may be paid, there shall be levied and collected annually on the taxable property of such person in the municipality a rate equal to 50 per cent of the rate to be levied in that year for general municipal purposes in the municipality.

(2) **Reserve account.**—The money raised under subsection (1) shall be deposited in a reserve account for public school purposes and may be invested in such securities as a trustee may invest in under the *Trustee Act*, and the earnings from such investments shall form part of the reserve account.

(3) **Use of money in account.**—Subject to subsection (4), where, in a municipality referred to in subsection (1), a public school board is organized and makes provision for the education of its resident pupils, the municipal council shall pay over to the board such money as is held by the municipality under this section, and such money,

(a) shall be used for such expenditures for permanent improvements for public school purposes as the board considers expedient; and
(b) in any one year, may be used to defray not more than one-third of the amount that would otherwise be required to be requisitioned by the board for public school purposes from such municipality.

(4) **Application in a school division.**—Where a municipality referred to in subsection (1) becomes part of a school division, the municipal council shall pay over to the divisional

board such money as is held by the municipality and such money shall be used as provided in clause (3)(b).

PART X

TEACHERS

Contracts

258. (1) **Full-time or part-time teacher.**—A full-time or part-time teacher who is employed by a board shall be employed as a permanent or probationary teacher with respect to those teaching duties with the board that are not related to the teacher's employment as an occasional teacher, a continuing education teacher or a continuing education instructor.

(2) **Memorandum of contract.**—A memorandum of every contract of employment between a board and a permanent teacher or a probationary teacher shall be made in writing in the form of contract prescribed by the regulations, signed by the parties, sealed with the seal of the board and executed before the teacher enters upon his or her duties, but if for any reason such memorandum is not so made, or has not been amended to incorporate any change made in the form of contract so prescribed, every contract shall be deemed to include the terms and conditions contained in the form of contract prescribed for a permanent teacher.

259. (1) **Continuing education teachers.**—A continuing education teacher shall be employed on a contract of employment in writing in the form of the continuing education teacher's contract prescribed by the regulations.

(2) **Application of subs. (1).**—Subsection (1) does not apply to an occasional teacher who is employed as a substitute for a continuing education teacher.

(3) **Contract.**—A continuing education teacher's contract shall be signed by the parties and sealed with the seal of the board before or after the teacher enters upon the duties of the teacher.

(4) **Full-time or part-time teacher and continuing education teacher.**—A teacher who is employed by a board as a continuing education teacher may be employed by another board as a full-time or part-time teacher.

(5) **Permanent or probationary teacher and continuing education teacher.**—Despite subsection (1), where a teacher and a board agree, a full-time or part-time teacher who is employed by the board as a permanent teacher and as a continuing education teacher or as a probationary teacher and a continuing education teacher may be employed under the teacher's contract as a permanent teacher or probationary teacher, as the case requires.

(6) **Permanent or probationary teacher as continuing education teacher only.**—Despite subsection (1), where a teacher and a board agree, a teacher employed by the board as a permanent teacher or as a probationary teacher with duties only as a continuing education teacher may be employed with respect to those duties under the teacher's contract as a permanent teacher or as a probationary teacher, as the case requires.

260. (1) **Salary of teacher.**—Unless otherwise expressly agreed and subject to subsections (3) to (6), a teacher is entitled to be paid his or her salary in the proportion that the total number of school days for which the teacher performs his or her duties in the school year bears to the total number of school days in the school year.

(2) **School days and school year.**—In subsection (1), a reference to school days in respect of a continuing education teacher shall be deemed to be a reference to the days upon which the class taught by the teacher is required to be taught and a reference to a school year is deemed to be a reference to the number of days during which the program of which the class is a part is scheduled by the board.

(3) **Payment for absence due to illness or dental condition.**—Subject to subsection (4), a permanent, probationary or temporary teacher is entitled to his or her salary for a total of twenty school days in any one school year in respect of absence from duty on account of the teacher's sickness certified to by a physician or on account of acute inflammatory condition of the teacher's teeth or gums certified to by a licentiate of dental surgery, but a board may in its discretion pay the teacher his or her salary for more than twenty days absence from duty on account of such sickness or such tooth or gum condition.

(4) **Part-time teacher.**—A part-time teacher is entitled to his or her salary for 10 per cent of the periods of instruction and supervision specified in the agreement for the teacher's employment in any one school year in respect of absence from duty on account of the teacher's sickness certified to by a physician or on account of acute inflammatory condition of the teacher's teeth or gums certified to by a licentiate of dental surgery, but a board may in its discretion pay the part-time teacher his or her salary for more than 10 per cent of the periods of instruction and supervision in respect of absence from duty on account of such sickness or such tooth or gum condition.

(5) **Absence of teacher in quarantine.**—Every teacher is entitled to his or her salary despite absence from duty in any case where, because of exposure to a communicable disease, the teacher is quarantined or otherwise prevented by the order of the medical health authorities from attending upon his or her duties.

(6) **Absence by reason of being a juror or witness.**—A teacher is entitled to his or her salary despite absence from duty by reason of a summons to serve as a juror, or a summons as a witness in any proceeding to which the teacher is not a party or one of the persons charged, provided that the teacher pays to the board any fee, exclusive of travelling allowances and living expenses, that the teacher receives as a juror or as a witness.

(7) **Award of salary by way of penalty.**—If it appears to the judge on the trial of an action for the recovery of a teacher's salary that there was not reasonable ground for the board disputing its liability or that the failure of the board to pay was from an improper motive, the judge may award as a penalty a sum not exceeding three months salary.

(8) **Failure of board to pay salary when no written agreement or contract.**—For the purposes of subsection (7), the failure of a board to pay a teacher's salary may be extended by a judge to include failure to pay a teacher's salary when an agreement for the teacher's employment has been made by the board but no written memorandum has been made and executed as required by section 258 or no contract has been entered into under section 259, if the judge is satisfied upon the evidence that the refusal of the board to pay the salary by reason of the absence of a memorandum in writing or a contract is without merit.

261. Probationary teacher.—A board shall not offer to a teacher, and no teacher shall accept, a contract as a probationary teacher for a period greater than,

(a) two years where the teacher has less than three years of experience; and
(b) one year where the teacher has at least three years of experience,

as a teacher in an elementary or secondary school in Ontario before the commencement of the contract.

262. (1) **Teachers to be qualified.**—Except as otherwise provided in this Act, no person shall be employed or act as a teacher in an elementary or secondary school unless the person is qualified as prescribed by the regulations.

(2) **Certificates.**—Subject to this Act, a certificate of qualification as a teacher may be awarded only to a person of good moral character and physically fit to perform the duties of a teacher, who passes the examinations prescribed by, and otherwise complies with, the regulations.

(3) **Idem.**—All certificates of qualification are valid for such periods as the regulations prescribe.

263. Termination of contract where welfare of school involved.—Despite the other provisions of this Part and despite anything in the contract between the board and the teacher, where a permanent or probationary teacher is employed by a board and a matter arises that in the opinion of the Minister adversely affects the welfare of the school in which the teacher is employed,

(a) the board or the teacher may, with the consent of the Minister, give the other party thirty days written notice of termination, and the contract is terminated at the expiration of thirty days from the date the notice is given; or
(b) the board may, with the consent of the Minister, give the teacher written notice of immediate termination together with one-tenth of the teacher's yearly salary in addition to the amount to which the teacher would otherwise be entitled, and the contract thereupon is terminated.

Duties

264. (1) **Duties of teacher.**—It is the duty of a teacher and a temporary teacher,
(a) **teach.**—to teach diligently and faithfully the classes or subjects assigned to the teacher by the principal;
(b) **learning.**—to encourage the pupils in the pursuit of learning;
(c) **religion and morals.**—to inculcate by precept and example respect for religion and the principles of Judaeo-Christian morality and the highest regard for truth, justice, loyalty, love of country, humanity, benevolence, sobriety, industry, frugality, purity, temperance and all other virtues;
(d) **co-operation.**—to assist in developing co-operation and co-ordination of effort among the members of the staff of the school;
(e) **discipline.**—to maintain, under the direction of the principal, proper order and discipline in the teacher's classroom and while on duty in the school and on the school ground;
(f) **language of instruction.**—in instruction and in all communications with the pupils in regard to discipline and the management of the school,
(i) to use the English language, except where it is impractical to do so by reason

of the pupil not understanding English, and except in respect of instruction in a language other than English when such other language is being taught as one of the subjects in the course of study, or

    (ii) to use the French language in schools or classes in which French is the language of instruction except where it is impractical to do so by reason of the pupil not understanding French, and except in respect of instruction in a language other than French when such other language is being taught as one of the subjects in the course of study;

(g) **timetable.**—to conduct the teacher's class in accordance with a timetable which shall be accessible to pupils and to the principal and supervisory officers;

(h) **professional activity days.**—to participate in professional activity days as designated by the board under the regulations;

(i) **absence from school.**—to notify such person as is designated by the board if the teacher is to be absent from school and the reason therefor;

(j) **school property.**—to deliver the register, the school key and other school property in the teacher's possession to the board on demand, or when the teacher's agreement with the board has expired, or when for any reason the teacher's employment has ceased; and

(k) **textbooks.**—to use and permit to be used as a textbook in a class that he or she teachers in an elementary or a secondary school,

    (i) in a subject area for which textbooks are approved by the Minister, only textbooks that are approved by the Minister, and

    (ii) in all subject areas, only textbooks that are approved by the board.

(1.1) **Sign language.**—Despite clause (1)(f), a teacher or temporary teacher may use American Sign Language or Quebec Sign Language in accordance with the regulations.

(2) **Refusal to give up school property.**—A teacher who refuses, on demand or order of the board that operates the school concerned, to deliver to the board any school property in the teacher's possession forfeits any claim that the teacher may have against the board.

(3) **Teachers, conferences.**—Teachers may organize themselves for the purpose of conducting professional development conferences and seminars. 1993, c. 11, s. 36.

265. Duties of principal.—It is the duty of a principal of a school, in addition to the principal's duties as a teacher,

(a) **discipline.**—to maintain proper order and discipline in the school;

(b) **co-operation.**—to develop co-operation and co-ordination of effort among the members of the staff of the school;

(c) **register pupils and record attendance.**—to register the pupils and to ensure that the attendance of pupils for every school day is recorded either in the register supplied by the Minister in accordance with the instructions contained therein or in such other manner as is approved by the Minister;

(d) **pupil records.**—in accordance with this Act, the regulations and the guidelines issued by the Minister, to collect information for inclusion in a record in respect of each pupil enrolled in the school and to establish, maintain, retain, transfer and dispose of the record; 1991, Vol. 2, c. 10, s. 6

(e) **timetable.**—to prepare a timetable, to conduct the school according to such timetable

PART X — TEACHERS   S. 266

and the school year calendar or calendars applicable thereto, to make the calendar or calendars and the timetable accessible to the pupils, teachers and supervisory officers and to assign classes and subjects to the teachers;

(f) **examinations and reports.**—to hold, subject to the approval of the appropriate supervisory officer, such examinations as the principal considers necessary for the promotion of pupils or for any other purpose and report as required by the board the progress of the pupil to his or her parent or guardian where the pupil is a minor and otherwise to the pupil;

(g) **promote pupils.**—subject to revision by the appropriate supervisory officer, to promote such pupils as the principal considers proper and to issue to each such pupil a statement thereof;

(h) **textbooks.**—to ensure that all textbooks used by pupils are those approved by the board and, in the case of subject areas for which the Minister approves textbooks, those approved by the Minister;

(i) **reports.**—to furnish to the Ministry and to the appropriate supervisory officer any information that it may be in the principal's power to give respecting the condition of the school premises, the discipline of the school, the progress of the pupils and any other matter affecting the interests of the school, and to prepare such reports for the board as are required by the board;

(j) **care of pupils and property.**—to give assiduous attention to the health and comfort of the pupils, to the cleanliness, temperature and ventilation of the school, to the care of all teaching materials and other school property, and to the condition and appearance of the school buildings and grounds;

(k) **report to M.O.H.**—to report promptly to the board and to the medical officer of health when the principal has reason to suspect the existence of any communicable disease in the school, and of the unsanitary condition of any part of the school building or the school grounds;

(l) **persons with communicable diseases.**—to refuse admission to the school of any person who the principal believes is infected with or exposed to communicable diseases requiring an order under section 22 of the *Health Protection and Promotion Act* until furnished with a certificate of a medical officer of health or of a legally qualified medical practitioner approved by the medical officer of health that all danger from exposure to contact with such person has passed;

(m) **access to school or class.**—subject to an appeal to the board, to refuse to admit to the school or classroom a person whose presence in the school or classroom would in the principal's judgment be detrimental to the physical or mental well-being of the pupils; and

(n) **visitor's book.**—to maintain a visitor's book in the school when so determined by the board.

Pupil Records

266. (1) **Definition.**—In this section, except in subsection (12), "record", in respect of a pupil, means a record under clause 265(d).

(2) **Pupil records privileged.**—A record is privileged for the information and use of supervisory officers and the principal and teachers of the school for the improvement of instruction of the pupil, and such record,

(a) subject to subsections (2.1), (3) and (5), is not available to any other person; and
(b) except for the purposes of subsection (5), is not admissible in evidence for any purpose in any trial, inquest, inquiry, examination, hearing or other proceeding, except to prove the establishment, maintenance, retention or transfer of the record,

without the written permission of the parent or guardian of the pupil or, where the pupil is an adult, the written permission of the pupil.

(2.1) **Information to medical officer of health.**—The principal of a school shall, upon request by the medical officer of health serving the area in which the school is located, give that medical officer of health the following information in respect of pupils enrolled in the school;

1. The pupil's name, address and telephone number.
2. The pupil's birthdate.
3. The name, address and telephone number of the pupil's parent or guardian.

(3) **Right of parent and pupil.**—A pupil, and his or her parent or guardian where the pupil is a minor, is entitled to examine the record of such pupil.

(4) **Idem.**—Where, in the opinion of a pupil who is an adult, or of the parent or guardian of a pupil who is a minor, information recorded upon the record of the pupil is,

(a) inaccurately recorded; or
(b) not conducive to the improvement of instruction of the pupil,

such pupil, parent or guardian, as the case may be, may, in writing, request the principal to correct the alleged inaccuracy in, or to remove the impugned information from, such record.

(5) **Reference where disagreement.**—Where the principal refuses to comply with a request under subsection (4), the pupil, parent or guardian who made the request may, in writing, require the principal to refer the request to the appropriate supervisory officer who shall either require the principal to comply with the request or submit the record and the request to a person designated by the Minister, and such person shall hold a hearing at which the principal and the person who made the request are the parties to the proceeding, and the person so designated shall, after the hearing, decide the matter, and his or her decision is final and binding upon the parties to the proceeding.

(6) **Use re further education or employment.**—Nothing in subsection (2) prohibits the use by the principal of the record in respect of a pupil to assist in the preparation of,

(a) a report required by this Act or the regulations; or
(b) a report,
   (i) for an educational institution or for the pupil or former pupil, in respect of an application for further education, or
   (ii) for the pupil or former pupil in respect of an application for employment,
   where a written request is made by the former pupil, the pupil where he or she is an adult, or the parent or guardian of the pupil where the pupil is a minor.

(7) **Information for Minister or board.**—Nothing in this section prevents the compilation and delivery of such information as may be required by the Minister or by the board.

(8) **No action re content.**—No action shall be brought against any person in respect of the content of a record.

(9) **Testimony re content.**—Except where the record has been introduced in evidence as provided in this section, no person shall be required in any trial or other proceeding to give evidence in respect of the content of a record.

(10) **Secrecy re contents.**—Except as permitted under this section, every person shall preserve secrecy in respect of the content of a record that comes to the person's knowledge in the course of his or her duties or employment, and no such person shall communicate any such knowledge to any other person except,

(a) as may be required in the performance of his or her duties; or
(b) with the written consent of the parent or guardian of the pupil where the pupil is a minor; or
(c) with the written consent of the pupil where the pupil is an adult.

(11) **Definition.**—For the purposes of this section, "guardian" includes a person, society or corporation who or that has custody of a pupil.

(12) **Application to former records.**—This section, except subsections (3), (4) and (5), applies with necessary modifications to a record established and maintained in respect of a pupil or retained in respect of a former pupil prior to the 1st day of September, 1972.

(13) **Use of record in disciplinary cases.**—Nothing in this section prevents the use of a record in respect of a pupil by the principal of the school attended by the pupil or the board that operates the school for the purposes of a disciplinary proceeding instituted by the principal in respect of conduct for which the pupil is responsible to the principal. 1991, Vol. 2, c. 10, s. 7.

Boards of Reference

267. Definitions.—In sections 268 to 277,

"contract".—"contract" means a contract of employment between a teacher and a board; ("contrat")

"employed".—"employed" means employed as a permanent teacher by a board; ("employé")

"judge".—"judge" means a judge of the Ontario Court (General Division); ("juge")

"teacher".—"teacher" means a person qualified to teach in an elementary or secondary school and employed by a board on the terms and conditions contained in the form of contract prescribed for a permanent teacher. ("enseignant")

268. (1) **Termination of contract by board.**—The dismissal of a teacher, or the termination of the contract of a teacher, by a board shall be by notice in writing, which shall state the reasons therefor, in accordance with the terms of the contract.

(2) **Termination of contract by teacher.**—Where a teacher is employed by a board, the termination of the contract by the teacher shall be by notice in writing in accordance with the terms of the contract.

(3) **Application for board.**—Where a teacher is dismissed or the contract of a teacher is terminated by the board or the teacher, the teacher or board if not in agreement with the

S. 269   EDUCATION ACT

dismissal or termination may at any time within twenty-one days after receiving the notice referred to in subsection (1) or (2), as the case may be, apply in writing by registered letter to the Minister for a Board of Reference, stating the disagreement.

(4) **Service of notice.**—The applicant shall send a copy of the application by registered mail to the other party to the disagreement on the same day as the application is sent to the Minister.

269. (1) **Appointment in place of teacher dismissed.**—A board shall not make a permanent appointment to take the place of a teacher who is dismissed or whose contract has been terminated in a manner not agreeable to the teacher until,

- (a) the time prescribed for applying for a Board of Reference has elapsed and the teacher has not applied for a Board of Reference and sent a copy of the application to the board, as provided in section 268;
- (b) the board has received from the teacher notice in writing that no application will be made under section 268;
- (c) the board has received from the Minister notice in writing that an application made by the teacher under section 268 has been withdrawn;
- (d) the board has received from the Minister notice in writing that the Minister has refused an application made by the teacher under section 268;
- (e) the board has received from the Minister notice in writing that the teacher, being the applicant, has failed to comply with the requirements of subsection 270(3); or
- (f) the board has received from the Minister a copy of the direction of the Board of Reference under section 273 directing the discontinuance of the contract,

whichever first occurs.

(2) **New contract after termination of contract by teacher.**—A teacher who terminates a contract in a manner not agreeable to the board shall not enter into a contract with another board after the teacher has received notice of the application of the board for a Board of Reference until,

- (a) the teacher has received from the Minister notice in writing that an application made by the board under section 268 has been withdrawn;
- (b) the teacher has received from the Minister notice in writing that the Minister has refused an application made by the board under section 268;
- (c) the teacher has received from the Minister notice in writing that the board, being the applicant, has failed to comply with the requirements of subsection 270(3); or
- (d) the teacher has received from the Board of Reference a copy of the direction of the Board of Reference under section 273 directing the discontinuance of the contract,

whichever first occurs.

270. (1) **Application for Board of Reference.**—Upon receipt of an application for a Board of Reference, the Minister shall cause notice of the application to be sent by registered mail to the other party to the disagreement and shall within thirty days of sending the notice inquire into the disagreement and shall, within the same time,

- (a) refuse to grant the Board of Reference; or
- (b) grant the Board of Reference and appoint a judge to act as chair thereof.

(2) **Appointment.**—Where, under subsection (1), a judge is appointed after the expiry of thirty days referred to therein to act as chair of a Board of Reference, the failure to make the

appointment within the thirty-day period does not invalidate the Board of Reference or the appointment of the judge as chair thereof, provided the Board of Reference is granted in accordance with subsection (1).

(3) **Naming of representatives.**—Upon appointing a judge to act as chair of a Board of Reference, the Minister shall cause notice thereof to be sent by registered mail to the board and teacher involved in the disagreement and the notice shall require each of them to name to the Board of Reference a representative who is not the teacher involved or a member of the board and to send or cause to be sent by hand or by registered mail to the Minister a notice of such nomination within twelve days of the sending of the notice by the Minister.

(4) **Failure to name representatives.**—If the applicant fails to comply with the requirements of subsection (3), the application shall be deemed to be abandoned and the Minister shall cause notice thereof to be sent by registered mail to the other party to the disagreement.

(5) **Idem.**—If the respondent fails to comply with the requirements of subsection (3), the Minister shall direct the continuance of the contract.

(6) **Failure of representatives to appear.**—If the representative of the board or the teacher, having been named, fails to appear at the hearing, the chair of the Board of Reference shall name a representative for the board or teacher, as the case may be.

(7) **Applicant deemed eligible.**—Where the Minister grants a Board of Reference, the applicant shall be deemed to have met the conditions precedent to the granting of a Board of Reference.

(8) **Death or withdrawal of representative.**—Where, after the hearing has commenced, the representative of the board or of the teacher dies, for any reason is unable to continue to act or withdraws from the Board of Reference, the other representative shall withdraw and the decision of the Board of Reference shall be made by the chair.

(9) **Death, etc., of chair before hearing.**—Where, before the hearing has commenced, the chair of a Board of Reference dies, disqualifies himself or herself, for any reason is unable to act or is prohibited from acting, the Minister shall appoint another judge to act as chair and the Board of Reference shall proceed in accordance with this Part except that for the purposes of section 271 the date of appointment of the chair is the date of appointment of the chair appointed to act under this section.

(10) **New Board of Reference after hearing commences.**—Where, after the hearing has commenced and before the chair of a Board of Reference reports to the Minister and to the parties,
 (a) the chair dies, disqualifies himself or herself, for any reason is unable to continue as chair, or is prohibited from acting; or
 (b) the Board of Reference is prohibited from acting or proceeding,
the Board of Reference is terminated and, where, within ninety days after the death, disqualification, inability to continue or prohibition referred to in clause (a) or (b), the person who applied for the Board of Reference requests the Minister in writing to grant another Board of Reference, the Minister may grant a new Board of Reference, in which case the provisions of this Part apply with necessary modifications except that the representatives named to the new Board of Reference shall not be the representatives named to the Board of Reference terminated under this subsection and the determination and direction of the costs under section 276 may

include the costs, if any, incurred in respect of the Board of Reference terminated under this subsection.

(11) **Procedure at new Board of Reference.**—Where a new Board of Reference is granted under subsection (10), the hearing shall proceed as if the hearing by the Board of Reference terminated under subsection (10) had not commenced.

271. Place and time of hearing.—The chair of the Board of Reference shall, within thirty days of his or her appointment, and upon reasonable notice thereof to the parties, convene the Board of Reference in any appropriate and convenient court house or municipal or school building and at such time as the chair may appoint.

272. Duty to inquire and powers of judge.—The Board of Reference shall inquire into the matter in dispute and for such purposes the chair has the powers of a commission under Part II of the *Public Inquiries Act*, which Part applies to such inquiry as if it were an inquiry under that Act.

273. (1) **Direction of Board of Reference to report.**—A Board of Reference shall direct the continuance of the contract or the discontinuance of the contract.

(2) **Chair of Board of Reference to report.**—The chair of a Board of Reference shall, within seven days after,

(a) the application for the Board of Reference is withdrawn; or
(b) the matter in dispute has been settled by the parties to the Board of Reference; or
(c) the completion of the hearing and the receipt of any written submissions required by the chair,

report to the Minister and the parties the disposition of the application.

274. New Board of Reference provided.—Where, pursuant to an application for judicial review under the *Judicial Review Procedure Act*, the report or the direction of a Board of Reference is set aside, the Minister may grant a new Board of Reference if the board or teacher applies therefor to the Minister by registered mail within fifteen days after the date of the order of the court setting aside the report or direction, and sections 267 to 277 apply with necessary modifications in respect of the new Board of Reference.

275. (1) **Direction of Board.**—The direction of the Board of Reference under section 273 is binding upon the board and the teacher.

(2) **Failure to comply with direction of Board.**—If a board fails to comply with the direction of the Board of Reference under section 273, the Minister may direct that any portion of the amounts then or thereafter payable to the board under the authority of any Act of the Legislature shall not be paid to the board until it has complied with the direction.

(3) **Idem.**—If a teacher fails to comply with the direction of the Board of Reference under section 273, the Minister may suspend the certificate of qualification of the teacher for such period as the Minister considers advisable.

276. Payment of costs.—Subject to the regulations made under section 277, the chair of the Board of Reference shall determine and direct the costs to be paid by either or both parties in the disagreement, and every such order may be enforced in the same manner as an order as to costs made in an action in the Ontario Court (General Division).

277. Regulations.—The Lieutenant Governor in Council may make regulations,

(a) fixing the remuneration of members of Boards of Reference and defining, prescribing

and limiting other items of expense, including travelling and living expenses, which shall be included in the costs of a Board of Reference;
(b) regulating the practice and procedure to be followed upon any reference; and
(c) respecting any matter necessary or advisable to carry out effectively the intent and purpose of sections 268 to 276.

PART XI

SUPERVISORY OFFICERS

278. Qualifications of supervisory officers.—Every supervisory officer appointed under this Part shall hold the qualifications required by the regulations for a supervisory officer.

279. Director of education.—A board of education that had an enrolment in its public and secondary schools of 2,000 or more on the 30th day of September of any year and does not have a director of education shall, on or before the 1st day of August of the year following, appoint a director of education, and he or she shall hold the qualifications required by the regulations for a supervisory officer who is responsible to the board for the development, implementation, operation and supervision of educational programs in the schools.

280. Director of education for separate school board.—A separate school board that had an enrolment in its schools of 2,000 or more on the 30th day of September of any year and does not have a director of education shall, on or before the 1st day of August of the year following, appoint a director of education, and he or she shall hold the qualifications required by the regulations for a supervisory officer who is responsible to the board for the development, implementation, operation and supervision of educational programs in the schools.

281. (1) [Repealed 1993, c. 11, s. 37.]

(2) **Idem.**—Two or more boards of education that each have an enrolment in its public and secondary schools of fewer than 2,000, two or more district school area boards or a board of education and a district school area board may with the approval of the Minister agree to appoint a supervisory officer as director of education to be responsible to the boards for the development, implementation, operation and supervision of educational programs in the schools of the boards.

(3) **Idem.**—Two or more county or district combined separate school boards that each has an enrolment in its schools of fewer than 2,000, two or more rural or combined separate school boards or a rural or combined separate school board and a district combined separate school board may with the approval of the Minister agree to appoint a supervisory officer as director of education to be responsible to the boards for the development, implementation, operation and supervision of educational programs in the schools of the boards.

282. (1) **Abolition of position.**—A board that is required by this Act to employ a director of education in any year or that appoints a director of education or a supervisory officer with the approval of the Minister shall not abolish the position of director of education or supervisory officer, as the case may be, without the approval of the Minister.

(2) **Idem.**—Where, before the 14th day of December, 1984, a board abolished a position mentioned in subsection (1), the Minister may require the board to re-establish the position and the board shall comply with the requirement forthwith.

283. (1) **Chief executive officer.**—A director of education is the chief education officer and the chief executive officer of the board by which he or she is employed and is a supervisory officer who qualified as such as a teacher.

(2) **Idem.**—The chief executive officer of a board shall, within policies established by the board, develop and maintain an effective organization and the programs required to implement such policies.

(3) **General report of chief executive officer.**—At the first meeting in December of each year, the chief executive officer of a board shall submit to the board a report in a format approved by the Minister on the action he or she has taken during the preceding 12 months under subsection (2) and a copy of such report shall be submitted to the Minister on or before the 31st day of January next following.

284. (1) **Supervisory officers and director of education.**—Every board that is required to appoint a director of education shall, subject to the regulations, employ such other supervisory officers as it considers necessary to supervise adequately all aspects of the programs under its jurisdiction.

(2) **English and French.**—English-speaking supervisory officers shall be appointed for schools and classes where English is the language of instruction and French-speaking supervisory officers shall be appointed for schools and classes where French is the language of instruction. 1993, c. 11, s. 38.

284.1 (1) **Supervisory officers, enrolment under 2,000.**—Subject to subsections (2) and (3), a board having an enrolment in its schools of fewer than 2,000 shall appoint one or more English-speaking supervisory officers for schools and classes where English is the language of instruction and one or more French-speaking supervisory officers for schools and classes where French is the language of instruction.

(2) **Agreements.**—With the approval of the Minister, a board may enter into an agreement with another board to obtain the services of an English-speaking or French-speaking supervisory officer appointed by the other board.

(3) **Same.**—A board other than a board of education or a county or district combined separate school board may enter into an agreement with the Minister to obtain the services of an English-speaking or French-speaking supervisory officer appointed by the Minister. 1993, c. 11, s. 39.

285. (1) **Responsibility of supervisory officer.**—A board with a supervisory officer,

(a) shall, subject to the regulations, designate the title and area of responsibility of the supervisory officer; and
(b) may assign to the supervisory officer such administrative duties, in addition to those prescribed in section 286 and the regulations, as the board considers expedient. 1993, c. 11, s. 40.

(2) **Confirmation by Minister.**—No person shall be appointed as a supervisory officer by a board until notice in writing of the proposed appointment and the area of responsibility to be assigned has been given to the Minister and the Minister has confirmed that the person to be appointed is eligible for the position.

PART XI — SUPERVISORY OFFICERS

286. (1) **Duties of supervisory officers.**—Subject to the regulations, a board or the Minister shall assign the following duties to its or the Minister's supervisory officer or officers,

(a) **assist teachers.**—to bring about improvement in the quality of education by assisting teachers in their practice;

(b) **co-operate with boards.**—to assist and co-operate with boards to the end that the schools may best serve the needs of the pupils;

(c) **visit schools.**—to visit schools and classrooms as the Minister may direct and, where the supervisory officer has been appointed by a board, as the board may direct;

(d) **prepare reports.**—to prepare a report of a visit to a school or classroom when required by the Minister and, where the supervisory officer has been appointed by a board, when required by the board and to give to a teacher referred to in any such report a copy of the portion of the report that refers to the teacher;

(e) **Acts and regulations.**—to ensure that the schools under his or her jurisdiction are conducted in accordance with this Act and the regulations;

(f) **annual report to Minister.**—to make a general annual report as to the performance of his or her duties and the condition of the schools in his or her area of jurisdiction when required by the Minister and, where the supervisory officer has been appointed by a board, when required by the board;

(g) **report to M.O.H.**—to report to the appropriate medical officer of health any case in which the school buildings or premises are found to be in an unsanitary condition;

(h) **report to the Minister.**—to furnish the Minister with information respecting any school in his or her area of jurisdiction whenever required to do so;

(i) **supervise business.**—to supervise the business functions of the board; and

(j) **supervise buildings and property.**—to supervise the use and maintenance of the buildings and property of the board.

(2) **Responsibility to Minister.**—Every supervisory officer appointed by the Minister is responsible to the Minister for the performance of his or her duties.

(3) **Responsibility to board.**—Every supervisory officer appointed by a board is responsible to the board through the chief executive officer for the performance of the duties assigned to the supervisory officer by the board.

(4) **Full-time position.**—Except as otherwise provided by this Act or the regulations, a supervisory officer shall not, without the approval of the Minister, hold any other office, have any other employment or follow any other profession or calling, during his or her tenure as a supervisory officer.

(5) **Access to books and records, etc.**—A provincial supervisory officer or a person designated by the Minister shall have access, as required by the Minister, to any school and to the books and records of a board or a school.

287. (1) **Suspension or dismissal of supervisory officer by board.**—A supervisory officer appointed by a board may be suspended or dismissed by the board, in accordance with the regulations, for neglect of duty, misconduct or inefficiency.

(2) **Notice re suspension or dismissal.**—Where a board suspends or dismisses a supervisory officer, the board shall forthwith notify in writing the supervisory officer and the Minister of the suspension or dismissal and the reasons therefor.

S. 288 EDUCATION ACT

PART XII

FRENCH LANGUAGE INSTRUCTION

Elementary

288. Definitions.—In this Part,

"**board**".—"board" means,

 (a) a board of education the members of which are elected under the *Municipal Elections Act,*

 (b) a county or district combined separate school board,

and includes,

 (c) for the purposes of section 289, a district school area board, a protestant separate school board, a rural separate school board and a combined separate school board,

 (d) for the purposes of section 291, a secondary school board and a board of education formed under section 67, and

 (e) for the purposes of sections 303 to 308, a board described in clause (c) or (d); ("conseil")

"**committee**".—"committee", except in sections 303 to 308, means a French-language advisory committee formed under section 292; ("comité")

"**French-language instructional unit**".—"French-language instructional unit" means a class, group of classes or school in which French is the language of instruction but does not include a class, group of classes or school established under paragraph 25 of subsection 8(1) (French-language instruction for English-speaking pupils); ("module scolaire de langue française")

"**French-speaking person**".—"French-speaking person" means a child of a person who has the right under subsection 23(1) or (2), without regard to subsection 23(3), of the *Canadian Charter of Rights and Freedoms* to have his or her children receive their primary and secondary school instruction in the French language in Ontario; ("francophone")

"**French-speaking ratepayer**".—"French-speaking ratepayer" means a person who is entitled to vote at an election of members of the board and who has the right under subsection 23(1) or (2), without regard to subsection 23(3), of the *Canadian Charter of Rights and Freedoms* to have his or her children receive their primary and secondary school instruction in the French language in Ontario. ("contribuable francophone") 1993, c. 27, *Schedule.*

289. (1) **Right to instruction in French-language instructional unit.**—Every French-speaking person who is qualified under this Act to be a resident pupil of a board has the right to receive elementary school instruction in a French-language instructional unit operated or provided by the board.

(2) **Duty of board to provide French-language instructional unit.**—Every board that has one or more resident pupils who exercise their right to receive instruction in a French-language instructional unit shall establish and operate one or more French-language instruc-

PART XII — FRENCH LANGUAGE INSTRUCTION **S. 290**

tional units for those pupils or shall enter into an agreement with another board to enable those pupils to receive instruction in a French-language instructional unit operated by the other board.

(3) **Meals, lodging and transportation.**—A board that provides a French-language instructional unit for elementary school instruction by means of an agreement with another board shall provide to each French-speaking resident pupil of the first-mentioned board who is a pupil in the French-language instructional unit and resides with the parent or other person who has lawful custody of the pupil more than twenty-four kilometres from the French-language instructional unit,

    (a) an allowance payable monthly in an amount set by the board for meals and lodging for each day of attendance as certified by the principal in respect of the French-language instructional unit and for transportation once a week from the pupil's residence to the lodging and return; or

    (b) daily transportation in a manner determined by the board from the pupil's residence to the French-language instructional unit and return, where the parent or other person who has lawful custody of the pupil elects to have daily transportation.

(4) **English as a subject of instruction.**—English may be a subject of instruction in any grade in a French-language instructional unit mentioned in subsection (1).

(5) **Idem, grades 5, 6, 7 and 8.**—English shall be a subject of instruction in grades 5, 6, 7 and 8 in every French-language instructional unit.

(6) **Admission of pupils other than French-speaking pupils.**—A board, on the request of the parent of a pupil of the board who is not a French-speaking person, or of a person who has lawful custody of a pupil of the board who is not a French-speaking person, or of a pupil of the board who is an adult and is not a French-speaking person, may admit the pupil to a French-language instructional unit if the admission is approved by majority vote of an admissions committee appointed by the board and composed of the principal of the school to which admission is requested, a teacher who uses the French language in instruction in the school and a French-speaking supervisory officer employed by the board or arranged for in accordance with subsection (7).

(7) **Where board has no French-speaking supervisory officer.**—Where a board does not employ a French-speaking supervisory officer, it shall arrange for a French-speaking supervisory officer employed by another board or by the Minister to serve as a member of the admissions committee.

(8) **English-language schools or classes.**—Where a board provides one or more French-language elementary schools, a resident pupil of the board has the right to receive instruction in the English language and subsections (1), (2) and (3) apply with necessary modifications in respect of the resident pupil and the board.

290. Duties and responsibilities of advisory committee in elementary schools.—Where a board has established a French-language advisory committee under section 292, or an English-language advisory committee under section 301, the committee has the same duties and responsibilities in respect of the French-language schools and classes or English-language schools and classes, as the case may be, that are provided in the elementary schools operated by the board as it has in respect of French-language instructional units or English-language schools and classes, as the case may be, for secondary school purposes.

S. 291 EDUCATION ACT

Secondary

291. (1) **Right to instruction in French-language instructional unit.**—Every French-speaking person who is qualified under this Act to be a resident pupil of a board has the right to receive secondary school instruction in a French-language instructional unit operated or provided by the board.

(2) **Duty of board to provide French-language instructional unit.**—Every board that has one or more resident pupils who exercise their right to receive instruction in a French-language instructional unit shall establish and operate one or more French-language instructional units for those pupils or shall enter into an agreement with another board to enable those pupils to receive instruction in a French-language instructional unit operated by the other board.

(3) **Meals, lodging and transportation.**—A board that provides a French-language instructional unit for secondary school instruction by means of an agreement with another board shall provide to each French-speaking resident pupil of the first-mentioned board who is a pupil in the French-language instructional unit and resides with the parent or other person who has lawful custody of the pupil more than twenty-four kilometres from the French-language instructional unit,

(a) an allowance payable monthly in an amount set by the board for meals and lodging for each day of attendance as certified by the principal in respect of the French-language instructional unit and for transportation once a week from the pupil's residence to the lodging and return; or

(b) daily transportation in a manner determined by the board from the pupil's residence to the French-language instructional unit and return, where the parent or other person who has lawful custody of the pupil elects to have daily transportation.

292. (1) **French-language advisory committee.**—A board by resolution shall establish a French-language advisory committee and provide for the holding of elections of members of the committee if,

(a) the board does not operate a French-language instructional unit;

(b) the board enters or has entered into an agreement or agreements with another board or boards to enable one or more resident pupils of the board to receive instruction in one or more French-language instructional units operated by the other board or boards;

(c) the calculated enrolment of resident pupils in respect of whom the agreement or agreements are entered into is less than 300 and is less than 10 per cent of the total calculated enrolment of resident pupils of the board; and

(d) ten or more French-speaking ratepayers apply in writing to the board for the establishment of the French-language advisory committee.

(2) **Definitions.**—In this section, "calculated enrolment", "resident pupil" and "total calculated enrolment" have the same meaning as in Part XIII.

(3) **Resolution.**—The board shall pass the resolution and the elections shall be held within two months after receiving the application.

(4) **Composition of committee.**—The committee shall consist of,

(a) not more than three persons appointed by the board from among the members of the board; and

PART XII — FRENCH LANGUAGE INSTRUCTION **S. 292**

(b) six French-speaking ratepayers who are not members of the board but have the qualifications to be elected to the board, elected by French-speaking ratepayers.

(5) **Qualifications.**—A person is qualified to be appointed or elected to the committee if the person is a French-speaking ratepayer and is qualified to be elected to the board.

(6) **Disqualification.**—A person who ceases to be qualified to be elected to a board is not qualified to act as a member of a committee.

(7) **Committee of less than nine members.**—A committee may meet and conduct business although fewer than three persons are appointed to it under clause (4)(a) or fewer than six persons are elected to it under clause (4)(b).

(8) **Application of s. 229.**—Section 229 applies with necessary modifications to a member of a committee under clause (4)(b).

(9) **Term of office.**—A member of a committee shall hold office during the term of the members of the board and until a new board is organized and a successor is appointed or elected, as the case may be.

(10) **Apportionment of members.**—The board, subject to subsections (13) and (14), shall apportion the number of members under clause (4)(b) among the municipalities and the localities, or among parts or groups of such municipalities or localities, within the jurisdiction of the board as nearly as is practicable in the proportion that the number of French-speaking persons who elect to receive their education in a French-language instructional unit from each such municipality, locality or part or group thereof bears to the total number of such pupils within the area of jurisdiction of the board.

(11) **Meetings of French-speaking ratepayers to elect committee members.**—The board shall make provision for a meeting of its French-speaking ratepayers in respect of each area to which one or more members are apportioned under subsection (10) for the purpose of electing such member or members to the committee, and shall advertise in each of its schools and in the public media serving the local population, the place, date and time of the meeting, and take such additional action to publicize the meeting as it considers expedient.

(12) **Idem.**—Where the election of members of a committee under subsection (1) would otherwise be held within three months before the date of the regular election of members of the board, the election required under subsection (1) shall be held in accordance with section 293.

(13) **Consultation with committee re apportionment.**—For the purpose of the second and subsequent elections of members to a committee, the board shall consult with the committee before making the apportionment referred to in subsection (10) and shall make such apportionment on or before the 1st day of November in the year of a regular election of the board.

(14) **Idem.**—Where a board has a committee that was established before the coming into force of this section and the board is required to establish a new committee under subsection (7), the board, for the purpose of making the first apportionments under subsection (10) for the new committee, shall consult with the existing committee before making the apportionment.

(15) **Dissolution.**—A committee is dissolved on the 1st day of December in a year, if no resident pupil of the board has received instruction in a French-language instructional unit operated by another board at some time in October or November of that year pursuant to an agreement described in clause (4)(b).

293. (1) **French-speaking ratepayers to elect subsequent members to committee.**—Where a committee has been established and a new board has been elected, a meeting provided under subsection 292(11) to elect a member or members to the committee shall be held not later than ten days following the first meeting of the newly-elected board commencing at 8 o'clock in the afternoon on such date and at such place as the board may determine, and such meeting may also consider any other matters brought before it, and the provisions of subsection 292(11) respecting the publicizing of the meeting apply.

(2) **Idem.**—The members of the committee to be appointed by the board shall be appointed not later than the date of the election meeting referred to in subsection (1).

294. (1) **Election of chair of meeting.**—The secretary of the board or a person appointed by the board shall call to order each meeting of French-speaking ratepayers under sections 292 and 293 and shall preside thereat for the purpose of electing a chair of the meeting.

(2) **Secretary of meeting.**—The chair of a meeting shall appoint a secretary who shall record the proceedings of the meeting and perform such other duties as are required by the chair.

(3) **Procedure at meeting.**—The chair of a meeting shall conduct the election of the member or members of the committee to be elected at such meeting and shall submit all motions to the meeting in the manner desired by the majority, and the chair is entitled to vote on any motion and, in the case of an equality of votes with respect to the election of a member of the committee, the chair shall provide for drawing lots to determine which of the candidates is elected and a motion on which there is an equality of votes is lost.

(4) **Notice of result of election.**—Notice in writing shall be given by the secretary of a meeting to the secretary of the board designating by their names and addresses the person or persons elected as members of the committee.

295. (1) **Chair and vice-chair of committee.**—At the first meeting of the committee, the members shall elect from among themselves a chair and a vice-chair.

(2) **Quorum.**—A majority of the members of the committee constitutes a quorum, and the vote of a majority of the members present at a meeting is necessary to bind the committee.

(3) **Vote of chair, equality of votes.**—On every motion, the chair may vote, and a motion on which there is an equality of votes is lost.

(4) **Special meeting.**—A special meeting of the committee may be called by the chair of the committee and shall be called by the chair upon the request in writing of two members of the committee who shall specify the objects for which the meeting is to be held, and the objects shall be stated in the notice calling the meeting.

296. (1) **Vacancies.**—Every vacancy on a committee for any cause shall be filled by appointment by the board from among the members of the board in the case of appointed members and by the elected members of the committee in the case of elected members and every person so appointed shall hold office for the unexpired term of the member whose seat has become vacant.

(2) **Application of s. 221(3).**—Subsection 221(3) applies with necessary modifications to the resignation of a member of a committee.

PART XII — FRENCH LANGUAGE INSTRUCTION **S. 298**

297. (1) **Recommendations.**—A committee is responsible for developing proposals designed to meet the educational and cultural needs of the French-speaking pupils and the French-speaking community and for such purpose may make recommendations in respect of,
- (a) the provision of suitable sites, accommodation and equipment;
- (b) the establishment, operation and management of French-language instructional units;
- (c) the use of the French language and of the English language in French-language instructional units;
- (c.1) the use of Quebec Sign Language as a language of instruction;
- (d) the recruitment and appointment of the required teaching, supervisory and administrative personnel;
- (e) the establishment of the course of study and the use of textbooks;
- (f) the development and establishment of special education programs;
- (g) the establishment of attendance areas for French-language instructional units;
- (h) the provision of transportation for pupils;
- (i) the entering into agreements with other boards in respect of the provision of instruction in the French language and supervisory and consultative services;
- (j) the provision of board, lodging, and transportation for pupils;
- (k) the development and establishment of adult education programs;
- (l) the use of any facility and means necessary to meet the educational and cultural needs of the French-speaking community;
- (m) the provision of summer school programs; and
- (n) any other matter pertaining to French-language education for French-speaking pupils.

(2) **Committee report to board.**—The committee shall report at each regular meeting of the board.

(3) **Board to seek advice of committee.**—The board shall seek the advice of the committee on all matters affecting the establishment, program, administration and termination of French-language instructional units or classes, groups of classes or schools in which Quebec Sign Language is the language of instruction before any final decision regarding such matters is taken by the board and shall provide adequate accommodation and staff to implement the decision of the board.

(4) **Consideration of recommendations by board.**—The board shall consider any recommendation submitted to it in writing by the committee and shall not refuse its approval without having given the committee an opportunity to be heard by the board or by any committee of the board to which such recommendation is referred and, where a board refuses a recommendation of the committee, it shall, within thirty days after receiving the recommendation of the committee, forward to the committee written reasons for its refusal.

(5) **Referral by committee to Languages of Instruction Commission.**—Upon receipt of a refusal and the reasons therefor under subsection (4), the committee may, by motion, refer the matter to the Languages of Instruction Commission of Ontario, in which case it shall send to the Commission and to the board copies of the motion, the recommendations of the committee and the written reasons of the board for its refusal. 1993, c. 11, s. 41.

298. (1) **Attendance of committee chair at board meetings.**—The chair of the committee has the right,

S. 299 EDUCATION ACT

(a) to attend meetings of the board in the same manner as a member of the board; and
(b) to participate in the discussion at a meeting of the board in respect of any matter that is within the jurisdiction of the committee under subsection 297(1).

(2) **Presentation of recommendations.**—The chair of the committee has the right to present recommendations of the committee to the board and to speak to the recommendations.

(3) **Designation of member by chair.**—The chair of the committee may designate a member of the committee to act in the place of the chair at any meeting of the board.

(4) **Attendance of committee chair at board committee meeting.**—The chair of the committee or a member of the committee designated by the chair of the committee has the right to attend a meeting of a committee of the board, including a committee of the whole board, and shall be given the opportunity to be heard at the meeting in respect of any matter that affects French-speaking pupils and that is within the jurisdiction of the committee of the board or the committee of the whole board, as the case may be.

(5) **Confidentiality.**—The chair of the committee or a member of the committee designated by the chair of the committee to attend a meeting of the committee of the whole board is subject to the same rule of confidentiality that applies to members of the board.

(6) **Distribution of administrative materials.**—Notices, agendas and minutes in respect of meetings of the board shall be distributed to members of the committee together with such supporting documents as may be agreed upon by the board and the committee.

(7) **Formation of sub-committees.**—The committee may, at its discretion, form sub-committees to assist it in its work.

(8) **Committee may hold public meetings.**—The committee may hold such public meetings to report upon its work as it considers necessary or desirable.

(9) **Declaration.**—Every person elected to a committee, on or before the day of the first meeting of the committee that he or she attends, shall make and subscribe a declaration in the same form with necessary modifications as subsections 209(1) and (2) require of a person elected to a board and, for the purpose,

(a) a reference to a person elected to a board shall be deemed to be a reference to a person elected to a committee;
(b) a reference to a person elected to fill a vacancy on a board shall be deemed to be a reference to a person elected to fill a vacancy on a committee;
(c) a reference to a meeting shall be deemed to be a reference to a meeting of the committee or, if the person is a member of the committee designated by the chair to attend a meeting of the board, a meeting of the committee or of the board; and
(d) a reference to the office of trustee shall be deemed to be a reference to the office of member of the committee.

(10) **Resignation.**—A member of a committee who fails to comply with subsection (9) shall be deemed to have resigned from the committee.

(11) **Filing.**—A member of a committee shall file his or her declaration with the secretary of the board within eight days after making and subscribing the declaration.

299. (1) **Resources and services to be provided by board.**—The board shall make available to the committee the resources and services provided for a committee of the board.

(2) **Annual report of committee.**—The chair of the committee shall cause to be prepared in French and English an annual report, and the report shall be included in that of the board where the board publishes a report.

(2.1) **Same.**—Where a committee is to be dissolved as a result of the operation of section 315.1 or 325.1, the annual report required by subsection (2) shall cover the part of the year that ends with the election.

(3) **Services of professional staff to be provided.**—The committee may, through the chief executive officer of the board, obtain the advice and assistance of such supervisory officers and teachers employed by the board as the committee may request. 1993, c. 41, s. 4.

300. (1) **Allowance.**—Where a board has determined to pay an allowance to members of the board under subsection 191(1), the board shall pay to each member of the committee who is not a member of the board an allowance in such amount as is determined by the board.

(2) **Attendance at meetings and conferences.**—The board may authorize a member of the committee to attend on the same basis as a member of the board such conferences and meetings as the board considers necessary or desirable for the effective functioning of the committee, and subsections 191(10) and (11) apply with necessary modifications to a member of the committee.

(3) **Provincial association membership fee.**—The board shall, on behalf of the members of the committee, pay all or part of a fee required for membership in a provincial association of French-language committees where the committee desires such membership.

301. (1) **English-language classes where French-language school or classes established.**—Where a board has provided one or more French-language secondary schools and a pupil of the board elects to be taught in the English language, section 291 applies with necessary modifications in respect of provision for the use of the English language in instruction.

(2) **English-language advisory committee.**—A board by resolution shall establish an English-language advisory committee and provide for the holding of elections of members of the committee if,

(a) the board does not operate an English-language instructional unit;
(b) the board enters or has entered into an agreement or agreements with another board or boards to enable one or more resident pupils of the board to receive instruction in one or more English-language instructional units operated by the other board or boards;
(c) the calculated enrolment of resident pupils in respect of whom the agreement or agreements are entered into is less than 300 and is less than 10 per cent of the total calculated enrolment of resident pupils of the board; and
(d) ten or more ratepayers apply in writing to the board for the establishment of the English-language advisory committee.

(3) **Application of ss. 291 to 302.**—Sections 291 to 302 apply with necessary modifications in respect of English-language advisory committees.

(4) **Definitions.**—In this section, "calculated enrolment", "resident pupil" and "total calculated enrolment" have the same meanings as in Part XIII.

302. (1) **Admission of pupils other than French-speaking pupils.**—A board, on the request of a pupil of the board who is not a French-speaking person or, where the pupil is a minor, of his or her parent or guardian, may admit the pupil to a French-language instructional unit if the pupil's admission is approved by a majority vote of an admissions committee appointed by the board and composed of the principal of the school in which the French-language instructional unit is operated, a French-language teacher of such school and, subject to subsection (2), a French-speaking supervisory officer employed by the board.

(2) **Where board has no French-speaking supervisory officer.**—Where the board does not employ a French-speaking supervisory officer, it shall arrange for a French-speaking supervisory officer employed by another board or by the Minister to serve as a member of the admissions committee.

Languages of Instruction Commission of Ontario

303. Definitions.—In this section and in sections 304 to 308,

"**Commission**".—"Commission" means the Languages of Instruction Commission of Ontario continued under this Part; ("Commission")

"**committee**".—"committee" means a French-language advisory committee or an English-language advisory committee established under section 292; ("comité")

"**ratepayer**".—"ratepayer", in respect of a board, means a person entitled to vote at an election of members of the board. ("contribuable")

304. (1) **Commission continued.**—The Languages of Instruction Commission of Ontario is continued under the name Languages of Instruction Commission of Ontario in English and Commission des langues d'enseignement de l'Ontario in French and shall be composed of nine members appointed by the Lieutenant Governor in Council, at least four of whom shall be French-speaking and at least four of whom shall be English-speaking, and one of the members shall be appointed as chair.

(2) **Term, reappointment and remuneration.**—Members of the Commission shall hold office for a term of one, two or three years as may be determined from time to time by the Lieutenant Governor in Council, may be reappointed and shall be paid such remuneration as is determined by the Lieutenant Governor in Council.

(3) **Vacancies.**—Where a vacancy occurs in the membership of the Commission, the vacancy may be filled for the unexpired portion of the term of the person whose office has become vacant.

(4) **Commission is responsible to the Minister.**—The Commission is responsible to the Minister for its operation and shall be assisted by such employees in the public service of Ontario as the Minister may assign for the purpose and may, as required from time to time, obtain the services of a lawyer.

(5) **Quorum.**—A quorum consists of three members of whom at least one shall be French-speaking and one English-speaking.

(6) **Recommendation.**—A recommendation of the Commission requires the approval of at least a majority of the members of the Commission.

(7) **Duties of Commission.**—The Commission shall consider matters referred to it by committees and requests for advice and assistance on questions in respect of which a committee may make recommendations, from boards and committees, and where there is no committee,

PART XII — FRENCH LANGUAGE INSTRUCTION S. 304

from a group of ratepayers of the board concerned determined by the Commission to be representative of the French-speaking or English speaking minority, as the case may be, within the jurisdiction of the board.

(7.1) **Same.**—Where the Commission has had a matter referred to it by a committee of a board and the committee has been replaced or is to be replaced by a French-language or English-language section established under Part XIII, the Commission shall take the establishment of the section into account in considering the matter.

(8) **Person to speak for group.**—A group referred to in subsection (7) shall name one of its members to speak for the group.

(9) **Referral to Commission by Minister.**—The Minister may refer to the Commission any matter relating to instruction in the French language or, where the pupils of a board who receive instruction in the English language are a minority of the pupils of a board, any matter relating to instruction in the English language.

(10) **Determination by Commission re establishment of advisory committee.**—Where, within the area of jurisdiction of a board, there is doubt as to whether the French-speaking or English-speaking pupils are in the minority, the Commission has the power to determine whether there shall be a French-language advisory committee or an English-language advisory committee, or both, and the board shall establish such committee or committees as the Commission determines.

(11) **Investigation of irregularity.**—Where, within thirty days of the election of a committee, the board or the committee requests the Commission to investigate an alleged irregularity respecting the election of a member of the committee, the Commission shall investigate such election and give the member an opportunity to make representation to the Commission and shall declare the member to be elected if the Commission finds the election and procedures to be substantially in accordance with this Part or declare the seat vacant if the Commission finds the election and procedures not to be substantially in accordance with this Part and shall send a copy of its decision and reasons therefor to the board or committee and to the member.

(12) **Deferral of action by board.**—When a matter is referred to the Commission, the board concerned shall defer action thereon until the matter has been resolved.

(13) **Commission shall request mediation or reject referral.**—When a matter is referred to the Commission it shall,

(a) forthwith appoint one or more mediators where it considers that the furtherance of such matter may be conducive to meeting the educational and cultural needs of the French-speaking or the English-speaking community; or

(b) except where a matter is referred by the Minister, take no further action where it considers that the furtherance of such matter is not conducive to meeting the educational and cultural needs of the French-speaking or the English-speaking community.

(14) **Where referral rejected.**—Where the Commission takes no further action on a referral it shall forthwith send notice in writing of its decision and of the reasons therefor to the board, the Minister and either the committee or the person named under subsection (8).

(15) **Notice of appointment of mediator.**—Where the Commission makes an appointment under subsection (13) it shall communicate the name and address of each mediator to,

(a) the Minister;

(b) the secretary of the board; and

(c) the chair of the committee,

and where a committee has not been established by a board, to the person named under subsection (8). 1993, c. 41, s. 5.

305. (1) **Remuneration.**—Mediators shall be paid such remuneration as the Lieutenant Governor in Council may determine.

(2) **Who not eligible as mediator.**—A mediator shall not be a member of the Commission.

(3) **Duties of mediator.**—The mediator or mediators shall, after inquiring into the matter referred for mediation and conferring with the parties involved, endeavour to bring about an agreement and shall, within twenty-one days of being appointed, report to the Commission the agreement that has been reached, or the failure to bring about agreement.

(4) **Extension of period of mediation.**—The period referred to in subsection (3) may be extended by the Commission or by agreement of the parties to the mediation.

306. (1) **Duties of Commission.**—Where the report of the mediator or mediators to the Commission indicates failure to bring about an agreement, the Commission shall consider and inquire into all pertinent aspects of the matter referred to mediation and shall, within twenty-one days of its receipt of the report, recommend to the board in writing a course of action that it considers appropriate to settle the matter and shall send copies of its recommendation to the Minister and either the committee or the person named under subsection 304(8).

(2) **Resolution by board.**—Within thirty days of the receipt by the board of the recommendation of the Commission, the board shall resolve either to implement the recommendation or not to implement the recommendation.

(3) **Notice to Commission.**—The board shall give to the Commission written notice of the resolution.

(4) **Where board resolves not to implement recommendation.**—A board that resolves not to implement the recommendation shall also give to the Minister written notice of the resolution and shall give to the Minister and to the Commission written reasons for the decision.

(5) **Time for notices and reasons.**—The board shall give the notices and reasons within the thirty day period mentioned in subsection (2).

307. (1) **Second resolution.**—A board that resolves not to implement the recommendation of the Commission may rescind the resolution and resolve to implement the recommendation.

(2) **Conflict with by-law.**—In the event of a conflict between subsection (1) and a by-law of the board, subsection (1) prevails.

(3) **Time for second resolution.**—A board must act under subsection (1) within sixty days after receiving the recommendation of the Commission.

308. (1) **Reconsideration by Commission.**—Where a board does not resolve to implement the recommendation of the Commission within the period of time mentioned in section 306 or 307, as the case requires, the Commission shall reconsider the matter and shall make a written report and recommendation to the Minister in respect of the matter.

(2) **Order by Minister.**—The Minister shall consider the report and recommendation of the Commission under subsection (1) and shall make such order to the board or the Commission, or both, to deal with the matter as the Minister considers appropriate in the circumstances.

(3) **Report and recommendation not binding on Minister.**—The report and recommendation of the Commission are not binding upon the Minister, and the Minister is not required to give to any person an opportunity to make submissions or to be heard before making an order under subsection (2).

(4) **Enforcement of order.**—An order by the Minister under subsection (2), exclusive of the reasons, if any, therefor may be filed in the Ontario Court (General Division), whereupon the order shall be entered in the same way as a judgment or order of that court and is enforceable as an order of that court.

(5) **Service of order.**—An order by the Minister under subsection (2),
  (a) to a board is effective according to its terms when a copy is served upon the secretary of the board; and
  (b) to the Commission is effective according to its terms when a copy is served upon the chair of the Commission.

PART XIII

GOVERNANCE OF FRENCH-LANGUAGE INSTRUCTION

309. (1) **Definitions.**—In this Part,

"**board**".—"board" means,
  (a) a board of education, other than a board of education for an area municipality in The Municipality of Metropolitan Toronto, the members of which are elected under the *Municipal Elections Act*, or
  (b) a county or district combined separate school board; ("conseil")

"**calculated enrolment**".—"calculated enrolment" means a number of pupils enrolled in French-language instructional units, calculated in accordance with the regulations; ("effectif calculé")

"**estimated revenues**".—"estimated revenues" means revenues from all sources receivable by a board as set out in the estimates prepared and adopted by the board; ("recettes prévues")

"**French-language**".—"French-language", in relation to a resident pupil, means a resident pupil enrolled in a French-language instructional unit; ("de langue française")

"**French-language instructional unit**".—"French-language instructional unit" means a class, group of classes or school under Part XII in which the French language is the language of instruction or a class, group of classes or school in which Quebec Sign Language is the language of instruction but does not include a class, group of classes or school established under paragraph 25 of subsection 8(1) (French-language instruction for English-speaking pupils); ("module scolaire de langue française")

"**regular election**".—"regular election" has the same meaning as in the *Municipal Elections Act*; ("élection ordinaire")

"resident pupil".—"resident pupil", in respect of a board, means a pupil who is registered on a register or registers prescribed by the Minister for the purposes of this Part and who is qualified to be a resident pupil of the board and is enrolled in a school,

(a) operated by the board, or
(b) operated by another board to which the first-mentioned board pays fees in respect of the pupil; ("élève résident")

"total calculated enrolment".—"total calculated enrolment" means a number of pupils calculated in accordance with the regulations. ("effectif total calculé")

(2) **French day nurseries.**—The establishment, operation and maintenance by a board of day nurseries in which French is the language ordinarily spoken is within the exclusive jurisdiction of the French-language section of the board.

(3) **Corporation.**—For the purpose of subsection (2) and the *Day Nurseries Act*, the French-language section shall be deemed to be a corporation. 1993, c. 11, s. 42; c. 27, *Schedule*.

310. Regulations.—The Lieutenant Governor in Council may by regulation prescribe the method of calculation of calculated enrolment and total calculated enrolment.

311. (1) **French-language section.**—Every board that operates a French-language instructional unit shall have a French-language section of the board.

(2) **300 resident pupils.**—Every board that enters or has entered into an agreement or agreements with another board or boards to enable a calculated enrolment of at least 300 resident pupils of the board to receive instruction in one or more French-language instructional units operated by the other board or boards shall have a French-language section of the board.

(3) **10 per cent enrolment.**—Every board that enters or has entered into an agreement or agreements with another board or boards to enable a calculated enrolment of at least 10 per cent of the resident pupils of the board to receive instruction in one or more French-language instructional units operated by the other board or boards shall have a French-language section of the board.

(4) **Minority.**—Subsections (1) to (3) apply only if the calculated enrolment of French-language resident pupils of the board is a minority of the total calculated enrolment of resident pupils of the board.

(5) **Exception.**—Despite any other provision of this Part, a French-language section of a board shall not be elected under section 315 or 325 at a regular election if on the first day of the school year commencing in the year in which the regular election is to be held, the board is not operating a French-language instructional unit and it is not providing education for at least 285 of its resident pupils or at least 9.50 per cent of its resident pupils pursuant to an agreement as described in subsection (2) or (3). 1993, c. 41, s. 6.

312. Authority of French-language section.—The French-language section of a board shall govern for the board the French-language instructional units of the board.

313. Qualifications of members of French-language section.—A person is qualified to be elected as a member of the French-language section of a board if,

(a) the person is qualified to be elected as a member of the board;
(b) the person has the right under subsection 23(1) or (2), without regard to subsection

PART XIII — GOVERNANCE OF FRENCH-LANGUAGE INSTRUCTION   S. 315

23(3), of the *Canadian Charter of Rights and Freedoms* to have his or her children receive their primary and secondary school instruction in the French language in Ontario; and

(c) the person chooses to vote only for members of the French-language section of the board and not for any other member of the board.

314. (1) **Elector.**—A person is qualified to be an elector in respect of a member of the French-language section of a board if,

(a) the person is qualified to vote in a regular election of members of the board;

(b) the person has the right under subsection 23(1) or (2), without regard to subsection 23(3), of the *Canadian Charter of Rights and Freedoms* to have his or her children receive their primary and secondary school instruction in the French language in Ontario; and

(c) the person chooses to vote only for members of the French-language section of the board and not for any other member of the board.

(2) **Idem.**—No person is entitled to vote in a regular election for both members of the French-language section of a board and other members of the board.

315. (1) **Election.**—The members of the French-language section of a board shall be elected in accordance with this section by the persons qualified to vote for members of the French-language section of the board.

(2) **General vote.**—Subject to subsections (3) to (6), the members of the French-language section of a board shall be elected by general vote.

(3) **Idem.**—For a regular election to be held in 1991, or thereafter, where a board has a French-language section, the section may divide the area of jurisdiction of the board into electoral areas for the purposes of electing the members of the next section and for filling vacancies therein and determine the representation for each electoral area.

(4) **Public meeting.**—Before passing a resolution under subsection (3), the French-language advisory committee, or French-language section of a board, as the case may be, shall hold at least one public meeting at which French-speaking ratepayers shall be given an opportunity to make representations on the proposed electoral areas.

(5) **Final determination.**—Following the public meeting or meetings held under subsection (4), the electoral areas may be fixed as originally proposed or with such amendments as the committee, council or section of a board, as the case may be, considers appropriate and without holding any further public meetings.

(6) **Idem.**—Where electoral areas have been established for an election, the members of the French-language section shall be elected by general vote in each electoral area.

(7) **Idem.**—A resolution to establish electoral areas is of no effect unless it is passed before the 1st day of August in the year of the regular election to which it relates and unless before that date a certified copy of the resolution is delivered to the clerks of the municipalities responsible for conducting the nominations of the members of the French-language section of the board.

(8) **Boundaries.**—The clerk of a municipality shall adjust a boundary of an electoral area so as to prevent the division of polling subdivisions established for the election.

S. 315.1 EDUCATION ACT

(9) **Election officers.**—The election of members of a French-language section of a board shall be conducted by the same officers and in the same manner as elections of members of the council of a municipality.

(10) **Idem.**—For the purpose of performing the function of returning officer, the secretary of the board shall be the clerk of each part of territory without municipal organization in the area of jurisdiction of the board that is deemed to be a district municipality for school purposes.

(11) **Information.**—A clerk described in subsection (7) shall provide to the clerks of the other municipalities, if any, in the area of jurisdiction of the board such information as is required by them to conduct the election of the members of the French-language section of the board.

(12) **Application of section 230.**—Despite subsections (1) to (11), the French-language section of a board may by resolution approved by a majority of the members of the section direct that an election of members to the section shall be subject to subsections 230(15) to (28).

1993, c. 27, *Schedule*.

315.1. (1) **Application of section.**—This section applies only where the calculated enrolment of French-language resident pupils of the board is a miunority of the total calculated enrolment of resident pupils of the board.

(2) **Special election of French-language section.**—Every board that does not have a French-Language section but that resolves to operate a French-language instructional unit shall, within three months of passing the resolution, hold a special election for a three member French-language section of the board.

(3) **Same.**—Despite subsection (2), if a regular election is to be held later in the calendar year in which the resolution was passed, the board shall not hold the special election.

(4) **Same.**—Despite subsection (3), a board may nevertheless resolve to hold the special election, so long as it is held before April 1 of the year in which the resolution was passed.

(5) **Non-application of sections 313 to 315.**—Sections 313 to 315 do not apply to special elections held under this section.

(6) **Qualifications of members of French-language section.**—A person is qualified to be elected under this section as a member of the French-language section of a board if,

(a) the person is qualified to be elected as a member of the board; and

(b) the person has the right under subsection 23(1) or (2), without regard to subsection 23(3), of the *Canadian Charter of Rights and Freedoms* to have his or her children receive their primary and secondary school instruction in the French language in Ontario.

(7) **Electors.**—A person is qualified to be an elector in an election under this section in respect of a member of the French-language section of a board if,

(a) the person is qualified to vote in a regular election of members of the board; and

(b) the person has the right under subsection 23(1) or (2), without regard to subsection 23(3), of the *Canadian Charter of Rights and Freedoms* to have his or her children receive their primary and secondary school instruction in the French language in Ontario.

(8) **Whether members to be apportioned by area.**—A board that is to hold an election under this section shall decide whether the three members of the French-language section are

PART XIII — GOVERNANCE OF FRENCH-LANGUAGE INSTRUCTION **S. 315.1**

to be elected for the board's area of jurisdiction as a whole or in accordance with an apportionment.

(9) **Apportionment of members**—A board that decides under subsection (8) that an election is to be held in accordance with an apportionment shall apportion the three members to be elected to the French-language section among geographic areas within the area of jurisdiction of the board as nearly as is practicable in the proportion that the number of resident pupils of the board receiving their education in a French-language instructional unit from each such area bears to the total number of such pupils from the total area of jurisdiction of the board.

(10) **Consultation with French-language advisory committee.**—The board shall consult with the French-language advisory committee of the board, if any, before making a decision under subsection (8) and before making an apportionment under subsection (9).

(11) **Meetings to elect French-language section members.**—A board that is to hold an election for the board's area of jurisdiction as a whole shall make provision for a meeting of electors for the purpose of electing by general vote the three members of the French-language section.

(12) **Same.**—A board that is to hold an election in accordance with an apportionment under subsection (9) shall make provision for a meeting of electors in respect of each area to which one or more members are apportioned for the purpose of electing by general vote the member or members of the French-language section apportioned to the area.

(13) **Same.**—A board shall advertise in each of its schools and in the public media serving the local population, the place, date and time of meetings under subsections (11) and (12) and shall take any additional action to publicize the meeting that it considers expedient.

(14) **Procedure at meeting**—Section 294 applies with necessary modifications to an election held under this section.

(15) **Appointments to French-language section by Minister.**—Where, following an election under this section, there are fewer than three members of the French-language section of a board, the Minister, by order, shall appoint as many qualified persons as members of the French-language section as are necessary to provide for a three member section.

(16) **Term of office.**—A person elected or appointed under this section to a French-language section of a board shall hold office during the term of the members of the board elected at the last regular election.

(17) **When French-language section deemed constituted.**—For the purposes of subsections (18) and (19), the French-language section of a board shall be deemed to be constituted when two of its members have been elected or appointed.

(18) **Taking office.**—Members elected or appointed under this section to the French-language section of a board shall take office in accordance with section 209 of the first Monday of the month following the constitution of the French-language section.

(19) **Same.**—Despite subsection (18), where a person is elected or appointed under this section after the constitution of the French-language section, the person shall take office immediately, in accordance with section 209.

S. 316 EDUCATION ACT

(20) **Dissolution of French-language advisory committee.**—The French-language advisory committee of a board under Part XII is dissolved when the members of the French-language section of the board take office under subsection (18). 1993, c. 41, s. 7.

316. Meetings, etc.—Sections 207 and 208, except subsection 208(11), apply with necessary modifications to a French-language section of a board.

317. (1) **Areas of representation.**—Where a board is required to have a French-language section and the areas to be represented by members of the board are fixed by or under this or any other Act, the Minister, after considering the recommendations, if any, of the board, may by order,

(a) change the areas to be represented by one or more members of the board who are not members of the French-language section; and

(b) prescribe a different method of determining the areas to be represented by one or more members of the board who are not members of the French language section.

(2) **Limitation.**—A member of a French-language section of a board shall not vote on any recommendations that the board proposes to make under subsection (1). 1993, c. 27, *Schedule*.

318. (1) **Jurisdiction.**—The following matters are within the exclusive jurisdiction of the French-language section of a board:

1. The planning and establishment of French-language instructional units, including the preparation and submission of capital expenditure forecasts in respect of such units to the board for submission to the Ministry.
2. The administration and the closing of French-language instructional units.
3. Admissions committees under subsection 289(6) and section 302.
4. The planning, establishment, implementation and maintenance of programs and courses for pupils enrolled in a French-language instructional unit.
5. The recruitment and assignment of teachers and administrative and supervisory personnel for French-language instructional units.
6. Entering into agreements under section 181 (provision of accommodation or services to another board), 184 (furnishing or obtaining education for pupils), 185 (public and separate school boards), 186 (furnishing or obtaining secondary school education for pupils) or 189 (adult basic education) in respect of pupils in French-language instructional units.

(2) **Excluded matters.**—The following matters are outside the jurisdiction of the French-language section of a board and its members:

1. The planning and establishment of schools that are not French-language instructional units, including the preparation and submission of capital expenditure forecasts to the board for submission to the Ministry in respect of such schools.
2. The administration and the closing of schools that are not French-language instructional units.
3. The planning, establishment, implementation and maintenance of programs and courses for pupils enrolled in a school or class that is not a French-language instructional unit.
4. The recruitment and assignment of teachers and administrative and supervisory personnel for schools and classes mentioned in paragraph 3.

PART XIII — GOVERNANCE OF FRENCH-LANGUAGE INSTRUCTION **S. 319**

5. Entering into agreements under section 181 (provision of accommodation or services to another board), 184 (furnishing or obtaining education for pupils), 185 (public and separate school boards), 186 (furnishing or obtaining secondary school education for pupils) or 189 (adult basic education) in respect of pupils in a school or class that is not under Part XII.

(3) **Common jurisdiction.**—In respect of any matter not referred to in subsection (1) or (2), including the employment of the director of education, a member of the French-language section of a board has the same powers, duties, rights and responsibilities as a member of the board who is not a member of the French-language section.

(4) **Quorum.**—The following rules apply with respect to quorums where a board has a French-language section:

1. The presence of a majority of all the members constituting the board is necessary to form a quorum when dealing with a matter that is not a matter to which paragraph 2 or 3 applies.
2. The presence of a majority of all the members of a French-language section of a board is necessary to form a quorum when dealing with matters within the exclusive jurisdiction of the French-language section of the board.
3. The presence of a majority of all members of a board who are not members of the French-language section of the board is necessary to form a quorum when dealing with matters outside the jurisdiction of the French-language section of the board.
4. Where the board is a board of education and the board, other than the French-language section, is composed, in part, of members who are elected by separate school electors, for the purposes of paragraph 3, when dealing with matters that affect public schools exclusively, the presence of a majority of the members elected to the board by the public school electors is necessary to form a quorum.
5. Subsection 208(11) does not apply.

(5) **Change of jurisdiction.**—If a majority of the members of the French-language section of a board and a majority of the other members of the board each resolve that a matter that is a centralized service, as defined in subsection 319(5), shall be within the exclusive jurisdiction of the French-language section of the board or outside the jurisdiction of the French-language section of the board and its members, subsections (1) and (2) shall be deemed to be modified accordingly in respect of the board, and the secretary of the board shall transmit to the Minister notice of the change of jurisdiction.

(6) **Reversion of jurisdiction.**—A resolution passed under subsection (5) shall cease to have effect at the end of the term of the members in office when the resolution was passed unless a majority of the members of the French-language section of the board and a majority of the other members of the board resolve that it shall cease to have effect at an earlier date.

319. (1) **Application.**—This section applies to every board that has a French-language section under this Part.

(2) **Allocation of estimated revenues.**—After the estimates of the board in respect of a year are approved or adopted, as the case requires, the board shall allocate the amounts of its estimated revenues for the year as follows:

1. Firstly, to the specific educational programs or specific schools or classes that generated a portion of the estimated revenues, in amounts equal to the amounts generated.

S. 320 EDUCATION ACT

    2.   Secondly, to the centralized services of the board, in amounts equal to the amounts set out for the centralized services in the estimates.

    3.   Thirdly, to all the schools and classes operated by the board.

(3) **Schools and classes.**—The board shall allocate the estimated revenues under paragraph 3 of subsection (2) to the schools and classes that are French-language instructional units in the ratio that the average daily enrolment in those schools and classes is to the average daily enrolment of the board in all schools and classes mentioned in the paragraph.

(4) **Balance of schools and classes.**—The board shall allocate the estimated revenues under paragraph 3 of subsection (2) to the balance of the schools and classes that are not French-language instructional units in the ratio that the average daily enrolment in those schools and classes is to the average daily enrolment of the board in all schools and classes mentioned in the paragraph.

(5) **Definition.**—In this section, ''centralized services'' means,

(a) salaries, benefits and professional development of employees but excluding employees whose recruitment and assignment is specified in this Part as either within the exclusive jurisdiction of the French-language section of the board or outside the jurisdiction of the French-language section of the board and its members,

(b) normal maintenance of and operational services and equipment required for school sites,

(c) school supplies other than instructional and learning materials,

(d) transportation of pupils to and from school and from school to school,

(e) allocation to reserve funds and the reserve for working funds,

(f) establishment and maintenance of the head office of the board, including services operated therefrom,

(g) permanent improvements other than the replacement for schools and classes of furniture, furnishings, library books and instructional equipment and apparatus, and

(h) expenditures that are not within clauses (a) to (g) but that are approved from time to time by the board.

320. (1) **Duty of board.**—Every board shall ensure that the matters that are within the exclusive jurisdiction and the matters that are outside the jurisdiction of the French-language section of the board are provided for when the board prepares and adopts its estimates and when the board allocates its estimated revenues.

(2) **Variation.**—Subject to subsection (1), a board may vary an allocation in order to accommodate a change in circumstances or assumptions upon which the estimates of the board were made.

321. (1) **Annual filing by boards.**—Every board shall file annually with the Ministry a report in the prescribed form in respect of the enrolment of resident pupils of the board in schools and classes operated as French-language instructional units and in respect of the enrolment of resident pupils of the board in schools and classes not operated as French-language instructional units.

(2) **Counting date.**—Every board shall compile the date mentioned in subsection (1) as of the 30th day of September in each year.

PART XIII — GOVERNANCE OF FRENCH-LANGUAGE INSTRUCTION   S. 324

322. (1) **Calculated enrolment.**—A determination of the calculated enrolment of a board and the total calculated enrolment of a board shall be made by the appropriate supervisory officer of the board.

(2) **When calculation made.**—The calculated enrolment and the total calculated enrolment shall be determined on or before the 1st day of February in the year in which a regular election will be held under the *Municipal Elections Act*.

(3) **Approval of calculation.**—On or before the 1st day of March in a year in which a regular election will be held under the *Municipal Elections Act*, the determination of the calculated enrolment and the total calculated enrolment made under subsection (1) shall be confirmed by resolution by,

(a) a majority of the members of the board who are members of the French-language section; and

(b) a majority of the members of the board who are not members of the French-language section.

(4) **Referral to the Languages of Instruction Commission of Ontario.**—If no determination is made under subsection (1) or a determination is not confirmed under subsection (3), the appropriate supervisory officer shall refer the matter to the Languages of Instruction Commission of Ontario on or before the 15th day of March in a year in which a regular election will be held under the *Municipal Elections Act*.

(5) **Idem.**—The Languages of Instruction Commission of Ontario shall determine the calculated enrolment and the total calculated enrolment of the board and shall notify the appropriate supervisory officer of its determination not later than twenty days after the referral under subsection (4).

(6) **Idem.**—If a determination is made under subsection (5), it shall be used in place of any other determination.

323. (1) **Liaison committee.**—Any two or more committees established by boards under Part XII or French-language sections of boards, or any combination of such committees and French-language sections, may establish a liaison committee which shall be known as a regional committee for French-language education.

(2) **Function.**—A regional committee for French-language education may consider and make recommendations to the French-language section of a board or to the committee established by a board under Part XII on any matter that affects French-language education.

324. (1) **Notice to Minister.**—Where a French-language section becomes aware that it will not be operating a French-language instructional unit and it will not be providing education for at least 285 resident pupils of the board or at least 9.50 per cent of the resident pupils of the board pursuant to an agreement as described in subsection 311(2) or (3), the French-language section shall forthwith notify in writing the full board of such fact and the effective date thereof and the board shall forthwith notify in writing the Minister.

(2) **Dissolution.**—Unless the notice to the Minister under subsection (1) is revoked, the French-language section of a board in respect of which a notice is required to be given to the Minister is dissolved on the thirtieth day next following the date upon which the section ceases

to operate a unit or provide the education referred to in subsection (1) and the members shall cease to hold office on that date.

(3) **Revocation of notice.**—A board, upon written request of the French-language section of the board that is received before the dissolution of the French-language section of the board, shall revoke by notice in writing delivered to the Minister, a notice given to the Minister under subsection (1).

(4) **Section 182 agreement distinguished.**—Where a public board agrees to transfer a secondary school established and operated under Part XII to a Roman Catholic school board under section 182, the agreement to transfer is not an agreement referred to in subsections 311(2) and (3).

(5) **Deemed application.**—Where a French-language section of a board is dissolved, at least ten French-speaking ratepayers, within the meaning of Part XII of the Act, shall be deemed to have applied to the board on the day of the dissolution for the establishment of a French-language advisory committee.

325. (1) **English as language of instruction.**—There shall be an English-language section of a board and this Part shall apply with necessary modifications in respect of the board and in respect of the English-language section of the board if the calculated enrolment of English-language resident pupils of the board is a minority of the total calculated enrolment of the resident pupils of the board and,

(a) the board operates an English-language instructional unit under Part XII;

(b) the board enters or has entered into an agreement or agreements with another board or boards to enable a calculated enrolment of at least 300 resident pupils of the board to receive instruction in one or more English-language instructional units operated by the other board or boards; or

(c) the board enters or has entered into an agreement or agreements with another board or boards to enable a calculated enrolment of at least 10 per cent of the resident pupils of the board to receive instruction in one or more English-language instructional units operated by the other board or boards.

(c.1) a reference in this Part or in a regulation under this Part to "Quebec Sign Language" shall be deemed to be a reference to "American Sign Language"; and

(2) **Interpretation.**—For the purposes of subsection (1),

(a) a reference in this Part or in a regulation under this Part to "French-speaking" shall be deemed to be a reference to "English-speaking";

(b) a reference in this Part, other than in subsection (3), or in a regulation under this Part to "French-language" shall be deemed to be a reference to "English-language";

(c) a reference in this Part or in a regulation under this Part to "French language" shall be deemed to be a reference to the "English language";

(c.1) a reference in this Part or in a regulation under this Part to "Quebec Sign Language" shall be deemed to be a reference to "American Sign Language"; and

(d) a reference in this Part, other than in subsection (3), to a person who has the right under subsection 23(1) or (2), without regard to subsection 23(3), of the *Canadian Charter of Rights and Freedoms* to have his or her children receive their primary and secondary school instruction in the French language in Ontario shall be deemed to

PART XIII — GOVERNANCE OF FRENCH-LANGUAGE INSTRUCTION **S. 325.1**

be a reference to a person who does not have that right and to be a reference to a person who has but elects not to exercise that right.

(3) **French as majority.**—Where a board has an English-language section other than an English-language section elected under section 325.1, the other members of the board must have the qualifications to be elected as a member of a French-language section of a board as described in section 313 and an elector of such other members must have the qualifications to be an elector in respect of a French-language section of a board as described in section 314.

1993, c. 11, s. 43; c. 41, s. 8.

325.1 (1) **Definitions.**—In this section,

"**calculated enrolment**".—"calculated enrolment" has the meaning given to it by section 309, except that the reference to "French-language instructional units" shall be deemed to be a reference to "English-language instructional units"; ("effectif calculé")

"**English-language instructional unit**".—"English-language instructional unit" means a class, group of classes or school in which the English language is the language of instruction and includes a class, group of classes or school established under paragraph 25 of subsection 8 (1). ("module scolaire de langue anglaise")

(2) **Application of section.**—This section applies only where the calculated enrolment of English-language resident pupils of the board is a minority of the total calculated enrolment of resident pupils of the board.

(3) **Special election of English-language section.**—Every board that does not have an English-language section but that resolves to operate an English-language instructional unit shall, within three months of passing the resolution, hold a special election for a three member English-language section of the board.

(4) **Same.**—Despite subsection (3), if a regular election is to be held later in the calendar year in which the resolution was passed, the board shall not hold the special election.

(5) **Same.**—Despite subsection (4), a board may nevertheless resolve to hold the special election, so long as it is held before April 1 of the year in which the resolution was passed.

(6) **Qualifications of members of English-language section.**—A person is qualified to be elected under this section as a member of the English-language section of a board if the person is qualified to be elected as a member of the board.

(7) **Electors.**—A person is qualified to be an elector in an election under this section in respect of a member of the English-language section of a board if the person is qualified to vote in a regular election of members of the board.

(8) **Application of subsections 315.1(5) and (8) to (20).**—Subsections 315.1(5) and (8) to (20) apply with necessary modifications where a board holds an election under this section.

(9) **Same.**—For the purposes of subsection (8),

(a) a reference in section 315.1 to a French-language advisory committee shall be deemed to be a reference to an English-language advisory committee;

(b) a reference in section 315.1 to a French-language instructional unit shall be deemed to be a reference to an English-language instructional unit; and

(c) a reference in section 315.1 to a French-language section shall be deemed to be a reference to an English-language section.

(10) **Non-application of subsection 325(3).**—Subsection 325 (3) does not apply where the English-language section is elected under this section. 1993, c. 41, s. 9.

326. (1) **Forms.**—The Minister may prescribe the form of the report under subsection 321(1) and require its use for the purposes of this Part.

(2) **Application of *Regulations Act*.**—An act of the Minister under subsection (1) is not a regulation within the meaning of the *Regulations Act*.

REGULATIONS UNDER THE EDUCATION ACT
TABLE OF CONTENTS

REGULATION 283 — CALCULATION OF AMOUNT OF RESERVE OR REDUCTION IN REQUIREMENT RESULTING FROM STRIKE OR LOCK-OUT 243
   1. General 243
   2. Calculation of reserve under s. 237(2) of the Act 243
   3. Calculation of reserve under s. 238(2) of the Act 244

REGULATION 284 — CONDITIONS FOR EXTENDED FUNDING 245
   1. Definitions 245
   2. Conditions 245

REGULATION 285 — CONTINUING EDUCATION 246

PART I

   1. Continuing education courses and classes 246
   2. Powers of board 247
   3. Teacher's qualification 247

PART II

   4. Definitions 247
   5. Establishment of programs 248
   6. French-speaking persons 249
   7. Daily limit 249
   8. Day classes at school 249
   9. Night classes 249
   10. Discontinuance of program 249

REGULATION 286 — COUNTY COMBINED SEPARATE SCHOOL ZONES 250
   1. List of county combined separate school zones 250

REGULATION 287 — DESIGNATION OF SCHOOL DIVISIONS 252
   1. Designation of school divisions 252
      Schedules 1-28   School divisions 252

REGULATION 288 — DESIGNATION OF SUPPORT STAFF 263
   1. Definitions 263
   2. Application 263
   3. Transferred school 263
   4. Identification of unrequired and surplus positions at public board 264
   5. Vacancies at Roman Catholic school board 264

REGULATIONS UNDER THE EDUCATION ACT

6.	Designation of voluntary transferees	264
7.	Provision of list of voluntary transferees	265
8.	Copies of list to parties in employee agreements	265
9.	Offer on vacancy at public board	265
10.	Objection	265

REGULATION 289 — DESIGNATION OF TEACHERS 266

1.	Definitions	266
2.	Application	266
3.	Identification of unrequired teachers	266
4.	Calculation of enrolment shift	267
5.	Determining staff reductions	269
6.	Vacancies at Roman Catholic school board	269
7.	Provision of list of voluntary transferees	269
8.	Designation of voluntary transferees	270
9.	Copies of list to branch affiliates	270
10.	Consultation with branch affiliates	270
11.	Agreements for transfer between Roman Catholic school boards	270
12.	Offer on vacancy at public board	270
13.	Objection	271
14.	Designation of all teachers at transferred school	271
15.	French-language schools	271
16.	Deemed designation	271

REGULATION 290 — DISTRICT COMBINED SEPARATE SCHOOL ZONES ... 272

| 1. | Designation of district combined separate school zones | 272 |
| 2. | Schedules 1-18   District combined separate school zones | 272 |

REGULATION 291 — DISTRICT SCHOOL AREAS 280

| 1.-12. | District school areas | 280 |
| | Schedules | 280 |

REGULATION 292 — FEES FOR MINISTRY COURSES 284

1.	Definition	284
2.	Tuition fee	284
3.	Non-attendance and withdrawal	284

REGULATION 293 — FEES FOR TRANSCRIPTS AND STATEMENTS OF STANDING AND FOR DUPLICATES OF DIPLOMAS, CERTIFICATES AND LETTERS OF STANDING 285

| 1.-4. | Fees | 285 |

REGULATION 294 — THE JAMES BAY LOWLANDS SECONDARY SCHOOL BOARD 286

| 1. | Definitions | 286 |

TABLE OF CONTENTS

2.	Board continued	286
3.	Members	286
4.	Disqualifications	287
5.	Meetings to elect members	287
6.	Apportionment	287
7.	Application of s. 235 of the Act	288
8.	Meeting of electors of secondary school district	288
	Schedule	288

REGULATION 295 — THE NORTHERN DISTRICT SCHOOL
AREA BOARD 289

1.	Definitions	289
2.	Board continued	289
3.	Members	289
4.	Meetings to elect members	289

REGULATION 296 — ONTARIO SCHOOLS FOR THE BLIND
AND THE DEAF 291

1.	Definitions	291
2.	Designations	291
3.-8.	Admissions	291
9.-12.	Fees	293
13.	Transportation	294
14.	Duties of pupils	294
15.	Duties of Teachers	294
16.	Duties of Residence Counsellors	295
17.	Parents	295
18.-21.	Duties of Superintendent	296
22.	Superintendent's Advisory Council	298
23.	Qualifications of Teachers	298

REGULATION 297 — ONTARIO TEACHER'S QUALIFICATIONS 299

1.	Definitions	299

PART I — BASIC QUALIFICATIONS

2.-3.	Qualification for Certificate and Record Card	301
4.	Language	302
4.1	Entry on record card	302
5.	Native ancestry	302
6.	Lack of entitlement	303
7.	Qualification for Provisional Letter of Standing	303
8.	Renewal of Provisional Letter of Standing	303
9.	Deemed Provisional Letter of Standing	304
10.	Granting of Certificate and Record Card	304

REGULATIONS UNDER THE EDUCATION ACT

11.-16.	Temporary Letters of Standing	304
17.	Granting of Certificate and Record Card	306
18.	Extension of Temporary Letter of Standing	306
19.	Permanent Letter of Standing to teach the deaf	307
20.-22.	Provisional and Permanent Letter of Standing to teach the trainable retarded	308
23.	Provisional Letter to teach a Native language as a second language	309
24.	Extension of Provisional Letter to teach a Native language as a second language	309
25.	Permanent Letter to teach a Native language as a second language	309
25.1	Provisional Letter to teach dance	310
25.2	Granting of Ontario Teacher's Certificate	311
26.	Deemed to hold Ontario Teacher's Certificate	311
27.	Qualifications of other miscellaneous teachers	312

PART II — ADDITIONAL QUALIFICATIONS FOR TEACHERS

28.	Minimum course length	313
29.-30.	Additional areas of concentration	313
31.	One session courses	314
32.-37.	Three-session specialist courses	315
38.-39.	One-session honour specialist course	317
40.-49.	Principal's qualifications	319

PART III — LETTERS OF PERMISSION

50.	Letters of permission	321

PART IV — TEMPORARY LETTERS OF APPROVAL

51.	Temporary letters of approval	321
	Schedule A Intermediate and Senior Division Options taken in English or French	322
	Schedule B Technological Studies Options taken in English or French	323
	Schedule C One-Session Qualifications taken in English or French	324
	Schedule D Three-Session Qualifications taken in English or French	325
	Schedule E Honour Specialist Qualifications taken in English or French	326
	Form 1 Ontario Teacher's Certificate	326
	Form 2 Ontario Teacher's Qualifications Record Card	327
	Form 3 Temporary Letter of Standing	328
	Form 4 Provisional Letter of Standing	329
	Form 5 Letter of Eligibility	330
	Form 6 Permanent Letter of Standing	333
	Form 7 Application for Letter of Permission	334
	Form 8 Application for Temporary Letter of Approval	335

TABLE OF CONTENTS

Form 9 Permanent Letter of Standing (for) Teacher of a Native Language as a Second Language ... 337
Form 10 Provisional Letter of Standing — Dance ... 338
Form 11 Permanent Letter of Standing — Dance ... 339

REGULATION 298 — OPERATION OF SCHOOLS — GENERAL ... 340
1. Definitions ... 340
2. Accommodation ... 340
3. Daily sessions ... 340
4. Opening or closing exercises ... 341
5. Flag ... 341
6. Emergency procedures ... 341
7. Textbooks ... 342
8. Elementary school boards ... 342
9.-10. Qualifications for Principals and Vice-principals ... 342
11. Duties of principals ... 344
12. Vice-principals ... 346
13. Principals, vice-principals and teachers in charge of schools and classes established under Part XII of the Act ... 346
14.-15. Teachers in charge of organizational units ... 347
16. Duties of teachers in charge of organizational units ... 348
17.-18. Subject and program supervision and co-ordination ... 348
19. Qualifications of teachers ... 349
20. Duties of teachers ... 352
21. Appointment to teach in the case of an emergency ... 353
22. Cancelled and suspended certificates ... 353
23. Requirements for pupils ... 353
24. Advertisements and announcements ... 354
25. Canvassing and fund-raising ... 354
26. Supervision ... 354
27.-29. Religion in schools ... 354
30.-31. Special education programs and services ... 355

REGULATION 299 — PAYMENT OF LEGISLATIVE GRANTS ... 357
1. Payment of legislative grants ... 357

REGULATION 300 — PRACTICE AND PROCEDURE — BOARDS OF REFERENCE ... 358
1. Definitions ... 358
2. Parties ... 358
3. Rules ... 358
4. Reference books ... 358
5. Documents to be filed with chair of Board ... 358
6. Order of presentation of evidence ... 359

REGULATIONS UNDER THE EDUCATION ACT

7.	Admissible evidence	360
8.	Record to be made	360
9.	Language	360
10.	Interpreter	360
11.	Judicial review acts as stay	360
12.	Adjudicator must hear evidence	360
13.	Remuneration	360
14.	Calling an opposite party as witness	361
15.	Examination of witness unable to attend	361
16.	Exclusion of witness or of evidence	361
17.	Forwarding of record to Minister	361

REGULATION 301 — PUPIL RECORDS 362
        REVOKED: O. Reg. 212/91 362

REGULATION 302 — PURCHASE OF MILK 362
1.	Authorization	362
2.	Conditions	362

REGULATION 303 — REGIONAL TRIBUNALS 363
1.	Composition	363
2.	Jurisdiction	363
3.-4.	Ineligibility for membership	364
5.	Language	364
6.	Arrangements	364

REGULATION 304 — SCHOOL YEAR AND SCHOOL HOLIDAYS 365
1.	Definitions	365
2.	School year, school holidays and professional activity days	365
3.	Examination days	366
4.	School calendars	366
5.	School calendars not following s. 2 of this Regulation	366
6.	Alteration	366
7.	Publication of school calendar	367
8.	Evaluation of professional activity days	367
9.	Remembrance Day	367

REGULATION 305 — SPECIAL EDUCATION IDENTIFICATION PLACEMENT AND REVIEW COMMITTEES AND APPEALS 368
1.	Definitions	368
2.	Establishment and conduct of committees	368
3.	Composition	369
4.	Appeal from committee decision	370
5.	Deficient notice deemed to be amended	370
6.	Placement with or without consent, unless appeal brought	371

TABLE OF CONTENTS

7.	Special Education Appeal Board	371
8.	Review of placement	372
9.	Notice to parent	372
10.	Evidence to be considered	373
11.	Appeal from review	373
12.	Notice of appeal	373

REGULATION 306 — SPECIAL EDUCATION PROGRAMS AND SERVICES 374

1.-2.	Special Education Plan	374
3.	Report on special education	374
4.-5.	Scope of plan	374
6.	Maintenance and review of plan	375

REGULATION 307 — SPECIAL GRANT 376

1.-3.	Special grant	376

REGULATION 308 — SUPERVISED ALTERNATIVE LEARNING FOR EXCUSED PUPILS 377

1.	Definitions	377
2.	Committee	377
3.	Application	378
4.	Review on parental request	378
5.	Appeal from committee decision	379
6.	Alteration	379
7.	Enforcement by school attendance counsellor	379
8.	Move to another jurisdiction	379
9.	Parental removal from jurisdiction	380
10.	Continuance of program	380

REGULATION 309 — SUPERVISORY OFFICERS 381

PART I — QUALIFICATIONS OF SUPERVISORY OFFICERS

1.	Definitions	381
2.	Qualifications	382
2.1-3.	Business Supervisory Officer	383
4.-6.	Deemed certificate holders	385

PART II — TRANSFER AND DISMISSAL

7.	Redundant positions	385
8.	Neglect, misconduct, inefficiency	386
9.	[Revoked.]	386
10.	[Revoked.]	386
11.	[Revoked.]	386

241

REGULATIONS UNDER THE EDUCATION ACT

12.	[Revoked.]	386
13.	[Revoked.]	386
14.	[Revoked.]	386
15.	[Revoked.]	386

REGULATION 310 — TEACHERS' CONTRACTS 387
   1. Form of contracts 387
   2. Payment of salaries 387
  Form 1 Permanent Teacher's Contract 387
  Form 2 Probationary Teacher's Contract 389
  Form 3 Continuing Education Teacher's Contract 390

REGULATION 311 — TERRITORY WITHOUT MUNICIPAL ORGANIZATION ATTACHED TO A DISTRICT MUNICIPALITY 392
   1. Territories without municipal organization in the Territorial District of Thunder Bay attached to a district municipality 392

REGULATION 312 — TRAINING ASSISTANCE 395
   1. Calculation of training assistance under s. 135/16 of the Act 395

REGULATION 313 — TRUSTEE DISTRIBUTION 397
   1. Definition 397
   2. Trustee distribution 397
   3. Combined municipalities 398

REGULATION 283
CALCULATION OF AMOUNT OF RESERVE OR REDUCTION IN REQUIREMENT RESULTING FROM STRIKE OR LOCK-OUT
R.R.O. 1990, Reg. 283

1. (1) The calculations under this Regulation shall be made for a board of education and for The Metropolitan Toronto School board separately for public and for secondary school purposes.

(2) Where actual financial data required for a calculation under this Regulation are not available when the calculation is required to be made, estimated data shall be used.

(3) In this Regulation, "salaries and wages" means the salaries and wages, including fringe benefits, that are in effect on the date that the strike or lock-out commences.

2. (1) The amount that a board shall place in a reserve under subsection 237(2) of the Act shall be calculated by,

(a) determining the excess of,
 (i) the total of the salaries and wages that are included in the estimates of the board in such year and that are not paid to employees of the board in respect of the period of a strike by or lock-out of such employees, or any of them, that occurs in such year,

over,

 (ii) the expenditures incurred in such year by the board that, in the opinion of the Minister, are attributable to the strike or lock-out; and

(b) subtracting from such excess the product of the percentage rate of grant for the board in respect of recognized ordinary expenditure, determined under the Regulation governing the payment of legislative grants for such year, and the reduction in the recognized ordinary expenditure for such year, as defined in such Regulation, in respect of the board, that results from such strike or lock-out.

(2) The amount that, under clause 237(3)(b) of the Act, shall be set out in a statement by the board, shall be calculated by,

(a) determining the excess of,
 (i) the amount of money,
  (A) that would normally be paid as salaries and wages but is not paid to employees of the board in respect of the period of a strike by or lock-out of such employees, or any of them, that occurred in such year prior to the adoption of the estimates, and
  (B) that is excluded from the estimates of the board,

over

 (ii) the expenditures incurred by the board in such year prior to the adoption of the estimates that, in the opinion of the Minister, are attributable to such strike or lockout; and

(b) subtracting from such excess the product of the percentage rate of grant for the board in respect of recognized ordinary expenditure, determined under the Regulation governing the payment of legislative grants for such year, and the reduction in the recognized ordinary expenditure for such year, as defined in such Regulation, in respect of the board, that results from such strike or lock-out.

3. (1) In this section,

"area municipality" means an area municipality as defined in the *Municipality of Metropolitan Toronto Act*;

"board" means a board of education of an area municipality;

"School Board" means The Metropolitan Toronto School Board.

(2) The amount that the School Board shall place in a reserve for public or secondary school purposes, as the case may be, under subsection 238(2) of the Act, shall be calculated by,

(a) determining the excess of,
  (i) the total of the salaries and wages of employees of the boards and of the School Board that are included in the estimates of the School Board in such year and that are not paid to such employees in respect of the period of a strike by or lock-out of such employees, or any of them, that occurs in such year,

  over,

  (ii) the total of the expenditures incurred by the boards and the School Board in such year that, in the opinion of the Minister, are attributable to the strike or lock-out; and

(b) subtracting from such excess the product of the percentage rate of grant for the School Board in respect of recognized ordinary expenditure, determined under the Regulation governing the payment of legislative grants for such year, and the reduction in the recognized ordinary expenditure for such year, as defined in such Regulation, in respect of the School Board, that results from such strike or lock-out.

(3) The amount that, under clause 238(5)(b) of the Act, shall be set out in a statement by the School Board for public or secondary school purposes, as the case may be, shall be calculated by,

(a) determining the excess of,
  (i) the amount of money,
    (A) that would normally be paid as salaries and wages but is not paid to employees of the boards and of the School Board in respect of the period of a strike by or lock-out of such employees, or any of them, that occurred in such year prior to the adoption of the estimates, and
    (B) that is excluded from the estimates of the School Board,

  over,

  (ii) the total of the expenditures incurred by the boards and the School Board in such year prior to the adoption of the estimates that, in the opinion of the Minister, are attributable to such strike or lock-out; and

(b) subtracting from such excess the product of the percentage rate of grant for the School Board in respect of recognized ordinary expenditure, determined under the Regulation governing the payment of legislative grants for such year, and the reduction in the recognized ordinary expenditure for such year, as defined in such Regulation, in respect of the School Board, that results from such strike or lock-out.

REGULATION 284
CONDITIONS FOR EXTENDED FUNDING
R.R.O. 1990, Reg. 284

1. In this Regulation,

"implementation plan" means the plan formulated and filed with the Planning and Implementation Commission under subsection 149(1) of the Act for the school year referred to in the plan and in respect of which the board has been given notice;

"notice" means notice of the Minister that the Roman Catholic school board is eligible to share in the legislative grants for secondary school purposes,
   (a) for the school year set out in the notice, and
   (b) in respect of the method and location, if any, set out in the notice, for the provision of instruction in the grade or grades set out in the notice.

2. The following conditions are prescribed for the purposes of subsection 128(2) of the Act:
   1. The Roman Catholic school board shall undertake in accordance with its implementation plan to provide in its schools or pursuant to an agreement with another board the grade or grades set out in the implementation plan.
   2. The Roman Catholic school board shall meet the criteria set out in subsection 151(2) of the Act with respect to the provision of the grade or grades set out in its implementation plan.

REGULATION 285
CONTINUING EDUCATION
R.R.O. 1990, Reg. 285; Fr. version O. Reg. 441/92

PART I

1. (1) The following classes or courses provided by a board other than as part of the day school program on an instructional day as defined in Regulation 304 of Revised Regulations of Ontario, 1990 (School Year and School Holidays) are continuing education courses or classes for the purpose of paragraph 31 of subsection 171(1) of the Act and the regulations:

1. A class or course that is designed to develop or to improve the basic literacy and numeracy skills of adults to a level that does not exceed the grade 8 level of competency.
2. A class or course in English or French for adults whose first language learned and still understood is neither English nor French and that is not a class in which a pupil may earn a credit in English or French as a second language.
3. A class or course in citizenship and, where necessary, in language instruction in the English or the French language for persons admitted to Canada as permanent residents under the *Immigration Act* (Canada).
4. A class or course in driver education in which a pupil may not earn a credit.
5. A class or course in the primary or junior division or in the first two years of the intermediate division in which a language other than English or French is the subject of instruction.
6. A class or course in which a pupil may earn a credit.
7. A class for the purpose of extending the knowledge of adults, for the purpose of improving the skills of adults, for the specific interest of adults or for the enhancement of the knowledge or skills of elementary or secondary school pupils beyond that expected or required of the pupils as part of the regular program in an elementary or secondary school,
    i. for which the board charges registration fees to persons taking the class and the fees are not calculated in accordance with the regulations, or
    ii. in which the work required for its successful completion is not acceptable to the Minister as partial fulfilment of the requirements for a diploma granted by the Minister.

(2) The following classes or courses provided by a board between the hours of 8.00 a.m. and 5.00 p.m. that start after the completion of one school year and that end before the next following school year are continuing education classes or courses for the purposes of paragraph 31 of subsection 171(1) of the Act and the regulations:

1. A class or course for remedial purposes for pupils who are enrolled in an elementary school operated by the board and that is,
    i. a class or course that the board is required or authorized to provide during the school day to pupils enrolled in elementary schools and, in the school year immediately preceding commencement of the class or course, was a class or course that was provided to its elementary school pupils, and

ii. approved by the Minister.
2. A class or course that is for trainable retarded pupils who are enrolled in an elementary school or school or class for trainable retarded pupils operated by the board.
3. A class or course in which a pupil may earn a credit.

2. (1) Subject to subsection (2) and Part II, a board that establishes continuing education courses or classes shall determine the courses to be given in each of its continuing education classes, the number of times that each continuing education course or class is held per week, the length of time per session of each continuing education course or class and the dates and the time of the day or evening upon which each continuing education course or class is given.

(2) An elementary school board may offer continuing education courses and classes only in courses of study that the board is authorized or required to provide in its day school program in the primary and junior divisions and the intermediate division.

(3) An elementary school board may, subject to Part II, offer as a subject a language other than English or French in the primary and junior divisions and in the first two years of the intermediate division in its continuing education courses and classes.

(4) The principal of a school shall be the principal of the continuing education courses and classes in the school unless the board appoints as principal thereof another person who holds the appropriate principal's qualifications set out in section 9 of Regulation 298 of Revised Regulations of Ontario, 1990 (Operation of Schools — General).

(5) A school site that was used for school purposes and a school site that is used as a school during the school year may be used for a continuing education course or class.

(6) Two or more boards may jointly establish continuing education courses and classes in a school or schools operated by one or more of the boards concerned and determine where such courses and classes shall be conducted.

3. (1) A valid certificate of qualification or a letter of standing is required to be held by a person,
    (a) who provides the classroom teaching in a continuing education course or class referred to in paragraph 6 of subsection 1(1) or in subsection 1(2); or
    (b) who is employed in respect of the development or co-ordination of the program of which a continuing education course or class referred to in clause (a) is a part.

(2) A board may employ a person who is not a teacher to provide instruction in a continuing education course or class, other than a continuing education course or class referred to in paragraph 6 of subsection 1(1) or in subsection 1(2), if the person holds qualifications acceptable to the board for such employment.

PART II

4. In this Part,

"board", other than in section 6, means a board of education, public school board, Roman Catholic separate school board or Protestant separate school board, The Metropolitan Toronto French-Language School Council and the public sector and the Roman Catholic sector of The Ottawa-Carleton French-language School Board;

"commencement date" means the last school day of the month of January or September, as the case requires;

"parent" includes guardian;

"program" means a program of instruction in a continuing education course or class referred to in paragraph 5 of subsection 1(1);

"qualified person", in respect of a board, means a person who is enrolled or is eligible to be enrolled in an elementary school, a kindergarten or a junior kindergarten operated by the board, and who is not enrolled or is not eligible to be enrolled in a secondary school operated by the board, but if the board does not operate a secondary school, does not include a person who is enrolled or is eligible to be enrolled in the last two years of the intermediate division.

5. (1) If a board is not providing a program and receives from parents written requests on behalf of twenty-five or more qualified persons of the board for the establishment of a program, the board shall establish the program requested.

(2) If a board is providing one or more programs and the board receives from parents written requests on behalf of twenty-five or more qualified persons of the board for the establishment of a program that the board is not providing, the board shall establish the program requested.

(3) Despite subsections (1) and (2), a board may enter into an agreement with another board for the other board to provide the program requested.

(4) A program established under this section shall start not later than the commencement date that first occurs ninety days or more after the date of the request.

(5) A board that establishes a program under this section shall provide a class or course in the program for all qualified persons of the board who wish to attend if at least ten qualified persons of the board attend the first scheduled class or course of the program.

(6) A program provided by a board shall be provided throughout the school year in which the program was established so long as a person attends the class or course in the program.

(7) If a board, other than a Roman Catholic separate school board or the Roman Catholic sector of The Ottawa-Carleton French-language School Board, establishes a program under this section, it shall admit to a class or course in the program a qualified person in respect of another board that is not a Roman Catholic separate school board or the Roman Catholic sector of The Ottawa-Carleton French-language School Board.

(8) If a Roman Catholic separate school board establishes a program under this section, it shall admit to a class or course in the program a qualified person in respect of another Roman Catholic separate school board or the Roman Catholic sector of The Ottawa-Carleton French-language School Board.

(9) If the Roman Catholic sector of The Ottawa-Carleton French-language School Board establishes a program under this section, it shall admit to a class or course in the program a qualified person in respect of a Roman Catholic separate school board.

(10) A board may admit to a class or course in a program a person who is enrolled or eligible to be enrolled in an elementary school, a kindergarten or a junior kindergarten operated by a board and the person is not enrolled or eligible to be enrolled in a secondary school

operated by a board, despite the fact that the board is not required to admit the person under this section.

6. (1) In this section,

"board" means the public sector and the Roman Catholic sector of The Ottawa-Carleton French-language School Board and The Metropolitan Toronto French-Language School Council;

"French-speaking person" means a child of a person who has the right under subsection 23(1) or (2), without regard to subsection 23(3), of the *Canadian Charter of Rights and Freedoms* to have his or her children receive their primary and secondary school instruction in the French language in Ontario.

(2) Despite section 5, a board shall not admit to a program that it operates or provides for another board a person who is not a French-speaking person.

(3) Subsection (2) does not apply to a person who is enrolled in an elementary school, a kindergarten or a junior kindergarten operated by the board or another board.

7. (1) Subject to subsections (2) and (3), a qualified person of a board may attend one or more programs provided in one or more languages by one or more boards.

(2) The maximum period in each week during the school year that a qualified person of a board may attend a program in any one language is two and one-half hours.

(3) The maximum period during a day that falls after the completion of one school year and before the commencement of the next following school year that a qualified person of a board may attend a program in any one language is two and one-half hours.

8. A board that provides a program before the end of the instructional program of a school day may do so only in a school site that is used for school purposes by the board during the school day.

9. (1) A board that provides a program following the end of the instructional program of a school day or on a day that is not a school day may provide a class or course in the program in a place that is not a school site.

(2) If a board conducts a class or course in a program in a place that is not used as a school site during the school day, the time that the class begins shall be not earlier than the time at which the instructional program of the board ends.

(3) A board that conducts a class or course in a program in a place that is not used as a school site during the school day shall allow an interval of time between the end of the instructional program and the beginning of the class sufficient to permit pupils enrolled in the instructional program to travel to the place in which the class is being conducted.

10. (1) A board may discontinue a program at the end of the school year if the number of qualified persons of the board enrolled in courses or classes provided under the program is fewer than twenty-five at the conclusion of the school year in which the program is provided.

(2) A board that proposes to discontinue a program shall advise any person who participated in the program to the end of the school year that the program will be discontinued and that the program may be re-established in accordance with this Part.

REGULATION 286
COUNTY COMBINED SEPARATE SCHOOL ZONES
R.R.O. 1990, Reg. 286; Fr. version O. Reg. 377/92

1. Each of the following areas is designated as an area that forms a county combined separate school zone:
1. The County of Brant, designated as "Brant".
2. The County of Elgin, designated as "Elgin".
3. The County of Essex including Pelee Island but excluding the City of Windsor, designated as "Essex"
4. The Regional Municipality of Halton, designated as "Halton".
5. The County of Kent, designated as "Kent".
6. The County of Lambton, designated as "Lambton".
7. That portion of The Regional Municipality of Niagara that was formerly the County of Lincoln, designated as "Lincoln".
8. The County of Middlesex, designated as "London and Middlesex".
9. The Regional Municipality of Durham except the Town of Newcastle, designated as "Durham Region".
10. The County of Oxford, designated as "Oxford".
11. The County of Renfrew, designated as "Renfrew".
12. The County of Simcoe, the towns of Bracebridge and Gravenhurst, the Township of Georgian Bay and the Township of Muskoka Lakes in The District Municipality of Muskoka, designated as "Simcoe".
13. The Regional Municipality of Waterloo, designated as "Waterloo".
14. That portion of The Regional Municipality of Niagara that was formerly the County of Welland, designated as "Welland".
15. The County of Wellington, designated as "Wellington".
16. The Regional Municipality of Hamilton-Wentworth, designated as "Hamilton-Wentworth".
17. The Regional Municipality of York, designated as "York Region".
18. The United Counties of Prescott and Russell, designated as "Prescott and Russell".
19. The United Counties of Stormont, Dundas and Glengarry, designated as "Stormont, Dundas and Glengarry".
20. The counties of Bruce and Grey, designated as "Bruce-Grey".
21. The County of Dufferin and The Regional Municipality of Peel, designated as "Dufferin-Peel".
22. The counties of Frontenac and Lennox and Addington, designated as "Frontenac-Lennox and Addington".
23. The Regional Municipality of Haldimand-Norfolk, designated as "Haldimand-Norfolk".
24. The counties of Hastings and Prince Edward and the Township of Airy and the geographic townships of Dickens, Lyell, Murchison and Sabine in the Territorial District of Nipissing, designated as "Hastings-Prince Edward".
25. The counties of Huron and Perth, designated as "Huron-Perth".

REGULATION 286　　　　　　　　　　　　　　　　　　　　　　　**S. 1**

26. The County of Lanark and the United Counties of Leeds and Grenville, designated as "Lanark-Leeds and Grenville".
27. The counties of Northumberland, Peterborough and Victoria and the Town of Newcastle, designated as "Peterborough-Victoria-Northumberland and Newcastle".
28. The City of Windsor, designated as "Windsor".
29. The City of Ottawa, the City of Vanier and the Village of Rockcliffe Park, designated as "Ottawa".
30. The Regional Municipality of Ottawa-Carleton except the City of Ottawa, the City of Vanier and the Village of Rockcliffe Park, designated as "Carleton".

REGULATION 287
DESIGNATION OF SCHOOL DIVISIONS
R.R.O. 1990, Reg. 287: am. O. Reg. 527/92, O. Reg. 413/93

1. (1) The area referred to in paragraph 1 of each Schedule is designated as a school division.

(2) The name set out in paragraph 2 of each Schedule is the name assigned to the divisional board that has jurisdiction in the school division referred to in paragraph of that Schedule.

Schedule 1

1. In the Territorial District of Algoma, being,
     i. the towns of Bruce Mines and Thessalon,
     ii. the Village of Hilton Beach,
     iii. the townships of Hilton, Jocelyn, Johnson, Laird, Plummer Additional, St. Joseph and Thessalon,
     iv. the Township of MacDonald, Meredith and Aberdeen Additional,
     v. the Township of Tarbutt and Tarbutt Additional, and
     vi. the geographic townships of Aberdeen, Bridgland, Galbraith, Gould, Haughton, Kirkwood, McMahon, Morin, Rose and Wells.
2. The Central Algoma Board of Education.

Schedule 2

1. In the Territorial District of Algoma, being the Township of Hornepayne.
2. The Hornepayne Board of Education.

Schedule 3

1. In the Territorial District of Algoma, being,
     i. the townships of Dubreuilville, Michipicoten and White River, and
     ii. the geographic townships of Chenard, Dunphy, Esquega, Fiddler, Finon and Huotari.
2. The Michipicoten Board of Education.

Schedule 4

1. In the Territorial District of Algoma, being,
     i. the town of Blind River and the City of Elliot Lake,
     ii. the Village of Iron Bridge,
     iii. the townships of Day and Bright Additional, The North Shore, Shedden and Thompson,
     iv. the geographic townships of Bright, Cobden, Gladstone, Grasett, Jogues, Juil-

REGULATION 287 **Sched. 7**

lette, Kamichisitit, Mack, Montgomery, Nouvel, Parkinson, Patton, Scarfe, Timmermans and the portion of the geographic township of Striker not included in the Township of The North Shore, and

  v. all the islands in the North Channel of Lake Huron lying south of the geographic townships of Bright, Cobden, and the portion of Striker that is not part of the Township of The North Shore.

2. The North Shore Board of Education.

Schedule 5

1. In the Territorial District of Algoma, being,
    i. the City of Sault Ste. Marie,
    ii. the Township of Prince,
    iii. the geographic townships of Archibald, Aweres, Dennis, Deroche, Fenwick, Fisher, Gaudette, Havilland, Herrick, Hodgins, Home, Jarvis, Kars, Kincaid, Ley, Peever, Pennefather, Rix, Ryan, Shields, Slater, Tilley, Tupper and VanKoughnet, and
    iv. the mining locations known as Montreal Mining Southern Location, Montreal Mining Northern Location, A. McDonnell Mining Location, Kincaid Mining Locations 5, 6, 7 and 8 and Rankin Mining Location.
2. The Sault Ste. Marie Board of Education.

Schedule 6

1. In the Territorial District of Cochrane, being,
    i. the towns of Cochrane and Iroquois Falls,
    ii. the townships of Black River-Matheson and Glackmeyer, and
    iii. the geographic townships of Aurora, Blount, Brower, Calder, Clute, Colquhoun, Fournier, Fox, Guibord, Hanna, Kennedy, Lamarche, Leitch, Mortimer, Munro, Newmarket, Ottaway, Pyne, St. John, Stimson and Teefy.
2. Cochrane-Iroquois Falls, Black River-Matheson Board of Education. O. Reg. 413/93, s. 1.

Schedule 7

1. In the Territorial District of,
    i. Cochrane, being,
        A. the Town of Hearst,
        B. the Township of Mattice-Val Côté, and
        C. the geographic townships of Barker, Casgrain, Hanlan, Irish, Kendall, Landry, Lowther, Stoddard, Studholme and Way, and
    ii. Algoma, being the geographic townships of Ebbs and Templeton.
2. The Hearst Board of Education.

Sched. 8 REGULATIONS UNDER THE EDUCATION ACT

Schedule 8

1. In the Territorial District of Cochrane, being,
    i. the towns of Kapuskasing and Smooth Rock Falls,
    ii. the townships of Fauquier-Strickland, Moonbeam, Opasatika and Val Rita-Harty,
    iii. the geographic townships of Haggart, McCowan, Nansen and O'Brien, and
    iv. the portion of the geographic Township of Owens that is not in the Township of Val Rita-Harty.
2. The Kapuskasing-Smooth Rock Falls and District Board of Education or Conseil de l'éducation de Kapuskasing-Smooth Rock Falls et de son district. O. Reg. 413/93, s. 2.

Schedule 9

1. In the Territorial District of Cochrane, being the City of Timmins.
2. The Timmins Board of Education.

Schedule 10

1. In the Territorial District of Kenora, being,
    i. the towns of Dryden and Sioux Lookout,
    ii. the townships of Barclay, Ignace and Machin,
    iii. the geographic townships of Britton, Buller, Colenso, Drayton, Eton, Hartman, Ilsley, Jordan, Ladysmith, Melgund, Mutrie, Redvers, Rowell, Rugby, Smellie, Southworth, Van Horne, Vermilion, Vermilion Additional, Wabigoon, Wainwright and Zealand,
    iv. that portion of the geographic township of Aubrey that is not part of the Township of Machin, and
    v. that portion of Block 10 lying south of the production easterly and westerly of the most northerly limit of the geographic township of Drayton.
2. The Dryden Board of Education.

Schedule 11

1. In the Territorial District of Kenora, being,
    i. the towns of Jaffray and Melick, Keewatin and Kenora,
    ii. the Township of Sioux Narrows,
    iii. the geographic townships of Boys, Kirkup, Pellatt and Redditt,
    iv. all the lands in unsurveyed territory in the vicinity of the station house of the Canadian National Railways at Minaki described as follows:

    Commencing at a point distant 4 kilometres measured east astronomically from the northeast corner of the said station house;

Thence north astronomically 4 kilometres;

Thence west astronomically 8 kilometres;

Thence south astronomically 8 kilometres;

Thence east astronomically 8 kilometres;

Thence north astronomically 4 kilometres to the point of commencement, and
  v. except for those parts of the mainland which are crossed by the said line, all lands lying north of a line extending from the southernmost extremity of the geographic Township of Boys to the southwest corner of the geographic Township of Kirkup and south of the southerly boundaries of the geographic townships of Boys and Pellatt, the towns of Jaffray and Melick, Keewatin and Kenora.
2. The Kenora Board of Education.

Schedule 12

1. In the Territorial District of Kenora, being,
    i. the townships of Ear Falls, Golden and Red Lake,
    ii. the geographic townships of Baird, Dome and Heyson,
    iii. all lands within an area of 6.4 kilometres in width and lying on both sides of the centre line of tertiary road Number 804 and within 3.2 kilometres of the said centre line measured at right angles thereto, and not in the Township of Ear Falls, and
    iv. all lands within an area of 6.4 kilometres in width and lying on both sides of the centre line of that part of the King's Highway known as Number 105 and within 3.2 kilometres of and measured at right angles to that portion of the centre line of the said part of the highway extending in a generally northerly and northwesterly direction from its intersection with the centre line of Pickerel Creek to its intersection with the southerly limit of the Township of Red Lake, and not in the Township of Ear Falls or referred to in subparagraph iii.
2. The Red Lake Board of Education.

Schedule 13

1. In the Territorial District of Manitoulin, being all of the said territorial district except the Township of Rutherford and George Island and the geographic townships of Carlyle, Humboldt and Killarney.
2. The Manitoulin Board of Education.

Schedule 14

1. In The District Municipality of Muskoka, being all of The District Municipality of Muskoka except the Freeman Ward of the area municipality of the Township of Georgian Bay.

Sched. 15 REGULATIONS UNDER THE EDUCATION ACT

2. The Muskoka Board of Education.

Schedule 15

1. In the Territorial District of Nipissing, being,
    i. the City of North Bay,
    ii. the towns of Cache Bay, Mattawa and Sturgeon Falls,
    iii. the townships of Bonfield, Caldwell, Calvin, East Ferris, Field, Mattawan, Papineau and Springer,
    iv. the Improvement District of Cameron, and
    v. the geographic townships of Badgerow, Bastedo, Beaucage, Blyth, Boyd, Clarkson, Commanda, Crerar, Deacon, Eddy, Falconer, French, Gibbons, Grant, Hugel, Jocko, Kirkpatrick, Lauder, Loudon, Lyman, Macpherson, Merrick, Notman, Pedley, Pentland, Phelps, Poitras and Wyse.
2. The Nipissing Board of Education.

Schedule 16

1. In the Territorial District of,
    i. Parry Sound, being
        A. the Township School Area of Burk's Falls,
        B. the Township School Area of Gurd, Patterson and Pringle,
        C. the Township School Area of Hardy, McConkey, Wilson, Mills and Pringle,
        D. the Township School Area of Kearney, Bethune and Proudfoot,
        E. the Township School Area of Laurier,
        F. the Township School Area of Magnetawan,
        G. the Township School Area of McMurrich,
        H. the Township School Area of Nipissing,
        I. that part of the Township School Area of North Himsworth and East Ferris, lying within the Township of North Himsworth,
        J. the Township School Area of South Himsworth,
        K. the Township School Area of Perry,
        L. the Township School Area of South River,
        M. the Township School Area of Sundridge,
        N. School Section No. 3, in the geographic townships of Bethune and Proudfoot,
        O. School Section No. 2, in the geographic Township of Monteith,
        P. the School Section of the Town of Powassan,
        Q. all other lands not designated in Schedule 17, and
    ii. Nipissing, being,
        A. the Town of Kearney, and
        B. the Township School Area of Chisholm.
2. The East Parry Sound Board of Education. O. Reg. 527/92, s. 1.

REGULATION 287 **Sched. 18**

Schedule 17

1. In,
    i. the Territorial District of Parry Sound, being,
        A. the Town of Parry Sound,
        B. the Village of Rosseau,
        C. the townships of Carling, Christie, Foley, Hagerman, Humphrey, McDougall, McKellar and The Archipelago,
        D. the geographic townships of Blair, Brown, Burton, East Burpee, Ferguson, Ferrie, Henvey, McKenzie, Mowatt and Wallbridge,
        E. those parts of the geographic townships of Croft and Spence which are not included in the Township School area of Magnetawan,
        F. those parts of the geographic townships of Harrison and Shawanaga that are not in the Township of The Archipelago, and
    ii. The District Municipality of Muskoka, being the Freeman Ward of the area municipality of the Township of Georgian Bay.
2. The West Parry Sound Board of Education.

Schedule 18

1. In the Territorial District of Rainy River, being,
    i. the Township of Atikokan,
    ii. the geographic townships of Asmussen, Baker, Bennett, Hutchinson, McCaul, Tanner and Trottier,
    iii. all the lands in unsurveyed territory described as follows:

    Commencing at the southwest corner of the geographic Township of Bennett;
    Thence south astronomically 9.6 kilometres;

    Thence east astronomically to a point distant 9.6 kilometres measured south astronomically from the southeast corner of the geographic Township of Baker;

    Thence north astronomically 9.6 kilometres more or less to the southeast corner of the geographic Township of Baker;

    Thence west astronomically to the point of commencement, and

    iv. all the lands in unsurveyed territory described as follows:

    commencing at the southwest corner of the geographic Township of McCaul;
    Thence south astronomically 9.6 kilometres;

    Thence east astronomically to a point distant 9.6 kilometres measured south astronomically from the southeast corner of the geographic Township of Trottier;

    Thence north astronomically 9.6 kilometres more or less to the southeast corner of the geographic Township of Trottier;

    Thence west astronomically to the point of commencement.
2. The Atikokan Board of Education.

Schedule 19

1. In the Territorial District of,
    i. Rainy River, being,
        A. the towns of Fort Frances and Rainy River,
        B. the townships of Alberton, Atwood, Blue, Chapple, Dilke, Emo, La Vallee, Morley, Morson and Worthington,
        C. the Township of McCrosson and Tovell,
        D. the Improvement District of Kingsford,
        E. the geographic townships of Claxton, Croome, Dance, Dewart, Farrington, Fleming, Griesinger, Halkirk, Mathieu, McLarty, Menary, Miscampbell, Nelles, Pratt, Rowe, Senn, Sifton, Spohn, Sutherland and Watten,
        F. the Wild Land Reserve,
        G. all lands in unsurveyed territory within an area the boundary sides of which are as follows:
            1. On the north side, the northerly limit of the Territorial District of Rainy River commencing at the point of intersection of the 49th degree parallel of north latitude with the International Boundary; thence due east 24 kilometres more or less along the 49th degree parallel of north latitude to the east shore of the Lake of the Woods; thence north easterly and northerly along the east shore of the Lake of the Woods and the south and east shores of Sabaskong Bay of the Lake of the Woods to the point of intersection of the westerly production of the north boundaries of the geographic townships of Claxton and McLarty; thence due easterly along the said north boundaries of the said geographic townships and along their production due east being along O.L.S. Gillon's base line of 1919 to the 24th mile post on O.L.S. Alexander Niven's 6th meridian line; thence due south along the said meridian line 9.6 kilometres to the 18th mile post thereon in latitude 49° 0' 6'' north; thence due east to the point of intersection of the production north of the east boundary of the geographic Township of Farrington.
            2. On the east side, the line formed by the east boundary of the geographic Township of Farrington, the production of the said east boundary due north to the north boundary of the Territorial District of Rainy River and the production due south of the said east boundary to the International Boundary.
            3. On the south side, the International Boundary from the mouth of the Rainy River easterly to the point of intersection on the International Boundary of the production due south of the east boundary of the geographic Township of Farrington.
            4. On the west side, the International Boundary from the mouth of the Rainy River northerly to the point of intersection on the International Boundary of the 49th degree parallel of north latitude, and

REGULATION 287 **Sched. 21**

    ii. Kenora, being,
- A. the geographic townships of Godson, Phillips and Tweedsmuir,
- B. all lands in unsurveyed territory within an area the boundary sides of which are as follows:
    1. On the west side, the International Boundary between the point of intersection thereon of the 49th degree parallel of north latitude and the point of intersection of the production westerly of the north boundary of the geographic Township of Tweedsmuir along the 4th base line.
    2. On the south side, the line described as commencing at the point of intersection of the 49th degree parallel of north latitude with the International Boundary; thence due east 24 kilometres more or less along the 49th degree parallel of north latitude to the east shore of the Lake of the Woods; thence north easterly and northerly along the east shore of the Lake of the Woods and the south and east shores of Sabaskong Bay of the Lake of the Woods to the point of intersection of the westerly production of the south boundary of the geographic township of Godson; thence due east along the said north boundary of the said geographic Township and along their production due east being along O.L.S. Gillon's base line of 1919 to the 24th mile post on O.L.S. Alexander Niven's 6th meridian line.
    3. On the east side, O.L.S. Alexander Niven's 6th meridian line between the 24th mile post thereon and the point of intersection on the said meridian line of the production due east along the 4th base line of the north boundary of the geographic Township of Tweedsmuir.
    4. On the north side, the production along the 4th base line westerly to the International Boundary and easterly to O.L.S. Alexander Niven's 6th meridian line of the north boundary of the geographic Township of Tweedsmuir.

2. The Fort Frances-Rainy River Board of Education.

Schedule 20

1. In the Territorial District of Sudbury, being,
    - i. the Township of Chapleau, and
    - ii. the geographic townships of Caverley, Chapleau, de Gaulle, Eisenhower, Gallagher, Genier, Halsey, Kaplan and Panet.
2. The Chapleau Board of Education.

Schedule 21

1. In the Territorial District of Sudbury, being,
    - i. the towns of Espanola, Massey and Webbwood,

Sched. 22 REGULATIONS UNDER THE EDUCATION ACT

  ii. the townships of Baldwin, Nairn and The Spanish River,
  iii. the geographic townships of Curtin, Foster, Gough, McKinnon, Merritt, Mongowin, Roosevelt, Shakespeare and Truman, and
  iv. the portion of the geographic Township of Hyman that is not part of the Town of Walden.
2. The Espanola Board of Education.

Schedule 22

1. In the Territorial District of,
    i. Sudbury, being,
        A. The Regional Municipality of Sudbury,
        B. the Township of Casimir, Jennings and Appleby,
        C. the Township of Cosby, Mason and Martland,
        D. the Township of Hagar,
        E. the Township of Ratter and Dunnet,
        F. the geographic townships of Allen, Awrey, Bigwood, Burwash, Cartier, Cascaden, Cherriman, Cleland, Cox, Davis, Delamere, Foy, Haddo, Hart, Harty, Hawley, Hendrie, Henry, Hess, Hoskin, Janes, Laura, Loughrin, Moncrieff, Scadding, Scollard, Secord, Servos and Street,
        G. the portions of the geographic townships of Dill, Eden and Tilton that are not part of The Regional Municipality of Sudbury,
        H. the portion of the geographic Township of Dryden that is not part of The Regional Municipality of Sudbury, and,
        I. the portion of the geographic Township of Trill that is not part of The Regional Municipality of Sudbury.
    ii. Manitoulin, being the Township of Rutherford and George Island.
2. The Sudbury Board of Education.

Schedule 23

1. In the Territorial District of Thunder Bay, being,
    i. the towns of Geraldton and Longlac,
    ii. the Township of Beardmore, and
    iii. the geographic townships of Ashmore, Daley, Errington, Houck, Leduc and Oakes.
2. The Geraldton Board of Education.

Schedule 24

1. In the Territorial District of Thunder Bay, being,
    i. the City of Thunder Bay,
    ii. the townships of Conmee, Gillies, Neebing, O'Connor, Oliver, Paipoonge and Shuniah,
    iii. the geographic townships of Blackwell, Conacher, Devon, Forbes, Fraleigh,

REGULATION 287 **Sched. 27**

Goldie, Golding, Gorham, Hagey, Laurie, Lismore, Lybster, Marks, Michener, Pearson, Robson, Scoble, Sibley, Strange and Ware,
    iv. the Dawson Road Lots, and
    v. the area bounded by the easterly boundary of Lot 1, concessions 1 and 2 of the Dawson Road Lots; the southerly boundary of the geographic Township of Forbes; the westerly shore of the Kaministiquia River (sometimes known as the Dog River) and the northerly shore of the Shebandowan River (sometimes known as the Matawin River).
2. The Lakehead Board of Education.

Schedule 25

1. In the Territorial District of Thunder Bay, being,
    i. the Town of Marathon,
    ii. the townships of Manitouwadge, Schreiber and Terrace Bay,
    iii. the geographic townships of Atikameg, Bomby, Brothers, Bryant, Byron, Cecil, Cecile, Coldwell, Cotte, Davies, Flood, Foote, Grain, Grenville, Herbert, Homer, Killraine, Knowles, Laberge, Lahontan, Lecours, McCron, McGill, Mikano, Nickle, O'Neill, Pic, Priske, Roberta, Shabotik, Spooner, Strey, Syine, Tuuri, Walsh, Wiggins and Yesno, and
    iv. all lands in unsurveyed territory within an area described as follows:
        A. on the north side, the extension of the north side of the geographic Township of Davies westerly to intersect with the boundary formed by extending the west side of the geographic Township of Wiggins northerly until it meets the said extension,
        B. on the east side, the extension of the east side of the geographic Township of Spooner southerly until the Canada-United States border,
        C. on the south side, the Canada-United States border, and
        D. on the west side, the extension of the west side of the geographic Township of Wiggins southerly until the Canada-United States border,
    excluding St. Ignace Island.
2. the Lake Superior Board of Education.

Schedule 26

1. In the Territorial District of Thunder Bay, being,
    i. the townships of Dorion and Nipigon,
    ii. the Township of Red Rock, and
    iii. the geographic townships of Boothe, Corrigal, Lyon and Stirling.
2. the Nipigon-Red Rock Board of Education.

Schedule 27

1. In the Territorial District of
    i. Timiskaming, being,

Sched. 28   REGULATIONS UNDER THE EDUCATION ACT

- A. the towns of Charlton, Cobalt, Englehart, Haileybury, Latchford and New Liskeard,
- B. the Village of Thornloe,
- C. the townships of Armstrong, Brethour, Casey, Chamberlain, Coleman, Dack, Dymond, Evanturel, Harley, Harris, Hilliard, Hudson, James and Kerns,
- D. the geographic townships of Auld, Barber, Barr, Bayly, Beauchamp, Brigstocke, Bryce, Cane, Chown, Coleman, Corkill, Davidson, Farr, Firstbrook, Gillies Limit, Haultain, Henwood, Ingram, Kittson, Lawson, Lorrain, Lundy, Marter, Mickle, Milner, Mulligan, Nicol, Pense, Roadhouse, Robillard, Savard, Sharpe, Smyth, South Lorrain, Truax, Tudhope, Willet and Willison,
- E. concessions 1 and 2 in the geographic townships of Catharine, Marquis and Pacaud, and

    ii. Nipissing, being,
    - A. the Township of Temagami, and
    - B. the geographic townships of Askin, Aston, Banting, Belfast, Best, Briggs, Canton, Cassels, Chambers, Cynthia, Eldridge, Flett, Gladman, Godderham, Hammell, Hartle, Hobbs, Joan, Kenny, Law, Le Roche, McCallum, McLaren, Milne, Olive, Phyllis, Riddell, Sisk, Thistle, Torrington, Vogt and Yates.

2. The Timiskaming Board of Education.

Schedule 28

1. In the Territorial District of,
    i. Timiskaming, being,
    - A. the Town Kirkland Lake,
    - B. the townships of Larder Lake and McGarry,
    - C. the improvement districts of Gauthier and Matachewan,
    - D. the geographic townships of Boston, Eby, Grenfell, Lebel, Maisonville, McElroy and Otto, and
    - E. concessions 3, 4, 5 and 6 in the geographic townships of Catharine, Marquis and Pacaud, and

    ii. Cochrane, being the portion of the geographic Township of Benoit that is not part of the Township of Black River-Matheson.
2. The Kirkland Lake Board of Education.

REGULATION 288
DESIGNATION OF SUPPORT STAFF
R.R.O. 1990, Reg. 288

1. In this Regulation,

"enrolment shift" means,

- (a) in the case of the elementary school pupils of a public board, the reduction in enrolment determined under subsection 4(6) of Regulation 289 of Revised Regulations of Ontario, 1990, and
- (b) in the case of the secondary school pupils of a public board, the enrolment shift determined under subsection 4(7) of Regulation 289 of Revised Regulations of Ontario, 1990;

"person" means a member of the support staff of the board;

"that is coterminous with the public board" means that has jurisdiction in an area that is also the area or part of the area of jurisdiction of the public board and "that is coterminous with the Roman Catholic school board" has a corresponding meaning.

2. (1) This Regulation applies to a public board in each of the first ten years or for the remainder of the ten-year period that commenced with the year in which a separate school board that is coterminous with the public board elects, with the approval of the Minister, to perform the duties of a secondary school board.

(2) This Regulation does not apply to a public board that has entered or enters into an agreement within the meaning of subsection 135(1) of the Act with respect to the designation of persons.

(3) This Regulation does not apply where a public board has part of the same area of jurisdiction as a Roman Catholic school board as a result of the fact that a separate school zone that comprises part of the county or district combined Roman Catholic school board for which the Roman Catholic school board was established has a centre that is situate within 4.8 kilometres of the boundary of the public board and is not situate within the area of jurisdiction of the public board.

(4) Nothing in this Regulation prevents a public board that has jurisdiction in an area that is also the area or part of the area of jurisdiction of two or more Roman Catholic school boards from having an agreement within the meaning of subsection 135(1) of the Act with one or more of the Roman Catholic school boards with respect to the designation of persons under section 135 of the Act while at the same time dealing with one or more of the Roman Catholic school boards under this Regulation.

(5) Each public board that operates a school or class under Part XII of the Act shall make the determinations and designations required to be made under this Regulation separately for,

- (a) the French-language schools and classes operated by it under Part XII of the Act; and
- (b) all schools and classes other than those referred to in clause (a) that it operates.

3. If a school operated by a public board under Part XII of the Act is transferred to a Roman Catholic school board and the transfer is approved by the Minister, the public board shall designate all persons employed in the school under section 135 of the Act.

4. (1) For the purpose of determining the persons that it shall designate under section 135 of the Act, every public board shall, on or before the 30th day of April in each year, identify,

   (a) the number of positions that it believes will not be required in the next following school year because of the anticipated enrolment shift; and
   (b) by seniority, the persons who in accordance with its agreements or board policy are surplus to the needs of the board because of the anticipated shift of enrolment.

(2) In identifying persons under clause (1)(b), each person who is employed on a part-time basis shall be counted towards the number of persons to be identified only to the proportion of a full-time employee that the person represents.

(3) The number of persons identified under clause (1)(b) shall be equal to or shall differ by less than one from the number of positions determined under clause (1)(a).

(4) The public board, on or before the 30th day of April in each year, shall provide to each of the parties with which it has agreements in respect of persons in its employ and to each Roman Catholic school board that is coterminous with the public board, a list of the names and positions of all persons identified under clause (1)(b).

5. (1) Every Roman Catholic school board shall, on or before the 30th day of April in each year, provide to each public board that is coterminous with the Roman Catholic school board, a list of the positions for persons that are expected to be vacant in the Roman Catholic school board in the following school year.

(2) A public board that receives a list under subsection (1) shall forthwith make the list known to all persons in the employ of the public board.

(3) A person employed by a public board may volunteer to transfer in accordance with subsection 6(1) to the Roman Catholic school board to fill a vacant position identified under subsection (1), whether or not the person is identified according to clause 4(1)(b).

6. (1) Every public board shall designate each year in accordance with section 135 of the Act the number of persons identified under clause 4(1)(a) according to the following rules:

1. Designate persons identified under clause 4(1)(b) who are willing to transfer voluntarily to the Roman Catholic school board to fill the vacant positions identified under subsection 5(1).
2. If there are vacant positions remaining to be filled after designating the persons referred to in paragraph 1, in order of seniority, designate the persons who have volunteered under subsection 5(3).
3. If there are positions remaining to be designated after designating the persons referred to in paragraphs 1 and 2, designate, in accordance with the public boards agreements, board policy or an understanding with its employees or their authorized representatives, from the persons identified under clause 4(1)(b), a number of persons equal to the remaining number of positions identified under clause 4(1)(a).

(2) A designation under paragraph 2 of subsection (1) shall only be made if the designation of the person leaves open a permanent position with the public board that is filled by a person identified under clause 4(1)(b) who has not volunteered to fill a vacancy in the Roman Catholic school board.

7. Each public board shall provide, within thirty days of receiving the list of vacant positions for persons in the Roman Catholic school board, to each Roman Catholic school board that is coterminous with the public board a list,

- (a) of all persons who have been identified under subsection 4(1) who are willing to transfer voluntarily to the Roman Catholic school board to fill the vacant positions of persons in the Roman Catholic school board; and
- (b) showing each person, in addition to those persons referred to in clause (a), who is willing to transfer voluntarily to the Roman Catholic school board to fill a vacancy in the Roman Catholic school board.

8. Each public board that makes a designation under this Regulation and each Roman Catholic school board that is coterminous with the public board shall provide a list of persons so designated to each of the parties with which it has agreements in respect of persons in its employ.

9. (1) If a position with a public board becomes vacant within the year in which a person is designated under section 5, up to and including the 31st day of May in the year next following, and no person employed or eligible to be employed under the recall provisions of a collective agreement with the public board in respect of persons is available to fill the position, the public board shall offer the right of first refusal with respect to the position to the designated person with the greatest seniority who is qualified to fill the position.

(2) If the person with the greatest seniority refuses or cannot fill the position referred to in subsection (1),

- (a) the position shall be offered to other designated persons with the qualifications to fill the position in descending order of seniority until the position is filled or there are no more designated persons; and
- (b) the public board shall not be obligated to continue offering positions to that person.

(3) If a person accepts an offer referred to in subsection (1), the Roman Catholic school board shall transfer the employment contract of the person to the public board and the public board shall treat the employment contract of the person as if the person had never left the employ of the public board.

(4) If a person accepts an offer referred to in subsection (1), the public board shall allow the Roman Catholic school board a reasonable length of time in the circumstances to fill the vacancy thus created before requiring the transfer of the person.

(5) If, as a result of a person accepting an offer referred to in subsection (1), a position becomes vacant in the Roman Catholic school board and there are still persons unemployed who were identified in accordance with clause 4(1)(b), the public board may designate the next person identified under clause 4(1)(b) to fill the position.

10. If a person files an objection under subsection 135(13) of the Act and the public board is of the opinion that the objection is made in good faith, the public board may designate another person in place of the person making the objection, in accordance with its agreements in respect of such persons or board policy.

REGULATION 289
DESIGNATION OF TEACHERS
R.R.O. 1990, Reg. 289

1. In this Regulation,

"agreement", other than an agreement within the meaning of subsection 135(1) of the Act, in relation to the employment of teachers, "branch affiliate" and "teacher" have the same meaning as in the *School Boards and Teachers Collective Negotiations Act*;

"non-resident pupil", "resident-internal pupil" and "resident-external pupil" have the same meaning as in Ontario Regulation 128/85 (General Legislative Grants);

"proportion of qualifications of teachers" means the relative number of teachers who have qualifications in the areas of general studies and technological studies;

"that is coterminous with the public board" means that has jurisdiction in an area that is also the area or part of the area of jurisdiction of the public board and "that is coterminous with the Roman Catholic school board" has a corresponding meaning.

2. (1) This Regulation applies to a public board in each of the first ten years commencing with the year in which a separate school board that is coterminous with the public board elects with the approval of the Minister to perform the duties of a secondary school board.

(2) This Regulation does not apply to a public board that has entered into an agreement within the meaning of subsection 135(1) of the Act.

(3) Two or more public boards that act jointly with each other for the purpose of making or renewing an agreement shall,

(a) although they are required to do certain things under this Regulation on or before the 30th day of April and on or before the 31st day of May, do those things on or before the 15th day of May and on or before the 30th day of June, as the case requires, and

(b) make the determinations and designations required to be made under this Regulation for all such public boards jointly as if they are one public board and the public boards shall not act individually.

3. (1) For the purpose of determining the persons on its elementary and secondary teaching staffs that it shall designate under section 135 of the Act, every public board shall, on or before the 30th day of April in each year, determine in accordance with its agreements or board policy,

(a) the number of teaching positions that it believes will not be required in the next following school year because of an anticipated reduction in the enrolment of pupils in that school year from the enrolment of pupils as of the 30th day of September in the previous year; and

(b) the identity of the teachers,
  (i) whose services may not be required at the end of the school year as a result of the calculation under clause (a), and
  (ii) who in accordance with its agreements are surplus to the needs of the board but who are still in the employ of the board.

(2) The public board, on or before the 30th day of April in each year, shall provide to its branch affiliates and to each Roman Catholic school board that is coterminous with the public board, a list of the names and qualifications of all teachers identified under clause (1)(b).

4. (1) Each Roman Catholic school board shall supply, on or before the 31st day of March in each year, for ten consecutive years commencing with the year in which it elects with the approval of the Minister to perform the duties of a secondary school board, to each public board that is coterminous with the Roman Catholic school board, the enrolment and other data necessary to enable the public board to carry out the calculations referred to in this section.

(2) Each board referred to in subsection (1) shall make copies of the data required under that subsection available to its branch affiliates.

(3) Each public board shall, on or before the 30th day of April in each year, make the following calculations in respect of each Roman Catholic school board that is coterminous with the public board for the purpose of determining the enrolment shift:

1. $R_g = \dfrac{E^0_g}{E^{-1}_{g-1}}$ for each of grades 9, 10, 11, 12 and 13 correct to four places of decimal where g means grade

2. $P^1_g = R_g \times E^0_{g-1}$ for each of grades 9, 10, 11, 12 and 13 where g means grade

3. $P^t_9 = R_9 \times E^{t-1}_8$ for each school year from 2 to 10 where t means school year

4. $P^t_g = R_g \times P^{t-1}_{g-1}$ for each of grades 10, 11, 12 and 13 and for each school year from 2 to 10 where g means grade and t means school year

5. $ES^t = \sum [(E^t_g - P^t_g) - (E^{t-1}_g - P^{t-1}_g)]$ for each school year from 1 to 10 where t means school year

where R_g is the retention rate of the Roman Catholic school board in respect of grade g, in the school year immediately preceding the school year in which the Roman Catholic school board has made an election under section 124 of the Act,

E^t_g is the number of pupils in grade g as of the 30th day of September of school year t who reside in the area of jurisdiction of the public board and who are enrolled in the Roman Catholic school board that is coterminous with the public board as,

  (a) resident-internal pupils,

  (b) resident-external pupils, other than resident-external pupils enrolled in the public board under subsection 144(2) of the Act, or

  (c) non-resident pupils who are qualified to be resident pupils of the public board and who

S. 4 REGULATIONS UNDER THE EDUCATION ACT

P^t_g enrol in the Roman Catholic school board under subsection 144(1) of the Act, and includes pupils enrolled in a private school the enrolment of which is to become or has become part of the enrolment of the Roman Catholic school board in accordance with the Act,

P^t_g is the projected number of pupils in grade g in the school year t to represent an estimate of the enrolment of the pupils assuming the Roman Catholic school board did not make an election under section 124 of the Act, and

ES^t is the enrolment shift in school year t, where the summation is made for all grades in respect of which the Roman Catholic school board receives grants in school year t under sections 129 and 130 of the Act,

where $t = 1$ represents the school year in which the Roman Catholic school board makes an election under section 124 of the Act, $t = 0$ and $t = -1$ represent each of the two preceding school years respectively and $t = 2, 3, 4, 5, 6, 7, 8, 9$ or 10 represents each of the succeeding nine school years following the election.

(4) Each public board shall, on or before the 30th day of April in each year, determine in respect of each Roman Catholic school board that is coterminous with the public board, the difference between the number of its elementary pupils who are expected to transfer in the next school year to the elementary schools operated by the Roman Catholic school board and the number of elementary pupils of the Roman Catholic school board who are expected to transfer to the elementary schools operated by the public board.

(5) The difference determined under subsection (4), if greater than zero, shall be the net number of elementary pupils anticipated to transfer to the Roman Catholic school board.

(6) The reduction in enrolment with respect to the elementary school pupils of the public board for the year for which the calculations are made that is attributable to the election of the Roman Catholic school board under section 124 of the Act shall be the net number of elementary pupils anticipated to transfer in the school year as calculated under subsection (4).

(7) The reduction in enrolment with respect to the secondary school pupils of the public board for the year for which the calculations are made that is attributable to the election of the Roman Catholic school board under section 124 of the Act shall be the enrolment shift for the year as determined under subsection (3).

(8) Despite subsection (3), where Rg is calculated to be lower than the average Rg from the previous five years, the Rg shall be the average Rg from the previous five years.

5. (1) Every public board shall, in the manner set out in clause 3(1)(a), determine the number of positions on each of the elementary and secondary teaching staffs of the board that are related to the reduction in its enrolment determined under subsections 4(6) and (7).

(2) The number of positions determined under subsection (1) shall be,

(a) adjusted to take into account,
  (i) the actual enrolment data as of the 30th day of September of the previous calendar year, and
  (ii) in respect of the previous calendar year, the difference between the number of positions calculated to one place of decimal under this section and the number of teachers designated under section 8;
(b) increased by one in respect of each position for which there is no designation under subsection 12(5); and
(c) increased to take into account the termination in the current calendar year of a secondment, sabbatical, leave of absence or any other scheme or plan acceptable under its agreements, board policy or an understanding with its branch affiliate or branch affiliates, where, pursuant to an agreement under subsection 135(1) of the Act, the public board in a previous calendar year, reduced, because of the secondment, sabbatical, leave of absence or other scheme or plan, the number of positions in respect of which it was required to make designations.

(3) The number of positions in respect of which teachers are to be designated under section 135 of the Act shall be the lesser of,

(a) the number determined under subsection (1) as adjusted under subsection (2), calculated to one place of decimal; and
(b) the number of positions determined under clause 3(1)(a).

(4) Where the number of teachers available for designation under clause 3(1)(b) is reduced by the employment, death or retirement of a teacher referred to in clause 3(1)(b) and is less than the number of teachers required to be designated under subsection (3), the determination under subsection (3) of the number of positions in respect of which teachers are to be designated under section 135 of the Act shall be reduced accordingly.

6. (1) Every Roman Catholic school board shall, on or before the 30th day of April in each year, provide to each public board that is coterminous with the Roman Catholic school board, a list of the positions on its elementary and secondary teaching staffs that are expected to be vacant in the Roman Catholic school board in the following school year.

(2) A public board that receives a list under subsection (1) shall forthwith make the list known to all teachers in the employ of the public board.

7. Each public board shall, within fifteen days of receiving the list of vacancies in the Roman Catholic school board, provide to each Roman Catholic school board that is coterminous with the public board a list,

(a) of all teachers who have been identified under clause 3(1)(b) who are willing to transfer voluntarily to the Roman Catholic school board to fill the vacancies in the Roman Catholic school board; and
(b) showing each teacher, in addition to those teachers referred to in clause (a), who is

willing to transfer voluntarily to the Roman Catholic school board to fill a vacancy in the Roman Catholic school board.

8. (1) Every public board shall, on or before the 31st day of May in each year, designate teachers under section 135 of the Act to the number of positions set out in subsection (4) as follows:

1. In order of seniority, designate the teachers identified under clause 7(a).
2. Where there are positions remaining to be designated after designating the teachers referred to in paragraph 1, in order of seniority, designate the teachers identified under clause 7(b) if the vacancy created in the public board can be filled by a teacher identified under clause 3(1)(b).
3. Where there are positions remaining to be designated after designating the teachers referred to in paragraphs 1 and 2, designate, in accordance with its agreements, board policy or an understanding with its branch affiliate or branch affiliates, an appropriate number of teachers from among the teachers identified in clause 3(1)(b), ensuring where possible that the proportion of qualifications of teachers designated is representative of the proportion of qualifications of teachers employed by the public board.

(2) In the absence of any agreement, board policy or understanding that deals with how teachers shall be designated, the public board shall designate teachers referred to in paragraph 3 of subsection (1) in order of seniority.

(3) In designating the teachers under this section, each teacher who is employed on a part-time basis shall be counted towards the number of teachers designated only to the proportion of a full-time employee that the teacher represents.

(4) The number of teachers designated under this section shall be equal to or shall differ by less than one from the number of positions determined under section 5.

9. Each public board that makes a designation under this Regulation and each Roman Catholic school board that is coterminous with the public board shall provide a list of the teachers so designated to each of its branch affiliates.

10. Each board shall consult with its branch affiliates in respect of any matter required or implemented under this Regulation.

11. Nothing in this Regulation prevents a public board that has jurisdiction in an area that is also the area or part of the area of jurisdiction of two or more Roman Catholic school boards from having an agreement within the meaning of subsection 135(1) of the Act with one or more of the Roman Catholic school boards with respect to the designation of teachers under section 135 of the Act while at the same time dealing with one or more of the Roman Catholic school boards under this Regulation.

12. (1) If a position with a public board becomes vacant in the year in which a teacher who is designated under section 8, up to and including the 31st day of May in the year next following, and no teacher employed or eligible to be employed under the recall provisions of the agreement of the public board is available to fill the position, the public board shall offer the right of first refusal with respect to the position to the designated teacher with the greatest seniority who holds the qualifications to fill the position.

(2) Where the teacher with the greatest seniority refuses or cannot fill the position referred to in subsection (1),

(a) the position shall be offered to other designated teachers with the qualifications to fill the position in descending order of seniority until the position is filled or there are no more designated teachers; and

(b) the public board shall not be obligated to continue offering positions to that teacher.

(3) Where a teacher accepts an offer referred to in subsection (1), the Roman Catholic school board shall transfer the teacher's contract of employment to the public board and the public board shall treat the teacher's contract of employment as if the teacher had never left the employ of the public board.

(4) Where a teacher accepts an offer referred to in subsection (1), the public board shall allow the Roman Catholic school board a reasonable length of time in the circumstances to fill the vacancy thus created before requiring the transfer of the teacher.

(5) If, as a result of a teacher accepting an offer referred to in subsection (1), a position becomes vacant in the Roman Catholic school board and there are still teachers unemployed who were identified in accordance with clause 3(1)(b), the public board may designate another teacher to fill the position in accordance with section 8.

13. (1) Where a teacher files an objection under subsection 135(13) of the Act and the public board is of the opinion that the objection is made in good faith, the public board shall designate another teacher in place of the teacher making the objection in accordance with its agreements or understanding with its branch affiliate or branch affiliates or board policy.

(2) In the absence of a provision in its agreements, board policy or understanding with its branch affiliate or branch affiliates with respect to the designation of another teacher, the public board shall designate a teacher under subsection (1) by taking into account the seniority of the teachers from among whom it is selecting and ensuring where possible that the proportion of qualifications of teachers designated is representative of the proportion of qualifications of teachers employed by the public board.

14. Where a school operated by a public board under Part XII of the Act is transferred to a Roman Catholic school board and the transfer is approved by the Minister, the public board shall designate under section 135 of the Act all teachers employed in the school.

15. Each public board that operates a school or class under Part XII of the Act shall make the determinations and designations required to be made under this Regulation separately for,

(a) the French-language schools and classes operated by it under Part XII of the Act; and

(b) for all schools and classes other than those referred to in clause (a) that it operates.

16. All teachers who are designated by a public board on and after the 24th day of June, 1986 up to and including the 12th day of February, 1987 shall be deemed to have been designated in accordance with this Regulation and the adjustments required under subsection 5(2) shall be made in respect of such designations.

REGULATION 290
DISTRICT COMBINED SEPARATE SCHOOL ZONES
R.R.O. 1990, Reg. 290: am. O. Reg. 526/92, O. Reg. 730/92, O. Reg. 412/93

1. The municipalities, geographic townships and localities referred to in paragraph 1 of each Schedule are designated as an area that forms a district combined separate school zone.

2. The name set out in paragraph 2 of each Schedule is the name designated for the area designated in paragraph 1 of that Schedule.

Schedule 1

1. In the Territorial District of Kenora, being,
    i. the towns of Jaffray and Melick, Keewatin and Kenora,
    ii. the Township of Sioux Narrows,
    iii. the geographic townships of Boys, Kirkup, Pellatt and Redditt,
    iv. all the lands in unsurveyed territory in the vicinity of the station house of the Canadian National Railways at Minaki described as follows:

    Commencing at a point distant 4 kilometres measured east astronomically from the northeast corner of the said station house;

    Thence north astronomically 4 kilometres;

    Thence west astronomically 8 kilometres;

    Thence south astronomically 8 kilometres;

    Thence east astronomically 8 kilometres;

    Thence north astronomically 4 kilometres to the point of commencement, and
    v. except for those parts of the mainland which are crossed by the said line, all lands lying north of a line extending from the southernmost extremity of the geographic Township of Boys to the southwest corner of the geographic Township of Kirkup and south of the southerly boundaries of the geographic townships of Boys and Pellatt, the towns of Jaffray and Melick, Keewatin and Kenora.
2. Kenora.

Schedule 2

1. In the Territorial District of Kenora, being,
    i. the towns of Dryden and Sioux Lookout,
    ii. the townships of Barclay and Machin,
    iii. the geographic townships of Britton, Buller, Colenso, Drayton, Eton, Hartman, Ilsley, Jordan, Ladysmith, Melgund, Mutrie, Redvers, Rowell, Rugby, Smellie, Southworth, Van Horne, Vermilion, Vermilion Additional, Wabigoon, Wainwright and Zealand,
    iv. that portion of the geographic Township of Aubrey that is not part of the Township of Machin, and

REGULATION 290 **Sched. 3**

    v. that portion of Block 10 lying south of the production easterly and westerly of the most northerly limit of the geographic Township of Drayton.
2. Dryden.

Schedule 3

1. In the Territorial District of,
    i. Rainy River, being,
        A. the towns of Fort Frances and Rainy River,
        B. the townships of Alberton, Atwood, Blue, Chapple, Dilke, Emo, La Vallee, Morley, Morson and Worthington,
        C. the Township of McCrosson and Tovell,
        D. the Improvement District of Kingsford,
        E. the geographic townships of Claxton, Croome, Dance, Dewart, Farrington, Fleming, Griesinger, Halkirk, Mathieu, McLarty, Menary, Miscampbell, Nelles, Pratt, Rowe, Senn, Sifton, Spohn, Sutherland and Watten,
        F. The Wild Land Reserve,
        G. all lands in unsurveyed territory within an area the boundary sides of which are as follows:
            1. On the north side, the northerly limit of the Territorial District of Rainy River commencing at the point of intersection of the 49th degree parallel of north latitude with the International Boundary; thence due east 24 kilometres more or less along the 49th degree parallel of north latitude to the east shore of the Lake of the Woods; thence north easterly and northerly along the east shore of the Lake of the Woods and the south and east shores of Sabaskong Bay of the Lake of the Woods to the point of intersection of the westerly production of the north boundaries of the geographic townships of Claxton and McLarty; thence due easterly along the said north boundaries of the said geographic townships and along their production due east being along O.L.S. Gillon's base line of 1919 to the 24th mile post on O.L.S. Alexander Niven's 6th meridian line; thence due south along the said meridian line 9.6 kilometres to the 18th mile post thereon in latitude 49° 0' 6'' north; thence due east to the point of intersection of the production north of the east boundary of the geographic Township of Farrington.
            2. On the east side, the line formed by the east boundary of the geographic Township of Farrington, the production of the said east boundary due north to the north boundary of the Territorial District of Rainy River and the production due south of the said east boundary to the International Boundary.
            3. On the south side, the International Boundary from the mouth of the Rainy River easterly to the point of intersection on the Inter-

Sched. 4 REGULATIONS UNDER THE EDUCATION ACT

national Boundary of the production due south of the east boundary of the geographic Township of Farrington.
4. On the west side, the International Boundary from the mouth of the Rainy River northerly to the point of intersection on the International Boundary of the 49th degree parallel of north latitude, and
  ii. Kenora, being,
   A. the geographic townships of Godson, Phillips and Tweedsmuir,
   B. all lands in unsurveyed territory within an area the boundary sides of which are as follows:
      1. On the west side, the International Boundary between the point of intersection thereon of the 49th degree parallel of north latitude and the point of intersection of the production westerly of the north boundary of the geographic Township of Tweedsmuir along the 4th base line.
      2. On the south side, the line described as commencing at the point of intersection of the 49th degree parallel of north latitude with the International Boundary; thence due east 24 kilometres more or less along the 49th degree parallel of north latitude to the east shore of the Lake of the Woods; thence north easterly and northerly along the east shore of the Lake of the Woods and the south and east shores of Sabaskong Bay of the Lake of the Woods to the point of intersection of the westerly production of the south boundary of the geographic Township of Godson; thence due east along the said north boundary of the said geographic Township and along its production due east being along O.L.S. Gillon's base line of 1919 to the 24th mile post on O.L.S. Alexander Niven's 6th meridian line.
      3. On the east side, O.L.S. Alexander Niven's 6th meridian line between the 24th mile post thereon and the point of intersection on the said meridian line of the production due east along the 4th base line of the north boundary of the geographic Township of Tweedsmuir.
      4. On the north side, the production along the 4th base line westerly to the International Boundary and easterly to O.L.S. Alexander Niven's 6th meridian line of the north boundary of the geographic Township of Tweedsmuir.
2. The Fort Frances-Rainy River.

Schedule 4

1. In the Territorial District of Thunder Bay, being,
   i. the City of Thunder Bay,
   ii. the townships of Conmee, Gillies, Neebing, O'Connor, Oliver, Paipoonge and Shuniah,
   iii. the geographic townships of Blackwell, Conacher, Devon, Forbes, Fraleigh,

REGULATION 290 **Sched. 8**

Goldie, Golding, Gorham, Hagey, Laurie, Lismore, Lybster, Marks, Michener, Pearson, Robson, Scoble, Sibley, Strange and Ware,
    iv. the Dawson Road Lots, and
    v. the area bounded by the easterly boundary of Lot 1, concessions 1 and 2 of the Dawson Road Lots; the southerly boundary of the geographic Township of Forbes; the westerly shore of the Kaministiquia River (sometimes known as the Dog River) and the northerly shore of the Shebandowan River (sometimes known as the Matawin River).
2. Lakehead.

Schedule 5

1. In the Territorial District of Thunder Bay, being,
    i. the towns of Geraldton and Longlac,
    ii. the Township of Beardmore, and
    iii. the geographic townships of Ashmore, Daley, Errington, Houck, Leduc and Oakes.
2. Geraldton.

Schedule 6

1. In the Territorial District of Algoma, being,
    i. the City of Sault Ste. Marie,
    ii. the Township of Macdonald, Meredith and Aberdeen Additional,
    iii. the Township of Tarbutt and Tarbutt Additional,
    iv. the townships of Johnson, Laird and Prince,
    v. the geographic townships of Archibald, Awres, Dennis, Deroche, Fenwick, Fisher, Gaudette, Havilland, Herrick, Hodgins, Home, Jarvis, Kars, Kincaid, Ley, Peever, Pennefather, Rix, Ryan, Shields, Slater, Tilley, Tupper and VanKoughnet, and
    vi. the mining locations known as Montreal Mining Southern Location, Montreal Mining Northern Location, A. McDonnell Mining Location, Kincaid Mining Locations 5, 6, 7 and 8 and Rankin Mining Location.
2. Sault Ste. Marie.

Schedule 7

1. In the Territorial District of Algoma, being the townships of Michipicoten and White River and the geographic townships of Esquega and Fiddler.
2. Michipicoten.

Schedule 8

1. In the Territorial District of,
    i. Algoma, being,
        A. the town of Blind River and Elliot Lake,

Sched. 9   REGULATIONS UNDER THE EDUCATION ACT

- B. the Village of Iron Bridge,
- C. the townships of Day and Bright Additional, The North Shore, Shedden and Thompson,
- D. the geographic townships of Bright, Cobden, Gladstone, Grasett, Jogues, Juillette, Kamichisitit, Mack, Montgomery, Nouvel, Parkinson, Patton, Scarfe and Timmermans,
- E. the portion of the geographic Township of Striker that is not part of the Township of The North Shore, and
- F. all the islands of the North Channel of Lake Huron lying south of the geographic townships of Bright, Cobden and the portion of Striker that is not part of the Township of The North Shore.

 ii. Sudbury, being.
- A. the towns of Espanola, Massey and Webbwood,
- B. the townships of Baldwin, Nairn and The Spanish River,
- C. the geographic townships of Curtin, Foster, Gough, McKinnon, Merritt, Mongowin, Roosevelt, Shakespeare and Truman, and
- D. the portion of the geographic Township of Hyman that is not part of the Town of Walden.

 iii. Manitoulin, being the Town of Little Current.
2. North Shore.

Schedule 9

1. In the Territorial District of,
    i. Sudbury, being,
    - A. The Regional Municipality of Sudbury,
    - B. the Township of Casimir, Jennings and Appleby,
    - C. the Township of Cosby, Mason and Martland,
    - D. the Township of Hagar,
    - E. the Township of Ratter and Dunnet,
    - F. the geographic townships of Allen, Awrey, Bigwood, Burwash, Cartier, Cascaden, Cherriman, Cleland, Cox, Davis, Delamere, Foy, Haddo, Hart, Harty, Hawley, Hendrie, Henry, Hess, Hoskin, Janes, Laura, Loughrin, Moncrieff, Scadding, Scollard, Secord, Servos and Street,
    - G. the portions of the geographic townships of Dill, Eden and Tilton that are not part of The Regional Municipality of Sudbury,
    - H. the portion of the geographic Township of Dryden that is not part of The Regional Municipality of Sudbury, and,
    - I. the portion of the geographic Township of Trill that is not part of The Regional Municipality of Sudbury.
    ii. Manitoulin, being the Township of Rutherford and George Island, and
    iii. Parry Sound, being the geographic Township of Henvey and Wallbridge.
2. Sudbury.

REGULATION 290 **Sched. 12**

Schedule 10

1. In the Territorial District of Sudbury, being,
    i. the Township of Chapleau, and
    ii. the geographic townships of Caverley, Chapleau, de Gaulle, Eisenhower, Gallagher, Genier, Halsey, Kaplan and Panet.
2. Chapleau.

Schedule 11

1. In the
    i. Territorial District of Nipissing, being,
        A. the City of North Bay,
        B. the towns of Cache Bay, Kearney, Mattawa and Sturgeon Falls,
        C. the townships of Bonfield, Caldwell, Calvin, Chisholm, East Ferris, Field, Mattawan, Papineau-Cameron and Springer,
        D. the geographic townships of Badgerow, Bastedo, Beaucage, Blyth, Boyd, Clarkson, Commanda, Crerar, Deacon, Eddy, Falconer, French, Gibbons, Grant, Hugel, Jocko, Kirkpatrick, Lauder, Loudon, Lyman, Macpherson, Merrick, Notman, Pedley, Pentland, Phelps, Poitras and Wyse, and
    ii. Territorial District of Parry Sound, being,
        A. the towns of Kearney, Powassan and Trout Creek,
        B. the villages of Burk's Falls, Magnetawan, Rosseau, South River and Sundridge,
        C. the townships of Armour, Chapman, Humphrey, Joly, Machar, McMurrich, Nipissing, North Himsworth, Perry, Ryerson, South Himsworth and Strong, and
        D. the geographic townships of Laurier, Lount, Monteith, Patterson and Pringle, and
    iii. District Municipality of Muskoka, being,
        A. the Town of Huntsville, and
        B. the Township of Lake of Bays.
2. Nipissing. O. Reg. 526/92, s. 1.

Schedule 12

1. In the Territorial District of,
    i. Cochrane, being the portion of the geographic Township of Benoit that is not part of the Township of Black River-Matheson,
    ii. Nipissing, being,
        A. the Township of Temagami, and
        B. the geographic townships of Askin, Aston, Banting, Belfast, Best, Briggs, Canton, Cassels, Chambers, Cynthia, Eldridge, Flett, Gladman, Gooderham, Hammell, Hartle, Hobbs, Joan, Kenny, Law, Le Roche, Mc-

Sched. 13 REGULATIONS UNDER THE EDUCATION ACT

              Callum, McLaren, Milne, Olive, Phyllis, Riddell, Sisk, Thistle, Torrington, Vogt and Yates, and
    iii. Timiskaming, being,
        A. the towns of Cobalt, Charlton, Englehart, Haileybury, Kirkland Lake, Latchford and New Liskeard,
        B. the Village of Thornloe,
        C. the townships of Armstrong, Brethour, Casey, Chamberlain, Coleman, Dack, Dymond, Evanturel, Harley, Harris, Hilliard, Hudson, James, Kerns, Larder Lake and McGarry,
        D. the improvement districts of Gauthier and Matachewan, and
        E. the geographic townships of Auld, Barber, Barr, Bayly, Beauchamp, Boston, Brigstocke, Bryce, Cane, Catharine, Chown, Coleman, Corkill, Davidson, Eby, Farr, Firstbrook, Gillies Limit, Grenfell, Haultain, Henwood, Ingram, Kittson, Lawson, Lebel, Lorrain, Lundy, Maisonville, Marquis, Marter, McElroy, Mickle, Milner, Mulligan, Nichol, Otto, Pacaud, Pense, Roadhouse, Robillard, Savard, Sharpe, Smyth, South Lorrain, Truax, Tudhope, Willet and Willison.
2.   Kirkland Lake – Timiskaming. O. Reg. 730/92, s. 1.

Schedule 13

[Revoked O. Reg. 730/92, s. 2.]

Schedule 14

1.   In the Territorial District of Cochrane, being,
    i. the towns of Cochrane and Iroquois Falls,
    ii. the townships of Black River-Matheson and Glackmeyer, and
    iii. the geographic townships of Aurora, Blount, Brower, Calder, Clute, Colquhoun, Fournier, Fox, Guibord, Hanna, Kennedy, Lamarche, Leitch, Mortimer, Munro, Newmarket, Ottaway, Pyne, St. John, Stimson and Teefy. O. Reg. 412/93, s. 1.
2.   Cochrane-Iroquois Falls, Black River-Matheson.

Schedule 15

1.   In the Territorial District of Cochrane, being,
    i. the towns of Kapuskasing and Smooth Rock Falls,
    ii. the townships of Fauquier-Strikland, Moonbeam, Opasatika and Val Rita-Harty,
    iii. the geographic townships of Haggart, McCowan, Nansen and O'Brien, and
    iv. the portion of the Township of Owens that is not part of the Township of Val Rita-Harty.
2.   Kapuskasing.

Schedule 16

1. In the Territorial District of,
    i. Cochrane, being,
        A. the Town of Hearst,
        B. the Township of Mattice-Val Côté, and
        C. the geographic townships of Barker, Casgrain, Hanlan, Irish, Kendall, Landry, Lowther, Stoddard, Studholme and Way, and
    ii. Algoma, being the geographic townships of Ebbs and Templeton.
2. Hearst.

Schedule 17

1. In the Territorial District of Cochrane, being the City of Timmins.
2. Timmins.

Schedule 18

1. In the Territorial District of Thunder Bay, being,
    i. the Town of Marathon,
    ii. the townships of Dorion, Manitouwadge, Nakina, Nipigon, Red Rock, Schreiber and Terrace Bay,
    iii. the geographic townships of Atikameg, Bomby, Boothe, Brothers, Bryant, Byron, Cecil, Cecile, Coldwell, Corrigal, Cotte, Davies, Flood, Foote, Grain, Grenville, Herbert, Homer, Killraine, Knowles, Laberge, Lahontan, Lecours, Lyon, McCron, McGill, Mikano, Nickle, O'Neill, Pic, Priske, Roberta, Shabotik, Spooner, Stirling, Strey, Syine, Tuuri, Walsh, Wiggins and Yesno,
    iv. all lands, excluding St. Ignace Island, in unsurveyed territory within an area described as follows:
        A. on the north side, the extension of the north side of the geographic Township of Davies westerly to intersect with the boundary formed by extending the west side of the geographic Township of Wiggins northerly until it meets the said extension,
        B. on the east side, the extension of the east side of the geographic Township of Spooner southerly until the Canada-United States border,
        C. on the south side, the Canada-United States border, and
        D. on the west side, the extension of the west side of the geographic Township of Wiggins southerly until the Canada-United States border,
2. North of Superior.

REGULATION 291
DISTRICT SCHOOL AREAS
R.R.O. 1990, Reg. 291

The Airy and Sabine District School Area

1. The Airy District School Area and The Sabine District School Area are combined into one district school area to be known as The Airy and Sabine District School Area.

The Caramat District School Area

2. The lands described in the following Schedule are formed into a district school area to be known as The Caramat District School Area:

Schedule

All and singular that tract of land in the Compact Rural Community of Caramat and surrounding area in the Territorial District of Thunder Bay more particularly described as follows:

Beginning at a point distant 2 miles measured north astronomically from the intersection of the northeasterly limit of the Canadian National Railway with the northerly limit of Location JK 320;

Thence west astronomically 2 miles;

Thence south astronomically 4 miles;

Thence east astronomically 4 miles;

Thence north astronomically 4 miles;

Thence west astronomically 2 miles, more or less, to the place of beginning.

The Collins District School Area

3. The lands described in the following Schedule are formed into a district school area to be known as The Collins District School Area:

Schedule

All and singular that tract of land situate in the Territorial District of Thunder Bay, having an area of one square mile and bounded as follows:

On the north by a line drawn due east and west astronomically through a point distant one half-mile measured due north astronomically from mile board 21 on the main line of the Canadian National Railway at the hamlet of Collins; on the east by a line drawn due north and south astronomically through a point distant one half-mile due east astronomically from the said mile board; on the south by a line drawn due east and west astronomically through a point distant one half-mile due south astronomically from the said mile board; and on the west by a line drawn due north and south astronomically through a point distant one half-mile due west astronomically from the said mile board.

The Connell and Ponsford District School Area

4. The part of the Improvement District of Pickle Lake in the Patricia Portion of the Territorial District of Kenora that is not within The Connell and Ponsford District School Area is added to such district school area.

The Kilkenny District School Area

5. The lands in the geographic Township of Kilkenny in the Territorial District of Thunder Bay described in the following Schedule that comprise The Kilkenny District School Area are altered by excluding therefrom the lands comprising the Rocky Bay Indian Reserve Number 1 and by adding thereto the portion of the geographic Township of Kilkenny not included in the Schedule:

Schedule

In the geographic Township of Kilkenny in the Territorial District of Thunder Bay, being that area originally comprising school section No. 1 MacDiarmid and being an area five miles square whose boundaries begin at a point one mile south from north latitude 49 degrees, 30 minutes and one mile west from 88 degrees west longitude and that extends five miles due west, then five miles due south, then five miles due east and then five miles due north to the point of beginning.

The McCullagh District School Area

6. The portion of The Connell and Ponsford District School Area that is in the geographic Township of McCullagh in the Patricia Portion of the Territorial District of Kenora, being all that portion of such district school area that is not in the Improvement District of Pickle Lake, is detached from The Connell and Ponsford District School Area and formed into The McCullagh District School Area.

The Moose Factory Island District School Area

7. The lands described in the following Schedule are formed into a district school area to be known as The Moose Factory Island District School Area:

Schedule

The area in the Territorial District of Cochrane consisting of the islands in the Moose River that are situate in their entirety north of the line formed by the projection easterly of the southerly boundary of the geographic Township of Horden to the westerly limit of Indian Reserve No. 68, except Indian Reserve No. 1 on Moose Factory Island.

The Moosonee District School Area

8. The following parts of the Territorial District of Cochrane are added to The Moosonee District School Area:
 1. The geographic Township of Caron.
 2. The parts of the geographic townships of Horden and Moose that are not in The Moosonee District School Area, except the parts of such geographic townships that are composed of islands and parts of islands in the Moose River.

The Northern District School Area

9. The Allanwater District School Area, The Armstrong District School Area, The Auden District School Area, The Ferland District School Area and The Savant Lake District School Area are combined into one district school area to be known as The Northern District School Area.

The Slate Falls District School Area

10. The lands described in the following Schedule are formed into a district school area to be known as The Slate Falls District School Area:

Schedule

All and singular that tract of land situate in the Patricia Portion of the Territorial District of Kenora, more particularly described as follows:

Beginning at the place of intersection of the Ninth Base Line and the Fourth Meridian; thence easterly along the Ninth Base Line a distance of six miles to a point; thence northerly and parallel to the Fourth Meridian a distance of six miles to a point; thence westerly and parallel to the Ninth Base Line to a point in the Fourth Meridian; thence southerly along the Fourth Meridian to the place of beginning.

The Sturgeon Lake District School Area

11. The lands described in the following Schedule are formed into a district school area to be known as The Sturgeon Lake District School Area:

Schedule

All and singular that tract of land situate in the Territorial District of Kenora being within an area four miles in width lying on both sides of the centre line of secondary highway No. 599 and within two miles of and measured at right angles to that portion of the said centre line extending from the easterly boundary of the Township of Ignace northeasterly a distance of forty-five miles.

The Summer Beaver District School Area

12. The lands described in the following Schedule are formed into a district school area to be known as The Summer Beaver District School Area:

Schedule

All and singular that tract of land situate in the Patricia Portion of the Territorial District of Kenora being within a radius of two miles from a point having a latitude of 52° 45' North and a longitude of 88° 30' West.

REGULATION 292
FEES FOR MINISTRY COURSES
R.R.O. 1990, Reg. 292

1. In this Regulation, "course" means a course provided by the Ministry leading to,
  (a) the Program Development and Implementation qualification;
  (b) the Program Supervision and Assessment qualification; and
  (c) the Principal's Refresher Course qualification.

2. Subject to section 3, the total tuition fee to be paid for a course shall be $390 which shall consist of,
  (a) a non-refundable amount of $40 payable upon application for admission to the course; and
  (b) an amount of $350 payable not later than thirty days prior to the commencement of the course.

3. (1) Where a person who has applied to take a course does not commence the course, no amount referred to in clause 2(b) is payable, and any amount referred to in clause 2(b) received for the course by or on behalf of such person shall be refunded to the person who paid it.

(2) Where a person who has commenced a course withdraws from the course during the first week of the course, other than for medical reasons or compassionate grounds, and gives notice in writing to the Ministry of the withdrawal, the amount referred to in clause 2(b) that is payable by or on behalf of such person shall be $87.50 and any amount in excess of $87.50 that was paid for the course by or on behalf of such person shall be refunded to the person who paid it.

(3) Where a person who has commenced a course withdraws from the course because of,
  (a) medical reasons evidenced by the certificate of a medical doctor; or
  (b) compassionate grounds acceptable to the Minister,

the amount referred to in clause 2(b) that is payable by or on behalf of such person shall be nil if the withdrawal is during the first week of the course and shall be reduced by $87.50 for each full week of the course that is subsequent to the withdrawal if the withdrawal is during the second or any subsequent week, and the appropriate amount shall be refunded to the person who paid the fee for the course.

(4) The fee to be paid under this Regulation by or on behalf of a teacher, principal or supervisory officer who was on active service in His or Her Majesty's forces in World War II or the Korean War and who produces proof of such services shall be nil.

REGULATION 293
FEES FOR TRANSCRIPTS AND STATEMENTS OF STANDING AND FOR DUPLICATES OF DIPLOMAS, CERTIFICATES AND LETTERS OF STANDING
R.R.O. 1990, Reg. 293: am. O. Reg. 341/92, O. Reg. 522/93

1. (1) The fee for a transcript of standing, or for a duplicate of a diploma or certificate, obtained in Ontario by a pupil is $20.

(2) The fee set out in subsection (1) shall be adjusted as follows:
1. As of October 1, 1993, to $21.
2. As of July 1, 1994, to $22.
3. As of July 1, 1995, to $23.
4. As of July 1, 1996, to $24. O. Reg. 341/92, s. 1; O. Reg. 522/93, s. 1.

2. (1) The fee for a duplicate of an Ontario Teacher's Certificate is $37.

(2) The fee set out in subsection (1) shall be adjusted as follows:
1. As of October 1, 1993, to $39.
2. As of July 1, 1994, to $41
3. As of July 1, 1995, to $43.
4. As of July 1, 1996, to $45. O. Reg. 341/92, s. 2; O. Reg. 522/93, s. 2.

3. (1) The fee for a duplicate of a letter of standing, or of a certificate of qualification as a teacher other than an Ontario Teacher's Certificate, is $20.

(2) The fee set out in subsection (1) shall be adjusted as follows:
1. As of October 1, 1993, to $21.
2. As of July 1, 1994, to $22.
3. As of July 1, 1995, to $23.
4. As of July 1, 1996, to $24. O. Reg. 341/92, s. 3; O. Reg. 522/93, s. 3.

4. (1) The fee for the preparation by the Ministry, on the request of a teacher, of a statement of standing obtained, and a description of courses completed, at a teacher's education institution in Ontario is $20.

(2) The fee set out in subsection (1) shall be adjusted as follows:
1. As of October 1, 1993, to $21.
2. As of July 1, 1994, to $22.
3. As of July 1, 1995, to $23.
4. As of July 1, 1996, to $24. O. Reg. 341/92, s. 4; O. Reg. 522/93, s. 4.

REGULATION 294
THE JAMES BAY LOWLANDS SECONDARY SCHOOL BOARD
R.R.O. 1990, Reg. 294

1. In this Regulation,

"board" means The James Bay Lowlands Secondary School Board;

"elector", in respect of an area for which one or more members of the board are to be elected, means a person who is the owner or tenant of property in, or a resident of, such area and who is a Canadian citizen or other British subject and of the full age of eighteen years;

"equalized assessment" for a municipality or a locality means the assessment upon which taxes are levied in the municipality or locality, as the case may be, in the year for which the apportionment is made as adjusted by the latest assessment equalization factor applicable thereto that is provided by the Minister.

2. The James Bay Lowlands Secondary School Board is continued and has jurisdiction in The James Bay Lowlands Secondary School District described in the Schedule.

3. (1) Subject to subsection (2), the board shall be composed of four members of whom,

 (a) two shall be elected by and from among the electors in respect of the mainland portion of the geographic townships of Caron, Horden and Moose;

 (b) one shall be elected by and from among the electors in respect of the islands in the Moose River that form part of the secondary school district except the portion of Factory Island that is an Indian Reserve; and

 (c) one shall be elected by and from among the electors of the Moose Band in respect of Indian Reserves 1 and 68.

(2) Where the board has agreed to negotiate an agreement under subsection 188(1) of the Act to provide tuition for Indian pupils,

 (a) from the Attawapiskat Band, the council of the Attawapiskat Band may appoint as a member of the board a member of the Band from Indian Reserve 91 or 91A if the council of the Attawapiskat Band passes a resolution requesting a member on the board and forwards a copy thereof to the secretary of the board;

 (b) from the Kashechewan community, the council of the Albany Band may appoint as a member of the board a member of the Band from the Kashechewan community of Indian Reserve 67 if the council of the Albany Band passes a resolution requesting a member on the board from the Kashechewan community and forwards a copy thereof to the secretary of the board; or

 (c) from the Fort Albany community, the council of the Albany Band may appoint as a member of the board a member of the Band from the Fort Albany community of Indian Reserve 67 if the council of the Albany Band passes a resolution requesting a member on the board from the Fort Albany community and forwards a copy thereof to the secretary of the board,

and a member appointed under this subsection is in addition to the number of members of the board provided for in subsection (1), and the term of office of such member terminates on the same date as the term of office of the elected members.

REGULATION 294   S. 6

4. (1) In addition to the disqualifications set out in the Act, a person is not qualified to be elected or to act as a member of the board who is a member of, or the secretary-treasurer of, The Moosonee Development Area Board.

(2) A member of the board who ceases to be an elector in respect of the area for which he or she was elected is thereupon disqualified to act as a member of the board.

5. (1) Meetings shall be held in the year 1982 and in every third year thereafter on such date in the month of November and at such places and times as the board may determine for the purpose of electing the members of the board referred to in subsection 3(1).

(2) The term of office of a member of the board shall be three years commencing on the 1st day of December next following his or her election to the board.

(3) Where a vacancy occurs from any cause in the office of an elected member of the board, the remaining members shall, subject to section 225 of the Act, forthwith hold a new election to fill the vacancy in the manner provided by this Regulation for holding an election of the board, except that the election shall be held only in respect of the area for which the vacancy occurs.

(4) At least six days before a meeting under this section, the secretary of the board shall post notice of the meeting in two or more of the most prominent places in the area from which one or more members are to be elected at the meeting and shall advertise the meeting in such other manner as the board considers expedient.

(5) A meeting under this section shall be conducted in the manner determined by the electors in respect of the area for which the meeting is held who are present at the meeting, by a presiding officer selected by such electors, but the election of the member or members of the board shall be by ballot, and the minutes of the meeting shall be recorded by a secretary who shall,

(a) in the case of the meeting to elect the members provided for in clause 3(1)(a), be the secretary of The Moosonee Development Area Board;
(b) in the case of the meeting to elect the member provided for in clause 3(1)(b), be the secretary of The Moose Factory Island Board of Education; and
(c) in the case of the meeting to elect the member provided for in clause 3(1)(c), be the chief of the Moose Band or a person designated by the chief.

(6) If objection is made to the right of a person to vote at a meeting under this section or section 8, the presiding officer shall require the person to make the following declaration:

I .... declare and affirm that,

1. I am of the full age of eighteen years.
2. I am a Canadian citizen or British subject.
3. I have a right to vote at this election (*or* on the question submitted to this meeting).

and after making such declaration, the person making it may vote.

(7) Subsections 92(9), (10), (12), (13), (17), (18), (19), (20) and (22) of the Act apply with necessary modifications to a meeting under this Regulation.

6. (1) The sum required by the board for secondary school purposes in each year shall be apportioned between the Moosonee Development Area and the remainder of the James Bay Lowlands Secondary School District in the ratio of the equalized assessment of the property rateable for secondary school purposes in the Moosonee Development Area to the equalized assessment of such property in the remainder of such secondary school district.

(2) For the purpose of subsection (1), the Moosonee Development Area is deemed to be a municipality and the portion of The James Bay Lowlands Secondary School District that is not in the Moosonee Development Area is deemed to be a locality.

7. (1) Subject to subsection (2), subsections 235(1) and (2) of the Act apply with necessary modifications to the board.

(2) The board may not apply to the Ontario Municipal Board in respect of the issue of debentures for a permanent improvement until such issue has been sanctioned at a special meeting of the electors of The James Bay Lowlands Secondary School District.

8. (1) A special meeting of the electors of the secondary school district shall be called by the secretary of the board when directed by the board or upon the request in writing of five such electors, by posting, at least six days before the meeting, notice of the meeting in three or more of the most prominent places in the secondary school district and such notice shall include the date, time, place and objects of the meeting, and the meeting shall be advertised in such other manner as the board considers expedient.

(2) A special meeting under this section shall be conducted in the manner determined by the electors of the secondary school district who are present at the meeting, by a presiding officer selected by such electors and the minutes of the meeting shall be recorded by the secretary of the board.

Schedule
The James Bay Lowlands Secondary School District

That part of the Territorial District of Cochrane comprised of the geographic townships of Caron, Horden and Moose and the unsurveyed territory consisting of the islands in the Moose River that are situate in their entirety north of a line formed by the projection easterly of the southerly boundary of the geographic Township of Horden to the westerly limit of Indian Reserve No. 68.

REGULATION 295
THE NORTHERN DISTRICT SCHOOL AREA BOARD
R.R.O. 1990, Reg. 295

1. In this Regulation,

"Board" means The Northern District School Area Board;

"elector", in respect of an area for which one or more members of the Board are to be elected, means a person who is a public school elector of such area as defined in subsection 61(1) of the Act.

2. The Board is continued with jurisdiction in The Northern District School Area set out in section 9 of Regulation 291 of Revised Regulations of Ontario, 1990.

3. (1) The Board shall be composed of eight members,
  (a) one of whom shall be elected by and from the electors of the school section formerly known as The Allanwater District School Area;
  (b) three of whom shall be elected by and from the electors of the school section formerly known as The Armstrong District School Area;
  (c) one of whom shall be elected by and from the electors of the school section formerly known as The Auden District School Area;
  (d) one of whom shall be elected by and from the electors of the school section formerly known as The Ferland District School Area; and
  (e) two of whom shall be elected by and from the electors of the school section formerly known as The Savant Lake District School Area.

(2) Where a member of the Board ceases to be an elector in respect of the area for which he or she was elected he or she ceases to be qualified to act as a member of the Board.

4. (1) Meetings of the Board shall be held in the year 1982 and in every third year thereafter on such date in the month of November and, subject to subsection (2), at such places and times as the Board may determine for the purpose of electing the members of the Board referred to in subsection 3(1).

(2) The members of the Board shall be elected at a general meeting of the electors of each former district school area held separately within each former district school area.

(3) The term of office of a member of the Board shall be three years commencing on the 1st day of December next following the member's election to the Board.

(4) Where a vacancy occurs from any cause in the office of a member of the Board, the remaining members shall, subject to section 225 of the Act, forthwith hold an election to fill the vacancy in the manner provided by this Regulation for holding an election of the Board, except that the election shall be held only in respect of the area for which the vacancy occurs.

(5) At least six days before holding a meeting under this section, the secretary of the Board shall post a notice of the meeting in two or more prominent places in the area from which a member or members is or are to be elected and shall, where instructed by the Board, advertise the meeting in such other manner as the Board considers expedient.

(6) A meeting under this section shall be conducted by a presiding officer selected by the electors in respect of the area for which the meeting is held and who are present at the meeting,

in such manner as the electors determine, provided that the election of the member or members of the Board shall be by ballot and the minutes of the meeting shall be recorded by a secretary selected by such electors.

(7) An elector is entitled to vote for as many candidates for the Board in his or her area as there are Board members to be elected in such area, but only once for each candidate.

(8) If objection is made to the right of a person to vote at a meeting under this section, the presiding officer shall require the person to make the declaration set out in subsection 62(7) of the Act and after making such declaration, the person making it is entitled to vote.

(9) Subsections 92(9), (10), (12), (13), (17), (18), (19), (20) and (22) of the Act apply with necessary modifications to a meeting under this Regulation.

REGULATION 296
ONTARIO SCHOOLS FOR THE BLIND AND THE DEAF
R.R.O. 1990, Reg. 296

Interpretation

1. In this Regulation,

"applicant" means an applicant for admission to a School;

"bursar" means the business administrator of a School;

"Director" means the Executive Director of the Regional Services Division of the Ministry;

"Indian" means,

    (a) an Indian as defined in the *Indian Act* (Canada), or

    (b) an Eskimo,

who is not qualified to be a resident pupil of a board;

"parent" includes a guardian;

"residence counsellor" means a person employed as a residence counsellor in a School;

"School" means a school referred to in section 2;

"Superintendent" means the Superintendent of a School.

Designations

2. (1) The Ontario School for the Blind, Brantford is designated as The W. Ross Macdonald School.

(2) The Ontario School for the Deaf, Belleville is designated as The Sir James Whitney School.

(3) The Ontario School for the Deaf, Milton is designated as The Ernest C. Drury School.

(4) The Ontario School for the Deaf, London is designated as The Robarts School.

Admissions

3. (1) Where an applicant who is not an Indian, or the parent of such applicant, submits to the Superintendent evidence satisfactory to the Superintendent that,

    (a) the applicant will be under the age of twenty-one years on the first day of the school year for which he or she seeks admission;

    (b) because of a visual or an auditory handicap, or both, as certified by a legally qualified medical practitioner, the applicant is in need of a special educational program in the School;

    (c) if the applicant is under eighteen years of age, the applicant's parent is a resident of Ontario; and

    (d) if the applicant is eighteen years of age or over, the applicant is a resident of Ontario, the Superintendent shall, subject to subsection (2) and subsection 8(1), admit the applicant to the School.

(2) An applicant who is qualified to be a resident pupil of a board that operates a day class for the hearing impaired that would be appropriate to the applicant shall not be admitted to an Ontario School for the Deaf except where in the opinion of the Minister the admission is in the best interests of the applicant.

(3) Where an applicant who is not an Indian and who will be twenty-one years of age or over on the first day of the school year for which he or she seeks admission submits to the Superintendent evidence satisfactory to the Superintendent under clauses (1)(b) and (d), and the Minister approves the admission of the applicant, the Superintendent shall admit the applicant to the School.

4. Where the minister of education for a province of Canada other than Ontario,
   (a) requests admission for an applicant,
      (i) whose parent resides in that province or who, being eighteen years of age or over, himself or herself resides in that province,
      (ii) to whom clause 3(1)(b) applies, and
      (iii) who is not inadmissible under subsection 8(1); and
   (b) agrees to pay such fees as are payable for the instruction and maintenance of the applicant, and the Minister approves the admission of the applicant, the Superintendent shall admit the applicant.

5. Where the Minister of Indian Affairs and Northern Development for Canada,
   (a) requests admission for an applicant who,
      (i) is an Indian to whom clause 3(1)(b) applies; and
      (ii) is not inadmissible under subsection 8(1); and
   (b) agrees to pay such fees as are payable for the instruction and maintenance of the applicant,

and the Minister approves the admission of the applicant, the Superintendent shall admit the applicant.

6. Where an applicant who is not an Indian and who,
   (a) has not attained the age of eighteen years and whose parent is not a resident of any province of Canada; or
   (b) has attained the age of eighteen years and is not a resident of any province of Canada,

submits to the Superintendent evidence satisfactory to the Superintendent under clause 3(1)(b), the Superintendent shall, where the Minister approves the admission of the applicant, admit the applicant to the School upon payment of a fee, determined by the Minister, that shall be not greater than the fee payable under section 10 or 11, as the case may be.

7. Where an applicant is eligible for admission under section 3, 4, 5 or 6, the Superintendent may admit him or her at any time during the school year provided that accommodation and a program are available.

8. (1) An applicant shall not be admitted to a School if he or she is unable to profit from instruction in a program at the School.

(2) Where, in respect of an applicant, doubt exists as to whether,

REGULATION 296   S. 11

   (a) evidence submitted under clause 3(1)(b) establishes that the applicant is in need of a special educational program; or
   (b) the applicant is able to profit from instruction in a program,

at the School, the admission of the applicant may be for a trial period.

(3) Upon the request of the Superintendent, or of the parent of an applicant, or of an applicant who is eighteen years of age or over, the Minister may appoint a committee to hear and determine any question concerning the eligibility for admission of the applicant.

Fees

9. No fee is payable in respect of a pupil admitted to a School under section 3.

10. (1) The fee payable in a fiscal year on behalf of a pupil who is admitted under section 4 or 5 to a School referred to in subsection 2(2), (3) or (4) and is in residence at such School shall be equal to the average of the quotients obtained by dividing, for each School,

   (a) the estimated operating costs of the School for such fiscal year, excluding where applicable the estimated costs of extension and resource services, teacher education, daily transportation of pupils, food services for the staff and for pupils who are not in residence, the summer course for parents, the media centre, the program for emotionally disturbed pupils and special projects,

by,

   (b) 425 in the case of The Sir James Whitney School and The Ernest C. Drury School, and 250 in the case of The Robarts School.

(2) The fee payable in a fiscal year on behalf of a pupil who is admitted under section 4 or 5 to a School referred to in subsection 2(2), (3) or (4) and is not in residence at such School shall be equal to the average of the quotients obtained by dividing, for each School,

   (a) the estimated operating costs of the School for such fiscal year, excluding where applicable the estimated costs of extension and resource services, teacher education, the laundry, residence counsellors and residence operating expenses, food services for the staff and for pupils who are in residence, the summer course for parents, the media centre, the program for emotionally disturbed pupils and special projects,

by,

   (b) 425 in the case of The Sir James Whitney School and The Ernest C. Drury School, and 250 in the case of The Robarts School.

11. (1) Subject to subsection (2), the fee payable in a fiscal year on behalf of a pupil who is admitted under section 4 or 5 to The W. Ross Macdonald School shall be equal to the quotient obtained by dividing by 275 the estimated operating costs of the School for such fiscal year, excluding the estimated costs of the deaf-blind program, the large-print library and the total stimulation program.

(2) The fee payable in a fiscal year on behalf of a deaf-blind pupil who is admitted under section 4 or 5 to The W. Ross Macdonald School shall be equal to the quotient obtained by dividing,

   (a) the sum of the amounts allocated in the estimates of such School for such fiscal year to salaries of teachers, counsellors and aides in the deaf-blind program and to transportation and communication services and supplies for pupils in such program,

by,

(b) the number of pupils enrolled in such program on the last school day in June of such fiscal year.

12. Where in any month a pupil for whom a fee is payable attends a School for only a part of the month, his or her fee for such month shall be reduced proportionately.

Transportation

13. (1) The Superintendent may provide daily transportation to and from a School for pupils of the school who are not in residence at the School.

(2) The Minister may pay all or part of the transportation costs for a pupil admitted to a School under section 3 where the board of which such pupil is qualified to be a resident pupil does not provide transportation to and from the School.

Duties of Pupils

14. A pupil at a School shall,
(a) except with the permission of the Superintendent, be in attendance on the first day in the school year and attend classes punctually and regularly during the school year;
(b) take such tests and examinations as may be required by the Superintendent;
(c) exercise self-discipline and accept such discipline as would be exercised by a kind, firm and judicious parent;
(d) be clean in his or her person and habits, diligent in his or her studies and courteous to other pupils and to the teaching and non-teaching staff of the School;
(e) be responsible to the Superintendent for his or her conduct on the school premises, on out-of-school activities and programs sponsored by the School and while travelling on a bus under contract to or owned by the Ministry;
(f) leave the school premises only under conditions specified by the Superintendent; and
(g) if the pupil is in residence at the School, participate in the programs provided by the residence counsellor for his or her residence area.

Duties of Teachers

15. A person employed to teach at a School shall, in addition to the duties of a teacher under the Act,
(a) be responsible for effective instruction in the subjects assigned to him or her by the Superintendent, the management of his or her classes and the discipline in his or her classroom;
(b) co-operate with officials of the Ministry and the Superintendent for the purposes of planning and evaluating the program of instruction;

(c) make adequate provision in his or her daily program for the individual differences of the pupils in his or her classes so that each pupil may experience a reasonable amount of success;
(d) prepare for use in his or her class or classes such teaching plans and outlines as are required by the Superintendent and submit the plans and outlines to the Superintendent on request;
(e) assist in maintaining discipline in the School and in fostering school spirit and morale; and
(f) carry out such supervisory duties as may be assigned by the Superintendent.

Duties of Residence Counsellors

16. A residence counsellor shall,
(a) be responsible for the residence area assigned to him or her by the Superintendent and provide for the safety, health, comfort and well-being of pupils in such area;
(b) plan and provide programs to encourage and promote the growth and development of each pupil in the residence area and evaluate such programs;
(c) make adequate provision for individual differences of the pupils in the programs that he or she provides;
(d) record the growth and development of each pupil in the residence area;
(e) assist in maintaining school spirit, morale and discipline;
(f) carry out such supervisory duties as may be assigned to him or her by the Superintendent; and
(g) co-operate with the Superintendent in all matters affecting the School.

Parents

17. (1) There shall be deposited with the bursar a sum of at least $20.00 to defray the personal incidental expenses of a pupil enrolled in a School.

(2) As a condition of admission of a pupil to a School, the parent of the pupil or the pupil, where he or she is over eighteen years of age, shall agree,
(a) to supply on request of the Superintendent personal items necessary to enable the pupil to participate in school programs;
(b) to provide transportation and escort for the pupil where necessary to ensure regular attendance if such transportation and escort is not otherwise provided;
(c) to authorize the Superintendent, upon recommendation of the school physician, to arrange in case of emergency for the admission of the pupil to a hospital for treatment or surgery;
(d) to permit such medical treatment of the pupil as may be recommended by the school physician, subject to any other consent that may be required;
(e) to guarantee payment for medical and dental services required by the pupil during the school year, except such services that are provided by the School; and
(f) to notify the Superintendent promptly of the reason for the absence of the pupil.

S. 18 REGULATIONS UNDER THE EDUCATION ACT

(3) The parent of a pupil may visit with the pupil at the School in which the pupil is enrolled as authorized by the Superintendent.

Duties of Superintendent

18. There shall be for each School a Superintendent who shall,
- (a) admit pupils in accordance with this Regulation;
- (b) determine the pupils who shall be in residence at the School and the pupils who shall reside in homes approved by him or her;
- (c) determine the mode of transportation to and from School to be used by a pupil for whom such transportation is provided by the School;
- (d) assign pupils to classes and programs;
- (e) transfer and promote such pupils as he or she considers proper;
- (f) establish and maintain, and retain, transfer and dispose of, a pupil record in respect of each pupil enrolled in the School, in the manner prescribed by the regulations;
- (g) at least once in every calendar year provide for a review of the placement of each pupil to ensure that the program is appropriate for the capabilities and needs of the pupil;
- (h) recommend for a Secondary School Graduation Diploma or a Secondary School Honour Graduation Diploma a pupil of the School who has completed the requirements for such diploma;
- (i) be in charge of the organization, management and discipline of the School and ensure that proper supervision is maintained at all times;
- (j) furnish to the Director, on his or her request, information on any matter affecting the interests of the School;
- (k) arrange for regular inspection of the school premises and report promptly to the Ministry of Government Services any repairs required to be made by that Ministry;
- (l) determine the times at which pupils may leave the school premises and the times at which they may be visited at the School;
- (m) notify the parent immediately if a pupil becomes seriously ill or requires hospital treatment off the school property;
- (n) notify the parent if a pupil damages or destroys school property and request suitable compensation;
- (o) hold emergency drills at the School and the residences at least six times during the school year and require that every pupil and staff member take part therein;
- (p) report promptly to the local medical officer of health and the Director any cases of infectious or contagious disease in the School; and
- (q) report at least once each term the progress of each pupil to his or her parent, or to the pupil where the pupil is eighteen years of age or over.

19. (1) The Superintendent may dismiss a pupil from a School or from a program in the School for a period not exceeding thirty days because of misconduct, persistent opposition to authority, habitual neglect of duty, the wilful destruction of school property, the use of profane or wilfully insulting language, or conduct injurious to the moral tone of the School or to the physical or mental well-being of others in the School and, where a pupil has been so dismissed, the Superintendent shall notify forthwith in writing the pupil, his or her teachers, the parent of the pupil and the Director of the dismissal, the reasons therefor and the right of appeal under subsection 2.

(2) The parent of a pupil who has been dismissed under subsection (1), or the dismissed pupil where the pupil is eighteen years of age or over, may, within seven days of the commencement of the dismissal, appeal to the Director against the dismissal, and the Director, after hearing the appeal or where no appeal is made, may remove, confirm or modify the dismissal and, where he or she considers it appropriate, may order that any record of the dismissal be expunged.

(3) The Director may dismiss a pupil permanently from a School on the ground that the pupil's conduct is so refractory that his or her presence is injurious to other pupils where,
- (a) the Superintendent so recommends;
- (b) the pupil and his or her parent have been notified in writing of,
  - (i) the recommendation of the Superintendent, and
  - (ii) the right of the pupil where the pupil is eighteen years of age or over, and otherwise of his or her parent, to make representations at a hearing to be conducted by the Director; and
- (c) such hearing has been conducted.

(4) The parties to a hearing under this section shall be the parent of the pupil, or the pupil where he or she is eighteen years of age or over, and the Superintendent.

20. (1) The Superintendent may discharge a pupil,
- (a) for failure to make progress satisfactory to the Superintendent; or
- (b) where the pupil is no longer in need of a special educational program in the School and another program placement would be more appropriate for the pupil.

(2) Where a pupil has been discharged under subsection (1), the Superintendent shall,
- (a) notify in writing the pupil and the parent of the pupil, of the discharge, the reason therefor and the right of appeal to the Director;
- (b) counsel the parent of the pupil, or the pupil where he or she is eighteen years of age or over, in respect of the opportunities available to the pupil; and
- (c) give supportive guidance to the parent and to the pupil where, in the opinion of the Superintendent, such guidance is necessary.

(3) The parent of a pupil who has been discharged under subsection (1), or the discharged pupil where he or she is eighteen years of age or over, may, within seven days of the discharge, appeal to the Director against the discharge, and the Director, after hearing the appeal or where no appeal is made, may confirm the discharge or order that the pupil be readmitted to the School.

(4) The parties to a hearing under this section shall be the parent of the pupil, or the pupil where he or she is eighteen years of age or over, and the Superintendent.

21. A Superintendent may cause a pupil to be sent home because of,
- (a) serious or continued ill-health of the pupil; or
- (b) the need of the pupil for medical treatment, certified by the school physician.

Superintendent's Advisory Council

22. (1) A Superintendent may establish a Superintendent's Advisory Council for his or her School to make recommendations to the Superintendent in respect of the organization, administration and government of the School.

(2) A Superintendent's Advisory Council established under subsection (1) shall be composed of at least six persons appointed by the Superintendent, and such Council shall meet at the call of the Superintendent at least twice during each school year.

(3) A member of a Superintendent's Advisory Council is entitled to be reimbursed for his or her expenses necessarily incurred to attend a meeting of the Superintendent's Advisory Council.

Qualifications of Teachers

23. (1) A teacher employed to teach the deaf at a School shall hold,
- (a) a certificate of qualification to teach in an elementary school or a secondary school in Ontario or a letter of standing; and
- (b) the Diploma in Deaf Education granted by the Minister or qualifications in education of the deaf that the Minister considers equivalent thereto.

(2) A deaf adult may be employed to teach the deaf at a School if he or she holds a Permanent Letter of Standing valid for the teaching of the deaf.

(3) A teacher employed to teach the blind at a School shall,
- (a) hold a certificate of qualification to teach in an elementary school or a secondary school in Ontario or a letter of standing; and
- (b) have completed, or be actively engaged in completing, the requirements for the specialist qualification for teaching the blind, or hold qualifications in education of the blind that the Minister considers equivalent thereto.

(4) A teacher employed to teach the deaf-blind at a School shall,
- (a) hold a certificate of qualification to teach in an elementary school or a secondary school in Ontario or a letter of standing; and
- (b) have completed, or be actively engaged in completing, the requirements for the specialist qualification for teaching the deaf-blind, or hold qualifications in education of the deaf-blind that the Minister considers equivalent thereto.

REGULATION 297
ONTARIO TEACHER'S QUALIFICATIONS
R.R.O. 1990, Reg. 297: am. O. Reg. 34/91, O. Reg. 415/91,
O. Reg. 243/92, O. Reg. 687/92, O. Reg. 559/93, O. Reg. 729/94

DEFINITIONS

1. In this Regulation,

"acceptable university degree" means a degree that is,
- (a) granted by an Ontario university that is an ordinary member of the Association of Universities and Colleges of Canada,
- (b) granted by a Canadian university in a province other than Ontario that is an ordinary member of the Association of Universities and Colleges of Canada, and is a degree that is considered by the Minister to be equivalent to a degree referred to in clause (a),
- (c) granted by a university in the United States that is recognized by,
    - (i) Middle States Association of Colleges and Schools,
    - (ii) New England Association of Schools and Colleges,
    - (iii) North Central Association of Colleges and Schools,
    - (iv) Northwest Association of Schools and Colleges,
    - (v) Southern Association of Colleges and Schools, or
    - (vi) Western Association of Schools and Colleges,

    and is considered by the Minister to be equivalent to a degree referred to in clause (a), and
- (d) granted by a university that is located in a country other than Canada and the United States and that is considered by the Minister to be equivalent to a degree referred to in clause (a);

"appropriate supervisory officer" means, in respect of a teacher, the supervisory officer assigned by a board in accordance with the Act and regulations or by the Minister to provide supervisory services in respect of the performance by the teacher of his or her duties under the Act and the regulations;

"approved program" means a program approved by the Minister;

"band" and "council of the band" have the same meaning as in the *Indian Act* (Canada);

"candidate" means a candidate for an Ontario Teacher's Certificate, a Letter of Standing or an additional qualification granted under this Regulation;

"Deputy Minister" means the Deputy Minister of Education;

"division" means the primary division, junior division, intermediate division or senior division;

"general studies" means the courses developed from curriculum guidelines that are issued by the Minister for the intermediate division and senior division and listed under a heading other than "Technological Studies" in Appendix B to OSIS;

"holds a degree" means, in respect of a candidate, that he or she has completed all the requirements for and has been approved for, the granting of a degree, regardless of whether or not the degree has been conferred;

"OSIS" means the circular entitled "Ontario Schools Intermediate and Senior Divisions Program and Diploma Requirements" issued by the Minister including any document issued by the Minister in accordance with paragraphs 1, 2, 3, 4 and 25 of subsection 8(1) of the Act;

"program of professional education" means a program approved by the Minister and conducted at a college, faculty or school of education in Ontario that includes,
- (a) a concentrated study of,
  - (i) the primary and junior divisions, with or without a focus on the teaching of French as a second language,
  - (ii) the junior division and one optional course from Schedule A that is in the intermediate division and a course related to grades 7 and 8 of the intermediate division,
  - (iii) the intermediate and senior divisions including two optional courses from Schedule A, or
  - (iv) technological studies, including a minimum of two optional courses from Schedule B at the basic level, or one optional course from Schedule B at the basic level and the other such course at the advanced level,
- (b) studies in education including learning and development throughout the primary, junior, intermediate and senior division,
- (c) teaching methods designed to meet the individual needs of pupils,
- (d) the acts and regulations respecting education,
- (e) a review of the curriculum guidelines issued by the Minister related to all of the divisions and a study of curriculum development,
- (f) a minimum of forty days of practical experience in schools or in other situations approved by the Minister for observation and practice teaching;

"technological qualifications" means, in respect of a candidate for the Ontario Teacher's Certificate or a Provisional or Temporary Letter of Standing,
- (a) the holding of the secondary school graduation diploma or the successful completion of courses that are considered by the Minister to be the equivalent of such diploma,
- (b) proof of his or her competence in the area or areas of technological studies selected as options in the program of professional education, and
- (c) one of,
  - (i) five years of wage-earning, business or industrial experience in the area or areas of technological studies selected as options in the program of professional education,
  - (ii) a combination of education related to the area or areas of technological studies selected as options in the program of professional education beyond that referred to in clause (a) and business or industrial experience in the area or areas of technological studies selected as options in the program of technological studies that totals five years, including at least two years of wage-earning

experience, no less than sixteen months of which is continuous employment, or

(iii) at least 3700 hours of wage-earning experience and successful completion of a post-secondary education program acceptable to the Minister that includes at least twenty-four months of academic studies, if the wage-earning experience and the education program are related to the area or areas of technological studies selected as options in the program of professional education.

"technological studies" means the courses developed from curriculum guidelines that are issued by the Minister for the intermediate division and the senior division and listed under the heading "Technological Studies" in Appendix B to OSIS;

"university course" means a one-year university course beyond the Grade 13 level, or the equivalent of such one-year university course, where the course is part of a program leading to an acceptable university degree;

"university credit" means a unit of recognition in respect of the successful completion of a university course, such that sixty such university credits are required to complete a four-year university program leading to an acceptable university degree. O. Reg. 243/92, s. 1; O. Reg. 559/93, s. 1.

PART I
BASIC QUALIFICATIONS

2. A candidate for the Ontario Teacher's Certificate shall submit to the dean of a college or faculty of education or the director of a school of education in Ontario,

(a) a certificate of birth or baptism, or other acceptable proof of the date and place of birth;

(b) in the case of a candidate who is a married woman who wishes to have her certificate issued in her married name, a certificate of marriage or other acceptable proof that she is the person referred to in the certificate or other document submitted under clause (a);

(c) a certificate of change of name where applicable;

(d) evidence satisfactory to such dean or director of his or her academic or technological qualifications;

(e) in the case of a person who was not born in Canada, the basis upon which the candidate is present in Canada;

(f) proof of freedom from active tuberculosis.

3. Where the dean of a college or faculty of education or the director of a school of education in Ontario reports to the Deputy Minister that a candidate,

(a) has complied with section 2;

(b) holds an acceptable university degree or qualifications the Minister considers equivalent thereto, or technological qualifications; and

(c) has successfully completed a program of professional education, the Minister may grant to the candidate an Ontario Teacher's Certificate in Form 1, and an Ontario Teacher's Qualifications Record Card in Form 2 that indicates the areas of concentration successfully completed.

4. (1) An entry on an Ontario Teacher's Qualifications Record Card in respect of a program successfully completed in Canada shall indicate by the language in which the entry is recorded whether the program was taken in English or in French.

(2) An entry on an Ontario Teacher's Qualifications Record Card in respect of a program successfully completed out of Canada shall indicate by the language in which the entry is recorded whether the qualification referred to is for teaching in schools and classes where English is the language of instruction or in French-language schools and classes established under Part XII of the Act.

(3) Despite section 13, qualifications valid in French-language schools and classes established under Part XII of the Act are valid in French-language classes where the teacher is otherwise qualified according to subsection 19(14) of Regulation 298 of Revised Regulations of Ontario, 1990.

4.1. An entry on an Ontario Teacher's Qualifications Record Card in respect of a program in International Languages shall specify which language was studied in the program. O. Reg. 243/92, s. 2.

5. Where the dean of a college or faculty of education or the director of a school of education in Ontario reports to the Deputy Minister that a candidate,

(a) has complied with section 2;
(b) is of native ancestry;
(c) holds the requirements for a Secondary School Graduation Diploma or standing the Minister considers equivalent thereto; and
(d) has successfully completed a program of professional education with concentration in the primary division and the junior division,

the Minister may grant to the candidate an Ontario Teacher's Certificate, in Form 1, and an Ontario Teacher's Qualifications Record Card in Form 2 that indicates the areas of concentration successfully completed.

(2) The Minister may grant to a candidate a Provisional Letter of Standing valid for one year for teaching in the primary division and junior division if the dean of a college or faculty of education or the director of a school of education in Ontario reports to the Deputy Minister that the candidate meets the qualifications of clauses (1)(a) to (c) and has successfully completed the first session of a program of professional education with concentration in the primary division and the junior division.

(3) The Provisional Letter of Standing granted under subsection (2) shall be in Form 4, if the program referred to in that subsection was taken in English, and in Form 4a, if the program was taken in French.

(4) The Minister may renew a candidate's Provisional Letter of Standing for one year for teaching in the primary division and junior division if the candidate submits to the Deputy Minister evidence that the candidate,

(a) holds a Provisional Letter of Standing granted under subsection (2) that has expired or is about to expire; and
(b) has an offer of a position as a teacher in the primary division or junior division from,
   (i) a board,
   (ii) a private school,
   (iii) the Provincial Schools Authority established under section 2 of the *Provincial Schools Negotiations Act*,
   (iv) the Department of Indian Affairs and Northern Development of the Government of Canada, or
   (v) a council of a band or an education authority, if the council of the band or the education authority is authorized by the Crown in right of Canada to provide education for Indians. O. Reg. 243/92, s. 3.

6. (1) Where the dean of a college or faculty of education or the director of a school of education in Ontario at the time of making a report under section 3, 5, 7 or 10 is of the opinion from the information provided under section 2 by the candidate in respect of whom the report is to be made, that the candidate is not entitled under the laws of Canada to obtain employment as a teacher in Canada, the dean or director at the time of making the report shall so inform the Minister.

(2) Where the Minister is informed as set out in subsection (1), the Minister may refuse to grant the certificate and record card referred to in section 3 or 5 or in subsection 10(2), as the case may be, or may withhold the Provisional Letter of Standing referred to in section 7 or its extension under subsection 10(1), until the candidate provides proof to the Minister that the candidate is entitled under the laws of Canada to obtain employment as a teacher in Canada.

7. Where the dean of a college or faculty of education or the director of a school of education in Ontario reports to the Deputy Minister that a candidate,
(a) has complied with section 2;
(b) holds an acceptable university degree or qualifications the Minister considers equivalent thereto or technological qualifications; and
(c) has successfully completed the first session of a program of professional education,

the Minister may grant to the candidate a Provisional Letter of Standing, in Form 4 where the session was taken in English and in Form 4a where the session was taken in French.

8. Where a person who is the holder of a Provisional Letter of Standing granted under section 7 that has expired, or is about to expire, submits to the Deputy Minister evidence that he or she has an offer of a position as a teacher from,
(a) a board;
(b) a private school;
(c) the Provincial Schools Authority established under section 2 of the *Provincial Schools Negotiations Act*;
(d) the Department of Indian Affairs and Northern Development of the Government of Canada; or
(e) a council of a band or an education authority where such council of the band or education authority is authorized by the Crown in right of Canada to provide education for Indians,

the Minister may renew the Provisional Letter of Standing for a period of one year.

9. For the purposes of section 10, a person who holds a Temporary Elementary School Certificate or a Temporary Secondary School Certificate is deemed to hold a Provisional Letter of Standing granted on the date of his or her Temporary Elementary School Certificate or his or her Temporary Secondary School Certificate.

10. (1) Where the dean of a college or faculty of education or the director of a school of education in Ontario reports to the Deputy Minister that a person who holds a Provisional Letter of Standing,
- (a) has taught successfully for one school year in Ontario as certified by the appropriate supervisory officer; and
- (b) has successfully completed the second session of a program of professional education where such second session is not the final session of the program,

the Minister may extend the person's Provisional Letter of Standing for one year.

(2) Where the dean of a college or faculty of education or the director of a school of education in Ontario reports to the Deputy Minister that a candidate who holds a Provisional Letter of Standing,
- (a) has taught successfully in Ontario, as certified by the appropriate supervisory officer, for one school year after the granting of a Provisional Letter of Standing and after its extension where it was extended; and
- (b) has successfully completed the final session of a program of professional education,

the Minister may grant to the candidate an Ontario Teacher's Certificate in Form 1, and an Ontario Teacher's Qualifications Record Card in Form 2 that indicates the areas of concentration successfully completed.

11. An applicant for a Temporary Letter of Standing who completed a teacher education program outside Ontario shall submit to the Deputy Minister with the application,
- (a) the items required to be submitted under section 2;
- (b) evidence of his or her academic or technological qualifications;
- (c) his or her teaching certificate and a transcript of his or her teacher education program;
- (d) a statement from the issuing authority that his or her teaching certificate has not been suspended or cancelled;
- (e) where the candidate is not a Canadian citizen or a permanent resident of Canada, evidence that the candidate is entitled under the laws of Canada to obtain employment in Canada as a teacher; and
- (f) such evidence as the Deputy Minister may require of successful teaching experience in schools and programs similar to those for which the Temporary Letter of Standing applied for is valid.

12. (1) Where an applicant for a Temporary Letter of Standing,
- (a) has complied with section 11;
- (b) has successfully completed in a Canadian province other than Ontario a teacher education program acceptable to the Minister; and
- (c) holds the academic or technological qualifications required for an Ontario Teacher's Certificate,

the Deputy Minister may issue to the applicant a Letter of Eligibility in Form 5 where the teacher education program was taken in English and in Form 5a where the program was taken in French.

(1.1) The Letter of Eligibility is valid for three years from its date of issue.

(2) Where an applicant who holds a Letter of Eligibility granted under this section submits to the Deputy Minister evidence that the applicant has an offer of a position as a teacher in Ontario from,

(a) a board;
(b) a private school;
(c) the Provincial Schools Authority established under section 2 of the *Provincial Schools Negotiations Act*;
(d) the Department of Indian Affairs and Northern Development of the Government of Canada; or
(e) a council of a band or an incorporated education authority established by two or more bands where such council of the band or education authority is authorized by the Crown in right of Canada to provide education for Indians,

and that the offer is subject to the applicant obtaining a Temporary Letter of Standing, the Minister may grant to the applicant a Temporary Letter of Standing in Form 3 or Form 3a, as the case may be, valid for six years from the date of issue. O. Reg. 729/94, s. 1.

13. (1) Where an applicant for a Temporary Letter of Standing,

(a) has complied with the requirements of section 11;
(b) has successfully completed outside Canada a teacher education program acceptable to the Minister; and
(c) holds the academic or technological qualifications required for an Ontario Teacher's Certificate,

the Deputy Minister may issue to the applicant a Letter of Eligibility in Form 5 or if the applicant wishes to become qualified to teach in French-language schools and classes established under Part XII of the Act, a Letter of Eligibility in Form 5a.

(2) The Letter of Eligibility is valid for three years from its date of issue. O. Reg. 729/94, s. 2.

14. Where an applicant who holds a Letter of Eligibility issued under section 13 in Form 5 or Form 5a submits to the Deputy Minister evidence that the applicant,

(a) has an offer of a position as a teacher in Ontario from,
   (i) a board,
   (ii) a private school,
   (iii) the Provincial Schools Authority established under section 2 of the *Provincial Schools Negotiations Act*,
   (iv) the Department of Indian Affairs and Northern Development of the Government of Canada, or
   (v) a council of a band or an incorporated education authority established by two or more bands where such council of the band or education authority is authorized by the Crown in right of Canada to provide education for Indians,

and such offer is subject to his or her obtaining a Temporary Letter of Standing; and
  (b) has successfully completed, subsequent to the date of such offer, an approved orientation program in English or French, as the case may be, for holders of Letters of Eligibility,

the Minister may grant to the applicant a Temporary Letter of Standing in Form 3 or Form 3a, as the case may be, valid for six years from the date of issue.

15. The Minister may grant a Temporary Letter of Standing, in Form 3 where the program of professional education was taken in English or in Form 3a where such program was taken in French, that is valid for a period of one year from the date of issue to a person who,

  (a) was the holder of a Letter of Standing that was issued under Parts I, II and IV of Ontario Regulation 295/73 and that had the force of an Interim Certificate referred to in subsection 26(1); and
  (b) is not the holder of an Ontario Teacher's Certificate or a Temporary Letter of Standing and who is offered a position as a teacher by,
   (i) a board,
   (ii) a private school,
   (iii) the Provincial Schools Authority established under section 2 of the *Provincial Schools Negotiations Act,*
   (iv) the Department of Indian Affairs and Northern Development of the Government of Canada, or
   (v) a council of a band or an education authority, where such council of the band or education authority is authorized by the Crown in right of Canada to provide education for Indians.

16. A Temporary Letter of Standing that was issued to a person on or after the 1st day of July, 1978 up to and including the 9th day of July, 1980 that was intended to be valid for six years ceases to be valid on the 10th day of July, 1987.

17. (1) Where a person who holds a Temporary Letter of Standing granted under section 12, 14 or 15 or a Temporary Letter of Standing to which section 16 applies, that is still valid or that has expired, submits to the Deputy Minister evidence that the person had, while the person was the holder of the Temporary Letter of Standing, at least ten months of successful teaching experience in Ontario as certified by the appropriate supervisory officer, the Minister may grant to the person an Ontario Teacher's Certificate in Form 1 and an Ontario Teacher's Qualifications Record Card in Form 2 that indicates the areas of concentration successfully completed.

(2) Where a Temporary Letter of Standing issued under section 12, 14 or 15 or a Temporary Letter of Standing to which section 16 applies expires, the person who is the holder of the Temporary Letter of Standing is not eligible for another Temporary Letter of Standing.

18. (1) Where a person who holds a Temporary Letter of Standing granted under section 12, 14 or 15 or a Temporary Letter of Standing to which section 16 applies, that has expired or is about to expire, submits to the Deputy Minister,

  (a) evidence that the person had while the person was the holder of the Temporary Letter of Standing, fewer than ten months of successful teaching experience in Ontario, as certified by the appropriate supervisory officer; and

(b) evidence that the person has an offer of a position as a teacher from,
  (i) a board,
  (ii) a private school,
  (iii) the Provincial Schools Authority established under section 2 of the *Provincial Schools Negotiations Act*,
  (iv) the Department of Indian Affairs and Northern Development of the Government of Canada, or
  (v) a council of a band or an incorporated education authority established by two or more bands where such council of the band or education authority is authorized by the Crown in right of Canada to provide education for Indians,

the Minister may, despite subsection 17(2), extend the period of validity of the Temporary Letter of Standing that has expired or is about to expire, as the case may be, for a period of one year.

(2) Where the Minister extends the period of validity of a Temporary Letter of Standing under subsection (1), the Temporary Letter of Standing issued to the person shall be altered to indicate the extended period of validity.

19. Where the dean of a college or faculty of education or the director of a school of education in Ontario reports to the Deputy Minister that a candidate,
  (a) has complied with section 2;
  (b) is entitled under the laws of Canada to obtain employment in Canada as a teacher, if the candidate is not a Canadian citizen or a permanent resident of Canada;
  (c) is unable to undertake a program leading to the Ontario Teacher's Certificate by reason of impaired hearing;
  (d) holds an acceptable university degree or qualifications the Minister considers equivalent thereto; and
  (e) has successfully completed an approved program of teacher education for teaching the deaf,

the Minister may grant to the candidate a Permanent Letter of Standing in Form 6 where such approved program was taken in English and in Form 6a where such approved program was taken in French that is valid in Ontario for teaching the deaf.

(2) The Minister may grant a Provisional Letter of Standing valid for one year for teaching the deaf to a candidate who has successfully completed an approved program of teacher education outside Ontario for teaching the deaf, if the candidate submits to the Deputy Minister,
  (a) evidence that the candidate has complied with section 2;
  (b) evidence that the candidate is deaf or hard of hearing;
  (c) evidence that the candidate is a Canadian citizen or a permanent resident of Canada or is entitled under the laws of Canada to obtain employment in Canada as a teacher;
  (d) evidence that the candidate holds an acceptable university degree or qualifications that the Minister considers equivalent to an acceptable university degree; and
  (e) if the candidate is qualified to teach outside Ontario,
    (i) the candidate's teaching certificate and a transcript of the candidate's teacher education program; and
    (ii) a statement from the authority that issued the candidate's teaching certificate that the certificate has not been suspended or cancelled.

(3) The Provisional Letter of Standing granted under subsection (2) shall be in Form 4, if the program for teaching the deaf referred to in that subsection was taken in English, and in Form 4a, if the program was taken in French.

(4) The Minister may extend a Provisional Letter of Standing granted under subsection (2) for one-year periods.

(5) The Minister may grant a Permanent Letter of Standing for teaching the deaf to a person who holds a Provisional Letter of Standing granted under subsection (2) if the person submits to the Deputy Minister evidence of at least one year of experience successfully teaching the deaf in Ontario since the granting of the Provisional Letter of Standing, as certified by the appropriate supervisory officer.

(6) The Permanent Letter of Standing granted under subsection (5) shall be in Form 6, if the program for teaching the deaf referred to in subsection (2) was taken in English, and in Form 6a, if the program was taken in French. O. Reg. 34/91, s. 1; O. Reg. 243/92, s. 4.

20. Where the principal of a course leading to the additional qualification of Part I Special Education, or the dean of a college or faculty of education or the director of a school of education in Ontario, reports to the Deputy Minister that a candidate,

- (a) holds one of,
    - (i) a Diploma in Pre-School Education obtained at Ryerson Polytechnical Institute,
    - (ii) a Diploma in Child Study obtained at the Institute of Child Study of the University of Toronto, or
    - (iii) a Diploma in Early Childhood Education obtained at an Ontario college of applied arts and technology;
- (b) has complied with section 2;
- (c) has successfully completed the program for Part I Special Education including Part I of the Teaching Trainable Retarded option; and
- (d) is entitled under the laws of Canada to obtain employment in Canada as a teacher, if the candidate is not a Canadian citizen or a permanent resident of Canada,

the Minister may grant to the candidate a Provisional Letter of Standing, in Form 4 where such program was taken in English and in Form 4a where such program was taken in French, that is valid for one year for teaching in schools or classes for the trainable retarded. O. Reg. 34/91, s. 2.

21. Where a person who is the holder of a Provisional Letter of Standing granted under section 20 that has expired, or is about to expire, submits to the Deputy Minister evidence that he or she has an offer of a position as a teacher in schools or classes for the trainable retarded, the Minister may renew the Provisional Letter of Standing for a period of one year.

22. Where the principal of a course leading to the additional qualification of Part II Special Education, or the dean of a college or faculty of education or the director of a school of education in Ontario reports to the Deputy Minister that a candidate,

- (a) holds a Provisional Letter of Standing granted under section 20;
- (b) has taught successfully for one year in Ontario in a school or class for the trainable retarded as certified by the appropriate supervisory officer;
- (c) is entitled under the laws of Canada to obtain employment in Canada as a teacher, if the candidate is not a Canadian citizen or a permanent resident of Canada; and

(d) has successfully completed the program for Part II Special Education including Part II of the Teaching Trainable Retarded option,

the Minister may grant to the candidate a Permanent Letter of Standing, in Form 6 where such program was taken in English, or in Form 6a where such program was taken in French, that is valid for teaching in schools or classes for the trainable retarded. O. Reg. 34/91, s. 3.

23. (1) The Minister may grant to a candidate a Provisional Letter of Standing valid for one year for teaching of a Native language as a second language if the dean of a college or faculty of education or the director of a school of education in Ontario reports to the Deputy Minister that the candidate,

(a) has demonstrated an acceptable degree of fluency in the Algonquin or Iroquoian language;
(b) has complied with section 2;
(c) has successfully completed the first session of an approved program for Teacher of a Native Language as a Second Language; and
(d) is entitled under the laws of Canada to obtain employment in Canada as a teacher, if the candidate is not a Canadian citizen or a permanent resident of Canada.

(2) A Provisional Letter of Standing granted under subsection (1) shall be in Form 4, where the program referred to in clause (1)(c) was taken in English, or in Form 4a, where the program was taken in French. O. Reg. 34/91, s. 4(1).

24. The Minister may extend a candidate's Provisional Letter of Standing for one year for the teaching of a Native language as a second language if the dean of a college or faculty of education or the director of a school of education in Ontario reports to the Deputy Minister that the candidate,

(a) holds a Provisional Letter of Standing granted under section 23;
(b) has submitted evidence of at least one year of successful teaching experience in a Native language as a second language, as certified by,
   (i) the appropriate supervisory officer, where the successful teaching experience was in Ontario and was not in a school operated on an Indian reserve, or
   (ii) the appropriate supervisory official, where the successful teaching experience was outside Ontario or in a school operated on an Indian reserve in Ontario; and
(c) has successfully completed the second session of an approved program for Teacher of a Native Language as a Second Language after completing the experience referred to in clause (b). O. Reg. 34/91, s. 4(2).

25. (1) The Minister may grant to a candidate a Permanent Letter of Standing for the teaching of a Native language as a second language if the dean of a college or faculty of education or the director of a school of education in Ontario reports to the Deputy Minister that the candidate,

(a) holds a Provisional Letter of Standing extended under section 24;
(b) has submitted evidence of at least one year of successful teaching experience in a Native language as a second language, following the completion of the teaching experience referred to in section 24, as certified by,
   (i) the appropriate supervisory officer, where the successful teaching experience was in Ontario and was not in a school operated on an Indian Reserve, or

S. 25.1 REGULATIONS UNDER THE EDUCATION ACT

- (ii) the appropriate supervisory official, where the successful teaching experience was outside Ontario or in a school operated on an Indian Reserve in Ontario; and
- (c) has successfully completed the third session of an approved program for Teacher of a Native Language as a Second Language after completing the successful teaching experience referred to in clause (b).

(2) The Permanent Letter of Standing granted under subsection (1) shall be in Form 9, where the program referred to in clause (1)(c) was taken in English, or in Form 9a, where the program was taken in French. O. Reg. 34/91, s. 4(3).

25.1 (1) The Minister may grant to a candidate a Provisional Letter of Standing valid for one year for teaching dance if the dean of a college or faculty of education or the director of a school of education in Ontario reports to the Deputy Minister that the candidate,

- (a) has complied with section 2;
- (b) holds a Secondary School Graduation Diploma or has qualifications that the Minister considers to be equivalent to a Secondary School Graduation Diploma;
- (c) has successfully completed, before the 31st day of August, 1995, the first session of the program in Dance referred to in Schedule E;
- (d) is competent to perform in the areas of dance taught in elementary and secondary schools; and
- (e) is entitled under the laws of Canada to obtain employment in Canada as a teacher, if the candidate is not a Canadian citizen or a permanent resident of Canada.

(2) A Provisional Letter of Standing granted under subsection (1) shall be in Form 10, if the program referred to in clause (1)(c) was taken in English, or in Form 10a, if the program was taken in French.

(3) The Minister may extend a candidate's Provisional Letter of Standing for one year for teaching dance if the dean of a college or faculty of education or the director of a school of education in Ontario reports to the Deputy Minister that the candidate,

- (a) holds a Provisional Letter of Standing granted under subsection (1);
- (b) has submitted evidence of at least one year of experience successfully teaching dance in Ontario since the granting of the Provisional Letter of Standing, as certified by the appropriate supervisory officer; and
- (c) has successfully completed, before the 31st day of August, 1996, the second session of the program in Dance referred to in Schedule D.

(4) The Minister may grant to a candidate a Permanent Letter of Standing for teaching dance if the dean of a college or faculty of education or the director of a school of education in Ontario reports to the Deputy Minister that the candidate,

- (a) holds a Provisional Letter of Standing granted under subsection (1);
- (b) has submitted evidence of at least one year of experience successfully teaching dance in Ontario following the experience referred to in clause (3)(b), as certified by the appropriate supervisory officer; and
- (c) has successfully completed, before the 31st day of August, 1997, the third session of the program in Dance referred to in Schedule D.

(5) The Permanent Letter of Standing granted under subsection (4) shall be in Form 11, if the program referred to in clause (4)(c) was taken in English, or in Form 11a, if the program was taken in French. O. Reg. 243/92, s. 5, *part.*

25.2 The Minister may grant to a candidate an Ontario Teacher's Certificate in Form 1 and an Ontario Teacher's Qualifications Record Card in Form 2 that indicates the areas of concentration successfully completed if the candidate submits to the Deputy Minister evidence that the candidate,

(a) holds a valid Permanent Letter of Standing;
(b) holds an acceptable university degree or qualifications that the Minister considers equivalent to an acceptable university degree; and
(c) has successfully completed an approved program of teacher education leading to qualifications in two areas of concentration in the primary division, junior division, intermediate division or senior division. O. Reg. 243/92, s. 5, *part.*

26. (1) A person who holds one of the following certificates and who is,

(a) a Canadian citizen; or
(b) a British subject who was granted the certificate prior to the 1st day of September, 1973,

is deemed to hold the Ontario Teacher's Certificate:

1. First Class Certificate valid in Secondary Schools.
2. High School Specialist's Certificate.
3. Interim Elementary School Teacher's Certificate.
4. Interim Elementary School Teacher's Certificate, Standard 1, 2, 3 or 4.
5. Interim Elementary School Teacher's Certificate, Standard 1, 2, 3 or 4 (French only).
6. Interim First Class Certificate.
7. Interim High School Assistant's Certificate.
8. Interim High School Assistant's Certificate, Type A.
9. Interim High School Assistant's Certificate, Type B.
10. Interim Occupational Certificate, Type A (Practical Subjects).
11. Interim Occupational Certificate, Type B (Practical Subjects).
12. Interim Primary School Specialist's Certificate.
13. Interim Second Class Certificate.
14. Interim Vocational Certificate, Type A.
15. Interim Vocational Certificate, Type B.
16. Occupational Specialist's Certificate (Practical Subjects).
17. Permanent Commercial-Vocational Certificate.
18. Permanent Elementary School Teacher's Certificate.
19. Permanent Elementary School Teacher's Certificate, Standard 1, 2, 3 or 4.
20. Permanent Elementary School Teacher's Certificate, Standard 1, 2, 3 or 4 (French only).
21. Permanent First Class Certificate.
22. Permanent High School Assistant's Certificate.
23. Permanent Occupational Certificate (Practical Subjects).
24. Permanent Primary School Specialist's Certificate.

25. Permanent Second Class Certificate.
26. Permanent Vocational Certificate.
27. Vocational Specialist's Certificate.

(2) The Minister shall grant to a person referred to in subsection (1) an Ontario Teacher's Certificate in Form 1, and an Ontario Teacher's Qualifications Record Card in Form 2 that indicates the qualifications held by the person.

(3) A person who holds an interim certificate referred to in subsection (1) continues to be qualified to teach in accordance with the certificate until the date to which the certificate is valid as shown thereon and the person may upon application be granted by the Minister an Ontario Teacher's Certificate in Form 1 and an Ontario Teacher's Qualifications Record Card in Form 2 that indicates the qualifications that he or she holds.

(4) Where a person who held a Letter of Standing granted before the 1st day of July, 1978 submits to the Deputy Minister evidence of at least ten months of successful teaching experience in Ontario on the Letter of Standing, as certified by the appropriate supervisory officer, in a division or subject for which the Letter of Standing is valid, the Minister may grant to the person an Ontario Teacher's Certificate in Form 1, and an Ontario Teacher's Qualifications Record Card in Form 2 that indicates the qualifications held by the person.

27. (1) A person who holds one of the following certificates or Letters of Standing that was valid on the 1st day of July, 1978 but who is not qualified for the Ontario Teacher's Certificate under this Regulation remains qualified to teach in the classes, schools and subjects in which he or she is qualified by the certificate or Letter of Standing:

1. Elementary Certificate in Teaching Trainable Retarded Children.
2. Elementary Instrumental Music Certificate, Type A.
3. Elementary Instrumental Music Certificate, Type B.
4. Elementary Vocal Music Certificate, Type A.
5. Elementary Vocal Music Certificate, Type B.
6. Interim Second Class Certificate (French only).
7. Interim Specialist Certificate in Instrumental Music.
8. Interim Specialist Certificate in Vocal Music.
9. Intermediate Certificate in Teaching Trainable Retarded Children.
10. Intermediate Industrial Arts Only Certificate.
11. Intermediate Instrumental Music Certificate, Type A.
12. Intermediate Instrumental Music Certificate, Type B.
13. Intermediate Vocal Music Certificate, Type A.
14. Intermediate Vocal Music Certificate, Type B.
15. Letter of Standing (Renewable).
16. Permanent Letter of Standing (Renewable).
17. Permanent Second Class Certificate (French only).
18. Permanent Specialist Certificate in Instrumental Music.
19. Permanent Specialist Certificate in Vocal Music.
20. Specialist Certificate as Teacher of the Blind.
21. Specialist Certificate as Teacher of the Deaf.
22. Supervisor's Certificate in Instrumental Music.
23. Supervisor's Certificate in Vocal Music.

24. Teacher of the Trainable Retarded.
25. Temporary Certificate as Teacher of French to English-speaking Pupils in Elementary Schools.

(2) Where the dean of a college or faculty of education or the director of a school of education in Ontario reports to the Deputy Minister that a candidate,

(a) has complied with section 2;
(b) is entitled under the laws of Canada to obtain employment in Canada as a teacher, if the candidate is not a Canadian citizen or a permanent resident of Canada;
(c) holds a certificate or Letter of Standing listed in subsection (1);
(d) holds an acceptable university degree or qualifications the Minister considers equivalent thereto, or technological qualifications or, in the case of a candidate for an Ontario Teacher's Certificate valid for teaching in French-language schools and classes established under Part XII of the Act, a Secondary School Honour Graduation Diploma; and
(e) has successfully completed approved programs with concentration in two divisions,

the Minister may grant to the candidate an Ontario Teacher's Certificate in Form and an Ontario Teacher's Qualifications Record Card in Form 2 that indicates the areas of concentration successfully completed.

(3) A person who holds a Deferred Elementary School Teacher's Certificate or a Deferred First Class Certificate that was valid on the 1st day of July, 1978 remains qualified to teach in the schools and classes for which he or she is qualified by the certificate and, upon submission to the Ministry of evidence of completion of the academic requirements for an Interim Elementary School Teacher's Certificate or an Interim First Class Certificate, as the case may be, in force at the time the deferred certificate was issued, the Minister may grant to the person an Ontario Teacher's Certificate in Form 1, and an Ontario Teacher's Qualifications Record Card in Form 2 that indicates the qualifications held by the person.

(4) A person who holds an Interim Commercial-Vocational Certificate that was valid on the 30th day of June, 1978, subject to the conditions and requirements pertaining to such certificate, remains qualified to teach in the schools and classes for which he or she is qualified by the certificate, and upon submission to the Ministry, on or before the 30th day of June, 1981, of evidence that he or she has met the requirements for a Permanent Commercial-Vocational Certificate in force at the time the interim certificate was issued, the Minister may grant to the person an Ontario Teacher's Certificate in Form 1 and an Ontario Teacher's Qualifications Record Card in Form 2 that indicates the qualifications held by the person. O. Reg. 34/91, s. 5.

PART II
ADDITIONAL QUALIFICATIONS FOR TEACHERS

28. A session of a course leading to an additional qualification shall consist of a minimum of 125 hours of work that is approved by the Minister.

29. Where the dean of a college or faculty of education or the director of a school of education in Ontario reports to the Deputy Minister that a candidate,

(a) holds or has been recommended by the dean or the director for an Ontario Teacher's Certificate, a Permanent Letter of Standing or a Temporary Letter of Standing;
(b) holds an acceptable university degree or qualifications the Minister considers equivalent thereto; and
(c) has successfully completed an approved program leading to qualifications in an additional area of concentration in the primary division, the junior division, the intermediate division in general studies or the senior division in general studies, or has qualifications that the Minister considers equivalent to the successful completion of such a program,

the Minister may have entered on the candidate's Ontario Teacher's Qualifications Record Card or the record of qualification in respect of such teacher held by the Ministry such additional area of concentration. O. Reg. 34/91, s. 6; O. Reg. 243/92, s. 6.

30. (1) Subject to subsection (2), where the dean of a college or faculty of education in Ontario reports to the Deputy Minister that a candidate,

(a) holds or has been recommended by the dean or the director for an Ontario Teacher's Certificate or a Temporary Letter of Standing;
(b) has successfully completed an approved program leading to additional qualifications in a subject listed in Schedule B, or has qualifications that the Minister considers equivalent to the successful completion of such a program;
(c) in the case of a candidate for a qualification listed in Schedule B at the advanced level, has produced evidence of,
   (i) twelve months of business or industrial experience in the area of the qualification,
   (ii) academic experience that the Minister considers equivalent to twelve months of business or industrial experience in the area of the qualification, or
   (iii) a combination of academic, business and industrial experience that the Minister considers equivalent to twelve months of business or industrial experience in the area of the qualification; and
(d) has demonstrated competence in the area referred to in clause (c),

the Minister may have entered on the candidate's Ontario Teacher's Qualifications Record Card or the record of qualification in respect of such teacher held by the Ministry the additional qualification in such subject.

(2) An additional qualification may not be entered under subsection (1) on the Ontario Teacher's Qualifications Record Card or the record of qualification in respect of such teacher held by the Ministry, of a candidate whose areas of concentration in the program of professional education that qualified him or her for the Ontario Teacher's Certificate were not in technological studies unless the candidate meets the requirements of clause (c) of the definition of "technological qualifications" in section 1. O. Reg. 34/91, s. 7.

One Session Courses

31. Where the principal of a single-session course leading to a qualification listed in Schedule C or the dean of a college or faculty of education or the director of a school of education in Ontario reports to the Deputy Minister that a candidate,

(a) holds or has been recommended by the dean or the director for an Ontario Teacher's Certificate or a Temporary Letter of Standing; and
(b) has successfully completed an approved program leading to additional qualifications in a subject listed in Schedule C, or has qualifications that the Minister considers equivalent to the successful completion of such a program,

the Minister may have entered upon the candidate's Ontario Teacher's Qualifications Record Card or the record of qualification in respect of such teacher held by the Ministry the additional qualification in such subject. O. Reg. 34/91, s. 8.

Three-Session Specialist Courses

32. The Minister may have entered on a candidate's Ontario Teacher's Qualifications Record Card or on the record of qualification held by the Ministry in respect of a candidate the Part I qualification in a subject listed in Schedule D if the principal of the first session of a three-session course leading to a specialist qualification in the subject, the dean of a college or faculty of education or the director of a school of education in Ontario reports to the Deputy Minister that the candidate,

(a) holds an Ontario Teacher's Certificate or a Temporary Letter of Standing;
(b) has successfully completed an approved program leading to the Part I qualification; and
(c) has an entry on the candidate's Ontario Teacher's Qualifications Record Card or the record of qualification held by the Ministry in respect of the candiate that shows,
 (i) qualifications in the primary division, the junior division, the intermediate division in general studies or the senior division in general studies, in the case of Part I qualification other than Primary Education, Junior Education or intermediate Education,
 (ii) an area of concentration for the corresponding division, in the case of a Part I qualification in Primary Education, Junior Education or Intermediate Education, or
 (iii) qualification in technological studies, in the case of a Part I qualification in one of the following:
    1. Computers in the Classroom.
    2. Co-operative Education.
    3. Design and Technology.
    4. English as a Second Language.
    5. Guidance.
    6. Media.
    7. Multiculturalism in Education.
    8. Music — Instrumental.
    9. Music — Vocal (Primary, Junior).
    10. Music — Vocal (Intermediate, Senior).
    11. Special Education.
    12. The Blind.
    13. The Deaf.

14. The Deaf/Blind.
15. Visual Arts. O. Reg. 559/93, s. 2.

33. Where the principal of the second session of a three-session course or the dean of a college or faculty of education or the director of a school of education in Ontario reports to the Deputy Minister that a candidate,

   (a) holds or is deemed to hold an Ontario Teacher's Certificate or a Temporary Letter of Standing;
   (b) has successfully completed the first session, or the equivalent thereof, of a course leading to an additional qualification in a subject listed in Schedule D;
   (c) has submitted evidence of at least one year of successful teaching experience in Ontario certified by the appropriate supervisory officer or of at least one year of successful teaching experience outside Ontario certified by the appropriate supervisory official; and
   (d) has successfully completed the approved program for the second session of the course after completing the experience referred to in clause (c),

the Minister may have entered upon the candidate's Ontario Teacher's Qualifications Record Card or the record of qualification in respect of such teacher held by the Ministry the Part II qualification in such subject. O. Reg. 34/91, s. 10.

34. Where the principal of the third session of a three-session course or the dean of a college or faculty of education or the director of a school of education in Ontario reports to the Deputy Minister that a candidate,

   (a) holds or is deemed to hold an Ontario Teacher's Certificate or a Temporary Letter of Standing;
   (b) has successfully completed the second session, or the equivalent thereof, of a course leading to an additional qualification in a subject listed in Schedule D;
   (c) submits evidence of at least two years of successful teaching experience, including at least one year of experience in Ontario in the subject referred to in clause (b), certified by the appropriate supervisory officer and, if some of the experience was outside Ontario, by the appropriate supervisory official; and
   (d) has successfully completed subsequent to the experience referred to in clause (c) the approved program for the third session of such course,

the Minister may have entered upon the candidate's Ontario Teacher's Qualifications Record Card or the record of qualification in respect of such teacher held by the Ministry the specialist qualification in such subject. O. Reg. 34/91, s. 11.

35. Where the dean of a college or faculty of education or the director of a school of education in Ontario or the principal of a course reports that a candidate who does not hold an Ontario Teacher's Certificate,

   (a) holds a Permanent Letter of Standing valid in Ontario for teaching the deaf only; and
   (b) has otherwise met the requirements of section 31, 32, 33, 34, 38, 43 or 44,

the Minister may grant to the candidate a letter indicating that the candidate holds the appropriate additional qualification.

36. (1) A teacher who holds or is deemed to hold an Ontario Teacher's Certificate and who, prior to the 1st day of October, 1978, began a Master of Education program approved by the Minister as leading to the Specialist Certificate in Guidance, may obtain the specialist qualification in Guidance by completing the requirements for such Certificate as they existed on the 30th day of June, 1978, and the Minister shall, upon submission to the Deputy Minister of evidence satisfactory to the Minister of the completion of such requirements, have entered on such teacher's Ontario Teacher's Qualifications Record Card the specialist qualification in Guidance.

(2) A teacher who holds or is deemed to hold an Ontario Teacher's Certificate and who, prior to the 1st day of October, 1978, began a Master of Library Science program approved by the Minister as leading to the Specialist Certificate in Librarianship, may obtain the specialist qualification in Librarianship by completing the requirements for such Certificate as they existed on the 30th day of June, 1978, and the Minister shall, upon submission to the Deputy Minister of evidence satisfactory to the Minister of the completion of such requirements, have entered on such teacher's Ontario Teacher's Qualifications Record Card the specialist qualification in Librarianship.

37. A teacher who holds a special certificate in a subject listed in Schedule C, D or E, or a special certificate no longer issued, continues to be qualified in accordance with such certificate, and the Minister shall have the additional qualification corresponding to such special certificate recorded on the teacher's Ontario Teacher's Qualifications Record Card where the teacher holds or is granted an Ontario Teacher's Certificate.

One-Session Honour Specialist Course

38. (1) Where the dean of a college or faculty of education in Ontario reports to the Deputy Minister that a candidate for an Honour Specialist qualification in a subject or subjects listed in Schedule E,

(a) holds or is deemed to hold an Ontario Teacher's Certificate or a Temporary Letter of Standing and the candidate's Ontario Teacher's Qualifications Record Card or the record of qualification in respect of such teacher held by the Ministry has an entry showing qualifications in the primary division, the junior division, the intermediate division in general studies or the senior division in general studies; and

(b) holds,
   (i) a degree of Bachelor of Arts or Bachelor of Science from an Ontario university in a program,
     (A) that requires four years of university study, or the equivalent thereof, to a total of at least sixty university credits, and
     (B) in which the candidate has obtained at least second class or equivalent standing in the subject or subjects in which the candidate seeks an Honour Specialist qualification, including, in the case of two subjects, at least forty-two university credits therein and not fewer than eighteen university credits in each subject or, in the case of one subject, at least twenty-seven university credits therein, or
   (ii) qualifications the Minister considers equivalent to the qualifications referred to in subclause (i);

(c) submits evidence of at least two years of successful teaching experience, including at least one year of experience in Ontario in the subject or one or both of the subjects in which the Honours Specialist qualification is sought, certified by the appropriate supervisory officer and, if some of the experience was outside Ontario, by the appropriate supervisory official; and

(d) has successfully completed subsequent to the experience referred to in clause (c) the approved program for the Honour Specialist qualification in the subject or subjects referred to in sub-subclause (b)(i)(B),

the Minister may have entered upon the candidate's Ontario Teacher's Qualifications Record Card or the record of qualification in respect of the teacher held by the Ministry the Honour Specialist qualification in such subject or subjects referred to in sub-subclause (b)(i)(B).

(2) A university credit that has been used to meet the requirements for an Honour Specialist qualification established by clause (1)(b) shall not be used to meet the requirements for another Honour Specialist qualification.

(3) For the purpose of clause (1)(b), a university credit in Anthropology, Psychology or Sociology shall be deemed to be a university credit in Individual and Society.

(4) Where the dean of a college or faculty of education in Ontario reports to the Deputy Minister that a candidate for the Honour Technological Studies Specialist Qualification,

(a) holds or is deemed to hold an Ontario Teacher's Certificate or a Temporary Letter of Standing;

(b) has entries on his or her Ontario Teacher's Qualifications Record Card or the record of qualification in respect of such teacher held by the Ministry indicating qualifications in at least,

(i) three of the subjects listed in Schedule B including at least one at both the basic and the advanced level, or

(ii) four of the subjects listed in Schedule B at the basic level and an entry indicating the Specialist qualification in one of the subjects in Schedule D listed as exceptions in subclause 32(a)(i);

(c) submits evidence of at least two years of successful teaching experience, including at least one year of experience in Ontario in technological studies, certified by the appropriate supervisory officer and, if some of the experience was outside Ontario, by the appropriate supervisory official;

(d) holds a Secondary School Honour Graduation Diploma or has successfully completed the equivalent of one year's full-time study in a program in respect of which a Secondary School Graduation Diploma or its equivalent is required for admission; and

(e) has successfully completed subsequent to the experience referred to in clause (c) the approved program for the Honour Technological Studies Specialist qualification,

the Minister may have entered upon the candidate's Ontario Teacher's Qualifications Record Card or the record of qualification in respect of such teacher held by the Ministry the Honour Technological Studies Specialist qualification.

(5) The entry on a candidate's Ontario Teacher's Qualifications Record Card or the record of qualification in respect of such teacher held by the Ministry indicating that he or she has completed successfully the first session of a three-session course leading to the Specialist qualification in Design and Technology or Computer Studies — Computer Technology is

deemed to be equivalent to one basic level entry for the purposes of clause (4)(b). O. Reg. 34/91, s. 12; O. Reg. 243/92, s. 9.

39. (1) Where a teacher who completed prior to the 1st day of September, 1979 the first session of a two-session course leading to an Interim Vocational Certificate, Type A or an Interim Occupational Certificate, Type A completes the requirements for such certificate as they existed on the 30th day of June, 1978, the Minister may have entered on the teacher's Ontario Teacher's Qualifications Record Card the appropriate qualification.

(2) Where a teacher who,
- (a) held an Interim High School Assistant's Certificate, Type A on the 1st day of July, 1978; or
- (b) completed at a college or faculty of education in Ontario prior to the 1st day of July, 1979 the requirements for such certificate as they existed immediately before the 1st day of July, 1978,

completes the requirements for the High School Specialist Certificate as they existed immediately before the 1st day of July, 1978, the Minister may have entered on the teacher's Ontario Teacher's Qualifications Record Card the appropriate Honours Specialist qualification.

Principal's Qualifications

40. (1) The Principal's Qualification Program shall consist of two one-session courses.

(2) A teacher holds principal's qualifications if the teacher's Ontario Teacher's Qualifications Record Card or the record of qualification in respect of the teacher held by the Ministry has an entry for Part II of the Principal's Qualification Program. O. Reg. 559/93, s. 3, *part*.

41. An applicant for admission to the Principal's Qualification Program must,
- (a) hold an acceptable university degree;
- (b) hold an Ontario Teacher's Certificate or Temporary Letter of Standing;
- (c) hold concentrations in three divisions including the intermediate division, as indicated on the applicant's Ontario Teacher's Qualifications Record Card or the record of qualification held by the Ministry in respect of the applicant;
- (d) provide evidence of at least five years of successful teaching experience in a school providing elementary or secondary education, as certified by the appropriate supervisory officer or, in the case of experience outside Ontario, by the appropriate supervisory official; and
- (e) hold or provide evidence of one of the following:
    1. A Specialist or Honour Specialist qualification as indicated on the applicant's Ontario Teacher's Qualifications Record Card or the record of qualification held by the Ministry in respect of the applicant, and,
        - i. successful completion of at least half the number of courses required to qualify for a master's degree that is an acceptable university degree, or
        - ii. an additional Specialist or Honour Specialist qualification as indicated on the applicant's Ontario Teacher's Qualifications Record Card or the record of qualification held by the Ministry in respect of the applicant.

2. A master's degree or doctorate that is an acceptable university degree.
3. Successful completion of such number of graduate university courses as is equivalent to the number of graduate university courses that are required to qualify for a master's degree that is an acceptable university degree. O. Reg. 559/93, s. 3, *part*.

42. If the principal of a course leading to qualifications in Part I of the Principal's Qualification Program reports to the Deputy Minister that a candidate has met the admission requirements of section 41 and has successfully completed the course, the Minister may have the Part I qualification entered on the candidate's Ontario Teacher's Qualifications Record Card or the record of qualification held by the Ministry in respect of the candidate. O. Reg. 559/93, s. 3, *part*.

43. An applicant for admission to a course leading to qualifications in Part II of the Principal's Qualification Program must have an entry on his or her Ontario Teacher's Qualifications Record Card or the record of qualification held by the Ministry in respect of the applicant showing qualifications in Part I of the program. O. Reg. 559/93, s. 3, *part*.

44. If the principal of a course leading to qualifications in Part II of the Principal's Qualification Program reports to the Deputy Minister that a candidate has met the admission requirements of section 43 or 48 and has successfully completed the course, the Minister may have the Part II qualification entered on the candidate's Ontario Teacher's Qualifications Record Card or the record of qualification held by the Ministry in respect of the candidate. O. Reg. 559/93, s. 3, *part*.

45. Where the principal of a Principal's Development Course reports to the Deputy Minister that a candidate,
 (a) holds principal's qualifications;
 (b) has two years of successful experience as a principal or vice-principal as certified by the appropriate supervisory officer; and
 (c) has successfully completed the Course,
the Minister may have entered on the candidate's Ontario Teacher's Qualifications Record Card the Principal's Development Course qualification. O. Reg. 559/93, s. 4.

46. A teacher who holds a High School Principal's Certificate, an Elementary School Principal's Certificate, a Secondary School Principal's Certificate, Type B, a Secondary School Principal's Certificate, Type A, a Secondary School Principal's Certificate or a Vocational School Principal's Certificate, whether such certificate is an interim certificate or a permanent certificate, remains qualified within the limitations of the certificate except that the interim qualification will not lapse after the five-year period of validity and such qualification shall be shown on his or her Ontario Teacher's Qualifications Record Card.

47. A teacher who holds an Elementary School Inspector's Certificate shall be deemed to hold an Elementary School Principal's Certificate.

48. Despite section 43, a teacher who holds or who is deemed to hold an interim or permanent Elementary School Principal's Certificate, or who holds an interim or permanent Secondary School Principal's Certificate, Type B, an interim or permanent Vocational School

Principal's Certificate, an interim Secondary School Principal's Certificate, or an interim Secondary School Principal's Certificate Type A, may be admitted to the course leading to the qualifications in Part II of the Principal's Qualification Program. O. Reg. 559/93, s. 5.

49. (1) Where a teacher held an interim Elementary School Principal's Certificate, an interim Secondary School Principal's Certificate, Type B, or an interim Secondary School Principal's Certificate, Type A, on the 1st day of July, 1978 and completes the requirements for the permanent certificate that corresponds thereto as they existed immediately before the 1st day of July, 1978, the Minister shall have entered on the teacher's Ontario Teacher's Qualifications Record Card the appropriate qualification.

(2) A teacher who holds a permanent Secondary School Principal's Certificate, Type A or a permanent Secondary School Principal's Certificate is deemed to hold principal's qualifications.

PART III
LETTERS OF PERMISSION

50. (1) The Minister may grant to a board a Letter of Permission for a period specified in the letter if the director of education or secretary of the board submits to the appropriate Regional Director of Education of the Ministry, in duplicate, an application in Form 7 or 7a together with evidence that,

(a) the board has publicly advertised, on at least three occasions, a position for which a teacher is required under the regulations;

(a.1) at least one advertisement was published in a daily newspaper having provincial circulation in Ontario;

(b) at least one advertisement appeared during the thirty days preceding the start of employment;

(c) seven days have passed since the date of the final advertisement; and

(d) no teacher has applied for the position or no teacher who has applied for the position has accepted it.

(2) The period for which a Letter of Permission is granted,

(a) shall not exceed one year; and

(b) shall not extend beyond the end of a school year unless,

　(i) the period begins after the end of a school year and ends before the beginning of the next school year.

　(ii) [Revoked O. Reg. 243/92, s. 10(2).] O. Reg. 34/91, s. 13; O. Reg. 243/92, s. 10; O. Reg. 559/93, s. 6.

PART IV
TEMPORARY LETTERS OF APPROVAL

51. (1) The Minister may grant to a board a Temporary Letter of Approval for a period

Sched. A REGULATIONS UNDER THE EDUCATION ACT

specified in the letter if the director of education or secretary of the board submits to the appropriate Regional Director of Education of the Ministry, in duplicate, an application in Form 8 or 8a certifying that,

    (a) the board finds it necessary to assign or appoint a teacher to teach a subject or hold a position who does not hold the qualifications required under the regulations for teaching the subject or holding the position; and

    (b) the teacher in respect of whom the application is made,

        (i) holds an Ontario Teacher's Certificate or a Letter of Standing, and

        (ii) is considered competent to teach the subject or hold the position.

(2) The period for which a Temporary Letter of Approval is granted,

    (a) shall not exceed one year; and

    (b) shall not extend beyond the end of a school year unless the period begins after the end of a school year and ends before the beginning of the next school year. O. Reg. 34/91, s. 14.

Schedule A
Intermediate and Senior Division Options taken in English or French

Business Studies — Accounting
Business Studies — Data Processing
Business Studies — Marketing and Merchandising
Business Studies — Information Management
Classical Studies — Greek
Classical Studies — Latin
Computer Science
Dance
Design and Technology
Dramatic Arts
Economics
English (First language)
English (Second language) — anglais
Environmental Science
Family Studies
French (Second language)
French (First language) — français
Geography
History
Individual and Society
International Languages
Law
Mathematics
Music — Instrumental
Music — Vocal
Native Language (Second language)

Native Studies
Politics
Physical and Health Education
Religious Education
Science — General
Science — Biology
Science — Chemistry
Science — Geology
Science — Physics
Visual Arts

O. Reg. 34/91, s. 15; O. Reg. 243/92, s. 11; O. Reg. 559/93, s. 7

Schedule B
Technological Studies Options Taken in English or French

BASIC LEVEL
Communications
  Art
  Communications Technology
  Computer Electronics
  Drafting Comprehensive
  Electronics
  Graphic Communications
  Music
  Photography

Construction
  Architectural Drafting
    and Design
  Construction Services
  Construction Technology
  Electricity
  Environmental Control
  Plumbing
  Sheet Metal
  Trowel Trades
  Woodworking

Manufacturing
  Control Systems
  Engineering Drafting
    and Design
  Foundry and Moulding
    Practice
  Industrial Electrics

ADVANCED LEVEL
Communications
  Art
  Communications Technology
  Computer Electronics
  Drafting Comprehensive
  Electronics
  Graphic Communications
  Music
  Photography

Construction
  Architectural Drafting
    and Design
  Construction Services
  Construction Technology
  Electricity
  Environmental Control
  Plumbing
  Sheet Metal
  Trowel Trades
  Woodworking

Manufacturing
  Control Systems
  Engineering Drafting
    and Design
  Foundry and Moulding
    Practice
  Industrial Electrics

Sched. C REGULATIONS UNDER THE EDUCATION ACT

Manufacturing Technology	Manufacturing Technology
Metal Fabrication	Metal Fabrication
Precision Machining	Precision Machining
Services	Services
Appliance Repair	Appliance Repair
Cosmetology	Cosmetology
Culinary Arts	Culinary Arts
Horticulture	Horticulture
Hospitality	Hospitality
Natural Resource Management	Natural Resource Management
Personal Care	Personal Care
Services Technology	Services Technology
Textile Maintenance	Textile Maintenance
Textiles and Clothing	Textiles and Clothing
Upholstery	Upholstery
Transportation	Transportation
Agricultural Equipment	Agricultural Equipment
Aircraft	Aircraft
Auto Body	Auto Body
Automotive	Automotive
Small Powered Equipment	Small Powered Equipment
Transportation Technology	Transportation Technology

O. Reg. 415/91, s. 1.

Schedule C
One-Session Qualifications taken in English or French

Adult Education
Associate Teacher
Childhood Education
Childhood Education in Great Britain
Community School Development
Computer Studies — Computer Technology
Driver Education Instructor
Integrated Arts
Law
Preschool Deaf Education
Teaching Children with Language Difficulties — Aphasia
Teacher of Cree
Teacher of Mohawk
Teacher of Native Children
Teacher of Ojibway
Teaching Writing

REGULATION 297 **Sched. D**

Schedule D
Three Session Qualifications taken in English or French

Business Studies — Accounting
Business Studies — Data Processing
Business Studies — Entrepreneurship Studies
Business Studies — Marketing and Merchandising
Business Studies — Information Management
Computer Studies — Computer Science
Computers in the Classroom
Co-operative Education
Dance
Design and Technology
Dramatic Arts
English as a Second Language
Environmental Science
Family Studies
French as a Second Language
Guidance
Intermediate Education
International Languages
Junior Education
Librarianship
Mathematics in Primary and Junior Education
Media
Multiculturalism in Education
Music — Instrumental
Music — Vocal (Primary, Junior)
Music — Vocal (Intermediate, Senior)
Native Language as a Second Language
Physical and Health Education (Primary, Junior)
Physical and Health Education (Intermediate, Senior)
Primary Education
Reading
Religious Education
Science in Primary and Junior Education
Special Education
The Blind
The Deaf
The Deaf/Blind
Visual Arts

O. Reg. 34/91, s. 16; O. Reg. 243/92, s. 12.

Sched. E REGULATIONS UNDER THE EDUCATION ACT

Schedule E
Honour Specialist Qualifications taken in English or French

Biology
Business Studies
Chemistry
Computer Science
Contemporary Studies
Dance
Dramatic Arts
English (First language)
English (Second language) — anglais
Environmental Science
Family Studies
French (Second language)
French (First language) — français
Geographic
Geology
Greek
History
International Languages
Latin
Mathematics
Music
Physical and Health Education
Physics
Religious Education
Science
Visual Arts

O. Reg. 34/91, s. 17; O. Reg. 243/92, s. 13; O. Reg. 559/93, s. 8.

FORM 1

FORMULE 1

Education Act
Loi sur l'éducation

ONTARIO TEACHER'S CERTIFICATE

BREVET D'ENSEIGNEMENT DE L'ONTARIO

THIS IS TO CERTIFY THAT   NOUS, SOUSSIGNÉS, CERTIFIONS QUE

....

Name in full   Prénoms et nom

326

REGULATION 297 **FORM 2**

having complied with the regulations made under the *Education Act* is hereby granted an

ayant satisfait aux exigences des règlements établis selon la *Loi sur l'éducation* reçoit par la présente un

ONTARIO TEACHER'S CERTIFICATE

BREVET D'ENSEIGNEMENT DE L'ONTARIO

valid in the schools of Ontario in accordance with the regulations made under the *Education Act*.

valide dans les écoles de l'Ontario d'après les règlements établis selon la *Loi sur l'éducation*.

Number ....
Numéro

Dated at Toronto this .... day of ...., 19......
Fait à Toronto, ce jour du mois de

....
DEPUTY MINISTER MINISTER OF EDUCATION
LE SOUS-MINISTRE LE MINISTRE DE L'ÉDUCATION

FORM 2

FORMULE 2

Education Act
Loi sur l'éducation

ONTARIO TEACHER'S QUALIFICATIONS RECORD CARD

CARTE DES QUALIFICATIONS DE L'ENSEIGNANT DE L'ONTARIO

Issued to: S.I.N.
Délivrée à .... N.A.S. ....
Date ....Degree (s) ....Date of Birth ....
 Grade(s) Date de naissance

DEPUTY MINISTER MINISTER OF EDUCATION
LE SOUS-MINISTRE LE MINISTRE DE L'ÉDUCATION

FORM 3 REGULATIONS UNDER THE EDUCATION ACT

BASIC QUALIFICATIONS QUALIFICATIONS DE BASE		ADDITIONAL QUALIFICATIONS QUALIFICATIONS ADDITIONNELLES	
Institution Attended Établissement fréquenté	Year Année	Qualifications	Year Année
....	....	....	....
		....	....
Areas of Concentration Secteurs de concentration	Year Année	....	....
		....	....
Initial		....	....
		....	....
....	....	....	....
....	....	....	....
....	....	....	....
			....
Additional Additionnel	Year Année	....	....
....	....		

FORM 3

Education Act

TEMPORARY LETTER OF STANDING

for

....
(Name in full)

In consideration of your academic or technological and professional training you are hereby granted a TEMPORARY LETTER OF STANDING valid until ...., for teaching in Ontario in schools and classes where English is the language of instruction. Professional education has been received in

....
....
....

....
NUMBER   DATE OF ISSUE

....
DEPUTY MINISTER   MINISTER OF EDUCATION

REGULATION 297 **FORM 4**

FORM 3a

Loi sur l'éducation

ATTESTATION TEMPORAIRE DE COMPÉTENCE

décernée à

....
(Prénoms et nom)

Eu égard à formation scolaire ou technologique et professionnelle, vous recevez par la présente une ATTESTATION TEMPORAIRE DE COMPÉTENCE valide jusqu'au ...., vous autorisant à enseigner en Ontario dans les écoles et les classes de langue française instituées en vertu de la *Loi sur l'éducation*, partie XII.

La formation professionnelle a été reçue

....
....
....

....
NUMÉRO DATE

....
Le sous-ministre Le ministre de l'Éducation
O. Reg. 687/92, s. 1.

FORM 4

Education Act

PROVISIONAL LETTER OF STANDING

THIS IS TO CERTIFY THAT

....

having complied with the regulations made under the *Education Act*, is hereby granted a PROVISIONAL LETTER OF STANDING valid until .... for teaching in Ontario in schools and classes where English is the language of instruction.

Professional education has been received in

....
....
....

Number ....

Dated at Toronto this .... day of ...., 19......

FORM 4a REGULATIONS UNDER THE EDUCATION ACT

....
                   Deputy Minister   Minister of Education

RENEWAL   MINISTER OF EDUCATION

1. ....

FORM 4a

Loi sur l'éducation

ATTESTATION PROVISOIRE DE COMPÉTENCE

NOUS, SOUSSIGNÉS, CERTIFIONS QUE

....

ayant satisfait aux exigences des règlements établis selon la *Loi sur l'éducation*, reçoit par la présente une ATTESTATION PROVISOIRE DE COMPÉTENCE valide jusqu'au .... pour enseigner en Ontario dans les écoles et les classes de langue française institutées en vertu de la *Loi sur l'éducation*, partie XII.

La formation professionnelle a été reçue

....
....
....

Numéro ....

Fait à Toronto le .... 19......

....
                 Le sous-ministre   Le ministre de l'Éducation

RENOUVELLEMENT   LE MINISTRE DE L'ÉDUCATION

1. ....

O. Reg. 687/92, s. 1.

FORM 5

Education Act

LETTER OF ELIGIBILITY

TO

....
(Name)

In consideration of your academic and professional education, you are hereby issued

S. 5a

a LETTER OF ELIGIBILITY, valid for three years under section ....of the Ontario Teacher's Qualifications
                              12(1) or 13
Regulation. When you have conformed with the requirements of section ...., you will qualify for a
                              12(2) or 14
Temporary Letter of Standing that shows professional education has been received in:
....
....

Dated at Toronto, this .... day of ...., 19......

....
Deputy Minister

Statement of Board Supervisory Officer

This is to certify that .... the holder of this Letter of Eligibility,
                                      (Name)
has been offered a position as a teacher with ....
                                                                                    (Name of Board)

for the school year ...., subject to the granting of a Temporary Letter of Standing, and further, that the applicant has adequate fluency in the use of the English language to carry out the duties and responsibilities of a teacher.

Dated at ...., this .... day of ...., 19......

....
Supervisory Officer

....
Position

O. Reg. 729/94, s. 3

FORM 5a

Loi sur l'éducation

ATTESTATION D'ADMISSIBILITÉ

DÉCERNÉE À

....
(nom)

Eu égard à votre formation scolaire et professionnelle, nous vous décernons par la présente

S. 5a REGULATIONS UNDER THE EDUCATION ACT

une ATTESTATION D'ADMISSIBILITÉ, valide pour trois ans, en vertu de l'article ....du Règlement sur la qualification
12(1) ou 13
requise de l'enseignant en Ontario. Lorsque vous aurez satisfait aux exigences de l'article ....,
12(2) ou 14
vous pourrez recevoir une attestation temporaire de compétence indiquant que vous avez reçu une formation professionnelle en:

....

....

Fait à Toronto, le ...., 19......

....

Le sous-ministre

Déclaration de l'agent de supervision du conseil scolaire

Je soussigné(e) certifie que ...., titulaire de la présente
(nom)
attestation d'admissibilité, a reçu une offre d'emploi comme enseignant du conseil scolaire

....
(nom du conseil scolaire)

pour l'année scolaire ...., sous réserve de l'obtention d'une attestation temporaire de compétence. Je certifie de plus que cette personne possède une maîtrise du français suffisante pour satisfaire aux tâches et aux exigences de sa profession d'enseignant.

Fait à ...., le ...., 19......

....

L'agent de supervision

....

Poste

O. Reg. 729/94, s. 3.

REGULATION 297   **FORM 6a**

FORM 6

Education Act

PERMANENT LETTER OF STANDING

THIS IS TO CERTIFY THAT

....
(Name)

having complied with the regulations made under the *Education Act*, is hereby granted a PERMANENT LETTER OF STANDING valid for the teaching of the

....in Ontario.
Deaf or Trainable Retarded

Number ....

Dated at Toronto this .... day of ...., 19 ....

....
      Deputy Minister   Minister of Education

FORM 6a

Loi sur l'éducation

ATTESTATION PERMANENTE DE COMPÉTENCE

NOUS, SOUSSIGNÉS, CERTIFIONS QUE

....
(nom)

ayant satisfait aux exigences des règlements établis selon la *Loi sur l'éducation*, reçoit par la présente une ATTESTATION PERMANENTE DE COMPÉTENCE pour enseigner aux .....
élèves sourds ou élèves déficients moyens

en Ontario.

Numéro ....

Fait à Toronto le .... 19 .....

....
      Le sous-ministre   Le ministre de l'Éducation

O. Reg. 687/92, s. 1.

FORM 7 REGULATIONS UNDER THE EDUCATION ACT

FORM 7

Education Act

APPLICATION FOR LETTER OF PERMISSION

To the Regional Director of Education of the Ministry:

On behalf of ....
(name of board)

A LETTER OF PERMISSION is requested to employ

....
(name in full)

Social Insurance Number ....

as a teacher of the ....divisions

at ....school.

from .... 19 .... to .... 19 ....

I certify and attach evidence that the Board has complied with section 52 of the Ontario Teacher's Qualifications Regulation, including a copy of the most recent advertisement of the position for which the Letter of Permission is required.

Date ....
Director of Education or Secretary of the Board

LETTER OF PERMISSION IS HEREBY GRANTED

Date ....
Regional Director of Education

FORM 7a

Loi sur l'éducation

DEMANDE DE PERMISSION INTÉRIMAIRE

Au directeur régional de l'éducation du ministère :

Au nom du ....
(nom du conseil scolaire)

UNE PERMISSION INTÉRIMAIRE est demandée pour l'emploi de

REGULATION 297 FORM 8

....
(prénoms et nom)

Numéro d'assurance sociale ....

en qualité d'enseignant aux cycles ....

à l'école ....

du .... 19 .... au .... 19 ....

    Je certifie et joins la preuve que le conseil scolaire a satisfait à l'article 52 du Règlement sur la qualification requise de l'enseignant en Ontario. Veuillez trouver ci-jointe une copie de l'annonce publicitaire la plus récente offrant le poste pour lequel on demande une permission intérimaire.

Date ....
                                                                          Le directeur de l'éducation ou
                                                                          le secrétaire du conseil scolaire

---

PERMISSION INTÉRIMAIRE ACCORDÉE PAR LA PRÉSENTE

Date ....
                                                                        Le directeur régional de l'éducation
                                                                          O. Reg. 687/92, s. 1.

FORM 8

Education Act

APPLICATION FOR TEMPORARY LETTER OF APPROVAL

To the Regional Director of Education of the Ministry:

On behalf of ....
                                  (name of board)

A TEMPORARY LETTER OF APPROVAL is requested to employ

....
                                  (name in full)

Social Insurance Number ....

Basic Certification ....

as a ....
                                  (teacher, principal, etc.)

FORM 8a REGULATIONS UNDER THE EDUCATION ACT

of ....
(subject, division, school)

from ....19 .... to ....19 ......
(date) (date)

I certify that the Board finds it necessary to appoint or assign the teacher named above who does not hold the qualifications required by the regulations for the position but is considered competent to carry out the duties of the position.

Date ....19 ....
Director of Education or Secretary of the Board

TEMPORARY LETTER OF APPROVAL IS GRANTED

Date ....19 ....
Minister of Education

O. Reg. 34/91, s. 18.

FORM 8a

Loi sur l'éducation

DEMANDE D'APPROBATION TEMPORAIRE

Au directeur régional de l'Éducation du ministère :

Au nom du ....
(nom du conseil scolaire)

Une APPROBATION TEMPORAIRE est demandée pour l'emploi de

....
(nom au complet)

Numéro d'assurance sociale ....

Brevet de base ....

en qualité de ....
(enseignant, directeur d'école, etc.)

de ....
(matière, cycle, école)

du ....19 .... au ....19 ......

Je certifie que le conseil scolaire estime nécessaire de nommer ou d'affecter à ce poste l'enseignant susnommé qui ne possède pas les qualifications requises par les règlements, mais qui est jugé compétent pour en exercer les fonctions.

REGULATION 297 **FORM 9a**

Date ....19.......   ....
                                                  Directeur de l'Éducation
                                                  ou secrétaire du conseil scolaire

LETTRE D'APPROBATION
TEMPORAIRE ACCORDÉE

Date ....19.......   ....
                                                  Ministre
                                                  de l'Education
                                                  O. Reg. 34/91, s. 18; O. Reg. 687/92, s. 1.

FORM 9

Education Act

PERMANENT LETTER OF STANDING
TEACHER OF A NATIVE LANGUAGE AS A SECOND LANGUAGE

THIS IS TO CERTIFY THAT

....
(Name)

having complied with the regulations made under the *Education Act*, is hereby granted a PERMANENT LETTER OF STANDING — TEACHER OF A NATIVE LANGUAGE AS A SECOND LANGUAGE valid for the teaching of,

.... in Ontario
(Algonquian, Iroquoian)

Number ....
Dated at Toronto, this .... day
of ...., 19 ....

....
DEPUTY MINISTER   MINISTER OF EDUCATION

FORM 9a

Loi sur l'éducation

ATTESTATION PERMANENTE DE COMPÉTENCE POUR L'ENSEIGNEMENT D'UNE
LANGUE AUTOCHTONE COMME LANGUE SECONDE

NOUS, SOUSSIGNÉS, CERTIFIONS QUE

....
(nom)

ayant satisfait aux exigences des règlements pris en application de la *Loi sur l'éducation*, reçoit

FORM 10   REGULATIONS UNDER THE EDUCATION ACT

par la présente une ATTESTATION PERMANENTE DE COMPÉTENCE POUR L'ENSEIGNEMENT D'UNE LANGUE AUTOCHTONE COMME LANGUE SECONDE pour enseigner l'une des deux langues suivantes :

.... en Ontario
(algonquin, iroquois)

Numéro ....
Fait à Toronto le ....
....19 ....

....
   Le sous-ministre   Le ministre de l'Éducation
                                                              O. Reg. 687/92, s. 1.

FORM 10

Education Act

PROVISIONAL LETTER OF STANDING — DANCE

This is to certify that ....,
having complied with the regulations made under the *Education Act*, is hereby granted a PROVISIONAL LETTER OF STANDING valid

until .... for teaching dance.

Number ....

Dated at Toronto, this .... day of ...., 19 ....

....
        Deputy Minister   Minister of Education
                                                                 O. Reg. 243/92, s. 14.

FORM 10a

Loi sur l'éducation

ATTESTATION PROVISOIRE DE COMPÉTENCE POUR L'ENSEIGNEMENT
DE LA DANSE

Nous, soussigné(e)s, certifions que ....,
ayant satisfait aux exigences des règlements pris en application de la *Loi sur l'éducation*, reçoit par la présente une ATTESTATION PROVISOIRE DE COMPÉTENCE valable jusqu'au
.... pour l'enseignement de la danse.

Numéro ....

REGULATION 297 **FORM 11a**

Fait à Toronto le ....19 ....

    Le sous-ministre,   Le ministre de l'Éducation,

....

                                                                      O. Reg. 243/92, s. 14.

FORM 11

Education Act

PERMANENT LETTER OF STANDING — DANCE

This is to certify that ....,
having complied with the regulations made under the *Education Act*, is hereby granted a PERMANENT LETTER OF STANDING valid for teaching dance.

Number ....

Dated at Toronto, this ....day of ...., 19 ....

....
      Deputy Minister   Minister of Education

                                                                        O. Reg. 243/92, s. 14.

FORM 11a

Loi sur l'éducation

ATTESTATION PERMANENTE DE COMPÉTENCE POUR L'ENSEIGNEMENT DE LA DANSE

Nous, soussigné(e)s, certifions que ....,
ayant satisfait aux exigences des règlements pris en application de la *Loi sur l'éducation*, reçoit par la présente une ATTESTATION PERMANENTE DE COMPÉTENCE valable pour l'enseignement de la danse.

Numéro ....

Fait à Toronto le ....19 ....

    Le sous-ministre,   Le ministre de l'Éducation,

....

                                                                      O. Reg. 243/92, s. 14.

REGULATION 298
OPERATION OF SCHOOLS — GENERAL

R.R.O. 1990, Reg. 298: am. O. Reg. 339/91 (Fr. version); O. Reg. 242/92

1. In this Regulation,

"business studies" means the courses in general studies that are developed from curriculum guidelines listed under the heading "Business Studies" in Appendix B to OSIS;

"division" means the primary division, the junior division, the intermediate division or the senior division;

"French as a second language" includes programs for English speaking pupils in which French is the language of instruction;

"general studies" means the courses developed from curriculum guidelines that are issued by the Minister for the intermediate division and senior division and listed under a heading other than "Technological Studies" in Appendix B to OSIS;

"OSIS" means the circular entitled "Ontario Schools Intermediate and Senior Divisions Program and Diploma Requirements" issued by the Minister including any document issued by the Minister in accordance with paragraphs 1, 2, 3, 4 and 25 of subsection 8(1) of the Act;

"parent" includes guardian;

"technological studies" means the courses developed from curriculum guidelines that are issued by the Minister for the intermediate division and senior division and listed under the heading "Technological Studies" in Appendix B to OSIS.

Accommodation

2. (1) A board shall file with the Ministry plans for the erection of, addition to, or alteration of a school building together with details of the site thereof.

(2) It is a condition of the payment of a legislative grant in respect of capital cost that the plans and details referred to in subsection (1) be approved by the Minister.

Daily Sessions

3. (1) The length of the instructional program of each school day for pupils of compulsory school age shall be not less than five hours a day excluding recesses or scheduled intervals between classes.

(2) The instructional program on a school day shall begin not earlier than 8 a.m. and end not later than 5 p.m. except with the approval of the Minister.

(3) Despite subsection (1), a board may reduce the length of the instructional program on each school day to less than five hours a day for an exceptional pupil in a special education program.

(4) Every board may establish the length of the instructional program on each school day for pupils in junior kindergarten and kindergarten.

(5) A scheduled interval between classes for the lunch break for pupils and teachers shall be not less than forty consecutive minutes.

(6) In the intermediate division and the senior division, a principal may, subject to the approval of the board, provide for recesses or intervals for pupils between periods.

(7) Every board shall determine the period of time during each school day when its school buildings and playgrounds shall be open to its pupils, but in every case the buildings and the playgrounds shall be open to pupils during the period beginning fifteen minutes before classes begin for the day and ending fifteen minutes after classes end for the day.

(8) There shall be a morning recess and an afternoon recess, each of which shall be not less than ten minutes and not more than fifteen minutes in length, for pupils in the primary and junior divisions.

Opening or Closing Exercises

4. (1) Every public elementary and secondary school shall hold opening or closing exercises.

(2) Opening or closing exercises shall include *O Canada* and may include *God Save The Queen*.

(3) Opening or closing exercises may include the following types of readings that impart social, moral or spiritual values and that are representative of Ontario's multicultural society:
1. Scriptural writings including prayers.
2. Secular writings.

(4) Opening or closing exercises may include a period of silence.

(5) No pupil enrolled in a public elementary or secondary school shall be required to take part in any opening or closing exercises where a parent or guardian of the pupil or the pupil, where the pupil is an adult, applies to the principal of the school that the pupil attends for exemption therefrom.

Flag

5. (1) Every school shall fly both the National Flag of Canada and the Provincial Flag of Ontario on such occasions as the board directs.

(2) Every school shall display in the school the National Flag of Canada and the Provincial Flag of Ontario.

Emergency Procedures

6. (1) In addition to the drills established under the fire safety plan required under Regulation 454 of Revised Regulations of Ontario, 1990 (Fire Code), every board may provide for the holding of drills in respect of emergencies other than those occasioned by fire.

(2) Every principal, including the principal of an evening class or classes or of a class or classes conducted outside the school year, shall hold at least on emergency drill in the period during which the instruction is given.

(3) When a fire or emergency drill is held in a school building, every person in the building shall take part in the fire or emergency drill.

Textbooks

7. (1) The principal of a school, in consultation with the teachers concerned, shall select from the list of the textbooks approved by the Minister the textbooks for the use of pupils of the school, and the selection shall be subject to the approval of the board.

(2) Where no textbook for a course of study is included in the list of the textbooks approved by the Minister the principal of a school, in consultation with the teachers concerned, shall, where they consider a textbook to be required, select a suitable textbook and, subject to the approval of the board, such textbook may be introduced for use in the school.

(3) In the selection of textbooks under subsection (2), preference shall be given to books that have been written by Canadian authors and edited, printed and bound in Canada.

(4) Every board shall provide without charge for the use of each pupil enrolled in a day school operated by the board such textbooks selected under subsections (1) and (2) as relate to the courses in which the pupil is enrolled.

Elementary School Boards

8. (1) Where the area of jurisdiction of a district school area board, a Roman Catholic separate school board, other than a Roman Catholic school board, or a Protestant separate school board is not within a secondary school district, the board shall provide instruction that would enable its resident pupils to obtain sixteen credits towards a secondary school graduation diploma or an Ontario secondary school diploma.

(2) A board referred to in subsection (1) that offers courses of instruction during July or August or both in any year may provide instruction that would enable its resident pupils to obtain two credits in addition to the sixteen credits referred to in subsection (1).

(3) Where a board referred to in subsection (1) provides,
(a) daily transportation for its resident pupils; or
(b) reimbursement for board and lodging and for transportation once a week to and from the places of residence of its resident pupils,

that it considers necessary to enable its resident pupils to attend a school operated by another board, the other board may provide such instruction as would enable such resident pupils to obtain the number of credits referred to in subsections (1) and (2).

(4) A Roman Catholic separate school board, other than a Roman Catholic school board, or a Protestant separate school board that has jurisdiction in a secondary school district may provide instruction for its resident pupils that would enable the pupils to obtain up to eighteen credits towards a secondary school graduation diploma or an Ontario secondary school diploma.

Qualifications for Principals and Vice-Principals

9. (1) The principal and vice-principal of a school having an enrolment greater than 125 shall each be a teacher who,

(a) holds or is deemed to hold, under Regulation 297 of Revised Regulations of Ontario, 1990, principal's qualifications; or
(b) holds a principal's certificate that is a qualification to be principal or vice-principal, as the case may be, in the type of school identified on the certificate, or is deemed under section 47 of Regulation 297 of Revised Regulations of Ontario, 1990 to hold such a certificate,

and, in the case of a school,

(c) in which English is the language of instruction; or
(d) that is established under Part XII of the Act and in which French is the language of instruction,

shall each be a person who is eligible to teach in such school under subsection 19(11), (12) or (13), as the case may be.

(2) Despite subsection (1), where a teacher who does not hold the degree of Bachelor of Arts or Bachelor of Science from an Ontario university or a degree that the Minister considers equivalent thereto was, prior to the 1st day of September, 1961, employed by a board as principal or vice-principal of an elementary school that had an enrolment of 300 or more pupils, the teacher shall be deemed to be qualified as principal or vice-principal, as the case may be, of any elementary school operated by that board or its successor board.

(3) Despite subsection (1), where a teacher who does not hold the qualifications referred to in subsection (1),

(a) was employed by a board prior to the 1st day of September, 1972 as principal of an elementary school that had an enrolment of 300 or more pupils and is employed by such board as principal of an elementary school on the 8th day of September, 1978;
(b) was employed by a board on the 1st day of September, 1978 as vice-principal of an elementary school that had an enrolment on the last school day in April, 1978 of 300 or more pupils; or
(c) was employed by a board on the 1st day of September, 1978 as principal or vice-principal of an elementary school that had an enrolment on the last school day in April, 1978 that was greater than 125 and less than 300,

such teacher shall be deemed to be qualified as principal or vice-principal, as the case may be, of any elementary school operated by that board or its successor board.

(4) A board may appoint a person who holds the qualifications required by subsection (1) as a supervising principal to supervise the administration of two or more elementary schools operated by the board and such person shall be subject to the authority of the appropriate supervisory officer.

(5) A supervising principal may be principal of only one school.

(6) Despite subsection (1), a teacher who, before the 1st day of September, 1970, held the necessary qualifications as principal of a secondary school continues to be qualified as principal or vice-principal of a secondary school.

10. (1) The principal and vice-principal of a school for trainable retarded pupils having an enrolment greater than 100 or of a school in which there are classes for trainable retarded pupils and the enrolment in such classes is greater than 100 shall each be a teacher who,

(a) holds or is deemed to hold, under Regulation 297 of Revised Regulations of Ontario,

1990, principal's qualifications, or holds a certificate referred to in section 46 of such Regulation or is deemed to hold such certificate under section 47 thereof; and

(b) holds an additional qualification in special education as recorded on the teacher's Ontario Teacher's Qualifications Record Card.

(2) The principal of an elementary or secondary school that includes one or more classes for trainable retarded pupils shall be the principal of such classes, and the vice-principal of such a school shall be the vice-principal of such classes except where a vice-principal is appointed to be in charge of such classes exclusively.

(3) Despite subsection (1), where a teacher who does not hold the qualifications referred to in subsection (1) was, on the 1st day of September, 1978 employed by a board as principal or vice-principal of a school for trainable retarded pupils that had an enrolment greater than 100 or of a school in which there were classes for trainable retarded pupils and the enrolment in such classes was greater than 100, the teacher shall be deemed to be qualified as principal or vice-principal, as the case may be, of a school for trainable retarded pupils or of a school in which there are classes for trainable retarded pupils the enrolment in which is greater than 100 that is operated by that board or its successor board.

Duties of Principals

11. (1) The principal of a school, subject to the authority of the appropriate supervisory officer, is in charge of,

(a) the instruction and the discipline of pupils in the school; and
(b) the organization and management of the school.

(2) Where two or more schools operated by a board jointly occupy or use in common a school building or school grounds, the board shall designate which principal has authority over those parts of the building or grounds that the schools occupy or use in common.

(3) In addition to the duties under the Act and those assigned by the board, the principal of a school shall, except where the principal has arranged otherwise under subsection 26(3),

(a) supervise the instruction in the school and advise and assist any teacher in cooperation with the teacher in charge of an organizational unit or program;
(b) assign duties to vice-principals and to teachers in charge of organizational units or programs;
(c) retain on file up-to-date copies of outlines of all courses of study that are taught in the school;
(d) upon request, make outlines of courses of study available for examination to a resident pupil of the board and to the parent of the pupil, where the pupil is a minor;
(e) provide for the supervision of pupils during the period of time during each school day when the school buildings and playgrounds are open to pupils;
(f) provide for the supervision of and the conducting of any school activity authorized by the board;
(g) where performance appraisals of members of the teaching staff are required under a collective agreement or a policy of the board, despite anything to the contrary in such collective agreement or board policy, conduct performance appraisals of members of the teaching staff;

(h) subject to the provisions of the policy of the board or the provisions of a collective agreement, as the case may be, in respect of reporting requirements for performance appraisals, report thereon in writing to the board or to the supervisory officer on request and give to each teacher so appraised a copy of the performance appraisal of the teacher;

(i) where the performance appraisals of members of the teaching staff are not required by board policy or under a collective agreement, report to the board or to the supervisory officer in writing on request on the effectiveness of members of the teaching staff and give to a teacher referred to in any such report a copy of the portion of the report that refers to the teacher;

(j) make recommendations to the board with respect to,
   (i) the appointment and promotion of teachers, and
   (ii) the demotion or dismissal of teachers whose work or attitude is unsatisfactory;

(k) provide for instruction of pupils in the care of the school premises;

(l) inspect the school premises at least weekly and report forthwith to the board,
   (i) any repairs to the school that are required, in the opinion of the principal,
   (ii) any lack of attention on the part of the building maintenance staff of the school, and
   (iii) where a parent of a pupil has been requested to compensate the board for damage to or destruction, loss or misappropriation of school property by the pupil and the parent has not done so, that the parent of the pupil has not compensated the board;

(m) where it is proposed to administer a test of intelligence or personality to a pupil, inform the pupil and the parent of the pupil of the test and obtain the prior written permission for the test from the pupil or from the parent of the pupil, where the pupil is a minor;

(n) report promptly any neglect of duty or infraction of the school rules by a pupil to the parent or guardian of the pupil;

(o) promote and maintain close co-operation with residents, industry, business and other groups and agencies of the community;

(p) provide to the Minister or to a person designated by the Minister any information that may be required concerning the instructional program, operation or administration of the school and inform the appropriate supervisory officer of the request;

(q) assign suitable quarters for pupils to eat lunch.

(4) A principal shall only make a recommendation to the board under subclause (3)(j)(ii) after warning the teacher in writing, giving the teacher assistance and allowing the teacher a reasonable time to improve.

(5) A principal of a school,

(a) in which there is a French-language instructional unit as defined in section 309 of the Act, who does not hold qualifications to teach in the French-language as required by subsection 19(12) or is qualified to teach in such unit only under subsection 19(13); or

(b) in which there is an English-language instructional unit as mentioned in subsection 325(1) of the Act, who does not hold qualifications to teach in the English language as required by subsection 19(11) or is qualified to teach in each unit only under subsection 19(13),

shall notify the appropriate supervisory officer in writing of the impracticability of the duty placed on the principal, having regard to the qualifications of the principal, to supervise the instruction, to conduct performance appraisals and to assist and advise the teachers referred to in the notice.

(6) Where arrangements are made under subsection 26(3), the principal is relieved from compliance with clauses (3)(a), (g), (h) and (i) to the extent that such duties are performed by another qualified person or persons.

(7) The other qualified person or persons who perform the duties shall be responsible to the board for the performance of such duties.

(8) The outlines of the courses of study mentioned in clause (3)(c) shall be written and provided,
- (a) in the French language in the case of courses of study provided in a French-language instructional unit operated under Part XII of the Act; and
- (b) in both the English and French languages in the case of a course of study in a program established in the school under paragraph 25 of subsection 8(1) of the Act.

(9) Where, after reasonable notice by the principal, a pupil who is an adult, or the parent of a pupil who is a minor, fails to provide the supplies required by the pupil for a course of study, the principal shall promptly notify the board.

(10) A principal shall transmit reports and recommendations to the board through the appropriate supervisory officer.

(11) A principal, subject to the approval of the appropriate supervisory officer, may arrange for home instruction to be provided for a pupil where,
- (a) medical evidence that the pupil cannot attend school is provided to the principal; and
- (b) the principal is satisfied that home instruction is required.

Vice-Principals

12. (1) A board may appoint one or more vice-principals for a school.

(2) A vice-principal shall perform such duties as are assigned to the vice-principal by the principal.

(3) In the absence of the principal of a school, a vice-principal, where a vice-principal has been appointed for the school, shall be in charge of the school and shall perform the duties of the principal.

Principals, Vice-Principals and Teachers in Charge of Schools and Classes Established Under Part XII of the Act

13. (1) Where, under section 289 of the Act, more than two classes where French is the language of instruction are established in an elementary school that is not a French-language elementary school, the board that operates the school shall appoint one of the teachers of such classes or a teacher who holds the qualifications required to teach such classes to be responsible to the principal for the program of education in such classes.

(2) Where the enrolment in classes established under section 291 of the Act in a secondary school that is not a French-language secondary school is more than seventy-five but not more than 200 pupils, the board that operates the school shall appoint one of the teachers of such classes or a teacher who holds the qualifications required to teach such classes to be responsible to the principal for the program of education in such classes.

(3) Where, in a secondary school, the enrolment in the classes referred to in subsection (2) is more than 200 pupils, the board shall appoint for such school a vice-principal who is qualified to teach in such classes and who shall be responsible to the principal for the program of education in such classes.

(4) Despite subsections (1), (2) and (3), where a teacher who does not hold the qualifications referred to in such subsections was, on the 8th day of September, 1978, employed by the board as a teacher or vice-principal, as the case may be, to carry out the responsibility referred to in such subsections, the teacher shall be deemed to be qualified for such position in any elementary or secondary school, as the case may be, operated by that board or its successor board.

(5) Subsections (1) to (4) apply with necessary modifications to schools or classes for English-speaking pupils established under sections 289 and 301 of the Act.

Teachers in Charge of Organizational Units

14. (1) The organization of a secondary school shall be by departments or other organizational units.

(2) A board shall appoint for each organizational unit of a secondary school a teacher to direct and supervise, subject to the authority of the principal, such organizational unit.

(3) Where a program of technological studies or business studies is offered in a secondary school, the board that operates the school shall appoint a teacher to be in charge of each program, subject to the authority of the principal.

(4) A teacher appointed under subsection (2) or (3) shall not be appointed to be in charge of more than one organizational unit.

(5) A teacher appointed under subsection (2) or (3) shall hold specialist or honour specialist qualifications in one or more of the subjects taught in the organizational unit for which the teacher is appointed.

15. (1) The organization of an elementary school may be by divisions or other organizational units.

(2) A board may appoint for each organizational unit of an elementary school a teacher to direct and supervise such organizational unit subject to the authority of the principal of the school.

(3) A teacher appointed under subsection (2) shall hold specialist or honour specialist qualifications in respect of the organizational unit for which the teacher is appointed.

(4) Despite subsection (3), a teacher who, on the 30th day of June, 1981, had been appointed by the board to direct and supervise an organizational unit shall be deemed to be qualified in respect of such organizational unit operated by that board or its successor board.

Duties of Teachers in Charge of Organizational Units

16. In addition to duties as a teacher under the Act and this Regulation, a teacher appointed under section 14 or 15 shall,
- (a) assist the principal, in co-operation with the teachers in charge of other organizational units or programs, in the general organization and management of the school;
- (b) assist the principal,
    - (i) by recommending appointments to the teaching staff of the organizational unit,
    - (ii) by recommending assignments and timetable allotments for the teaching staff of the organizational unit,
    - (iii) in co-ordinating and supervising the teaching and in implementing the instructional program of the organizational unit,
    - (iv) in maintaining close co-operation with the community, and
    - (v) in assembling information that the principal may be required to provide in accordance with clause 11(3)(1);
- (c) file with the principal up-to-date copies of outlines of courses of study for the organizational unit or program, with sufficient detail to permit the effective co-ordination of the courses of study;
- (d) assist teachers in the organizational unit or program in improving their methods of instruction, in maintaining proper standards for instruction, and in keeping records of the work and achievement of pupils;
- (e) ensure that there is reasonable supervision of pupils who are engaged in activity authorized by the board that is performed off school property and that is part of the organizational unit or program; and
- (f) ensure that equipment for use in courses and activities in the organizational unit or program is maintained in safe working order.

Subject and Program Supervision and Co-Ordination

17. (1) A board may, in respect of one or more subjects or programs in the schools under its jurisdiction, appoint a teacher to supervise or co-ordinate the subjects or programs or to act as a consultant for the teachers of the subjects or programs.

(2) A teacher appointed under subsection (1) shall hold specialist or honour specialist qualifications, if such are available, in one or more of the subjects or programs in respect of which the teacher is appointed.

(3) Despite subsection (1), a teacher who, on the 8th day of September, 1978, was employed by a board to supervise or co-ordinate a subject or program in its schools or to act as a consultant shall be deemed to be qualified for such position in the schools operated by that board or its successor board.

18. (1) Subject to the authority of the appropriate supervisory officer, a teacher appointed in a subject or program under section 17 shall assist teachers in that subject or program in maintaining proper standards and improving methods of instruction.

(2) A teacher appointed under section 17 in performing duties in a school is subject to the authority of the principal of that school.

Qualifications of Teachers

19. (1) A teacher in a school shall, subject to subsection (2), be a person who holds or is deemed under Regulation 297 of Revised Regulations of Ontario, 1990 to hold an Ontario Teacher's Certificate and shall, subject to subsections (4), (5), (11) and (12), be assigned or appointed to teach according to a qualification recorded on the teacher's Ontario Teacher's Qualifications Record Card or the record of qualification in respect of such teacher held by the Ministry.

(2) A teacher who does not hold and is not deemed under Regulation 297 of Revised Regulations of Ontario, 1990 to hold an Ontario Teacher's Certificate but who,

(a) holds a Temporary Letter of Standing or a Provisional Letter of Standing or a Permanent Letter of Standing; or

(b) holds a certificate or Letter of Standing referred to in subsection 26(3) or 27(1) of Regulation 297 of Revised Regulations of Ontario, 1990,

may teach in a school in a subject or program for which the Letter of Standing or certificate is valid or in which the teacher has received professional education as indicated on the Temporary Letter of Standing or Provisional Letter of Standing.

(3) A person who does not hold any of the qualifications referred to in subsection (2) but who holds a Letter of Eligibility issued under section 12 or 13 of Regulation 297 of Revised Regulations of Ontario, 1990 may be employed by a board as an occasional teacher only,

(a) in classes where English is the language of instruction if the Letter of Eligibility is in Form 5 to Regulation 297 of Revised Regulations of Ontario, 1990; or

(b) in classes where French is the language of instruction if the Letter of Eligibility is in Form 5a to Regulation 297 of Revised Regulations of Ontario, 1990.

(4) Subject to subsections (6), (11), (12), (14) and (15), and with due regard for the safety and welfare of the pupils and the provision of the best possible program, a teacher whose Ontario Teacher's Qualifications Record Card, or the record of qualification in respect of such teacher held by the Ministry, indicates qualification in the primary division, the junior division, the intermediate division in general studies or the senior division in general studies may, by mutual agreement of the teacher and the principal of a school and with the approval of the appropriate supervisory officer, be assigned or appointed to teach in a division or a subject in general studies for which no qualification is recorded on the teacher's Ontario Teacher's Qualifications Record Card or the record of qualification in respect of such teacher held by the Ministry.

(5) Subject to subsections (11), (12) and (15), and with due regard for the safety and welfare of the pupils and the provision of the best possible program, a teacher whose Ontario

Teacher's Qualifications Record Card, or the record of qualification in respect of such teacher held by the Ministry, has entries indicating qualifications in technological studies may by mutual agreement of the teacher and the principal of a school, with the approval of the appropriate supervisory officer, be assigned or appointed to teach a subject in technological studies for which no qualification is recorded on the Ontario Teacher's Qualification Record Card or the record of qualification in respect of such teacher held by the Ministry.

(6) Subject to subsections (7), (8), (9) and (10), a teacher who does not hold an acceptable university degree as defined in the definition of "acceptable university degree" in section 1 of Regulation 297 of Revised Regulations of Ontario, 1990 shall not be assigned or appointed to teach general studies in a secondary school, except that where the teacher is qualified to teach in the primary division, the junior division and the intermediate division of an elementary school and,

(a) on the 30th day of June, 1981 was teaching in a secondary school; or
(b) on or before the 2nd day of October, 1981 was assigned or appointed to teach general studies in a secondary school, and on the 30th day of June, 1982 was teaching in a secondary school,

the teacher may be assigned or appointed to teach general studies to pupils enrolled in a modified or basic level course by that board or its successor board.

(7) Despite subsection (1), a teacher who holds,

(a) a commercial-vocational qualification; or
(b) technological studies qualifications in any one or more of clerical practice, merchandising or warehousing,

may be assigned or appointed to teach the courses in business studies equivalent to the courses in business studies shown on the teacher's Ontario Teacher's Qualifications Record Card or the record of qualification in respect of the teacher held by the Ministry.

(8) A teacher who holds qualifications in technological studies in sewing and dressmaking, or textiles and clothing, or home economics may be assigned or appointed to teach in a secondary school the clothing portion of the family studies course.

(9) A teacher who holds qualifications in technological studies in food and nutrition or home economics may be assigned or appointed to teach in a secondary school the food and nutrition portion of the family studies course.

(10) A teacher who holds qualifications in technological studies in vocational art, instrumental music or vocal music may be assigned or appointed to teach art, instrumental music or vocal music, as the case may be, in general studies in a secondary school.

(11) A teacher who has not received basic teacher education in the English language or who is not otherwise qualified under the regulations for such assignment or appointment shall not be assigned or appointed to teach in classes where English is the language of instruction.

(12) A teacher who has not received basic teacher education in the French language or who is not otherwise qualified under the regulations for such assignment or appointment shall not be assigned or appointed to teach in schools or classes established under Part XII of the Act where French is the language of instruction.

(13) Despite subsections (11) and (12), a teacher who holds qualifications to teach in the intermediate division and the senior division may be assigned or appointed to teach in either or both of such divisions in classes where English or French is the language of instruction.

(14) No teacher shall,
- (a) be assigned, or appointed to teach, in any of grades 9, 10, 11, 12 and 13 in any one school year for more than the time required for two courses that are recognized for credit in art, business studies, guidance including counselling, family studies, instrumental music, vocal music or physical education; or
- (b) be placed in charge of,
    - (i) a school library program,
    - (ii) a guidance program, or
    - (iii) special education; or
- (c) be assigned or appointed to teach,
    - (i) French as a second language,
    - (ii) English as a second language,
    - (iii) design and technology,
    - (iv) subject to subsections (5) and (15), technological studies,
    - (v) in a special education class,
    - (vi) in a class for deaf, hard of hearing, blind or limited vision pupils, or
    - (vii) as a resource or withdrawal teacher in special education programs,

unless,
- (d) the teacher's Ontario Teacher's Qualifications Record Card or the record of qualification in respect of such teacher held by the Ministry indicates qualifications in the subject or program to which the teacher is to be assigned or appointed or placed in charge; or
- (e) the teacher is qualified for such assignment, appointment or placement under subsection (2) or (16) or deemed to be qualified therefor under subsection (17).

(15) On or after the 1st of September, 1982, no teacher shall be assigned or appointed to teach courses in the senior division in technological studies at the General or Advanced levels unless the teacher's Ontario Teacher's Qualifications Record Card or the record of qualification in respect of such teacher held by the Ministry indicates advanced level qualifications in the area of technological studies to which the teacher is to be assigned or appointed.

(16) A teacher in a school or class for trainable retarded pupils shall,
- (a) have an entry on the teacher's Ontario Teacher's Qualifications Record Card or on the record of qualification in respect of such teacher held by the Ministry, indicating qualifications in the area of teaching the trainable retarded; or
- (b) hold one of the following:
    1. Elementary Certificate in Teaching Trainable Retarded Children.
    2. Intermediate Certificate in Teaching Trainable Retarded Children.
    3. Certificate as Teacher of the Trainable Retarded.
    4. Provisional or Permanent Letter of Standing valid for the teaching of the trainable retarded.

(17) A teacher who, on the 8th day of September, 1978, was employed by a board to teach,

(a) French as a second language or English as a second language in an elementary school or a secondary school; or
(b) industrial arts in an elementary school,

and is not qualified for such position under subsection (14), shall be deemed to be qualified for such position in the elementary schools or the secondary schools, as the case may be, that are operated by that board or its successor board.

(18) Where a teacher's Ontario Teacher's Qualifications Record Card or record of qualification has entries indicating qualifications both in technological studies and in guidance, the teacher may be assigned or appointed to teach guidance and counselling in general studies in a secondary school.

(19) The provision of subsection (14) that no teacher shall be assigned or appointed to teach in a special education class or program unless the teacher holds qualifications in special education does not apply to the teaching of classes in general studies or technological studies in what was formerly designated a special vocational or occupational program until the 1st day of September, 1985.

(20) A teacher may be assigned or appointed to teach those courses that are equivalent to those courses that appear on the teacher's Ontario Teacher's Qualifications Record Card or the record of qualification in respect of the teacher held by the Ministry. O. Reg. 243/92, s. 1.

Duties of Teachers

20. In addition to the duties assigned to the teacher under the Act and by the board, a teacher shall,

(a) be responsible for effective instruction, training and evaluation of the progress of pupils in the subjects assigned to the teacher and for the management of the class or classes, and report to the principal on the progress of pupils on request;

(b) carry out the supervisory duties and instructional program assigned to the teacher by the principal and supply such information related thereto as the principal may require;

(c) where the board has appointed teachers under section 14, 15 or 17, co-operate fully with such teachers and with the principal in all matters related to the instruction of pupils;

(d) unless otherwise assigned by the principal, be present in the classroom or teaching area and ensure that the classroom or teaching area is ready for the reception of pupils at least fifteen minutes before the commencement of classes in the school in the morning and, where applicable, five minutes before the commencement of classes in the school in the afternoon;

(e) assist the principal in maintaining close co-operation with the community;

(f) prepare for use in the teacher's class or classes such teaching plans and outlines as are required by the principal and the appropriate supervisory officer and submit the plans and outlines to the principal or the appropriate supervisory officer, as the case may be, on request;

(g) ensure that all reasonable safety procedures are carried out in courses and activities for which the teacher is responsible; and

(h) co-operate with the principal and other teachers to establish and maintain consistent disciplinary practices in the school.

Appointment to Teach in the Case of an Emergency

21. (1) Where no teacher is available, a board may appoint, subject to section 22, a person who is not a teacher or a temporary teacher.

(2) A person appointed under subsection (1) shall be eighteen years of age or older and the holder of an Ontario secondary school diploma, a secondary school graduation diploma or a secondary school honour graduation diploma.

(3) An appointment under this section is valid for ten school days commencing with the day on which the person is appointed.

Cancelled and Suspended Certificates

22. (1) A board shall not appoint a person whose teaching certificate is cancelled or under suspension to teach under section 21 or in accordance with a Letter of Permission.

(2) A person whose teaching certificate is cancelled or under suspension ceases to hold teacher's qualifications during the period of cancellation or suspension and shall not be appointed as a teacher.

Requirements For Pupils

23. (1) A pupil shall,
(a) be diligent in attempting to master such studies as are part of the program in which the pupil is enrolled;
(b) exercise self-discipline;
(c) accept such discipline as would be exercised by a kind, firm and judicious parent;
(d) attend classes punctually and regularly;
(e) be courteous to fellow pupils and obedient and courteous to teachers;
(f) be clean in person and habits;
(g) take such tests and examinations as are required by or under the Act or as may be directed by the Minister; and
(h) show respect for school property.

(2) When a pupil returns to school after an absence, a parent of the pupil, or the pupil where the pupil is an adult, shall give the reason for the absence orally or in writing as the principal requires.

(3) A pupil may be excused by the principal from attendance at school temporarily at any time at the written request of a parent of the pupil or the pupil where the pupil is an adult.

(4) Every pupil is responsible for his or her conduct to the principal of the school that the pupil attends,
(a) on the school premises;

(b) on out-of-school activities that are part of the school program; and
(c) while travelling on a school bus that is owned by a board or on a bus or school bus that is under contract to a board.

Advertisements and Announcements

24. No advertisement or announcement shall be placed in a school or on school property or distributed or announced to the pupils on school property without the consent of the board that operates the school except announcements of school activities.

Canvassing and Fund-Raising

25. (1) It is the duty of a pupil to ensure that any canvassing or fund-raising activity on school property by the pupil is carried on only with the consent of the board that operates the school.

(2) No principal, vice-principal or teacher, without the prior approval of the board that operates the school at which they are employed, shall authorize any canvassing or fund-raising activity that involves the participation of one or more pupils attending the school.

Supervision

26. (1) The appropriate supervisory officer, in addition to the duties under the Act, may, during a visit to a school, assume any of the authority and responsibility of the principal of the school.

(2) Psychiatrists, psychologists, social workers and other professional support staff employed by a board shall perform, under the administrative supervision of the appropriate supervisory officer, such duties as are determined by the board and, where such persons are performing their duties in a school, they shall be subject to the administrative authority of the principal of that school.

(3) A supervisory officer who is notified under subsection 11(5) shall forthwith notify the French-language education council or section, English-language education council or section or majority language section of the board, as the case requires, and arrange for,

(a) the provision of supervision of instruction;
(b) assistance and advice to the teachers in respect of whom the supervisory officer was given notice under subsection 11(5); and
(c) the conducting of performance appraisals, where appropriate, of the teachers in respect of whom the supervisory officer was given notice under subsection 11(5),

in the language in which the instruction is provided.

Religion in Schools

27. Sections 28 and 29 do not apply to a separate school board or to the Roman Catholic sector of The Ottawa-Carleton French-Language School Board.

28. (1) A board may provide in grades one to eight and in its secondary schools an optional program of education about religion.

(2) A program of education about religion shall,
- (a) promote respect for the freedom of conscience and religion guaranteed by the *Canadian Charter of Rights and Freedoms*; and
- (b) provide for the study of different religions and religious beliefs in Canada and the world, without giving primacy to, and without indoctrination in, any particular religion or religious belief.

(3) A program of education about religion shall not exceed sixty minutes of instruction per week in an elementary school.

29. (1) Subject to subsections (2) and (3), a board shall not permit any person to conduct religious exercises or to provide instruction that includes indoctrination in a particular religion or religious belief in a school.

(2) A board may enter into an agreement with a separate school board or the Roman Catholic sector of The Ottawa-Carleton French-Language School Board that permits the separate school board or the Roman Catholic sector to use space and facilities to conduct religious exercises or provide religious instruction for the purposes of the separate school board or the Roman Catholic sector.

(3) A board may permit a person to conduct religious exercises or to provide instruction that includes indoctrination in a particular religion or religious belief in a school if,
- (a) the exercises are not conducted or the instruction is not provided by or under the auspices of the board;
- (b) the exercises are conducted or the instruction is provided on a school day at a time that is before or after the school's instructional program, or on a day that is not a school day;
- (c) no person is required by the board to attend the exercises or instruction; and
- (d) the board provides space for the exercises or instruction on the same basis as it provides space for other community activities.

(4) A board that permits religious exercises or instruction under subsection (3) shall consider on an equitable basis all requests to conduct religious exercises or to provide instruction under subsection (3).

Special Education Programs and Services

30. A hearing-handicapped child who has attained the age of two years may be admitted to a special education program for the hearing-handicapped.

31. The maximum enrolment in a special education class shall depend upon the extent of the exceptionalities of the pupils in the class and the special education services that are available to the teacher, but in no case shall the enrolment in a self-contained class exceed,
- (a) in a class for pupils who are emotionally disturbed or socially maladjusted, for pupils who have severe learning disabilities, or for pupils who are younger than compulsory school age and have impaired hearing, eight pupils;

S. 31 REGULATIONS UNDER THE EDUCATION ACT

(b) in a class for pupils who are blind, for pupils who are deaf, for pupils who are trainable retarded, or for pupils with speech and language disorders, ten pupils;

(c) in a class for pupils who are hard of hearing, for pupils with limited vision, or for pupils with orthopaedic or other physical handicaps, twelve pupils;

(d) in a class for pupils who are educable retarded children, twelve pupils in the primary division and sixteen pupils in the junior and intermediate divisions;

(e) in an elementary school class for pupils who are gifted, twenty-five pupils;

(f) in a class for aphasic or autistic pupils, or for pupils with multiple handicaps for whom no one handicap is dominant, six pupils; and

(g) on and after the 1st day of September, 1982, in a class for exceptional pupils consisting of pupils with different exceptionalities, sixteen pupils.

REGULATION 299
PAYMENT OF LEGISLATIVE GRANTS
R.R.O. 1990, Reg. 299

1. A board may be paid a sum on account of a legislative grant for educational purposes for a year prior to the filing of a regulation prescribing the conditions governing the payment of legislative grants for educational purposes for the year, if the sum does not exceed the sum of,

 (a) 30 per cent of the grant payable to the board for the preceding year in respect of a legislative grant other than an amount referred to in clause (b); and

 (b) the amount allocated to the board for the year in respect of which an allocation is made under the Capital Grant Plan established and maintained by the Minister.

REGULATION 300
PRACTICE AND PROCEDURE — BOARDS OF REFERENCE
R.R.O. 1990, Reg. 300

1. In this Regulation,

"applicant" means a person in respect of whose application the Minister has granted a Board;

"Board" means a Board of Reference that is granted by the Minister under section 270 of the Act;

"reference" means proceedings before a Board; and

"respondent" means a party to a reference other than the applicant.

2. the parties to a reference shall be,
- (a) where a board is the applicant, the board and the teacher who terminated his or her contract; and
- (b) where a teacher is the applicant, the teacher and the board that dismissed the teacher or terminated his or her contract.

3. Except as provided by section 7, the minimum rules for proceedings provided in Part I of the *Statutory Powers Procedure Act*, apply to a reference.

4. The chair of the Board shall cause three reference books to be prepared from the documents filed with him or her under section 5.

5. (1) Where a teacher is the applicant, the teacher shall file with the chair of the Board three copies of each of,
- (a) the contract of the teacher with the board where the teacher holds a copy of the contract, or an affidavit that the teacher does not hold a copy of the contract;
- (b) the notice of dismissal or termination of contract;
- (c) the statement of the disagreement with the dismissal or termination of contract as sent to the Minister;
- (d) the notice from the Minister that he or she has directed a judge to act as chair of the Board; and
- (e) the notice of the nomination by the teacher of a representative to the Board.

(2) Where a teacher is the applicant, the board shall file with the chair of the Board three copies of each of,
- (a) the contract of the teacher with the board;
- (b) the resolution, if any, of the board dismissing the teacher or terminating his or her contract;
- (c) the copy of the application for a Board provided by the applicant;
- (d) the notice of the application for a Board provided by the Minister;
- (e) the notice from the Minister that he or she has directed a judge to act as chair of the Board; and
- (f) the notice of the nomination by the board of a representative to the Board.

(3) The Minister shall cause to be filed with the chair of the Board three copies of each of,
- (a) the application for a Board;

(b) the notice of the application for a Board sent to the respondent; and
(c) the Order-in-Council authorizing the judge to act as chair of the Board.

(4) Where a board is the applicant, the teacher shall file with the chair of the Board three copies of each of,

(a) the contract of the teacher with the board where the teacher holds a copy of the contract, or an affidavit that the teacher does not hold a copy of the contract;
(b) the copy of the application for a Board provided by the applicant;
(c) the notice of the application for a Board provided by the Minister;
(d) the notice from the Minister that he or she has directed a judge to act as chair of the Board; and
(e) the notice of the nomination by the teacher of a representative to the Board.

(5) Where a board is the applicant, the board shall file with the chair of the Board three copies of each of,

(a) the contract of the teacher with the board;
(b) the notice of termination of contract;
(c) the statement of the disagreement with the termination of the contract as sent to the Minister;
(d) the notice from the Minister that he or she has directed a judge to act as chair of the Board; and
(e) the notice of the nomination by the board of a representative to the Board.

(6) The documents to be filed with the chair under this section shall be filed with him or her not less than three days before the day upon which the hearing is to begin.

(7) A copy of the documents filed with the chair by an applicant shall be served by the applicant upon the respondent and a copy of the documents filed with the chair by a respondent shall be served by the respondent upon the applicant, and such service shall be made by personal service or by registered mail upon the party or upon the solicitor of the party to be served and shall be made not less than three days before the day upon which the hearing is to begin.

(8) A reference shall not be defeated by any error or omission in the supply of the documents referred to in this section, but the chair may require any such error or omission to be corrected upon such terms as to adjournment, costs and otherwise as he or she may determine.

6. (1) At a reference, the respondent shall begin and at the conclusion of the case for the respondent,

(a) where the applicant states an intention not to adduce evidence and the applicant has not adduced evidence, the respondent has the right to sum up the evidence and the applicant has the right to reply; and
(b) where the applicant wishes to adduce evidence, the applicant has the right to open the applicant's case and after the conclusion of such opening to adduce evidence and, when all the evidence is concluded, to sum up the evidence, and the respondent has the right to reply.

(2) Where a party to a reference is represented by counsel or an agent, a right conferred upon the party by subsection (1) may be exercised by the party's counsel or agent at the option of the party.

(3) Where, for any reason, a party to a reference omits or fails to adduce evidence that is material, the Board, at the request of such party made prior to the giving of the direction of the Board, may permit the party to adduce such evidence upon such conditions in respect of cross-examination, introduction of rebuttal evidence, reply, costs and any other matters as the chair may direct.

7. Despite section 15 of the *Statutory Powers Procedure Act*, the findings of fact of the Board shall be based exclusively on evidence admissible under the law of evidence and on matters of which notice may be taken under section 16 of that Act.

8. (1) The evidence before a Board shall be recorded by a person approved and appointed by the chair of the Board and who, before acting, shall make an oath or affirmation that he or she will truly and faithfully record the evidence to the best of his or her abilities.

(2) It is not necessary to transcribe the evidence recorded at a reference unless,

(a) the chair orders that it be done, in which case the costs thereof shall be included in the costs of the reference; or

(b) a party to the reference requests that it be done and pays the costs of the preparation of the transcript.

(3) Where evidence at a reference is transcribed, the transcript shall be accompanied by an affidavit or affirmation of the person recording the evidence that it is a true report of the evidence.

9. A reference shall be conducted, and the report and direction of the Board shall be, in the English language, except where the Board and the parties to the reference agree that the reference be conducted in the French language, in which case the report and direction of the Board may, at the option of the Board, be in the French language.

10. (1) The chair may, and if required by a party to the reference shall, appoint a person to act as an interpreter at the reference, and such person before acting shall make an oath or affirmation that he or she will truly and faithfully translate the evidence to the best of his or her abilities.

(2) The costs of an interpreter shall be included in the costs of the reference.

11. (1) An application for judicial review of a decision of the Board operates as a stay in the reference.

(2) Where an application for judicial review of a decision of the Board is made where the reference was conducted in the French language, the decision of the Board and the reasons therefor, where reasons have been given, and the transcript, if any, of the oral evidence given at the hearing, shall be translated into the English language, and the costs thereof shall be included in the costs of the reference.

12. A member of a Board who participates in a decision of the Board shall have been present throughout the reference.

13. (1) The remuneration of members of a Board other than the chair shall not be less than $85 per day or greater than $150 per day.

(2) In addition to the remuneration under subsection (1), a member of a Board is entitled to his or her actual travelling and living expenses incurred while engaged in his or her duties as a member of the Board.

(3) Counsel fees, interpreter fees, fees in respect of the recording and transcribing of the evidence, allowances to court attendants and other costs incurred in respect of a reference shall be at the rate for such fees, allowances and costs in matters before a county or district court.

14. A party to a reference who desires to call as a witness an opposite party may either request the Board to summons the party or give the party or the party's solicitor at least five days notice of the intention to examine the party as a witness, paying at the same time the amount proper for attendance money, and, if such opposite party does not attend on such summons or notice, the reference may be postponed at the direction of the chair of the Board.

15. The chair of the Board may, where it appears necessary for the purposes of the reference, make an order for the examination on oath or affirmation before any person and at any place of a person who has knowledge respecting the matters before the Board and who, because of illness or other reasonable cause, is unable to attend the reference and may permit such deposition to be placed in evidence.

16. The chair of the Board at a reference may,
- (a) order a witness who is not a party to the reference to be excluded from the reference until called to give evidence; and
- (b) exclude the testimony of any person who does not comply with an order made under clause (a).

17. A record of a reference, compiled by a Board shall be forwarded as soon as practicable by the chair of the Board to the Minister, and such record shall be retained by the Minister for a period of at least two years after which time it may be destroyed without the necessity of notice thereof being given to either party to the reference.

REGULATION 301
PUPIL RECORDS
R.R.O. 1990, Reg. 301; rev. O. Reg. 212/91

Revoked.

REGULATION 302
PURCHASE OF MILK
R.R.O. 1990, Reg. 302

1. A board is authorized to purchase milk for free distribution to pupils in schools under its jurisdiction.

2. The authority of a board may be exercised on condition that,

(a) the distribution is effected only on school days between 8.45 a.m. and 4.00 p.m. and under the supervision and direction of the principal; and

(b) the milk is consumed on the school premises.

REGULATION 303
REGIONAL TRIBUNALS
R.R.O. 1990, Reg. 303; Fr. version O. Reg. 666/91

1. A regional tribunal shall consist of three members appointed by the Minister, one of whom shall be designated by the Minister as the chair of the regional tribunal.

2. A regional tribunal referred to in Column 1 of the Table may be established for the region described opposite thereto in Column 2 of the Table and has jurisdiction in that region.

TABLE

Item	Column 1 Regional Tribunal	Column 2 Region
1.	North Western Region (English) North Western Region (French)	The territorial districts of Kenora, Rainy River and Thunder Bay
2.	Midnorthern Western Region (English) Midnorthern Western Region (French)	The territorial districts of Algoma, Manitoulin and Sudbury
3.	North Eastern Region (English) North Eastern Region (French)	The territorial districts of Cochrane, Muskoka, Nipissing, Parry Sound and Timiskaming
4.	Western Region (English) Western Region (French)	The counties of Bruce, Elgin, Essex, Grey, Huron, Kent, Lambton, Middlesex, Oxford and Perth
5.	Central Region (English) Central Region (French)	The Municipality of Metropolitan Toronto, the regional municipalities of Durham, Haldimand-Norfolk, Halton, Hamilton-Wentworth, Niagara, Peel, Waterloo and York and the counties of Brant, Dufferin, Haliburton, Hastings, Northumberland, Peterborough, Prince Edward, Simcoe, Victoria and Wellington

6.	Eastern Region (English) Eastern Region (French)	The Regional Municipality of Ottawa-Carleton and the counties of Dundas, Frontenac, Glengarry, Grenville, Lanark, Leeds, Lennox and Addington, Prescott, Renfrew, Russell and Stormont

3. No person is eligible to be a member of a regional tribunal unless he or she resides in the region in which the regional tribunal has jurisdiction.

4. No person who has had any prior involvement with the determination under appeal is eligible to be a member of a regional tribunal that hears the appeal.

5. Where an appeal is taken to a regional tribunal in respect of the identification or placement of an exceptional pupil enrolled in a school or class established under Part XII of the Act and the parent or guardian of the pupil requests that the appeal be heard in the French language or the English language, as the case may be,
- (a) the persons appointed by the Minister as members of the tribunal shall be French-speaking or English-speaking, as required; and
- (b) the appeal shall be heard in the French language or in the English language, as the case may be.

6. Upon receiving notification of the names of the members of a regional tribunal appointed by the Minister, the secretary of the tribunal shall,
- (a) fix a date for hearing the appeal and shall so advise the parties to the hearing;
- (b) require the Regional Director of Education for the administrative region of the Ministry within which the board that is a party to the hearing has jurisdiction to make, in cooperation with the parties to the hearing, arrangements for a suitable place and time at which the hearing shall be held; and
- (c) advise in writing the parties to the hearing of the arrangements that have been made.

REGULATION 304
SCHOOL YEAR AND SCHOOL HOLIDAYS
R.R.O. 1990, Reg. 304; Fr. version 664/91

1. (1) In this Regulation,

"instructional day" means a school day that is designated as an instructional day on a school calendar and upon which day an instructional program that may include examinations is provided for each pupil whose program is governed by such calendar;

"professional activity" includes evaluation of the progress of pupils, consultation with parents, the counselling of pupils, curriculum and program evaluation and development, professional development of teachers and attendance at educational conferences;

"professional activity day" means a school day that is designated as a day for professional activities on a school calendar;

"school day" means a day that is within a school year and is not a school holiday;

"school year" means the period prescribed as such by or approved as such under this Regulation.

(2) A board may designate half a school day an instructional program and the remainder of the day for professional activities, but such a day constitutes a half-day in determining the number of instructional days in the school year.

2. (1) Subject to section 5, the school year shall commence on or after the 1st day of September and end on or before the 30th day of June.

(2) Subject to section 5, a school year shall include a minimum of 194 school days of which up to 9 days may be designated by the board as professional activity days and the remaining school days shall be instructional days.

(3) Despite subsection (2), where a board designates more than 9 professional activity days, the number of days in excess of 9 shall be added to the number of instructional days identified on the school calendar.

(4) Subject to section 5, the following are school holidays:

1. Every Saturday and Sunday.
2. When the school is open during July, Canada Day.
3. Labour Day.
4. A day appointed by the Governor General or the Lieutenant Governor as a public holiday or for Thanksgiving.
5. A Christmas vacation consisting of fourteen consecutive days commencing on the Monday next following the Friday preceding the 21st day of December, but when the 21st day of December is a Thursday or a Friday, commencing on the Monday next following.
6. Five consecutive days commencing on the Monday next following the Friday preceding the 14th day of March.
7. Good Friday.
8. Easter Monday.
9. Victoria Day.

3. (1) A board may designate up to fifteen instructional days as examination days.

(2) Despite subsection (1), where a board designates more than fifteen instructional days as examination days, the number of days in excess of fifteen shall be added to the number of instructional days identified on the school calendar.

(3) Where a school has a policy of granting exemptions to pupils from the writing of examinations, such exemptions may be granted only from the final examinations in a course and only where at least one other set of examinations has been held.

(4) The teaching staff shall be in school during regular school hours on examination days and accessible to pupils, unless the board directs otherwise.

4. (1) In each year every board shall, except in respect of a school or class for which the board has submitted a proposed school calendar under section 5, prepare, adopt and submit to the Minister on or before the 1st day of May in respect of the school year next following, the school calendar or school calendars to be followed in the schools under its jurisdiction, and each such school calendar shall,

  (a) state the school or schools in which the calendar is to be followed;
  (b) conform to section 2; and
  (c) identify each day of the school year as an instructional day, a professional activity day or a school holiday.

(2) In preparing a school calendar under subsection (1), the board shall ensure that some of the professional activity days are designated for the purposes of curriculum development, implementation and review.

(3) A school calendar submitted under subsection (1) shall be accompanied by a general outline of the activities to be conducted on the professional activity days identified on the calendar.

5. (1) For one or more schools under its jurisdiction a board may designate a school year and school holidays that are different from those prescribed in section 2 and, where a board does so, the board shall submit to the Minister on or before the first day of March a proposed school calendar for the school year next following in respect of such school or schools, identifying thereon each day of the school year as an instructional day, a professional activity day or a school holiday, and the board may, upon approval thereof by the Minister, implement such school calendar.

(2) Where the Minister informs a board that he or she does not approve the school calendar submitted under subsection (1), the board may amend its proposed school calendar and submit to the Minister a revised school calendar and, upon approval thereof by the Minister, the board may implement the revised school calendar.

(3) Where a board has submitted a proposed school calendar under subsection (1) and the Minister has not approved on or before the 15th day of April such calendar or a revision thereof submitted under subsection (2), the board shall, on or before the 1st day of May, prepare, adopt and submit to the Minister a school calendar in accordance with section 4.

6. (1) Where in the opinion of the board it is desirable to alter the date of a professional activity day or an examination day on a school calendar that has been submitted under section 4 or subsection 5(3) or approved and implemented under subsection 5(1) or (2), the board may alter the school calendar.

(2) Where, the board alters a school calendar under subsection (1), the board shall notify the parents concerned and the Minister of the altered date as far in advance as possible.

(3) The prior approval of the Minister is required for changes other than to the date of a professional activity day or an examination day.

(4) Where,
(a) a school or class is closed for a temporary period because of failure of transportation arrangements, inclement weather, fire, flood, a breakdown of the school heating plant or a similar emergency, or a school is closed under the *Health Protection and Promotion Act* or the *Education Act*; and
(b) the school calendar is not altered under subsection (1),

the day on which the school or class is closed remains an instructional day or a professional activity day, as the case may be, as designated on the school calendar applicable to such school or class.

7. (1) Every board shall publish annually its school calendar or school calendars and ensure that copies thereof are available at the beginning of the school year for the information of parents and pupils.

(2) A school calendar or school calendars published under subsection (1) shall, in addition to the information required to be listed under subsection 4(1), indicate in a general manner the activities to be conducted on professional activity days.

8. In each year, every board shall undertake an annual evaluation of the activities of the professional activity days of the previous year and retain such evaluations on file.

9. (1) A Remembrance Day service shall be held in every school on the 11th day of November or, when the 11th day of November is a Saturday or a Sunday, on the Friday preceding the 11th day of November.

(2) Subsection (1) does not apply where the school participates in a service of remembrance at a cenotaph or other location in the community.

REGULATION 305
SPECIAL EDUCATION IDENTIFICATION PLACEMENT AND REVIEW COMMITTEES AND APPEALS
R.R.O. 1990, Reg. 305; Fr. version O. Reg. 663/91

1. In this Regulation,

"Appeal Board" means a Special Education Appeal Board established by a board under section 4;

"committee" means a Special Education Identification, Placement and Review Committee established under this Regulation and includes a Special Education Program Placement and Review Committee heretofore established under the regulations that meets the requirements of this Regulation for a Special Education Identification, Placement and Review Committee;

"parent" includes a guardian of a pupil.

2. (1) Where a board has established or establishes special education programs or provides special education services for its exceptional pupils it shall establish in accordance with section 3 one or more Special Education Identification, Placement and Review Committees and shall determine the jurisdiction that each such committee shall have.

(2) A principal,
- (a) may upon written notification to a parent of a pupil; or
- (b) shall at the written request of a parent of a pupil,

refer the pupil to the committee or, having regard to the jurisdiction of the committees where more than one committee has been established, refer the pupil to the committee that the principal considers to be the most appropriate in respect of the pupil.

(3) Where a committee is engaged in identifying a pupil as an exceptional pupil or in determining the recommended placement of such a pupil, the committee shall obtain and consider an educational assessment of the pupil and,

- (a) where the committee determines that a health assessment or a psychological assessment or both of the pupil are required to enable the committee to make a correct identification or determination in respect of the pupil and with the written permission of the parent, obtain and consider a health assessment of the pupil by a legally qualified medical practitioner and obtain and consider a psychological assessment of the pupil;
- (b) where, in the opinion of the committee, it is practicable so to do, the committee shall, with the consent of a parent of the pupil, interview the pupil;
- (c) unless the parent waives or refuses to participate in an interview, the committee shall interview a parent of the pupil; and
- (d) the committee shall cause to be sent to a parent of the pupil and to the principal who has made the referral, as soon as possible after the making of its determination, a written statement of,
  - (i) the identification it has made of the needs of the pupil,
  - (ii) where, in the opinion of the committee the pupil is an exceptional pupil, the recommendation made in respect of the placement of the pupil, and

(iii) the date the committee proposes to notify the board of its determination.

(4) A parent of a pupil may, prior to the date set out in a statement under subclause (3)(d)(iii) in respect of the pupil, upon written notice to the principal, request in writing a meeting with the committee to discuss the statement and the committee shall arrange to meet with the parent and the principal for such purpose.

(5) Each committee shall notify the director of education of the board, or the secretary of the board where the board does not have a director of education,

(a) on or after the date set by the committee as set out in the statement; or
(b) after the discussion of the statement held under subsection (4),

of the determination made by the committee as set out in the statement and the change, if any, made in the determination as a consequence of such discussion and shall send a copy of such notice to the parent and the principal.

(6) A board may establish procedures in addition to the requirements set out in subsection (3) that shall be followed by a committee.

(7) Each board that has established one or more committees shall prepare a guide for the use and information of parents that,

(a) describes the circumstances in which and the procedures under which a pupil may be referred to a committee;
(b) outlines the procedures referred to in subsection (3) and any additional procedures required by the board under subsection (6) that are required to be followed by a committee in identifying a pupil as an exceptional pupil and determining the recommended placement of the pupil;
(c) explains the function of and the right to appeal determinations of a committee to the Appeal Board; and
(d) sets out the provisions of section 6 of this Regulation,

and shall ensure that copies thereof are available at each school within the jurisdiction of the board and at the head office of the board and shall provide copies for the appropriate Regional Director of Education of the Ministry.

(8) Where a board provides schools or classes under Part XII of the Act, the board shall ensure that the guide referred to in subsection (7) is available in the English or French language as the case may be.

3. (1) A committee shall consist of such number of members, not fewer than three, as the board that establishes the committee may determine, all of whom, subject to subsection (2), shall be appointed by the board and one of whom shall be a supervisory officer or a principal employed by the board, except that where the board does not employ a supervisory officer and employs only one principal, one of such members shall be a person approved by the appropriate Regional Director of Education.

(2) A supervisory officer referred to in subsection (1) may designate a person to act in his or her place as a member of the committee without the approval of the board.

(3) A member or trustee of the board is not eligible to be appointed as a member of a committee.

(4) Where an identification, placement or review of a placement under consideration by a committee is in respect of a secondary school pupil admitted to secondary school from a

separate school, or in respect of a trainable retarded pupil of a divisional board whose parent is a separate school supporter, the board that operates the secondary school, or the divisional board, as the case may be, shall advise the separate school board of the identification, placement or review under consideration and when requested so to do by the separate school board shall appoint as an additional member of the committee for the purpose only of such consideration,

(a) a supervisory officer or a principal of the separate school board from among the supervisory officers and principals designated for such purpose by the separate school board; or
(b) a provincial supervisory officer or other person designated by the Regional Director of Education for the region in which the head office of the secondary school or divisional board, as the case may be, is situate where the separate school board has appointed only one principal and does not employ a supervisory officer.

(5) Where a board provides a school or class under Part XII of the Act and is required to establish one or more committees under section 2 of this Regulation, it shall establish one or more additional committees,

(a) comprised of members who are French-speaking where French is the language of instruction in such school or class; or
(b) comprised of members who are English-speaking where English is the language of instruction in such school or class,

and where a pupil who is enrolled in such school or class is referred to a committee and a parent of the pupil so requests, the committee whose members are French-speaking or English-speaking, as the case may be, shall consider the identification, the placement and any review of the placement of the pupil.

4. (1) A parent of a pupil who disagrees with,

(a) the identification of the pupil as an exceptional pupil;
(b) the decision that the pupil is not an exceptional pupil; or
(c) the placement of the pupil as an exceptional pupil,

as determined by a committee, may give to the secretary of the board within fifteen days of the discussion referred to in subsection 2(4), or in subsection 10(3), as the case may be, a written notice of appeal of the determination of the committee and the board shall within thirty days of the receipt of the notice of appeal by the secretary establish and, subject to subsections 7(1) to (5), appoint the members of an Appeal Board.

(2) Where the parent of a pupil gives notice of appeal under subsection (1), the notice shall indicate whether the disagreement with the decision of the committee is in respect of the matter referred to in clause (1)(a), (b) or (c) or in respect of both of the matters referred to in clauses (1)(a) and (c), as the case may be, and shall include a statement that sets out the parent's disagreement with the decision.

5. An Appeal Board shall not reject or refuse to deal with an appeal by reason of any actual or alleged deficiency in the statement referred to in subsection 4(2) or in the failure of the parent, in the opinion of the Appeal Board, to accurately indicate in the notice of appeal the subject of the disagreement, and where, during the meeting referred to in subsection 7(7), the true nature of the disagreement and the reasons therefor are ascertained, the notice of appeal shall be deemed to be amended accordingly and shall be so reported to the secretary of the board under subsection 7(10).

6. (1) An exceptional pupil shall not be placed in a special education program without the written consent of a parent of the pupil.

(2) Where a parent of an exceptional pupil,
   (a) refuses or fails to consent to the placement recommended by a committee and to give notice of appeal under section 4; and
   (b) has not instituted proceedings in respect of the determinations of the committee within thirty days of the date of the written statement prepared by the committee,

the board may direct the appropriate principal to place the exceptional pupil as recommended by the committee and to notify a parent of the pupil of the action that has been taken.

7. (1) A Special Education Appeal Board shall consist of three members none of whom shall have had any prior involvement with the matter under appeal.

(2) Where a pupil in respect of whom an appeal is brought under section 4 is enrolled in a school or class established under Part XII of the Act, a parent of the pupil may request that the appeal be conducted before an Appeal Board comprised of members who are French-speaking or English-speaking, as the case may be, and the board shall ensure that the request is complied with by appointing where necessary, a chair and members of the Appeal Board who are French-speaking or English-speaking as required, and this subsection applies even though the parent may not have requested that the identification, the placement or review of the placement of the pupil have been conducted by members of a committee who were French-speaking or English-speaking, as the case may be.

(3) The chair of the Appeal Board, who shall be designated as such by the board, shall not be, or have been,
   (a) a member or a trustee of the board; or
   (b) an employee or former employee of the board.

(4) One member of the Appeal Board shall hold qualifications as a supervisory officer.

(5) Where an appeal is brought in respect of a pupil, one member of the Appeal Board shall be,
   (a) a member of a local association as defined in subsection 206(1) of the Act that is designated by a parent of the pupil;
   (b) a representative of the local association referred to in clause (a) who is resident in the area of jurisdiction of the board and nominated by the local association; or
   (c) where no local association referred to in clause (a) has been established in the area of jurisdiction of the board, a member of the local community nominated by a parent of the pupil.

(6) Each board shall provide each Appeal Board with secretarial and administrative services required by the Appeal Board.

(7) A chair of an Appeal Board shall forthwith arrange with a parent of the pupil where an appeal is brought in respect of a pupil, for a meeting with the Appeal Board at a convenient time and place for a discussion of the disagreement of the parent with the determination of the committee and the relevant issues under appeal.

(8) Any person who in the opinion of an Appeal Board may be able to contribute information with respect to the matters before the Appeal Board shall be invited to attend the discussion and the discussion shall be conducted in an informal manner.

(9) Where in the opinion of an Appeal Board all the opinions, views and information that bear upon the matters under appeal have been presented to the Appeal Board, the Appeal Board shall adjourn the discussion and within three days thereafter may,
- (a) agree with the committee and dismiss the appeal;
- (b) disagree with the committee and refer the matter back to the committee stating the reasons for the disagreement; or
- (c) where the Appeal Board is satisfied that a pupil in respect of whom an appeal is brought is not in need of a special education program or special education services, set aside the determination of the committee that the pupil is an exceptional pupil.

(10) An Appeal Board shall report its decision in writing to a parent of a pupil in respect of whom an appeal is brought, the committee and the secretary of the board, with reasons therefor where demanded.

(11) The board within thirty days after receiving the report referred to in subsection (10) shall accept or reject such decision and the secretary of the board shall notify in writing a parent of the pupil and the committee of the decision of the board and in such notice shall inform the parent of the provisions of section 37 of the Act.

(12) Each board shall, in accordance with its own policies, pay the travelling and living expenses and other costs of the members of the Appeal Board incurred while engaged on their duties as members of the Appeal Board.

8. (1) Where an exceptional pupil is placed by a committee,
- (a) a committee shall review the placement of the pupil at least once every twelve months or pursuant to an application made under clause (b), whichever first occurs;
- (b) a parent of the pupil or the principal of the school at which the special education program is provided may, at any time after the placement has been in effect for three months, apply in writing to the chief executive officer of the board, or to the secretary of the board where the board has no chief executive officer, for a review by a committee of the placement of the pupil; and
- (c) the placement of the pupil shall not be changed by a committee without,
  - (i) prior notification in writing of the proposed change in placement to a parent of the pupil,
  - (ii) a discussion of the proposed change in placement between the committee and a parent of the pupil, and
  - (iii) the consent in writing of a parent of the pupil.

(2) Subsection 6(2) applies with necessary modifications to the refusal or failure of a parent to consent to a recommended change in placement under clause (1)(c).

9. A board that provides an exceptional pupil with a special education program or services shall cause a parent or guardian of the pupil to be advised in writing of the reviews, notices and discussions referred to in section 8 that are to be provided in accordance with this Regulation and the provisions of subsection 8(2).

10. (1) Where a committee is engaged in the review of a placement of an exceptional pupil it shall,

(a) obtain and consider an educational assessment of the exceptional pupil; and
(b) consider on the basis of written reports, and other evidence including the evidence of a parent of the exceptional pupil whether the placement of the pupil appears to meet the needs of the pupil.

(2) Where the committee is satisfied with the suitability of the placement of an exceptional pupil it shall in writing confirm the placement and so report to a parent of the exceptional pupil and to the principal of the school where the exceptional pupil attends.

(3) If a parent of an exceptional pupil who is the subject of a review so requests in writing, the committee shall within fifteen days of the receipt of the request by the board meet with the parent to discuss the report.

11. A parent of an exceptional pupil who disagrees with a placement or the refusal to change a placement recommended by a committee as a result of a review referred to in clause 8(1)(a) may appeal to an Appeal Board in accordance with section 4.

12. (1) A notice of appeal under section 4 acts as a stay of proceedings of a committee in relation to the placement of a pupil.

(2) For the purposes of this Regulation, where a statement, report or notice is sent by mail it shall be sent by first class mail and it shall be deemed to have been received by the person to whom it was sent on the fifth day next following the date on which it was mailed.

(3) Where a parent of an exceptional pupil refuses in writing to discuss the statement or report of a committee with the committee and wishes to appeal to the Appeal Board, the discussion shall for the purposes of section 4 be deemed to have been held on the day such written refusal is received by the committee.

REGULATION 306
SPECIAL EDUCATION PROGRAMS AND SERVICES
R.R.O. 1990, Reg. 306

1. A Special Education Program Placement and Review Committee heretofore established by a board under the regulations shall be deemed to be a committee referred to in subparagraph iii of paragraph 5 of subsection 11(1) of the *Education Act* for the purposes of identifying exceptional pupils and making and reviewing placements of exceptional pupils.

2. (1) In this Regulation, "special education plan" means,

(a) in respect of the school year 1985-86, a plan in effect during the school year prepared by a board that discloses the methods by which and the time within which the board will be in compliance with paragraph 7 of section 170 of the Act; and

(b) in respect of a school year that commences in September in the year 1986 or any year thereafter, a plan in effect during the school year 1985-86 that is reviewed from year to year in accordance with subsection (3).

(2) Every board shall maintain the special education plan in respect of the board and ensure that the special education plan is amended from time to time to meet the current needs of the exceptional pupils of the board.

(3) Every board shall ensure that the special education plan of the board is reviewed annually by the board and that the review is completed prior to the 15th day of May in each year.

(4) In any year where the special education plan is amended by the board, the amendment shall be submitted to the Minister for review on or before the 15th day of May in that year.

(5) The Minister may at any time require a board to amend its special education plan in a manner that the Minister considers necessary so as to ensure that the board provides special education programs and special education services that meet the current needs of the exceptional pupils of the board.

3. (1) Commencing with the school year 1986-87 and in every second school year thereafter, every board shall, in accordance with procedures provided by the Minister, prepare and approve a report on the provision by the board of special education programs and special education services.

(2) The report referred to in subsection (1) shall be submitted to the Minister for review not later than the 15th day of May in the year 1987 and in every second year thereafter.

4. (1) Every board shall ensure that the special education plan of the board provides for the enrolment and placement of each trainable retarded child who is,

(a) in attendance at a day nursery licensed under the *Day Nurseries Act* that has a program for developmentally handicapped children; and

(b) qualified to be a resident pupil of the board.

(2) A copy of the provisions of the special education plan referred to in subsection (1) shall be submitted to the Minister where required by the Minister.

5. (1) Every board shall ensure that the special education plan of the board provides for the enrolment and placement of each person under the age of twenty-one years who is qualified to be a resident pupil of the board and who resides or is lodged within the area of jurisdiction of the board in a centre, facility, home, hospital or institution, other than a private school, that is approved, designated, established, licensed or registered under any Act, and in which no education program is provided by the Ministry or the Ministry of Correctional Services.

(2) Where the centre, facility, home, hospital or institution referred to in subsection (1) is situate within the area of jurisdiction of the board, the board shall make provision in its special education plan for the enrolment and placement of each person under the age of twenty-one years who,

    (a) is a resident in such centre, facility, home, hospital or institution; and
    (b) would be qualified to be a resident pupil of the board if the person's parent or guardian was also resident within the area of jurisdiction of the board.

6. Every board shall ensure that the special education plan of the board is maintained and reviewed in accordance with this Regulation and implemented by the board in accordance with the terms of the plan as to the dates by which and the extent to which special education programs and special education services shall be established or provided for its exceptional pupils.

REGULATION 307
SPECIAL GRANT
R.R.O. 1990, Reg. 307

1. Subject to the approval of the Lieutenant Governor in Council, the Minister may pay in any year, pursuant to a request from a board, in addition to the grant payable under the General Legislative Grants Regulation for such year, a special grant to such board where the General Legislative Grant otherwise payable to the board has placed or will place, in the opinion of the Minister, an undue burden upon all the ratepayers or supporters of the board or upon such of them as are assessed in a particular municipality or locality within the area of jurisdiction of the board.

2. A board to which a special grant is paid in a year under section 1 is not precluded from applying for receiving a special grant in a subsequent year.

3. The Minister, subject to the approval of the Lieutenant Governor in Council, shall prescribe the purpose to which a special grant paid under this Regulation is to be applied, and the amount of such special grant is recoverable in the year next following the year in which it is made if it is not applied as prescribed.

REGULATION 308
SUPERVISED ALTERNATIVE LEARNING FOR EXCUSED PUPILS
R.R.O. 1990, Reg. 308; Fr. version O. Reg. 665/91

1. In this Regulation,

"achievement report" means a written communication on the progress of a pupil between a parent of the pupil and the principal of the school at which the pupil is enrolled or the principal of such other school designated by a committee;

"approved work station" means the place of work approved by a committee where the pupil is employed during school hours when the pupil is excused from attendance at school either full-time or part-time under subsection 3(4);

"child" means a person of compulsory school age who has attained the age of fourteen years;

"committee" means a Supervised Alternative Learning for Excused Pupils Committee established under section 2;

"parent" includes a guardian;

"program" means a supervised alternative learning program in respect of a pupil that is approved by a committee and that may include one or more of,
 (a) full-time or part-time employment at an approved work station for such term or period of time as is fixed or determined under the program,
 (b) completion of a life-skills course, and
 (c) such continuing studies or other activity directed towards the pupil's needs and interests as may be acceptable to the committee,

pursuant to which a pupil is excused from attendance at school either full-time or part-time and by which regular contact with the pupil is maintained by a teacher or other staff member who is employed at or associated with the school where the pupil is enrolled, or such other school as may be designated by the committee, to ensure that the pupil continues to conform to the program;

"pupil" means a child for whom a program has been prescribed under subsection 3(4).

2. (1) A board shall establish a committee to be known as the Supervised Alternative Learning for Excused Pupils Committee for the purposes of this Regulation and designate the secretary of it.

(2) A committee shall be composed of such persons, not fewer than three, as may be appointed by a board in each year, and a quorum of a committee shall consist of,
 (a) a member of the board;
 (b) a supervisory officer who qualified as such as a teacher and is employed by the board, or, where the board does not employ a supervisory officer, the appropriate provincial supervisory officer for the area in which the board has jurisdiction; and
 (c) at least one person who is not an employee of the board in addition to those referred to in clauses (a) and (b).

(3) A committee shall designate a member as chair.

(4) Where a committee considers that it is in the best interests of a pupil, it may designate a school for the purposes of a program that is not the school where the pupil is enrolled.

3. (1) A parent of a child may apply in writing to the principal of the school where the child is enrolled or has a right to attend to have the child participate in a program and the parent shall state in the application why he or she considers that the child should participate in a program.

(2) Where an application is made under subsection (1), the principal shall forthwith forward the application to the secretary of the committee and a copy thereof to the school attendance counsellor, and the committee shall consider the application and any oral or written submission made by any person in support thereof or in opposition thereto and may require the principal and any other employee of the board to report to the committee upon the child in respect of whom the application is made and to make recommendations in respect of the application.

(3) The parent of a child may examine the written reports and recommendations, if any, in respect of the child made under subsection (2).

(4) The committee shall, after interviewing the child, his or her parent and, where the committee considers it appropriate, any other person,

   (a) reject the application, in which case the child shall attend school as required by subsection 21(1) of the Act; or
   (b) approve the application, in which case the committee shall prescribe a program directed towards the child's needs and interests,

and the secretary of the committee shall notify in writing the principal, the school attendance counsellor, the child and the parent of the decision of the committee.

4. (1) Where the parent of a child disagrees with the determination of the committee to reject the application under clause 3(4)(a) and wishes to bring further relevant information to the attention of the committee, or disagrees with the program prescribed by the committee and notifies the secretary in writing of the disagreement setting out the reasons therefor, the committee may review the decision with which the parent disagrees and, as the case requires, with or without hearing the parent,

   (a) approve the application and prescribe a program;
   (b) confirm or alter the program; or
   (c) refuse to review its determination or the program that it has prescribed,

and the committee shall notify in writing the principal, the school attendance counsellor, the child and the parent of the decisions it has taken in respect of the notification given by the parent.

(2) A pupil shall conform to the program as prescribed for the pupil by the committee under subsection 3(4) or subsection (1) of this section or as altered under subsection 6(2), and the pupil is excused from attendance at school so long as the pupil conforms to the program.

(3) A pupil who is excused from attendance at school either full-time or part-time as determined by the committee under subsection 3(4) or subsection (1) of this section or as altered under subsection 6(2), shall be recorded as a full-time pupil on the register of the school in which the pupil is enrolled or of such other school as was designated by the committee, until the pupil is no longer of compulsory school age.

5. (1) Where the parent of a child disagrees with the determination of the committee to,
   (a) reject the application under clause 3(4)(a); or
   (b) refuse to review its determination under clause 4(1)(c),
the parent may in writing notify the provincial school attendance counsellor of his or her disagreement and the reasons therefor, and the provincial school attendance counsellor may,
   (c) inquire into the validity of the parent's request to have a program prescribed for the child and recommend that the child attend school as required by subsection 21(1) of the Act; or
   (d) recommend, where he or she is satisfied that the child should be excused from attendance at school under this Regulation, that a program be prescribed for the pupil and remit the application to the committee for reconsideration,
and a copy of the recommendation shall be delivered to the board, the principal, the school attendance counsellor, the child and the parent.

(2) Where the provincial school attendance counsellor remits an application to the committee under clause (1)(d), the committee shall reconsider the application.

6. (1) Where a parent of a pupil or a pupil wishes to alter the program prescribed for the pupil under subsection 3(4) or 4(1), the parent may apply in writing to the secretary of the committee for approval of such alteration by the committee.

(2) Where a parent applies under subsection (1) or where a report is made under subsection 7(2), the committee may, after discussion of the application or the report with the pupil and his or her parent, alter the program prescribed for the pupil and shall notify in writing the principal, the school attendance counsellor, the pupil and the parent of the decision of the committee.

7. (1) The school attendance counsellor shall have the same powers and shall perform the same duties in respect of a pupil as in the case of a child who is not excused from attendance at school.

(2) The teacher or other staff member responsible for maintaining regular contact with the pupil shall report to the committee when requested by the committee, and the principal of the school where the pupil is enrolled or of such other school as was designated by the committee shall report to the parent whenever achievement reports are issued by the principal.

(3) A school attendance counsellor of a board shall report as required by the board to the appropriate supervisory officer of the board who shall report to the provincial school attendance counsellor through the chief executive officer of the board on or before the 30th day of September in each year on the number of pupils who under this Regulation during the preceding school year,
   (a) were excused from attendance at school;
   (b) were required to attend school on a part-time basis only;
   (c) returned to full-time attendance at school; and
   (d) ceased to be excused from attendance under section 8.

(4) The parent of a pupil may examine a report in respect of the pupil under subsection (2).

8. Where a pupil and his or her parent move from the area of jurisdiction of the board under which the program is prescribed for the pupil to the area of jurisdiction of another board, the pupil shall be removed from the roll on which he or she was included under subsection 4(3), and the board of which the pupil is then qualified to be a resident pupil shall refer to its committee the question of whether the pupil should be excused from attendance at a school operated by it, and the committee shall make the determination in accordance with subsections 3(2) and (4) and may prescribe a program for the pupil in accordance with subsection 3(4), and for such purpose the committee shall, where it has obtained the consent in writing of the parent, have access to all reports, recommendations and submissions made to the committee of the board that previously prescribed a program for the pupil.

9. Where a pupil resides within the area of jurisdiction of the board under which the program for the pupil is administered but ceases to be a resident pupil of such board by reason of the parent of the pupil ceasing to reside within the area of jurisdiction of the board, the pupil shall continue in the program in accordance with this Regulation without payment of a fee.

10. Where a pupil has ceased to reside within the area of jurisdiction of the board under which the program for the pupil was prescribed and the pupil is not qualified to be a resident pupil of the board in whose area of jurisdiction he or she has taken up residence, the pupil is not excused from attendance at school unless the pupil continues to conform to the program that was prescribed for him or her and, where the pupil continues to conform to the program the pupil shall do so without the payment of a fee and shall remain enrolled as a full-time pupil of the school where the pupil was enrolled immediately before his or her change of residence and the school attendance counsellor for the board that has jurisdiction in the area in which the pupil resides shall give such assistance and cooperation to the teacher or other staff member who makes the reports to the committee under subsection 7(2) as the committee may require.

REGULATION 309
SUPERVISORY OFFICERS
R.R.O. 1990, Reg. 309: am. O. Reg. 665/92, O. Reg. 162/93

PART I

QUALIFICATIONS OF SUPERVISORY OFFICERS

1. (1) In this Part,

"acceptable university degree" means a degree from an Ontario university or post-secondary institution that is an ordinary member of the Association of Universities and Colleges of Canada or a degree that is equivalent thereto from a university other than such Ontario university or post-secondary institution;

"architect" means a person who is an architect within the meaning of the *Architects Act*;

"certified general accountant" means a member of the Certified General Accountants Association of Ontario;

"certified management accountant" means a registered or certified member of The Society of Management Accountants of Ontario;

"chartered accountant" means a member of The Institute of Chartered Accountants of Ontario;

"lawyer" means a member of the Law Society of Upper Canada;

"Principal's Certificate" means a permanent principal's certificate;

"professional engineer" means a person who is a professional engineer within the meaning of the *Professional Engineers Act*;

"program in school board management" means two compulsory graduate courses approved by the Minister that are offered by a university, one of which is a course in school board finance and the other in school board administration, and four optional graduate courses approved by the Minister that are offered by a university in education, public administration or political science;

"university" means,

    (a) an Ontario university or post-secondary institution that is an ordinary member of the Association of Universities and Colleges of Canada,

    (b) a Canadian university in a province other than Ontario that is an ordinary member of the Association of Universities and Colleges of Canada,

    (c) a university in the United States that is recognized by,

        (i) Middle States Association of Colleges and Schools,

        (ii) New England Association of Schools and Colleges,

        (iii) North Central Association of Colleges and Schools,

        (iv) Northwest Association of Schools and Colleges,

        (v) Southern Association of Colleges and Schools,

        (vi) Western Association of Schools and Colleges, or

    (d) a university that is located in a country other than Canada or the United States and that is a member of the association of Commonwealth Universities or the International Association of Universities.

(2) A person who holds or who under this Regulation is deemed to hold a Supervisory Officer's Certificate is, subject to subsection 6(1), qualified as a supervisory officer for the purposes of the Act and this Regulation.

(3) A person referred to in subsection 3(4) who is employed by a board is qualified as a business supervisory officer for the purposes of the Act and this Regulation for the period during which the person is employed by the board in a position referred to in that subsection.

(4) For the purposes of this Regulation, a person who is the holder of a Master's degree that is an acceptable university degree and who successfully completes a graduate course, either as part of or in addition to the courses necessary to obtain the degree, in each of school board finance and school board administration at a university shall be deemed to have completed a program in school board management.

(5) For the purposes of this Regulation, a person who is the holder of an acceptable university degree and who is a certified general accountant, a certified management accountant or a chartered accountant shall be deemed to be a person who has completed the four optional graduate courses as part of a program in school board management.

O. Reg. 665/92, s. 1.

2. On application, the Minister shall issue a Supervisory Officer's Certificate to a person who meets the following qualifications:

1. The person has at least seven years of successful teaching experience in a school providing elementary or secondary education.
2. The person holds an Ontario Teacher's Certificate or a Temporary Letter of Standing.
3. The person holds qualifications to teach in the intermediate division and at least two other divisions that are indicated on the person's Ontario Teacher's Qualifications Record Card or on the person's record of qualifications held by the Ministry.
4. The person holds an acceptable university degree.
5. The person holds a master's degree from a university.
6. The person meets one or more of the following criteria:
    i. The person holds,
        A. an Elementary School Principal's Certificate,
        B. a Secondary School Principal's Certificate, Type A,
        C. a Secondary School Principal's Certificate, Type B, or
        D. a Secondary School Principal's Certificate.
    ii. The person holds an Ontario Teacher's Qualifications Record Card indicating qualifications in Program Development and Implementation and in Program Supervision and Assessment.
    iii. The person holds specialist or honours specialist qualifications in one or more subjects and has, in addition to the experience required by paragraph 1, at least two years of successful experience as a teacher appointed by a board under section 17 of Regulation 298 of Revised Regulations of Ontario, 1990 to supervise or co-ordinate a subject or program or to act as a consultant for the teachers of a subject or program, as certified by the appropriate supervisory officer.
    iv. The person has, in addition to the experience required by paragraph 1, at least two years of experience,

A. as an education officer employed by the Ministry, as certified by a regional or branch director of the Ministry,
B. as an employee outside Ontario in a position that is equivalent in the Minister's opinion to the position of supervisory officer of a school board, as certified by a person acceptable to the Minister, or
C. as a program consultant seconded to the Ministry for French language, English language or Native language programs, as certified by a regional or branch director of the Ministry.

7. The person has successfully completed the supervisory officer's qualifications program described in section 2.2 within five years after starting the program. O. Reg. 665/92, s. 2, *part.*

2.1 (1) On application, the Minister shall issue a Business Supervisory Officer's Certificate to a person who meets the following qualifications:
1. The person has at least seven years of successful experience in business administration, including at least three years in a managerial role relevant to the role of business supervisory officer.
2. The person holds an acceptable university degree.
3. The person,
    i. holds a master's degree from a university, or
    ii. is qualified to practise as an architect, certified general accountant, certified management accountant, chartered accountant, lawyer or professional engineer, or is qualified to practise in another professional capacity that, in the opinion of the Minister, provides experience appropriate for the position of business supervisory officer.
4. The person has successfully completed a program in school board management.
5. The person has successfully completed the business supervisory officer's qualifications program described in section 2.2 within five years after starting the program.

(2) A person shall be deemed to meet the qualifications set out in paragraphs 1 to 4 of subsection (1) if, not later than the 31st day of December, 1997, the person obtains the qualifications that were required of a candidate for a Business Supervisory Officer's Certificate under subsection 2(3) of this Regulation as it read immediately before the 6th day of November, 1992. O. Reg. 665/92, s. 2, *part.*

2.2 The supervisory officer's qualifications program referred to in section 2 and the business supervisory officer's qualifications program referred to in section 2.1 shall have the following features:
1. The program shall be provided by an organization or institution that has entered into a contract with the Minister to provide the instruction and arrange for the practical experience referred to in paragraphs 3 and 4.
2. No person shall be admitted to the program unless the person has submitted proof to the organization or institution that provides the program that the person meets the qualifications set out in paragraphs 1 to 6 of section 2 or paragraphs 1 to 4 of subsection 2.1(1).
3. The program shall consist of,
    i. four instructional modules, each consisting of at least fifty hours of instruction, and

ii. one module consisting of at least fifty hours of practical experience in the workplace.
4. The instructional modules shall provide instruction that, in the opinion of the Minister, is relevant to the position of supervisory officer or business supervisory officer, as the case may be, in the following subject areas:
   i. Statutes, regulations and government policies affecting education in Ontario.
   ii. Curriculum guidelines and other reference material pertaining to elementary and secondary education in Ontario.
   iii. Theories and practices of supervision, administration and business organization. O. Reg. 665/92, s. 2, *part.*

3. (1) A supervisory officer responsible for the development, implementation, operation and supervision of educational programs in schools shall,
   (a) hold a Supervisory Officer's Certificate; or
   (b) be a person who is deemed to hold a Supervisory Officer's Certificate under section 4.

(2) A senior business official who,
   (a) reports to a director of education;
   (b) reports to an assistant director of education or associate director of education; or
   (c) is employed by a board that has an enrolment of more than 600 pupils and that does not employ a director of education,

shall, subject to subsections (4) and (5), be a person who holds, or who under this Regulation is deemed to hold, a Business Supervisory Officer's Certificate.

(3) A business official who;
   (a) is assigned one or more of the duties of a supervisory officer;
   (b) reports to a senior business official referred to in subsection (2); and
   (c) has been appointed to a position designated by a board as superintendent, assistant superintendent, comptroller, assistant comptroller, business administrator or assistant business administrator or to a position that the board considers equivalent thereto and that has been approved by the Minister,

shall, subject to subsection (4), be a person who holds, or who under this Regulation is deemed to hold, a Business Supervisory Officer's Certificate.

(4) A board may appoint a person who does not hold or who under this Regulation is not deemed to hold a Business Supervisory Officer's Certificate as a senior business official referred to in subsection (2) or as a business official referred to in subsection (3) for a term of not more than two years if the person,
   (a) holds an acceptable university degree or is qualified to practise as an architect, certified general accountant, certified management accountant, chartered accountant, lawyer or professional engineer, or in another professional capacity that, in the opinion of the Minister, provides experience appropriate for the position of business supervisory officer; and
   (b) has entered into an agreement in writing with the Board that sets out that the person will endeavour to obtain a Business Supervisory Officer's Certificate within the term of the appointment. O. Reg. 665/92, s. 3(2).

(5) Despite subsection (4), a board may employ a person appointed under that subsection for an additional period of not more than two years if the person continues to make progress towards obtaining a Business Supervisory Officer's Certificate.

(6) A person who was appointed under subsection (4) before the 6th day of November, 1992 may, by agreement with the board, amend the agreement under clause (4)(b) to be consistent with the new requirements of that clause. O. Reg. 655/92, s. 3(3).

4. A person who, prior to the 1st day of July 1974,

(a) held an Elementary School Inspector's Certificate, a Public School Inspector's Certificate, a Secondary School Principal's Certificate, or a Secondary School Principal's Certificate, Type A; or

(b) served as a provincial inspector of secondary schools or a municipal inspector of secondary schools,

is deemed to hold a Supervisory Officer's Certificate.

5. (1) A person who was in the employ of a board on the 31st day of August, 1975, in a position referred to in subsection 3(2) or (3), is deemed to hold a Supervisor Officer's Certificate.

(2) A person employed in the Ministry on the 31st day of August, 1975, in a position that the Minister considers similar to one of those referred to in subsection 3(2) or (3) is deemed to hold a Supervisory Officer's Certificate.

6. (1) A person who,

(a) holds a Supervisory Officer's Certificate and was not required, at the time the certificate was obtained, to have seven years of successful teaching experience;

(b) is deemed to hold a Supervisory Officer's Certificate under section 5; or

(c) holds a Business Supervisory Officer's Certificate,

is qualified as a supervisory officer under this Regulation for business administration purposes only.

(2) A supervisory officer other than a supervisory officer referred to in subsection (1) who, on the 30th day of September, 1986, was performing the duties,

(a) of a senior business official referred to in clause 3(2)(c) and who reports as referred to in clauses 3(2)(a) and (b); or

(b) of a business official referred to in clause 3(3)(c) who reports to a senior business official referred to in subsection 3(2),

is deemed to hold a Business Supervisory Officer's Certificate. O. Reg. 665/92, s. 4.

PART II

TRANSFER AND DISMISSAL

7. (1) In this section, "redundant" in respect of the position of a supervisory officer means no longer required to be filled by reason of,

(a) the implementation by a board of a long range organizational plan of operation in respect of schools or of supervisory services that eliminates the position or merges it with another position;

(b) a reduction in the number of classes or in the business functions of the board for which supervision is required; or

(c) a change in duties or requirements placed upon boards by or under any Act that renders a supervisory service unnecessary or reduces the need for such service.

(2) Where a board declares the position of a supervisory officer redundant, the board shall,

(a) give the supervisory officer at least three months' notice in writing that the position has been declared redundant;

(b) transfer the supervisory officer to a position for which he or she is qualified, with supervisory and administrative responsibilities as similar as possible to those of his or her previous position; and

(c) pay the supervisory officer for at least one year following the date of the transfer with no reduction in his or her rate of salary.

8. (1) A board shall not suspend or dismiss a supervisory officer without first giving the supervisory officer reasonable information about the reasons for the suspension or dismissal and an opportunity to make submissions to the board.

(2) A supervisory officer who wishes to make submissions to the board may make them orally or in writing. O. Reg. 162/93, s. 1.

9. [Revoked O. Reg. 162/93, s. 1.]

10. [Revoked O. Reg. 162/93, s. 1.]

11. [Revoked O. Reg. 162/93, s. 1.]

12. [Revoked O. Reg. 162/93, s. 1.]

13. [Revoked O. Reg. 162/93, s. 1.]

14. [Revoked O. Reg. 162/93, s. 1.]

15. [Revoked O. Reg. 162/93, s. 1.]

REGULATION 310
TEACHERS' CONTRACTS
R.R.O. 1990, Reg. 310

Form of Contracts

1. (1) Every contract between a board and a permanent teacher shall be in Form 1.

(2) Every contract between a board and a probationary teacher shall be in Form 2.

(3) Except where otherwise provided under subsection 259(5) or (6) of the Act, every contract between a board and a continuing education teacher shall be in Form 3.

Payment of Salaries

2. (1) Subject to subsection (4), a board shall pay the salary of a teacher under contract in Form 1 or Form 2 in the number of payments set out in the contract.

(2) Subject to subsection (4), a board shall pay the salary of a teacher under contract in Form 3 in the number of payments or on the dates set out in the contract.

(3) In the case of a contract in Form 1 or Form 2, the contract shall provide for not fewer than ten salary payments.

(4) Where during the term of a contract between a board and a teacher the salary of the teacher is changed by mutual agreement in writing between the board and the teacher, the contract shall be deemed to be varied accordingly.

FORM 1

Education Act

PERMANENT TEACHER'S CONTRACT

This Agreement made in duplicate this .... day of ...., 19 ...., between ....

hereinafter called the "Board" and .... of
(   )
(the .... of .... in the County   )
(   )
((or as the case may be) of ....   )
(   )

hereinafter called the "Teacher".

1. The Board agrees to employ the Teacher as a permanent teacher and the Teacher agrees to teach for the Board commencing the .... day of .... , 19 ....

FORM 1   REGULATIONS UNDER THE EDUCATION ACT

at a yearly salary of .... Dollars, subject to any changes in salary mutually agreed upon by the Teacher and the Board, payable in ....
(not fewer than ten)
payments, less any lawful deduction, in the following manner:

    i. Where there are ten payments, one-tenth on or before the last teaching day of each teaching month.

    ii. Where there are more than ten payments, at least one-twelfth on or before the last teaching day of each teaching month, any unpaid balance being payable on or before the last teaching day of June, or at the time of leaving the employ of the Board, whichever is the earlier.

2. This Agreement is subject to the Teacher's continuing to hold qualifications in accordance with the Acts and the regulations administered by the Minister.

3. The Teacher agrees to be diligent and faithful in his or her duties during the period of employment, and to perform such duties and teach such subjects as the Board may assign under the Acts and the regulations administered by the Minister.

4. Where the Teacher attends an educational conference for which the school has been legally closed and his or her attendance at it is certified by the supervisory officer concerned or by the chair of the conference, the Board agrees to make no deductions from the Teacher's salary for his or her absence during that attendance.

5. Where an Act of Ontario or a regulation thereunder authorizes the Teacher to be absent from school without loss of pay, the Board agrees that no deduction from his or her pay will be made for the period of absence so authorized.

6. This Agreement may be terminated,

(a) at any time by the mutual consent in writing of the Teacher and the Board;

(b) on the 31st day of December in any year of the Teacher's employment by either party giving written notice to the other on or before the last preceding 30th day of November; or

(c) on the 31st day of August in any year of the Teacher's employment by either party giving written notice to the other on or before the last preceding 31st day of May.

7. The Teacher agrees with the Board that if the Teacher enters into an agreement with another board he or she will within forty-eight hours notify the Board in writing of the termination of this Agreement unless the notice has already been given.

8. Where the Teacher is to be transferred by the Board from a school in one municipality to a school in another municipality, the Board agrees to notify the Teacher in writing on or before the 1st day of May immediately prior to the school year for which the transfer is effective, but nothing in this paragraph prevents the transfer of a teacher at any time by mutual consent of the Board and the Teacher.

9. This Agreement shall remain in force until terminated in accordance with any Act administered by the Minister or the regulations thereunder.

REGULATION 310 **FORM 2**

In witness whereof the Teacher has signed and the Board has affixed hereto its corporate seal attested by its proper officers in that behalf.

....
(signature of Chair of the Board)

....
(signature of Secretary of the Board)

....
(signature of Teacher)

FORM 2

Education Act

PROBATIONARY TEACHER'S CONTRACT

This Agreement made in duplicate this .... day of ...., 19 ...., between .... hereinafter called the "Board" and .... of
(   )
(the .... of .... in the County   )
(   )
((or as the case may be) of ....)
(   )

hereinafter called the "Teacher".

1. The Board agrees to employ the Teacher as a probationary teacher for a probationary period of .... years and the Teacher agrees to teach for the Board commencing the .... day of ...., 19 .... at a yearly salary of .... Dollars, subject to any changes in salary mutually agreed upon by the Teacher and the Board, payable in ....
(not fewer than ten)
payments, less any lawful deduction, in the following manner:

      i. Where there are ten payments, one-tenth on or before the last teaching day of each teaching month.

      ii. Where there are more than ten payments, at least one-twelfth on or before the last teaching day of each teaching month, any unpaid balance being payable on or before the last teaching day of June, or at the time of leaving the employ of the Board, whichever is the earlier.

2. This Agreement is subject to the Teacher's continuing to hold qualifications in accordance with the Acts and regulations administered by the Minister.

FORM 3 REGULATIONS UNDER THE EDUCATION ACT

3. The Teacher agrees to be diligent and faithful in his or her duties during the period of employment, and to perform such duties and teach such subjects as the Board may assign under the Acts and regulations administered by the Minister.

4. Where the Teacher attends an educational conference for which the school has been legally closed and his or her attendance at it is certified by the supervisory officer concerned or by the chair of the conference, the Board agrees to make no deductions from the Teacher's salary for his or her absence during that attendance.

5. Where an Act of Ontario or a regulation thereunder authorizes the Teacher to be absent from school without loss of pay, the Board agrees that no deduction from his or her pay will be made for the period of absence so authorized.

6. Despite anything in this contract this Agreement may be terminated,
   (a) at any time by the mutual consent in writing of the Teacher and the Board;
   (b) on the 31st day of December in any year of the Teacher's employment by either party giving written notice to the other on or before the last preceding 30th day of November; or
   (c) on the 31st day of August in any year of the Teacher's employment by either party giving written notice to the other on or before the last preceding 31st day of May.

7. The Teacher agrees with the Board that if the Teacher enters into an agreement with another board he or she will within forty-eight hours notify the Board in writing of the termination of this Agreement unless the notice has already been given.

8. Where this Agreement is not terminated under paragraph 6 at the conclusion of the probationary period in paragraph 1, the Teacher is deemed to be employed as a permanent teacher by the Board.

In witness whereof the Teacher has signed and the Board has affixed hereto its corporate seal attested by its proper officers in that behalf.

....
(signature of Chair of the Board)

....
(signature of Secretary of the Board)

....
(signature of Teacher)

FORM 3

Education Act

CONTINUING EDUCATION TEACHER'S CONTRACT

This Agreement made in duplicate this ....

day of ...., 19 ....
between ....hereinafter
called the "Board" and .... of

REGULATION 310 **FORM 3**

(the .... of .... in the county)
(or as the case may be) of ....)
hereinafter called the "Teacher".

1. For the session commencing on the .... day of ...., 19 ...., and ending on the .... day of ...., 19 ...., the Board agrees to employ the Teacher as a continuing education teacher and the Teacher agrees to teach for the Board as a continuing education teacher at a salary of $ ....
(specify amount per hour or per session)

2. The salary specified in paragraph 1, subject to any changes in salary mutually agreed upon by the Teacher and the Board, is reduced by any lawful deductions and is payable as follows:

....
(specify number of payments or dates of payment)

3. This Agreement is subject to the Teacher continuing to hold qualifications in accordance with the Acts and the regulations administered by the Minister.

4. During the session specified in paragraph 1, the Teacher agrees to perform such duties as the Board may assign under the Acts and the regulations administered by the Minister and to be diligent and faithful in the performance of the Teacher's duties.

5. Despite anything in this contract, this Agreement may be terminated prior to the end of the session mentioned in paragraph 1,
   (a) at any time by mutual consent in writing of the Teacher and the Board;
   (b) if the Teacher has entered upon the teaching duties referred to in paragraph 4, at any time by either party giving written notice to the other not less than forty-eight hours before the date of termination specified in the notice; or
   (c) by the Board at any time without advance notice to the Teacher where, before the commencement of the course or class or teaching in the subject, the Board has resolved not to offer the course, class or subject in the session mentioned in paragraph 1.

IN WITNESS WHEREOF the Teacher has signed and the Board has affixed hereto its corporate seal attested by its proper officers.

....
....
....
(signature of Teacher)

REGULATION 311
TERRITORY WITHOUT MUNICIPAL ORGANIZATION ATTACHED TO A DISTRICT MUNICIPALITY
R.R.O. 1990, Reg. 311

1. (1) Those portions of the territory without municipal organization situate in the Territorial District of Thunder Bay being,

(a) the geographic townships of Atikameg, Bomby, Brothers, Bryant, Cecil, Cecile, Davies, Flood, Foote, Grenville, Herbert, Knowles, Laberge, McCron, McGill, Mikano, Nickle, Roberta, Shabotik and Spooner; and

(b) all lands in unsurveyed territory within an area the boundary sides of which are as follows:

1. On the east side, the easterly boundary of the Territorial District of Thunder Bay.
2. On the south side, the International Boundary.
3. On the west side, the line described as commencing at the point of intersection of the 86th Meridian and the International Boundary, extending northerly along the said Meridian until it meets the 48th Parallel, then easterly along the said Parallel until it meets the high water mark on the shoreline of the geographic Township of Homer, then southerly and southeasterly along the said high water mark to the intersection of the easterly boundary of the geographic Township of Homer, then northerly along the said easterly boundary of the geographic Township of Homer to the intersection of the boundary of Pukaskwa National Park, then northeasterly and along the boundary of the said National Park to the northerly boundary of the said National Park, thence westerly along the said northerly boundary to the point of intersection thereof with the 86th Meridian, then northerly along the said Meridian until it meets the southerly boundary of the geographic Township of Lecours to the southwest angle of the geographic Township of Bomby, then northerly along the said westerly boundary of the geographic Township of Bomby to the northwest angle of the said Township, then westerly along the northerly boundary of the geographic Township of Lecours to the point of intersection with the 86th Meridian, then northerly along the said Meridian until it meets the southerly boundary of the geographic Township of Grenville, then westerly along the southerly boundary of the geographic Township of Grenville to the southwest angle thereof, then northerly along the westerly boundary of the geographic townships of Grenville and Davies to the northwest angle of the geographic Township of Davies.
4. On the north side, the lien formed by the northerly boundary of the Township of Manitouwadge and the extension westerly of the northerly boundary of the Township of Manitouwadge to the northwest angle of the geographic Township of Davies and the extension easterly of the northerly boundary of the Township of Manitouwadge along the northerly boundary of the geographic townships of Nickle, Herbert and Foote to the easterly boundary of the District of Thunder Bay,

are attached to the Township of Manitouwadge.

(2) Those portions of the territory without municipal organization situate in the Territorial District of Thunder Bay being,

(a) the geographic Township of Pic not included in former school section No. 1. Pic; and
(b) the geographic Township of Coldwell not included in former school section No. 1. Port Coldwell,

are attached to the Town of Marathon.

(3) Those portions of Territory without municipal organization situate in the Territorial District of Thunder Bay being,

(a) the geographic townships of Byron, Cotte, Grain, Homer, Lecours and O'Neill; and
(b) all lands in unsurveyed territory within an area the boundary sides of which are described as follows:
1. On the east side, the line described in paragraph 3 of clause (1)(b).
2. On the south side, the International Boundary.
3. On the west side, the Meridian 86°30'.
4. On the north side, the line former by the projection westerly of the northerly boundary of the geographic Township of Davies until it meets the Meridian 86°30',

are attached to the Town of Marathon.

(4) The portion of the territory without municipal organization comprising the geographic Township of Syine not included in the former school section No. 1. Jackfish is attached to the Township of Terrace Bay.

(5) Those portions of the territory without municipal organization situate in the Territorial District of Thunder Bay being,

(a) the geographic townships of Strey, Tuuri and Walsh;
(b) all lands in unsurveyed territory within an area the boundary sides of which are described as follows:
1. On the east side, the Meridian 86°30'.
2. On the south side, the International Boundary.
3. On the west side, the line described as commencing at the intersection of the southeast angle of the Township of Terrace Bay and the International Boundary, then northerly along the easterly limit of the Township of Terrace Bay to the northeast angle thereof, then westerly along the northerly boundary of the Township of Terrace Bay to the point of intersection thereon of the easterly limit of the geographic Township of Strey, then continuing along the northerly limit of the Township of Terrace Bay and the southerly limit of the geographic Township of Strey to the southwest angle of the geographic Township of Strey, then northerly along the westerly limit of the geographic Township of Strey and its projection northerly parallel to the 87th Meridian to the point of intersection with a line that is the projection westerly of the northerly limit of the geographic Township of Davies.
4. On the north side, a line that is the projection westerly of the northerly limit of the geographic Township of Davies,

are attached to the Township of Terrace Bay.

(6) The portion of territory without municipal organization comprising the geographic Township of Lahontan not included in former school section No. 1. Rossport is attached to the Township of Schreiber.

S. 1 REGULATIONS UNDER THE EDUCATION ACT

(7) Those portions of the territory without municipal organization situate in the Territorial District of Thunder Bay being,
- (a) the geographic townships of Killraine, Priske, Wiggins and Yesno; and
- (b) all lands in unsurveyed territory, exclusive of St. Ignace Island, within an area the boundary sides of which are described as follows:
1. On the east side, the line described in paragraph 3 of clause (5)(b).
2. On the south side, the International Boundary.
3. On the west side, a line that is the extension southerly to the International Boundary of the westerly limit of the geographic Township of Wiggins, the said westerly limit of the said geographic Township of Wiggins and the line that is the projection northerly of the said westerly limit of the geographic Township of Wiggins to the point of intersection of a line that is the projection westerly of the northerly limit of the geographic Township of Davies.
4. On the north side, a line that is the projection westerly of the northerly limit of the geographic Township of Davies,

are attached to the Township of Schreiber.

REGULATION 312
TRAINING ASSISTANCE
R.R.O. 1990, Reg. 312

1. (1) For the purposes of subsection 135(16) of the Act, during the period of twenty months commencing on the date upon which the transfer of employment of the designated person becomes effective under subsection 135(11) of the Act, where the retraining of the designated person requires the attendance of the person at an educational institution in Ontario other than a school operated by the Roman Catholic school board to which the teaching contract, employment contract or employment relationship of the person is transferred, the following, subject to subsections (2), (3), (4) and (5), is prescribed as training assistance:

training assistance $= x + y$

where $x =$ the cost of,

(a) tuition at the institution;
(b) educational material required or recommended for the designated person by the institution; and
(c) incidental expenses incurred by the designated person that are payable to the institution as a result of enrolment and attendance at the institution.

$y =$ where the campus of the institution that the designated person attends or the place at which the designated person is required to attend to obtain practical experience that is part of the program of the institution in which the designated person is enrolled is situate,

(a) in a municipality other than the municipality in which the designated person resides or a municipality adjoining the municipality or locality in which the designated person resides; and
(b) more than eight kilometres further by road or rail than the distance by road or rail from the residence of the designated person to the place at which the designated person was required to perform services for the public board immediately prior to being designated under section 135 of the Act,

an amount,

(c) where the designated person travels daily to the campus or the place, that does not exceed $75 per day for each day that the designated person is in attendance at the campus or place, in respect of,
   (i) the actual cost of daily transportation to and from the residence of the designated person or the cost of daily transportation calculated at a rate per kilometre determined by the Roman Catholic school board, and
   (ii) the actual cost of meals or the cost of meals calculated at the rate that the Roman Catholic school board ordinarily pays for employees who are engaged in performing duties for the board; or
(d) where daily transportation to and from the residence of the designated person is impracticable by reason of distance or the lack of suitable transportation, of $450 per week for each week or part thereof that the designated person is in attendance at the campus or place, in respect of,

(i) the cost of board and lodging in the municipality in which the campus or place is situate, and

(ii) the actual cost of transportation once a week to and from the lodging and the residence of the designated person or the cost of transportation once a week calculated at a rate per kilometre determined by the Roman Catholic school board,

and reimbursement for all necessary living and household expenses of an extraordinary nature in respect of the maintenance and support of dependants of the designated person incurred during the period of the board and lodging as a direct result of the designated person finding it necessary to obtain the board and lodging.

(2) A Roman Catholic school board that enters into a collective agreement that covers the designated person and that provides for the payment of an amount in respect of retraining during the period referred to in subsection (1) that exceeds the maximum amount of $75 per day or the $450 per week set out in subsection (1) or the $10,000 set out in subsection (4) shall pay the amount set out in the collective agreement and not the amount set out in subsection (1) or (4), as the case may be.

(3) The amount determined under subsection (1) shall be reduced by the net amount after taxes and employment related deductions of remuneration earned by the designated person as a result of obtaining practical experience as part of the retraining program or otherwise taking part in the retraining program.

(4) The maximum amount that is required to be paid under subsection (1) for training assistance for a designated person is $10,000 in addition to the salary and benefits to which the designated person is entitled under section 135 of the Act.

(5) Where the amount calculated under subsection (1) exceeds $10,000, the Roman Catholic school board may pay the total amount calculated in respect of x under subsection (1) and apply the balance, if any, to the amount calculated in respect of y under subsection (1) or the converse as is agreed upon by the board and the designated person.

REGULATION 313
TRUSTEE DISTRIBUTION

R.R.O. 1990, Reg. 313: am. O. Reg. 47/91, Fr. version O. Reg. 378/92; O. Reg. 143/94

1. In this Regulation, "major part" means, with respect to a county or regional municipality, an area in the county or regional municipality that is larger than 50 per cent of the geographic area of the county or regional municipality.

2. (1) Subject to subsections (2) to (4), a determination and a distribution under Part VIII of the Act with respect to a board shall be made by the clerks of the three municipalities within the area of jurisdiction of the board having successively the greatest population.

(2) Where the area of jurisdiction of a board comprises fewer than three municipalities, the clerk of the municipality having the largest population, in consultation with the clerk of the other municipality, where applicable, shall make a determination and a distribution.

(3) If the area of jurisdiction of a board is composed of all or the major part of two counties, a determination and a distribution shall be made by the clerks of the municipalities having the largest population in each county and the clerk of the municipality having the next largest population.

(3.1) If the area of jurisdiction of a board is composed of all or the major part of three counties, a determination and a distribution shall be made by the clerks of the municipalities having the largest population in each county.

(4) Where the area of jurisdiction of a board comprises a county or the major part of a county and a regional municipality or the major part of a regional municipality, a determination and a distribution shall be made by the clerk of the municipality having the largest population in the county and the clerk of the municipality having the largest population in the regional municipality and the clerk of the municipality, in the area of jurisdiction of the board, having successively the next largest population.

(5) The director of education of a board shall take the necessary steps to convene a meeting of the persons required to make the determination and distribution for the board and shall be consulted during the process of making a determination of or a distribution for the members of the board.

(6) A determination and a distribution under Part VIII of the Act shall be made before the 15th day of March in the year of a regular election under the *Municipal Elections Act* or, if the determination of the calculated enrolment and the total calculated enrolment of the board is referred to the Languages of Instruction Commission of Ontario under subsection 322(4) of the Act, before the 15th day of April in that year.

(7) If the members of a board who represent an electoral group direct that an alternative distribution be made, the alternative distribution shall be made before the 31st day of March in the year of a regular election under the *Municipal Elections Act* or, if the determination of the calculated enrolment and the total calculated enrolment of the board is referred to the Languages of Instruction Commission of Ontario under subsection 322(4) of the Act, before the 30th day of April in that year.

(8) The clerk of the municipality having the largest population shall send the Minister, the secretary of the board and the clerks of all municipalities and regional municipalities that are wholly or partly within the area of jurisdiction of the board,

   (a) a copy of the final determination and the final distribution made under Part VIII of the Act;
   (b) a copy of any resolution under rule 6 of subsection 230(8) of the Act approving an increase in the number of members of the board;
   (b.1) a copy of any resolution under subsection 230(14.1) of the Act approving a decrease in the number of members to be elected by an electoral group of the board.
   (c) a copy of any resolution under subsection 230(17) of the Act directing that an alternative distribution be made; and
   (d) a copy of the data and calculations by which the final determination and final distribution were made.

(9) The copies required to be sent under subsection (8) shall be sent by registered mail not later than the 31st day of March in the year of a regular election under the *Municipal Elections Act* or, if the determination of the calculated enrolment and the total calculated enrolment of the board is referred to the Languages of Instruction Commission of Ontario under subsection 322(4) of the Act, not later than the 30th day of April in that year.

(10) Where a municipality is divided into electoral areas for the election of board members, other than electoral areas established under section 315 of the Act, and the clerk of the municipality is not a person prescribed to make a distribution, the clerk may make recommendations on the distribution to be made to electoral areas within the municipality.

(11) [Revoked O. Reg. 47/91, s. 1(4)]

(12) [Revoked O. Reg. 47/91, s. 1(4)]

(13) [Revoked O. Reg. 47/91, s. 1(4)]

3. (1) If two or more municipalities are combined for the election of one or more members, the nominations shall be submitted to the returning officer of the municipality having the largest population.

(2) Where all or part of two or more municipalities are included in an electoral area established under section 315 of the Act, the nominations shall be submitted to the returning officer of the municipality that has the greatest population.

(3) The returning officer who conducts the nominations shall send, by registered mail within forty-eight hours after the closing of nominations, to the clerk of each municipality that is included in the combination of municipalities or that is situated all or partly within the electoral area, as the case may be, the names of the candidates who have qualified.

(4) The clerk of a municipality shall be the returning officer for the vote to be recorded in the municipality.

(5) The clerk of a municipality shall report the vote recorded to the returning officer to whom nominations were submitted under subsection (1) or (2) and the returning officer shall prepare the final summary and announce the result of the vote.

(6) For the purposes of this section, the secretary of a board shall be the clerk of each part of territory without municipal organization that is deemed a district municipality in the area of jurisdiction of the board.

(7) In this section, "municipality" includes territory without municipal organization that is deemed to be a district municipality under subsection 53(3) or 103(1) of the Act.

IMMUNIZATION OF SCHOOL PUPILS ACT

TABLE OF CONTENTS

1.	Definitions	403
2.	Purpose of Act	403
3.	Duty of parent	403
4.	Offence	404
5.	Certificate by M.O.H. as evidence	404
6.	Order for suspension re designated diseases	404
7.	Term of suspension	404
8.	Service of copy of order upon parent	404
9.	Rescission of order	405
10.	Statement by physician	405
11.	Record of immunization	405
12.	Order by M.O.H.	405
13.	Hearing and submissions	406
14.	Notice of transfer of pupil	406
15.	Notice	406
16.	Appeal to court	407
17.	Regulations	407
18.	Service	408

IMMUNIZATION OF SCHOOL PUPILS ACT
R.S.O. 1990, c. I.1

1. Definitions.—In this Act,

"Board."—"Board" means the Health Protection Appeal Board under the *Health Protection and Promotion Act*; ("Commission")

"board".—"board" means a "board" as defined in the *Education Act*; ("conseil")

"designated diseases."—"designated diseases" means diphtheria, measles, mumps, poliomyelitis, rubella and tetanus; ("maladies désignées")

"immunization record."—"immunization record" means a record of immunization maintained by a medical officer of health under this Act; ("dossier d'immunisation")

"medical officer of health."—"medical officer of health" means "medical officer of health" as defined in the *Health Protection and Promotion* Act; ("médecin-hygiéniste")

"parent."—"parent" includes an individual or a corporation that has the responsibilities of a parent; ("père ou mère")

"person."—"person" includes a board; ("personne")

"physician."—"physician" means legally qualified medical practitioner; ("médecin")

"prescribed."—"prescribed" means prescribed by the regulations; ("prescrit")

"pupil."—"pupil" means a pupil who is a minor; ("élève")

"regulations."—"regulations" means regulations made under this Act; ("règlements")

"school."—"school" means a "private school" and a "school" as defined in the *Education Act* and includes a kindergarten, a junior kindergarten and a beginners class within the meaning of the Education Act; ("école")

"school day."—"school day" means "school day" as defined in the *Education Act*; ("jour de classe")

"statement of conscience or religious belief."—"statement of conscience or religious belief" means a statement by affidavit in the prescribed form by a parent of the person named in the statement that immunization conflicts with the sincerely held convictions of the parent based on the parent's religion or conscience; ("déclaration de conscience ou de croyance religieuse")

"statement of medical exemption."—"statement of medical exemption" means a statement in the prescribed form signed by a physician stating that the prescribed program of immunization in relation to a designated diseases,

(a) may be detrimental to the health of the person named in the statement, or

(b) is unnecessary in respect of the person named in the statement by reason of past infection or laboratory evidence of immunity. ("déclaration d'exemption médicale")

2. Purpose of Act.—The purpose of this Act is to increase the protection of the health of children against the diseases that are designated diseases under this Act.

3. Duty of parent.—(1) The parent of a pupil shall cause the pupil to complete the prescribed program of immunization in relation to each of the designated diseases.

(2) **Exception**—Subsection (1) does not apply to the parent of a pupil in respect of the prescribed program of immunization in relation to a designated disease specified by a physician in a statement of medical exemption filed with the proper medical officer of health and, where the physician has specified an effective time period, only during the effective time period.

(3) **Idem.**—Subsection (1) does not apply to a parent who has filed a statement of conscience or religious belief with the proper medical officer of health.

(4) **Idem.**—Subsection (1) does not apply to a parent who, before the coming into force of this section, has filed with the proper medical officer of health a statement of religious belief in the form prescribed before the coming into force of this section.

4. Offence.—Every person who contravenes section 3 is guilty of an offence and on conviction is liable to a fine of not more than $1,000.

5. Certificate by M.O.H. as evidence.—In proceedings under section 4, as certificate by a medical officer of health as to whether or not he or she has received a statement of medical exemption, a statement of conscience or religious belief or a statement of religious belief is admissible in evidence as proof in the absence of evidence to the contrary of the facts stated therein without proof of the appointment or signature of the medical officer of health.

6. Order for suspension re designated diseases.—(1) A medical officer of health, in the circumstances mentioned in subsection (2), by a written order may require a person who operates a school in the area served by the medical officer of health to suspend from attendance at the school a pupil named in the order.

(2) **Grounds for order re designated diseases.**—The circumstances mentioned in subsection (1) are,

- (a) that the medical officer of health has not received,
    - (i) a statement signed by a physician showing that the pupil has completed the prescribed program of immunization in relation to the designated diseases,
    - (ii) a statement of medical exemption in respect of the pupil or, where the medical officer of health has received a statement of medical exemption, the effective time period specified in the statement has expired and the medical officer of health has not received a further statement of medical exemption, or
    - (iii) a statement of conscience or religious belief in respect of the pupil; and
- (b) that the medical officer of health is not satisfied that the pupil has completed, has commenced and will complete or will commence and complete the prescribed program of immunization in relation to the designated diseases.

7. Term of suspension.—A suspension under an order by a medical officer of health under section 6 is for a period of twenty school days.

8. Service of copy of order upon parent.—(1) A medical officer of health who makes an order under section 6 shall serve a copy of the order upon a parent of the pupil.

(2) **Written reasons.**—An order under section 6 is not valid unless written reasons for the order are included in or attached to the order.

(3) **Repeated orders.**—A medical officer of health may make orders under section 6 from time to time in respect of a pupil where the circumstances specified in the section for making the order continue to exist.

9. Rescission of order.—A medical officer of health who has made an order under section 6 shall rescind the order where the circumstances for making the order no longer exist.

10. Statement by physician.—Every physician who administers an immunizing agent to a child in relation to a designated disease shall furnish to a parent of the child a statement signed by the physician showing that the physician has administered the immunizing agent to the child.

11. Record of immunization.—(1) Every medical officer of health shall maintain a record of immunization in the form and containing the information prescribed by the regulations in respect of each pupil attending school in the area served by the medical officer of health.

(2) **Review of record.**—A medical officer of health shall keep under review the immunization record maintained by the medical officer of health in respect of a pupil who has not completed the prescribed program of immunization in relation to the designated diseases.

12. Order by M.O.H.—A medical officer of health, in the circumstances mentioned in subsection (2), by a written order may require a person who operates a school located in the health unit served by the medical officer of health to exclude from the school a pupil named in the order.

(2) **Grounds for order.**—The circumstances mentioned in subsection (1) are,

(a) that the medical officer of health is of the opinion, upon reasonable and probable grounds, that there is an outbreak or an immediate risk of an outbreak of a designated disease in the school at which the pupil attends; and
(b) that the medical officer of health has not received,
  (i) a statement of immunization signed by a physician showing, or is not otherwise satisfied, that the pupil has completed the prescribed program of immunization in relation to the designated disease, or
  (ii) a statement of medical exemption in the prescribed form signed by a physician stating that the prescribed program of immunization in relation to the designated disease is unnecessary in respect of the pupil by reason of past infection or laboratory evidence of immunity.

(3) **Term of order.**—An order under subsection (1) remains in force until rescinded in writing by the medical officer of health.

(4) **Rescission of order.**—A medical officer of health who makes an order under subsection (1) shall rescind the order as soon as the medical officer of health is satisfied that the outbreak or the immediate risk of the outbreak of the designated disease has ended.

(5) **Service of copy of order.**—The medical officer of health shall serve a copy of the order under subsection (1) upon a parent of the pupil and, where the pupil is sixteen or seventeen years of age, upon the pupil.

(6) **Service of copy of rescinding order.**—The medical officer of health shall serve a rescinding order made under subsection (4) upon the person who operates the school and shall serve a copy of the order upon a parent of the pupil and, where the pupil is sixteen or seventeen years of age, upon the pupil.

(7) **Written reasons.**—An order under subsection (1) shall include written reasons for the making of the order.

13. Hearing and submissions.—A medical officer of health need not hold or afford to any person an opportunity for a hearing or afford to any person an opportunity to make submissions before making an order under this Act.

14. Notice of transfer of pupil.—(1) Where a pupil transfers from a school, the person who operates the school shall give notice of the transfer in the prescribed form to the medical officer of health serving the area in which the school is located.

(2) **Transmittal of copy of immunization record.**—Where the notice under subsection (1) states that the pupil is transferring to a school in an area under the jurisdiction of another medical officer of health, the medical officer of health shall send a copy of the immunization record of the pupil to the other medical officer of health.

15. Notice.—(1) Where a medical officer of health makes an order under this Act requiring the suspension of a pupil or requiring that a pupil be excluded from a school due to an outbreak or an immediate risk of an outbreak of a designated disease, the medical officer of health shall serve upon a parent of the pupil or, where the pupil is sixteen or seventeen years of age, upon the pupil a notice of entitlement to a hearing.

(2) **Idem.**—A notice under subsection (1) shall inform the parent or pupil, as the case may be, that the parent or pupil is entitled to a hearing by the Board if the parent or pupil mails or delivers to the medical officer of health, to the Board and to the person who operates the school, within fifteen days after the notice is served on the parent or pupil, notice in writing requiring a hearing and the parent or pupil may so require such a hearing.

(3) **Opportunity to show compliance and to examine documents.**—Where a hearing by the Board is required in accordance with this section, the medical officer of health shall afford to the parent or pupil requiring the hearing a reasonable opportunity before the hearing,

(a) to show or to achieve compliance with all lawful requirements concerning the subject-matter of the hearing; and

(b) to examine any written or documentary evidence that will be produced or any report the contents of which will be given in evidence at the hearing.

(4) **Powers of Board where hearing.**—Where a hearing is required in accordance with this section, the Board shall appoint a time and place for and hold the hearing and the Board by order may confirm, alter or rescind the decision or order of the medical officer of health and for such purposes the Board may substitute its finding for that of the medical officer of health.

(5) **Time for hearing.**—The Board shall hold a hearing under this section within fifteen days after receipt by the Board of the notice in writing requiring the hearing and the Board may, from time to time at the request or with the consent of the person requiring the hearing, extend the time for holding the hearing for such period or periods of time as the Board considers just.

(6) **Parties.**—The medical officer of health, the parent or pupil who has required the hearing and such other persons as the Board may specify are parties to the proceedings before the Board.

(7) **Effect of order.**—Despite the fact that a hearing is required in accordance with this section, an order under this Act by a medical officer of health takes effect when it is served on the person to whom it is directed.

(8) **Members holding hearing not to have taken part in investigation, etc.**—Members of the Board holding a hearing shall not have taken part before the hearing in any investigation or consideration of the subject-matter of the hearing and shall not communicate directly or indirectly in relation to the subject-matter of the hearing with any person or with any party or representative of the party except upon notice to and opportunity for all parties to participate, but the Board may seek legal advice from an adviser independent from the parties and in such case the nature of the advice shall be made known to the parties in order that they may make submissions as to the law.

(9) **Recording of evidence.**—The oral evidence taken before the Board at a hearing shall be recorded and, if so required, copies or a transcript thereof shall be furnished upon the same terms as in the Ontario Court (General Division).

(10) **Findings of fact.**—The findings of fact of the Board pursuant to a hearing shall be based exclusively on evidence admissible or matters that may be noticed under sections 15 and 16 of the *Statutory Powers Procedure Act*.

(11) **Only members at hearing to participate in decision.**—No member of the Board shall participate in a decision of the Board pursuant to a hearing unless he or she was present throughout the hearing and heard the evidence and argument of the parties and, except with the consent of the parties, no decision of the Board shall be given unless all members so present participate in the decision.

(12) **Release of documentary evidence.**—Documents and things put in evidence at a hearing shall, upon the request of the person who produced them, be released to the party by the Board within a reasonable time after the matter in issue has been finally determined.

16. Appeal to court.—(1) Any party to the proceedings before the Board under this Act may appeal from its decision or order to the Divisional Court in accordance with the rules of court.

(2) **Record to be filed in court.**—Where any party appeals from a decision or order of the Board under this Act, the Board shall forthwith file in the Ontario Court (General Division) the record of the proceedings before it in which the decision was made, which, together with the transcript of evidence if it is not part of the Board's record, shall constitute the record in the appeal.

(3) **Powers of court on appeal.**—An appeal under this section may be made on questions of law or fact or both and the court may affirm or may rescind the decision of the Board and may exercise all powers of the Board to confirm, alter or rescind the order that is the subject of the appeal and to substitute its findings for that of the person who made the order as the court considers proper and for such purposes the court may substitute its opinion for that of the person who made the order or of the Board, or the court may refer the matter back to the Board for rehearing, in whole or in part, in accordance with such directions as the court considers proper.

17. Regulations.—The Lieutenant Governor in Council may make regulations,
(a) prescribing any matter referred to in this Act as prescribed by the regulations;
(b) prescribing forms and providing for their use and requiring that statements of conscience or religious belief be in the form of affidavits;

(c) governing the custody, recording, inspection and destruction of records in respect of immunizations in relation to designated diseases;

(d) prescribing programs of immunization in respect of designated diseases, including specifying immunizing agents and the number and timing of dosages of immunizing agents;

(e) classifying children, pupils or persons and exempting any such class from any provision of this Act or the regulations and prescribing conditions to which such exemption shall be subject;

(f) requiring and governing reports by persons who operate schools to medical officers of health in respect of records and documentation related to the immunization of children applying for admission to the schools and pupils and former pupils in the schools;

(g) respecting any other matter that the Lieutenant Governor in Council considers necessary or advisable to carry out effectively the intent and purpose of this Act.

18. Service.—(1) Any notice, order or other document under this Act or the regulations is sufficiently given, served or delivered if delivered personally or sent by ordinary mail addressed to the person to whom it is to be given, served or delivered at his or her last known address.

(2) **When service deemed made.**—A notice, order or other document sent by ordinary mail in accordance with subsection (1) shall be deemed to be given, served or delivered on the seventh day after the day of mailing, unless the person to whom it is sent establishes that, acting in good faith, the person did not receive the notice, order or other document until a later date through absence, accident, illness or other cause beyond the person's control.

REGULATION UNDER THE IMMUNIZATION OF SCHOOL PUPILS ACT

REGULATION 645 — GENERAL	411
1. Record of immunization	411
2. Statement of medical exemption	411
3. Statement of conscience or religious belief	411
4. Notice of transfer of pupil	411
5. Schedule	411
Form 1	412
Form 2	414
Form 3	415

REGULATION 645
GENERAL
R.R.O. 1990, Reg. 645

1. A record of immunization maintained by a medical officer of health with respect to a pupil shall contain,

- (a) the name of the pupil in full;
- (b) the date of birth of the pupil;
- (c) the sex of the pupil;
- (d) the name of the school attended by the pupil;
- (e) a record of all the pupil's immunization against designated diseases showing,
    - (i) the type of vaccine given,
    - (ii) the date of administration of the vaccine, and
    - (iii) any reactions to the vaccine;
- (f) any statement of medical exemption that pertains to the pupil showing the effective time period on the statement; and
- (g) any statement of religious belief that pertains to the pupil.

2. A statement of medical exemption shall be in Form 1.

3. A statement of conscience or religious belief shall be in Form 2.

4. A notice of transfer of pupil referred to in section 14 of the Act shall be in Form 3.

5. The following program of immunization in respect of designated diseases in prescribed:

Schedule

Item	Disease	Type of Vaccine to be Used	Minimum Number of Doses Accepted	Recommended Schedule of Primary Immunization	Interval Between Booster Doses
1.	Diphtheria	TOXOID	3	Two injections, 1 to 2 months apart with a further dose one year later. Children immunized in infancy require three doses 1 to 2 months apart, a further dose one year later and a booster dose at age 4–6.	10 years
2.	Tetanus	TOXOID	3	Two injections, 1 to 2 months apart with a further dose one year later. Children immunized in infancy require three doses 1 to 2 months apart, a further dose one year later and a booster dose at age 4–6.	10 years

FORM 1   IMMUNIZATION OF SCHOOL PUPILS ACT REGULATIONS

3. Poliomyelitis	Inactivated Polio vaccine (IPV) or	3	Two injections, 1 to 2 months apart with a further dose one year later. Children immunized in infancy require three doses 1 to 2 months apart, a further dose one year later and a booster dose at age 4–6.	10 years
	Live Oral Polio vaccine (OPV)	3	Two doses 1 to 2 months apart with a further dose 2 to 12 months later. Children immunized in infancy require a booster dose at age 4–6.	NONE required
4. Measles	Live attenuated virus vaccine	1 after one year of age	One dose after the first birthday.	NONE required
5. Mumps	Live attenuated virus vaccine	1 after one year of age	One dose after the first birthday.	NONE required
6. Rubella	Live attenuated virus vaccine	1 after one year of age	One dose after the first birthday.	NONE required

FORM 1

Immunization of School Pupils Act

STATEMENT OF MEDICAL EXEMPTION

PUPIL'S NAME: ....
                           Last Name   First Name

ADDRESS: ....

DATE OF BIRTH: .... / .... / ....
                     Year   Month   Day

SCHOOL: .... Class or Grade : ....

I, ..., certify that, for medical reasons indicated below, the above named pupil should be exempted from the requirements of the Act.

The specific reasons and length of exemptions are checked in the boxes below. The time periods for temporary medical exemptions are indicated.

REGULATION 645 **FORM 1**

Disease	Immunity		Contraindication	Length of Exemption	
	Physician diagnosed prior disease	Test evidence of Immunity	Detrimental to Health	Permanent	Temporary From To
Diphtheria		☐	☐	☐	☐ ...... / ......
Tetanus		☐	☐	☐	☐ ...... / ......
Poliomyelitis		☐	☐	☐	☐ ...... / ......
Measles	☐	☐	☐	☐	☐ ...... / ......
Mumps	☐	☐	☐	☐	☐ ...... / ......
Rubella		☐	☐	☐	☐ ...... / ......

Use this space to define evidence of immunity: ....

....

....

Use this space for explanations of contraindications detrimental to health: ....

....

....

....

Physician's Signature ....

Address: ....

Date: ....

FORM 2 IMMUNIZATION OF SCHOOL PUPILS ACT REGULATIONS

FORM 2

Immunization of School Pupils Act

STATEMENT OF CONSCIENCE OR RELIGIOUS BELIEF

AFFIDAVIT

I, ..., parent of the following named pupil:

PUPIL'S NAME: ....
                      Last Name   First Name

ADDRESS: ....

DATE OF BIRTH: ..../ ..../ ....
                Year   Month   Day

SCHOOL: .... Class or Grade: ....,

make oath or solemnly affirm and say as follows:

The requirements of the *Immunization of School Pupils Act*, conflict with my sincerely held convictions based on my religion or conscience.

I understand that section 12 of the Act provides that the Medical Officer of Health may order that the above named pupil be excluded from school if there is an outbreak or immediate risk of an outbreak of a designated disease in the school at which the pupil attends where the following have not been received:—

    1. A statement of immunization or other satisfactory evidence of immunization.

    2. A statement of medical exemption stating that immunization is unnecessary because of evidence of immunity.

SWORN OR SOLEMNLY AFFIRMED before me at)
the

.... of ....)

Municipality of .... this ....)

)   ....
)   Parent's Signature

day of ...., 199.....)

....)
      A commissioner, etc.   )

REGULATION 645   **FORM 3**

FORM 3

Immunization of School Pupils Act

NOTICE OF TRANSFER FROM A SCHOOL

To the Medical Officer of Health ....
Health Agency

Notice is hereby given that the following pupils have transferred from:

....School, ...
Address

Date	Name of Pupil	Sex	Date of Birth	Grade	Transferring to	
					School	School Board

Signed ....

for ....
Operator of School

MUNICIPAL CONFLICT OF INTEREST ACT

TABLE OF CONTENTS

1.	Definitions	419
2.	Indirect pecuniary interest	420
3.	Interest of certain relatives deemed that of member	420

EXCEPTIONS

4.	Where s. 5 does not apply	421

DUTY OF MEMBER

5.	When present at meeting at which matter considered	421

RECORD OF DISCLOSURE

6.	Disclosure to be recorded in minutes	422

REMEDY FOR LACK OF QUORUM

7.	Quorum deemed constituted	422

ACTION WHERE CONTRAVENTION ALLEGED

8.	Who may try alleged contravention of s. 5 (1-3)	423
9.	Who may apply to judge	423
10.	Power of judge to declare seat vacant, disqualify member and require restitution	423
11.	Appeal to Divisional Court	423
12.	Proceedings not invalidated but voidable	423
13.	Other Procedures prohibited	424

GENERAL

14.	Insurance	424
15.	Conflict with other Acts	424

MUNICIPAL CONFLICT OF INTEREST ACT
R.S.O. 1990, c. M.50; repealed S.O. 1994, c. 23, s. 2 (not yet in force)*

1. Definitions.—In this Act,

"child."—"child" means a child born within or outside marriage and includes an adopted child and a person whom a parent has demonstrated a settled intention to treat as a child of his or her family; ("enfant")

"controlling interest."—"controlling interest" means the interest that a person has in a corporation when the person beneficially owns, directly or indirectly, or exercises control or direction over, equity shares of the corporation carrying more than 10 per cent of the voting rights attached to all equity shares of the corporation for the time being outstanding; ("intérêts majoritaires")

"council."—"council" means the council of a municipality other than an improvement district and means the board of trustees of a municipality that is an improvement district; ("conseil")

"elector."—"elector" means,

(a) in respect of a municipality, or a local board thereof, other than a school board, a person entitled to vote at a municipal election in the municipality, and

(b) in respect of a school board, a person entitled to vote at the election of members of the school board; ("électeur")

"interest in common with electors generally."—"interest in common with electors generally" means a pecuniary interest in common with the electors within the area of jurisdiction and, where the matter under consideration affects only part of the area of jurisdiction, means a pecuniary interest in common with the electors within that part; ("intérêt commun à tous les électeurs")

"judge."—"judge" means a judge of the Ontario Court (General Division); ("juge")

"local board."—"means a school board, board of directors of a children's aid society, committee of adjustment, committee of management of a community recreation centre, conservation authority, court of revision, land division committee, public utilities commission, public library board, board of management of an improvement area, board of park management, board of health, police services board, planning board, district welfare administration board, trustees of a police village, board of trustees of a police village, board or committee of management of a home for the aged, suburban roads commission or any other board, commission, committee, body or local authority established or exercising any power or authority under any general or special Act in respect of any of the affairs or purposes, including school purposes, of a municipality or of two or more

---

* Editor's Note: Pursuant to section 2(2) of the Planning and Municipal Statute Law Amendment Act, 1994, S.O. 1994, c. 23, this Act is to be repealed and will essentially be replaced by the Local Government Disclosure of Interest Act, 1994, which is set out in Schedule B to the Planning and Municipal Statute Law Amendment Act, 1994 (see section 2(1)). As of the date of publication, the relevant legislation provisions were not yet proclaimed in force. In this Consolidation, the text of the new legislation follows the Municipal Conflict of Interest Act.

municipalities or parts thereof, but does not include a committee of management of a community recreation centre appointed by a school board, a local roads board, a local services board or a negotiating committee appointed under the *Municipal Boundary Negotiations Act*; ("conseil local")

"meeting."—"meeting" includes any regular, special, committee or other meeting of a council or local board, as the case may be; ("réunion")

"member."—"member" means a member of a council or of a local board; ("membre")

"municipality."—"municipality" means the corporation of a county, city, town, village, township or improvement district or of a metropolitan, regional or district municipality and a board, commission or other local authority exercising any power in respect of municipal affairs or purposes, including school purposes, in territory without municipal organization, but does not include a committee of management of a community recreation centre appointed by a school board, a local roads board or a local services board; ("municipalité")

"parent."—"parent" means a person who has demonstrated a settled intention to treat a child as a member of his or her family whether or not that person is the natural parent of the child; ("père ou mère")

"school board."—"school board" means a board of education, public school board, secondary school board, Roman Catholic separate school board or Protestant separate school board and includes a divisional board of education; ("conseil scolaire")

"senior officer."—"senior officer" means the chair or any vice-chair of the board of directors, the president, any vice-president, the secretary, the treasurer or the general manager of a corporation or any other person who performs functions for the corporation similar to those normally performed by a person occupying any such office; ("dirigeant")

"spouse."—"spouse" means a person of the opposite sex to whom the person is married or with whom the person is living in a conjugal relationship outside marriage. ("conjoint")

2. Indirect pecuniary interest.—For the purposes of this Act, a member has an indirect pecuniary interest in any matter in which the council or local board, as the case may be, is concerned, if,

    (a) the member or his or her nominee,
        (i) is a shareholder in, or a director or senior officer of, a corporation that does not offer its securities to the public,
        (ii) has a controlling interest in or is a director or senior officer of, a corporation that offers its securities to the public, or
        (iii) is a member of a body,
    that has a pecuniary interest in the matter; or
    (b) the member is a partner of a person or is in the employment of a person or body that has a pecuniary interest in the matter.

3. Interest of certain relatives deemed that of member.— For the purposes of this Act, the pecuniary interest, direct or indirect, of a parent or the spouse or any child of the member shall, if known to the member, be deemed to be also the pecuniary interest of the member.

Exceptions

4. Where s. 5 does not apply.—Section 5 does not apply to a pecuniary interest in any matter that a member may have,

- (a) as a user of any public utility service supplied to the member by the municipality or local board in like manner and subject to the like conditions as are applicable in the case of persons who are not members;
- (b) by reason of the member being entitled to receive on terms common to other persons any service or commodity or any subsidy, loan or other such benefit offered by the municipality or local board;
- (c) by reason of the member purchasing or owning a debenture of the municipality or local board;
- (d) by reason of the member having made a deposit with the municipality or local board, the whole or part of which is or may be returnable to the member in like manner as such a deposit is or may be returnable to all other electors;
- (e) by reason of having an interest in any property affected by a work under the *Drainage Act* or under the *Local Improvement Act*;
- (f) by reason of having an interest in farm lands that are exempted from taxation for certain expenditures under the *Assessment Act*;
- (g) by reason of the member being eligible for election or appointment to fill a vacancy, office or position in the council or local board when the council or local board is empowered or required by any general or special Act to fill such vacancy, office or position;
- (h) by reason only of the member being a director or senior officer of a corporation incorporated for the purpose of carrying on business for and on behalf of the municipality or local board or by reason only of the member being a member of a board, commission, or other body as an appointee of a council or local board;
- (i) in respect of an allowance for attendance at meetings, or any other allowance, honorarium, remuneration, salary or benefit to which the member may be entitled by reason of being a member or under a by-law passed pursuant to section 256 of the *Municipal Act*, or as a member of a volunteer fire brigade, as the case may be;
- (j) by reason of the member having a pecuniary interest which is an interest in common with electors generally; or
- (k) by reason only of an interest of the member which is so remote or insignificant in its nature that it cannot reasonably be regarded as likely to influence the member.

Duty of Member

5. When present at meeting at which matter considered.—(1) Where a member, either on his or her own behalf or while acting for, by, with or through another, has any pecuniary interest, direct or indirect, in any matter and is present at a meeting of the council or local board at which the matter is the subject of consideration, the member,

- (a) shall, prior to any consideration of the matter at the meeting, disclose the interest and the general nature thereof;

(b) shall not take part in the discussion of, or vote on any question in respect of the matter; and

(c) shall not attempt in any way whether before, during or after the meeting to influence the voting on any such question.

(2) **Where member to leave closed meeting.**—Where the meeting referred to in subsection (1) is not open to the public, in addition to complying with the requirements of that subsection, the member shall forthwith leave the meeting or the part of the meeting during which the matter is under consideration.

(3) **When absent from meeting at which matter considered.**—Where the interest of a member has not been disclosed as required by subsection (1) by reason of the member's absence from the meeting referred to therein, the member shall disclose the interest and otherwise comply with subsection (1) at the first meeting of the council or local board, as the case may be, attended by the member after the meeting referred to in subsection (1).

Record of Disclosure

6. Disclosure to be recorded in minutes.—(1) Every declaration of interest and the general nature thereof made under section 5 shall, where the meeting is open to the public, be recorded in the minutes of the meeting by the clerk of the municipality or secretary of the committee or local board, as the case may be.

(2) **Idem.**—Every declaration of interest made under section 5, but not the general nature of that interest, shall, where the meeting is not open to the public, be recorded in the minutes of the next meeting that is open to the public.

Remedy for Lack of Quorum

7. Quorum deemed constituted.—(1) Where the number of members who, by reason of the provisions of this Act, are disabled from participating in a meeting is such that at that meeting the remaining members are not of sufficient number to constitute a quorum, then, despite any other general or special Act, the remaining number of members shall be deemed to constitute a quorum, provided such number is not less than two.

(2) **Application to judge.**—Where in the circumstances mentioned in subsection (1), the remaining number of members who are not disabled from participating in the meeting is less than two, the council or local board may apply to a judge without notice for an order authorizing the council or local board, as the case may be, to give consideration to, discuss and vote on the matter out of which the interest arises.

(3) **Power of judge to declare s. 5 not to apply.**—The judge may, on an application brought under subsection (2), by order, declare that section 5 does not apply to the council or local board, as the case may be, in respect of the matter in relation to which the application is brought, and the council or local board thereupon may give consideration to, discuss and vote on the matter in the same manner as though none of the members had any interest therein, subject only to such conditions and directions as the judge may consider appropriate and so order.

Action Where Contravention Alleged

8. Who may try alleged contravention of s. 5(1-3).—The question of whether or not a member has contravened subsection 5(1), (2) or (3) may be tried and determined by a judge.

9. Who may apply to judge.—(1) Subject to subsection (3), an elector may, within six weeks after the fact comes to his or her knowledge that a member may have contravened subsection 5(1), (2) or (3), apply to the judge for a determination of the question of whether the member has contravened subsection 5(1), (2) or (3).

(2) **Contents of notice of application.**—The elector in his or her notice of application shall state the grounds for finding a contravention by the member of subsection 5(1), (2) or (3).

(3) **Time for bringing application limited.**—No application shall be brought under subsection (1) after the expiration of six years from the time at which the contravention is alleged to have occurred.

10. Power of judge to declare seat vacant, disqualify member and require restitution.—(1) Subject to subsection (2), where the judge determines that a member or a former member while he or she was a member has contravened subsection 5(1), (2) or (3), the judge,

 (a) shall, in the case of a member, declare the seat of the member vacant; and
 (b) may disqualify the member or former member from being a member during a period thereafter of not more than seven years; and
 (c) may, where the contravention has resulted in personal financial gain, require the member or former member to make restitution to the party suffering the loss, or, where such party is not readily ascertainable, to the municipality or local board of which he or she is a member or former member.

(2) **Saving by reason of inadvertence or error.**—Where the judge determines that a member or a former member while he or she was a member has contravened subsection 5(1), (2) or (3), if the judge finds that the contravention was committed through inadvertence or by reason of an error in judgment, the member is not subject to having his or her seat declared vacant and the member or former member is not subject to being disqualified as a member, as provided by subsection (1).

(3) **Member not to be suspended.**—The authority to disqualify a member in subsection (1) does not include the right to suspend a member.

11. Appeal to Divisional Court.—(1) An appeal lies from any order made under section 10 to the Divisional Court in accordance with the rules of court.

(2) **Judgment or new trial.**—The Divisional Court may give any judgment that ought to have been pronounced, in which case its decision is final, or the Divisional Court may grant a new trial for the purpose of taking evidence or additional evidence and may remit the case to the trial judge or another judge and, subject to any directions of the Divisional Court, the case shall be proceeded with as if there had been no appeal.

(3) **Appeal from order or new trial.**—Where the case is remitted to a judge under subsection (2), an appeal lies from the order of the judge to the Divisional Court in accordance with the provisions of this section.

12. Proceedings not invalidated but voidable.—The failure of any person to comply with subsection 5(1), (2) or (3) does not of itself invalidate any proceedings in respect of any such matter but the proceedings in respect of such matter are voidable at the instance of the municipality or of the local board, as the case may be, before the expiration of two years from the date of the passing of the by-law or resolution authorizing such matter unless to make void the proceedings would adversely affect the rights of any person acquired under or by virtue of the proceedings who acted in good faith and without actual notice of the failure to comply with subsection 5(1), (2) or (3).

13. Other Proceedings prohibited.—Proceedings to declare a seat vacant or to disqualify a member or former member for conflict of interest, or to require a member or former member to make restitution where a contravention has resulted in personal financial gain, shall be had and taken only under this Act.

General

14. Insurance.—(1) Despite section 252 of the *Municipal Act*, the council of every municipality may at any time pass by-laws,

(a) for contracting for insurance;

(b) despite the *Insurance Act*, to enable the municipality to act as an insurer; and

(c) for exchanging with other municipalities in Ontario reciprocal contracts of indemnity or inter-insurance in accordance with Part XIII of the *Insurance Act*,

to protect a member of the council or of any local board thereof who has been found not to have contravened section 5, against any costs or expenses incurred by the member as a result of a proceeding brought under this Act, and for paying on behalf of or reimbursing the member for any such costs or expenses.

(2) **Insurance Act does not apply.**—The *Insurance Act* does not apply to a municipality acting as an insurer for the purposes of subsection (1).

(3) **Surplus funds.**—Despite subsections 387(1) and (2) of the *Insurance Act*, any surplus funds and the reserve fund of a municipal reciprocal exchange may be invested only in such securities as a municipality may invest in under subsection 163(2) of the *Municipal Act*.

(4) **Reserve funds.**—The money raised for a reserve fund of a municipal reciprocal exchange may be expended or pledged for, or applied to, a purpose other than that for which the fund was established if two-thirds of the municipalities that are members of the exchange together with two-thirds of the municipalities that previously were members of the exchange and that may be subject to claims arising while they were members of the exchange agree in writing and if section 386 of the *Insurance Act* is complied with.

(5) **Local boards.**—A local board has the same powers to provide insurance for or to make payments to or on behalf of its members as are conferred upon the council of a municipality under this section in respect of its members.

(6) **Former members.**—A by-law passed under this section may provide that it applies to a person who was a member at the time the circumstances giving rise to the proceeding occurred but who, prior to the judgment in the proceeding, has ceased to be a member.

15. Conflict with other Acts.—In the event of conflict between any provision of this Act and any provision of any general or special Act, the provision of this Act prevails.

LOCAL GOVERNMENT DISCLOSURE OF INTEREST ACT, 1994

(Not Yet Proclaimed in Force)

TABLE OF CONTENTS

1. Purpose 427
2. Definitions 427
3. Exceptions 428
4. Duty of member 429
5. Gifts 430
6. Financial disclosure requirement 430
7. Commissioner 431
8. Applications 431
9. Power of court 432
10. Appeal to Divisional Court 432
11. Proceedings not invalidated 433
12. Other procedures prohibited 433
13. Quorum 433
14. Minutes 434
15. Register 434
16. Prohibition re information 434
17. Offence 434
18. Insurance 434
19. By-laws 435
20. Community economic development corporations 435
21. Regulations 435
22. Regulations 435
23. Conflict 435
24. Short title 435

LOCAL GOVERNMENT DISCLOSURE OF INTEREST ACT, 1994

S.O. 1994, c. 23, Schedule B*
(Not Yet Proclaimed in Force)

1. Purpose.—The purpose of this Act is to preserve the integrity and accountability of local government decision-making.

2. (1) **Definitions.**—In this Act,

"board".—"board" means,
  (a) a local board as defined in the *Municipal Affairs Act*,
  (b) boards, agencies, corporations or other entities or classes of them established in relation to local, municipal or school purposes as may be prescribed in the regulations; ("commission")

"child".—"child" means a child under 18 years of age born within or outside marriage and includes an adopted child and a person whom a parent has demonstrated a settled intention to treat as a child of his or her family; ("enfant")

"commissioner".—"commissioner" means the commissioner appointed under this Act; ("commissaire")

"committee".—"committee" means any advisory or other committee or subcommittee composed of members of one or more boards or councils; ("comité")

"council".—"council" means the council of a municipality other than an improvement district and the board of trustees of an improvement district; ("conseil")

"meeting".—"meeting" includes any regular, special, committee or other meeting of a council or board; ("réunion")

"member".—"member" means a member of a council or of a board; ("membre")

"Minister".—"Minister" means the Minister of Municipal Affairs; ("ministre")

"municipality".—"municipality" means a local municipality, county, improvement district, metropolitan, regional or district municipality and the County of Oxford; ("municipalité")

"pecuniary interest".—"pecuniary interest" includes a direct or indirect pecuniary interest of a member and a pecuniary interest deemed to be that of a member; ("intérêt pécuniaire")

"prescribed".—"prescribed" means prescribed by regulations made under this Act; ("prescrit")

"senior officer".—"senior officer" means the chair or any vice-chair of the board of directors, the president, any vice-president, the secretary, the treasurer or the general manager of a corporation or any other person who performs functions for the corporation similar to those normally performed by a person occupying any such office; ("dirigeant")

"spouse".—"spouse" means a spouse as defined in Part III of the *Family Law Act*. ("conjoint")

---

* Editor's Note: On proclamation, this Act will replace the Municipal Conflict of Interest Act, R.S.O. 1990, c. M.50. See S.O. 1994, c. 23, sections 2(3)-(5) for transitional provisions.

S. 3 DISCLOSURE OF INTEREST ACT

(2) **Non-application.**—This Act does not apply to a committee of management of a recreation centre appointed by a school board, to a local roads board or to a local services board.

(3) **Pecuniary interest.**—For the purposes of this Act, a member shall be deemed to have a pecuniary interest in a matter in which a council or board is concerned, if,

    (a) the member or his or her nominee,
- (i) is a shareholder in, or a director or senior officer of, a corporation that does not offer its securities to the public,
- (ii) has a controlling interest in, or is a director or senior officer of, a corporation that offers its securities to the public,
- (iii) is a partner or agent of a person,
- (iv) is a member of a body,

that has a pecuniary interest in the matter;

    (b) the member or the member's spouse or child is an employee of a person or body and the member knows that the person or body has a pecuniary interest in the matter;

    (c) the member knows that the member's spouse or child has a direct or indirect pecuniary interest in the matter; or

    (d) the member knows that the member's spouse or child,
- (i) is a shareholder in, or a director or senior officer of, a corporation that does not offer its securities to the public,
- (ii) has a controlling interest in, or is a director or senior officer of, a corporation that offers its securities to the public,
- (iii) is a partner or agent of a person,
- (iv) is a member of a body,

that has a pecuniary interest in the matter.

(4) **Definition.**—In subsection (3), "controlling interest" means the interest that a person has in a corporation when the person beneficially owns, directly or indirectly, or exercises control or direction over, equity shares of the corporation carrying more than 10 per cent of the voting rights attached to all equity shares of the corporation for the time being outstanding.

3. Exceptions.—Section 4 does not apply to a pecuniary interest in any matter that a member may have,

    (a) as a user of any public utility service supplied to the member by the municipality or board under similar conditions as other users;

    (b) as a recipient of any service or commodity or any subsidy, loan or other benefit offered by the municipality or board on terms common to other persons;

    (c) as a purchaser or owner of a debenture of the municipality or board;

    (d) as a depositor with the municipality or board, if the whole or part of the deposit is or may be returnable to the member in like manner as a deposit is or may be returnable to other persons under similar conditions;

    (e) in any property affected by a work under the *Drainage Act* or under the *Local Improvement Act*;

    (f) in farm land that is exempt from taxation for certain expenditures under the *Assessment Act*;

    (g) as a director or senior officer of a corporation incorporated by the municipality or to

carry on business on behalf of the municipality or board or as a person nominated by the council as a director or officer of a corporation;
(h) as a member or office holder of a council, board or other body when it is required by law or by virtue of office or results from an appointment by a council or board;
(i) as a recipient of an allowance for attendance at meetings, or any other allowance, honorarium, remuneration, salary or benefit to which the member may be entitled as a member;
(j) in common with persons generally within the area of jurisdiction or, if the matter under consideration affects only part of the area, in common with persons within that part;
(k) as a member or volunteer for a charitable organization or a non-for-profit organization with objects substantially similar to those provided by section 118 of the *Corporations Act* if the member receives no remuneration or other financial benefit from the organization and the pecuniary interest is in common with other persons in the organization;
(l) as a recipient of remuneration, consideration or an honorarium under section 256 of the *Municipal Act* or as a volunteer firefighter;
(m) that is so remote or insignificant in its nature that it cannot reasonably be regarded as likely to influence the member.

4. (1) **Duty of member.**—If a member has a pecuniary interest in any matter and is or will be present at a meeting at any time at which the matter is the subject of consideration, the member,

(a) shall, before any consideration of the matter at the meeting, orally disclose the interest and its general nature;
(b) shall not, at any time, take part in the discussion of, or vote on, any question in respect of the matter;
(c) shall not, at any time, attempt, either on his or her own behalf or while acting for, by or through another person, to influence the voting on any such matter or influence employees of or persons interested in a contract with the council or board in respect of the matter;
(d) shall immediately leave the meeting and remain absent from it at any time during consideration of the matter; and
(e) shall, as soon as possible, complete and file with the clerk of the municipality or secretary of the board a written disclosure, in the prescribed form, setting out the interest and its general nature.

(2) **When absent from meeting.**—If a member is absent from all or part of a meeting in which he or she has a pecuniary interest in a matter being considered, other than an absence due to compliance with clause (1)(d), clause (1)(c) applies to that member and he or she shall,

(a) disclose the interest in the manner described in clause (1)(a) at the next meeting of the council or board that the member attends;
(b) in the case of a committee meeting, disclose the interest in the manner described in clause (1)(a) at the next meeting of the committee that the member attends; and
(c) file a written disclosure in the manner described in clause (1)(e) as soon as possible after the next meeting that the member attends.

(3) **Limitation.**—A disclosure under this section is not required to disclose that the member has a spouse or child or the name of the member's spouse or child.

(4) **Interest of member.**—Where a disclosure omits reference to a member's spouse or child, the interest shall be stated as being that of the member.

(5) **Filing.**—If a member of a committee is required to file a written disclosure under this section, the member shall file it in the manner described in clause (1)(e) with the clerk of the council or secretary of the board that appointed the member.

5. (1) **Gifts.**—A member shall not, either directly or through another person, accept a fee, gift or personal benefit except compensation authorized by law that is connected with the performance of his or her duties of office.

(2) **Exception.**—Subsection (1) does not apply to,

(a) a gift or personal benefit that is received as an incident of the protocol or social obligations that normally accompany the responsibilities of office; or

(b) a contribution that is authorized under the *Municipal Elections Act* made to a member who is a registered candidate under that Act.

(3) **Disclosure.**—A member shall complete and file a disclosure statement with the clerk of the municipality or secretary of the board as soon as possible after receiving a gift or personal benefit described under clause (2)(a) if,

(a) the value of the gift or benefit exceeds the lower of the amount prescribed or provided by by-law or resolution; or

(b) the total value received directly or indirectly from one source in one calendar year exceeds the lower of the amount prescribed or provided by by-law or resolution.

(4) **Contents.**—A disclosure statement filed under subsection (3) shall state the nature of the gift or benefit, its source and the circumstances under which it was given or accepted.

6. (1) **Financial disclosure requirement.**—This section applies only to members of,

(a) a council;

(b) a school board as defined in section 210.1 of the *Municipal Act*;

(c) a public utility commission; and

(d) a police village.

(2) **Filing form.**—Every member shall, within 60 days of being elected or appointed, file with the clerk of the municipality or the secretary of the board a financial disclosure statement in the prescribed form.

(3) **Omissions.**—The member may with the consent of the commissioner omit or delete from the financial disclosure statement information if,

(a) disclosure would reveal a source of income for the member or the member's spouse or child from services that are customarily provided on a confidential basis; or

(b) the possibility of serious harm to a person or business justifies a departure from the general principle of public disclosure.

(4) **Changes.**—The member shall file a supplementary financial disclosure statement during the month of December of every calendar year except an election year.

(5) **Limitation.**—A financial disclosure statement under this section is not required to disclose that the member has a spouse or child or the name of the member's spouse or child.

(6) **Interest of member.**—Where a financial disclosure statement omits reference to a member's spouse or child, the financial information shall be stated as being that of the member.

7. (1) **Commissioner.**—The Minister may appoint a commissioner to exercise the powers and perform the duties set out in this Act.

(2) **Assistant commissioner.**—The commissioner may appoint one or more assistant commissioners who may exercise such powers and duties of the commissioner as the commissioner delegates to them.

(3) **Restriction.**—The commissioner and any assistant commissioner shall not be a member of the Legislative Assembly, a council or a board.

(4) **Guidelines.**—The commissioner may provide such guidelines for the proper administration of this Act as he or she considers necessary for the guidance of members, boards and municipalities.

8. (1) **Applications.**—Any person may apply in writing to the commissioner for an investigation to be carried out of an alleged contravention by a member of section 4, 5 or 6.

(2) **Timing.**—An application may only be made within 90 days after the person became aware of the alleged contravention.

(3) **Fees.**—The commissioner may establish fees in respect of applications under subsection (1) and may waive any fee in cases of hardship.

(4) **Contents.**—An application shall set out the reasons for believing that the member has contravened section 4, 5 or 6 and include a statutory declaration attesting to the fact that the person became aware of the contravention not more than 90 days before the date of the application.

(5) **Investigation.**—The commissioner, upon receiving an application, may conduct such investigation as he or she considers necessary.

(6) **Same.**—For the purpose of conducting an investigation, the commissioner,

(a) has the right of access, at all reasonable hours, to all relevant books, papers or documents of the member or applicant and of a municipality or board; and

(b) has the powers of a commission under Part II of the *Public Inquiries Act* which Part applies to the investigation as if it were an inquiry under that Act.

(7) **Timing.**—The commissioner shall complete the investigation within 180 days of receiving the completed application.

(8) **Completion.**—Upon completion of the investigation, the commissioner,

(a) shall, if he or she considers it appropriate, apply to the Ontario Court (General Division) for a determination as to whether the member has contravened section 4, 5 or 6; or

(b) shall advise the applicant that the commissioner will not be making an application to the court.

(9) **Court determination.**—The question of whether or not a member has contravened section 4, 5 or 6 may be tried and determined by the Ontario Court (General Division).

(10) **Application.**—Any person may apply to the court for a determination under subsection (9).

(11) **Requirement.**—No application may be made to the court unless the application includes a statutory declaration attesting to the fact that the person became aware of the contravention not more than 90 days before the date of the application to the commissioner under subsection (4).

(12) **Restriction.**—Despite subsection (10), no person other than the commissioner shall make an application to the court unless the person has submitted an application to the commissioner under subsection (1) and,

- (a) the commissioner has notified the applicant that he or she will not be carrying out an investigation;
- (b) the commissioner has failed to complete the investigation within 180 days of receiving the application; or
- (c) the commissioner has notified the applicant that the commissioner will not be making an application to the court under clause (8)(b).

(13) **Limitation.**—No application shall be brought to the court under this section after the expiration of two years from the date on which the contravention is alleged to have occurred.

9. (1) **Power of court.**—If the court determines that a member or a former member while he or she was a member has contravened section 4, 5 or 6, the court,

- (a) shall suspend the member without pay and benefits for a period of not more than 90 days;
- (b) may, in the case of a member, declare the seat of the member vacant;
- (c) may disqualify the member or former member from being a member for a period of not more than seven years; and
- (d) may, where the contravention has resulted in personal financial gain, require the member or former member to make restitution to the party suffering the loss, or, where such party is not readily ascertainable, to the municipality or board of which he or she is a member or former member.

(2) **Restrictions.**—A member suspended from a council or board under subsection (1) shall not during the period of the suspension,

- (a) participate in any meeting of the council or board as a member or otherwise;
- (b) participate in any meeting of any body,
    - (i) to which the member has been appointed by the council or board, or
    - (ii) on which the member is required by law to sit by virtue of the member's office on the council or board;
- (c) participate in any meeting of any other council or board that appointed or approved the appointment of the member to the council or board; or
- (d) in the case of suspension from a council, participate in any meeting of any other council of which the member is also a member.

(3) **No vacancy.**—Clause 38(c) of the *Municipal Act* and section 229 of the *Education Act* do not apply to the seat of a member if the member is absent due to a suspension under clause 9(1)(a).

10. (1) **Appeal to Divisional Court.**—An appeal lies to the Divisional Court from a determination made under section 9 as to whether a contravention has occurred or not.

(2) **Judgment or new trial.**—The Divisional Court may give any judgment that ought to have been pronounced, in which case its decision is final, or the Divisional Court may grant a new trial for the purpose of taking evidence or additional evidence and may remit the case to the Ontario Court (General Division) and, subject to any directions of the Divisional Court, the case shall be proceeded with as if there had been no appeal.

(3) **Further appeal.**—If the case is remitted to the Ontario Court (General Division) under subsection (2), the appeal lies from the order of the court to the Divisional Court in accordance with this section.

11. Proceedings not invalidated.—The failure of any member to comply with section 4 does not of itself invalidate any proceedings in respect of any matter but the proceedings are voidable at the instance of the municipality or of the board, as the case may be, before the expiration of two years from the date of the passing of the by-law or resolution authorizing the matter unless to make void the proceedings would adversely affect the rights of any person acquired under or by virtue of the proceedings who acted in good faith and without actual notice of the failure to comply with section 4.

12. Other procedures prohibited.—The following proceedings in respect of disclosure of interest shall be taken only under this Act:

1. To suspend a member without pay or benefits.
2. To declare a seat vacant.
3. To disqualify a member or former member.
4. To require a member or former member to make restitution where a contravention has resulted in personal gain.

13. (1) **Quorum.**—If the number of members who, by reason of this Act, are disabled from participating in a meeting is such that there is no quorum, despite any other Act, any number that is not less than one-third of the total number of members of the council or board shall be deemed to constitute a quorum, but the number shall not be less than two unless an order is made under subsection (3) authorizing it.

(2) **Same.**—When the remaining number of members under subsection (1) is two, the concurrent votes of both are necessary to carry any resolution, by-law or other measure.

(3) **Order.**—If the remaining number of members who are not disabled from participating in the meeting is less than one-third of the total number of members or less than two, as the case may be, the council or board may apply to the commissioner without notice for an order authorizing the council or board to give consideration to, discuss and vote on the matter out of which the pecuniary interests arise.

(4) **Declaration.**—The commissioner may declare that section 4 does not apply to a matter that is the subject of consideration by a council or board if,

(a) the council or board applies to the commissioner under subsection (3); and
(b) the council or board submits a copy of the written disclosure statements of the members who are disabled from participating.

(5) **Conditions.**—As part of a declaration given under subsection(4), the commissioner may require the council or board to comply with any conditions the commissioner considers appropriate.

(6) **Effect.**—If a declaration is made, section 4 does not apply and the council or board may give consideration to the matter in the same manner as though none of the members had a pecuniary interest in it, subject to any conditions the commissioner sets out in the declaration.

14. Minutes.—Every oral declaration made under section 4 shall be recorded in the minutes of the meeting by the clerk of the municipality or secretary of the committee or board, as the case may be.

15. (1) **Register.**—The clerk of a municipality and the secretary of a board shall maintain a register of disclosures for the members of the council or board, respectively.

(2) **Contents.**—The register shall contain,

(a) the written disclosures of pecuniary interests under section 4;
(b) disclosure statements and supplementary disclosure statements of financial information under section 6; and
(c) disclosure statements of gifts or personal benefits under section 5.

(3) **Inspection.**—All documents in the register are public documents and may be inspected by any person under request at the office of the clerk or the secretary during normal office hours.

(4) **Copies.**—Any person may make extracts from the documents and is entitled to copies of them upon payment of such fees as may be charged by the municipality or board for the preparation of copies of other documents.

(5) **Retention of records.**—Despite section 116 of the *Municipal Act*, a municipality or local board shall not destroy the documents in the register until after the prescribed period.

16. Prohibition re information.—A member or former member shall not use or disclose information that is gained in the execution of his or her office and is not available to the general public to further or seek to further his or her pecuniary interests or the pecuniary interests of any other person.

17. Offence.—Every person who contravenes section 16 is guilty of an offence.

18. (1) **Insurance.**—Despite section 252 of the *Municipal Act*, the council of every municipality may pass by-laws,

(a) for contracting for insurance;
(b) despite the *Insurance Act*, to enable the municipality to act as an insurer; and
(c) for exchanging with other municipalities in Ontario reciprocal contracts of indemnity or inter-insurance in accordance with Part XIII of the *Insurance Act*,

to protect a member who has been found not to have contravened section 4, 5 or 6, against any costs or expenses incurred by the member as a result of a proceeding brought under this Act, and for paying on behalf of or reimbursing the member for the costs or expenses.

(2) *Insurance Act* **does not apply.**—The *Insurance Act* does not apply to a municipality acting as an insurer for the purposes of subsection (1).

(3) **Surplus funds.**—Despite subsections 387(1) and (2) of the *Insurance Act*, any surplus funds and the reserve fund of a municipal reciprocal exchange may be invested only in such securities as a municipality may invest in under subsection 163(2) of the *Municipal Act*.

(4) **Reserve funds.**—The money raised for a reserve fund of a municipal reciprocal exchange may be spent or pledged for, or applied to, a purpose other than that for which the

fund was established if two-thirds of the municipalities that are members of the exchange together with two-thirds of the municipalities that previously were members of the exchange and that may be subject to claims arising while they were members of the exchange agree in writing and if section 386 of the *Insurance Act* is complied with.

(5) **Boards.**—A board has the same powers to provide insurance for or to make payments to or on behalf of its members as are conferred on a municipality under this section in respect of its members.

(6) **Former members.**—A by-law or resolution passed under this section may provide that it applies to a person who was a member at the time the circumstances giving rise to the proceeding occurred but who, before the judgment in the proceeding, had ceased to be a member.

19. By-laws.—A municipality or board may pass by-laws or resolutions providing for the maximum amount of a single gift or benefit and of the combined value of gifts and benefits under section 5.

20. Community economic development corporations.—If a director of a community economic development corporation is required to file a written disclosure or a disclosure statement under this Act, the director shall file it with the clerk of the municipality that nominated or appointed the person.

21. Regulations.—The Lieutenant Governor in Council may make regulations prescribing,

(a) financial information or classes of financial information that must be disclosed or that is exempt from being disclosed in a financial disclosure statement under section 6;

(b) the maximum amount of a single gift or benefit and of the combined value of gifts and benefits under section 5.

22. Regulations.—The Minister may make regulations,

(a) prescribing the duties of the commissioner;

(b) prescribing procedures for applications to the commissioner under section 13;

(c) prescribing forms or requiring that information required be on a form provided by the Ministry;

(d) prescribing boards, agencies, corporations or other entities or classes of them to which this Act applies;

(e) prescribing the period for the purposes of subsection 15(5).

23. Conflict.—In the event of conflict between a provision of this Act and a provision of any other Act, the provision of this Act prevails.

24. Short title.—The short title of this Act is *Local Government Disclosure of Interest Act, 1994*.

SCHOOL BOARDS AND TEACHERS COLLECTIVE NEGOTIATIONS ACT

TABLE OF CONTENTS

PART I

GENERAL

1. Definitions 441
2. Purpose of Act 442
3. Application of Act 442
4. Joint negotiations 442
5. Representation of teachers by branch affiliate 443
6. Negotiating group 443
7. Parties may obtain assistance 443

PART II

NEGOTIATIONS

8. Subject-matter of negotiations 443
9. Notice of desire to negotiate 443
10. Notice of desire to negotiate for renewal of agreement 443
11. Obligation to negotiate 444
12. Parties may choose procedures to reach agreement 444
13. Where Commission may assign person to assist parties 444

PART III

FACT FINDING

14. Appointment of fact finder 444
15. Parties may proceed to make agreement or to arbitration or selection procedure 445
16. Persons prohibited as fact finder 445
17. Vacancy 445
18. Notice of appointment of fact finder 445
19. Notice of matters agreed upon and matters in dispute 445
20. Duty of fact finder 445
21. Matters that may be considered by fact finder 446
22. Procedure of fact finder 446
23. Submission of report of fact finder 446
24. Report not binding 446

COLLECTIVE NEGOTIATIONS ACT

25.	Assignment of assistance	446
26.	Where report confidential	446
27.	Parties may agree to refer matters in dispute	446

PART IV

VOLUNTARY BINDING ARBITRATION

28.	Parties to give notice to Commission where arbitration agreed upon	447
29.	Persons prohibited as arbitrator or members of chair of board of arbitration	448
30.	Vacancy	448
31.	Notice of matters agreed upon and matters in dispute	449
32.	Procedure	449
33.	Powers of arbitrator or board of arbitration	449
34.	Duty of arbitrator or board of arbitration	449
35.	Time for report of arbitrator or board of arbitration	450
36.	Preparation and execution of document by parties	450

PART V

FINAL OFFER SELECTION

37.	Parties to give notice to Commission where selection agreed upon	450
38.	Persons prohibited as selector	451
39.	Selector unable to act	451
40.	Notice of matters agreed upon and matters in dispute	451
41.	Notice of final offer	451
42.	Final offer of opposite party	451
43.	Written response	451
44.	Hearing	451
45.	Parties may dispense with hearing	452
46.	Procedure	452
47.	Selection of final offer	452
48.	Effect of decision	452
49.	Preparation and execution of document by parties	453

PART VI

AGREEMENTS

50.	Term of agreement	453
51.	Conflict	453
52.	Resolution of matters arising out of agreement	453
53.	Provision against strikes and lock-outs	454
54.	Agreement to form part of contract of employment	454

TABLE OF CONTENTS

55.	Notice of agreement	454
56.	Where agreement reached	454
57.	Notice to Commission of execution of agreement	454
58.	Binding effect of agreement	454

PART VII

EDUCATION RELATIONS COMMISSION

59.	Commission continued	455
60.	Duties of Commission	456
61.	Testimony by member of Commission	456
62.	Money	456

PART VIII

STRIKES AND LOCK-OUTS

63.	Notice of strike	456
64.	Principals and vice-principals	457
65.	Unlawful strike	457
66.	Unlawful lock-out	457
67.	Declaration of unlawful strike	457
68.	Lock-out	458
69.	Participation in lawful strike	458
70.	Resignation, etc., by teacher	458

PART IX

MISCELLANEOUS

71.	Copies of notice to be given to Commission	459
72.	Decisions, etc., of Commission and others not subject to review	459
73.	Service of notice	459
74.	Costs	459
75.	Statement as to officers of branch affiliate	460
76.	Where vote by secret ballot required	460
77.	Contravention by teacher or trustee	460
78.	Style of prosecution	461
79.	Vicarious responsibilities	461
80.	Application	461
81.	Compellability of witnesses	461

SCHOOL BOARDS AND TEACHERS COLLECTIVE NEGOTIATIONS ACT
R.S.O. 1990, c. S.2

PART I
GENERAL

1. Definitions.—In this Act,

"affiliate."—"affiliate" means one of the following bodies:
1. L'Association des Enseignants Franco-Ontariens.
2. The Federation of Women Teachers' Associations of Ontario.
3. The Ontario English Catholic Teachers' Association.
4. The Ontario Public School Teachers' Federation.
5. The Ontario Secondary School Teachers' Federation; ("organisation d'enseignants")

"agreement."—"agreement" means a written collective agreement made after the 18th day of July, 1975 and pursuant to this Act between a board and a branch affiliate or branch affiliates or between two or more boards and two or more branch affiliates covering matters negotiable under this Act; ("convention")

"board."—"board" means a board of education, public school board, secondary school board, Roman Catholic separate school board or Protestant separate school board and includes a divisional board of education; ("conseil")

"branch affiliate."—"branch affiliate" means an organization composed of all the teachers employed by a board who are members of the same affiliate; ("section locale")

"Commission."—"Commission" means the Education Relations Commission; ("Commission")

"Council."—"Council" means the Ontario School Trustees' Council; ("Conseil")

"Federation."—"Federation" means the Ontario Teachers' Federation; ("Fédération")

"lock-out."—"lock-out" means the suspension of employment of, or the refusal to assign work to, teachers other than principals and vice-principals in a school or schools by a board with the view to compelling the cessation of a strike or preventing the resumption of a strike or with the view to inducing or persuading the branch affiliate that represents the teachers to enter into or renew an agreement; ("lock-out")

"member association."—"member association" means one of the following bodies:
1. L'Association française des conseils scolaires de l'Ontario.
2. Northern Ontario Public and Secondary School Trustees' Association.
3. Ontario Public School Trustees' Association.
4. Ontario Separate School Trustees' Association; ("association de conseillers scolaires")

"party."—"party" means a board or a branch affiliate; ("partie")

"principal."—"principal" means a principal as defined in the *Education Act*; ("directeur d'école") "**strike.**"—"strike" includes any action or activity by teachers in combination or in concert or in accordance with a common understanding that is designed to curtail, restrict, limit or interfere with the operation or functioning of a school program or school programs or of a school or schools including, without limiting the foregoing,

(a) withdrawal of services,
(b) work to rule,
(c) the giving of notice to terminate contracts of employment; ("grève")

"**teacher.**"—"teacher" means a person,

(a) who holds a valid certificate of qualification as a teacher in an elementary or secondary school in Ontario,
(b) who holds a letter of standing granted by the Minister under the *Education Act*,
(c) in respect of whom the Minister has granted a letter of permission under the *Education Act*,

and who is employed by a board under a contract of employment as a teacher in the form of contract prescribed by the regulations under the *Education Act*, but does not include a supervisory officer as defined in the *Education Act*, an instructor in a teacher-training institution or a person employed to teach in a school for a period not exceeding one month; ("enseignant")

"**vice-principal.**"—"vice-principal" means a vice-principal within the meaning of the regulations under the *Education Act*; ("directeur adjoint")

"**vote by secret ballot.**"—"vote by secret ballot" means a vote by ballots cast in such a manner that a person expressing his or her choice cannot be identified with the choice expressed. ("scrutin secret")

2. Purpose of Act.—The purpose of this Act is the furthering of harmonious relations between boards and teachers by providing for the making and renewing of agreements and by providing for the relations between boards and teachers in respect of agreements.

3. Application of Act.—(1) This Act applies to all collective negotiations between boards and teachers in respect of any term or condition of employment put forward by either party for the purpose of making or renewing an agreement.

(2) **Negotiations to be in accordance with Act.**—No such collective negotiations shall be carried on between a board and the teachers employed by the board except in accordance with this Act.

4. Joint negotiations.—(1) In negotiations and procedures under this Act to make or renew an agreement or agreements, two or more boards may act jointly as a party and two or more branch affiliates may act jointly as a party, where both the boards and branch affiliates involved so agree, to make or renew an agreement between the boards and the branch affiliates or to make or renew a separate agreement between each of the boards and a branch affiliate that represents teachers employed by the board.

(2) **Idem.**—A separate agreement between a board and a branch affiliate made pursuant to subsection (1) may include terms and conditions of employment in addition to and consistent with those terms and conditions which are part of the agreement between all the boards acting as a party and all the branch affiliates acting as a party.

(3) **Branch affiliates may negotiate as one party.**—Despite subsection (1), two or more branch affiliates may act as one party in negotiations and procedures under this Act to make or renew an agreement or agreements with the same board.

(4) **Agreements between individual boards and branch affiliates.**—Where two or more boards act jointly as a party and two or more branch affiliates act jointly as a party pursuant to subsection (1), any negotiations and proceedings and resulting agreement pursuant to subsection (2) between one of the boards and a branch affiliate shall be deemed to be part of the joint negotiations and agreement in accordance with subsection (1).

(5) **Continuation of agreement to act jointly.**—A board or branch affiliate that agrees to act jointly with another board or branch affiliate pursuant to subsection (1), shall continue to act jointly with such other board or branch affiliate until an agreement is made or renewed between the parties.

5. Representation of teachers by branch affiliate.—A branch affiliate shall, in negotiations and procedures under this Act, represent all the teachers composing its membership.

6. Negotiating group.—In negotiations to make or renew an agreement, a party shall be represented by only one group of persons but may at any time increase, decrease or change the composition of the group.

7. Parties may obtain assistance.—At any time during negotiations or procedures under this Act,

(a) a board that is a party may obtain assistance from the Council, a member association or another board;
(b) a branch affiliate that is a party may obtain assistance from the Federation, an affiliate or another branch affiliate; and
(c) a party may obtain assistance from one or more advisors, agents, counsel or solicitors.

PART II

NEGOTIATIONS

8. Subject-matter of negotiations.—Negotiations shall be carried out in respect of any term or condition of employment put forward by either party.

9. Notice of desire to negotiate.—Where there is no agreement in force between a board and a branch affiliate, the branch affiliate may give to the board or the board may give to the branch affiliate written notice of its desire to negotiate with the view to making an agreement.

10. Notice of desire to negotiate for renewal of agreement.—(1) Either party to an agreement may give written notice to the other party within the month of January in the year in which the agreement expires of its desire to negotiate with the view to the renewal, with or without modification, of the agreement then in operation.

(2) **Where notice not given of desire to negotiate renewal of agreement.**—Where an agreement exists between a board or boards and a branch affiliate or branch affiliates and no party to the agreement gives notice in accordance with this Act of its desire to negotiate with the view to the renewal of the agreement, the agreement continues in operation and is renewed

from year to year, with each yearly period expiring on the 31st day of August, until the year, if any, in which notice is given in accordance with this Act of desire to negotiate with the view to the renewal, with or without modification, of the agreement.

(3) **Working conditions may not be altered.**—Where notice has been given of desire to negotiate to make or renew an agreement, the terms and conditions of the agreement, other than a term or condition that prevents a strike, that was in force at the time of giving the notice shall not be altered until either,

(a) an agreement or a new agreement comes into force or the agreement is renewed, as the case may be; or

(b) subject to subsection 27(2) and subsection 68(5), sixty days have elapsed after the Commission has made public the report of the fact finder as provided in section 26,

whichever first occurs.

11. Obligation to negotiate.—The parties shall meet within thirty days from the giving of the notice and they shall negotiate in good faith and make every reasonable effort to make an agreement or to renew the agreement, as the case requires.

12. Parties may choose procedures to reach agreement.—(1) The parties, at any time during negotiations to make or renew an agreement, may agree to,

(a) request the Commission to assign a person to assist the parties to make or renew the agreement;

(b) request the Commission to appoint a fact finder as provided in Part III; or

(c) refer all matters remaining in dispute between them that may be provided for in an agreement to,

(i) an arbitrator or a board of arbitration for determination as provided in Part IV, or

(ii) a selector for determination as provided in Part V.

(2) **Effect of choice of procedure.**—Where the parties refer all matters remaining in dispute between them to an arbitrator or a board of arbitration or to a selector pursuant to clause (1)(c), no teacher who is a member of a branch affiliate that is a party shall engage in a strike against the board that is a party and the board shall not lock out or declare a state of lock-out to exist against members of the branch affiliate that is a party.

13. Where Commission may assign person to assist parties.—The Commission may, in the exercise of its own discretion, at any time assign a person to assist the parties to make or renew an agreement.

PART III

FACT FINDING

14. Appointment of fact finder.—The Commission shall appoint forthwith a person as a fact finder during negotiations to make or renew an agreement if the parties have not referred all matters remaining in dispute between them to an arbitrator or board of arbitration as provided in Part IV or a selector as provided in Part V and,

(a) one or both of the parties gives notice to the Commission that an impasse has been

reached in the negotiations and requests the appointment of a fact finder, and the Commission approves the request;
(b) the Commission is of the opinion that an impasse has been reached in the negotiations; or
(c) the agreement that was in operation in respect of the parties expires during negotiations between the parties to make or renew an agreement, and fact finding has not taken place as provided in this Part.

15. Parties may proceed to make agreement or to arbitration or selection procedure.—The parties to negotiations to make or renew an agreement may, despite the appointment of a fact finder,
(a) make or renew the agreement; or
(b) agree to refer all matters remaining in dispute between them to,
(i) an arbitrator or a board of arbitration for determination as provided in Part IV, or
(ii) a selector for determination as provided in Part V,
and upon the giving of notice to the Commission by the parties that they have so acted, the appointment of the fact finder is terminated.

16. Persons prohibited as fact finder.—No person shall be appointed a fact finder who has a direct pecuniary interest in the matters coming before him or her or who is acting or has, within the period of six months immediately before the date of his or her appointment, acted as solicitor, counsel, negotiator, advisor or agent of either of the parties, but no person shall be deemed to have a direct pecuniary interest by reason only of being a ratepayer within the area of jurisdiction of the board that is a party.

17. Vacancy.—Where a fact finder ceases to act by reason of withdrawal, death or otherwise before submitting his or her report to the Commission, the Commission shall appoint another person in the fact finder's stead and such person shall commence the work of the fact finder anew.

18. Notice of appointment of fact finder.—Where the Commission appoints a fact finder, the Commission shall give written notice to each of the parties of the appointment of and the name and address of the fact finder.

19. Notice of matters agreed upon and matters in dispute.—(1) Within seven days after the receipt of notice from the Commission of the appointment of the fact finder, each party shall give written notice to the fact finder and to the other party setting out all the matters that the parties have agreed upon for inclusion in an agreement and all the matters remaining in dispute between the parties.

(2) **Where notice not given.**—Where a party fails to comply with subsection (1), the fact finder may make a determination of the matters mentioned in subsection (1) and may then proceed pursuant to this Part.

20. Duty of fact finder.—(1) It is the duty of a fact finder to confer with the parties and to inquire into, ascertain and make a report setting out the matters agreed upon by the parties for inclusion in an agreement and the matters remaining in dispute between the parties.

(2) **What report may contain.**—A fact finder may, in his or her report, include findings in respect of any matter that he or she considers relevant to the making of an agreement between

the parties and recommend terms of settlement of the matters remaining in dispute between the parties.

21. Matters that may be considered by fact finder.—In inquiring into and ascertaining the matters remaining in dispute between the parties, the fact finder amy inquire into and consider any matter that the fact finder considers relevant to the making of an agreement between the parties including, without limiting the foregoing,

(a) the conditions of employment in occupations outside the public teaching sector;
(b) the effect of geographic or other local factors on the terms and conditions of employment;
(c) the cost to the board of the proposal of either party;
(d) the interests and welfare of the public.

22. Procedure of fact finder.—The fact finder shall determine his or her own procedure under guidelines established by the Commission and, where the fact finder requests information from a party, the party shall provide the fact finder with full and complete information.

23. Submission of report of fact finder.—The fact finder shall submit his or her report to the Commission within thirty days after the date of his or her appointment or within such longer period of time as the Commission, with the agreement of the parties, may direct and the Commission shall forthwith give a copy of the report to each of the parties.

24. Report not binding.—The report of the fact finder is not binding on the parties but is made for the advice and guidance of the parties and upon receipt of the report the parties shall endeavour, in good faith, to make an agreement or to renew the agreement, as the case may be.

25. Assignment of assistance.—(1) Where the Commission has given a copy of the report of the fact finder to each of the parties and the Commission is of the opinion that the parties will or are likely to benefit from assistance, the Commission may assign a person to assist the parties to make or renew, as the case may be, the agreement.

(2) **Idem.**—Where the Commission has given a copy of the report of the fact finder to each of the parties and both of the parties request assistance from the Commission, the Commission shall assign a person to assist the parties to make or renew, as the case may be, the agreement.

26. Where report confidential.—(1) If the parties make or renew, as the case may be, an agreement within fifteen days after the Commission has given a copy of the report to each of the parties, the report shall not be made public by the Commission, either of the parties or by any person.

(2) **Release of report.**—If the parties do not make an agreement, or renew the agreement, as the case may be, within the period of time specified in subsection (1), the Commission shall make public the report of the fact finder.

(3) **Deferral of release.**—Despite subsections (1) and (2), where both parties agree and the Commission approves, the Commission may defer making public the report of the fact finder for an additional period of not more than five days.

27. Parties may agree to refer matters in dispute.—(1) If the parties do not make or renew, as the case may be, an agreement within fifteen days after the Commission has given a copy of the report of the fact finder to each of the parties, the parties may agree to refer all matters in dispute between them that may be provided for in an agreement to,

    (a) an arbitrator or a board of arbitration for determination as provided in Part IV; or

    (b) a selector for determination as provided in Part V.

(2) **Effect of choice of procedure.**—Where, pursuant to subsection (1), the parties refer all matters remaining in dispute between them that may be provided for in an agreement to an arbitrator or a board of arbitration or refer all such matters to a selector and either of the parties submits its final offer to the selector,

    (a) the terms of the agreement, if any, in force between the parties at the time of the giving of notice of desire to negotiate pursuant to subsection 10(1) or (2), shall not be altered until an agreement is made or renewed between the parties; and

    (b) no teacher who is a member of a branch affiliate that is a party shall engage in a strike against the board that is a party and the board shall not lock out or declare a state of lock-out to exist against members of the branch affiliate that is a party.

PART IV

VOLUNTARY BINDING ARBITRATION

28. Parties to give notice to Commission where arbitration agreed upon.—(1) Where the parties agree to refer all matters remaining in dispute between them that may be provided for in an agreement to an arbitrator or a board of arbitration, the parties shall jointly give written notice to the Commission that they have so agreed and the notice shall state,

    (a) that the parties agree to refer the matters to an arbitrator and,

        (i) the date of appointment and the name and address of the arbitrator, or

        (ii) that the parties have not appointed the arbitrator and that the parties request the Commission to appoint the arbitrator; or

    (b) that the parties agree to refer the matters to a board of arbitration and,

        (i) that the parties have each appointed a person as a member of the board of arbitration and shall set out the names and addresses of the two members so appointed, or

        (ii) that both of the parties or one of them, as the case may be, has not appointed a person as a member of the board of arbitration and that the parties request the Commission to appoint the members or member, as the case may be, of the board,

and the notice shall state that the decision of the arbitrator or board of arbitration will be accepted by the parties as binding upon them.

(2) **Parties not to withdraw.**—Except as provided in section 56, a party shall not withdraw from arbitration proceedings under this Part after notice is given to the Commission in accordance with subsection (1).

(3) **Where appointments made by Commission.**—Where the parties, in the notice mentioned in subsection (1), request the Commission to appoint the arbitrator or the members or one of the members of the board of arbitration, the Commission shall make the appointment

or appointments and shall forthwith thereafter give notice thereof to the parties setting out the name and address of the appointee or the names and addresses of the appointees, as the case may be, together with the date of the appointment or appointments.

(4) **Appointment of chair by members.**—Where the parties agree to refer all matters remaining in dispute between them to a board of arbitration, the two members of the board of arbitration shall, within ten days after the giving of notice of their appointment by the parties or by the Commission, as the case may be, appoint a third person to be chair of the board of arbitration and the chair shall forthwith give written notice to the Commission of his or her appointment.

(5) **Where Commission to appoint chair.**—Where the two members of the board of arbitration are unable to appoint or to agree on the appointment of the chair of the board of arbitration within the period of time set out in subsection (4), the Commission shall appoint the chair and shall give notice of the appointment to the two members and to the parties and the notice shall set out the name and address of the person appointed and the date of the appointment.

29. Persons prohibited as arbitrator or members or chair of board of arbitration.—No person shall be appointed an arbitrator or member or chair of a board of arbitration who has a direct pecuniary interest in the matters coming before him or her or who is acting or has, within the period of six months immediately before the date of his or her appointment, acted as solicitor, counsel, negotiator, advisor or agent of either of the parties, but no person shall be deemed to have a direct pecuniary interest by reason only of being a ratepayer within the area of jurisdiction of the board that is a party.

30. Vacancy.—(1) Where a member of a board of arbitration is unable to enter on or to carry on his or her duties so as to enable a decision to be rendered within the period of time required by subsection (2) or ceases to act by reason of withdrawal or death before the board of arbitration has completed its work, a replacement shall be appointed by the body that appointed the member, and the board of arbitration shall continue to function as if such member were a member of the board of arbitration from the beginning.

(2) **Where chair unable to act.**—Where the chair of a board of arbitration is unable to enter on or to carry on his or her duties so as to enable a decision to be rendered within sixty days after his or her appointment or within such longer period of time as may be provided in writing by the board of arbitration and consented to by the Commission or ceases to act by reason of withdrawal or death, the Commission shall give notice thereof to the members of the board of arbitration who shall within seven days of the giving of the notice appoint a person to be the chair and if the appointment is not so made by the members it shall be made by the Commission, and after the chair is appointed the arbitration shall begin anew.

(3) **Where arbitrator unable to act.**—Where an arbitrator is unable to enter on or to carry on his or her duties so as to enable a decision to be rendered within sixty days after his or her appointment or within such longer period of time as may be provided in writing by the arbitrator and consented to by the Commission or ceases to act by reason of withdrawal or death, the Commission shall give notice thereof to the parties who shall within seven days of the giving of the notice appoint a person to be the arbitrator and if the appointment is not so made it shall be made by the Commission and after the arbitrator is appointed the arbitration shall begin anew.

PART IV — VOLUNTARY BINDING ARBITRATION

31. Notice of matters agreed upon and matters in dispute.—Within seven days after the giving of notice that the arbitrator or the chair of the board of arbitration, as the case may be, has been appointed, each party shall give written notice to the arbitrator or chair and to the other party setting out all the matters that the parties have agreed upon for inclusion in an agreement and all the matters remaining in dispute between the parties.

32. Procedure.—(1) The arbitrator or board of arbitration shall determine his, her or its own procedure but shall give full opportunity to the parties to present their evidence and make their submissions.

(2) **Idem.**—If the members of a board of arbitration are unable to agree among themselves on matters of procedure or as to the admissibility of evidence, the decision of the chair governs.

(3) **Decision.**—The decision of a majority of a board of arbitration is the decision of the board, but if there is no majority, the decision of the chair is the decision of the board.

33. Powers of arbitrator or board of arbitration.—(1) The arbitrator or board of arbitration has power,

   (a) to summon any person,
       (i) to give oral or written evidence on oath or affirmation to the arbitrator or board of arbitration, or
       (ii) to produce in evidence for the arbitrator or board of arbitration such documents and other things as the arbitrator or board of arbitration may specify;
   (b) to administer oaths and affirmations;
   (c) to accept for or exclude from consideration any oral testimony, document or other thing, whether admissible in a court of law or not.

(2) **Stated case for contempt for failure to attend, etc.**—Where any person without lawful excuse,

   (a) on being duly summoned under subsection (1) as a witness before the arbitrator or board of arbitration, as the case may be, makes default in so attending;
   (b) being in attendance as a witness before the arbitrator or board of arbitration, as the case may be, refuses to take an oath or to make an affirmation legally required by the arbitrator or board of arbitration to be taken or made, or to produce any document or thing in his or her power or control legally required by the arbitrator or board of arbitration to be produced, or to answer any question to which the arbitrator or board of arbitration may legally require an answer; or
   (c) does any other thing that would, if the arbitrator or board of arbitration had been a court of law having power to commit for contempt, have been contempt of that court,

the arbitrator or board of arbitration may state a case to the Divisional Court setting out the facts and that court may, on the application of the arbitrator or board of arbitration, inquire into the matter and, after hearing any witnesses who may be produced against or on behalf of that person and after hearing any statement that may be offered in defence, punish or take steps for the punishment of that person in like manner as if the person had been guilty of contempt of the court.

34. Duty of arbitrator or board of arbitration.—(1) The arbitrator or board of arbitration shall inquire into, consider and decide on all matters remaining in dispute between the parties.

(2) **Matters that may be considered by arbitrator or board of arbitration.**—In the conduct of proceedings and in reaching a decision in respect of a matter in dispute, the arbitrator or board of arbitration may inquire into and consider any matter that the arbitrator or board of arbitration considers relevant to the making of an agreement between the parties.

35. **Time for report of arbitrator or board of arbitration.**—(1) The arbitrator or board of arbitration shall complete the consideration of all matters in dispute between the parties and shall report in writing the decision of the arbitrator or board of arbitration on the matters to the parties and to the Commission within sixty days after the giving of notice of the appointment of the arbitrator or of the appointment of the chair of the board of arbitration, as the case may be, or within such longer period of time as may be provided in writing by the arbitrator or board of arbitration and consented to by the Commission.

(2) **Effect of decision.**—The decision of the arbitrator or board of arbitration is binding upon the parties and they shall comply in good faith with the decision.

36. **Preparation and execution of document by parties.**—(1) Within thirty days after receipt by the parties of the report of the arbitrator or board of arbitration, as the case may be, the parties shall prepare a document giving effect to all matters agreed upon by the parties and the decision of the arbitrator or board of arbitration and shall execute the document and thereupon it constitutes an agreement.

(2) **Where arbitrator or board of arbitration to prepare document.**—If the parties fail to execute the document within the period of time mentioned in subsection (1), the arbitrator or board of arbitration, as the case may be, shall prepare the document and submit it to the parties and shall fix the time within which and the place where the parties shall execute the document.

(3) **Failure to execute document.**—If the parties or either of them fail to execute the document within the time fixed by the arbitrator or the board of arbitration, the document shall be deemed to be in effect as though it had been executed by the parties and the document thereupon constitutes an agreement.

PART V

FINAL OFFER SELECTION

37. **Parties to give notice to Commission where selection agreed upon.**—(1) Where the parties agree to refer all matters remaining in dispute between them that may be provided for in an agreement to a selector, the parties shall jointly give written notice to the Commission that they have so agreed and the notice shall state that the parties agree to refer the matters to a selector and,
   (a) the date of appointment and the name and address of the selector; or
   (b) that the parties have not appointed the selector and that the parties request the Commission to appoint the selector.

(2) **Statement by parties.**—The parties shall, together with the notice mentioned in subsection (1), give to the Commission a written statement signed by the parties setting out that neither party will withdraw from the proceedings after the final offers of the parties have

PART V — FINAL OFFER SELECTION **S. 44**

been submitted to the selector and that the decision of the selector will be accepted by the parties as binding upon them.

(3) **Parties not to withdraw.**—Except as provided in section 56, where the parties give to the Commission a written statement in accordance with subsection (2), a party shall not withdraw from the proceedings after the final offer of either of the parties has been submitted to the selector.

(4) **Where Commission appoints selector.**—Where the parties request the Commission to appoint the selector, the Commission shall make the appointment and give notice of the appointment of the selector to the parties and the notice shall set out the name and address of the person appointed and the date of the appointment.

38. Persons prohibited as selector.—No person shall be appointed a selector who has a direct pecuniary interest in the matters coming before him or her or who is acting or has, within the period of six months immediately before the date of his or her appointment, acted as solicitor, counsel, negotiator, advisor or agent of either of the parties, but no person shall be deemed to have a direct pecuniary interest by reason only of being a ratepayer within the area of jurisdiction of the board that is a party.

39. Selector unable to act.—Where a selector is unable to enter on or to carry on his or her duties so as to enable a decision to be rendered within the time specified by this Act or such longer period of time as may be provided in writing by the selector and consented to by the Commission or ceases to act by reason of withdrawal or death, the Commission shall give notice thereof to the parties who shall within seven days of the giving of the notice appoint a person to be the selector, and if the appointment is not so made by the parties it shall be made by the Commission, and after the selector is appointed, the selection procedure shall begin anew.

40. Notice of matters agreed upon and matters in dispute.—Within seven days after the giving of notice that the selector has been appointed, the parties shall jointly give written notice to the selector setting out all matters that the parties have agreed upon for inclusion in an agreement and all the matters remaining in dispute between the parties.

41. Notice of final offer.—Within fifteen days after the giving of notice that the selector has been appointed, each party shall give written notice to the selector setting out the final offer of the party on all the matters remaining in dispute between the parties and may submit with the notice a written statement in support of the final offer set out in the notice.

42. Final offer of opposite party.—Upon receiving the notices of the parties setting out the final offer of each party, the selector shall forthwith give to each party a copy of the notice setting out the final offer of the opposite party on all the matters remaining in dispute between the parties together with a copy of the statement, if any, of the opposite party submitted in support of the final offer of the opposite party.

43. Written response.—Each party may, within ten days after being given a copy of the final offer and supporting statement, if any, of the opposite party, give to the selector a written reply and the selector shall forthwith give a copy of the reply of each party to the opposite party.

44. Hearing.—Within fifteen days after each party has been given a copy of the final offer and supporting statement, if any, of the opposite party, or within such longer period of time as may be provided in writing by the selector and consented to by the Commission, the selector shall hold a hearing in respect of the matters remaining in dispute between the parties and may, before making a selection, hold a further hearing or hearings.

45. Parties may dispense with hearing.—The parties may agree to dispense with a hearing by the selector and in such case may jointly give written notice to the selector that they have so agreed, and the selector, upon receipt of the notice, shall not hold a hearing but shall proceed to his or her decision.

46. Procedure.—(1) The selector shall determine his or her own procedure but, in holding a hearing, shall give full opportunity to the parties to present their evidence and make their submissions.

(2) **Powers of selector.**—The selector has power,
- (a) to summon any person,
    - (i) to give oral or written evidence on oath or affirmation to the selector, or
    - (ii) to produce in evidence for the selector such documents and other things as the selector may specify;
- (b) to administer oaths and affirmations;
- (c) to accept for or exclude from consideration any oral testimony, document or other thing, whether admissible in a court of law or not.

(3) **Stated case for contempt for failure to attend, etc.**—Where any person without lawful excuse,
- (a) on being duly summoned under subsection (2) as a witness before the selector makes default in so attending;
- (b) being in attendance as a witness before the selector, refuses to take an oath or to make an affirmation legally required by the selector to be taken or made, or to produce any document or thing in his or her power or control legally required by the selector to be produced, or to answer any question to which the selector may legally require an answer; or
- (c) does any other thing that would, if the selector had been a court of law having power to commit for contempt, have been contempt of that court,

the selector may state a case to the Divisional Court setting out the facts and that court may, on the application of the selector, inquire into the matter and, after hearing any witnesses who may be produced against or on behalf of that person and after hearing any statement that may be offered in defence, punish or take steps for the punishment of that person in like manner as if the person had been guilty of contempt of the court.

47. Selection of final offer.—The selector shall, within fifteen days after the conclusion of the hearing or hearings or within fifteen days after the giving of the notice by the parties that they have agreed to dispense with a hearing, as the case may be, or within such longer period of time as may be provided in writing by the selector and consented to by the Commission, make a decision selecting all of one of the final offers on all matters remaining in dispute between the parties given to the selector by one or the other of the parties.

48. Effect of decision.—The decision of the selector is binding upon the parties and they shall comply in good faith with the decision.

49. Preparation and execution of document by parties.—(1) Within thirty days after receipt of notice of the decision of the selector, the parties shall prepare a document giving effect to all matters agreed upon by the parties and the decision of the selector and shall execute the document and thereupon it constitutes an agreement.

(2) **Where selector to prepare document.**—If the parties fail to execute the document within the period of time mentioned in subsection (1), the selector shall prepare the document and submit it to the parties and shall fix the time within which and the place where the parties shall execute the document.

(3) **Failure to execute document.**—If the parties or either of them fail to execute the document within the time fixed by the selector, the document shall be deemed to be in effect as though it had been executed by the parties and the document thereupon constitutes an agreement.

PART VI

AGREEMENTS

50. Term of agreement.—Every agreement shall,
(a) provide for a term of operation of not less than one year;
(b) state that it is effective on and after the 1st day of September in the year in which it is to come into operation; and
(c) state that it expires on the 31st day of August in the year in which it ceases to operate.

51. Conflict.—(1) Where a conflict appears between a provision of an agreement and a provision of an Act or regulation, the provision of the Act or regulation prevails.

(2) **Application of *Constitution Act, 1867*—**The provisions of this Act shall not be construed as to prejudicially affect the rights and privileges with respect to the employment of teachers enjoyed by Roman Catholic and Protestant separate school boards under the *Constitution Act, 1867*.

52. Resolution of matters arising out of agreement.—(1) Unless an agreement otherwise provides for the final and binding settlement of all differences between the parties arising from the interpretation, application, administration or alleged contravention of the agreement, the agreement is deemed to include a provision to the following effect:

> Where a difference arises between the parties relating to the interpretation, application or administration of this agreement, or where an allegation is made that this agreement has been contravened, either of the parties may, after exhausting any grievance procedure established by this agreement, notify the other party in writing of its desire to submit the difference or allegation to arbitration and the notice shall contain the name of the first party's appointee to an arbitration board. The recipient of the notice shall within five days inform the other party either that it accepts the other party's appointee as a single arbitrator or inform the other party of the name of its appointee to the arbitration board. Where two appointees are so selected they shall, within five days of the appointment of the second of them, appoint a third person who shall be the chair. If the recipient of the notice fails to appoint an arbitrator or if the two

appointees fail to agree upon a chair within the time limited, the appointment shall be made by the Commission upon the request of either party. The single arbitrator or the arbitration board, as the case may be, shall hear and determine the difference or allegation and shall issue a decision and the decision is final and binding upon the parties and upon any employee or employer affected by it. The decision of a majority is the decision of the arbitration board, but, if there is no majority, the decision of the chair governs. The arbitrator or arbitration board, as the case may be, shall not by his, her or its decision add to, delete from, modify or otherwise amend the provisions of this agreement.

(2) **Enforcement of arbitration decision.**—Where a party or a teacher fails to comply with any of the terms of a decision of an arbitrator or arbitration board, any party or any teacher affected by the decision may file with the Ontario Court (General Division) a copy of the decision of the arbitrator or arbitration board, exclusive of the reasons therefor and certified by the arbitrator or the chair of the arbitration board to be a true copy of the decision, whereupon the decision shall be entered in the same way as an order of that court and is enforceable as such.

53. Provision against strikes and lock-outs.—Every agreement shall be deemed to provide that there will be no strike or lock-out during the term of the agreement or of any renewal of the agreement.

54. Agreement to form part of contract of employment.—(1) An agreement between a board and a branch affiliate shall be deemed to form part of the contract of employment between the board and each teacher who is a member of the branch affiliate.

(2) **Conflict.**—Where a conflict appears between a provision of any other part of a contract of employment and a provision of the agreement referred to in subsection (1), the provision of the agreement prevails, but no agreement shall conflict with the form of contract prescribed by the regulations under the *Education Act*.

55. Notice of agreement.—Where the parties agree on all the matters to be included in an agreement, whether during or at the conclusion of negotiations or other proceedings under this Act, the chief executive officer of the board or of each of the boards, as the case may be, that is a party shall forthwith give notice thereof to the Commission.

56. Where agreement reached.—Where the parties agree on all the matters to be included in an agreement, whether during or at the conclusion of negotiations or other proceedings under this Act, they shall prepare a document incorporating all the matters agreed upon and shall execute the document and the document thereupon constitutes an agreement.

57. Notice to Commission of execution of agreement.—Upon the execution of an agreement, each party to the agreement shall forthwith give notice thereof, together with a copy of the agreement, to the Commission.

58. Binding effect of agreement.—An agreement is binding upon the board and upon the branch affiliate that is a party to it and upon the teachers employed by the board who are members of the branch affiliate.

PART VII

EDUCATION RELATIONS COMMISSION

59. Commission continued.—(1) The Education Relations Commission is continued under the name Education Relations Commission in English and Commission des relations de travail en éducation in French.

(2) **Composition.**—The Commission shall be composed of five persons who shall be appointed by the Lieutenant Governor in Council.

(3) **Chair and vice-chair.**—The Lieutenant Governor in Council shall designate a chair and a vice-chair from among the members of the Commission.

(4) **Acting chair.**—In the case of the absence or inability to act of the chair or of there being a vacancy in the office of the chair, the vice-chair shall act as and have all the powers of the chair and in the absence of the chair and vice-chair from any meeting of the Commission, the members of the Commission present at the meeting shall appoint an acting chair who shall act as and have all the powers of the chair during the meeting.

(5) **Term of office.**—The members of the Commission shall be appointed for a term of one, two or three years so that as nearly as possible one-third of the members shall retire each year.

(6) **Vacancy.**—Every vacancy on the Commission caused by the death, resignation or incapacity of a member may be filled by the appointment by the Lieutenant Governor in Council of a person to hold office for the remainder of the term of such member.

(7) **Reappointment.**—Each of the members of the Commission is eligible for reappointment upon the expiration of his or her term of office.

(8) **Quorum.**—Three members of the Commission constitute a quorum and are sufficient for the exercise of all the authority of the Commission.

(9) **Exercising powers.**—The powers of the Commission shall be exercised by resolution and the Commission may pass resolutions governing the calling of and the proceedings at meetings and specifying the powers and duties of employees of the Commission and generally dealing with the carrying out of its duties.

(10) **Remuneration.**—The members of the Commission shall be paid such remuneration and expenses as are determined by the Lieutenant Governor in Council.

(11) **Employees.**—Subject to the approval of the Lieutenant Governor in Council, the Commission may,
   (a) establish job classifications, salary ranges and terms and conditions of employment for its employees; and
   (b) appoint and pay such employees as are considered proper.

(12) **Pension plan.**—The Commission shall be deemed to have been designated by the Lieutenant Governor in Council under the *Public Service Pension Act* as a commission whose permanent employees are required to be members of the Public Service Pension Plan.

(13) **Professional and other assistance.**—The Commission may engage persons other than those employed pursuant to subsection (11) to provide professional, technical or other

assistance to or on behalf of the Commission, and may prescribe the terms of engagement and provide for payment of the remuneration and expenses of such persons.

60. Duties of Commission.—(1) It is the duty of the Commission,

(a) to carry out the duties imposed on it by this Act and such other functions as may, in the opinion of the Commission, be necessary to carry out the intent and purpose of this Act;

(b) to maintain an awareness of negotiations between teachers and boards;

(c) to compile statistical information on the supply, distribution, professional activities and salaries of teachers;

(d) to provide such assistance to parties as may facilitate the making or renewing of agreements;

(e) to select and, where necessary, to train persons who may act as mediators, fact finders, arbitrators or selectors;

(f) to determine, at the request of either party or in the exercise of its discretion, whether or not either of the parties is or was negotiating in good faith and making every reasonable effort to make or renew an agreement;

(g) to determine the manner of conducting and to supervise votes by secret ballot pursuant to this Act; and

(h) to advise the Lieutenant Governor in Council when, in the opinion of the Commission, the continuance of a strike, lock-out or closing of a school or schools will place in jeopardy the successful completion of courses of study by the students affected by the strike, lock-out or closing of the school or schools.

(2) **Provision of information.**—The Commission may request a board to provide information necessary to compile the statistical information referred to in subsection (1) and a board shall comply with such a request within a reasonable period of time.

(3) **Annual report.**—The Commission shall annually prepare a report on the affairs of the Commission for the preceding year and the report shall be tabled in the Legislature.

61. Testimony by member of Commission.—No member of the Commission shall be required to give testimony in any proceeding under this Act with regard to information obtained in the discharge of his or her duties as a member of the Commission.

62. Money.—The money required for the purposes of the Commission shall be paid out of the money appropriated therefor by the Legislature.

PART VIII

STRIKES AND LOCK-OUTS

63. Notice of strike.—No teacher shall take part in a strike against the board that employs the teacher unless,

(a) there is no agreement in operation that is deemed under this Act to form part of the contract of employment between the board and the teacher;

(b) notice of desire to negotiate to make or renew an agreement has been given by either party;

(c) all the matters remaining in dispute between the board and the branch affiliate that represents the teacher have been referred to a fact finder and fifteen days have elapsed after the Commission has made public the report of the fact finder;

(d) the offer of the board in respect of all matters agreed upon by the parties and in respect of all matters remaining in dispute between the parties last received by the branch affiliate that represents the teacher is submitted to and rejected by the teachers composing the branch affiliate by a vote by secret ballot conducted under the supervision of and in the manner determined by the Commission;

(e) the teachers composing the branch affiliate that represents the teacher have voted, not earlier than the vote referred to in clause (d) and not before the end of the fifteen-day period referred to in clause (c), in favour of a strike by a vote by secret ballot conducted under the supervision of and in the manner determined by the Commission; and

(f) after a vote in favour of a strike in accordance with clause (e), the branch affiliate that represents the teacher gives to the board written notice of the strike and of the date on which the strike will commence at least five days before the commencement of the strike.

64. Principals and vice-principals.—(1) A principal and a vice-principal shall be members of a branch affiliate.

(2) **Idem, membership in branch affiliate.**—Despite subsection (1), in the event of a strike by the members of a branch affiliate each principal and vice-principal who is a member of the branch affiliate shall remain on duty during the strike or any related lock-out or state of lock-out or closing of a school or schools.

65. Unlawful strike.—(1) The Federation shall not and no affiliate or branch affiliate shall call or authorize or threaten to call or authorize an unlawful strike.

(2) **Idem.**—No officer, official or agent of the Federation, an affiliate or a branch affiliate or member of a branch affiliate shall counsel, procure, support or encourage an unlawful strike or threaten an unlawful strike.

66. Unlawful lock-out.—(1) The Council shall not and no member association or board shall call or authorize or threaten to call or authorize an unlawful lock-out.

(2) **Idem.**—No officer, official or agent of the Council, a member association or a board or member of a board shall counsel, procure, support or encourage an unlawful lock-out or threaten an unlawful lock-out.

67. Declaration of unlawful strike.—(1) Where the Federation, an affiliate or a branch affiliate calls or authorizes a strike or teachers take part in a strike against a board that the board, a member association, the Council or any person normally resident within the jurisdiction of the board alleges is unlawful, the board, member association, Council or person may apply to the Ontario Labour Relations Board for a declaration that the strike is unlawful, and the Board may make the declaration.

(2) **Declaration of unlawful lock-out.**—Where the Council, a member association or a board calls or authorizes a lock-out of members of a branch affiliate that the branch affiliate, an affiliate, the Federation or any person normally resident within the jurisdiction of the board

alleges is unlawful, the branch affiliate, affiliate, Federation or person may apply to the Ontario Labour Relations Board for a declaration that the lock-out is unlawful, and the Board may make the declaration.

(3) **Direction by O.L.R.B.**—Where the Ontario Labour Relations Board makes a declaration under subsection (1) or (2), the Board in its discretion may, in addition, direct what action, if any, a person, teacher, branch affiliate, affiliate, the Federation, a board, member association or the Council and their officers, officials or agents shall do or refrain from doing with respect to the unlawful strike or unlawful lock-out.

(4) **Enforcement of direction by court.**—The Ontario Labour Relations Board shall file with the Ontario Court (General Division) a copy of a direction made under subsection (3), exclusive of the reasons therefor, whereupon the direction shall be entered in the same way as an order of the court and is enforceable as such.

68. Lock-out.—(1) Where a lawful strike takes place against a board, the board may lock out or declare a state of lock-out to exist against all members, other than principals or vice-principals, of the branch affiliate that represents teachers engaged in the strike.

(2) **Idem.**—No board shall lock out or declare a state of lock-out to exist or close a school or schools unless and until the proposal of the branch affiliate in respect of all matters agreed upon by the parties and in respect of all matters remaining in dispute between the parties last received by the board has been presented to a meeting of the board in public session.

(3) **Idem.**—Except as provided in subsection (1), a board shall not lock out a teacher.

(4) **Closing of school.**—Where a lawful strike takes place against a board, the board may close a school or schools where the board is of the opinion that,

(a) the safety of students may be endangered;
(b) the school building or the equipment or supplies therein may not be adequately protected during the strike; or
(c) the strike will substantially interfere with the operation of the school.

(5) **Payment of teachers.**—A teacher shall not be paid his or her salary in respect of the days on which,

(a) the teacher takes part in a strike, other than a strike as defined in clause (b) of the definition of "strike" in section 1;
(b) the teacher is locked out; or
(c) the school in which the teacher is employed is closed pursuant to subsection (4).

(6) **Resumption of strike or new strike.**—Where a lawful strike is terminated without an agreement coming into effect, no teacher shall take part in a resumption of the strike or take part in a new strike except after the provisions of clauses 63(d), (e) and (f) have again been complied with in respect of such resumption or new strike.

(7) **Application of section.**—This section applies despite any provision of the *Education Act*.

69. Participation in lawful strike.—The contract of employment or position of a teacher shall not be terminated by reason of his or her participation in a lawful strike.

70. Resignation etc. by teacher.—Nothing in this Act precludes a teacher,

PART IX — MISCELLANEOUS   S. 74

(a) from terminating his or her employment with a board in good faith in accordance with the provisions of his or her contract of employment;
(b) from withdrawing a voluntary service in good faith on an individual basis.

PART IX

MISCELLANEOUS

71. Copies of notice to be given to Commission.—Where, under this Act, a party is required to give notice to another party, the party giving the notice shall also within the same time limit, if any, give a copy of the notice to the Commission.

72. Decisions, etc., of Commission and others not subject to review.—Except in respect of section 51, no decision, order, determination, direction, declaration or ruling of the Commission, a fact finder, an arbitrator or board of arbitration, a selector or the Ontario Labour Relations Board shall be questioned or reviewed in any court, and no order shall be made or process entered, or proceedings taken in any court, whether by way of injunction, declaratory judgment, certiorari, mandamus, prohibition, quo warranto, application for judicial review or otherwise, to question, review, prohibit or restrain the Commission, fact finder, arbitrator or board of arbitration, selector or the Ontario Labour Relations Board or the proceedings of any of them.

73. Service of notice.—Any notice or document required or authorized by this Act to be given shall,

(a) where it is to be given to the Commission, be delivered to the office of the Commission;
(b) where it is to be given to a board, be delivered to the office of the board;
(c) where it is to be given to a branch affiliate, be delivered to an officer of the branch affiliate;
(d) where it is to be given to an affiliate, the Council, the Federation or a member association, be delivered to the office of the affiliate, the Council, the Federation or the member association, as the case requires;
(e) where it is to be given to an arbitrator or selector, be delivered to the arbitrator or selector; and
(f) where it is to be given to a board of arbitration, be delivered to the chair or either of the other two members of the board of arbitration.

74. Costs.—(1) The expenditures incurred by a party in respect of a person appointed or retained by the party for the purpose of making or renewing an agreement shall be borne by the party and all other expenses, including fees for a single arbitrator, a selector or a chair of a board of arbitration shall be shared equally by the parties and such expenditures and fees shall be paid within sixty days after the agreement or renewal of agreement is executed or is deemed in effect as though it had been executed by the parties.

(2) **Idem.**—The fees and expenses, if any, of persons assigned by the Commission to assist parties to make or renew an agreement and of fact finders appointed by the Commission shall be paid by the Commission.

75. Statement as to officers of branch affiliate.—Where the Commission so directs, a branch affiliate shall file with the Commission, within the time prescribed in the direction, a statement signed by its president or secretary setting out the names and addresses of its officers.

76. Where vote by secret ballot required.—(1) Subject to subsection (2), a vote conducted by a branch affiliate to give approval to the terms of an agreement shall be a vote by secret ballot.

(2) **Idem.**—A vote conducted by a branch affiliate for the purpose of section 63 or for the purpose of giving approval to the terms of an agreement after the commencement of a strike shall be a vote by secret ballot conducted under the supervision of and in the manner determined by the Commission.

77. Contravention by teacher or trustee.—(1) Every person who contravenes any provision of this Act is guilty of an offence and on conviction is liable to a fine of not more than $1,000 for each day upon which the contravention occurs or continues.

(2) **Contravention by Council or Federation.**—The Council and every member association and every board and the Federation and every affiliate and every branch affiliate that contravenes any provision of this Act is guilty of an offence and on conviction is liable to a fine of not more than $25,000 for each day upon which such contravention occurs or continues.

(3) **Contravention of decision, etc.**—The contravention of a decision, order, determination, direction, declaration or ruling made under this Act is deemed, for the purposes of this section, to be a contravention of this Act.

(4) **Where officers also guilty of offence.**—Where the Council or a member association or the Federation or an affiliate or a branch affiliate is guilty of an offence under this Act, every officer or representative thereof, and where a board is guilty of an offence under this Act every member of the board, who assents to the commission of the offence shall be deemed to be a party to and guilty of the offence and is liable to a fine under subsection (1) as if he or she had been convicted of an offence under subsection (1).

(5) **Information.**—An information in respect of a contravention of any provision of this Act may be for one or more offences and no information, warrant, conviction or other proceedings in any such prosecution is objectionable or insufficient by reason of the fact that it relates to two or more offences.

(6) **Consent to prosecution.**—No prosecution for an offence under this Act shall be instituted except with the consent of the Ontario Labour Relations Board which may only be granted after affording an opportunity to the person or body seeking the consent and the person or body sought to be prosecuted to be heard.

(7) **Practice and procedure of O.L.R.B.**—The Ontario Labour Relations Board shall determine its own practice and procedure but shall give full opportunity to the parties to any proceedings to present their evidence and to make their submissions, and the Ontario Labour Relations Board may, subject to the approval of the Lieutenant Governor in Council, make rules governing its practice and procedure and the exercise of its powers and prescribing such forms as are considered advisable.

(8) **Decision of O.L.R.B.**—The decision of the majority of the members of the Ontario Labour Relations Board present and constituting a quorum is the decision of the Ontario Labour Relations Board, but, if there is no majority, the decision of the chair or vice-chair governs.

PART IX — MISCELLANEOUS S. 81

78. Style of prosecution.—A prosecution for an offence under this Act may be instituted against any body, association or organization in the name of the body, association or organization whether or not the body, association or organization is a body corporate and, for the purposes of any such prosecution, any unincorporated body, association or organization shall be deemed to be a body corporate.

79. Vicarious responsibilities.—Any act or thing done or omitted by an officer, official or agent of the Federation, an affiliate, a branch affiliate, the Council, a member association or a board or by a member of a board within the apparent scope of his or her authority to act on behalf of the Federation, affiliate, branch affiliate, Council, member association or board shall be deemed to be an act or thing done or omitted by the Federation, affiliate, branch affiliate, Council, member association or board, as the case may be.

80. Application.—(1) The *Arbitrations Act* does not apply to proceedings under this Act.

(2) **Idem.**—The *Statutory Powers Procedure Act* does not apply to proceedings under this Act other than in respect of a determination referred to in clause 60(1)(f).

(3) **Idem.**—Despite subjection (2), but subject to section 72, the *Statutory Powers Procedure Act* applies to proceedings before the Ontario Labour Relations Board under this Act.

81. Compellability of witnesses.—Despite any other provision of this Act,

(a) the Minister of Education;
(b) the Deputy Minister of Education;
(c) the chair, a vice-chair or a member of the Ontario Labour Relations Board;
(d) an arbitrator or member or chair of a board of arbitration; or
(e) a selector,

is not a compellable witness in any proceeding under this Act.

TEACHING PROFESSION ACT

TABLE OF CONTENTS

1. Definitions 465
2. Body corporate 465
3. Objects 465
4. Membership in Federation 465
5. Board of Governors 466
6. Executive 466
7. President and vice-presidents 466
8. Secretary-treasurer 467
9. Functions of executive 467
10. Conferences 467
11. Collection of fees 467
12. Regulations 468

TEACHING PROFESSION ACT
R.S.O. 1990, c. T.2, as am. S.O. 1991, Vol. 2, c. 52

1. Definitions.—In this Act,

"Board of Governors."—"Board of Governors" means the Board of Governors of the Federation; ("conseil d'administration")

"board of trustees."—"board of trustees" means a board of education, board of secondary school trustees, board of public school trustees, board of separate school trustees or divisional board of education; ("assemblée des conseillers scolaires")

"executive."—"executive" means the executive of the Federation; ("bureau")

"Federation."—"Federation" means The Ontario Teachers' Federation; ("Fédération")

"member."—"member" means a member of the Federation; ("membre")

"Minister."—"Minister" means the Minister of Education; ("ministre")

"Ministry."—"Ministry" means the Ministry of Education; ("ministère")

"regulations."—"regulations" means the regulations made under this Act; ("règlements")

"teacher."—"teacher" means a person who is legally qualified to teach in an elementary or secondary school and is under contract in accordance with Part X of the *Education Act* but does not include a supervisory officer, an instructor in a teacher-training institution or a person employed to teach in a school for a period not exceeding one month. ("enseignant")

2. Body corporate.—The federation of teachers known as The Ontario Teachers' Federation is continued as a body corporate, under the name The Ontario Teachers' Federation in English and Fédération des enseignantes et enseignants de l'Ontario in French.

3. Objects.—(1) The objects of the Federation are,

(a) to promote and advance the cause of education;

(b) to raise the status of the teaching profession;

(c) to promote and advance the interests of teachers and to secure conditions that will make possible the best professional service;

(d) to arouse and increase public interest in educational affairs;

(e) to co-operate with other teachers' organizations throughout the world having the same or like objects; and

(f) to represent all members of the pension plan established under the *Teachers' Pension Act* in the administration of the plan and the management of the pension fund.

4. Membership in Federation.—(1) Every teacher is a member of the Federation except,

(a) a teacher who has withdrawn from membership under subsection 4(1) or (2) of *The Teaching Profession Act*, being chapter 64 of the Statutes of Ontario, 1944;

(b) a teacher who,
  (i) at any time during World War II was a member of Her Majesty's forces or engaged on special war service designated by the regulations, and
  (ii) at the time of entering the forces or becoming engaged on such service was a teacher or was training to be a teacher at a provincial normal school or the Ontario College of Education, and

(iii) notifies the Minister and the secretary of the Board of Governors of his or her withdrawal from membership by registered letter posted not later than six months after he or she ceases to be in the forces or on special war service.

(2) **Associate members.**—Every student in a teachers' college or in a college of education in Ontario is an associate member of the Federation.

(3) **Persons receiving pension.**—Every person who was a member of the Federation upon retirement and who is receiving a pension or an allowance under the *Teachers' Pension Act* may, on request, be an associate member of the Federation.

5. Board of Governors.—(1) There shall be a Board of Governors of the Federation, which shall be composed of fifty members consisting of the immediate past president, the president, the first vice-president, the second vice-president and the secretary-treasurer of each of, The Ontario Secondary School Teachers' Federation, The Federation of Women Teachers' Associations of Ontario, The Ontario Public School Teachers' Federation, the Association des enseignantes et des enseignants franco-ontariens and The Ontario English Catholic Teachers' Association, and five representatives of each of such federations or associations, who shall be elected annually at the annual meeting of the federation or association from among its members.

(2) **Term of office.**—The members of the Board of Governors shall take office at the conclusion of the annual meeting of the Federation and shall hold office until their successors take office.

(3) **Vacancies.**—If a vacancy occurs on the Board of Governors, it shall be filled by the executive of the affiliated body that the person who vacated the office represented and the person so named to fill the vacancy shall hold office for the remainder of the term of the person who vacated the office.

6. Executive.—(1) There shall be an executive of the Federation, which shall be composed of eleven members as follows,

(a) the immediate past president, the president, the first vice-president, the second vice-president and the third vice-president of the Federation;

(b) one representative of The Ontario Secondary School Teachers' Federation, one representative of The Federation of Women Teachers' Associations of Ontario, one representative of The Ontario Public School Teachers' Federation, one representative of the Association des enseignantes et des enseignants franco-ontariens and one representative of The Ontario English Catholic Teachers' Association, who shall be elected annually at the annual meeting of the Board of Governors from among its members; and

(c) the secretary-treasurer of the Federation.

(2) **Term of office.**—The members of the executive shall take office at the conclusion of the annual meeting of the Federation and shall hold office until their successors take office.

(3) **Vacancies.**—If a vacancy occurs on the executive, it may be filled by the Board of Governors from among its members who represent the affiliated body that the person who vacated the office represented, and the person so named shall hold office for the remainder of the term of the person who vacated the office.

7. President and vice-presidents.—There shall be a president, a first vice-president, a second vice-president and a third vice-president of the Federation who shall be elected annually at the annual meeting of the Board of Governors from among its members in such a manner that the officers of the immediate past president, president, first vice-president, second vice-president and third vice-president shall represent each of the affiliated bodies.

8. Secretary-treasurer.—There shall be a secretary-treasurer of the Federation appointed by the Board of Governors who may be a member of the Board of Governors and who shall receive such remuneration as may be fixed by the Board of Governors.

9. Functions of executive.—The executive is responsible for carrying on the business of the Federation and may,

- (a) subject to the approval of the Minister, acquire and hold in the name of the Federation such real and personal property as may be necessary for the purposes of the Federation and may alienate, mortgage, lease or otherwise dispose of such property as occasion may require;
- (b) invest the funds of the Federation in any securities in which a trustee is authorized to invest money under the *Trustee Act*;
- (c) make such grants as it considers advisable to organizations having the same or like objects as the Federation;
- (d) act as the representative of the members of the pension plan established under the *Teachers' Pension Act* including carrying out the following functions:
    1. Appointing persons to be members of the Ontario Teachers' Pension Plan Board created under that Act.
    2. Entering into agreements as described in that Act.
    3. Negotiating, agreeing to or directing amendments to the plan as permitted under that Act or an agreement entered into under that Act.
    4. Entering into an agreement on behalf of the Federation to indemnify a member of the Ontario Teachers' Pension Plan Board or a member of a committee of the Board against any costs sustained with respect to legal proceedings arising out of an act or omission done in the execution of his or her duties as a member of the Board or committee.

1991, Vol. 2, c. 52, s. 9.

10. Conferences.—In the interests of the advancement of education and the improvement of teaching conditions in Ontario, the Board of Governors shall meet annually and confer with the Minister and the senior officials of the Ministry on matters touching and concerning the objects of the Federation, and the Board of Governors shall at such meeting and may at any other time make such representations and recommendations either of a general nature or which relate to any particular school, teacher or matter as it considers advisable and as are in keeping with the objects of the Federation.

11. Collection of fees.—The prescribed membership fee shall be deducted by the board of trustees from the salary of each teacher,

- (a) where a single deduction is made, once in the month of November, or in the first full month thereafter in which the teacher begins a term of employment; or
- (b) where instalment deductions are made,
    - (i) where a teacher is employed for ten months or more, in not fewer than ten instalments, and

S. 12 TEACHING PROFESSION ACT

(ii) where a teacher is employed for fewer than ten months, in fewer than ten instalments,

and shall be forwarded to the treasurer of the Federation.

12. Regulations.—Subject to the approval of the Lieutenant Governor in Council, the Board of Governors may make regulations,

- (a) prescribing a code of ethics for teachers;
- (b) prescribing the fees to be paid by members of the Federation and the dates by which they are to be forwarded to the treasurer of the Federation;
- (c) providing for voluntary membership in the Federation of persons who are not members thereof and prescribing the duties, responsibilities and privileges of voluntary members;
- (d) prescribing the duties, responsibilities and privileges of associate members;
- (e) providing for the suspension and expulsion of members from the Federation and other disciplinary measures;
- (f) designating the services and organizations that shall be deemed to be special war services for the purposes of clause 4(1)(b);
- (g) providing for the holding of meetings of the Board of Governors and of the executive and prescribing the manner of calling and the notice to be given in respect of such meetings;
- (h) prescribing the procedure to be followed at meetings of the Board of Governors and of the executive;
- (i) providing for the payment of necessary expenses to the members of the Board of Governors and the executive;
- (j) conferring powers upon or extending or restricting the powers of and prescribing the duties of the Board of Governors and of the executive;
- (k) providing for the appointment of standing and special committees;
- (l) providing for the establishment of branches of the Federation or of the recognition by the Federation of local bodies, groups or associations of teachers which shall be affiliated with the Federation.

REGULATION MADE UNDER THE TEACHING PROFESSION ACT

TABLE OF CONTENTS

1.	Affiliated bodies	471
2.	Voluntary membership	471
3.	Application for membership by a former member	471
4.	Fees	472
5.	Meetings of the Board of Governors	473
6.	Meetings of executive	473
7.	Nominating committee	474
8.	Relations and Discipline Committee	474
9.	Standing committees	474
10.	Special committees	474
11.	Procedure at annual meeting of Board of Governors	474
12.	Expenses	475
13.	General duties of members	475
14.	Duties of a member to his pupils	475
15.	Duties of a member to educational authorities	475
16.	Duties of a member to the public	476
17.	Duties of a member to the Federation	476
18.	Duties of a member to fellow members	476
19.-28.	Relations and discipline procedure	476
29.	Evidencing Regulations and Resolutions	479
30.	Effective date and transitional provisions	480

REGULATION MADE UNDER THE TEACHING PROFESSION ACT*

[Updated to December 31, 1994]

Affiliated Bodies

1. The Ontario Secondary School Teachers' Federation, the Federation of Women Teachers' Association of Ontario, the Ontario Public School Teachers' Federation, l'Association des enseignantes et des enseignants franco-ontariens and the Ontario English Catholic Teachers' Association shall be affiliated with the Federation and known as "affiliated bodies."

Voluntary Membership

2. (1) The Board of Governors shall grant voluntary membership in the Federation to a person who,

    (a) is not a member thereof;
    (b) holds a teacher's certificate;
    (c) is engaged in an educational capacity;
    (d) is a member of an affiliated body; and
    (e) makes application to the Board of Governors for voluntary membership in the Federation.

(2) The Board of Governors shall grant voluntary membership in the Federation to a person who is not a member thereof and who is from outside Ontario and is on an assignment of two years or less as a teacher in Ontario under a teacher exchange program.

(3) The duties of a voluntary member shall be the same as those of a member under Sections 13 to 18.

(4) A voluntary member shall have such privileges as are common to all members of the Federation.

Application for Membership by a Former Member

3. (1) A teacher who has withdrawn from membership under subsection (1) or (2) of Section 4 of the *Teaching Profession Act, 1944*, may make application to the Board of Governors for reinstatement as a member.

(2) The Board of Governors shall refer the application to the proper affiliated body for its opinion of the application.

---

* Editor's Note: Section 1 of the Regulations Act, R.S.O. 1990, c. R.21 expressly excludes regulations made pursuant to the Teaching Profession Act from the application of the Regulations Act, R.S.O. 1990, c. R.21, and as such, they are not required to be published in the Ontario Gazette. Accordingly, the Regulation Made Under the Teaching Profession Act does not have a conventional "R.S.O. 1990, Reg. ***" or an "O. Reg. ***/9*" citation.

The text noted below was updated by verifying its accuracy with the Ontario Teachers' Federation. Section 12 of the Teaching Profession Act gives the Board of Governors of that organization the authority to pass regulations pursuant to that Act.

(3) Where the Board of Governors, after considering the opinion of the affiliated body, accepts the application, the secretary-treasurer of the Federation shall notify the Minister and the applicant forthwith.

Fees

4. (1) Subject to subsections 2 and 4, a member shall pay the Federation an annual membership fee as follows:

1. A secondary school teacher, 1.18 per cent of total annual salary.
2. A statutory member of the Ontario Public School Teachers' Federation $100.00 plus 1.2 per cent of the total annual salary of the member.
3. A female public school teacher,
    (i) working more than half-time, $650.00,
    (ii) working half-time or less, $325.00.
4. A separate school teacher,
    (i) working more than half-time, $660.00,
    (ii) working half-time or less, an amount which bears the same relation to $660.00 as does the teacher's total annual salary the teacher would earn if full-time.
5. A teacher in a French-language school or class who is a member of L'Association des enseignantes et des enseignants franco-ontariens, 1.5% of the teacher's total annual salary;

where "total annual salary" means salary in accordance with the terms and conditions under which the member is employed, and includes a cost of living or other similar bonus.

(2) A member who is employed by a board exclusively in respect of the continuing education classes provided by the board shall pay the Federation an annual membership fee as follows:

1. A secondary school teacher, 1.18 per cent of the salary attributable to such teaching.
2. A statutory member of the Ontario Public School Teachers' Federation, 1.15 per cent of the salary attributable to such teaching.
3. A female public school teacher $0.20 in respect of each day on which the teacher performs teaching duties to a maximum amount of $4.00 for each month in which the teacher performs such teaching duties.
4. A separate school teacher, 1.25 per cent of the salary attributable to such teaching duties.
5. A teacher of a French-language school or class who is a member of L'Association des enseignantes et des enseignants franco-ontariens, 1.5 per cent of the salary attributable to such teaching duties.

(3) A member to whom subsection (1) applies who is also employed for the purpose of a class referred to in subsection (2) shall pay an annual membership fee that is the sum of the annual membership fee applicable to the member under subsection (1) and the annual membership fee that would be applicable to the member under subsection (2), if the member were a person employed exclusively for the purpose of a class referred to in subsection (2).

(4) Where a fee, or a portion thereof, that is payable under subsection (1) is not based upon salary, such fee or portion thereof shall be reduced, in the case of a teacher who is not

REGULATION MADE UNDER THE TEACHING PROFESSION ACT **S. 6**

employed for the full school year, by multiplying such fee or portion thereof by the ratio of the number of full and part months that the teacher was employed in the school year to ten.

(5) A board of trustees, in respect of a teacher employed by the board, shall,

(a) where a single deduction is made, remit to the secretary-treasurer of the Federation the full annual fee,
   (i) by the 30th day of November, or
   (ii) in the case of a teacher whose employment commences after the first school day in November, by the last day of the first full month that the teacher is employed by the board; and
(b) where deductions are made in instalments, place the instalment fee on deposit with the Federation on or before the 15th day of the month immediately following the month of deduction.

Meetings of the Board of Governors

5. (1) The annual meeting of the Board of Governors shall be held in each year on the days during the three weeks next preceding Labour Day that are, and at a time and place that is, determined by the president.

(2) Subject to subsection (5), there shall be a special meeting of the Board of Governors on the days during or within two weeks following each of the Christmas vacation and the Easter vacation that are, and at a time and place that is, determined by the president.

(3) The Board of Governors shall meet at such other dates and times as the executive may by resolution determine.

(4) A member of the Board of Governors shall be allowed a leave of absence not exceeding four days a year to attend meetings of the Board of Governors referred to in subsections (2) and (3).

(5) Upon the recommendation of the executive and with the approval of at least thirty-two members of the Board of Governors, the Board of Governors may, by resolution, waive the holding of one of the meetings under subsection (2).

(6) The secretary-treasurer of the Federation shall send to members of the Board of Governors a written notice of the date, time and place of a meeting of the Board of Governors,

(a) at least fourteen days before the date of a meeting under subsection (1) or (2); and
(b) at least three days before the date of a meeting under subsection (3).

(7) A quorum at a meeting of the Board of Governors shall be thirty-two members thereof.

Meetings of Executive

6. (1) The executive shall meet immediately before and immediately after a meeting of the Board of Governors.

(2) The secretary-treasurer of the Federation shall send to members of the executive at least seven days in advance of a meeting of the executive written notice of date, time and place of the meeting under subsection (1).

(3) The president of the Federation may at any time call a special meeting of the executive.

(4) A quorum at any meeting of the executive shall be six members thereof.

S. 7 REGULATION MADE UNDER THE TEACHING PROFESSION ACT

Nominating Committee

7. (1) At the meeting of the executive immediately before the annual meeting of the Board of Governors, the executive shall appoint a nominating committee and include thereon a representative of each of the affiliated bodies.

(2) The nominating committee shall meet on the first day of the annual meeting of the Board of Governors to prepare nominations for the executive for the year next following.

(3) The nominating committee shall present the report of its nominations to the Board of Governors and, upon these and other nominations which may be submitted from the floor by any member of the Board of Governors, a secret ballot shall be taken.

Relations and Discipline Committee

8. There shall be a Relations and Discipline Committee appointed by the Board of Governors.

Standing Committees

9. (1) There shall be standing committees as follows:

1. Educational finance
2. Educational Studies
3. Legislation
4. Pension
5. Teacher Education

(2) A committee under subsection (1) shall,

(a) be composed of the chairman or a member of the corresponding committee of each affiliated body, together with the president and secretary-treasurer of the Federation; and

(b) be convened by a member designated by the executive, following the annual meeting of the Board of Governors.

(3) The Board of Governors may, by by-law, establish such standing committees, in addition to those set out in subsection (1), as it considers expedient, and terminate any standing committee so established.

(4) A by-law passed under subsection (3) establishing a standing committee shall make provision for the composition of the committee.

(5) Clause (b) of subsection (2) applies to a standing committee established under subsection (3).

Special Committees

10. The Board of Governors or the executive may, by resolution, appoint such special committees as it considers necessary from time to time.

Procedure at Annual Meeting of Board of Governors

11. (1) The order of procedure at the annual meeting of the Board of Governors shall be as follows:

REGULATION MADE UNDER THE TEACHING PROFESSION ACT   **S. 15**

1. Call to order.
2. Appointment of committees.
3. Reading and confirming the minutes of the next preceding meeting.
4. Business arising from the minutes.
5. Reading of correspondence and action thereon.
6. Reports of officers.
7. Reception of delegations.
8. Reports from affiliated bodies.
9. Reports of standing and special committees.
10. General business.
11. Elections.
12. Installation of officers.
13. Adjournment.

(2) The Board of Governors may omit one or more items of the order of procedure from the agenda of the annual meeting.

Expenses

12. The Federation shall pay such necessary expenses as members of the Board of Governors and of the executive incur in carrying out their duties under the Act and this Regulation.

General Duties of Members

13. A member shall strive at all times to achieve and maintain the highest degree of professional competence and to uphold the honour, dignity, and ethical standards of the teaching profession.

Duties of a Member to His Pupils

14. A member shall,
(a) regard as his first duty the effective education of his pupils and the maintenance of a high degree of professional competence in his teaching;
(b) endeavour to develop in his pupils an appreciation of standards of excellence;
(c) endeavour to inculcate in his pupils an appreciation of the principles of democracy;
(d) show consistent justice and consideration in all his relations with pupils;
(e) refuse to divulge beyond his proper duty confidential information about a pupil; and
(f) concern himself with the welfare of his pupils while they are under his care.

Duties of a Member to Educational Authorities

15. (1) A member shall,
(a) comply with the Acts and regulations administered by the Minister;
(b) co-operate with his educational authorities to improve public education;
(c) respect the legal authority of the board of trustees in the management of the school and in the employment of teachers;
(d) make in the proper manner such reports concerning teachers under his authority as may be required by the board of trustees; and

(e) present in the proper manner to the proper authorities the consequences to be expected from policies or practices which in his professional opinion are seriously detrimental to the interests of pupils.

(2) A member shall not,

(a) break a contract of employment with a board of trustees;
(b) violate a written or oral agreement to enter into a contract of employment with a board of trustees; or
(c) while holding a contract of employment with a board of trustees, make application for another position the acceptance of which would necessitate his seeking the termination of his contract by mutual consent of the teacher and the board of trustees, unless and until he has arranged with his board of trustees for such termination of contract if he obtains the other position.

Duties of a Member to the Public

16. A member shall,

(a) endeavour at all times to extend the public knowledge of his profession and discourage untrue, unfair or exaggerated statements with respect to teaching; and
(b) recognize a responsibility to promote respect for human rights.

Duties of a Member to the Federation

17. A member shall co-operate with the Federation to promote the welfare of the profession.

Duties of a Member to Fellow Members

18. (1) A member shall,

(a) avoid interfering in an unwarranted manner between other teachers and pupils;
(b) on making an adverse report on another member, furnish him with a written statement of the report at the earliest possible time and not later than three days after making the report;
(c) refuse to accept employment with a board of trustees whose relations with the Federation are unsatisfactory; and
(d) where he is in an administrative or supervisory position, make an honest and determined effort to help and counsel a teacher before subscribing to the dismissal of that teacher.

(2) Under clause (c) of subsection (1), the onus shall be on the member to ascertain personally from the Federation whether an unsatisfactory relationship exists.

(3) A member shall not attempt to gain an advantage over other members by knowingly underbidding another member, or knowingly applying for a position not properly declared vacant, or by negotiating for salary independently of his local group of fellow-members.

Relations and Discipline Procedure

19. (1) In this section and Sections 20 to 28

REGULATION MADE UNDER THE TEACHING PROFESSION ACT S. 20

(a) "Committee" means the Relations and Discipline Committee of the Ontario Teachers' Federation;

(b) "teaching certificate" means an Ontario Teacher's Certificate or other qualification to teach prescribed under Regulation 269 as amended and revised from time to time.

(2) The Committee shall be composed of ten members who are teachers, appointed by the Board of Governors, two of whom shall be from each affiliated body.

(3) A person is not eligible for appointment to the Committee who,

(a) holds office on a disciplinary body of an affiliated body;

(b) holds office on the executive of an affiliated body; or

(c) is employed by either an affiliated body or the Federation.

(4) The Committee shall appoint one of the members of the Committee to be chairman.

(5) The chairman of the Committee may assign a panel of five members of the Committee to hold a hearing.

(6) Three members of the panel assigned under subsection (5) constitute a quorum for a hearing and all disciplinary decisions require the vote of a majority of members of the Committee present at the hearing.

(7) The secretary-treasurer of the Federation shall act as secretary to the Committee but shall not participate in any decision of the Committee.

20. (1) The Committee shall,

(a) consider complaints regarding professional misconduct or unethical conduct of a member;

(b) consider applications for reinstatement of the teaching certificate of a former member or the lifting of a suspension thereof.

(2) A hearing of the Committee shall be held in camera unless the member requests otherwise by notice delivered to the Committee not later than the day before the day fixed for the hearing, in which case the Committee shall conduct the hearing in public except when,

(i) matters involving public security may be disclosed; or

(ii) the possible disclosure of intimate financial or personal matters outweighs the desirability of holding the hearing in public.

(3) No hearing in respect of alleged professional misconduct or unethical conduct shall be conducted by the Committee unless,

(a) a written signed complaint has been filed in the office of the secretary-treasurer of the Federation;

(b) a copy thereof has been served on the member whose conduct is being investigated; and

(c) the member whose conduct is being investigated has been served with notice of the time, place and purpose of the hearing.

(4) The secretary-treasurer of the Federation shall,

(a) prepare and complete or cause to be completed a written complaint and file it in the office of the secretary-treasurer of the Federation;

(b) serve upon the member whose conduct is being investigated,

(i) a copy of the complaint; and
(ii) a notice of the hearing which shall include,
   A. a statement of the time, place and purpose of the hearing;
   B. a reference to the statutory authority under which the hearing will be held;
   C. a statement that if the party notified does not attend at the hearing the Committee may proceed in his absence and he will not be entitled to any further notice of the proceedings; and
   D. a statement that the member may,
      1. be represented by counsel or an agent;
      2. call and examine witnesses;
      3. present arguments and submissions; and
      4. conduct cross-examination of witnesses as reasonably required for full and fair disclosure of the facts in relation to which they have given evidence; and
(c) make all necessary arrangements for the conduct of the hearing including,
   (i) the appointment of counsel for the Federation;
   (ii) the arrangement for oral evidence to be recorded; and
   (iii) the notification to all members of the Committee of the time and place of the hearing.

21. In proceedings before the Committee, the Federation and the member whose professional misconduct or unethical conduct, or reinstatement is being investigated shall be parties to the proceedings.

22. (1) A member whose professional misconduct or unethical conduct or reinstatement is being investigated shall be afforded an opportunity to examine, before the hearing, any written or documentary evidence that will be produced or any report, the contents of which will be given in evidence at the hearing.

(2) Members of the Committee conducting the hearing shall not,
(a) have taken part before the hearing in the investigation of the subject matter of the complaint;
(b) have taken part in any previous hearing involving the member whose professional misconduct, unethical conduct or reinstatement is being investigated; or
(c) communicate directly or indirectly in relation to the subject matter of the hearing with any person or with any party or representative of a party, except upon notice to and opportunity for all parties to participate.

23. (1) The evidence before the Committee shall be recorded by a person appointed by the chairman of the Committee.

(2) Nothing is admissible in evidence before the Committee that would be inadmissible in a civil case and the findings of the Committee shall be based exclusively on evidence before it.

(3) No member of the Committee shall participate in the decision of the Committee unless he has been present throughout the hearing.

24. At a hearing before the Committee, a party to the proceedings may,
(a) be represented by counsel or an agent;

(b) call and examine witnesses;
(c) present arguments and submissions; and
(d) conduct cross-examination of witnesses as reasonably required for full and fair disclosure of the facts in relation to which they have given evidence.

25. (1) A member may be found guilty by the Committee of a professional misconduct or unethical conduct if in the opinion of the Committee he has contravened any of the provisions of Sections 13 to 18.

(2) In the case of hearings into complaints of professional misconduct and unethical conduct, the Committee shall,
(a) consider the allegations, hear the evidence and ascertain the facts of the case;
(b) determine whether upon the evidence and the facts so ascertained the allegations have been proved;
(c) determine whether in respect of the allegations so proved, the member is guilty of professional misconduct or unethical conduct; and
(d) determine the penalty to be imposed, as hereinafter provided, in cases in which it finds a member guilty of professional misconduct or unethical conduct.

(3) Where the Committee finds a member guilty of professional misconduct or unethical conduct, it shall,
(a) recommend to the Minister the cancellation of the teaching certificate of the member;
(b) recommend to the Minister the suspension for a stated fixed period of the teaching certificate of the member; or
(c) reprimand the member,
or proceed with any combination of the foregoing.

26. (1) Where the Federation receives a request for a recommendation in respect of the reinstatement of a teaching certificate of a former member or the lifting of the suspension thereof, the secretary-treasurer shall refer the matter to the Committee for a hearing.

(2) Following a hearing under subsection (1), the Committee shall recommend to the Minister that the teaching certificate be reinstated or the suspension lifted, or that the teaching certificate remain cancelled or the suspension not be lifted, as the case may be.

27. (1) The Committee shall give its decision and recommendation, if any, under subsections 25.(3) or 26.(2) in writing and shall give reasons in writing, therefor, if requested by a party.

(2) The decision of the Committee shall be served upon the parties.

28. Any notice or other document required to be served by this regulation may be served by prepaid first class mail addressed to the person to whom notice is to be given at his last known address and where notice is served by mail, the service shall be deemed to have been made on the fifth day after the day of mailing unless the person to whom the notice is given establishes that he, acting in good faith, due to absence, accident, illness or other cause beyond his control, did not receive the notice or did not receive the notice until a later date.

Evidencing Regulations and Resolutions

29. Regulations made by and resolutions passed by the Board of Governors may be evidenced by the signatures of the president and the secretary-treasurer of the Federation.

S. 30 — REGULATION MADE UNDER THE TEACHING PROFESSION ACT

30. (1) This Regulation comes into force on the 1st day of January 1986, and applies in respect of any complaint of professional misconduct or unethical conduct filed in the office of the secretary-treasurer of the Federation on or after that date, and in respect of a request referred to in Section 26 received by the Federation on or after that date.

(2) The provisions of the Regulation made under the Teaching Profession Act that are revoked by this Regulation shall continue to apply to any matter or proceeding brought thereunder and not disposed of prior to the 1st day of January 1986 notwithstanding the coming into force of this Regulation.

INDEX

References are to sections of the Education Act unless otherwise indicated. Reg. — Education Act regulation; ISPA — Immunization of School Pupils Act; MCIA — Municipal Conflict of Interest Act; RTPA — Regulation Made Under the Teaching Profession Act; SBTCNA — School Boards and Teachers Collective Negotiations Act; TPA — Teaching Profession Act.

Absence. *see also* **Attendance.**
pupil
    habitual absenteeism, 30
    prosecutions, 31
teacher
    duty to notify, 264

Accounts. *see also* **Finances.**
inspection, 207

Adjoining
defined, 1

Admission. *see also* **Attendance, Resident pupil.**
adult, 40
age requirement, 33
alternative course or program, 42
beginner's class, 34
by right, 32
change of residence, 38
child in custody of corporation, 47
Children's Aid Society, 46
different secondary school
    by right, 41
    fee, 49
enrolment requirement, 40
evening classes, 42
fee, 47, 49
French-language instructional unit
    non-French-speakers, 289, 302
Indian school, 184
junior kindergarten, 34
kindergarten, 34
more accessible school, 39
on promotion, 43
Ontario School for the Blind, Reg 296, ss. 3-8
Ontario School for the Deaf, Reg. 296, ss. 3-8
other jurisdiction
    from, 42
    into, 48
parents in Canada unlawfully, 49.1
public school pupil, 33
regulations, 11
residency requirement, 33, 40
residents on tax-exempt property, 45
secondary school, 40, 43
separate school pupil, 33
sole support by one parent, 44
tax exempt land, 45
ward of training school, 46

Adult basic education. *see also* **Continuing education, Adult pupils.**
agreement with college, 189
agreement with community group, 189
defined, 189
Minister, 8

Adult education. *see* **Continuing education, Adult basic education, Adult pupils.**

Adult pupils. *see also* **Adult basic education, Continuing education.**
Minister, 11
parental authority, 1
schools for trainable retarded pupils, 71
secondary school admission, 40
vocational courses, 174

Advertisement
consent, Reg. 298, s. 24

Advisory body. *see also* **Committee.**
ministerial appointment, 10

481

INDEX

Advisory committee. *see* **Committee.**

Affiliate. *see also* **Branch affiliate, Negotiations, Collective agreement.**
defined, SBTCNA s. 1
negotiations with board, SBTCNA
offence, SBTCNA s. 77
officer, official or agent, SBTCNA s. 79
unlawful strike, SBTCNA s. 65

Affirmative action
designation of unrequired staff, 135
ministerial policy, 8

Agreement. *see also* **Contract, Collective agreement.**
between boards, 181, 184, 185, 186
between Ontario Teachers' Federation and Crown, TPA s. 9
between public and separate school boards, 185
between public school boards, 184
between secondary school boards, 186
between separate school boards, 184
re accommodation and services, 181
re adult basic education, 189
re continuing education, Reg. 285, s. 5
re federal establishments, 187
re Indian pupils, 188
re multi-use building, 195
re out-of-classroom program sites, 197
re pupils at Indian schools, 184
re teacher education, 14
re teachers' pension, T.P.A. s. 9
with land, 188
with Canada
    bursaries of scholarships, 12
    physical fitness, 12
    pupils at Indian schools, 12
    general, 187, 188
    learning materials, 12
    with colleges, 14, 189
    with conservation authorities, 197
    with municipality, 183
    with university, 14

Allowance
advisory committees, 191
board members, 191
board officers, 191
French-language advisory committee, 300
retirement, 179
vocational course advisory committee, 175

Alternative learning
approval, Reg. 308, s. 3
change in board, Reg. 308, s. 8, 10
general, Reg. 308
parent, Reg. 308, s. 9
program change, Reg. 308, s. 6
provincial school attendance counsellor, Reg. 308, s. 5
request, Reg. 308, s. 3
review procedures, Reg. 308, ss. 4, 5
school attendance counsellor, Reg. 308, s. 6
committee, Reg. 308, s. 2

Announcements
consent, Reg. 298, s. 24

Annual Report
Education Relations Commission, SBTCNA, s. 60
French-language committee, 299
Minister, 3

Appeal. *see also* **Court.**
electoral group distribution, 231
factors in determining school rate, 117
order: re designated disease, ISPA, s. 16
secondary school admission, 43
special education, Reg. 307, 4-12
suspension of pupil, 23

Appointment
board
    duty, 170
    powers, 171

Apportionment
adjusted, 240
exceptions, 240
grants, 240

INDEX

Apportionment — *continued*
regulations, 240
review procedures, 240
separate school board, 242
territory without municipal organization, 240

Arbitrations Act, **R.S.O. 1990, c. A.24,** 142, SBTCNA, s. 80

Arbitrator. *see* **Arbitration.**

Arbitration. *see also* **Mediation, Negotiations, Designation.**
board/branch affiliate negotiation dispute, SBTCNA, ss. 12, 27, 28-36
collective agreement dispute, SBTCNA, s. 52
Combined separate school zone boundary alteration, 99
designation dispute
   Arbitrations Act, 142
   arbitrator unable to act, 138
   fees and expenses, 141
   general, 137-142
   mothers, 139
   report, 140
   vacancy on arbitration board, 138
district school area boundary alteration, 59
expenses, 210
fees, 210
general, 210
liabilities for costs, 210
municipal treasurers, 210

Arrears
district school area with territory without municipal organization, 65
separate school in territory without municipal organization, 92

Assessment. *see also* **Assessment Commissioner, Rates, Assessment roll.**
commercial, 248
corporation or partnership, 112, 113
description, 251

equalying factor
   regulations, 11
municipality, 249
public school exemption, 162
residential and farm, 248
separate school
   not sharing in public school, 122, 162
   trustees, 118

Assessment Act, **R.S.O. 1990, c. A.31,** 109, 112, 113, 251, MCIA, s. 4

Assessment Commissioner. *see also* **Assessment.**
corporation or partnership, 112, 113
defined, 1
determination of electoral groups, 230
notification
   district school area formed or altered, 59
   separate school zone established, 80

Assessment Roll. *see also* **Assessment, Rates.**
annual statement
   separate school supporters, 119
correction of mistake, 109
name not listed
   admission to school, 38
Protestant Separate School Trustee
   authorized to make copy, 163

L'Association des enseignantes et des enseignants Franco-ontariens
"affiliate", SBTCNA s. 1
Ontario Teachers' Federation, TPA, s. 5, 6

L'Association Francaise des conseils scolaires de L'Ontario
member association, SBTCNA s. 1

Athletics. *see also* **Physical fitness, Recreation, Gymnasium classes.**
boards, 171

Attendance. *see also* **Resident pupil, Alternative learning, Admission, School**

483

INDEX

attendance counsellors, Absenteeism, Closing, Provincial attendance counsellor.
age, 21
alternative learning, Reg. 308, s. 4
bond, 30
child in custody of corporation, 47
Children's Aid Society wards, 46
compulsory, 21
deemed, 5
discretion of board, 32
excused, 21, Reg. 298, s. 23
distant from school, 190
employment of pupil, 30
expulsion, 23
general, 18-48
habitual absence, 30
blind, deaf, handicapped, 21
parental duty, 21, 30, Reg. 298, s. 23
principal, 28, 265, Reg. 298, s. 12
prosecution, 31
Provincial School Attendance Counsellor, 24
reason for absence, Reg. 298, s. 23
regulations on exceptions to compulsory attendance, 11
school attendance counsellors, 25-29
suspension, 23
underage child, 21
without payment of fee, 32

Attendance area
board, 171

Auditors. *see also* **Board finances.**
appointment
    board, 234
    district school area, 65
    rural separate school board, 90
    secondary school outside school divisions in territorial districts, 67
    separate school boards, 96
dismissal, 234
disqualification, 234
duties, 234
evidence, 234
meetings, 234
rights, 234
withholding reports on information from, 214

Author. *see also* **Book.**
promotion on sale of books, 217

Average daily enrolment
defined, 1

Award. *see also* **Scholarships, Bursaries, Prizes.**
Minister, 8

Bachelor of Education
Minister, 8

Ballot
form, 92
marking, 92

Band. *see also* **Indian.**
agreement with board, 188
defined, 1
representative, 188
separate school board representative, 188

***Bank Act*, R.S.C. 1985, c. B-1,** 121, 171

Banker's acceptance. *see also* **Borrowing.**
borrowing, 245

Beginner's class
admission, 34

Benefits
accident insurance
    board members, 176
    employees, 177
    work-experience programs, 176
general, 176-180
hospital insurance, 177
insurance contributions, 177
life insurance, 155
pensions, 178
property damage insurance, 176
public liability insurance, 176
retired person, 177

INDEX

Benefits — *continued*
retirement allowances, 178
sick leave credits, 180

Bill of exchange. *see also* **Borrowing.**
borrowing, 245

Blind pupils. *see also* **Ontario School for the Blind.**
compulsory attendance, 21
transportation, 190

Board. *see also* **Board duties and powers, Meeting, Board members, Finances, Officers, Employees, Property, Divisional board, District school areas, Board of Education, Separate School Board, Roman Catholic School Board.**
advisory committee reports, 205
agreements with other boards, 181
allowance, 191
benefits, 176
boundary changes, 230
debt obligations
  limits on, 235.3
collective agreements, SBTCNA
conduct of schools, 170
declaration, 209
defined, 1
dissolution, 216
duties, 170
election, 226, 228, 230
electoral groups, 230
French-language section, 311-326
general, 170-218
head office, 170
name, 55, 58, 80, 102, 172
negotiations with branch affiliates, SBTCNA
number of members, 230
oath of allegiance, 209
powers, 171
separate existence, 221
signatures, 171
three-member, 223
travel expenses, 191

vacancy
  appointment, 227
  declaration, 218
  election, 226
  electoral group, 222
  general, 222, 225-227
  when filled, 225
when deemed constituted, 208

Board duties and powers
duties
  appoint officers, 170 ¶1
  appoint principal, 170 ¶12
  appoint teachers, 170 ¶12
  bus and vehicle insurance, 170 ¶14
  conduct of school as required, 170 ¶10
  head office, 170 ¶5
  instruction and accommodation, 170 ¶6
  insurance, 170 ¶9
  meetings, 170 ¶4
  Ministerial requirements, 170 ¶18
  notify Minister of teacher convicted of offence that puts pupils at risk, 170 ¶12.1
  open school, 170 ¶11
  operate junior kindergarten, 170 ¶6.2
  operate kindergartens, 170 ¶6.1
  payment of bills, 170 ¶3
  repair property, 170 ¶8
  reports as required, 170 ¶16
  report unenrolled children, 170 ¶15
  security from officers, 170 ¶2
  special education, 170 ¶7
  statement of sick leave credits, 170 ¶17
  text books, 170 ¶13
powers
  activities and programs, 171(1) ¶28
  agreement with university or college use of facilities, 171(1) ¶44
  appointments, 171(1) ¶3
    employees, 171(1) ¶3
    guidance teachers, 171(1) ¶29
    officers, 171(1) ¶3
    psychiatrists, 171(1) ¶6
    psychologists, 171(1) ¶6

INDEX

Board duties and powers — *continued*
    supervisors, 171(1) ¶5
    teachers, 171(1) ¶3
  athletics, 171(1) ¶27
  attendance areas, 171(1) ¶7
  bonds, 171(1) ¶20
  borrowing, 171(1) ¶22
  cadet corps, 171(1) ¶26
  cafeteria for staff and pupils, 171(1) ¶37
  child care facilities, 171(1) ¶48
  closing of schools, 171(1) ¶7
  committees of board members, 171(1) ¶1
  committees with non-board members, 171(1) ¶2
  computer use agreement, 171(1) ¶9
  continuing education, 171(1) ¶31
  courses, 171(1) ¶8
  current expenditures
    designation as ordinary expenditures, 171(1) ¶47
  day nurseries, 171(1) ¶49
  deposits for text books, 171(1) ¶31.1
  debentures, 171(1) ¶20
  determine number and kind of schools, 171(1) ¶7
  duties of employees, 171(1) ¶3
  educational associations, 171(1) ¶17
    attendance at meetings grants, 171(1) ¶17
  educational program
    centre, facility, home, hospital or institute, 171(1) ¶40
    charitable organization, 171(1) ¶39
    hospital school, 171(1) ¶42
    sanatorium school, 171(1) ¶42
    treatment centre school, 171(1) ¶42
  election recounts, 171(1) ¶45
  establishment of schools, 171(1) ¶7
  evening classes, 171(1) ¶33
  fence, 171(1) ¶34
  field trips, 171(1) ¶28
  guaranteed investment certificate, 171(1) ¶20
  guidance counselling, 171(1) ¶29
  gymnasium classes, 171(1) ¶11
  instruction, 171(1) ¶8
  insurance, 171(1) ¶46
  interest rate payment, 171(1) ¶22
  investments, 171 (1) ¶19-21, ¶49
  junior kindergarten, 171(1) ¶15
  legal action to recover fees, 171(1) ¶23
  legal costs, 171(1) ¶18
  libraries, 171(1) ¶14
  maternity leave, 171(1) ¶41
  membership fees, 171(1) ¶17
  milk purchase, 171(1) ¶12
  minor physical defect of children, 171(1) ¶25
  notes, 171(1) ¶20
  park, 171(1) ¶10
  playground, 171(1) ¶10
  promissory notes, 171(1) ¶20
  public lectures, 171(1) ¶30
  records management, 171(1) ¶38
  reserve fund investments, 171(1) ¶21
  resource centre, 171(1) ¶14
  rink, 171(1) ¶10
  salaries, 171(1) ¶3
  school fairs, 171(1) ¶35
  school games, 171(1) ¶27
  school grounds, 171(1) ¶10
  school supplies, 171(1) ¶13
  securities, 171(1) ¶21
  signatures mechanically reproduced, 171(1) ¶16
  student activities, 171(1) ¶36
  student fees, 171(1) ¶23
  surgical treatment, 171(1) ¶25
  supervision for gymnasium classes, 171(1) ¶11
  supervision for park, playground, rinks, 171(1) ¶10
  teachers' courses, 171(1) ¶32
  term and other deposits, 171(1) ¶20
  terms of employment, 171(1) ¶3

Board duties and powers — *continued*
  territory without municipal organization
    recreation committee, 171(1) ¶43
    recovery of rates, 171(2)
    travelling expenses, 171(1) ¶17
    use of building and premises, 171(1) ¶24, 44
    use of school bus, 171(1) ¶24
    vocational counselling, 171(1) ¶29
    voluntary assistants, 171(1) ¶4
    wall, 171(1) ¶34

Board members. *see also* **Trustees, Board, Election, Employees, Finances, Officers, Meeting, Conflict of interest.**
absence, 229
appointment, 227
candidature, 220
conviction, 229
disqualification, 213, 220, 229
election, 222, 223
electoral group vacancy, 222
eligibility, 220
employee, 219
general, 219-229
ineligibility, 219
mental illness, 229
number, 230
qualifications, 220
resignation, 221
term of office, 221

Board of Education. *see also* **Board.**
defined, 1
establishment and status, 58
general, 58

Board of Reference
application, 268, 270
costs, 276
direction
  binding power, 275
  contract, 272
  failure to comply, 275

documents
  filing, Reg. 300, s. 5
  reference books, Reg. 300, s. 3
  service, Reg. 300, s. 5
duty and powers, 272
evidence
  full hearing, Reg. 300, s. 12
  presentation, Reg. 300, s. 6
examination, Reg. 300, s. 15
exclusion of witnesses, Reg. 300, s. 16
general, 267-277
interpretation, 267
interpreter, Reg. 300, s. 11
judicial review, 272-274, Reg. 300, s. 11
judge, 272-274, Reg. 300, s. 11
language, Reg. 300, s. 9
minimum rules, Reg. 300, s. 3
new board, 270, 274
parties, Reg. 300, s. 2
place and time, 271
practice and procedure, Reg. 300
record, Reg. 300, ss. 8, 17
regulations, 277
remuneration, Reg. 300, s. 13
report, 273
representatives, 270
restriction on entering new contract, 269
submissions
  by board, Reg. 300, s. 5
  by Minister, Reg. 300, s. 5
  by teacher, Reg. 300, s. 5
termination, 270
witness and attendance, Reg. 300, s. 14

Boarding. *see* **Meals and Lodging.**

Bond
boards, 171
to ensure attendance, 30(2)

Book. *see also* **Author, Permanent improvements.**
approval, 8
prohibition on promotion or sale, 217
publication of list, 8

INDEX

Book — *continued*
purchase, 11
selection, 8
textbook selection and provision, Reg. 298, s. 7

Borrowing
authorization, 245
banker's acceptance, 245
bill of exchange, 245
debt charges, 245
limitation on amount, 245
powers of board, 171
promissory note, 245
separate schools, 121
separate school trustees, 121

Branch affiliate. *see also* **Negotiations, Collective agreement, Affiliate.**
defined, SBTCNA s. 1
exclusive representation of teachers, SBTCNA, s. 5
list of officers, SBTCNA s. 75
negotiations with board, SBTCNA
offence, SBTCNA, s. 77
officer, official or agent, SBTCNA, s. 80
unlawful strike, SBTCNA, s. 65

Boundaries
change
    disposition of assets and liabilities, 57, 59, 99, 100
    separate school zone, 86
zones, 78

Building and site. *see also* **Permanent improvements, Closing, Property, Out-of-classroom program.**
announcements and advertisements, Reg. 298, s. 24
appropriation by board of education, 191
canvassing and fund raising, Reg. 298, s. 25
disposal, 194
erection, addition or alteration, 195, 197, 207, Reg. 298, s. 2
expropriation, 195
insurance, 170
lease, 195
Ministerial approval, 195
multi-use building, 195
purchase, 195
principal, 265
school site defined, 1
rural separate school board
    acquisition, 90
use
    by municipalities, 183
    for lawful purposes, 171
    practice teaching, 14
when open, Reg. 298, s. 3

Bursaries. *see also* **Awards, Scholarships, Prizes.**
agreement with Canada, 12
awarded by board, 173
established by person, 173
Minister, 8
variation, 17

Bus. *see also* **Permanent improvements.**
insurance, 170
permission to use, 171
purchase, 190

Business administrator. *see* **Board officers.**

By-laws
publication of notice
    borrowing money
        separate school zone, 121

Cabinet. *see* **Lieutenant-Governor in Council.**

Cadet corps
boards, 171

Cafeteria
boards, 171

Calendar. *see also* **Year, Holidays.**
publication, Reg. 304, s. 7
submission to Minister, Reg. 304, s. 4, 5

INDEX

Canada. *see* **Crown land, Federal government.**

Canvassing
consent of board, Reg. 298, s. 25
Minister, 8

Certificate. *see also* **interim certificate, Diploma, Ontario Teacher's Certificate, Qualifications.**
Minister, 8
regulations, 11

Charitable organization
boards, 171

Charter of Rights and Freedoms, 230, 313, 325, Reg. 298, s. 28

Chief education officer. *see* **Officers.**

Chief executive officer. *see* **Officers.**

***Child and Family Services Act,* R.S.O. 1990, c. C.11,** 190

Child Care Facility
boards, 171
Minister, 8
regulations, 11

Citizenship classes
permanent residents, Reg. 285, s. 1

Civil action. *see* **Court.**

Cleanliness. *see* **Principal.**

Clergy
visiting school, 52, 123

Clerk
index book, 108

Closing of school
below minimum attendance, 66
civic holiday, 20
deemed attendance, 5
emergency, 19
guidelines, 8
strike, SBTCNA, s. 68
transfer of pupils, 184
transportation failure, 19

Collective agreement. *see also* **Contract, Negotiations, Education relations commission, Strike, Lock-out.**
agreement on unrequired staff, 135
arbitration, SBTCNA, s. 52
binding effect, SBTCNA, s. 58
constitutional rights of separate schools preserved, SBTCNA, s. 51
costs, SBTCNA, s. 74
deemed dispute resolution provision, SBTCNA, s. 52
deemed strike or lock-out prohibition, SBTCNA, s. 53
defined, SBTCNA, s. 1
document, SBTCNA, s. 56
general, SBTCNA
individual contract, SBTCNA, s. 54
notice to commission, SBTCNA, ss. 55, 57, 71
offence, SBTCNA, s. 77
O.L.R.B. application, SBTCNA, s. 77
service of documents, SBTCNA, s. 73
statutory conflict, SBTCNA, s. 51
terms, SBTCNA, s. 50
voting, SBTCNA, s. 76
witness compellability, SBTCNA, s. 81

Collector
district school area board, 65

College. *see also* **Teachers' college.**
adult basic education, 189
agreement re teacher education, 14

Combined separate school zone. *see also* **County combined separate school zone, District combined separate school zone.**
boards, 97
boundary alteration
    arbitration, 99
    disposition of property, 100
    employment contracts, 100

INDEX

Combined separate school zone — *continued*
general, 99
referral to judge, 99
continuance of school, 101
deemed district municipalities, 103
defined, 1
designation of district zone, 98
dissolution of board, 97
district and county, 97
election in improvement district, 103
election, 94, 104
electors, 95
name, 102
regulations, 97
trustees, 95, 104
votes, 104
voters' list, 95
territory without municipal organization, 103

Commission of inquiry. *see also* **Languages of instruction commission of Ontario, Education relations commission.**
appointment, 10

Committee. *see* **Allowance, School board advisory committee, Vocation courses, Special education, Trainable retarded pupils, French-language advisory committee, English-language instruction, Regional committee for French-language education.**
ability of pupil to profit from instruction, 35
allowances, 191
board, 171
French-language, 292-301
school board advisory, 201-205
schools for trainable retarded children, 72-74
special education, 206

Communicable disease. *see* **Principal, Immunization, Health.**

Community cooperation. *see* **Principal, Teacher.**

Community group
adult basic education, 189

Community Recreation Centre
grant, 183

Computers
board, 171

Confidentiality. *see* **Pupil records.**

Conflict of interest
alleged contravention, , MCIA ss. 8-13
appeal, MCIA, s. 12
application to judge, MCIA, ss. 8-9, 13
controlling interest
defined, MCIA, s. 1
disclosure
meeting, MCIA, s. 5
on record, MCIA, s. 5
indirect pecuniary interest
child, MCIA, s. 3
controlling interest, MCIA, s. 2
director, MCIA, s. 2
employee, MCIA, s. 2
officer, MCIA, s. 2
parent, MCIA, s. 3
partner, MCIA, s. 2
shareholder, MCIA, s. 2
spouse, MCIA, s. 3
interest in common with electors generally, MCIA, s. 1
insurance, MCIA, s. 14
lack of quorum, MCIA, s. 7
meeting
closed
leaving, MCIA, s. 5
disclosure of interest, MCIA, s. 5
not participating, MCIA, s. 5
not voting, MCIA, s. 5
powers of judge, MCIA, s. 10
statutory conflict, MCIA, s. 15
where no pecuniary interest

INDEX

Conflict of interest — *continued*
    certain property interests, MCIA, s. 4
    debenture purchaser or owner, MCIA, s. 4
    deposition, MCIA, s. 4
    eligibility for office, MCIA, s. 4
    entitled recipient of allowance, MCIA, s. 4
    entitled recipient of benefit on common terms, MCIA, s. 4
    member, officer or director of board, MCIA, s. 4
    pecuniary interest in common with electors generally, MCIA, s. 4
    public utility user, MCIA, s. 4
    remote or insignificant interest, MCIA, s. 4
    tax exempt farm lands, MCIA, s. 4

Conservation authorities
Out-of-classroom programs, 197

Constitution. *see* **Charter.**

***Constitution Act*, 1867,** SBTCNA, s. 51

Continuing education
board
    agreement with other board, Reg. 285, s. 5
    general, 171
    powers and duties, Reg. 285, s. 2
    separate school, Reg. 298, s. 5
day classes, Reg. 285, s. 8
defined, Reg. 285, s. 1
discontinuance, Reg. 285, s. 10
entitlement to enrol, 43
establishment, Reg. 285, s. 5
evening classes, Reg. 285, s. 8
French-language schools, Reg. 285, s. 6
general, Reg. 285
instructor
    defined, 1
    qualifications, Reg. 285, s. 3
joint classes, Reg. 285, s. 2
language classes, Reg. 285, s. 2
maximum course load, Reg. 285, s. 7
principal, Reg. 285, s. 2
regulation, 11
school site, Reg. 285, s. 2
teacher
    contract, 259, Reg. 310, Form 3
    defined, 1
    qualifications, Reg. 285, s. 3

Contract
boundary alteration, 57, 100
collective agreement, SBTCNA, s. 54
continuing education teacher, 259, Reg. 310, Form 3
deemed terms and conditions, 258
divisional board, 57
form, 258, Reg. 310, s. 1
formalities, 258
formalities not complied with, 260
full-time teacher, 258
general, 258-263, Reg. 310
memorandum of, 258
nature of employment, 258
part-time teacher, 258
permanent teacher, Reg. 310, Form 1
probationary teacher, 261, Reg. 310, Form 2
regulations, 11
resignation in good faith, SBTCNA, s. 70
salary, 260, Reg. 310, s. 2
student-aid loan
    regulation, 11
termination, 263, 268
termination because of strike, SBTCNA, s. 69
withdrawal of voluntary services, SBTCNA, s. 170

Cooperation. *see* **Principal, Teacher.**

Copyright
Minister, 8

Corporation
employment of pupil, 30
employment of teacher, 217

Corporation — *continued*
indirect pecuniary interest, MCIA, s. 2
separate school supporter, 112

Correspondence courses
Minister, 8

Costs. *see also* **Fees, Court.**
education if student out of province for medical reasons, 8(1) ¶35
legal
    board, 171
teacher education, 14

County
defined, 1

County and district combined Roman Catholic separate school zone. *see* **Combined separate school zone.**

County combined separate school zones. *see also* **Combined separate school zones.**
defined, 1
general, 97-105
list and designations, Reg. 286, s. 1

Courses for pupils. *see also* **Alternative learning, Correspondence courses, Credit, Evening classes.**
Minister, 8

Courses for teachers. *see also* **Qualifications, Teacher, Teachers' college, Supervisory officer.**
board, 171
Minister, 8

Court. *see also* **Appeal, Offence.**
Order re: designated disease, ISPA, s. 16
Boards of reference, 274, Reg. 300, s. 11
collective agreement, SBTCNA, s. 72
combined separate school zone, 99
conflict of interest, MCIA, ss. 8-13
failure to take security, 198
formation of school section, 1

lack of quorum because of conflict of interest, MCIA, s. 7
Minister's submission of case for legal opinion, 10
regulations, SBTCNA, s. 72
recovery of unpaid student fees, 171
strike or lock-out, SBTCNA, s. 72
vacancy on board, 218
territory without municipal organization recovery of rates, 171

Credit
defined, 1

Crown land. *see also* **Canada, Federal government, Indian band.**
boards, 68
exemption from school division, 53
regulations, 11

Current expenditure
defined, 1

Current revenue
defined, 1

Day. *see also* **Calendar, Year.**
school day defined, 1
length of instructional program, Reg. 298, s. 3

Deaf pupils. *see also* **Ontario School for the Deaf.**
attendance, 21
special education, Reg. 298, s. 30
transportation, 190

Debenture. *see also* **Borrowing, Finances.**
board, 171, 235.1
bus purchase, 190
debt charges, 235
district school area, 65
divisional board, 235
general, 235
guarantee, 6
interest rate, 7
limitation, 18

Debenture — *continued*
Minister making payments on, 235.1 — 235.2
separate school, 121
temporary advances, 235
withholding to pay debt charges, 235

Debt charge. *see also* **Borrowing, Debenture.**
borrowing, 245
debenture, 235
defined, 1

Declaration
board members, 209
false, 211
objection to right to vote, 92
vacancy on board, 218

Demonstration school
general, 13
transportation, 190

Department. *see* **Department heads.**

Department heads
appointment, Reg. 298, s. 14
duties, Reg. 298, s. 14
    community cooperation, Reg. 298, s. 16(b)
    cooperation, Reg. 298, s. 16(a)
    information gathering, Reg. 298, s. 16(b)
    instruction, Reg. 298, s. 16(b)
    instruction methods and standards, Reg. 298, s. 16(d)
    maintenance of equipment, Reg. 298, s. 16(f)
    organization and management, Reg. 298, s. 16(a)
    outlines, Reg. 298, s. 16(c)
    supervision of instruction, Reg. 298, s. 16(b)
    pupil records, Reg. 298, s. 16(d)
    recommend appointments, Reg. 298, s. 16(b)
    recommend assignments and timetable allotments, Reg. 298, s. 16(b)
    safety, Reg. 298, s. 16(f)
    supervision of activity off school property, Reg. 298, s. 16(e)
    general, Reg. 298, ss. 14-16
regulations, 11

Designation of unrequired staff. *see also* **Arbitration.**
arbitration, 137-142
collective agreement, 135
compensation rate, 135
condition, 136
dispute resolution, 137
gratuity, 135
hearing, 137
public board staff, 135
regulations, 135
seniority, 135
sick leave, 135
similar employment, 135
support staff, Reg. 288
teachers, Reg. 289
training assistance, 135, Reg. 312
transmittal of lists, 135
voluntary transfers, 135

***Developmental Services Act*, R.S.O. 1990, c. D.11,** 190

Diocesan Council
school board advisory committee, 202

Diploma. *see also* **Certificate.**
fees for duplicate, Reg. 293
Minister, 8

Director of Education. *see also* **Officers, Supervisory officers.**
abolition of position, 282
additional supervisory officers, 284
chief education officer, 283
chief executive officer, 283
qualifications, 279
regulations, 11

INDEX

Director of Education — *continued*
responsibilities, 283
separate school board, 280
suspension or dismissal, 287

Discipline. *see also* **Principal, Teacher.**
duty to maintain, 264, 265
expulsion, 23
principal, 265, Reg. 298, s. 12
pupil, Reg. 298, s. 23
suspension, 23
teacher, 264, Reg. 298, s. 21

Dismissal. *see* **Teacher.**

Dispute. *see* **Court, Negotiation, Mediation, Agreement, Arbitration, Contract, Collective agreement.**

Disqualification. *see also* **Qualifications.**
board member, 220
failure to deliver up books and money, 216

District combined separate school zone. *see also* **Combined separate school zone.**
defined, 1
general, 97-105
list, descriptions and names, Reg. 290

District municipality
defined, 1

District school areas
arbitration, 59
assets and liabilities, 60
auditors, debentures and estimates, 65
board
    composition, 61
    declared inactive, 66
    dissolved, 66
    elections, 61-63
    general, 59-61
    meetings, 62
    name, 59
    special meetings, 62
    term of office, 61
combined
    elections, 64
defined, 1
formation and alteration, 59, 60
list, Reg. 291
new, 60
notification of assessment commissioner, 59
rates in municipality, 65
tax

Disturbance
offence, 212

Divisional board. *see also* **Board.**
alteration of boundaries, 57
Crown land exemption, 53
defined, 1
employment contracts, 57
establishment, 56
general, 53-57
improvement district, 54
name, 55
new school division, 55
powers and duties, 56, 235.1
territory without municipal organization, 53-54
trustees, 56

***Drainage Act*, R.S.O. 1990, c. D.17,** MCIA, s. 4

Driver education
continuing education, Reg. 285, s. 1

Duties
board, 170
collector, 65, 91
Minister, 2
parents, 21
principals, 265
secretary, 198
separate school board, 90, 96
supervisory officers, 286
teachers, 264
treasurer, 198

Education authority
defined, 1

INDEX

Education relations commission. *see also* **Negotiations.**
annual report, SBTCNA, s. 60
appointment of fact finder, SBTCNA, s. 12, 18
appointment of selector, SBTCNA, s. 37
assignment of assistant, SBTCNA, ss. 12, 13, 25
composition, SBTCNA, s. 59
continued, SBTCNA, s. 59
copy of notice, SBTCNA, s. 70
duties, SBTCNA, s. 60
employees, SBTCNA, s. 59
general, SBTCNA, ss. 59-62
information from board, SBTCNA, s. 60
judicial review, SBTCNA, s. 72

Education research
Minister, 8

Educational advancement programs
Minister, 8

Elections. *see also* **Electors, Electoral groups, Electoral areas, Ballots, Poll, Polling lists, Scrutineers.**
corrupt practices, 218
district school area board, 62
general, 62-66
validity, 218

Electoral areas. *see also* **Election, Electors, Electoral groups.**
creation *or* alteration, 233, 317
French-language section, 315, 317

Electoral group. *see also* **Election, Electors, Electoral areas.**
appeal of distribution, 231
application for determination or distribution, 232
defined, 230
determination of population, 230
distribution, 230
election, 230
English language, 230
French-language, 230

number of members, 230
vacated board position, 222

Electors. *see also* **Elections, Electoral areas, Electoral groups.**
separate school, 87-89, 95

Elementary school
credits to secondary school diploma, Reg. 298, s. 8
defined, 1
French-language instruction, 288-290
on Crown land
    regulations, 11
practice teaching, 14
regulations, 11

Emergency
closing of school, 19
requirement for procedures, Reg. 298, s. 6

Employee. *see also* **Board, Trustees, Officers, Teacher, Designation, Employment, Conflict of interest.**
board, 171
indirect pecuniary interest, MCIA, s. 2
insurance, 177
medical examinations
    Minister, 8
pension, 178
retirement allowance, 179
sick leave credits, 180

Employment
of pupil during school hours, 30
of teacher to promote or sell, 217

English-language instruction
advisory committee
    elementary school, 290
    secondary school, 301
by right
    elementary schools, 289
    secondary schools, 301
duty to provide
    elementary schools, 289
    secondary schools, 301
English-language section, 325

495

INDEX

English-language instruction — *continued*
meals, lodging and transportation
    elementary schools, 289
    secondary schools, 301

Enrolment shift. *see* **Designation of unrequired staff.**

Establishment of school
regulation, 11
separate schools
    Protestant, 158
    Roman Catholic, 80

Estimates
equalized assessment, 236
French-language instructional units, 319
general, 236
permanent improvements, 236
preparation and adoption, 236
reserve fund, 236
Roman Catholic school board, 133
separate school board, 114
trainable retarded children, 236

Evening classes. *see also* **Continuing education.**
admission, 42
board, 171
regulations, 11

Examination
days
    alteration, Reg. 304, s. 6
    number, Reg. 304, s. 3
examiners' fees, 11

Exceptional pupil. *see also* **Special education.**
defined, 1

Exchange program
fee, 49

Exchange teachers
regulations, 11

Excusion. *see* **Immunization, Meeting.**

Exemptions
separate school supporters, 50, 106, 159

Expenses
board members, 171, 191
committees, 191, 300, 301
officers, 171, 191
teachers, 171, 191

Expropriation
school site, 195

***Expropriations Act*, R.S.O. 1990, c. E.26,** 153

Expulsion. *see also* **Attendance.**
on refractory conduct, 23
use of pupil record, 266

Extended funding
conditions, Reg. 284

Fact finder. *see* **Negotiations.**

Fairs
board, 171

False statement
declaration, 211
notice of intent to operate private school, 16, 106, 159
registers, 213
reports, 213

Federal government. *see* **Crown land, Indian, Band**
agreement with board, 187, 188
apportionment of federal grants, 8
federal establishments, 187

Fédération des Associations de parents francophones
school board advisory committee, 202

Federation of catholic parent-teacher associations of Ontario
school board advisory committee, 202

Federation of women teachers' associations of Ontario
affiliate, SBTCNA, s. 1
Ontario Teachers' Federation, TPA, s. 5, 6

496

INDEX

Fee
admission, 47
arbitrators, 210
boards, 171
determination, 11
different school, 49
diploma or certificate duplicate, Reg. 293
diplomat, 49
distance to school, 49
Education Relations Commission assignee, SBTCNA, s. 74
exchange program, 49
general, 49, Reg. 292
Indian pupils, 188
Indian school, 184
letter of standing duplicate, Reg. 293
not payable, 32, 38, 40, 46, Reg. 292, s. 3
OTF membership, TPA, s. 11, RTPA, s. 4
Ontario School for the Blind, Reg. 296, ss. 9-12
Ontario School for the Deaf, Reg. 296, ss. 9-12
Ontario Teachers' Certificate duplicate, Reg. 293
payable
    by boards, 39, 48, 49, 68, 70, 71, 75, 246
    by persons, 45, 47, 49, 68
principal's refresher course, Reg. 292
program development and implementation course, Reg. 292
program supervision and assessment course, Reg. 292
public and separate schools, 185
refugee, 49
refundable, Reg. 292, s. 3
school in other jurisdiction, 49
tax exempt lands, 68
transcript, Reg. 293
tuition, Reg. 292, s. 2
veteran, Reg. 292, s. 3
Visiting Forces Act, 49

Fences. *see also* **Building and site.**
boards, 171

Finances. *see also* **Board, Fees, Tax, Rates, Assessment expenses, Property, Borrowing, Auditors, Debentures, Debt charge, Financial statement.**
assets, liabilities, etc., 58
board
    bonds, 171
    borrowing, 171
    debentures, 171
    fees and expenses, 171
    inspecting of books and accounts, 207
    insurance, 171
    investments, 171
    legal costs, 171
    limits on debt obligations, 235.3
    promissory notes, 171
    term deposits, 171
general, 234-257
separate schools, 106-122

Financial assistance
accounting statement, 9

Financial statement
alternative to publication, 234
filing, 234
publication, 234
treasurer, 234

Flag
requirements, Reg. 298, s. 5

Forms
teachers' contract, Reg. 310
teachers' qualifications, Reg. 297

French-language advisory committee. *see also* **French-language instruction, French-language section, Committee.**
elementary schools
    responsibilities and duties, 290
provincial association membership fee, 300
secondary school
    allowances, 300
    annual report, 299
    apportionment of members, 292
    composition, 292

French-language advisory committee — *continued*
  conduct, 298
  election, 292-294
  establishment and dissolution, 292
  members, 292
  recommendations, 298
  resources and services, 299
  vacancies, 296
  voting, 295

French-language instruction. *see also* **French-language section, French-language advisory committee.**
admission
  non-French-speakers
    elementary schools, 289
    secondary schools, 302
annual report on enrolment, 321
by right
  elementary school, 289
  secondary school, 291
calculation of enrolment, 322
continuing education, Reg. 285, s. 6
duty to provide
  elementary school, 289
  secondary school, 291
elementary schools, 288-290
English as a subject, 289
English-speaking pupils
  Minister, 8
general, 288-321
meals, lodging and transportation
  elementary school, 289
  secondary school, 291
Minister, 8
regulations, 11
responsible person, Reg. 298, s. 13
Roman Catholic school board, 130
secondary schools, 291-302
transfer between boards, 182
transportation, 190

French-language instructional unit. *see* **French-language instruction, French-language section, French-language advisory committee.**

French-language schools. *see* **French-language instruction, French-language section, French-language advisory committee.**

French-language section. *see also* **French-language instruction, French-language advisory committee.**
allocation of estimated revenues, 319, 320
day nurseries and, 309
dissolution, 324
elections, 315, 315.1, 325.1
elector qualifications, 314
electoral areas, 315
establishment, 312
jurisdiction, 318, 320
meetings, 316
public meetings, 315
quorum, 318

Fundraising
consent of board, Reg. 298, s. 25

Government of Canada. *see* **Federal government.**

Grant
French-language schools, 130
general, Reg. 299
instalment payments, 8
payment, Reg. 299
Protestant separate schools, 162
reduction of requisition or rates, 247
Roman Catholic school board, 128
separate school, 122
special, Reg. 307

Guarantee Companies Securities Act, **R.S.O. 1990, c. G.11,** 198

Guardian. *see also* **Parent, Adult pupil, Ward.**
defined, 1
expulsion of pupil, 23

Guardian — *continued*
liability
pupil attendance, 30
suspension of pupil, 23

Guidance teachers
board, 171

Gymnasium classes. *see also* **Athletics, Recreation, Physical fitness.**
board, 171

Handicapped pupil. *see* **Blind pupil, Deaf pupil, Exceptional pupil, Special education.**

Head office
defined, 1

Health. *see also* **Immunization.**
surgical treatment
board, 171
medical examinations
board employees
Minister, 8
medical officer
pupil records, 266
principal, 265

Health Insurance Act, **R.S.O. 1990, c. H.6,** 177

Health Protection and Promotion Act, **R.S.O. 1990, c. H.7,** ISPA, s. 1

Holidays. *see also* **Remembrance Day.**
general, Reg. 304
permitted, Reg. 304, s. 2

Home and school council
school board advisory committee, 202

Home instruction
principal, Reg. 298, s. 11

Human Rights Code, **R.S.O. 1990, c. H.19.** *see also* **Charter of Rights and Freedoms.** 136

Immigration Act, **R.S.C. 1985, c. I-2,** 49, Reg. 285, s. 1

Immunization
designated diseases
defined, ISPA, s. 1
evidence re statement
certificate by medical officer of health, ISPA, s. 5
general, ISPA
order for suspension
appeal, ISPA, s. 16
hearing, ISPA, s. 15
re designated diseases, ISPA, ss. 6-9, 13
order of exclusion
appeal, ISPA, s. 16
hearing, ISPA, s. 15
re designated diseases, ISPA, s. 12, 13
parental duty, ISPA, s. 3, 4
record
defined, ISPA, s. 1
maintenance and review, ISPA, s. 11
transfer, ISPA, s. 14
regulations
any matter, ISPA, s. 17
classification and exemption, ISPA, s. 17
forms and affidavits, ISPA, s. 17
records, ISPA, s. 17
reports, ISPA, s. 17
programs, agents, dosages, ISPA, s. 17
service of documents, ISPA, s. 18
statement by physician, ISPA, s. 10
statement of conscience or religious belief
defined, ISPA, s. 1
filing by parent, ISPA, s. 3
statement of medical exemption
defined, ISPA, s. 1
filing by physician, ISPA, s. 3
transfer, ISPA, s. 14

Implementation plan. *see* **Planning and Implementation Commission**

Improvement district
elections, 54, 103

Index book
general, 108
Protestant separate school, 161

Indian. *see also* **Band, Qualifications.**
agreements, 188
defined, 1
pupils
    board, 188
    enrolment, 188
    fees, 188
    Ontario School for the Blind, Reg. 296, s. 5
    Ontario School for the Deaf, Reg. 296, s. 5
    representative, 188
    separate school board representative, 188
    trustee, 188
school
    admission, 184
    fees, 184
teacher
    native languages, Reg. 297, ss. 23-25
    qualification, Reg. 297, s. 5

Indian Act, **R.S.C. 1985, c. I-5,** 184

Institutions
boards, 171

Instruction
board, 171
inability to profit from, 35
language of
    regulations, 11

Insurance
board employees, 177
boards, 170, 171, 176
conflict of interest, MCIA, s. 14

Insurance Act, **R.S.O. 1990, c. I.8,** 171, 176, 177, MCIA, s. 14

Intelligence test. *see also* **Psychiatrist.**
principal, Reg. 298, s. 11

Interest Rate
payable on debentures, 7

Interim certificate. *see also* **Certificate, Ontario Teachers' Certificate.**
continuing to teach, Reg. 297, s. 26

Intermediate division
defined, 1

Investment
board power re
    general, 171 (1) ¶19-21
    joint, 171 (1) ¶49, 171 (4)-(5), 171.1

Joint committees
combined, 134
shared jurisdiction, 134

Judge. *see also* **Court, Appeal.**
defined, 1

Judicial review. *see* **Court.**

Junior division
defined, 1

Junior kindergarten. *see also* **Kindergarten.**
admission, 34
board, 171

Jury duty
entitlement to salary, 260

Kindergarten. *see also* **Junior kindergarten.**
admission, 31
board, 171

Land. *see* **Building and site, Property.**

Language. *see also* **English-language, French-language.**
adult classes, Reg. 285, s. 1
classes, Reg. 285, s. 1
regulations, 11

INDEX

Languages of Instruction Commission of Ontario
continued, 304
deferral by board, 304
dispute over enrolment calculation, 322
duties and powers, 304
English-language advisory committee, 304
French-language advisory committee, 304
general, 303-308
mediator, 304, 305
members, 304
recommendations to board, 306
recommendations to Minister, 308
referral by Minister, 304

Leadership training camp
Minister, 15
regulations, 11

Learning materials. *see also* **Books.**
agreements with Canada, 12
care, 265
development and production, 8
principal, 265

Legislative Assembly
member
    visiting schools, 52, 123

Legislative grants. *see* **Grants.**

Legal costs
board, 171

Legal opinion
Minister, 10

Letter of approval. *see also* **Letter of Standing**
temporary
    application, Reg. 297, Form 8
    Minister, 8
    regulations, 11
    unqualified teacher, Reg. 297, s. 50

Letter of eligibility
form, Reg. 297, Form 5
teacher educated outside Canada, Reg. 297, ss. 13, 14
teacher educated outside Ontario, Reg. 297, ss. 11, 12

Letter of permission
application form, Reg. 297, Form 7
Minister, 8
regulation, 11
unqualified teacher, Reg. 297, s. 50

Letter of standing. *see also* **Letter of approval**
permanent
    native languages teacher, Reg. 297, s. 25, Form 9
    special education teacher, Reg. 297, s. 22
        teaching dance, Reg. 297, s. 25.1, Form 11
        teaching the deaf, Reg. 297, s. 19, Form 6
    Ontario Teacher's Certificate equivalent, Reg. 297, s. 26
provisional
    deemed to hold, Reg. 297, s. 9
    extension, Reg. 297, s. 10
    form, Reg. 297, Form 4
    general, Reg. 298, s. 19
    grant, Reg. 297, s. 7
    native languages teacher, Reg. 297, ss. 23-24, Form 4
    renewal, Reg. 297, s. 8
    special education, Reg. 297, ss. 20, 21
    teaching dance, Reg. 297, s. 25.1, Form 10
qualified to continue teaching, Reg. 297, s. 27
temporary
    education outside Canada, Reg. 297, ss. 13, 14
    education outside Ontario, Reg. 297, ss. 11, 12
    extension, Reg. 297, s. 18
    form, Reg. 297, Form 3
    general, Reg. 298, s. 19
    interim certificate, Reg. 297, s. 15
    unqualified teacher, Reg. 297, s. 15

INDEX

Levy. *see also* **Rates.**
transportation
    non-resident secondary school pupils, 116

Library
board, 171
public
    territory without municipal organization, 254
regulations, 11

Lieutenant-Governor in Council
appointment
    Provincial School Attendance Officer, 24
approval
    agreements with Crown, 12
    closing of school or class, 5
    regulations, 11
    teachers' college, 14
assignment of responsibility
    to Minister, 2
authorization
    Treasurer, 6, 7
establishment
    Special Education Tribunals, 36
regulatory power
    board debt and financial obligation limits, 235.3
    district school area board, 64
    school divisions, 55
    Special Education Tribunals, 37
    uniting of area to form separate school zone, 97
submission to
    Minister's annual report, 3
variance of terms and conditions
    scholarships and awards, 17

Literacy classes
adults, Reg. 285, s. 1

***Loan and Trust Corporation Act*, R.S.O. 1990, c. L.25,** 121, 171

Loans. *see* **Borrowing, Debt charge, Debenture.**

Local associations
Ontario Association for Community Living, 69
special education and advisory committees, 206

***Local Improvement Act*, R.S.O. 1990, c. L.26,** MCIA, s. 4

Locality
defined, 1

Lock-out. *see also* **Strike, Contract, Collective agreement.**
conditions, SBTCNA, s. 68
declaration of unlawful lock-out, SBTCNA, s. 67
defined, SBTCNA, s. 1
lawful, SBTCNA, s. 68
offence, SBTCNA, s. 77
OLRB application, SBTCNA, ss. 67, 72, 77
prohibition, SBTCNA, s. 53
reserve
    calculation of amount, Reg. 283, ss. 1-3
    regulations, 239
    tax reduction, 237, 238
resignation in good faith, SBTCNA, s. 70
unlawful, SBTCNA, s. 66
withdrawal of voluntary services, SBTCNA, s. 70

Lodging. *see* **Meals and lodging.**

Lunch
length, Reg. 298, s. 3
place, Reg. 298, s. 13

Maternity leave
boards, 171

Meals and lodging. *see also* **Transportation.**
English-language instruction, 289, 301
French-language instruction, 289, 291

INDEX

Meals and lodging — *continued*
long distance from schools, 190
out-of-classroom program, 197

Mediation. *see also* **Arbitration.**
Languages of Instruction Commission of Ontario, 304, 305
Planning and Implementation Commission, 152

Meeting. *see also* **Board, Finances, Employees, Trustees, Officers, Divisional board, District school area board, Conflict of interest.**
access, 207
chair and vice-chair, 208
exclusion of persons, 207
first, 208
general, 170, 207, 208
improper conduct, 207
presiding officer, 208
quorum, 208
secretary, 208
special, 208
voting, 208

Member association
defined, SBTCNA, s. 1
offence, SBTCNA, s. 77
officer, official or agent, SBTCNA, s. 79
unlawful lock-out, SBTCNA, s. 66

Mentally-handicapped pupils. *see also* **Exceptional pupil, Special education.**
compulsory school attendance, 20
transportation, 190

Metropolitan Toronto
school board
application of regulations, 11
evening classes, 11

Milk
purchase for free distribution, Reg. 302

Minister. *see also* **Ministry.**
additions to enrolment, 4
annual report, 3
authority, 2
closing of school or class, 5
delegation, 2
out-of-classroom program sites, 197
Planning and Implementation Commission, 148
powers
  adult basic education, 8(2)
  advisory body, 10
  affirmative action policy, 8(1) ¶29
  antiracism policy, 8(1) ¶29.1
  application of *Workers' Compensation Act*, 8(1) ¶9
  appointment of federal grants, 8(1) ¶21
  assessment equalization factors, 8(1) ¶30
  approval of board agreements, 8(1) ¶33
  attendance register, 8(1) ¶8
  awards, 8(1) ¶28
  book list publication, 8(1) ¶7
  book selection and approval, 8(1) ¶6
  book selection procedures, 8(1) ¶4
  child care facility construction, 8(1) ¶34
  classes, courses and programs, 8(2)
  closing guidelines, 8(1) ¶26
  commission of inquiry, 10
  copyright, 8(1) ¶23.1
  correspondence courses, 8(1) ¶17
  courses for teachers, administrators and counsellors, 8(1) ¶16
  courses of study, 8(1) ¶2
  courses and areas of study, 8(1) ¶3
  diplomas and certificates, 8(1) ¶1
  drug education, 8(1) ¶29.2
  educational research, 8(1) ¶24
  employment equity, 8(1) ¶29
  equivalent qualification, 8(1) ¶14
  exchange program funding, 8(1) ¶22
  French language programs, 8(1) ¶25
  learning materials, 8(1) ¶23
  legal opinion, 10
  legislative grant installment payments, 8(1) ¶32

503

Minister — *continued*
- letter of permission, 8(1) ¶10
- medical examinations, 8(1) ¶15
- professional development funding, 8(1) ¶22
- program effectiveness, 8(1) ¶3.1
- pupil records, 8(1) ¶27
- scholarships and bursaries, 8(1) ¶18
- schools for deaf and blind, 8(1) ¶20
- special education, 8(3)
- suspend, cancel, re-instate qualification, 8(1) ¶13
- teachers' college, 8(1) ¶19
- temporary letter of approval, 8(1) ¶11
- textbook purchase and distribution, 8(1) ¶5
- weighting and adjustment factors, 8(1) ¶31
- withdrawal of letter, 8(1) ¶12

regulations
- accommodation & equipment, 11(1) ¶9
- admission, 11(1) ¶2
- apportionment and distribution of funds, 11(3)
- assessment equalization factor, 11(3)
- assistance, 11(3)
- average daily enrolment, 11(3)
- book purchase, 11(1) ¶8
- child care facilities' funds, 11
- compulsory attendance, 11(8)
- continuing education, 11(1) ¶17, 18
- contract, 11(1) ¶14
- Crown land schools, 11(1) ¶15
- demonstration schools, 13
- evening classes, 11(1) ¶7
- examiners' fees, 11(1) ¶19
- exchange teachers, 11(1) ¶22
- fee determination, 11(3)
- fees, 11(9)
- forms, 11(1) ¶30
- general, 11(1) ¶1
- language of instruction, 11(1) ¶21
- language programs, 11(1) ¶36
- leadership training camp funding, 11(3)
- legislative grants, 11(3)
- letter of permission, 11(1) ¶13
- meals, lodging, transportation funding, 11(3)
- nominations and elections, 11(11)
- Ontario School for the Blind, 13
- Ontario School for the Deaf, 13
- payments to board, 11(3)
- practice teaching, 11(1) ¶25
- private sector competition, 11(1) ¶35
- procedure at hearings, 11(1) ¶32
- pupil duties, 11(1) ¶27
- pupil records, 11(1) ¶¶3, 4
- qualifications, 11(1) ¶11
- record cards, 11(1) ¶12
- recreation programs, 11(1) ¶10
- religious exercises and education, 11(1) ¶20
- school libraries, 11(1) ¶23
- school year, terms and holidays, 11(7)
- sign language, 11(1) ¶21.1
- special education, 11(1) ¶¶5, 6
- supervisory officer, 11(1) ¶¶33, 34
- supervisory officers' examinations, 11(1) ¶16
- teachers, administrators & counsellors, 11(1) ¶26
- teachers college, 11(9)
- teaching qualifications, 11(1) ¶29
- temporary letter of approval, 11(1) ¶13
- textbooks, 11(1) ¶24
- trainable retarded children, 11(1) ¶28
- transportation, 11(1) ¶31

resolution of language-related matters, 308
responsibility, 2
site or property, 194

Ministry. *see also* **Minister.**
annual report, 3
continued, 2
general, 2-17

Minutes
election meeting
- district school area electors, 62
- rural separate school supporters, 92

inspection, 207

INDEX

Municipal Act, **R.S.O. 1990, c. M.45,** 54, 103, 113, 114, 121, 178, 244, MCIA, s. 4, MCIA, s. 14

Municipal Affairs Act, **R.S.O. 1990, c. M.46,** 171, 180

Municipal conflict of interest. *see* **Conflict of interest.**

Municipal Elections Act, **R.S.O. 1990, c. M.53,** 61, 63, 89, 93, 97, 218, 220, 222, 226, 227, 230, 309, 322, Reg. 313

Municipal Tax Sales Act, **R.S.O. 1990, c. M.60,** 65

Municipality. *see also* **Rates, Assessment.**
agreement, 183
arbitrators, 210
defined, 1
out-of-classroom program sites, 197
use of facilities, 183

Native. *see* **Indian, Band, Qualifications.**

Native languages. *see* **Indian, Qualifications.**

Natural science program. *see* **Out-of-classroom program.**

Negotiations. *see also* **Collective agreement, Education Relations Commission.**
assistant to parties, SBTCNA, ss. 7, 12, 13, 25, 74
branch affiliate
  exclusive representation of teachers, SBTCNA, s. 5
collective, SBTCNA, s. 3
costs, SBTCNA, s. 74
fact-finder
  agreed upon matters, SBTCNA, s. 19
  appointment, SBTCNA, ss. 12, 14
  confirmed negotiations, SBTCNA, s. 15
  duty, SBTCNA, s. 20
  general, SBTCNA, s. 14
  jurisdiction, SBTCNA, s. 21
  notice of appointment, SBTCNA, s. 18
  procedure, SBTCNA, s. 22
  prohibited, SBTCNA, s. 16
  report, SBTCNA, ss. 23, 24, 26
  vacancy, SBTCNA, s. 17
final offer selection
  agreed upon matters, SBTCNA, s. 40
  contempt, failure to attend, etc., SBTCNA, s. 46
  decision, SBTCNA, ss. 47, 48
  final offers and responses, SBTCNA, ss. 41-43
  hearing, SBTCNA, ss. 44, 45
  notice to commission, SBTCNA, s. 37
  powers, SBTCNA, s. 46
  preparation of agreement, SBTCNA, s. 49
  procedure, SBTCNA, s. 46
  prohibited as selector, SBTCNA, s. 38
  unable to act, SBTCNA, s. 39
good faith, SBTCNA, s. 11
joint, SBTCNA, s. 4
judicial review, SBTCNA, s. 72
negotiating group, SBTCNA, s. 6
notice of desire to negotiate, SBTCNA, s. 9
notice of desire to renew an agreement, SBTCNA, s. 10
notice to Commission, SBTCNA, s. 71
obligation to negotiate, SBTCNA, s. 11
offence, SBTCNA, s. 77
OLRB application, SBTCNA, s. 77
reference to arbitrator, SBTCNA, ss. 12, 27
reference to selector, SBTCNA, ss. 12, 27
service, SBTCNA, s. 73
subject matter, SBTCNA, s. 8
voluntary binding arbitration
  agreed upon matters, SBTCNA, s. 31
  appointments, SBTCNA, s. 28
  contempt, failure to attend, etc., SBTCNA, s. 33
  duty, SBTCNA, s. 34
  jurisdiction, SBTCNA, s. 34
  notice to commission, SBTCNA, s. 28
  powers, SBTCNA, s. 33

Negotiations — *continued*
   preparation of agreement, SBTCNA, s. 36
   procedure, SBTCNA, s. 32
   prohibited as arbitrators, SBTCNA, s. 29
   report, SBTCNA, s. 35
   vacancy, SBTCNA, s. 30
   voting, SBTCNA, s. 76
   witness compellability, SBTCNA, s. 81

Night School. *see* **Evening classes, Continuing education.**

Northern Ontario Public and Secondary School Trustees' Association
member association, SBTCNA, s. 1

Notice
election meeting, 62, 90
Protestant separate school support, 159, 160
separate school support, 106, 107
trailer fees, 256

Oath. *see also* **Declaration.**
board members, 209

Occasional teacher. *see also* **Teacher.**
defined, 1

Offence
acting while disqualified, 213
disturbances, 212
employment of pupils, 30
employment to promote or sell books, 217
failure to deliver up books and money, 215, 216
false reports and registers, 213
false statement, 211
habitual absenteeism, 30
labour-related, SBTCNA, s. 77
operation of private school, 16
parental neglect
   child's attendance, 30
   immunization, ISPA, s. 4
promotion or sale of books, etc., 217
trailers, 256

withholding information from auditors, 214

Officers. *see also* **Director of Education, Supervisory officers, Board employees, Finances, Trustees, Property meeting.**
allowance, 191
business administrator, 198
chief education officer, 283
chief executive officer, 199, 283
Director of Education, 279-284
general, 170, 198
personal liability, 198
responsibility, 199
secretary
   board to appoint, 170
   defined, 1
   duties, 198
   failure to deliver up books and money, 215, 216
secretary-treasurer
   board to appointment, 171
   defined, 1
   duties, 198
   security, 170
treasurer
   board, 170, 171
   defined, 1
   duties, 198
   failure to deliver up books and money, 215, 216
   financial statements, 234
   security, 198

One-session course. *see also* **Qualifications, Three-session course.**
honour specialist
   qualifications, Reg. 297, ss. 38, 39
   subjects, Reg. 297, Sched. E
subjects, Reg. 297, Sched. C
qualification, Reg. 297, s. 31

Ontario Association for Community Living
local association, 69
transportation, 190

INDEX

Ontario English Catholic Teachers' Association
"affiliate", SBTCNA, s. 1
Ontario Teachers' Federation, TPA, ss. 5, 6

Ontario Labour Relations Board. *see* **Strike, Lock-out, Negotiations, Collective agreement.**
prosecution of offence, SBTCNA, s. 77
payment during strike, SBTCNA, s. 68

Ontario Municipal Employees' Retirement System Act, **R.S.O. 1990, c. O.29,** 178

Ontario Parent Council

members
  appointment, 17.1
  remuneration, 17.1
  term, 17.1
powers and duties, 17.1

Ontario Public School Teachers' Federation
"affiliate", SBTCNA, s. 1
Ontario Teachers' Federation, TPA, ss. 5, 6

Ontario Public School Trustees' Association
member association, SBTCNA, s. 1

Ontario School for the Blind
admission, Reg. 296, ss. 3-8
continued, 13
designation, Reg. 296, s. 2
discharge, Reg. 296, s. 20
dismissal, Reg. 296, s. 19
fees, Reg. 296, ss. 9-12
general, 13, Reg. 296
Indian pupils, Reg. 296, s. 5
Minister, 13
parents, Reg. 296, s. 17
pupils' duties, Reg. 296, s. 14
regulations, 13
residence counsellors' duties, Reg. 296, s. 16
return home, Reg. 296, s. 21
Superintendent's Advisory Council, Reg. 296, s. 22
Superintendent's duties, Reg. 296, s. 18
teacher qualifications, Reg. 296, s. 23
teacher's duties, Reg. 296, s. 15
transportation, 190, Reg. 296, s. 13

Ontario School for the Deaf
admission, Reg. 296, ss. 3-8
continued, 13
designations, Reg. 296, s. 2
discharge, Reg. 296, s. 20
dismissal, Reg. 296, s. 19
fees, Reg. 296, ss. 9-12
general, 13, Reg. 296
Indian pupils, Reg. 296, s. 5
Minister, 13
parents, Reg. 296, s. 17
pupils' duties, Reg. 296, s. 14
regulations, 13
residence counsellors' duties, Reg. 296, s. 16
return home, Reg. 296, s. 21
Superintendent's Advisory Council, Reg. 296, s. 22
superintendent's duties, Reg. 296, s. 18
teacher qualifications, Reg. 296, s. 23
teacher's duties, Reg. 296, s. 15
transportation, 190, Reg. 296, s. 13

Ontario School Trustees' Council
offence, SBTCNA, s. 77
officer, official or agent, SBTCNA, s. 79
unlawful lock-out, SBTCNA, s. 66

Ontario Secondary School Teachers' Federation
"affiliate", SBTCNA, s. 1
Ontario Teachers' Federation, TPA, ss. 5, 6

Ontario Separate School Trustees' Association
member association, SBTCNA, s. 1

Ontario Teacher's Certificate. *see also* **Qualification.**
criteria for qualification, Reg. 297, ss. 2, 3

Ontario Teacher's Certificate — *continued*
deemed holder, Reg. 297, s. 26
fees for duplicate, Reg. 293
form, Reg. 297, Form 1
grant, Reg. 297, ss. 10, 25.2
holder of temporary letter of standing, Reg. 297, s. 17
interim certificate holder eligible, Reg. 297, s. 26
letter of standing holder eligible, Reg. 297, s. 26
non-Canadian, Reg. 297, s. 27

Ontario Teachers' Federation
affiliated bodies, RTPA, s. 1
annual conferences with Ministry, TPA, s. 10
associate membership, TPA, s. 4
Board of Governors
    annual meeting, RTPA, ss. 5, 11
    expenses, RTPA, s. 12
    generally, TPA, s. 5
body corporate, TPA, s. 2
committees
    nominating, RTPA, s. 7
    Relations and Discipline, RTPA, ss. 8, 19-27
    special, RTPA, s. 10
    standing, RTPA, s. 9
duties of members
    educational authorities, to, RTPA, s. 15
    fellow members, to, RTPA, s. 18
    general, RTPA, s. 13
    Ontario Teachers' Federation, to, RTPA, s. 17
    public, to, RTPA, s. 16
    pupils, to, RTPA, s. 14
executive
    expenses, RTPA, s. 12
    generally, TPA, s. 6
    meetings, RTPA, s. 6
fees, TPA, s. 11, RTPA, s. 4
general, TPA
membership
    application for, RTPA, s. 3
    fees, RTPA, s. 4
    mandatory, TPA, s. 4
    voluntary, RTPA, s. 2
name, TPA, s. 2
objects, TPA, s. 3
offence, SBTCNA, s. 77
officer, official or agent, SBTCNA, s. 79
president, TPA, s. 7
regulations
    associate membership, TPA, s. 12
    branches, TPA, s. 12
    code of ethics, TPA, s. 12
    committees, TPA, s. 12
    discipline, TPA, s. 12
    evidence of, RTPA, s. 29
    expenses, TPA, s. 12
    fee amounts and due dates, TPA, s. 12
    local affiliated bodies, groups or associations, TPA, s. 12
    meetings, TPA, s. 12
    powers and duties of Board and executive, TPA, s. 12
    special war services, TPA, s. 12
    voluntary membership, TPA, s. 12
Relations and Discipline Committee
    procedure, RTPA, ss. 19-22
responsibilities
    appointments to Ontario Teachers' Pension Plan Board, TPA, s. 9
    grants, TPA, s. 9
    investment, TPA, s. 9
    pension agreement, TPA, s. 9
    pension plan amendments, TPA, s. 9
    property, TPA, s. 9
    representation of pension plan members, TPA, s. 9
secretary-treasurer, TPA, s. 8
students, TPA, s. 4
unlawful strike, SBTCNA, s. 65
vice-presidents, TPA, s. 7

Ontario Teacher's Qualifications Record Card. *see also* **Qualification.**
additional qualification entry, Reg. 297, ss. 29, 30

INDEX

Ontario Teacher's Qualifications Record Card — *continued*
form, Reg. 297, Form 2
grant, Reg. 297, s. 10
language, Reg. 297, s. 4
qualification entry, Reg. 298, s. 19

Opening exercises
exemption, Reg. 298, s. 4
requirement, Reg. 298, s. 4

Operation of schools
accommodation, Reg. 298, s. 2
daily session, Reg. 298, s. 3
emergency procedures, Reg. 298, s. 6
flags, Reg. 298, s. 5
general, Reg. 298
opening or closing exercises, Reg. 298, s. 4
textbooks, Reg. 298, s. 7
acquisition of land, 197
board and lodging, 197
building erection, addition, alteration, 197
conservation authorities, 197
municipal taxation, 197
separate school boards, 197
shared use, 197
site maintenance, 197

Organizational unit

Out-of-classroom program

Parcel of land
defined, 1

Parent
attendance, 21
consent for surgical treatment, 171
immunization, ISPA, ss. 3, 4
liability, 30
notification, Reg. 298, s. 1
pupil over 18 years, 1
remuneration, 190

Part-time teacher. *see also* **Teacher.**
defined, 1

Partnership
indirect pecuniary interest, MCIA, s. 2
separate school supporter, 112

Partnerships Act, **R.S.O. 1990, c. P.5,** 112

Pecuniary interest. *see* **Conflict of interest.**

Pensions
board employees, 178
Ontario Teachers' Federation, TPA, s. 9
teachers, TPA, s. 9

Permanent improvements. *see also* **Building and site, Books, Bus.**
defined, 1
estimates, 236

Permanent teacher. *see also* **Teacher.**
defined, 1

Personality test. *see* **Intelligence test.**

Physical fitness. *see also* **Athletics, Recreation, Gymnasium classes.**
agreement with Canada, 12

Planning and Implementation Commission
advisory role, 148
assistance, 152
condition for extended funding, Reg. 284, ss. 1-2
criteria, 151
defined, 1
general, 147
mediator appointment, 152
plans, 149
public meetings, 150
reports, 148

Playground
board, 171

Poll
book, 92
district school areas, 62
rural separate schools, 92

509

INDEX

Polling list
defined, 1

Population
defined, 1

Practice teaching
permission, 14
regulations, 11

Prepaid Hospital and Medical Services Act,
R.S.O. 1990, c. P.21, 177

Primary Division
defined, 1

Principal
continuing education, Reg. 285, s. 2
defined, 1
duties, 265, Reg. 298, s. 11
    assign classes and subjects, 265(e)
    assign duties, Reg. 298, s. 3(b)
    cleanliness of school, 265(j)
    communicable disease, 265(k), (l)
    community cooperation, Reg. 298, s. 11(3)(o)
    condition and appearance of school, 265(j)
    conduct school as per timetable and calendar, 265(e)
    counselling teacher, Reg. 298, s. 11(4)
    department heads, Reg. 298, s. 3(a), (b)
    develop cooperation, 265(b)
    discipline, 265(a), Reg. 298, s. 11(1)(a)
    examinations, 265(f)
    health and comfort of pupils, 265(j)
    home instruction, Reg. 298, s. 11(11)
    information to Minister, Reg. 298, s. 11(3)(p)
    inspection of premises, Reg. 298, s. 11(3)(l)
    instruction, Reg. 298, s. 11(1)(a), 3(a), (k)
    intelligence texts, Reg. 298, s. 11(m)
    lunch place for pupils, Reg. 298, s. 11(3)(q)
    maintenance staff inattentiveness, Reg. 298, s. 11(3)(e)
    management of school, Reg. 298, s. 11(1)(b)
    organization of school, Reg. 298, s. 11(1)(b)
    outline accessibility, Reg. 298, s. 11(3)(d)
    outline retention, Reg. 298, s. 11(3)(c), (8)
    parent's failure to make compensation, Reg. 298, s. 11(3)(l)
    performance appraisals of teachers, Reg. 298, s. 11(3)(g)-(i)
    personality test, Reg. 298, s. 11(3)(m)
    promote pupils, 265(g)
    pupil's inability to provide own supplies, Reg. 298, s. 11(9)
    pupil misconduct, Reg. 298, s. 11(3)(n)
    pupil records, 265(d)
    record attendance, 265(c)
    register pupils, 265(c)
    recommendations on teachers, Reg. 298, s. 11(3)(j)
    refuse access, 265(m)
    repairs, Reg. 298, s. 11(3)(l)
    report, 265(i)
    report disease or unsanitary conditions, 265(l)
    report on premises, Reg. 298, s. 11(3)(l)
    report pupil progress, 265(f)
    report to parent, Reg. 298, s. 11(3)(n)
    report through supervisory officer, Reg. 298, s. 11(10)
    statement on promotion, 265(g)
    supervision, Reg. 298, s. 11(3)(f)
    teaching materials, 265(j)
    temperature and ventilation, 265(j)
    textbooks, 265(h)
    timetables and calendars accessibility, 265(e)
    timetable preparation, 265(e)
    vice-principals, Reg. 298, s. 3(b)
    visitor's book, 265(o)

INDEX

Principal — *continued*
    when principal not language qualified,
        Reg. 298, ss. 11(5)-(7), 26(3)
    qualifications, Reg. 297, ss. 40-49, Reg. 298, s. 9
    qualification equivalents, Reg. 297, ss. 46, 47
    trainable retarded children, Reg. 298, s. 10

Principal's refresher course
    fees, Reg. 292
    qualification, Reg. 297, s. 45

Private School
    defined, 1
    general, 16

Privilege. *see* **Pupil records.**

Prizes. *see also* **Awards, Bursaries, Scholarships.**
    establishment, 173

Probationary teacher. *see also* **Teacher.**
    defined, 1

Professional Activity Days
    alteration, Reg. 304, s. 6
    described in calendar, Reg. 304, s. 7
    evaluation, Reg. 304, s. 7
    number per year, Reg. 304, s. 2
    school calendar, Reg. 304, ss. 4, 5

Program Development and Implementation Course
    admission, Reg. 297, s. 41
    fees, Reg. 292

Program Supervision and Assessment Course
    admission, Reg. 297, s. 42
    fees, Reg. 292

Promissory note. *see also* **Borrowing.**
    boards, 171
    borrowing, 245

Property. *see also* **Board, Learning materials, Employees, Finances, Trustees, Officers, Building and site.**
    agreement for multi-use building, 195
    appropriation, 193
    buildings, 195
    disposal, 194
    expropriation, 195
    leave, 194
    out-of-classroom programs, 17
    possession, 193
    purchase, 195
    removal of restrictions on use, 194
    repair, 170
    sale, 194
    vesting of school lands, 192

Protestant separate school
    board
        discontinuing, 168
        name, 166
        powers, 167
        trustee qualification, 164
    establishment, 158
    exemption from public school rates, 159
    general, 158-169
    index book, 161
    legislative grants, 162
    notice of support, 159
    reports, 163
    voter qualification, 164
    withdrawal of support, 159

Provincial Offences Act, **R.S.O. 1990, c. P.33,** 30

Provincial school attendance counsellor. *see also* **School attendance counsellor.**
    alternative learning, Reg. 308, s. 5
    general, 24
    notification
        appointment of school attendance counsellor, 25
    trustee, 29

INDEX

Provincial Supervisory Officer
defined, 1

Psychiatric facility
transportation, 190

Psychiatrist. *see also* **Intelligence test.**
board, 171
duties, Reg. 298, s. 26

Psychologist. *see* **Psychiatrist, Intelligence test.**

Public lectures
board, 171

Public school
board
    agreements, 184, 185
    defined, 1
elector
    defined, 1
    territory without municipal organization, 61
general, 50-76
Roman Catholic school board pupil, 144

Pupil. *see also* **Attendance, Admission, Exceptional pupil, Expulsion, Suspension, Trainable retarded pupil, Blind pupil, Deaf pupil, Adult pupil.**
conduct, Reg. 298, s. 23
duties
    fundraising, Reg. 298, s. 25
    regulations, 11
requirements, Reg. 298, s. 23
responsibilities, Reg. 298, s. 23

Pupil records
confidentiality, 266
Minister, 8
legal privilege, 266
regulation's, 11
secrecy, 266
use, 266

Qualifications of teachers. *see also* **One-session course, Three-session course, Ontario Teacher's Certificate.**
additional qualifications, Reg. 297, ss. 28-49
approved program, Reg. 297, s. 29
art and music studies, Reg. 298, s. 19
business or industrial experience, Reg. 297, s. 30
business studies, Reg. 298, s. 19
certificate
    cancellation and suspension, Reg. 298, s. 22
    equivalent, 8, Reg. 297, s. 26
    fee for duplicate, Reg. 293
    Ontario Teacher's Certificate, Reg. 298, s. 19
    to whom awarded, 262
deaf and blind pupils, Reg. 298, s. 19
deaf teacher, Reg. 297, ss. 19, 20
emergency, Reg. 298, s. 21
family studies, Reg. 298, s. 19
general, 262, Reg. 297, Reg. 298, s. 19
general studies, Reg. 298, s. 19
intermediate and senior division, Reg. 297, Sched. A
language of instruction, Reg. 298, s. 19
letter of approval, Reg. 297, s. 50
letter of permission, Reg. 297, s. 50
letter of standing, Reg. 297, ss. 7, 27, Form 9
minimum course length, Reg. 297, s. 28
Minister, 8
native ancestry, Reg. 297, s. 5
native languages, Reg. 297, ss. 23-25, Form 9
one-session courses, Reg. 297, s. 31
one-session honour specialist course, Reg. 297, ss. 38, 39
principal's qualifications, Reg. 297, ss. 40-49
regulations, 11
special education, Reg. 297, ss. 20-22, Reg. 298, s. 19
technological studies, Reg. 297, Sched. B, Reg. 298, s. 19

Qualifications of teachers — *continued*
three-session specialist courses, Reg. 297, ss. 32-37
trainable retarded children, Reg. 298, s. 19
unqualified teacher, 8, Reg. 297, ss. 50, 51, Reg. 298, s. 21

Rates. *see also* **Assessment.**
adjustment, 247
assessment data, 249
assessment for school purposes, 251
calculation, 117
collection, 244
determination, 250
district school areas, 65
divisional board, 243, 254
public/separate distinction, 110
equalizing factor, 117
error connection, 244
exemption
    pupil entitlement to continue, 143
    separate school supporter, 106
fees for trailers, 255
general, 243-257
grant to board, 247
installment payment, 243
levy, 243, 247, 252
municipality
    accountability, 244
    payment to board, 243
over-levy, 247
owner/occupant agreement, 111
public library, 254
public school board, 65, 243
responsibility for determination, 250
Roman Catholic school board, 133
secondary school
    boards, 65, 243
    exemption for separate school supporter, 132
separate schools
    annual statement of supporters, 119
    assessment of non-residents, 106
    copy of municipal assessment roll, 118
    corporate supporters, 112
    distinguishing, 110
    duties of board, 96
    estimates, 114
    exemption, 106
    factors, 117
    index book, 108
    levy for meals, lodging and transportation, 116
    liability, 111
    liability of non-resident supporter, 106
    mistakes in assessment, 109
    municipal collection, 243
    request to municipality, 120
    supporters, 106
    trustee powers, 115
    withdrawal of support, 107
statutory conflict, 253
tax notice, 244
under-levy, 247
where no public school, 257

Recess
requirement, Reg. 298, s. 3

Records. *see also* **Pupil records.**
discontinued separate school board, 86
dissolved district school area board, 66
board, 171
regulation, 11

Recreation. *see also* **Athletics, Community recreation centre.**
board, 171
facilities, 171
program, 11

Regional Committee for French-language Education
establishment, 323

Regional tribunal
composition, Reg. 303, s. 1
convening, Reg. 303, s. 6
establishment, Reg. 303, s. 2
general, Reg. 303
language, Reg. 303, s. 5
membership criteria, Reg. 303, ss. 3, 4

Regulations. *see also* **Minister.**
defined, 1

Religion
exemption from study, 144
optional program, Reg. 298, s. 28
prohibition on indoctrination, Reg. 298, s. 29
public schools, 51
regulation, 11
separate school board, Reg. 298, s. 29
when indoctrination allowed, Reg. 298, s. 29

Remembrance Day. *see also* **Holiday.**
service, Reg. 304, s. 9

Reports
board
    children not enrolled, 170
    Languages of Instruction Commission recommendation, 306
    transmission to Minister, 170
board member
    false, 213
French-language advisory committee, 299
Minister, 3
principal, 23, 28
school attendance counsellor, 10, 26

Reserve
account, 257
fund
    defined, 1
    estimates allocation, 236
    expenditure, 236
strike or lock-out
    calculation of amount, Reg. 283, ss. 1-3
    regulations, 239
    tax reduction, 237, 238

Resident pupils. *see also* **Admission, Attendance.**
beginners' class, 34
elementary, 33
junior kindergarten, 34
kindergarten, 34
public school, 33
right to attend
    any secondary school, 41
    more accessible school, 39
    school in another jurisdiction, 48
    school without fee, 32, 33, 35, 40
    trainable retarded school, 48
secondary, 40
separate schools, 33
trainable retarded child, 33, 40
transportation, 190
where one parent sole support, 44

Resignation
board member, 221

Retarded children. *see* **Trainable retarded pupils, Special education, Exceptional pupils.**

Retirement allowance. *see* **Allowance.**

Roman Catholic
defined, 1

Roman Catholic School Board. *see also* **Board, Roman Catholic, Separate schools, Roman Catholic separate schools, Separate school boards.**
conditions for extended funding, Reg. 284, ss. 1-2
defined, 1
eligibility, 131
estimates, 133
grades, 129, Reg. 284, s. 2
legislative grants
    French-language schools, 130
powers and duties, 126
rates, 133
secondary school pupil
    entitlement, 144
    exchange, 127
voluntary transfer to, Reg. 288, Reg. 289

Roman Catholic separate schools. *see also* **Roman Catholic school board, Combined separate school zone, Rural separate school, Separate school.**
general, 77-157

INDEX

Roman Catholic separate schools —
continued
secondary school education, 124-246
tax and finances, 106-122
zones, 78-86

Rural separate school
annual meeting, 92
annual report, 90
auditor, 90
board meetings, 89-90
board vacancy before incorporation, 224
collector
defined, 1
duties of board, 90
election conducted by municipality, 93
election of board, 92
electors, 89
general, 89-93
site, 90
trustees, 89
zone defined, 1

Safety. *see* **Principal, Teacher.**

Salary
contract, Reg. 310, s. 2
deduction for OTF membership, TPA, s. 11
defined, 1

Scholarship. *see also* **Prizes, Bursary, Awards.**
agreement with Canada, 12
establishment, 173
Minister, 8
variation, 17

School. *see also* **Demonstration school, Building and site, Admission, Crown land.**
defined, 1

School Attendance Counsellors. *see also* **Provincial school attendance counsellors, Attendance.**
appointment, 25
board, 26
general, 25-29
inquiries, 26
jurisdiction, 25, 28
powers, 26
principal, 28
responsibilities, 26
vacancy, 25

School Board Advisory Committee
appointment, 202
budget and expenditures, 204
composition, 202
establishment, 201
general, 200-205
limitations on powers, 205
meetings, 203
members, 202
powers, 205
reports and recommendations, 205
separate school board, 202

School building. *see* **Building and site.**

School bus. *see* **Bus.**

School calendar. *see* **Calendar.**

School closing. *see* **Closing.**

School day. *see* **Day.**

School divisions
defined, 1
formation and alteration, 1, 55
list, Reg. 287, s. 1
names, Reg. 287, s. 1

School facilities. *see* **Building and site.**

School fairs. *see* **Fairs.**

Schools for trainable retarded children. *see* **Trainable retarded pupils.**

School holidays. *see* **Holidays.**

School hours. *see* **Day.**

School library. *see* **Library.**

School property. *see* **Property, Building and site.**

INDEX

School section
defined, 1
formation, alteration, dissolution
   validity of proceedings, 1

School site. *see* **Building and site.**

School supplies
board, 171

School visitors. *see* **Visitors.**

Scrutineers
rural separate school board, 92

Secondary school
agreements, 186
defined, 7
district
   agreement, 186
   boards
      auditors, 67
      name, 67
      regulations, 67
      tax collection, 65, 67
      estimates, 67
      powers and duties, 67
   defined, 1
election by separate school board, 124
exempt land, 68
French-language instruction, 291-302
general, 50-76
Roman Catholic school board pupils, 127
Roman Catholic separate schools, 124-146
territorial districts outside school divisions, 67

Secretary. *see* **Officers.**

Secretary-treasurer. *see* **Officers.**

Securities
interest rate, 7

***Securities Act*, R.S.O. 1990, c. S.5,** 113

Security
collector, 198
failure to take, 198
form, 198

Selection of final offer. *see* **Negotiations.**

Senior division
defined, 1

Separate school. *see also* **Roman Catholic separate school, Roman Catholic school board, Rural separate school, Combined separate school, separate school supporter, Separate school board, Separate school zone.**
elector
   defined, 1
   general, 87
legislative grants, 122
municipal grants, 122
number of voter, 92
rights continued, 1
visitors, 122

Separate School Board. *see also* **Board, Separate school, Separate school zone, Rural separate school, Combined separate school board, Roman Catholic school board.**
accounts, 96
agreements, 184, 185
appointment of auditors, 96
appointment of officers, 96
collection of rates, 96
defined, 1
duties and powers
   general, 96
   designation of teachers, Reg. 289
   designation of support staff, Reg. 288
election
   secondary school board duties, 124, 125
estimates
   preparation, 114
property, 193
religious education, 96

516

INDEX

Separate school supporter. *see* **Separate school, Roman Catholic.**
corporation, 112
correction in assessment, 109
defined, 1
exemption from rates, 106, 132
index book, 108
non-resident, 106
partnership, 112
rates imposed before school established, 106, 107
resident, 106
trustees, 119
withdrawal of support, 107

Separate school zone. *see also* **Separate school, Separate school board.**
boundaries, 78
centres, 78
combined, 79, 85
deemed inclusion, 78
defined, 1
description, 78
detachment, 85
discontinuance, 86
establishment
    combined, 84
    election of trustees, 81
    meeting, 80
    legislative grants, 83
    name, 80
    powers of trustees, 81
    right to vote, 82
general, 78-86
geographic township, 78
levy
    transportation, board, lodging, 116
municipality, 78
two or more municipalities
    rates, 117
unorganized territory, 79

Separated town
defined, 1

Sick leave credits
board employees, 180

Sinking funds
interest rate, 7

Site. *see* **Building and site.**

Small Claims Court
enforcement of fee payment, 171
service of summons by bailiff, 215, 216

Social worker
duties, Reg. 298, s. 26
defined, 1

Special education. *see also* **Trainable retarded pupils, Deaf pupils, Blind pupils, Exceptional pupils, Special Education Advisory Committee, Special education identification, Placement and Review Committee.**
general, Reg. 306
hearing handicapped, Reg. 298, s. 30
maximum enrolment, Reg. 298, s. 31
minister, 8
placement, Reg. 305
program
    defined, 1
regulations, 11
teachers qualifications, Reg. 297, ss. 20-22, Reg. 298, s. 19

Special Education Advisory Committee. *see also* **Special education.**
composition, 206
establishment, 206
language requirements, 206
local associations, 206
Ontario Association for Community Living, 206
recommendations re special education programs, 206
requirements, 206

Special Education Appeal Board. *see also* **Special education tribunal.**
composition, Reg. 305, s. 7

INDEX

Special education identification, Placement and Review Committee. *see also* **Special education.**
appeal, Reg. 305, ss. 4-7, 12
appeal from review of placement, Reg. 305, s. 11
composition, Reg. 305, s. 3
duties, Reg. 306, ss. 4-5
establishment, Reg. 305, s. 2
evidence, Reg. 305, s. 2
parental guide, Reg. 305, s. 2
procedures, Reg. 305, s. 2
pupil referral, Reg. 305, s. 2
report, Reg. 306, s. 3
review of placement, Reg. 305, ss. 8-10
special education plan, Reg. 306, ss. 2, 4

Special education tribunal. *see also* **Special Education Appeal Board.**
establishment, 36, 37

Special grant. *see* **Grant.**

Statutory Powers Procedure Act, **R.S.O. 1990, c. S.22,** Reg. 300, ss. 3, 7, Reg. 309, s. 13, SBTCNA, s. 80

Strike. *see also* **Lock-out, Strike, Collective agreement.**
conditions on participation, SBTCNA, s. 63
declaration of unlawful strike, SBTCNA, s. 67
defined, SBTCNA, s. 1
offence, SBTCNA, s. 77
OLRB application, SBTCNA, ss. 67, 72, 77
principals and vice-principals, SBTCNA, s. 64
prohibition, SBTCNA, s. 53
reserve
 calculation of amount, Reg. 283, ss. 1-3
 regulations, 239
 tax reduction, 237, 238
resignation in good faith, SBTCNA, s. 70
restrictions on participation, SBTCNA, s. 63
resumption, SBTCNA, s. 68
voting, SBTCNA, s. 76
termination, SBTCNA, s. 69

unlawful, SBTCNA, s. 65
withdrawal of voluntary services, SBTCNA, s. 70

Subjects and programs. *see also* **Supervisory officer.**
supervisor, co-ordinator and consultant
 appointment, Reg. 298, s. 17
 duties, Reg. 298, s. 18

Summer school
board, 171
elementary school pupils, Reg. 285, s. 1
pupils, Reg. 285, s. 1
trainable retarded pupils, Reg. 285, s. 1

Summons
failure to deliver up books and money, 215, 216
service, 215, 216

Supervisory officer. *see also* **Director of Education, Subjects and programs.**
abolition of position, 282
access, 286
additional administrative duties, 285
appointment, 281, 285
defined, 1
designation, 285
director of education, 279, 280
dismissal, Reg. 309, s. 8
duties, 286, Reg. 298, s. 26
examinations, 11
general, 278-287, Reg. 309
language, 285, Reg. 298, s. 26
ministerial approval, 285
neglect, a misconduct, inefficiency, 287, Reg. 309, s. 8
other employment, 286
qualifications, 278, Reg. 309, ss. 1-6
redundancy of position, Reg. 309, s. 7
regulations, 11
requirement to employ, 284
responsibilities, 286
severance allowance, Reg. 209, ss. 11, 15
suspension, 287, Reg. 309, s. 12

INDEX

Support staff. *see also* **Designation of unrequired staff.**
defined, 1

Surgical treatment. *see* **Health.**

Surplus money
board, 171

Suspension. *see also* **Attendance, Immunization.**
appeal, 23
general, 23
designated disease
    general, ISPA, ss. 6-9, 13
    appeal, ISPA, s. 16
    hearing, ISPA, s. 15
use of pupil records, 266

Tax. *see also* **Rates, Assessment.**
exemption for separate school supporters, 50
general, 243-257
tax-exempt land, 45, 68

Teacher. *see also* **Qualifications, Contract, Negotiations, Board of Reference, Salary, Principal.**
appointment, 269
bursaries
    Minister, 8
conferences, 264
contract, 11
defined, 1
dismissal, 268, 269
disqualification
    membership on own board, 219
duties, 264, Reg. 298, s. 20
    actions in absence, 264(1)(i)
    assigned instructional program, Reg. 298, s. 20(b)
    assigned supervision tasks, Reg. 298, s. 20(b)
    class management, Reg. 298, s. 20(a)
    community cooperation, Reg. 298, s. 20(e)
    cooperate with department heads, Reg. 298, s. 20(c)
    develop cooperation, 264(1)(d)
    discipline, 264(1)(e), Reg. 298, s. 20(h)
    encourage learning, 264(1)(b)
    evaluation of pupil, Reg. 298, s. 20(a)
    inculcate highest regard for virtue, 264(1)(c)
    inculcate respect for religion, 264(1)(c)
    preparation of class, Reg. 298, s. 20(d)
    presence in class, Reg. 298, s. 20(d)
    professional activity days, 264(1)(h)
    report on pupil progress, Reg. 298, s. 20(a)
    return school property, 264(1)(j)
    safety procedures, Reg. 298, s. 20(g)
    sign language, 264(1.1)
    teach, 264(1)(a), Reg. 298, s. 20(a)
    teaching plans and outlines, Reg. 298, s. 20(f)
    timetable, 264(1)(g)
    use approved textbooks, 264(1)(k)
    use English or French, 264(1)(f)
education, 14
employment, 258
false registers or return, 213
general, 258-277
illness, 260
jury duty, 260
morals and character, 262, 264
part-time, 258, 260
permanent, 258
powers
    conferences and seminars, 264(3)
    professional development, 264(3)
probationary, 258, 261
promotion or sale of books, 217
recommendation on appointment and promotion, Reg. 298, s. 11
recommendation on demotion or dismissal, Reg. 298, s. 11
regulations, 11
refusal to give up school property, 215
salary, 260
sickness, 260
termination
    by board, 268

519

INDEX

Teacher — *continued*
by teacher, 268
certificate of qualification
  cancellation or suspension, 8, 262
letter of standing
  cancellation or suspension, 8, 262
replacement, 269

Teacher education centre
permanent letter of standing, Reg. 297, s. 19

Teachers' college. *see also* **College.**
agreement with university, 14
establishment, 14
Minister, 8
regulations, 11

***Teachers' Pension Act*, R.S.O. 1990, c. T.1,**
179, TPA, ss. 3, 9

Teaching materials. *see* **Learning materials, Principal, Teacher.**

Temperature. *see* **Principal.**

Temporary teacher
defined, 1

Territorial districts
grants, 240
secondary schools outside school divisions, 67

Territory without municipal organization
appointment, 240
district combined separate school zone, 103
district school area board, 65
divisional board, 53-54
list, Reg. 311
objection to voter, 62
public school electors, 61
trailer licence fees, 256

Textbook. *see* **Book.**

Three-session course. *see also* **Qualification, One-session course.**
specialist qualification, Reg. 297, ss. 32-37

subjects, Reg. 297, Sched. D

Trailer License Fees
exception for municipal trailer camps, 255
payment of share, 255
territory without municipal organization, 256

Trainable retarded pupils
principals and vice-principals, Reg. 298, s. 10
summer classes, Reg. 285, s. 1
teaching qualification, Reg. 297, ss. 20-22, Reg. 298, s. 19

Training-assistance. *see also* **Designation of unrequired staff.**
designated person, Reg. 312

Transcript
fees, Reg. 293

Transfer. *see* **Designation of unrequired staff.**

Transportation. *see also* **Meals and lodging.**
contracted, 190
English-language instruction, 301
failure of arrangements, 19
French-language instruction, 289
hearing-handicapped children, 190
levy in separate school zone, 116
long distance from school, 190
provision by board, 190
regulations, 11
where impracticable, 190
Ontario School for the Blind, Reg. 296, s. 13
Ontario School for the Deaf, Reg. 296, s. 13

Treasurer. *see* **Officers.**

Treasurer of Ontario
fixing interest rate, 7
guarantee of debentures, 6

Treatment centre schools
board, 171

INDEX

Trespassers
principal
　duty to refuse admission, 265
school site, 1

Trustee. *see also* **Board member, Board, Offence.**
allowance, 191
benefits, 176
board of education, 58
borrowing, 121
chair, 191, 208
combined separate school zone, 95, 104
declaration, 209, 211
determination, Reg. 313
disqualification, 220
distribution
　candidate for one seat only, 104
　general, Reg. 313
　improvement district, 103
　re-election of retiring trustee, 104
divisional board, 56
duties, 170, 90, 96
election, Reg. 313, s. 3
expenses, 191
first meeting, 208
general, 230-233
Indian pupils, 188
lack, 221
powers, 90, 96
Protestant separate school board, 165
quorum, 208
resignations, 221
separate school
　assessment roll, 118
　board, 114
　borrowing powers, 121
　rural
　zone, 80-81

Trustee Act, **R.S.O. 1990, c. T.23**, 171, TPA, s. 9

Unorganized territory. *see* **Territory without municipal organization.**

Urban school section
defined, 1

Urban municipality
defined, 1

Vacancy in office
board member convicted, 229
board of education, 222
district school area board, 223, 228
no qualified person
　appointment of trustee, 227
public and secondary boards, 222
separate school, 222, 224
within month of election, 225

Ventilation. *see* **Principal.**

Vice-principal. *see also* **Supervisory officers, Principals.**
duties, Reg. 298, s. 12
qualifications, Reg. 298, ss. 9, 10

Visiting Forces Act, **R.S.C. 1985, c. V-2**
fee, 49

Visitors
book, 265
principal, 265
public and secondary schools, 52
separate school, 123

Vocational courses. *see also* **Vocational school.**
advisory committee, 175
general, 174, 175

Vocational school. *see also* **Vocational courses.**
defined, 1

Voluntary assistants
board, 171

Voluntary transfer. *see* **Designation of unrequired staff.**

Ward
admission, 46

521

Workers' Compensation Act, **R.S.O. 1990, c. W.11,** 8

Year. *see also* **Day, Holidays, Remembrance Day.**
dates, Reg. 304, s. 2
defined, 1
general, Reg. 304
minimum length, Reg. 304, s. 2
regulations, 11
where varied, 22